Offshoring

Causes and Consequences at the Firm and Worker Level

World Scientific Studies in International Economics
(ISSN: 1793-3641)

World Scientific Studies in International Economics includes works dealing with the theory, empirical analysis, and evaluation of international economic policies and institutions, with topics covering international macroeconomics and finance, international trade theory and policy, as well as international legal and political economy. Monographs and edited volumes will comprise the core of the publications.

Vol. 71 *Offshoring: Causes and Consequences at the Firm and Worker Level*
edited by Holger Görg (Kiel Institute for the World Economy, Germany) & Aoife Hanley (Kiel Institute for the World Economy, Germany)

Vol. 70 *Policy Externalities and International Trade Agreements*
by Nuno Limão (University of Maryland, USA)

Vol. 69 *Economic Analysis of the Rules and Regulations of the World Trade Organization*
edited by Kamal Saggi (Vanderbilt University, USA)

Vol. 68 *International Trade, Capital Flows and Economic Development*
edited by Francisco L. Rivera-Batiz (Columbia University, USA) & Luis A. Rivera-Batiz (University of Puerto Rico, USA)

Vol. 67 *Megaregionalism 2.0: Trade and Innovation within Global Networks*
edited by Dieter Ernst (East-West Center, USA & The Centre for International Governance Innovation/CIGI, Canada) & Michael G. Plummer (The Johns Hopkins University, SAIS, Italy)

Vol. 66 *International and Interregional Migration: Theory and Evidence*
edited by Francisco L. Rivera-Batiz (Columbia University, USA)

Vol. 65 *International Trade Theory and Competitive Models: Features, Values, and Criticisms*
by Ronald W. Jones (University of Rochester, USA)

Vol. 64 *Information Spillovers and Market Integration in International Finance: Empirical Analyses*
by Suk-Joong Kim (University of Sydney, Australia)

Vol. 63 *Dimensions of Trade Policy*
by Martin Richardson (Australian National University, Australia)

The complete list of the published volumes in the series can be found at
https://www.worldscientific.com/series/wssie

71 World Scientific Studies in International Economics

Offshoring

Causes and Consequences at the Firm and Worker Level

editors

Holger Görg • Aoife Hanley

Kiel Institute for the World Economy, Germany

World Scientific

NEW JERSEY • LONDON • SINGAPORE • BEIJING • SHANGHAI • HONG KONG • TAIPEI • CHENNAI • TOKYO

Published by

World Scientific Publishing Co. Pte. Ltd.
5 Toh Tuck Link, Singapore 596224
USA office: 27 Warren Street, Suite 401-402, Hackensack, NJ 07601
UK office: 57 Shelton Street, Covent Garden, London WC2H 9HE

British Library Cataloguing-in-Publication Data
A catalogue record for this book is available from the British Library.

World Scientific Studies in International Economics — Vol. 71
OFFSHORING
Causes and Consequences at the Firm and Worker Level

ISBN 978-981-3239-42-5

For any available supplementary material, please visit
https://www.worldscientific.com/worldscibooks/10.1142/10969#t=suppl

Desk Editor: Alisha Nguyen

Typeset by Stallion Press
Email: enquiries@stallionpress.com

Printed in Singapore

About the Authors

Holger Görg is Director of the *Kiel Centre for Globalization* at the Institute for the World Economy, Kiel, Germany. He has been Professor of International Economics at the Kiel Institute and the University of Kiel, Germany, since 2008. He is also affiliated with the Tuborg Research Centre for Globalisation and Firms, Aarhus University, the Centre for Research on Globalisation and Economic Policy at the University of Nottingham, and IZA. Before joining Kiel he was on the staff at the University of Nottingham, the University of Ulster at Jordanstown and University College Cork. He completed a Ph.D. in Economics in 1999 at Trinity College Dublin. His research interests are in empirical international trade and industrial organisation focusing in particular on the activities of multinational companies, foreign direct investment, and international outsourcing. He has published widely in international journals, including the *Review of Economics and Statistics*, *Journal of International Economics*, *European Economic Review*, and *Economic Journal*. Professor Görg has also worked as consultant for, among others, The World Bank, European Commission, UN Economic Commission for Africa, UN Industrial Development Organization, Inter-American Development Bank, and various governments.

Aoife Hanley was Associate Professor at the University of Nottingham before taking up her position at Kiel's Institute for the World Economy in 2008 where she is currently Professor for Applied Economics of the Firm. Her previous work explores the impact of exporting, outsourcing or work practices changes on the innovation or productivity of firms. She also focusses on CSR and knowledge transfer in global value chains.

Table of Contents

Introduction

Holger Görg and Aoife Hanley[1]

Offshoring has increased substantially over the last three decades or so and is arguably one of the defining characteristics of the current age of globalization. In a nutshell, offshoring means the breaking up of the production chain where the production of the various components can be relocated across the globe. Examples abound of goods that are made up of components that are being produced in many parts of the world, think of computing equipment or cars, to mention just the very obvious ones. A well-studied example is the Apple iPhone, where inputs from a number of countries, including Germany, South Korea, Japan and the US are assembled in China, and the almost-finished product is then shipped to the US for final marketing and sales (Xing and Detert, 2010).

Going beyond case-studies, precisely measuring the importance of offshoring is tricky. Should one look at imports of intermediate inputs, or activities of multinational companies? If the former, how can "intermediate inputs" be measured in aggregate trade data? If the latter, does that not leave out a substantial proportion of offshoring through arm's-length relationships?[2] Be that as it may, commonly used aggregate data on various indicators generally show the importance of offshoring.

In Figure 1, we present some data on offshoring from Görg and Hanley (2017). This is measured as shares of foreign value added in total exports for various countries, in the spirit of Johnson and Noguera (2012). The

[1]The authors are grateful to Antonia Birkeneder for excellent research assistance.
[2]We discuss these issues in some more detail in Görg and Hanley (2017).

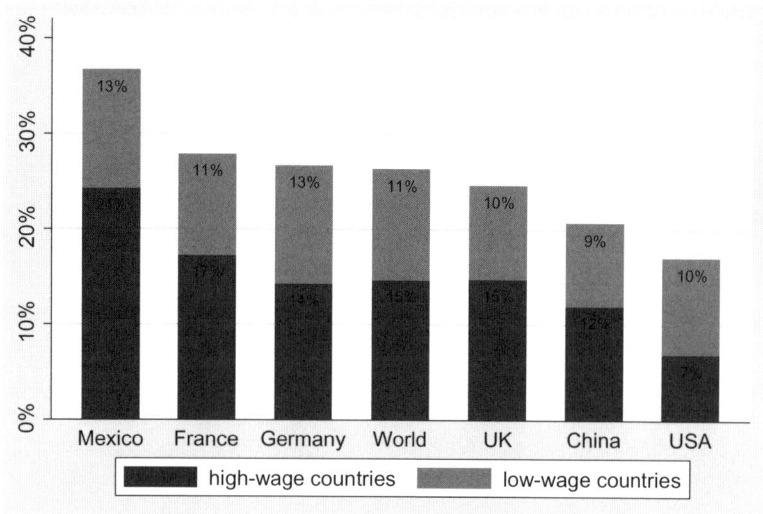

Figure 1: Proportion of Foreign Value Added
Source: Görg and Hanley (2017)

information in the table is calculated using data from the World Input-Output Database.[3] The use of the data can be illustrated using a simple example: A country may generate $40 billion in export sales, but only half of these sales might have been produced by firms in the domestic economy. In this case, we can say that 50 percent of the value added of the country derives from production in other countries; i.e., the foreign value added. This value can be used a measure of production offshoring.

Accordingly, the data in Figure 1 illustrate the value created by firms in foreign countries in the overall value of exported output. For example, the value created by foreign enterprises amounts to 27 percent of the value of exports in Germany. In other words, imported intermediates from foreign firms contributed 27 percent of the total value added of German exports. Interestingly, the US conducts substantially less offshoring than the world average or, indeed, China.

The data in Figure 1 only relate to one point in time, namely 2011 — the latest year for which we have WIOD data available. To get an idea of the dynamics in offshoring over the last decade or so, Figure 2 demonstrates

[3]Available at www.wiod.org, see Timmer *et al.* (2015) for a description of the database.

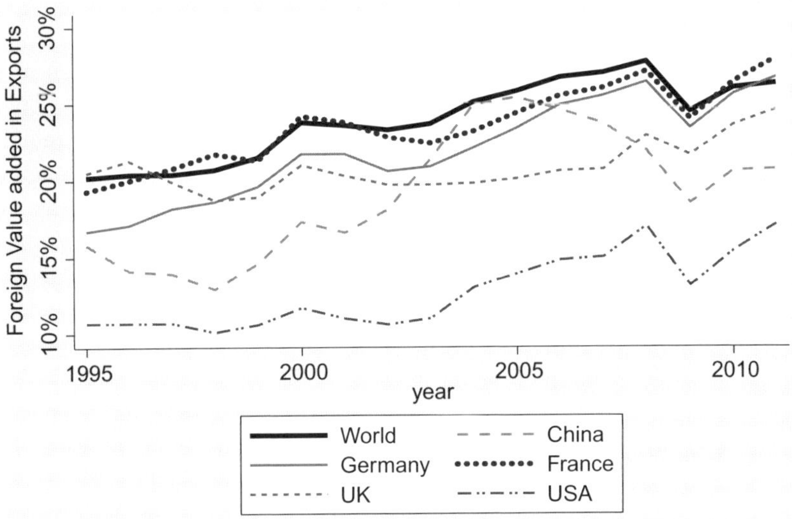

Figure 2: Development of Foreign Value Added Over Time
Source: Görg and Hanley (2017)

the changes that have occurred in offshoring over the years from 1995 to 2011.

Looking at the figure, it is clear that the overall trajectory is slightly upwards. The 2008 Financial Crisis prompted a dip in offshoring rates that are now returning to their pre-crisis levels. Once again, it is evident that the US conducts comparatively less offshoring than the other economies shown in the figure.

Mindful of these changes that have taken place, this volume collects a number of papers that we have written, either together or with other co-authors, on the topic of offshoring. Here a brief explanatory note might help to avoid confusion later on: Most of the papers included in this volume refer to "international outsourcing" instead of "offshoring". While the phenomenon remains essentially the same, these differences in terminology just reflect how the 'official' definition of this activity in the literature has changed down the years. In the 1990s, "offshoring" was frequently referred to as "fragmentation", the early 2000s saw a move to use the term" international outsourcing", while the next decade decided to call the activity "offshoring". As this volume is a child of the late 2010s, we apply the expression "offshoring" in this introduction, though most of the papers (which were written in the early to mid-2000s) refer to the phenomenon as "international outsourcing".

The papers included here are all empirical studies based on firm, individual or industry level data, which are published in various journals. They are grouped into three broad topics: First, the causes and motives of offshoring for firms. Second, the implications of the offshoring decision for firm performance, in particular productivity and innovation, as well as profitability and labour demand at the level of the firm. Third, the consequences of offshoring for individuals' wages and job security, as well as the relative demand for skills in an economy.

We attempt to summarize the main points of the papers in the remainder of this introduction.

Part I: Causes and Motives for Offshoring

Explanations for the rise in offshoring generally centre around two broad aspects. The first is changes in technology, which enables offshoring. The second, closely related point, is transport costs. Over the last three decades or so, production technologies have changed substantially. Consider the introduction and rise of the internet and increases in computing power. The impact of these technological changes has had a knock-on effect on how goods are produced within firms and traded between firms. Specifically, these technology changes have also substantially reduced the cost of transporting goods and services and the communication costs between production facilities in different locations. Accordingly, offshoring has become more viable. The papers in the first part of this volume consider some aspects of the motives and causes for offshoring, using empirical studies at the level of the firm.

An early paper by Jones and Kierzkowski (1990) was among the first to propose that the fragmentation of production needs well-functioning services, such as transportation, communication, finance, etc. Paper I.1 takes this as a starting point and investigates the link between the availability of services and firms' offshoring in a formal monopolistic competition model, which makes clear the mechanism at play in the services–offshoring nexus. The implications of the model are then investigated using firm level panel data for Irish manufacturing firms, offshoring being a widespread business practice in Ireland. In the empirical analysis, a firm's value of imported intermediates (as a proxy for offshoring) is related to the availability of services inputs in the adjacent local economy. The degree to which services inputs are available, is inferred from the firm's geographic region.

The empirical analysis shows that the availability of local services induces manufacturing firms to import more inputs, which is in line with the basic intuition developed in the theoretical model. This result holds, especially for purely domestic firms — i.e. firms that are not part of a foreign-owned multinational. This suggests that these non-multinational firms may be too small or inefficient to internalize the provision of services or to use services from a parent company abroad and may therefore depend more strongly on local service market conditions.

Paper I.2 is also concerned with the link between local availability of services and offshoring, but looks at this relationship from a somewhat different angle. The paper examines whether the availability of local services in the home country is important for a firm's decision to open affiliates abroad. Accordingly, this paper applies a different indicator of offshoring. Rather than considering imports of intermediate goods, it looks at operations of multinationals abroad. The empirical analysis is conducted using firm level panel data for France.

The paper shows robust evidence that improvements in the availability of services in the region in which a firm is located have a positive impact on a firm's decision to invest abroad. This effect is strongest for firms that are small, in the sense of having fewer domestic affiliates. These are likely to be firms that are less likely to internalize the provision of business services inputs, similar to the finding in Paper I.1. Taking the two papers together, the research shows that improvements in the availability of services — for reasons that include increased liberalization of the services sector — have the potential to enhance the efficiency of firms by allowing them to link more easily into the global economy through offshoring.

In Paper I.3 we look at the availability of the internet as a very specific aspect of technology-enabled offshoring. The question that is addressed in the paper, is whether firms that start using the internet for business purposes become more heavily engaged in offshoring (importing intermediates) as a result. To motivate the empirical analysis, the paper starts off with a theoretical model. This shows that access to the internet may, on the one hand, benefit offshoring as firms have access to a wider variety of suppliers at lower cost. However, there is also a dampening effect for offshoring, as firms sourcing through the internet are faced with lower reliability and, perhaps, reduced input quality.

The empirical analysis is carried out using a similar data set to the one used in Paper I.1 for firms in the Republic of Ireland. The paper focusses on firms that switch to using the internet, compared to a control group of firms that do not perform such a switch. The results show that the switchers experience a growth in their imported inputs which is around 60 percent higher than firms that do not use the internet. However, we do not find any such positive effect for the offshoring of material inputs. This may suggest that improved access to the internet may be likely to contribute significantly more to the tradability of services inputs.

Paper I.3 raises the following question: how does a technology change like internet adoption trigger increased numbers of firms to switch into offshoring some or part of their production from overseas suppliers? Internet adoption may be a key facilitator of offshoring. But the rise of the internet is only part of a more multi-faceted picture. Other advancements in technology, not just internet use, have permitted firms to transact with one another at arm's length.

Accordingly, technology improvements have helped to boost the rate at which firms offshore parts of their production chain. But are firms content to offshore every aspect of their production to overseas suppliers? Consider the implications of offshoring for firms offshoring part of their production chain. Offshoring firms permit foreign suppliers — some of whom become future competitors — to manufacture inputs on their behalf. Consequently, it makes sense that firms pick and choose which inputs to offshore and which inputs to produce within the four walls of the firm. Paper 1.4 deals with this thorny issue, namely how property rights considerations (patents, trademarks, brands etc.) and investments made by firms in R&D and machinery, influence the firm's willingness to offshore production to an outside firm.

Using data for over 8,000 firms from the UK Community Innovation Survey, the paper finds that property rights considerations indeed cause firms to shy away from offshoring. While firms might be unwilling to offshore activities related to the *final product* to outsiders, firms are more willing to involve outsiders in the supply of goods and services related to the *production process.*

What are the implications of this finding for our investigation into offshoring? We can see empirically, that firms do indeed pick and choose the type of inputs to offshore. Ancillary inputs (e.g. legal advice, logistics, and engineering services) can be offshored without any loss to the firm. However, it would be unwise for firms to offshore core inputs. The reason: firms need to retain control over core inputs in order to appropriate the profits arising from investments they have made in research, capital and employees. Our findings echo similar work by Veugelers and Cassiman (1999) that firms prefer to retain control over firm-specific investments. While offshoring can allow firms to reap cost advantages by allowing suppliers to specialize, produce more cost-effectively and pass on these cost savings to industrial buyers, such cost savings are ill-advised if they come at the cost of eroding the firm's unique assets and accordingly, the firm's competitive position.

Part II: Implications for Firm Performance

Having discussed the causes and motives for offshoring, we now shift our focus to the implications of offshoring for firms. In particular, the focus is on how offshoring affects productivity, innovation activity, but we also consider profitability and labour demand. A priori, one may expect the firm offshoring production to be able to benefit from the ability to reorganize production to concentrate on the most efficient stages in the home country. Also, offshoring allows access to intermediates abroad at lower prices or higher quality. The quality aspect may be particularly important for offshoring to industrialized countries, while the price effect may be more likely to materialize when offshoring to lower income countries. This restructuring due to offshoring should lead firms to improve their productivity, and to be able to invest more resources in innovation activity (e.g., Glass and Saggi, 2001). This may also have implications for profitability and labour demand. These questions are analysed empirically with firm level data in the seven papers in Part II.

We start off in Paper II.1 with an analysis of a firm's decision to outsource parts of the production chain. This paper is not about "offshoring" as considered in all other papers in this volume, but "outsourcing". It does not distinguish whether the production activity is relocated to some other supplier abroad (which we define as offshoring) or domestically. Still, it provides important insights into the implications of restructuring in the firm due to outsourcing, which is also informative for the other studies presented in this Part II of the volume. The empirical analysis in the paper is carried out using establishment level panel data for UK manufacturing industries for the period 1980 to 1992.

The paper firstly considers differences in outsourcing activity across different establishments. The empirical results suggest that higher wages in a firm are positively related to the decision to outsource production, suggesting that the cost saving motive is important. We also find that foreign-owned firms have higher levels of outsourcing than domestic establishments. In the second part of the paper, the focus is on the subsequent changes in productivity following the decision to outsource. Here results show that an establishment's outsourcing intensity is positively related to its labour productivity and total factor productivity growth. This effect is found to be more pronounced for foreign establishments than for firms with purely domestic ownership.

Paper II.1 thus reveals differences in productivity outcomes for foreign-owned and domestic plants deciding to fragment the production chain. Additionally, the study underscores the cost-saving motive of outsourcing. Paper II.2 takes these ideas further. Here we look at what features of foreign-owned plants might have given rise to these productivity differences. Foreign-owned firms, are by nature of their FDI investments, embedded in foreign markets. Domestic firms, at least those domestic firms that export, are also engaged in foreign markets. The question arises — can this higher embeddedness/engagement with foreign markets allow firms to leverage higher productivity benefits from offshoring? There is a strong intuition for arguing that exporting and international outsourcing have one major thing in common, namely transaction with a foreign stakeholder. It therefore makes sense, that there are productivity externalities from international outsourcing, for firms that are already transacting with foreign stakeholders. We find this is indeed the case: foreign-owned exporters report significantly higher productivity from their international outsourcing activities than domestic firms with no such global engagement. On a positive note for domestic firms — domestic firms too can capture positive productivity benefits from international outsourcing, if these domestic firms are also export-active. Note that this effect for domestic exporters was only seen to hold for the international outsourcing of materials.

The latter results for Paper II.2 were obtained for data from the Republic of Ireland. A reader might ask: are results obtained for international outsourcing based on data for the Republic of Ireland generalizable to other economies? Mindful of the need to broaden the research focus beyond one country, Paper II.3 reports findings for the productivity effects of international outsourcing for the UK, Ireland and Sweden. This analysis focusing on foreign services imports, represents one of the first attempts for a consortium of researchers with access to enterprise data for different countries, to work together in applying the same methodology and time-period. The overall result for total factor productivity, reveals mildly significant productivity premia to firms employing international outsourcing. A stronger finding is the common selection effect observed for firms across all three economies: firms engaged in international outsourcing tend to be large, foreign, pay higher wages and tend to be multinational in orientation.

So far we have noted the largely positive effects for international outsourcing, materials and services, on a firm's productivity. What we have not done, is examine more closely, the mechanisms by which this activity affects the firm. When we talk of "mechanisms", we include an examination of the firm's innovation and profits. The theoretical Glass and Saggi (2001) model posits that firms outsource activities due to lower factor costs abroad. Accordingly, outsourcing firms should report reduced costs and higher profits. These profits, subsequently, can be reinvested in R&D which in turn, might be expected to raise the firm's innovation rates.

Paper II.4 examines this "outsourcing-profit" channel in detail. The analysis considers the returns to outsourcing firms from purchasing services from domestic vis-à-vis international suppliers. Outsourcing firms report higher innovation from purchasing service inputs from local vis-à-vis international suppliers. Importantly, innovation returns are highest when firms purchase from the latter. The innovation premium from international outsourcing may well be driven by the wider choice of prices available from international suppliers. Accordingly, outsourcing firms can pick and choose from a wider menu of prices on foreign markets, than if they were to restrict their choice to domestic suppliers. The resulting cost savings can be invested back into R&D, with implications for the firm's innovation capability.

So far, we have discussed international outsourcing as though it takes place within an institutional vacuum. Firms negotiate and set up supply relationship with no reference to the legal aspects of the buyer-supplier relationship. For example, what happens when the outsourcing firm is unhappy with the timeliness and quality of intermediates? What happens if the supplier firm leaks proprietary information from its offshoring customer or otherwise abuses its position of trust? We know from Paper 1.4 that the safeguarding of property rights is very important for firms engaged in international outsourcing. Paper II.5 examines this issue of institutional context in greater depth, applying data for emerging economies within Eastern Europe. The choice of emerging economies for this study is not arbitrary. Emerging economies are still working to harmonize their legal and financial systems with the international standard set by developed economies. As such, this study focuses on a set of economies where trust in institutions may be lacking. Accordingly, the quality of institutional frameworks in these economies would be expected to be more critical in facilitating exchanges between firms across international boundaries. The paper finds that good institutions that mediate the legal underpinnings for property rights and the quantity of suppliers, significantly boost the benefits to international outsourcers active in the economy. The importance of the institutional environment is further underscored by the significance of EU membership. International outsourcers can expect to report even higher innovation outcomes when they transact with suppliers from an EU economy vis-à-vis a non-EU economy. Therefore, we should not be left in any doubt: international outsourcing requires trust between partner firms and trust requires a trustworthy institutional context.

The previous papers, especially II.4, have highlighted this "outsourcing-profit" channel in detail. Paper II.6 sheds light on the "outsourcing-profit" channel by zooming in on a burgeoning high-growth sector: Ireland's Electronics sector. The latter is dominated by affiliates of foreign-owned firms, e.g. Intel. Interestingly, from a policy perspective, foreign firms were actively solicited by Irish trade groups because of the potential for firms in this sector to get involved in supply relationships with Irish firms (linkages). Using data for 12 sub-sectors within the Electronics sector, we can examine detailed information relating to the purchases of materials and services by outsourcing firms. Importantly, this analysis corroborates the earlier finding reported in II.3 that plant size plays a key role in mediating the outsourcing relationship. Specifically, we find that the 'outsourcing-profit' channel is highly sensitive to plant size, large firms appropriating higher profits from their outsourcing activities than their small firm counterparts. Although there may be several reasons for this result, we conjecture that this finding hints at the existence of non-trivial transactions costs. Small plants are likely to face lower bargaining power when transacting with suppliers and incur higher, per unit search costs. A similar transactions-cost argumentation underpins the Grossman and Helpman (2002) theoretical paper. Accordingly, Paper II.6, by highlighting important plant size interactions in the "outsourcing-profit" channel, chimes with these earlier theoretical predictions regarding the role of transactions costs.

The last issue we consider in this Part II is the implication of offshoring for labour demand at the level of the firm. Intuitively, the restructuring taking place in an establishment may, in the short run, destroy jobs as part of the production that was previously carried out in-house is now gone.

However, the re-organization towards productivity enhancing activities, including innovation, may lead to new jobs being generated. Whether or not the latter outweigh the former is an empirical question that is addressed in Paper II.7 using plant level panel data for the electronics sector in Ireland.

The paper focuses on short run employment effects in the offshoring plants. To do so, a dynamic model of plant level labour demand is estimated. Overall, the estimation results suggest that, in the short run, there are significant reductions in plant level labour demand due to the use of offshoring. Distinguishing materials and services offshoring also suggests that the negative effects appear to be stronger from offshoring of materials than services. It is important to point out, however, that the nature of the estimation technique implies that only short run effects are captured. Of course, in the medium or longer run, plants may increase labour demand due to increased competitiveness following offshoring. This cannot be captured with the data used in the paper.

Part III: Labour Market Consequences at the Worker Level

Given this somewhat unsatisfactory analysis in Paper II.7, the third part of the volume now zooms in in much more detail on labour market effects of offshoring. We move away from the firm or plant as unit of analysis and consider workers instead. After all, these are the ultimate recipients when it comes to labour market effects, as it is their jobs and their wages that may be affected.

While many globalization critics usually argue that offshoring necessarily implies lower wages and job losses in the offshoring economy, this caveat by no means clear cut. The forces at work are neatly summarized in the theoretical paper by Grossman and Rossi-Hansberg (2008).[4] They distinguish between the offshoring of low-skill and high-skill activities and evaluate the effects of offshoring on wages for both low-skilled and high-skilled workers. Their theoretical framework identifies three types of effects.

Firstly, some firms may experience a positive boost to productivity due to offshoring. Considering low skill workers first, as firms will offshore the least productive low skill tasks, firms that use low skill labour intensively experience an improvement in productivity, as the productivity of the remaining low skill workers will increase. This allows them to expand

[4]There are, of course, also other theoretical contributions that highlight negative and positive effects of offshoring. See, Feenstra and Hanson (1996), Kohler (2004), Deardorff (2001), and Jones and Kierzkowski (2001) to mention but a few.

production. In turn, this implies that these firms increase their labour demand domestically to carry out the tasks that cannot be easily offshored. Consequently, labour demand for low skill labour increases bringing with it an *increase* in the wage rate. This positive effect is generally overlooked in the public debate on offshoring.

However, there are two other effects that work against this. As offshoring leads to greater cost savings in industries using relatively high intensities of low skilled labour, the relative price of goods in these low-skill industries is bound to fall relative to the price of goods in high-skill industries. This leads to a fall in the relative wage of low skill labour. Moreover, as offshoring frees up domestic low skill labour, this increases the labour supply of this type of workers which, ceteris paribus, further depresses the wage rate of these workers. The wage effect of offshoring on low skill labour is, hence, ambiguous. By contrast, the latter two effects imply unambiguously positive effects for high skill workers, if low skill tasks are offshored.

The opposite is true if high skill tasks are offshored. In this case, the wage implications for high skill workers are not clear in theory, as the positive productive effect is balanced against the adverse relative price and labour supply effects. In this case, however, low skill workers unambiguously gain.

On balance, the outcome of offshoring for wages in this model depends on the skill levels of workers, the relative strength of the three diverting effects, and on whether offshored activities are low-skill or high-skill intensive. The empirical papers collected in this part of the volume look at various aspects of the link between offshoring and wages.

Paper III.1 starts off with presenting some evidence based on aggregate industry level data for the United Kingdom for the period 1984 to 1995. This period has seen both increases in wage inequality as well as offshoring activity in the UK. Expanding on Feenstra and Hanson (1996a), the paper estimates relative factor demand equations derived from short-run cost functions. Skills are measured using the Standard Occupational Classification, distinguishing skilled, semi-skilled and unskilled workers at the industry level. Corresponding measures of offshoring at the industry level are generated as imported intermediate inputs from the UK Input-Output tables. The results from estimating the factor share equations show that offshoring has had a significant negative impact on the relative demand for low skilled workers in the UK. By contrast, demand for semi- or high-skilled workers remained unaffected. Instead, factor biased technological change, proxied by industry level R&D expenditure, appears to have increased the demand for skilled labour.

There are a number of drawbacks with such aggregate studies. Firstly, the factor demand is estimated as the cost share of the factor used in production, which combines the price of the factor (i.e., the wage for workers) with the level of factor usage. Whether changes in factor demand are due to changes in wages or employment of the factor is difficult to disentangle. Secondly, and relatedly, the decrease in the relative demand for low skilled workers observed in Paper III.1 may be due to decreases in the absolute demand for low skills, increases in the absolute demand for other factors, or both. These mechanisms cannot be pinned down with sufficient precision using aggregate data.

In order to get a better idea about winners and losers from offshoring, the remaining papers in Part III turn to analysing individual level data combined with offshoring information at the industry level. Paper III.2 is one of the first to have taken this approach in the literature. The paper estimates the impact of industry level offshoring on individual level wages using detailed micro data. This allows us to control for individual level heterogeneity in terms of skills and other demographic characteristics. Thus, we can answer the question as to whether individuals working in industries with high offshoring activity experience a different development of wages than comparable workers in other industries. Furthermore, we can investigate whether these wage effects differ for workers depending on their skill levels, as suggested by theory.

The analysis uses data for Germany from the German Socio Economic Panel (GSOEP) over the period 1991 to 2000. As for the UK, Germany experienced substantial increases in offshoring activity as measured using data on imported manufacturing inputs from input-output tables. Partly, this is due to the opening up of the Iron Curtain and subsequent offshoring of activity to Eastern European countries. The paper distinguishes three types of skills: high, medium and low. These are measured using two alternative definitions. Firstly, educational attainment based on the International Standard Classification of Education (ISCED) and, second, a survey measure based on required on the-job skills.

The results from estimating wage regressions at the individual level show that offshoring had a marked impact on wages. There is evidence for a negative effect of offshoring on the real wage for low-skilled workers, while high-skilled workers appear to gain from outsourcing in terms of receiving higher wages. These results are robust to the definition of skills. Using the estimation results, the paper also calculates the economic significance of the offshoring impact. On average, a 1 percentage point increase in offshoring reduced the wage for workers in the lowest skill categories by up to 1.5 percent, while it increased wages for high-skilled workers by up to 2.6 percent.

These results are, of course, country specific. Paper III.3 provides some international comparison, using individual level data for three countries, namely, Denmark, Germany and the UK for the period 1991 to 2000. The paper also focuses on the effects on individual wages of offshoring at the industry level. In order to be able to apply an appropriate comparison point, the paper distinguishes between high and low skilled workers using educational attainment, but unlike the previous paper, assigns all workers into these two skill categories and does not apply a 'medium skill' category. The paper expands on Paper III.2 by establishing whether the wage impact of offshoring differs across countries with different types of welfare states and, in particular, labour market institutions. The three countries represent the three different welfare state types we can find in Europe: the Scandinavian, the Central European, and the Anglo-Saxon system. All three substantially differ in terms of institutions and legislation particularly with respect to employment protection, unemployment benefits, minimum wages or the role of unions.

While one may expect some differences in the wage effects of offshoring across these three countries, the empirical analysis, based on estimating the same empirical specification on similar data, shows that the effects are, actually, quite similar and fairly small. Low-skilled workers experience reductions in real wages, in particular through outsourcing to Central and Eastern European Countries, while there is some evidence that high-skilled workers benefit through higher wages, at least in the UK. The strong positive effect of offshoring for high skilled workers in Germany as found in Paper III.2 does not materialize in this paper. This is most likely due to the different definition of skills used in this paper compared to Paper III.2.

In Paper III.4, we look at the implications of offshoring for workers not of different skills, but of different employment contracts. In particular, we consider differences between workers on temporary or permanent contracts. The data are again for Germany, where the GSOEP data also provides information on the type of employment contract. This is used to investigate whether industry level offshoring differently affects wages and also the probability of job losses of workers. In order to investigate the latter, the paper uses the GSOEP data to look at individual employment spells. Job losses are then defined as an individual moving from employment in period t to unemployment in period $t + 1$.

Interestingly, the paper does not find any strong systematic differences between temporary and permanent workers when it comes to wages. Or to put it differently, the contract type does not matter for the wage effects of offshoring. This is somewhat different when considering the risk of moving into unemployment, however. In this case, offshoring is associated with an increase in the unemployment risk for all low skilled workers, but this effect is stronger for those with temporary contracts compared to permanent contracts. The risk of moving into unemployment is lowered with increasing offshoring for high and medium skill workers, and there is no difference between temporary and permanent contracts. Hence, contract types play a role for unskilled workers, where the negative employment effects are somewhat cushioned for workers with a permanent as opposed to a temporary contract.

Traditional offshoring in manufacturing in industrialized countries is seen to be biased towards harming low skill workers while high skilled workers may gain. This is also borne out by the findings in the papers mentioned thus far. Since the early 2000s another aspect of offshoring grew rapidly, namely, offshoring of services. These may be activities that are high skill intensive — US hospitals offshoring the interpretation of x-rays to India is an example that was cited frequently. This type of offshoring may, thus, potentially harm high skilled workers and benefit low skills, as also pointed out by Grossman and Rossi-Hansberg (2008).

Paper III.5 looks at the implications of services offshoring (measured as imported intermediate services inputs) for individual wages using a similar set up as in Paper III.2. This analysis is done using data for the United Kingdom, where services trade plays a particularly important role, covering the period 1992 to 2004. Interestingly, the results pretty much reflect the impact of manufacturing offshoring: Low and medium skilled workers are affected negatively in terms of wages, while high skilled workers benefit from services offshoring. This suggests that, in the case of the UK, it is low to medium skill intensive services that are offshored, rather than high skill services as in the x-ray example.

Similar to Paper III.4, the final paper in this volume again questions the idea that only skills matter for the labour market effects of offshoring. More recent work has stressed that it is perhaps more instructive to look at tasks, i.e., the actual activity carried out by workers, rather than the skill level of workers. Coming back to the x-ray example above, the (high skill) task of reading the x-ray can be easily offshored using IT, while the lower skill task of driving a taxi cannot (at least with current technology). Paper III.6 connects to this debate and estimates the wage impact of offshoring, paying particular attention to the tasks carried out as well as the skill levels (educational attainment) of individuals.

The main data source is again the GSOEP micro data for Germany. This is combined with information on the tasks content of occupations. Measuring such tasks is not trivial. The paper uses data from another survey of individuals, the German Qualification and Career Survey. In this survey, respondents provide information about their occupation and also state the tasks they perform on the job and the work tools they use. Based on this information, we generate indices of the task content of occupations, which are then mapped back into the GSOEP data. The paper considers two types of task classifications, namely routine vs non-routine tasks, and interactive vs non-interactive tasks. One would expect that routine tasks are more easily offshorable than non-routine tasks, while tasks not involving any interaction with customers, suppliers, or colleagues are also more offshorable than those that are highly interactive.

The paper has one other novel aspect. Most of the empirical literature, and indeed all the papers in Part III reviewed thus far, calculate offshoring measures at the level of the industry in which an individual is employed. In other words, the research looks at within industry offshoring effects. Paper III.6 calculates offshoring measures also at the level of the occupation, and thus allows for within occupation (rather than industry) offshoring effects. The intuition is simple: For example, electrical engineers in the automobile industry may of course be affected by offshoring in the automobile industry — the within industry effect. However, they may also be affected if jobs for electrical engineers in the, say, computer industry are offshored, as this may increase the supply of electrical engineers that may potentially be employed in automobile production.

The results in the paper show that the within-industry impact of offshoring on individual wages is rather modest or non-existent. However, we find substantial negative wage effects of within occupation offshoring for low- and high-skilled workers. Furthermore, the magnitude of these effects very much depends on the type of tasks workers perform. The negative wage effect of offshoring for low-skilled workers carrying out tasks with the lowest degree of non-routine content — the tasks that can most easily be offshored — is significantly higher than the wage effect for low skilled workers with the highest degree of non-routine content.

Conclusions

Fragmentation of production across borders — or offshoring — is an important aspect of today's globalized world. Firms are increasingly operating in global value chains, with production facilities located in many countries. This is likely to remain important even though the current political climate seems to be set more towards anti-globalization than even just a few years ago.

The papers in this volume show that such offshoring has exerted profound effects on firms and workers. Firms engaged in offshoring have a productivity and technology advantage. Workers can benefit or lose from this process, depending on their skills and the actual tasks they carry out.

For the reasons mentioned above, offshoring has become increasingly politicized. Politicians with nationalist agendas in industrialized economies or opponents of neo-liberalism have held offshoring responsible for many of modern society's woes. Some of these include the widespread perception that offshoring inevitably leads to income inequality and unemployment. In developing and emerging economies, the backlash against offshoring stems from a different set of reasons: offshoring is held responsible for the, sometimes, appalling working practices observed in low-cost suppliers. And not even the firms themselves have been unequivocally happy with the practice. Some firms have engaged in "reverse-offshoring", where input production is shifted back to within the firm's four walls or outsourced to a supplier, closer to home.

Notwithstanding the criticisms, offshoring remains a ubiquitous business practice that appears set to stay. The question is: "How to live with offshoring?" This question has prompted researchers to turn their attention to the dynamics of value chains, to define the winners and losers, to identify, which if any, knowledge transfers and skill upgrading is taking place. Finally, the study of offshoring can be positioned in the wider debate on corporate social responsibility. It remains for future research to reveal whether offshoring is a viable strategy for socially responsible firms.

References

Deardorff, A.V. (2001a). Fragmentation across cones. In Arndt, S.W. and H. Kierzkowski (eds.), *Fragmentation: New Production Patters in the World Economy.* Oxford, UK: Oxford University Press.

Feenstra, R. and G. H. Hanson (1996). Foreign investment, outsourcing and relative wages. In R. C. Feenstra, G. M. Grossman and D. A. Irwin (eds.),

The Political Economy of Trade Policy: Papers in Honor of Jagdish Bhagwati. Boston, MA: MIT Press.

Feenstra, R. C. and G. H. Hanson (1996a). Globalization, outsourcing, and wage inequality. *American Economic Review*, 86(2), 240–245.

Glass, A. and K. Saggi (2001). Innovation and wage effects of international outsourcing. *European Economic Review*, 45, 67–86.

Görg, H. and A. Hanley (2017). Offshoring and transport costs. In B. Blonigen and W. Wilson (eds.), *Handbook of International Trade and Transportation.* London, UK: Edward Elgar.

Grossman, G. M. and E. Rossi-Hansberg (2008). Trading tasks: A simple theory of offshoring. *American Economic Review*, 98(5), 1978–1997.

Johnson, R. C. and G. Noguera (2012). Fragmentation and trade in value added over four decades, NBER Working Paper 18186.

Jones, R. W. and H. Kierzkowski (1990). The role of services in production and international trade: A theoretical framework. In Jones, R. W. and A. O. Krueger (eds.), *The Political Economy of International Trade: Essays in Honor of Robert B. Baldwin.* Cambridge, MA: Blackwell, pp. 31–48.

Jones, R. W. and H. Kierzkowski (2001). Globalization and the consequences of international fragmentation. In Calvo, G. A. *et al.* (eds.), *Money, Capital Mobility and Trade: Essays in Honor of Robert A. Mundell.* Cambridge, MA: MIT Press.

Kohler, W. (2004). International outsourcing and factor prices with multistage production.*Economic Journal*, 114, C166–C185.

Timmer, M. P., E. Dietzenbacher, B. Los, R. Stehrer and G. J. de Vries (2015). An illustrated user guide to the world input–output database: The case of global automotive production. *Review of International Economics*, 23, 575–605.

Veugelers, R. and B. Cassiman (1999). Make and buy in innovation strategies: Evidence from Belgian manufacturing firms. *Research Policy*,28(1), 63–80.

Xing, Y. and N. Detert (2010). How the iPhone widens the United States trade deficit with the People's Republic of China. ADBI Working Paper Series No. 257.

Part I

Causes and Motives for Offshoring

Chapter I.1

Greasing the wheels of international commerce: how services facilitate firms' international sourcing

Peter Debaere *Darden School of Business, University of Virginia*
Holger Görg *Kiel Institute for the World Economy*
Horst Raff *Department of Economics, University of Kiel*

Abstract. We use plant-level data to study the link between the local availability of services and the decision of manufacturing firms to source materials from abroad. We develop a model to generate predictions about how the intensity of international sourcing of materials depends on the availability of services and firm characteristics. These predictions are supported by the data. Greater availability of services across regions, industries, and time increases firms' foreign sourcing of materials relative to sales. The impact of services differs by firm type. National firms' sourcing responds to changes in regional service conditions, whereas multinationals tend to be less affected. JEL classification: F12, L23

Lubrifier les rouages du commerce international: comment les services facilitent l'approvisionnement international. A l'aide de données au niveau des établissements, on étudie le lien entre la disponibilité locale de services et la décision des entreprises manufacturières de s'approvisionner en biens à l'étranger. On développe un modèle pour engendrer des prédictions quant à savoir jusqu'à quel point l'intensité de l'approvisionnement en biens à l'étranger dépend de la disponibilité des services et des caractéristiques de l'entreprise. Ces prédictions sont supportées par les données. Une plus grande disponibilité de services à travers les régions, les industries et le temps accroît l'approvisionnement en biens à l'étranger des entreprises en pourcentage des ventes. L'impact des services diffère selon le type de firme. L'approvisionnement à l'étranger des entreprises domestiques répond

Debaere is also affiliated with CEPR. Görg is also affiliated with Department of Economics, University of Kiel, GlobID at Aarhus School of Bussiness, and CEPR, Raff is also affiliated with Kiel Institute for the World Economy and CESifo. The paper was started while Peter Debaere visited the Kiel Institute for the World Economy. The authors benefited from suggestions by Giorgio Barba Navaretti, Ed Davis, Peter Egger, Mary Lovely, James Harrigan, John McLaren, Gal Raz, and audiences at various conferences and workshops. Peter Debaere benefited from support by the Darden Foundation. Holger Görg gratefully acknowledges financial support through the European Commission as part of the 7th Framework Programme, Grant Agreement No. 244 552 (SERVICEGAP). Horst Raff acknowledges financial support from the German Science Foundation. Email: debaerep@darden.virginia.edu; holger.goerg@ifw-kiel.de; raff@econ-theory.uni-kiel.de;

Canadian Journal of Economics / Revue canadienne d'Economique, Vol. 46, No. 1
February / février 2013. Printed in Canada / Imprimé au Canada

aux variations régionales dans les conditions de service, alors que les entreprises plurinationales tendent à être moins affectées.

1. Introduction

International sourcing plays a very important role in global production. As a matter of fact, the growth in intermediate-goods trade is often referred to as a factor that distinguishes the current wave of globalization from previous ones.[1] Just consider the many sources of inputs for an iPod, sold by the U.S. company Apple. Dedrick, Kraemer, and Linden (2010) show that the hard drive is produced by the Japanese company Toshiba using affiliates based in China. The display module and display driver are produced in Japan, while some smaller inputs are supplied from Korea. The final assembly is carried out by a Taiwanese company in a plant in China. Furthermore, U.S. suppliers provide the video/multimedia processor as well as the portal player CPU.

Firms' international sourcing (also referred to as offshoring) decisions and their implications have been the subject of much recent theoretical and empirical analysis.[2] This is not surprising in light of public concerns about the impact of offshoring on domestic wages and especially on low-skilled labour employment. This concern, in part, also feeds the need to better understand what drives offshoring, which inevitably is linked to studying the different forms in which firms are organizing their production globally.

In this paper, we investigate an aspect of offshoring that, so far, has received little attention in the economics literature. We study the role that services play in organizing and optimizing manufacturing firms' sourcing processes.[3] With an increasingly important service sector worldwide and with growing research on services, this lack of attention is somewhat surprising. There are, however, a few notable exceptions. Francois (1990), Deardorff (2001), Jones and Kierzkowski (1990), as well as Golub, Jones, and Kierzkowski (2001) were among the first to emphasize how the increased availability of more differentiated or more affordable services can trigger international fragmentation of production. In particular, services can make it easier for firms in non-service sectors, irrespective of whether they are multinationals or not, to exploit the international division of labour and to split production into parts that can be made in different locations. Also the literature on multinational corporations has, to some extent, highlighted the link between services and offshoring in that multinationals' headquarter services help

1 See, for instance, Hummels, Ishii, and Yi (2001). Yi (2003) has hypothesized that the increased fragmentation of production and the resulting trade in intermediates is a key factor behind the growth of international trade.

2 See Helpman (2006) for a recent survey of the literature.

3 Our focus is primarily on the demand for producer services and how it relates to the production side of the economy. Note that there is an older literature that analyzes the demand for consumer services in an open economy. Much of that literature relates to the Balassa-Samuelson effect and the 'Baumol disease.' See Francois and Hoekman (2010).

rationalize multinationals' sourcing decisions (See Helpman 2006; Antras and Helpman 2004). At this point, however, there is little empirical evidence to link manufacturing firms' sourcing decisions to services beyond the general observation that any reduction in service-related costs will, just like any reduction in transportation costs, increase trade.

While the link between services and international sourcing has not received much attention in the economics literature, the business literature, for some time now, has emphasized the importance of services for organizing a firm's production. Supply-chain management, in particular, sees the challenge exactly in coordinating and integrating an increasingly sliced-up-value chain (See Gachon and Terwiesch 2009; Corbett 2004). Offshoring and outsourcing have matured, it is often argued, and the main question is no longer whether or not a well-defined intermediate input should be produced by an affiliate or stand-alone firm abroad or at home. Rather, the current focus is on managing and integrating the whole process of production across its different stages from the purchase of raw materials to the distribution to the customer. It is in this process that service firms, and in particular those providing business and computing services, have a vital role to play.

Consider, for example, a car producer with an extended supply chain of hundreds of suppliers. These suppliers send their parts at different times, through different channels and in different packages to the car manufacturer. Not only is it important that the parts eventually reach the car producer, but there is ample room to optimize this process. The time and arrival of parts have to be coordinated, damage and losses have to be minimized, international customs paperwork has to be taken care of for the pieces coming from abroad, and parts have to be warehoused before being shipped to the manufacturer. There are ample opportunities for third-party service providers to get involved in this process.[4] Moreover, many service firms have extended their operations into the IT sphere and become increasingly more involved in the manufacturer's operations; they can set up a tracking system where companies can see in real time where their supplies are and make suggestions for the optimal bunching of suppliers.

To study the link between the availability of services and firms' sourcing of intermediate manufacturing goods, we use the rich, but tractable, monopolistic competition setting of Melitz and Ottaviano (2008) that introduces heterogeneity through differences in firm productivity while allowing for variable markups. Subsequently, we test the predictions of the model with firm-level data. Exploiting the variation in service availability across regions, time, and industry, we show how the increased availability of services raises the ratio of imported intermediates to sales, which confirms the general intuition that services should grease the

4 The business literature sometimes refers to third-party service providers as third-party logistics firms. There are ample case studies of such third-party logistics firms, including UPS (http://www.ups-scs.com/solutions) in the United States, and Accenture in Ireland ('Guide to strategic outsourcing in Ireland,' http://www.accenture.com/xdoc/ir/locations/ireland/insights/guide.pdf).

wheels of international commerce. More important, however, we find that the impact of more services differs by firm type. National firms' sourcing, in particular, responds to changes in regional service conditions, whereas multinationals tend to be less affected. This result confirms our prediction that the specific way in which services are provided matters. It makes a difference whether services are provided locally by a third party or whether they are provided in-house or attracted from abroad. Our findings thus bring together the earlier hypotheses by Deardorff (2001), Jones and Kierzkowski (2001), and others on the impact of services on offshoring and the theory of the multinational. Indeed, multinationals by definition internalize some company-wide services through their headquarter services, and affiliates of multinationals can easily draw on these services from afar. It can thus be argued that the reason why we find that multinationals are less affected by local service conditions is exactly that they are large and productive enough to incur the fixed cost of setting up their own company-wide service operation or to draw on foreign services, which shields them somewhat from local service conditions.

To investigate the empirical relevance of our predictions about the sourcing behaviour of firms, we use an unbalanced panel of Irish plants from the *Annual Business Survey of Economic Impact* that runs from 2000 to 2004. The data set is quite unique in that it documents the sourcing behaviour in great detail, explicitly distinguishing between materials and services as well as between domestic and international sources. Note that for Irish firms domestic and international sourcing are just a fact of life: In our sample, around 90% of manufacturers source some foreign-produced materials and virtually all manufacturing firms (94%) source materials in the Irish economy, which is why we focus on how much is offshored, rather than whether there is any offshoring occurring at all.[5]

As far as services go, the *Survey* focuses on business and computing services, which are directly relevant for our study. In the empirical analysis, we exploit a particular feature of the data to get at the impact of services on the extent of material imports of firms. The *Survey* indicates whether a plant is located in one of three of Ireland's relatively different regions: the capital Dublin, the South, and the rest of the country. In our analysis we investigate how variations in the availability of services across regions, time and/or industry affect the international sourcing intensity of Irish plants, specifically the ratio of off-shored inputs to sales. We rationalize this focus on the local availability of service with the distinguishing characteristics of services: As Oldenski (2010) documents, services are much more dependent on face-to-face contact than manufacturing. Our

5 Görg, Hanley, and Strobl (2008) show, using similar firm-level data, that the level of international sourcing has positive effects on firm productivity. Examining how much firms offshore rather than whether they offshore or not is one way in which our analysis differs from Antras and Helpman (2004). A second difference is that we do not deal with the question of whether the production of materials is done in-house or by independent suppliers. Rather, we focus on the question of how firms procure the services needed for importing materials.

empirical analysis utilizes various estimation strategies to establish the robustness of our results: pooled data, fixed effects, and instrumental variables estimation.

Ireland is singularly fit for studying the questions that we are investigating. First, it is a small open economy with a trade to GDP ratio of over 80% that is widely regarded as a very well-positioned entry point into the European market. Ireland has attracted multiple well-known multinational corporations in electronics, pharmaceuticals, and medical appliances and more recently in services, some of which have chosen it as a base for offshoring.[6] Moreover, in terms of services and service trade Ireland has clearly excelled. In spite of its size, Ireland was, according to the OECD (2009), in absolute terms about the world's ninth largest exporter of services in 2007. Second, Ireland wants to promote itself increasingly as an area that is especially well suited for supply chain management. As a matter of fact, the Irish Development Agency (IDA), which tries to promote Ireland's image abroad, explicitly links Ireland with supply chain management in its publications.[7] Moreover, the Irish success story has been built to a large extent on sectors that should be especially conducive to supporting offshoring in goods: Ireland has an impressive IT sector, and has increasingly been able to attract financial, insurance, R&D and headquarter services.

The rest of the paper is structured as follows. In the next section, we lay out the model. Comparative static effects are derived in section 3. In section 4, we present the empirical model, and in section 5 we describe the data set. The results of our estimation are reported in section 6 and section 7 concludes. A technical appendix, available at the CJE online archive at cje.economics.ca, contains formal proofs and additional robustness checks.

2. The model

In this section, we develop a stylized model in which we integrate the material-input sourcing decision into the Melitz/Ottaviano (2008) model of monopolistic competition and firm heterogeneity.[8] To some extent, we tailor the setup to the data that we have available to test the predictions of the model.

There is a continuum of manufacturing firms selling their finished products in the domestic (Irish or European) market. From the consumers' point of view, these products are differentiated varieties. We index firms by $i \in \Omega$, and assume

6 A good reference on the service discussion in Ireland is *Catching the Wave. A service Strategy for Ireland, Report of the Service Strategy Group, 2008*; http://www.forfas.ie/publications/forfas080912/forfas080912_services _strategy.pdf

7 For a discussion of supply chain management in Ireland, see Sweeney et al. (2008).

8 The model builds also on Raff and Schmitt (2012), who study sourcing decisions of retail firms, and on Bas (2009), who studies the effect of trade barriers in input and final goods markets on production and exporting decisions.

that all consumers share the same quasi-linear utility function:

$$U = \alpha \int_{i\in\Omega} q_i^c di - \frac{1}{2}\beta \int_{i\in\Omega} \left(q_i^c\right)^2 di - \frac{1}{2}\gamma \left(\int_{i\in\Omega} q_i^c di\right)^2 + y, \tag{1}$$

where q_i^c denotes the quantity per capita bought from firm i, and y the consumption of the numeraire good. Parameter β describes the degree of substitutability within the set of different varieties of manufactures, Ω.

Assuming that the demand for the numeraire is positive, and denoting by L the number of consumers and by N the mass of active firms, the market demand faced by firm i can be expressed as a function of the firm's own price, p_i, and the average price in the market, $\bar{p}$:

$$q_i(p_i) \equiv Lq_i^c = \frac{\alpha L}{\gamma N + \beta} - \frac{L}{\beta}p_i + \frac{\gamma N}{\gamma N + \beta}\frac{L}{\beta}\bar{p}. \tag{2}$$

Firms are monopolistically competitive. That is, they take N and $\bar{p}$ as given when deciding on prices. In what follows, we will drop firm subscripts whenever possible.

Labour, the only factor of production, is inelastically supplied and perfectly mobile across sectors. Since the numeraire good is produced by a competitive industry under constant returns and a unit labour requirement of one, the price of labour in the economy is equal to one. All costs can therefore be expressed in terms of labour requirements.

Since we are particularly interested in firms' sourcing decisions, we assume that finished goods are produced using labour (l) and a composite material input (x) according to the Leontief technology $q = \min\{l/c, x\}$, where $1/c$ represents labour productivity.[9] The composite material input (x) combines domestic materials (z) and imported materials (m) according to the CES production function $x = (z^\phi + m^\phi)^{\frac{1}{\phi}}$, where $0 < \phi < 1$. Domestic and imported materials are hence imperfect substitutes, with an elasticity of substitution equal to $\theta = 1/(1 - \phi)$. For simplicity we assume that both z and m are produced using one unit of labour per unit of output, which is tantamount to having prices of z and m equal to one.

Firms first decide whether to enter the market and thus whether to incur the sunk cost F_E. Upon entering, each firm learns its labour productivity $1/c$. We assume that $1/c$ follows a Pareto distribution, so that the cumulative distribution of the marginal labour cost is $G(c) = (c/c_M)^k$, with $k \geq 1$ and support on $[0, c_M]$.

Then follows the decision on what price to charge and how to procure materials. Sourcing materials from abroad requires services of the type described in the introduction. We distinguish two ways in which these services can be provided.

9 The assumption that labour and materials are complements is made for analytical convenience. Our results would go through even if labour and materials were substitutes, provided that the elasticity of substitution is not too big.

Firms can either buy services from local service providers or they can instead choose to provide these services themselves or buy them from abroad. When a firm takes the first option and buys services from local service providers, we refer to these firms as mode-D firms. In this case, we assume that the margin paid to local service firms is $\delta - 1$ per unit of imported materials with $\delta > 1$. Since imported materials trade at a price of unity, the gross price of imported materials in mode-D (including the service margin) is δ. In the empirical section, we will take mode-D firms as the benchmark case against which we will evaluate mode-I firms, that is, firms that provide services internally or import them from abroad. We will use a measure of local services availability to proxy for the service margin $\delta - 1$. The idea is that a greater availability of local services leads to lower service prices and greater service variety, which implicitly reduces the cost of using local service providers.[10]

A firm that chooses mode I incurs a fixed cost, F_I, associated with operating an own service department, or with identifying and communicating with foreign service providers. Incurring this fixed cost, however, means that the margin on service purchases is reduced below $\delta - 1$; for simplicity, we normalize this margin to zero, so that imported materials in mode I carry a gross unit price of one. Mode D is hence associated with a higher variable cost than mode I. A trade-off occurs in the choice of mode because mode I involves a fixed cost.

Cost minimization by a manufacturer implies the following conditional demands for imported materials depending on the sourcing mode:

$$m^D(q) = \delta^{\frac{1}{\phi-1}} \left(1 + \delta^{\frac{\phi}{\phi-1}}\right)^{-\frac{1}{\phi}} q \tag{3}$$

$$m^I(q) = (2)^{-\frac{1}{\phi}} q. \tag{4}$$

The total cost of materials is hence given by

$$C^D(q) = \Delta_D q \tag{5}$$

$$C^I(q) = \Delta_I q + F_I, \tag{6}$$

where $\Delta_D \equiv (1 + \delta^{\frac{\phi}{\phi-1}})^{\frac{\phi-1}{\phi}}$ and $\Delta_I \equiv (2)^{\frac{\phi-1}{\phi}}$ represent the variable costs of materials under the two modes, and $\Delta_D > \Delta_I$.

A firm that uses mode $j = D, I$ then sets its price to maximize $(p - c)q(p) - C^j(q)$. Defining $c_D \equiv \frac{\beta\alpha + \gamma N\bar{p}}{\gamma N + \beta} - \Delta_D$, we can use (2) to show that the price elasticity

10 The motivation for choosing firms that use services locally as a benchmark is entirely pragmatic. It is much harder to observe and measure internally provided services, as well as measure the complete set of internationally available services.

of demand is given by

$$\eta \equiv -\frac{dq(p)}{dp}\frac{p}{q} = \frac{p}{c_D + \Delta_D - p}. \tag{7}$$

The profit-maximizing price of a firm with marginal labour cost c choosing mode D, respectively I, is hence given by

$$p^D(c) = \Delta_D + \frac{1}{2}(c_D + c) \tag{8}$$

$$p^I(c) = \frac{1}{2}(c_D + c + \Delta_D + \Delta_I). \tag{9}$$

The corresponding maximized profits are

$$\pi^D(c) = \frac{L}{4\beta}(c_D - c)^2 - F_E \tag{10}$$

$$\pi^I(c) = \frac{L}{4\beta}(c_D - c + \Delta_D - \Delta_I)^2 - F_E - F_I. \tag{11}$$

Since the entry cost is sunk, only firms able to cover their marginal labour and material costs and, in case of mode I, the fixed cost F_I are active in the market. (10) indicates that the critical value of the marginal labour cost at which a firm that has chosen mode D earns zero operating profit and hence is indifferent between being active and becoming inactive is c_D. A firm that has chosen mode I has a lower marginal cost of materials than a mode-D firm, as $\Delta_D > \Delta_I$. A comparison of (10) and (11) confirms that mode I yields a higher variable profit than mode D, but also requires an additional fixed outlay of F_I. Mode I is hence only attractive to firms whose output, and hence variable profit, is sufficiently big to allow them to offset F_I. These are the firms that have drawn a sufficiently high labour productivity, $1/c$. By equating $\pi^D(c)$ and $\pi^I(c)$, we can derive the critical value of the marginal labour cost, denoted by c_I, at which a firm is indifferent between modes D and I:

$$c_I = c_D + \frac{(\Delta_D - \Delta_I)}{2} - \frac{2\beta F_I}{L(\Delta_D - \Delta_I)}. \tag{12}$$

In order to make sure that not all entrants prefer mode I to mode D we have to assume that F_I is sufficiently large. On the other hand, we do not want F_I to be too large so that not even the most efficient firm (with $c = 0$) would choose mode

I. Hence, we assume

$$\frac{L}{4\beta}(\Delta_D - \Delta_I)^2 < F_I < \frac{L}{4\beta}((\Delta_D - \Delta_I)^2 + 2c_D(\Delta_D - \Delta_I)). \tag{13}$$

This assumption, together with the quadratic form of the profit functions, ensures that the value of c_I solving (12) is unique and lies strictly between zero and c_D. The two cut-off values of the marginal cost, c_D and c_I, thus define three categories of firms. Firms whose labour productivity is sufficiently high ($c \leq c_I$) choose mode I; firms whose labour productivity is in the middle range ($c_I < c \leq c_D$) opt for mode D; and firms with very low labour productivity ($c > c_D$) are inactive because they are not able to cover their marginal costs. Note that this classification of firms is quite intuitive. Stylized facts confirm, for example, that larger firms, such as multinationals, tend to be more productive firms. At the same time, they are more likely to provide company-wide internal services, and they are also known to import more services.

Finally, in equilibrium the mass of entrants has to be large enough so that the expected profit of a firm at the entry stage is equal to zero:

$$\int_0^{c_I} \pi^I(c)dG(c) + \int_{c_I}^{c_D} \pi^D(c)dG(c) + \int_{c_D}^{c_M} (-F_E)dG(c) = 0. \tag{14}$$

In the next section we explore the equilibrium of the model, focusing on those comparative static effects that allow us to formulate testable hypotheses.

3. Comparative statics

We are interested in understanding the variation in international sourcing across firms and, in particular, in figuring out how this variation is related to differences in local services availability (and thus the size of local service margins) and to firm characteristics. The variables that we observe at the firm level include the spending by a firm on domestic materials (z), the spending on imported materials (m), the value of the firm's sales (pq), and the status of a firm as either a multinational or a national firm. We can thus investigate directly how, in equilibrium, the ratio of imported materials to sales ($m/(pq)$) changes with δ as well as with the firm's labour productivity, $1/c$. In the empirical implementation we will proxy for mode-D firms with domestic firms and, by construction, equate mode-I firms with multinationals, which is why we also want to investigate how the imported materials ratio varies by mode. A formal proof of the results is relegated to the technical appendix.

Consider first the effect of a marginal change in δ. A mode-D firm's ratio of imported materials to sales can be computed using (3) and (8):

$$\frac{m^D}{p^D q^D} = \frac{\delta^{\frac{1}{\phi-1}}\left(1+\delta^{\frac{\phi}{\phi-1}}\right)^{-\frac{1}{\phi}}}{\Delta_D + \frac{1}{2}(c_D + c)}. \tag{15}$$

The numerator of (15) corresponds to m^D/q^D, and it is easily verified that $d(m^D/q^D)/d\delta < 0$, as an increase in δ leads to a substitution of domestic materials, z, for imported materials, m. The denominator of (15) represents p^D. A marginal increase in δ raises p^D in two ways, namely, by raising the marginal cost of materials, Δ_D, and by lowering the price elasticity of demand, η. The effect on η works through changes in c_D and Δ_D, as can be seen in (7). First, a higher δ implies a lower c_D, which boosts η. The reason why an increase in δ decreases c_D is that it lowers the profits of mode-D firms, thus forcing the least efficient mode-D firms to become inactive. Second, a rise in δ increases Δ_D, which reduces η. This second effect dominates the first, so that $d\eta/d\delta < 0$.

As $dp^D/d\delta > 0$ and $d(m^D/q^D)/d\delta < 0$, we have $d(m^D/(p^D q^D))/d\delta < 0$. Thus, a marginal increase in the cost of local services reduces material imports of mode-D firms relative to their sales. We now compare this outcome with the effect of a marginal increase in the cost of local services on the material imports of mode-I firms.

In the case of mode-I firms, we can use (4) and (9) to obtain

$$\frac{m^I}{p^I q^I} = \frac{(2)^{-\frac{1}{\phi}}}{\frac{1}{2}(c_D + c + \Delta_D + \Delta_I)}. \tag{16}$$

Obviously, the numerator, m^I/q^I, does not depend on δ. But a rise in δ affects mode-I firms indirectly, since, as shown above, it decreases the price elasticity of demand, η, and thus induces them to raise p^I. As a result, $d(m^I/(p^I q^I))/d\delta < 0$, so that a marginal increase in the cost of local services also implies a smaller ratio of imported materials to sales for mode-I firms. Mode-I firms should, of course, be less affected by changes in δ than mode-D firms, because their cost of material imports is independent of δ, and because the price response of mode-I firms is smaller: $dp^I/d\delta < dp^D/d\delta$. After all, mode-$I$ firms raise prices only in reaction to the decrease in the demand elasticity, whereas mode-D firms also raise prices because they experience an increase in the marginal cost of imported materials. A sufficient condition for $m^I/(p^I q^I)$ to react less to a change in δ than $m^D/(p^D q^D)$ is for δ to be sufficiently close to 1. For reference, with CES preferences, as, for example, in Antras and Helpman (2004), prices and outputs of mode-I firms would be a constant mark-up over their own marginal cost and hence would not react to changes in δ at all. In sum, we expect both types of firm to be affected by changes in δ,but mode-D firms more so than mode-I firms. This is a prediction we can test empirically.

Next, consider how the ratio of imported materials to sales depends on labour productivity, $1/c$. Since $m^I/q^I > m^D/q^D$ and $p^I < p^D$, it has to be the case that $m^I/(p^I q^I) > m^D/(p^D q^D)$. Given that mode-$I$ firms have strictly greater labour productivity than mode-D firms, it follows directly that firms with a higher labour productivity import more materials relative to sales than firms with low labour productivity, which we can check empirically. This prediction can be refined still further, since, even within each mode, firms with lower labour productivity (higher c) will set higher prices than more productive firms; that is, $d(m^D/(p^D q^D))/dc < 0$ and $d(m^I/(p^I q^I))/dc < 0$. Hence, the ratio of material imports to sales unambiguously rises with the firm's labour productivity, which we can also investigate in our empirical analysis.

Lastly, notice that a change in δ affects c_I. In particular, a fall in the cost of locally provided services raises c_I and hence induces some mode-I firms to switch to mode D. This also implies that mode-I firms will have a greater labour productivity premium over mode-D firms the lower is the cost of local services.

4. Empirical model

We now turn to the empirical investigation. As pointed out in the previous section, we do not directly observe the cost of services, δ, in our data. Instead, we use a measure of the availability of local services as a proxy. The reasoning for this proxy is that a greater availability of locally available services implies lower prices and greater service variety, which implicitly reduces the cost of using local service providers.

The aim is to investigate how the international sourcing of firms is influenced by the availability of services and firm productivity. To do so we estimate variants of the following empirical model based on the theoretical ideas developed in the previous sections:

$$\ln(m/(pq))_{it} = \ln(services)_{jrt}\beta_1 + LP_{it}\beta_2 + X_{it}\beta_3 + d_t + d_j + d_r + \epsilon_{it},$$

where $m/(pq)$ is the ratio of imported materials over sales for manufacturing plant i at time t, and *services* is a vector of variables capturing the availability of services in industry j and region r in which plant i operates.[11] LP is labour productivity (calculated as total wage bill per employee).[12] X is a vector of control variables to account for heterogeneity at the plant, industry, and regional levels. We also include a full set of time, 3-digit industry and region dummies (d_t, d_j, d_r, respectively), while ϵ_{it} denotes the final error term.

11 In order to avoid taking the log of zero, the variable is calculated as $\ln((m/pq) + 1)$. The same goes for all other logged variables in the empirical model.

12 Unfortunately, we do not have capital stock or investment data, so we cannot estimate production functions to calculate total factor productivity.

We calculate for our baseline estimation the number of services firms located in region r at time t as the measure of the availability of local services. This is a proxy for the pool of service providers in the region in which plant i is located and to which it has easy access in the domestic economy. Note that this variable has no variation across the industry dimension for different is, as this represents the total availability of services for all firms in manufacturing industries. Hence, the implicit assumption is that all manufacturing firms in the region have access to, and use in the same intensity, the same pool of services providers.

In order to show that the lack of variation along the industry dimension does not pose a problem for our econometric analysis, we also calculate an alternative measure that varies across industries, based on input-output linkages between manufacturing and services sectors. Utilizing plant-level information on the location and 2-digit sector of services firms we are able to calculate for each region r the number of services firms in service sector s, n_s. From the Irish input-output table for 2000, we use the input coefficients a_{js}, which give us the amount of inputs from service sector s used in manufacturing industry j as percentage of output of industry j.

Our alternative measure is then calculated as an 'effective services availability,'

$$effective\_services_{jrt} = \left(\sum_s a_{js} * n_{st}\right) / n_{mt}.$$

We scale this variable using the number of manufacturing firms in region r, n_m.[13]

In the baseline model, we include a number of control variables at the firm level in order to be able to properly identify the effect of services availability on material imports. We control for plant size (measured in terms of employment) as well as dummy variables for exporters, foreign multinationals, and domestic multinationals in our sample. These variables control for aspects of plant-level heterogeneity that have been highlighted in the recent theoretical and empirical literature.[14] The information on multinationals, however, also allows us to link our analysis back to the theoretical model, which shows that there are differences in the importance of local services availability for mode-I and -D firms. In other words, the coefficient β_1 is likely to differ for mode-I and mode-D firms. Multinationals are more likely to internalize service provision within their company structure. In addition, they are also the ones that most heavily rely on imported services. Therefore, multinationals are likely to be mode-I firms, and we can

13 In the technical appendix we present some summary statistics on the variation of the effective availability measure within and across regions. We see that, as is true for the standard thickness measure, Dublin has the highest values and BMW the lowest. There is also substantial variation within regions, as indicated by the standard deviation.

14 In extensions to our baseline model below, we also include further observable region-, time-, and industry-varying covariates in addition to a battery of fixed effects in order to aid identification of the coefficients on the services measures and address endogeneity concerns.

compare their sourcing behaviour and its sensitivity to changes in the availability of local services with that of national firms.

Note that we also include a whole battery of dummies. Time dummies should capture the effect of time-varying factors, such as, for example, changing factor prices, on firms' sourcing behaviour. The inclusion of regional and industry dummies is essential to control for systematic differences in sourcing behaviour that are related to the different production processes in various industries or regions. In addition, these dummies allow us to address some concerns about endogeneity of services availability. For example, firms may decide to locate in regions in which there are many firms in order to benefit from agglomeration economies. This would potentially introduce a correlation between the services measures and the error term. In short panels such as ours, where the location of firms does not change over time, it is a reasonable assumption that we can proxy this unobserved part of the error term using time-invariant regional dummies. To be on the safe side, we also include a set of time-varying regional variables. A similar argument could be made for unobserved effects at the industry level. If certain industries use services heavily, and if this is not fully captured by our time-varying industry variables, then this may lead to an endogeneity problem. Since, in our data, no firm switches industries, this is captured using the industry dummies.

In the first instance, we estimate our baseline model using simple OLS, allowing the error term to be clustered at the regional level, as our key variable of interest varies only at the regional level. This estimation technique allows us to utilize both the cross-section as well as time variation in our data. However, as a downside, it does not control adequately for plant-specific time-invariant unobserved effects. In order to control for such effects, we also estimate the model using a fixed-effects estimator. This has the additional advantage that the plant fixed effect also allows us to control further for potential endogeneity problems in the empirical model. If there are common factors at the plant level that drive the left- as well as right-side variables in the model, these will be taken care of, as long as they are assumed to be time invariant. We also relax this assumption and estimate the model using an instrumental variables approach.

5. Description of the data

We use recent plant-level data from the Republic of Ireland. These data are collected by Forfás, the Irish policy and advisory board with responsibility for enterprise, trade, science, and technology. Specifically, our data source is the *Annual Business Survey of Economic Impact* (ABSEI), covering the period 2000 until 2004. This is an annual survey of plants with at least 10 employees, although a plant, once it is included, is generally still surveyed even if its employment level falls below the 10-employee cut-off. The survey includes plants in manufacturing as well as services. In terms of services, the focus is on internationally tradeable services; firms in other services industries are neglected.

In particular, the focus is on NACE sectors 72 (computing services) and 74 (business services). These non-financial services are directly relevant for our analysis. They include a wide range of professional business services, including management consultancy, market research, and technical services such as engineering, hardware and software consulting. In 2004, out of 538 service-sector firms in the total sample, roughly 82% were in NACE sectors 72 and 74.

The data set provides information at the plant level on materials and services purchases, distinguishing imported and domestically procured materials and services.[15] Further data available from this source that are relevant to the current paper are total sales, employment, exports, nationality of ownership, 3-digit sector of production, and region of location. Within Ireland, a relatively small country, three regions are distinguished: Greater Dublin (the capital), South West & South East, and Borders/Midlands/West (BMW). There is substantial heterogeneity in economic development across these three regions, with most of economic activity concentrated in Dublin; the South is also fairly well developed, while there is less manufacturing industry in the BMW region.

The information on nationality of ownership allows us to establish whether a plant is an affiliate of a foreign-owned multinational. This information is recorded as a binary variable indicating whether a plant is under majority ownership of a foreign owner or not. The recent literature has highlighted that identifying foreign multinationals is only one part of the picture. In order to have a complete idea about the importance of multinationals, domestic firms with affiliates abroad also need to be recognized. In 2000, Forfás, as part of the ABSEI survey, also asked firms whether they had affiliates abroad. We use this unique information and classify those domestic firms that have affiliates abroad as domestic multinationals.[16]

In 2004, our sample contains 1,206 manufacturing plants. Of these, 343 are affiliates of foreign multinationals, 108 are domestic multinationals, 557 are domestic exporters, and 198 are domestic without exports or foreign affiliates.

Table 1 describes the development of material imports over sales, and the main measure of local services availability, on aggregate over the time period covered in our sample. On average, Irish plants import intermediates worth about 20% of sales, and there are about 150 services providers in the average region. On aggregate, these figures have not changed much over the five-year period.

15 Unfortunately, however, we do not know what type of materials or service are purchased.

16 Girma, Görg, and Strobl (2004) use this data to investigate productivity differentials between domestic multinationals, exporters, and purely domestic firms. To the best of our knowledge, there are no other studies that have been able to identify domestic multinationals in Ireland in large micro-level data sets. In the technical appendix we report descriptive regressions, which show that there are productivity and size premia for exporters and multinationals, as would be expected from the firm-level heterogeneity literature. We also find that exporters and multinationals have higher material import ratios. This is consistent with our theoretical model, which predicts that this ratio should be higher for high-productivity establishments.

TABLE 1
Development of (imported materials/sales) and service availability measure over time

Year	Imported materials/sales		Services firm availability	
	Mean	Std. dev.	Mean	Std. dev.
2000	0.212	0.147	135.23	1.71
2001	0.200	0.151	150.96	1.77
2002	0.188	0.149	163.20	1.73
2003	0.181	0.147	175.21	1.68
2004	0.190	0.146	149.16	1.64

NOTES: Services firm availability is defined as number of services firms in region r at time t.

TABLE 2
Summary statistics across regions, 2004

Region	Dublin	South West & East	Borders/Midlands/West
Imported materials/sales	0.182	0.210	0.200
	(0.172)	(0.178)	(0.169)
# of services firms	289	174	75
# of MNC services firms	72	64	20
# of domestic services firms	217	110	55
# of manufacturing firms	242	586	378
Services sales/total regional sales	0.458	0.116	0.078
Services employment/total regional employment	0.478	0.136	0.137

NOTES: Table reports means and standard deviations in parentheses. Imported materials/sales is defined as total value of imported materials over total value of sales.

However, the aggregate figures hide substantial heterogeneity across industries and plants, as indicated by the high standard deviation.

Table 2 provides some evidence on regional variations in our main variables of interest in 2004. While firms have on average imported material intensities of around 20%, there is variation across regions in this variable. In particular, the import share is lowest in the Dublin region, which is the region with the highest number of services firms. At the same time, it is the smallest region in terms of manufacturing firms. In order to investigate the link between imported materials and services at the firm level, it therefore appears necessary to control for such differences in regional characteristics.

Table 2 also illustrates the relative importance of services compared with manufacturing. In particular, in the Dublin region services firms slightly outnumber manufacturing firms. These services activities contribute to just under half of regional sales and employment. However, this is different in the two other regions. There are about three times as many manufacturing firms as services firms, and these services firms contribute to around 10% of sales and 13% of employment in both regions.

TABLE 3
Variation of (imported materials/sales) and service availability measure over sectors, year 2004

NACE description	Imported materials/sales		Services firm availability	
	Mean	Std. dev.	Mean	Std. dev.
Food & beverages	0.119	0.128	151.11	1.69
Tobacco	0.189	0.144	129.15	2.03
Textiles	0.264	0.134	128.38	1.71
Apparel	0.273	0.131	159.49	1.82
Leather	0.221	0.126	123.72	1.82
Wood products	0.152	0.140	115.12	1.65
Pulp & paper	0.226	0.163	199.94	1.68
Publishing & printing	0.143	0.135	222.29	1.69
Coke & petrol	0.232	0.071	75.19	1.09
Chemicals	0.238	0.142	184.56	1.64
Rubber & plastic	0.243	0.151	135.10	1.71
Non-metallic minerals	0.144	0.128	141.74	1.73
Basic metals	0.203	0.182	161.42	1.59
Fabricated metals	0.180	0.150	157.28	1.65
Machinery	0.208	0.145	149.90	1.67
Office machinery	0.230	0.184	170.89	1.78
Electrical machinery	0.230	0.162	157.43	1.73
Radio & communications	0.224	0.161	177.15	1.62
Medical & optical instruments	0.203	0.133	145.33	1.68
Vehicles	0.265	0.119	124.21	1.57
Other transport equipment	0.258	0.136	215.94	1.60
Other manufacturing	0.186	0.126	146.64	1.79

In table 3, we depict differences across industries. The first columns show means and standard deviations of the imported-materials-to-sales ratio by 2-digit industry for the year 2004. The means range from 12% (NACE 15—Food) to 27% (NACE 34—Transport Equipment). The subsequent columns also show summary statistics for the number of services firms in the region. Again, the statistics show differences across industries and firms. For these summary statistics there is a negative raw pairwise correlation between the ratio of imported materials to sales and the number of services firms. However, the correlation coefficients are not statistically significant. This suggests again that it is important to control for plant-level heterogeneity in order to uncover the relationship between material imports and services availability at the plant level.

6. Empirical results

We now turn to the estimation of our empirical model described in section 4. Table 4 provides results for our baseline model, where the availability of services is calculated using the simple measure of the number of services firms located in region r at time t. The specification also includes time, region and industry

TABLE 4
Baseline model for all firms
Dependent variable: ln (imported materials/sales)

	(1) All	(2) All	(3) All	(4) Irish MNEs	(5) Foreign MNEs	(6) Domestic
Services firm availability	0.129					
	(0.022)**					
Foreign MNC services firm availability		0.043	0.050	0.221	0.043	0.013
		(0.013)*	(0.012)*	(0.095)	(0.005)**	(0.022)
Domestic services firm availability		0.087	0.084	0.082	0.026	0.085
		(0.009)**	(0.009)**	(0.041)	(0.009)	(0.010)**
Labour productivity	0.003	0.003	−0.018	−0.017	−0.049	−0.005
	(0.005)	(0.005)	(0.004)*	(0.034)	(0.014)*	(0.007)
Dummy domestic MNC			0.020			
			(0.002)**			
Dummy foreign MNC			0.051			
			(0.006)**			
Dummy exporter			0.051	0.179	0.047	0.051
			(0.009)**	(0.050)*	(0.038)	(0.006)**
Firm size			0.008	0.030	0.001	0.010
			(0.003)	(0.016)	(0.007)	(0.005)
Observations	5478	5478	5478	466	1527	3485
R-squared	0.16	0.16	0.20	0.38	0.19	0.21

NOTES: Regressions with year, 3-digit industry, and region dummies. Robust standard errors, clustered around regions, are in parentheses. * Significant at 10%; ** significant at 5%. Regressions include constant term. Services firm availability is defined as the number of services firms in region r at time t. Foreign MNC services firm availability and domestic services firm availability are defined as the number of foreign and domestic services firms in region r at time t, respectively.

dummies, and is estimated using OLS. Hence, this estimation approach allows us to use the variation across establishments and time to identify the effect of services availability on the ratio of material imports to sales. Column (1) presents the most basic version of the empirical model, including the measure of the availability of services firms in the same region as plant i. The results show that, when unobserved heterogeneity at the industry and region levels are controlled for, greater services availability is associated with a higher ratio of materials imports to sales by manufacturing establishments. This is in line with our theoretical model, whereby services are needed to facilitate the successful import of materials. While we also find a positive coefficient on labour productivity, as predicted by the model, this is statistically insignificant in the baseline specification.

One aspect we need to take into account is the empirical importance of multinationals also for the provision of services inputs. It could be the case that our results not so much reflect the importance of the domestic provision of services by local firms) as they just pick up the importance of multinationals for linking up firms with suppliers abroad. Our data allow us to look into this in more detail. We calculate our service availability measures separately for domestic establishments and foreign multinationals and include these as separate regressors in the model. The results, reported in column (2), indicate that the availability of domestic providers of services seems more important than the presence of foreign multinational service firms, judging by the size and statistical significance of the two coefficients.

The results in columns (3) to (6) allow us to dig deeper into plant-level heterogeneity. First, we control for establishment status by including dummies for foreign multinationals, Irish multinationals, and exporters. Furthermore, in columns (4) to (6) we run the regression separately for domestic multinationals, foreign multinationals, and domestic plants. These specifications also allow us to investigate whether the effect of services availability differs between mode-*I* and mode-*D* firms. As argued above, multinationals are more likely to internalize service provision within their company structure, and they rely most heavily on imported services. Therefore, multinationals are more likely to be mode-*I* firms, and national firms are likely to be mode-*D* firms.

What is especially noteworthy in the results is that the availability of local service providers matters only for purely domestic establishments. Irish or foreign multinationals, by contrast, are not affected by the presence of domestic services. This is consistent with the theoretical model, assuming that multinationals are more likely to be internalizers of services provision. Moreover, this finding squares well with the observation in the data that of all manufacturing firms, multinationals import services most intensively.[17] Furthermore, there is evidence that foreign multinationals' international sourcing is positively correlated with the availability of services provided by foreign firms. However, this result is not robust to changes in specifications. Once we add firm fixed effects and additional sectoral covariates, this coefficient changes in sign and significance (see tables 6 to 8 below).

We also find that the coefficient on productivity is still statistically insignificant for domestic multinationals and purely domestic firms, but negative and significant for foreign multinationals. However, this result is difficult to interpret, since it may reflect other aspects of plant heterogeneity that are not controlled for. It should also be kept in mind that the coefficient on labour productivity is conditional on other covariates. In particular, the model includes size, which is likely to be correlated with productivity (but does not feature in our theoretical model). Note that size consistently returns a positive coefficient; that is, larger plants have higher ratios of imported materials.

Overall, our baseline results are in line with the theoretical idea that services are needed to 'grease the wheels of international commerce.' In what follows we check how robust our baseline results are to changes in the specification of the

17 The regression results showing this are reported in the technical appendix. Some fraction of the imported intermediates by multinationals will be intra-firm trade. By definition, stand-alone firms are not involved in intra-firm trade. Our data do not allow us to distinguish between intra-firm and arms' length trade of multinationals. However, anecdotal evidence suggests that intra-firm trade is significant for services.

TABLE 5
Baseline model for exporters only
Dependent variable: ln (imported materials/sales)

	(1) All	(2) Irish MNEs	(3) Foreign MNEs	(4) Domestic
Foreign MNC services firm availability	0.056	0.239	0.05	0.019
	(0.009)**	(0.101)	(0.004)***	(0.023)
Domestic services firm availability	0.092	0.090	0.031	0.103
	(0.010)**	(0.038)	(0.006)**	(0.015)**
Labour productivity	−0.025	−0.018	−0.048	−0.009
	(0.001)**	(0.037)	(0.016)*	(0.012)
Dummy domestic MNC	0.025			
	(0.001)**			
Dummy foreign MNC	0.051			
	(0.002)**			
Firm size	0.009	0.033	0.002	0.010
	(0.003)	(0.017)	(0.007)	(0.005)
Observations	4496	454	1469	2573
R-squared	0.19	0.37	0.18	0.22

NOTES: Regressions with year, 3-digit industry, and region dummies. Robust standard errors, clustered around regions, are in parentheses. * Significant at 10%; ** significant at 5%. Regressions include constant term. For a definition of service availability measures see table 4.

model.[18] For instance, the availability of services may affect not only imports of materials but also exports of firms, which is a feature not captured by our theoretical model. In order to take this into account, we include only exporters in our regression sample. In table 5 we replicate table 4 but for exporters. The result indicating the importance of services availability for domestic establishments holds.

One may be worried about endogeneity of our service availability measures, which may bias our results obtained thus far. We attempt to deal with endogeneity in the further analysis. First, as pointed out above, we argue that in a short panel plant fixed effects, which also capture time invariant industry and regional characteristics, take care of this to a large extent. Another concern is that the services measure is region specific and may therefore just pick up any region specific time-varying characteristic. In order to alleviate these concerns, we estimate the model with firm fixed effects and include further time-varying variables at the region and industry level, which may capture any potential correlation between

18 One hypothesis from our theory that we have not considered yet is that (low-productivity) mode-D firms should react more strongly to changes in the availability of services providers than (high productivity) mode-I firms. In order to investigate this empirically, we report in the technical appendix regressions, where we interact the service thickness variables with plant-level labour productivity. While we still find the importance of local services availability for domestic firms, the interaction terms do not turn out-to be statistically significant. The lack of statistical significance either may reflect that our sample splits cover adequately the distinction into I and D firms, or it may signal that we are asking too much of our service variables.

TABLE 6
Extended model with additional covariates, for exporters only
Dependent variable: ln (imported materials/sales)

	(1) Irish MNEs	(2) Foreign MNEs	(3) Domestic
Foreign MNC services firm availability	0.241	−0.088	0.009
	(0.046)**	(0.018)**	(0.016)
Domestic services firm availability	0.098	−0.024	0.103
	(0.069)	(0.014)	(0.006)**
Labour productivity	−0.025	0.016	0.017
	(0.019)	(0.014)	(0.015)
Firm size	−0.033	0.039	0.013
	(0.010)*	(0.011)*	(0.007)
Industry total services intensity	−0.016	0.005	−0.001
	(0.026)	(0.008)	(0.013)
Industry local services intensity	0.164	−0.143	−0.028
	(0.035)**	(0.085)	(0.018)
# of foreign MNC manufacturing firms in region	−0.027	0.003	−0.000
	(0.075)	(0.025)	(0.019)
# of domestic manufacturing firms in region	−0.006	0.011	−0.017
	(0.031)	(0.030)	(0.022)
Region size	0.064	−0.006	0.007
	(0.041)	(0.005)	(0.012)
Observations	454	1469	2573
# of firms	205	482	966
R-squared	0.10	0.05	0.02

NOTES: Regressions with firm fixed effects. R-squared for regression on within transformed variables, any impact of time invariant explanatory variables is purged. Robust standard errors, clustered around regions, in parentheses. * Significant at 10%; ** significant at 5%. Regressions include constant term and year dummies. For a definition of availability measures see table 4.

our services availability measure and the error term. At the regional level, we include the number of manufacturing firms (foreign and domestic) as well as total sales in the region. The former is included in order to address the possibility that the service availability measure just captures general agglomeration effects, which may influence firms' sourcing decisions. The second measure is included in order to capture the size of a region. At the industry level, we control for the service intensity of the industry (value of total services inputs over total sales in the industry) as well as the intensity with which the industry uses locally sourced services (value of locally sourced services over total services inputs). These measures allow us to control for heterogeneity in the use and sourcing of services inputs in different industries.

The results are reported in table 6. Some points are particularly noteworthy. First, the result that the availability of local services firms matters for sourcing decisions of domestic establishments holds. Second, as alluded to above, we now find that the availability of foreign multinational services firms negatively affects the sourcing decisions of foreign multinationals and positively affects those of

TABLE 7
Extended model with effective availability measure, for exporters only
Dependent variable: ln (imported materials/sales)

	(1) Irish MNEs	(2) Foreign MNEs	(3) Domestic
Foreign MNC services firm availability	−0.001	−0.001	0.000
	(0.001)	(0.001)	(0.001)
Domestic services firm availability	0.000	−0.000	0.001
	(0.000)	(0.000)	(0.000)*
Labour productivity	−0.027	0.017	0.017
	(0.019)	(0.014)	(0.015)
Firm size	−0.026	0.039	0.014
	(0.008)*	(0.010)*	(0.007)
Industry total services intensity	−0.021	0.005	−0.000
	(0.024)	(0.009)	(0.015)
Industry local services intensity	0.134	−0.152	−0.027
	(0.027)**	(0.083)	(0.018)
# of foreign MNC manufacturing firms in region	−0.018	0.003	0.005
	(0.065)	(0.026)	(0.021)
# of domestic manufacturing firms in region	0.015	−0.002	−0.007
	(0.024)	(0.027)	(0.023)
Region size	0.072	−0.024	−0.035
	(0.055)	(0.010)	(0.009)*
Observations	454	1469	2573
# of firms	205	482	966
R-squared	0.08	0.05	0.01

NOTES: Regressions with firm fixed effects. R-squared for regression on within transformed variables, any impact of time invariant explanatory variables is purged. Robust standard errors, clustered around regions, in parentheses. * Significant at 10%; ** significant at 5%. Regressions include constant term and year dummies. For a definition of effective availability measures see section 4.

Irish multinationals. However, these effects are not robust to further changes to the model; hence, we do not place much emphasis on them.

The services measure employed thus far varies only across regions and time. In order to deal with this, we use the 'effective service availability' measure described in section 4. It is based on multiplying the number of services firms in a region and 2-digit service sector by the input use coefficient of the 2-digit service in manufacturing industry *j* and summing over region and industry *j*.

Using this alternative measure we re-estimate the empirical model in table 7. The results show a statistically significant and positive coefficient on the the availability of local services for domestic establishments. As before, we do not find any evidence that the availability of local services matters for domestic or foreign multinationals in Ireland. Furthermore, the coefficients on the availability of services provided by foreign multinationals are now statistically insignificant.

Arguably, the inclusion of plant fixed effects as well as of a number of time-varying firm, industry, and regional variables is likely to be sufficient to alleviate endogeneity concerns, especially in our short panel. Still, we proceed further and test whether, conditional on the inclusion of all these covariates, the service availability measures are likely to be endogenous in our empirical model. To do so, we re-estimate the models presented in table 7 using an IV estimator. Our main excluded instrument is an annual regional house price index for Ireland.[19] We use the lag of this variable as instrument. This can be assumed to be highly correlated with the availability of services (i.e., be a relevant instrument), considering that services firms may be responsive in their location decisions to the cost of buying or renting premises. Hence, we expect a negative correlation between availability of services and the house price index. On the other hand, we may assume this to be a valid instrument in that it is unlikely to be correlated with the error term in the estimating equation. In other words, the lagged average house price in a region is unlikely to have a direct effect on sourcing at the firm level, conditional on the covariates included in the empirical model. In order to aid identification we also include two further instruments, namely, the interaction of the lagged house price index with the lagged dependent variable. Assuming validity of the lagged house price index, we can test orthogonality of these additional two instruments using a Sargan test. The estimations are reported in table 8. Note that the overidentification tests suggest that these are valid instruments, while the first stage F-tests suggest strongly that they are also relevant.[20] The results support our earlier findings on the importance of services availability for domestic firms only.[21]

7. Conclusion

It is a well-known fact that most developed countries are, to a large extent, service economies. Only a small percent of their labour force is employed in agriculture, some 20% to 30% work in manufacturing, and the rest, between 60% and 70% work in services. Still, the vast majority of international trade is in goods, not services. These basic facts beg the question of how international goods trade can be linked to services and whether services grease the wheels of international commerce.

There are various ways in which international trade and services are linked. We chose to focus on the sourcing behaviour of firms in the ongoing process of

19 The annual regional house price index data are available at http://www.esri.ie/irish_economy/permanent_tsbesri_house_p/ (accessed 26 October 2010). Note that the index distinguishes only two regions, Dublin and outside Dublin. Hence, the interaction terms add additional variation to the instrument set.

20 The first-stage results (not reported here to save space) also show that the three instrumental variables candidates are individually highly statistically significant. There is a negative correlation between changes in house prices and domestic services firms, and a positive correlation for the number of foreign services firms. Note also that the endogeneity tests do not allow us to reject the null hypothesis of exogeneity of regressors in two out of three cases.

21 In the technical appendix we present IV estimations using the simple measure of services availability used in tables 4 to 6. The results are similar to those presented in table 8.

TABLE 8
Instrumental variables estimation with effective availability measure, for exporters only
Dependent variable: ln (imported materials/sales)

	(1) Irish MNEs	(2) Foreign MNEs	(3) Domestic
Foreign MNC services firm availability	0.007	0.000	−0.002
	(0.003)**	(0.001)	(0.001)
Domestic services firm availability	0.000	−0.001	0.001
	(0.001)	(0.000)*	(0.000)*
Labour productivity	−0.036	−0.063	−0.014
	(0.023)	(0.013)**	(0.009)
Firm size	0.029	0.003	0.014
	(0.008)**	(0.004)	(0.003)**
Industry total services intensity	−0.022	−0.015	−0.023
	(0.055)	(0.022)	(0.022)
Industry local services intensity	0.068	−0.122	0.058
	(0.219)	(0.114)	(0.100)
# of foreign MNC manufacturing firms in region	−0.087	−0.004	−0.011
	(0.026)**	(0.021)	(0.010)
# of domestic manufacturing firms in region	−0.094	0.063	−0.012
	(0.029)**	(0.020)**	(0.012)
Region size	0.120	0.009	0.005
	(0.134)	(0.076)	(0.056)
Observations	306	987	1644
First-stage Shea Partial R2 (Foreign MNC services firm availability)	0.55	0.61	0.58
First-stage Shea Partial R2 (Domestic services firm availability)	0.36	0.50	0.49
Sargan (p-value)	0.27	0.10	0.05
Endogeneity (p-value)	0.14	0.65	0.91

NOTES: IV regressions. Services firm availability is endogenous variables. Instruments are lagged regional house price index and interaction of lagged house price index with lagged endogenous variable. Standard errors are in parentheses. * Significant at 10%; ** significant at 5%. Regressions include constant term, 3 digit industry, regional and year dummies. For a definition of effective availability measures see section 4.

fragmentation of production and to investigate the extent to which services facilitate this process. We specifically examined what effect services have on offshoring in manufacturing at the micro-level. With firm-level data from the Republic of Ireland we have shown that the availability of local services induces manufacturing firms to source more material inputs from abroad, which confirms the basic intuition that services should grease the wheels of international commerce. We found, however, that the availability of local services matters, especially for purely domestic firms. This finding is robust to a number of estimation techniques, in particular controlling for endogeneity of the services measures. Our result is quite intuitive and of particular interest. It indicates that firms, such as non-multinationals, that are too small or inefficient to internalize the provision of services or to attract services from abroad will depend more clearly on local service market conditions. Our finding thus brings together the earlier hypotheses on the impact of services on offshoring and the theory of the multinational, since multinationals, by definition, internalize some company-wide services through the headquarter services they provide and since affiliates of multinationals can easily draw on these services from afar.

In a way, it could be argued that our current approach looks only at one side of the service-sourcing link. It is true that we consciously only look at the side of the service-sourcing link that, from an empirical point of view, is most easily observable. Indeed, we establish that services matter for firms by looking at the local market and by showing that local services affect non-multinational firms that are very dependent on local conditions. Our finding that these local services do not matter much for multinationals' offshoring behaviour does not imply that services as such are not important for multinationals. On the contrary, only because multinationals internalize services and only because they can draw more easily on foreign services are local service conditions not all that critical for them. It would be nice to directly tackle the link between services and offshoring from the angle of the multinationals themselves and the total (international) services that they face, especially since multinationals tend to be larger and more important for international trade. Needless to say, however, with multinationals' services spread all over the globe, this is, from an empirical perspective, an almost impossible task given the current data availability.

References

Antras, Pol, and Elhanan Helpman (2004) 'Global sourcing,' *Journal of Political Economy* 112, 552–80

Bas, Maria (2009) 'Trade, foreign inputs and firms' decisions: theory and evidence,' CEPII Working Paper 2009-35

Corbett, Michael (2004) *The Outsourcing Revolution: Why It Makes Sense and How To Do It Right*. Dearborn Trade Publishing

Deardorff, Alan (2001) 'The international provision of trade services, trade and fragmentation,' *Review of International Economics* 9, 233–48

Dedrick, Jason, Kenneth L. Kraemer, and Greg Linden (2010) 'Who profits from innovation in global value chains? A study of the iPod and notebook PCs,' *Industrial and Corporate Change* 19, 81–116

Francois, Joseph (1990) 'Trade in producer services and returns due to specialization under monopolistic competition,' *Canadian Journal of Economics* 23, 109–24

Francois, Joseph, and Bernard Hoekman (2010) 'Services trade and policy,' *Journal of Economic Literature* 48, 642–92

Gachon, Gerard, and Christina Terwiesch (2009) *Matching Supply and Demand: An Introduction to Operations Management*. McGraw-Hill

Girma, Sourafel, Holger Görg, and Eric Strobl (2004) 'Exports, international investment, and plant performance: evidence from a non-parametric test,' *Economics Letters* 83, 317–24

Golub, Stephen, Ronald Jones, and Henryk Kierzkowski (2007) 'Globalization and country-specific service links,' *Journal of Economic Policy Reform* 10, 63–88

Görg, Holger, Aoife Hanley, and Eric Strobl (2008) 'Productivity effects of international outsourcing: evidence from plant level data,' *Canadian Journal of Economics* 41, 670–88
Helpman, Elhanan (2006) 'Trade, FDI and the organization of the firm,' *Journal of Economic Literature* 44, 589–630
Hummels, David L., Jun Ishii, and Kei-Mu Yi (2001) 'The nature of growth of vertical specialization in world trade,' *Journal of International Economics* 54, 75–96
Jones, Ronald, and Henryk Kierzkowski (1990) 'The role of services in production and international trade: a theoretical framework.' In *The Political Economy of International Trade: Essays in Honor of Robert E. Baldwin*, ed. R. Jones and A. Krueger. Cambridge, MA: Blackwell
Long, Ngo V., Raymond Riezman, and Antoine Soubeyran (2005) 'Fragmentation and services,' *North American Journal of Economics and Finance* 16, 137–52
Melitz, Marc J., and Gianmarco I.P. Ottaviano (2008) 'Market size, trade and productivity,' *Review of Economic Studies* 75, 295–316
OECD (2009) *OECD Factbook: Economic, Environmental and Social Statistics.* Paris: OECD
Oldenski, Lindsay (2010) 'Export versus FDI: a task-based approach,' Mimeo, Georgetown University
Raff, Horst, and Nicolas Schmitt (2012) 'Imports and the structure of retail markets,' *Canadian Journal of Economics* 45, 431–55
Sweeney, Eric, Claudia-Maria Wagner, and Bernd Huber (2008) 'Supply chain management diffusion among firms in the Republic of Ireland,' *International Journal of Logistics: Research and Applications* 11, 347–58
Yi, Kei-Mu (2003) 'Can vertical specialization explain the growth of world trade?' *Journal of Political Economy* 111, 52–102

Chapter I.2

Availability of Business Services and Outward Investment: Evidence from French Firms

*Holger Görg and Liza Jabbour**

Abstract

This paper considers the link between the local availability of services in a home country and a firm's decision to become a multinational. This is a highly topical issue, given that many industrialized countries are increasingly becoming service economies and firms become increasingly more globalized. In an analysis of rich firm level data for France we find evidence that the availability of services in the home country indeed has a positive impact on firms' decisions to become multinationals. This is robust to endogeneity concerns. The result can be interpreted in a simple set-up where the local availability of business services improves firm efficiency and, hence, allows firms to overcome sunk costs of investing abroad more easily.

1. Introduction

It is well known that most developed countries are increasingly becoming service economies. For example, Francois and Hoekman (2010) show that services have increased between 1977 and 2007 as a fraction of gross domestic product (GDP) from 58% to 74% for high-income Organisation for Economic Co-operation and Development (OECD) countries, and from 55% to 70% for the world as a whole. Still, research in the international trade literature has only started to investigate the potential interconnectedness between services and manufacturing.

At the firm level, it is apparent that firms classified as manufacturers also produce and export services (Breinlich and Criscuolo, 2011; Hijzen et al., 2011b; Kelle, 2013; Malchow-Møller et al., 2015). There are also links between manufacturing and services at the sectoral level. For example, Arnold et al. (2011) show that trade liberalization in the services sector has positive effects on productivity growth in manufacturing firms, while Breinlich et al. (2014) show that trade liberalization in manufacturing leads manufacturing firms to switch into producing services. Fernandes and Paunov (2012) investigate the positive links between foreign direct investment (FDI) in the services sector and manufacturing productivity. Most closely related to our paper, Debaere et al. (2013) argue and provide evidence that services play an important role for the international sourcing activities of manufacturing firms. The better the availability of services in the local economy (such as transportation, finance, or insurance) the higher a firm's engagement in international sourcing of inputs.

---

* Görg: Kiel Institute for the World Economy, University of Kiel, Kiellinie 66, 24105 Kiel, Germany. E-mail: holger.goerg@ifw-kiel.de. Jabbour: Birmingham Business School, University of Birmingham, University House, Birmingham, B15 2TT, UK. Görg is also affiliated with the Tuborg Centre for Globalisation and Firms at Aarhus University, Jabbour with the Kiel Institute for the World Economy, and both authors with the Globalisation and Economic Policy Centre (GEP) at the University of Nottingham. We are grateful to Ron Davies, Aoife Hanley, Frances Ruane, Dan Trefler, participants at the Festschrift workshop in Nottingham, the joint Kiel Institute/World Bank workshop on Trade in Services in Washington DC, and seminars at the University of Tübingen, University College Dublin and ESRI Dublin for very helpful comments.

In this paper we contribute further to this growing literature. We study whether the availability of local services in the home country is important for a firm's decision to open affiliates abroad and become a multinational. In doing so we bring together two strands of literature. On the one hand, there are papers that look at firms' decisions to engage in international activities and, more specifically, to become a multinational, in the framework of models of trade with heterogeneous firms (Helpman, 2006; Greenaway and Kneller, 2007). On the other hand, there is a new economic geography literature that looks at the location of headquarter activities, showing that availability of services play an important role (e.g. Henderson and Ono, 2008; Davis and Henderson, 2008; Strauss-Kahn and Vives, 2009).

We combine insights from these two, largely separate, strands of literature in our empirical analysis of comprehensive French firm level data. We investigate empirically the importance of the availability of local services in the home country for the probability of a domestic firm becoming a multinational, i.e. starting to open up affiliates abroad.[1]

The theoretical motivation for our empirical work is as follows. From the literature on heterogeneous firms we know that operations abroad involve substantial sunk costs. Combined with some aspect of firm heterogeneity (usually in terms of productivity or size), this implies that only a certain set of firms will choose to operate abroad and become a multinational (e.g. Helpman et al., 2004). The sunk costs of investing abroad are largely related to services, more specifically business services. There are costs of market research, communication costs between foreign affiliate and headquarters, legal costs for contracting, etc. Hence, firms deciding whether to become multinational or not, need access to business services firms that specialize in these activities.[2]

Assume that firms are final good producers, using business services as inputs. In a Dixit–Stiglitz world, a greater local provision of services, implying a larger variety of services inputs, improves efficiency of the final good producer using these services as inputs. The local provision is important as services require face-to-face contact and customer interaction. This is the mechanism identified in the new economic geography literature on the importance of services for headquarter locations (e.g. Davis and Henderson, 2008).

Adapted to our purposes this mechanism implies that the local availability of business services, improving firm efficiency, allows firms to overcome sunk costs of investing abroad more easily. Hence, if we assume two identical firms, one located in an environment with easy access to local business services, and one not, then we would assume that the former firm is more easily able to overcome sunk costs and invest abroad, while the absence of services' providers makes it harder for the latter firm to become a multinational. This is the issue we investigate empirically in the remainder of this paper, using rich firm level data for France.

We are, to the best of our knowledge, the first to look at this. However, the question is not just of academic interest but also addresses an important policy concern. In a globalized economy it is important for firms to be active on international markets in order to improve their competitiveness. We know that only the most productive firms invest abroad (Helpman et al., 2004) and that these firms grow not only abroad but also in their domestic operations (Hijzen et al., 2011a). We also know that developed economies are intensive in the production of services. Hence, the relationship between service activities and firms' ability to become multinationals provide important insights for policy makers.

To preview our results, we find indeed that the local availability of business services in the home country has a positive impact on firms' decisions to invest abroad and become multinationals. We obtain this finding when looking specifically at "new multinationals," i.e. firms that switch status from purely domestic to being a multinational. Furthermore, access to local services is more relevant to smaller domestic parents, suggesting that domestic parent firms that control a large network of domestic affiliates are more likely to internalize the production of their needed business services and may be less reliant on existing suppliers in the market. Our result is robust to dealing with endogeneity in an instrumental variable set-up, where we use information that may explain the formation of a local services sector as instruments.

The remainder of the paper is structured as follows. Section 2 presents the data set and shows some descriptive statistics. Section 3 presents the core of the paper, which is the empirical analysis of the link between local availability of services and a firm's decision to go multinational. Section 4 concludes.

2. Data, Variables and Descriptive Evidence

Our analysis is based on firm level data for France. We combine two data sets at the firm level, namely the *Financial Links Survey* and the *Firm Annual Survey*. In both datasets, each firm is identified with a unique registration code (Code Siren). This code is used to merge the two data sets. Both data sets cover the period 1990–2001.

The Financial Links ("Liaisons Financières") Survey

The data on FDI activities by French firms are extracted from the financial links' survey. This survey provides information on the structure of groups in the French Economy. It is an annual survey carried out by the French National Statistical Office (INSEE). The survey is not exhaustive, it is addressed to firms satisfying at least one of the following criteria: having more than 500 employees, having a value of stocks higher than €1.2 million, being identified as a parent company in the previous year, directly controlled by a foreign company in the previous year, or having a turnover value higher than €30 million.

Each firm, covered by the framework of the survey, has to report the financial links it has with other firms within France or abroad as well as its affiliation to a group. The firm has also to report the identity (unique registration code) and the country of location of all the firms that it directly controls. Moreover, each firm has to report the identity as well as the country of origin of the parent firm.[3]

The financial links survey allows the identification of several categories of firms: single firms, affiliates of a group, parent firms of domestic groups, and parents of multinational groups. For each parent company, it is possible to identify domestic and foreign affiliates. The panel structure of the financial links survey allows tracking the changes in the structure of groups and the identification of new domestic and foreign investments.

The survey also identifies the country of location of foreign affiliates of French multinationals. We use this information to classify countries depending on their links with France and the degree of openness of their business services sector.

The Firm Annual Survey ("Enquête Annuelle D'Entreprises")

We complement the data from the Financial Links Survey with information on firm characteristics extracted from the Firm Annual Survey. This is an exhaustive survey that covers all firms with more than 20 employees in manufacturing and service industries. The survey provides information on the activity of the firm: production, sales, investment, value-added, number of employees, wage bill, etc. The firm annual survey allows the construction of control variables at the firm level, the identification of the industry (four-digit French classification) where the firm mainly operates, and the geographic region where the firm is located.

The combination of the financial links and firm annual surveys results in an unbalanced panel of over 794,000 observations for the period 1990–2001. Table 1 presents the number of observations in each two-digit industry. About a quarter of firms in our sample (23%) is active in the business services sector and almost 14% of firms operate in the operational services sector. The business services sector encompasses activities like accounting, advertising, architecture, market studies, legal services, business consulting, IT services and engineering controls. Operational services encompasses other activities that firms tend to outsource like recruitment and hiring of employees, rental of vehicles and transport equipment, security and cleaning services, etc. For the remainder of the paper we aggregate business services and operational services and refer to them for brevity as "business services."

In the empirical analysis we look at whether the availability of business services plays a role in determining a firms' decision to become a multinational and open affiliates abroad. In our dataset we can distinguish three types of domestic firms:

(1) *Single firms*: domestic firms that are not affiliated to a group and that do not control any domestic or foreign affiliates. A large share (98%) of the firms in our sample correspond to single firms.
(2) *Domestic Parent*: domestic firms that control at least one affiliate, but control exclusively affiliates located within France. In our sample we indentify 2961 Domestic Parent firms.
(3) *Multinational*: French-owned firms that control at least one affiliate located abroad. Our sample contains 923 Multinational Parent firms. Of those, 463 firms are new multinationals, i.e. invested abroad for the first time during the sample period. Of these new multinationals, more than half invest in only one foreign affiliate, at the year of entry, and around 20% establish two foreign affiliates. Very few new multinationals control more than three foreign affiliates.

In the empirical analysis we try to identify an effect of the local availability of business services on multinationals by looking at these "new multinationals" only. In other words, we are interested in what determines a decision of a firm to switch from being purely domestic to becoming a multinational, i.e. opening up affiliates abroad.

The main variable of interest is the local availability of business services in the home country. As argued above, we would expect that, all other things equal, a greater availability of business services locally makes a firm more likely to overcome sunk costs of investing abroad and, hence, establish affiliates abroad. We assume that the benefits that a firm can extract from available business services require certain proximity between firms and providers of business services.

We follow Debaere et al. (2013) and use firm level information on the location of service firms to create a measure of the effective availability of business services in each region r as the number of business service firms, within the same region, multiplied by an input coefficient based on the input–output table for French industries provided by the French Statistical Office (INSEE). The input coefficient α_{js} represents the purchases of inputs from the business services sector s, used by industry j as a share of the total output of industry j. Specifically, our measure is calculated as

Table 1. Distribution of Firms by Industry

	Single firm		Domestic parent		Multinational		New multinational	
Industry (two-digits)	*Obs*	%	*Obs*	%	*Obs*	%	*Obs*	%
Wearing Apparel	23,850	3	137	1.58	79	2.16	17	3.67
Printing and Publishing	20,125	2.53	381	4.39	76	2.08	11	2.38
Pharmaceutical	5,440	0.69	57	0.66	112	3.07	13	2.81
Domestic Appliances	16,696	2.1	129	1.49	155	4.25	22	4.75
Motor Vehicles	5,963	0.75	36	0.41	49	1.34	7	1.51
Other Transport Equipment	3,130	0.39	14	0.16	54	1.48	3	0.65
Machinery and Equipment	41,716	5.25	166	1.91	190	5.21	21	4.54
Computer, Electronic, Optical Products, and Electrical Motors and Generators	12,584	1.58	99	1.14	44	1.21	12	2.59
Mineral Products	13,493	1.7	159	1.83	69	1.89	9	1.94
Textile	16,340	2.06	192	2.21	119	3.26	12	2.59
Wood and Paper	14,654	1.85	120	1.38	52	1.43	9	1.94
Chemicals, Plastic and Rubber	20,729	2.61	168	1.94	199	5.45	27	5.83
Basic Metals and Fabricated Metal Products	39,408	4.96	251	2.89	126	3.45	25	5.4
Electrical Products	8,660	1.09	48	0.55	94	2.58	8	1.73
Coke and Refined Petroleum Products	734	0.09	1	0.01	10	0.27	1	0.22
Water, Gas, and Electricity	1,745	0.22	51	0.59	34	0.93	0	0
Transportation and Storage	8,059	1.01	35	0.4	32	0.88	6	1.3
Financial and Insurance Activities	7,637	0.96	35	0.4	11	0.3	2	0.43
Real Estate Activities	83,213	10.48	798	9.19	91	2.49	14	3.02
Postal, Courier activities, and Telecommunication Activities	4,317	0.54	11	0.13	16	0.44	3	0.65
Business Services	179,852	22.65	4,579	52.74	1,782	48.84	202	43.63
Operational Services	111,883	14.09	562	6.47	150	4.11	23	4.97

Table 1. Continued

Industry (two-digits)	*Single firm*		*Domestic parent*		*Multinational*		*New multinational*	
	Obs	%	*Obs*	%	*Obs*	%	*Obs*	%
Hotels and Restaurants	99,889	12.58	453	5.22	30	0.82	7	1.51
Audiovisual Activities	24,371	3.07	175	2.02	74	2.03	9	1.94
Personal Services	29,615	3.73	25	0.29	1	0.03	0	0
Total	794,103	100	8,682	100	3,649	100	463	100

$$effective\ business\ services_{jrt} = \alpha_{js} * n_{srt}.$$

We follow the French administrative classification of regions and consider that metropolitan France consists of 96 different geographic locations located within 22 provinces.

Before we move on to the empirical estimation, we briefly present descriptive statistics on the characteristics of French new multinationals to relate our data to work on multinationals and heterogeneity. Table 2 presents some summary statistics by firm type on the key variables included in the empirical analysis. It shows, as expected, that multinationals are on average larger and more productive than non-multinationals. We also find that, compared with all multinationals, new multinationals—i.e. firms that started to become multinationals during the sample period—are smaller and less productive.[4]

We analyze further the heterogeneity of new multinationals by estimating the premia of being a new multinational based on several characteristics of the firm. We focus on total factor productivity (estimated using the Olley and Pakes (1996) methodology), output per worker, value-added per worker, scale (number of employees), exports and profits. This analysis corresponds to the estimation of the following equation:

$$Ln\ X_{it} = \beta_1 New\ Multinational_{it} + \beta_2\ LnScale_{it} + f_t + f_j + f_r + \varepsilon$$

where X represents the firm's characteristic, "New Multinational" is a dummy indicating whether the firm is a new multinational at time t and has switched from being a domestic firm to being a multinational at time t or earlier during the sample's time period. f_t, f_j and f_r are time and industry (three-digit) and province fixed effects.

Table 3 shows that French new multinationals are significantly more productive, larger in terms of employment and turnover, more export oriented and more profitable than the remaining categories of French firms.[5] The advantage of new multinationals is robust when we compare firms within the same size, within the same three-digit industry, and within the same geographical province. This is in line with findings for other countries, as in Helpman et al. (2004) and Mayer and Ottaviano (2007).

3. Availability of Business Services and Multinationality

We now turn to analyzing the link between the availability of business services in a firm's region and internationalization through opening up affiliates abroad. More precisely, we investigate whether a higher availability of business services within a region increases the likelihood of outward investment by firms located within the same region.

To start with, Table 4 presents the top five regions, in 2001, in terms of the number of business service firms, the number of multinational parents, and the number of new multinationals. Note that the regions Hauts-de-Seine and Val-de-Marne are suburbs of Paris. The other regions in the list include the largest French cities; Marseille (Bouches-du-Rhone), Lyon (Rhone) and Lille (Nord). The table highlights a co-agglomeration of business service and multinational firms in these locations.

It is not surprising to have an agglomeration of activity around large cities and in regions that have historically hosted a significant share of the production activity of a country. The co-agglomeration between business service firms and multinational

Table 2. Summary Statistics by Type of Firm

	Single			Domestic parent			Multinational			New multinational		
Variable	Obs	Mean	Std. Dev.	Obs	Mean	Std. Dev.	Obs	Mean	Std. Dev.	Obs	Mean	Std. Dev.
Scale	821,529	64.44	653.51	8,456	161.09	524.99	2,079	2,511.29	12,895.77	2,347	312.59	944.37
Labor Productivity	601,149	627.77	7351.5	6,524	1,400.04	7,730.40	1,787	4,202.14	30,416.10	2,006	2,165.42	7,153.34
Output per Worker	601,149	377.1	2,718.22	6,524	686.21	3,449.50	1,787	1,315.84	5,915.27	2,006	723.58	2,554.78
TFP	266,638	4.58	0.94	3,554	4.9	1.04	1,239	5.02	1.08	1,516	4.83	1
Output	644,926	63,850.1	742,548.7	7,138	144,836.1	507,889.6	1,863	3,887,592	20,500,000	2,070	399,018.6	1,176,627
Sales	374,139	111,248.4	1,069,086	3,663	195,824.1	475,679.5	1,417	4,780,487	23,000,000	1,449	467,101.3	1,246,737
Profits	644,926	1,618.55	66,282.71	7,138	7,109.23	111,596	1,863	274,226.1	1,341,870	2,070	18,627.07	199,035
Exports	581,816	20,907.87	382,814.6	6,892	16,123.32	98,048.8	1,856	1,204,701	8,025,094	2,051	157,534.3	566,326.7

Table 3. Heterogeneity of New Multinational Firms

	New multinational		*Scale*		*Constant*		*Year and*		
Dependent variables	*Coefficient*	*SE*	*Coefficient*	*SE*	*Coefficient*	*SEs*	*Industry dummies*	*Observations*	*Number of firms*
TFP	0.08***	0.02			4.64***	0.004	No	274,483	43,143
TFP	0.05**	0.02			4.4***	0.18	Yes	274,483	43,143
TFP	0.06***	0.02	−0.03***	0.002	4.5***	0.18	Yes	274,483	43,143
Labor Productivity	−0.01	0.02			5.33***	0.002	No	615,721	157,313
Labor Productivity	0.02	0.01			2.9***	0.15	Yes	615,721	157,313
Labor Productivity	0.04**	0.01	−0.07***	0.001	3.02***	0.15	Yes	615,721	157,313
Output per Worker	0.23***	0.02			5.7***	0.006	No	392,310	78,248
Output per Worker	0.14***	0.02			4.3***	0.22	Yes	392,310	78,248
Output per Worker	0.14***	0.02	0.04***	0.002	4.2***	0.22	Yes	392,310	78,248
Scale	0.16***	0.01			1.8***	0.003	No	786,151	198,346
Scale	0.23***	0.01			1.3***	0.15	Yes	786,151	198,346
Sales	0.38***	0.01			10.1***	0.005	No	326,822	57,052
Sales	0.19***	0.01			9.7***	0.17	Yes	326,822	57,052
Sales	0.1***	0.01	0.78***	0.001	6.7***	0.11	Yes	325,991	56,873
Exports	0.76***	0.04			7.01***	0.01	No	236,567	52,891
Exports	0.48***	0.04			6.7***	2.3	Yes	236,567	52,891
Exports	0.3***	0.04	0.9***	0.005	5.1***	2.1	Yes	234,348	51,523
Profits	0.55***	0.04			6.4***	0.007	No	288,235	60,317
Profits	0.45***	0.03			3.65***	0.33	Yes	288,235	60,317
Profits	0.32***	0.04	0.68***	0.004	1.37***	0.29	Yes	284,603	59,335

Note: SE=standard errors. *,**,***Denote significance at the 10%, 5% and 1% levels, respectively.

Table 4. Top Five Regions in terms of Business Services and Multinational Parents, 2001

Region	*Business services firms*	*Region*	*Multinational parents*	*Region*	*New multinationals*
Nord	1,058	Val de Marne	13	Rhone	2
Bouches du Rhone	1,174	Nord	13	Val de Marne	3
Rhone	1,325	Rhone	15	Bouches du Rhone	3
Hauts de Seine	2,886	Hauts de Seine	63	Hauts de Seine	7
Paris	6,569	Paris	118	Paris	11

parent firms may simply reflect the "natural" advantages of certain regions (Ellison et al., 2010; Davis and Henderson, 2008).[6]

In order to identify an effect of the availability of local business services on the decision of a firm to become a multinational our strategy is to focus on "new multinationals," i.e. firms that are domestic in t and become multinationals in $t+1$. We compare these switchers with parent firms that remain domestic firms throughout the sample period. That is, our control group consists of domestic parents—firms that own at least one affiliate, but only in France. We drop single firms that are not affiliated to a group in order to eliminate one potential source of firm heterogeneity that may otherwise bias our results.[7]

We estimate an empirical model:

$$Pr(New\ Multinational = 1) = f(Effective\ Business\ Services,\ Firm\ Characteristics,\ Regional\ Controls)$$

where the dependent variable is a dummy variable equal to zero for firms that have no foreign affiliate. The dummy is equal to 1 once a firm switches from being a domestic firm to becoming a multinational, i.e. when it opens up the first foreign affiliate in time t, and as long as the firm maintains its international investments. The dummy variable switches to zero if the firm exits the international market. We drop from our sample firms that are multinationals at the start of the time period. On the right-hand side, the variable "effective business services" is the measure of the availability of business services in the region in which the firm is located.

The empirical challenge is to identify a relationship between the availability of business services and the probability of becoming a multinational. In other words, we need to ensure that our business services variable does not merely reflect the impact of other related factors. Or to be more precise, we need to avoid a correlation of the business services variable with the error term. As a first step towards aiding identification of the effect of business services we introduce a vector of control variables. The model includes a number of firm and region level controls as well as full sets of time dummies, three-digit industry dummies, and region level dummies to control for unobserved heterogeneity along those lines.

Firm heterogeneity is likely to play an important role in determining the decision to become a multinational (see Helpman et al., 2004). Hence, in our empirical analysis, we control for the *scale* of the firm measured as the number of employees and for the productivity of the firm. We use *labor productivity* measured as the ratio of value-added over the number of employees.[8] We also control for the size of the domestic

Table 5. Summary Statistics of the Main Variables

Variable	*No. of observations*	*Mean*	*SD*	*Within variation*	*Between variation*
New Multinational	7,477	0.06	0.24	0.22	0.14
Multinational	7,477	0.19	0.40	0.30	0.25
Effective Business Services	7,477	201.65	318.53	115.75	330.22
No. Local Affiliates	7,477	4.06	6.31	3.66	4.97
Labor Productivity	6,043	566.71	1,517.48	992.88	1,567.38
Scale	7,477	175.81	412.33	163.80	263.99
Multinationals_Regions	7,477	79.78	97.01	14.90	96.83
Multinationals_Industry	7,477	58.28	66.10	17.15	65.62
Agglomeration	7,477	9.87	12.86	2.15	12.23
Business Services_All Regions	7,477	172.57	298.64	108.72	309.42

group by taking into account the number of local affiliates (*No. Local Affiliates*) controlled by the domestic parent company. Everything else being equal, we would expect domestic parent firms that control a larger network of domestic affiliates to find it easier to invest overseas and become multinationals as they may be more likely to internalize the provision of business service inputs (see Debaere et al., 2013).

At the region level, we account for the presence of general agglomeration forces that could influence the capacity of firms to internationalize through FDI (Mayer et al., 2010). Such agglomeration effects are likely to be correlated with the business services variable (Ellison et al., 2010) and their omission may therefore lead to a biased estimation of the impact of business services on firms' FDI decisions. We measure agglomeration (*Agglomeration*) as the share of employment in the firm's region in the total employment of the firm's industry at the three-digit level.

We also control for the general attractiveness of a region as a location for multinationals and general exogenous shocks that might influence activities by multinationals in a given industry. To do so, we include two variables; *Multinationals_Region* measures the number of domestic multinationals within a certain region in a given year, and *Multinationals_Industry*, measures the number of multinationals in a three-digit industry in a given year. These variables also control for any spillover or competition effects from existing domestic multinationals at the region and industry levels (e.g. Görg and Greenaway, 2004)

Table 5 presents summary statistics for the main variables included in the empirical analysis, based on the sample of firms used in the subsequent regression analysis.[9]

The use of additional covariates aids identification of the effect of locally available business services only under the assumption that there are no other time varying regional characteristics that may be correlated with the explanatory variable. While we would argue that this is unlikely to be the case, we also go one step further and implement an instrumental variables (IV) strategy, using information that may explain the formation of a local services sector as instruments. We discuss the IV approach, and the instrument used in detail below.

Table 7 presents the estimation results from our baseline model, where the availability of business services is measured as the weighted number of services firms in the region. The model is estimated using a complementary log–log estimator using data for firms in manufacturing and service firms.[10]

Table 6. Random Effects Probit Estimations

	(1)
Effective Business Services	0.74**
	(0.37)
No. Local Affiliates	4.47***
	(0.75)
EBS×No. Local Affiliates	−0.38**
	(0.17)
Multinationals_Regions	−0.27
	(0.24)
Multinationals_Industry	−0.25
	(0.18)
Labor Productivity	0.25**
	(0.1)
Scale	0.42***
	(0.1)
Agglomeration	−0.02
	(0.02)
Constant	−11.97***
	(2.5)
No. of observations	5,184

Notes: All specifications include constant, time, region and three-digit industry fixed effects. Standard errors (in parenthesis) are clustered at the region-industry level. *,**,***Denote significance at the 10%, 5% and 1% levels, respectively.

The four columns in the table differ in terms of the definition of the dependent variable. We estimate four versions of our empirical model in order to allow for differences in the effects depending on characteristics of the host country. In the first specification we take into account investments in all countries, as described above. In the following three columns, we distinguish between three types of investments: investments in countries with no past colonial links with France, investments in countries with no common language ties with France, and investments in countries that have significant restrictions to international trade in services.

The first two distinctions (no colonial links, no common language) allow us to abstract from country heterogeneity in terms of "gravity variables." Countries with colonial ties and or common language may be more attractive host countries *per se*, and services may potentially play less of a role for the decision to invest there.

Distinguishing countries by their level of restrictions for services trade allows us to consider, in an indirect way at least, whether the availability of services in the host country may distort our estimates on the importance of the provision of services in the home country. If a country is more closed to trade in business services, this may imply a lower quantity and/or quality of services in the host country. In that case, French firms may have to rely even more on services provision in the home country. In order to measure such restrictions, we use the *Services Trade Restrictions Database* of the World Bank to identify countries that impose restrictions on international trade in services (see Borchert et al., 2014).[11] More than 80% of new multinationals invest in a country that does not share colonial links or language links with France. Also, less than 50% invest in a country with trade restrictions in the business services sector.

Table 7. Business Services and New Multinationals—Baseline estimations

	(1) *All countries*	*(2)* *No colony*	*(3)* *No common language*	*(4)* *Closed to BS*
Effective Business Services	0.8***	0.88***	0.95***	1.34***
	(0.2)	(0.2)	(0.2)	(0.3)
No. Local Affiliates	1.3***	1.24***	1.25***	1.5***
	(0.08)	(0.09)	(0.1)	(0.1)
Multinationals_Regions	−0.35***	−0.2	−0.31**	−0.6**
	(0.13)	(0.14)	(0.13)	(0.2)
Multinationals_Industry	−0.55***	−0.5***	−0.53***	−0.86***
	(0.1)	(0.1)	(0.1)	(0.1)
Labor Productivity	0.28***	0.3***	0.32***	0.57***
	(0.09)	(0.09)	(0.1)	(0.16)
Scale	0.28***	0.35***	0.36***	0.55***
	(0.05)	(0.06)	(0.05)	(0.06)
Agglomeration	−0.002	−0.008	−0.01	−0.006
	(0.01)	(0.01)	(0.01)	(0.01)
Constant	−7.463***	−7.838***	−8.109***	−40.04***
	(1.1)	(1.3)	(1.2)	(2.8)
No. of observations	5,184	5,115	5,011	3,707
Predicted probability	0.13***	0.09***	0.1***	0.03***
	(0.009)	(0.008)	(0.009)	(0.005)
Business Services (Marginal Effect)	0.09***	0.08***	0.09***	0.05***
	(0.02)	(0.02)	(0.02)	(0.01)

Note: Details as per footnote to Table 6.

Accordingly, we define three different dependent variables for the analyses in columns (2)–(4): *No Colony* is a dummy equal to 1 once a firm switches from being a domestic firm to becoming a multinational with at least one affiliate in a foreign country with no past colonial links with France in time *t*, and as long as the firm maintains its international investments in these countries. The dummy variable switches to zero if the firm exits non-colonial international markets. Similarly the variables *No Common Language* and *Closed to Business Services* are dummy variables indicating whether a domestic firm has started and maintained at least one investment in a country with no-common language ties with France and a country that applies restrictions to the international trade of business services respectively. In all specifications standard errors are clustered at the regional three-digit industry level.

Firm heterogeneity in terms of size and productivity is included in all regressions. We find positive coefficients on these two variables, indicating that larger and more productive firms are more likely to open affiliates abroad. This is in line with expectations based on heterogeneous firm models such as Helpman et al. (2004). We also find that firms with a larger number of domestic affiliates are more likely to become multinationals. Conditional on other variables in the model and on region fixed effects, the coefficient on the agglomeration variable is statistically insignificant in all specifications. We also control for the presence of multinationals in the region and the industry to capture potential spillovers. We find statistically significant negative effects of these variables, particularly the variable measuring spillovers at the industry level. This

Table 8. Countries with Trade Restriction in the Services Sector

Mode 1

Albania	Hungary	Namibia
Algeria	India	Nepal
Argentina	Iran	Pakistan
Armenia	Italy	Paraguay
Bahrain	Japan	Peru
Bangladesh	Kenya	Philippines
Belarus	Republic of Korea	Portugal
Botswana	Kuwait	Saudi Arabia
Brazil	Lebanon	Senegal
Cambodia	Madagascar	Thailand
China	Malawi	Tunisia
Costa Rica	Malaysia	Turkey
Cote d'Ivoire	Mauritius	Uganda
Czech Republic	Mexico	Uzbekistan
Ethiopia	Mongolia	Zimbabwe
Guatemala	Morocco	
Honduras	Mozambique	

result points to a competition effect, not unusual in the literature on spillovers from multinationals (e.g. Görg and Greenaway, 2004). Here, French firms in industries with a high presence of existing domestic multinationals tend to be less likely to start becoming multinationals themselves.

Turning to our main variable of interest, we find that the local availability of business services is positively associated with a firm's decision to start becoming a multinational. The coeffecient is positive and statistically significant in all specifications. The point estimates in columns (1)–(3) are fairly similar, while the estimate in column (4)—where we only consider investments in countries with high restrictions on services trade—is higher. This is in line with our conjecture that the provision of services in such host countries may be poorer than in other host countries and that therefore the availability of local services in the home country is more important.

It can be argued that firms do not necessarily rely on external providers of business services to support their internationalization activities and it is important to distinguish between firms that rely on the market and those that are more likely to integrate these activities. While we do not have information in the data on production of services inputs by firms themselves, we conjecture that larger parent firms, in particular those with multiple production plants, may be more likely to produce services themselves (see Debaere et al., 2013). In the further analysis we, therefore, assume that domestic parent firms that control a large network of domestic affiliates are more likely to internalize the production of their needed business services within their own network, and may be less reliant on existing suppliers in the market.

Table 9 presents estimations of the model where we allow for an interaction between number of local affiliates of a domestic parent and the *Effective Business Services* variable. Table 9 shows that this interaction is negative and significant in all specifications. Moreover, the coefficient on the *Effective Business Services* variable increases in magnitude in comparison with the results presented in Table 7. Hence, these results are in line with our assumption that local business services are more relevant to domestic parents with smaller networks of affiliates. This is also in line with

Table 9. Business Services and New Multinationals—Including Interactions

	(1)	*(2)*	*(3)*	*(4)*
	All countries	*No colony*	*No common language*	*Closed to BS*
Effective Business Services	1.05***	1.14***	1.2***	1.58***
	(0.2)	(0.2)	(0.2)	(0.2)
No. Local Affiliates	2.2***	2.3***	2.3***	2.7***
	(0.17)	(0.2)	(0.17)	(0.23)
EBS×No. Local Affiliates	−0.2***	−0.24***	−0.25***	−0.27***
	(0.03)	(0.04)	(0.03)	(0.04)
Multinationals_Regions	−0.37***	−0.22	−0.32**	−0.65**
	(0.14)	(0.15)	(0.14)	(0.27)
Multinationals_Industry	−0.54***	−0.5***	−0.5***	−0.82***
	(0.09)	(0.11)	(0.11)	(0.13)
Labor Productivity	0.28***	0.32***	0.32***	0.6***
	(0.08)	(0.09)	(0.11)	(0.16)
Scale	0.29***	0.35***	0.37***	0.57***
	(0.05)	(0.05)	(0.05)	(0.07)
Agglomeration	−0.0001	−0.004	−0.01	−0.007
	(0.01)	(0.01)	(0.01)	(0.01)
Constant	−8.64***	−9.3***	−9.4***	−38.92***
	(1.1)	(1.3)	(1.2)	(2.2)
No. of observations	5,184	5,115	5,011	3,707
Predicted Probability	0.12***	0.09***	0.09***	0.03***
	(0.009)	(0.008)	(0.008)	(0.005)
Business Services (Marginal Effect)	0.12***	0.1***	0.11***	0.05***
	(0.02)	(0.02)	(0.02)	(0.01)

Note: Details as per footnote to Table 6.

the finding by Debaere et al. (2013), who show that availability of services matter for the outsourcing decision of firms, but only for small purely domestic non-multinational firms. Taken together, these sets of results suggest that firms that are too small to internalize the provision of services rely more on local services markets.

While Table 9 shows the coefficients from the nonlinear complementary log–log model, we also calculate marginal effects and predicted probabilities, which are reported at the bottom of the table. In column (1), an increase in business services by one standard deviation leads to an increase in the probability of investing abroad of 12% for firms with no domestic affiliate. This, thus, represents a doubling in the overall probability to invest abroad, which is also predicted at 12%. Hence, this suggests that the effect is not only statistically significant but also economically meaningful. The larger the number of affiliates, the less the parent firm benefits from the availability of business services, however.

Our interpretation of the positive coefficient on business services as a causal effect on a firm's decision to become a multinational relies on the assumption that, conditional on the covariates in the model, there are no unobserved time varying effects that are correlated with business services and multinationality that may be driving the results. However, if the forces that draw firms to particular locations are not captured by our spillover and agglomeration variables and the fixed effects at the region level, then our results could still suffer from endogeneity and, hence, be biased. In order to

Table 10. IV regressions

	(1)	(2)	(3)	(4)
	All Countries	No Colony	No Common Language	Closed to BS
Effective Business Services	0.05**	0.04	0.05**	0.021
	(0.02)	(0.02)	(0.02)	(0.02)
No. Local Affiliates	0.25***	0.24***	0.27***	0.16***
	(0.03)	(0.03)	(0.03)	(0.03)
EBS×No. Local Affiliates	−0.01*	−0.01**	−0.02***	−0.01
	(0.007)	(0.008)	(0.007)	(0.007)
Multinationals_Regions	−0.02	−0.01	−0.02	−0.017
	(0.02)	(0.02)	(0.02)	(0.016)
Multinationals_Industry	−0.05***	−0.04**	−0.03*	−0.04***
	(0.02)	(0.017)	(0.018)	(0.015)
Labor Productivity	0.03**	0.027**	0.024**	0.027***
	(0.01)	(0.01)	(0.01)	(0.009)
Scale	0.03***	0.037***	0.035***	0.035***
	(0.008)	(0.008)	(0.007)	(0.007)
Agglomeration	−0.0006	−0.001	−0.002	−0.0005
	(0.001)	(0.001)	(0.001)	(0.001)
Constant	−0.06	−0.02	−0.02	0.05
	(0.06)	(0.06)	(0.05)	(0.04)
No. of observations	5344	5344	5344	4670
R^2	0.3	0.29	0.296	0.276

Notes: All specifications include constant, time, province and three-digit industry fixed effects. We have also included two additional controls at the regional level, a dummy indicating the presence of a port and a dummy indicating the presence of an airport with international flights. Both these variables are insignificant. In all specifications standard errors (in parenthesis) are clustered at the region-industry level. Significances as per Table 6.

make further progress in identifying an effect of local business services on the probability of being a multinational, we now turn to instrumental variable techniques.

The main instrument we use is the size of the active population in each region, as this is likely to be an important variable to explain the formation of a local services sector. We use historic information from 1968, available from the population census data provided by the French Statistical Office (INSEE) to measure this. Historic population size is likely to be a relevant instrument as, for example, Davis and Henderson (2008) show that business services are disproportionally located in large cities. Historic information may therefore be a good proxy for the formation of a local business services sector, but is unlikely to be correlated with contemporaneous decisions of firms to become a multinational, conditional on the other covariates in the model.[12] Because these instruments are time-invariant within each region, we are not able to add region fixed effects with the IV specification. Instead we control for province level fixed effects and add two additional controls at the region level, *Port* and *International Airport*, which control for the availability of infrastructure related to internationalization. The first variable is a dummy variable that indicates the presence of a maritime port in the region. The second variable is a dummy variable that indicates the presence of an airport with international flights in the region.

Table 11. First Stage IV Regressions

	Effective business services				*EBS×No. local affiliates*			
	(1)	*(2)*	*(3)*	*(4)*	*(5)*	*(6)*	*(7)*	*(8)*
	All countries	*No colony*	*No common language*	*Closed to BS*	*All countries*	*No colony*	*No common language*	*Closed to BS*
No. Local Affiliates	−0.08	−0.08	−0.08	−0.11	−17.77***	−17.77***	−17.77***	−17.09***
	(0.11)	(0.11)	(0.11)	(0.12)	(0.64)	(0.64)	(0.64)	(0.7)
Multinationals_Regions	0.17***	0.17***	0.17***	0.16***	0.15***	0.15***	0.15***	0.11**
	(0.01)	(0.01)	(0.01)	(0.01)	(0.05)	(0.05)	(0.05)	(0.05)
Multinationals_Industry	0.33***	0.33***	0.33***	0.32***	0.51	0.51	0.51	0.45***
	(0.02)	(0.02)	(0.02)	(0.02)	(0.04)	(0.04)	(0.04)	(0.04)
Labor Productivity	0.004	0.004	0.004	0.01	0.01	0.01	0.01	0.01
	(0.008)	(0.008)	(0.008)	(0.008)	(0.02)	(0.02)	(0.02)	(0.02)
Scale	−0.01*	−0.01*	−0.01*	−0.01**	−0.01	−0.01	−0.01	−0.02
	(0.005)	(0.005)	(0.005)	(0.005)	(0.01)	(0.01)	(0.01)	(0.01)
Agglomeration	0.007***	0.007***	0.007***	0.007***	0.002	0.002	0.002	0.003
	(0.001)	(0.001)	(0.001)	(0.001)	(0.004)	(0.004)	(0.004)	(0.004)
Port	−0.24***	−0.24***	−0.24***	−0.22***	−0.43**	−0.43**	−0.43**	−0.43**
	(0.05)	(0.05)	(0.05)	(0.05)	(0.19)	(0.19)	(0.19)	(0.2)
International Airport	−0.19***	−0.19***	−0.19***	−0.2***	−0.35***	−0.35***	−0.35***	−0.31***
	(0.03)	(0.03)	(0.03)	(0.03)	(0.09)	(0.09)	(0.09)	(0.1)
Total Population Region	1.27***	1.27***	1.27***	1.28***	−0.51***	−0.51***	−0.51***	−0.4***
	(0.03)	(0.03)	(0.03)	(0.03)	(0.11)	(0.11)	(0.11)	(0.11)
*Total Population Region*No. Local Affiliates*	0.006	0.006	0.006	0.008	1.74***	1.74***	1.74***	1.7***
	(0.009)	(0.009)	(0.009)	(0.009)	(0.05)	(0.05)	(0.05)	(0.05)
F-statistics	4,763.6***	4,763.6***	4,763.6***	1,060.17***	54.46***	54.46***	54.46***	164.25***
Exogeneity test	1.9	1.9	1.9	1.4	1.9	1.9	1.9	1.4

Note: Standard errors in parentheses. Significances as per Table 6.

Table 12. *Business Services and New Multinationals—Excluding the Ile de France Province*

	(1)	(2)	(3)	(4)
	All countries	*No colony*	*No common language*	*Closed to BS*
Effective Business Services	1.2***	1.3***	1.2***	1.7***
	(0.3)	(0.3)	(0.3)	(0.4)
No. Local Affiliates	2.8***	2.9***	2.9***	3.5***
	(0.2)	(0.27)	(0.25)	(0.45)
EBS×No. Local Affiliates	−0.4***	−0.4***	−0.43***	−0.47***
	(0.06)	(0.06)	(0.07)	(0.14)
Multinationals_Regions	−0.3*	−0.19	−0.25	−0.7*
	(0.189)	(0.194)	(0.193)	(0.398)
Multinationals_Industry	−0.3**	−0.3**	−0.25	−0.46***
	(0.14)	(0.15)	(0.16)	(0.17)
Labor Productivity	0.09	0.14	0.18	0.3
	(0.13)	(0.15)	(0.15)	(0.31)
Scale	0.3***	0.41***	0.48***	0.6***
	(0.1)	(0.11)	(0.09)	(0.11)
Agglomeration	0.005	−0.03	−0.03	0.05
	(0.05)	(0.05)	(0.05)	(0.05)
Constant	−6.9***	−7.75***	−8.5***	−8.5***
	(1.4)	(1.6)	(1.5)	(2.06)
No. of observations	2,786	2,723	2,710	1,803
Predicted Probability	0. 12***	0. 09***	0. 09***	0.03***
	(0.01)	(0.01)	(0.01)	(0.01)
Effective Business Services (Marginal Effect)	0.13***	0.11***	0.1***	0.04***
	(0.04)	(0.03)	(0.03)	(0.01)

Notes: All specifications include constant, time, region and three-digit industry fixed effects. In all specifications standard errors (in parenthesis) are clustered at the region-industry level.

Table 10 presents the results from the instrumental variable estimations. We use population size on its own and interacted with the number of foreign affiliates as excluded instruments. The IV approach is implemented in a linear regression model. Reassuringly, the business services variable maintains its positive and significant coefficient in most specifications. Table 11 presents the result from the first stage of the IV estimations and the tests of exogeneity. Note that our instrument is highly relevant as indicated by the first stage F-test. Based on this instrument set, we cannot reject the assumption of exogeneity of the business services variable, conditional on the covariates included in the empirical model. Hence, we prefer the models based on the complementary log–log estimator.

Tables 12–14 present a series of further robustness checks. In Tables 12 and 13 we look specifically at the role of the Ile de France province that includes Paris and its suburbs. Table 4 indicates that a large number of French multinationals are located within the Ile de France province and that this province is top ranking in terms of the number of firms in the business services sector. Table 12 excludes the Ile de France province while Table 13 focuses exclusively on this specific province. Both tables report results that are similar to Table 9; the availability of business services at the

Table 13. Business Services and New Multinationals—within the Ile de France Province

	(1) All countries	*(2)* No colony	*(3)* No common language	*(4)* Closed to BS
Effective Business Services	1.3***	1.8***	1.9***	3.3***
	(0.44)	(0.44)	(0.46)	(0.79)
No. Local Affiliates	2.7***	3.05***	2.8***	2.4***
	(0.54)	(0.7)	(0.6)	(0.8)
*EBS*No. Local Affiliates*	−0.25***	−0.33***	−0.29***	−0.2
	(0.08)	(0.12)	(0.1)	(0.13)
Multinationals_Regions	−0.17	−0.07	−0.5	−1.2
	(0.38)	(0.38)	(0.44)	(0.89)
Multinationals_Industry	−0.77***	−0.84***	−1.01***	−1.99***
	(0.18)	(0.21)	(0.21)	(0.4)
Labor Productivity	0.45***	0.48***	0.4***	0.74***
	(0.08)	(0.1)	(0.09)	(0.1)
Scale	0.31***	0.41***	0.36***	0.48***
	(0.08)	(0.07)	(0.07)	(0.12)
Agglomeration	−0.01	−0.02	−0.03**	−0.023
	(0.01)	(0.01)	(0.01)	(0.02)
Constant	−24.8***	−27.5***	−26.11***	−28.08***
	(2.4)	(2.44)	(2.43)	(4.03)
No. of observations	1,957	1,893	1,870	1,495
Predicted Probability	0.1***	0.09***	0.07***	0.02***
	(0.01)	(0.02)	(0.01)	(0.004)
Business Services (Marginal effect)	0.13***	0.16**	0.15**	0.08***
	(0.04)	(0.03)	(0.05)	(0.02)

Notes: All specifications include constant, time, region and three-digit industry fixed effects. In all specifications standard errors (in parenthesis) are clustered at the region-industry level.

region level enhances the probability of becoming and remaining a multinational and this effect declines with the number of domestic affiliates.

It can be argued that it is restrictive to limit the availability of business services to the boundaries of the region where the firm is located. In Table 14 we relax this assumption and allow firms to benefit from the availability of business services in all metropolitan French regions. We introduce a new variable representing the availability of business services to a firm located in region r: *Effective Business Services_All Regions*. This variable is a weighted sum of measures of business services availabilities in all regions, including region r, where the weight is the inverse of the road distance separating two regions. Specifically, our measure is calculated as:

$$\textit{Effective Business Service all regions}_{jrt} = \sum_{s} w_{sr}\ \textit{Effective Business Services}_{jst}$$

where s represents regions including region r and w_{sr} is the inverse of the road distance betwen regions s and r (Combes et al., 2005). To account for internal distance, we follow Combes et al. (2005) and consider that each region is a disk where all production concentrates at the center and consumers are uniformly distributed on a given

Table 14. Business Services and New Multinationals—Distance Weighted Measures

	(1) All countries	(2) No colony	(3) No common language	(4) Closed to BS
Effective Business Services_All Regions	1.4***	1.47***	1.6***	2.07***
	(0.29)	(0.3)	(0.34)	(0.4)
No. Local Affiliates	1.89***	1.95***	2.03***	2.31***
	(0.15)	(0.17)	(0.16)	(0.22)
EBS_AR×No. Local Affiliates	−0.15***	−0.18***	−0.2***	−0.2***
	(0.02)	(0.03)	(0.02)	(0.03)
Multinationals_Regions	−0.36***	−0.21	−0.31**	−0.6**
	(0.13)	(0.14)	(0.13)	(0.25)
Multinationals_Industry	−0.6***	−0.57***	−0.58***	−0.93***
	(0.11)	(0.12)	(0.13)	(0.14)
Labor Productivity	0.28***	0.32***	0.32***	0.58***
	(0.08)	(0.09)	(0.1)	(0.1)
Scale	0.28***	0.35***	0.37***	0.57***
	(0.05)	(0.05)	(0.05)	(0.06)
Agglomeration	−0.001	−0.006	−0.01	−0.006
	(0.01)	(0.01)	(0.01)	(0.01)
Constant	−9.6***	−10.2***	−10.6***	−39.1***
	(1.3)	(1.5)	(1.5)	(2.2)
No. of observations	5,184	5,115	5,011	3,707
Predicted Probability	0.12***	0.09***	0.09***	0.03***
	(0.009)	(0.008)	(0.008)	(0.005)
Effective Business Services_ All Regions (Marginal effect)	0.16***	0.13***	0.14***	0.06***
	(0.03)	(0.03)	(0.03)	(0.01)

Note: Details as per footnote to Table 6.

proportion of the total land area of the region. Combes et al. (2005) use a proportion of 1/6 and calculate internal distance as $d_{rr}=1/6\sqrt{A/\pi}$ where A is the land area of region r.[13] Results reported in Table 14 are consistent with those reported in Table 9.

4. Conclusion

This paper considers, to the best of our knowledge for the first time, the link between the local availability of services and a firm's decision to become a multinational. This is a highly topical issue, given that many industrialized countries are increasingly becoming service industry economies and firms become increasingly more globalized. Hence, this begs the question as to how the internationalization of manufacturing can be linked to services. While there are many ways in which the globalization of manufacturing and services can be linked, we focus on firms' decisions to locate affiliates abroad.

In an analysis of rich firm level data for France we find robust evidence that the availability of services has a positive impact on firms' decisions to become multinationals. We also find that the effect of locally available services is strongest for firms that are small, in the sense of having fewer domestic affiliates. These are likely to be firms that are less likely to internalize the provision of business service inputs. These results hold when taking account of the potential endogeneity of the business services variable. In order to deal with this, we implement an instrumental variable strategy, using variables that capture factors of the formation of a local services sector as instruments.

Our result is quite intuitive and indicates that firms rely on the provision of local services when deciding to invest abroad.[14] This is particularly so if firms are too small to produce their needed business services themselves. The results can be interpreted in a simple theoretical set-up where the local availability of business services improves firm efficiency and, hence, allows firms to overcome sunk costs of investing abroad more easily.

Our research may provide some further input into the discussion on the advantages from liberalization in the services industries. As Borchert et al. (2014) argue, professional services (which are included in our measure of business services) are among the most protected in both industrialized and developing countries. Hence, further liberalization in these sectors could potentially improve the efficiency of firms by allowing them to link more easily into the global economy through opening up affiliates abroad.

References

Arnold, J. M., B. S. Javorcik, and A. Mattoo, "Does Services Liberalization Benefit Manufacturing Firms? Evidence from the Czech Republic," *Journal of International Economics* 85 (2011):136–46.

Borchert, I., B. Gootiiz, and A. Mattoo, "Policy Barriers to International Trade in Services: Evidence from a New Database," *World Bank Economic Review* 28 (2014):162–88.

Breinlich, H. and C. Criscuolo, "International Trade in Services: A Portrait of Importers and Exporters," *Journal of International Economics* 84 (2011):188–206.

Breinlich, H., A. Soderbery, and G. C. Wright, "From Selling Goods to Selling Services: Firm Responses to Trade Liberalization," CEPR discussion paper 10116, London (2014).

Combes, P. P., M. Lafourcade, and T. Mayer, "The Trade-creating Effects of Business and Social Networks: Evidence from France," *Journal of International Economics* 66 (2005):1–29.

Davis, J. C. and J. V. Henderson, "The Agglomeration of Headquarters," *Regional Science and Urban Economics* 38 (2008):445–60.

Deardorff, A., "The International Provision of Trade Services, Trade and Fragmentation," *Review of International Economics* 9 (2001):233–48.

Debaere, P., H. Görg, and H. Raff, "Greasing the Wheels of International Commerce: How Services Facilitate Firms' International Sourcing," *Canadian Journal of Economics* 46 (2013): 78–102.

Ellison, G., E. Glaeser, and W. R. Kerr, "What Causes Industry Agglomeration? Evidence from Coagglomeration Patterns," *American Economic Review* 100 (2010):1195–213.

Fernandes, A. M. and C. Paunov, "Foreign Direct Investment in Services and Manufacturing Productivity: Evidence for Chile," *Journal of Development Economics* 97 (2012):305–21.

Francois, J. and B. Hoekman, "Services Trade and Policy," *Journal of Economic Literature* 48 (2010):642–92.

Görg, H. and D. Greenaway, "Much Ado About Nothing? Do Domestic Firms Really Benefit from Foreign Direct Investment?" *World Bank Research Observer* 19 (2004):171–97.

Greenaway, D. and R. A. Kneller, "Firm Heterogeneity, Exporting and Foreign Direct Investment," *Economic Journal* 117, no. 517(2007):F134–61.

Henderson, J. V. and Y. Ono, "Where do Manufacturing Firms Locate their Headquarters?" *Journal of Urban Economics* 63 (2008):431–50.

Helpman, E., "Trade, FDI and the Organization of the Firm," *Journal of Economic Literature* 44 (2006):589–630.

Helpman, E., M. J. Melitz, and S. R. Yeaple, "Export versus FDI with Heterogeneous Firms, *American Economic Review* 94 (2004):300–16.
Hijzen, A., S. Jean, and T. Mayer, "The Effects at Home of Initiating Production Abroad: Evidence from Matched French Firms," *Review of World Economics/Weltwirtschaftliches Archiv* 147 (2011a):457–83.
Hijzen, A., M. Pisu, R. Upward, and P. W. Wright, "Employment, Job Turnover, and Trade in Producer Services: UK Firm-level Evidence," *Canadian Journal of Economics* 44 (2011b): 1020–43.
Jenkins, S. P., "Survival Analysis," unpublished paper, University of Essex, Colchester (2005).
Jones, R. and H. Kierzkowski, "The Role of Services in Production and International Trade: A Theoretical Framework," in R. Jones and A. Krueger (eds), The Political Economy of International Trade: Essays in Honor of Robert E. Baldwin, Oxford: Basil Blackwell (1990).
Kelle, M., "Crossing Industrial Borders: German Manufacturers as Services Exporters," *The World Economy* 36 (2013):1494–515.
Malchow-Møller, N., J. R. Munch, and J. R. Skaksen, "Services Trade, Goods Trade and Productivity Growth: Evidence from a Population of Private Sector Firms," *Review of World Economics/Weltwirtschaftliches Archiv* 151 (2015):197–229.
Mayer, T. and G. Ottaviano, The Happy Few: The Internationalisation of European Firms, Brussels: Bruegel Blueprint Series (2007)
Mayer, T., I. Mejean, I., and B. Nefussi, "The Location of Domestic and Foreign Production Affiliates by French Multinational Firms," *Journal of Urban Economics* 68 (2010):115–28.
Olley, S. and A. Pakes, "The Dynamics of Productivity in the Telecommunications Equipment Industry," *Econometrica* 64 (1996):1263–97.
Strauss-Kahn, V. and X. Vives, "Why and Where do Headquarters Move?" *Regional Science and Urban Economics* 39 (2009):168–86.

Notes

1. A related literature looks at the determinants of the location of foreign affiliates, e.g. Mayer et al. (2010) for France. We are not concerned with this, rather, we look at data for the home country (France in our case) and investigate the switch a firm makes from being a domestic firm to having affiliates abroad, i.e. becoming a multinational.
2. Of course, firms may also internalize the provision of such services inputs. This is the focus of Debaere et al. (2013) and also an issue we get back to in the empirical analysis. For the intuitive discussion here, it suffices to assume that at least some services inputs need to be sourced from local providers.
3. In case the firm is not affiliated to a group or if the firm is the parent company of a group, the identity of the parent firm is the identity of the firm itself.
4. In Table 2, the category "New Multinational" considers all observations from the moment a firm switches from domestic to multinational.
5. Table 3 includes "old" multinationals in the control group. The results are robust to the exclusion of these types of firms.
6. "Natural" advantages do not necessarily mean natural resources but reflect everything that is specific to a region and that makes it attractive for industrial activity.
7. We drop firms that remain single throughout the time period. New multinationals that were previously single are included in our sample.
8. As an alternative measure of productivity we estimate total factor productivity (TFP) using the semi-parametric method of Olley and Pakes (1996). However, owing to unavailability of data on the capital stock in many instances, this variable can only be calculated for a relatively small number of firms (see Table 3). Hence, we prefer labor productivity in the empirical estimation.
9. All independent variables, except for agglomeration are expressed in natural logarithm in the regressions.

10. The cloglog estimator is the discrete time version of the proportional hazard model. See Jenkins (2005) for an excellent overview of complementary log–log and proportional hazard models. This estimation does not include firm specific time-invariant effects. We also estimated the model using random effects probit, which controls for such unobserved firm heterogeneity. Results, which are available upon request, are comparable with the results reported in Table 7.

11. The database covers 103 countries and for each country considers five major service sectors encompassing 19 subsectors. It presents four indices of trade openness, an overall index and three different modes: mode 1 covering financial services, transportation and professional services, mode 3 covering all subsectors and mode 4 covering professional services. The database defines 5 degrees of trade openness: completely open with a score equal to zero, virtually open with minor restrictions with a score equal to 25, major restrictions with a score equal to 50, virtually closed with limited opportunities to enter and operate with a score equal to 75 and completely closed with a score equal to 100. We focus on mode 1 and we assume that countries with a score higher than 25 are closed to international trade in business services. Table 8 provides a list of countries that are considered closed to business services trade based on this definition.

12. We also experimented with two additional instruments, namely, the share of entrepreneurs and managers in the active population of each region, or a measure of the total demand for business services within each region. The share of entrepreneurs and managers is extracted from historical population census data. Total demand for business services corresponds to a weighted sum of two-digit industry level employment in each region where the weights represent the share of business services output sold as input to each industry. The weights are extracted from the input–output tables for French industries provided by the French Statistical Office (INSEE). Contemporaneous demand is again an important variable to explain the formation of the services sector. However, it is unlikely to be correlated with an individual firm's decision to open affiliates abroad. Our results are robust to the use of several of these instruments in each specification; however, the Sargan tests rejected the overidentification restrictions.

13. Our results are robust to the use of an internal distance equal to one.

14. This is in line with an earlier literature that emphasized that the increased availability of services inputs can trigger international fragmentation of production (e.g. Jones and Kierzkowski, 1990; Deardorff, 2001).

Chapter I.3

Outsourcing Foreign Services and the Internet: Evidence from Firm Level Data

HOLGER GÖRG*
Institut für Weltwirtschaft, Kiel, Germany
Christian Albrechts University, Kiel, Germany

AOIFE HANLEY
Institut für Weltwirtschaft, Kiel, Germany
Christian Albrechts University, Kiel, Germany

INGRID OTT
Institut für Weltwirtschaft, Kiel, Germany
Karlsruhe Institute of Technology (KIT), Germany

Abstract: We analyse the link between internet use and foreign sourcing of services and materials inputs. In our empirical analysis using firm level data for Ireland we find, among firms that *a priori* all purchase inputs abroad, that those who commenced outsourcing from suppliers over the internet ("Adopters") experience significantly higher growth rates of services offshoring. This result shows in a variety of econometric methods (OLS, Propensity Scoring (Kernel, Nearest Neighbour and Caliper Matching)). Adopting the internet for outsourcing induced an increase in the share of foreign services by 3.2-4.0 per cent.

I BACKGROUND

The introduction of internet-enabled outsourcing since the turn of the century is seen by many as a breakthrough for reducing the transaction cost of outsourcing services to firms. Miroudot *et al.* (2009) demonstrate that trade in intermediate services inputs (a frequently used measure for international outsourcing) in the OECD increased between 1995 and 2006 at

* Institut für Weltwirtschaft, Kiellinie 66, 24105 Kiel, Germany.
Email: holger.goerg@ifw-kiel.de

an average annual growth rate of 7 per cent. Examples of these internationally traded services include advertising, IT and logistics. An OECD (2006) report from the same period points out, however, that little has been done by researchers to investigate the full impacts of these changes for many aspects of the firms operations. The same report goes on to state that the choice of services open to outsourcers is wider than ever before:

> Rapid advances in Information and Communication Technologies (ICTs), combined with continuing efforts to liberalise international trade and investment in services, have increased the tradability of services and created new types of tradable services. (OECD, 2006, p. 4)

The menu of services available to firms is widening up to the present day. The cost of transacting these services decrease with the launch of new internet delivered platforms that enable firms to transact with suppliers. What remains to be seen is how such cost reductions arising have affected the foreign versus domestic mix of services bought in by firms. Additionally, the advances in the platforms used by firms to transact with suppliers online may have affected the choices of outsourcing firms.

It is not easy, however, to investigate empirically these changes on firms' outsourcing behaviour. This is because in a world of heterogeneous firms, firms are different from one another in terms of previous outsourcing behaviour, size, activity and other characteristics. The differences could be correlated with the changing outsourcing preferences of firms. A further problem for researchers is to identify an appropriate experimental frame. Specifically, rarely do researchers have the opportunity to compare the outsourcing patterns of outsourcing firms which apply a novel, internet-enabled outsourcing technology and outsourcing firms which do not. In other words, it is difficult to find an appropriate baseline against which to measure the impact of novel internet-enabled outsourcing tools on the outsourcing behaviour of firms.

The purpose of our paper is to investigate how the adoption of internet-enabled outsourcing technology by firms can bring about changes in the firm's outsourcing behaviour. Specifically, we investigate the change in the foreign outsourcing intensity (ratio of foreign/total outsourced services) for firms which switch to adopting an internet-enabled outsourcing technology (Adopters) versus firms choosing not to adopt such a technology (non-Adopters). To do this, our analysis applies data for more than 800 firms based in Ireland in the period 2002-2004 when international and Irish domestic service providers had commenced delivering their services to outsourcing firms using internet-based technologies – as distinct to transacting over the telephone or using e-mail correspondence. We apply a variety of estimation procedures (OLS and various forms of propensity score matching) to estimate the link between the adoption of internet-enabled outsourcing and the choices made by outsourcers. We find that the effect of adopting the internet for outsourcing induced an increase in the share of foreign services by 3.2 to 4.0 per cent, depending on the estimation method used.

Our paper relates to a small but growing literature on the causes and effects of international outsourcing, or more generally imported inputs at the firm level (e.g., Lileeva and van Biesebroeck, 2013; Hijzen *et al.*, 2010; Goldberg *et al.*, 2009). Looking specifically at the case of Ireland, Görg and Hanley (2004, 2011) and Görg *et al.* (2008) show that firms which increase their level of internationally outsourced inputs can potentially raise their productivity and innovation levels. However, the impact on profitability is ambiguous. In this paper, we shift the focus away from the consequences of the foreign sourcing decision for the firm, and look at one important potential driver of outsourcing, namely, technological progress or, more specifically, the use of the internet.

The rest of the paper is structured in the following way. We outline in Section II, some key studies on the effect of the internet on the outsourcing behaviour of firms. Section III briefly describes our research methodology. In Section IV we describe the Irish data used to investigate the research question. This is followed by an analysis in Section V and our findings are summarised in Section VI.

II BACKGROUND

Many firms have traditionally relied on other firms to provide specialised legal, technical and other services. Changes in telecommunications have radically changed the interface between service buyers and service providers. Specifically, advances in how the internet helps outsourcing firms to interface with services providers, is argued to have made the provision of services cheaper. Several researchers highlight the higher visibility and tradability of international traded services (Abramovsky and Griffith, 2006; Abramovsky and Griffith, 2009; Bartel *et al.*, 2014; 2012 and Sako, 2006).[1]

As a consequence of improved business-to-business internet platforms, the cut in the price of transacting with suppliers is expected to shift firms'

[1] An example of a highly specialised internationally traded service is the maritime insurance sector where a handful of London based firms have a developed specialisation over the years. Few domestic non-UK suppliers of maritime insurance could hope to compete with such a specialised supplier.

outsourcing behaviour. Jones and Kierzkowski (2001) argue that it is now easier and cheaper for (1) outsourcing firms to outsource foreign services and that (2) more services are being exchanged at arm's length than before. The UNCTAD (2004) *World Investment Report* shares this view.

What does the theory have to say about the effect of internet-enabled outsourcing on changes to the mix of foreign and domestic services outsourced by firms? To our knowledge, all models assume that firms make initial investments in Information and Communications Technology (ICT) in order to use internet-enabled outsourcing. The outlay of this investment must be balanced against the reduction in the firm's marginal cost of having adopted the internet-enabled technology. Abramovsky and Griffith (2006) argue that the overall cost of adopting internet-enabled outsourcing technology is comprised of several components, such as the adjustment cost where the services provided by external suppliers will never perfectly match the services of the firm's own in-house team of dedicated staff, and a transaction cost which rises with higher input specificity. Additionally, there are the costs of monitoring/writing a service contract and the search cost incurred by the firm when searching out the most appropriate supplier. The Abramovsky and Griffith (2006) model posits that exogenous rises in ICT spending should be accompanied by a higher use of outsourced services, as the marginal cost of these outsourced services falls.

A more recent model by Bartel *et al.* (2014) frames the decision to outsource production (as opposed to producing the input in-house) as being largely conditioned by the speed of technological change. When the technological pace of change in providing a service such as internet design is fast, then the firm will outsource the service to a service provider. The Bartel *et al.* (2014) model and the accompanying analysis follows in the path of earlier work by Grossman and Helpman (2005). The latter argue that technology will modify the relative cost of in-house production versus outsourcing.

It should be clear that these papers see a role for the speed of technological change and/or technology investments in raising the attractiveness of services which are supplied from outside of the firm. None of these models considers the relative attractiveness of foreign versus domestic supplied services. Hanley and Ott (2012) attempt to address this gap in the literature by considering a model where firms can either (1) choose to remain purchasing their inputs in conventional ways or (2) elect to purchase some or all of their inputs on an online buyer/supplier interface. The model describes the effect of improvements in online technologies on the pricing of inputs and ultimate demand for inputs. For all firms (those remaining with conventional outsourcing methods and those choosing to use a buyer/supplier interface), improvements in the internet cause a reduction in the price of services. This reduction in the price of services is largely due to a "competition" effect. This effect can be explained by increased competition among service providers as potential customers (firms) become more aware about the price and availability of services on offer and can choose the service which offers the best value for money. There is now a thicker market for services, in line with the stylised fact that the internet made many services such as professional services (auditing, legal, insurance, architecture etc.) tradable. Not all firms will continue to outsource services in conventional ways. There is a subgroup of firms that will start adopting internet-enabled outsourcing. Such firms invest in the buyer/supplier internet interface, an investment that does not guarantee a positive return. The effect on the ultimate amount of services outsourced is ambiguous due to a "dampening" effect, which captures the uncertainty of using the new method in a risk premium. Overall, the model predicts growth in the volume of foreign services transacted due to the competition effect where the market for international services is now more transparent and domestic buyers can pick and choose from a wider menu of suppliers. The growth in international traded services is in line with what other economists have observed for the period following the internet revolution (e.g., see Miroudot *et al.* 2009; Amiti and Wei, 2009).

III EMPIRICAL METHODOLOGY

The aim of this paper is to examine what happens to the intensity of foreign outsourcing when a firm adopts internet-enabled technologies for outsourcing. In doing so, we face a standard selection problem. If firms adopting internet-based tools to procure their services from suppliers ("Adopters") have, on average, different outsourcing intensities to begin with (compared with other firms which use conventional outsourcing methods), we might expect to see *ex post* differences in the intensities of foreign services for Adopters and non-Adopters even if Adopters had not started to adopt internet-based outsourcing tools. Adopting firms would then self-select into the Adopter group, in which case, the impact on the growth in foreign services would have less to do with the adoption of internet-based outsourcing and more to do with the inherent characteristics of the Adopter group.

The lack of statistically relevant and intuitively compelling instruments for online switching (factors prompting firms to switch to online outsourcing but which do not directly affect outsourcing growth) makes it difficult to deal with self-selection. The first step towards identifying an effect of switching to internet purchasing is, therefore, to define Adopters and Non-Adopters. To do so, we drop from our sample all firms that use the internet already in 2002. Among the remaining firms we defined Adopters as those who start using the internet in 2003. As a second step, we investigate the impact on foreign outsourcing *growth* rather than *levels*, allowing us to abstract from unobserved firm effects correlated with the level of outsourcing.

Following Heckman *et al.* (1997), we can calculate the average effect of switching to online outsourcing on subsequent outsourcing growth.

$$E\{y^1 - y^0 \mid ADOPT_{it}^1 = 1\} = E\{y^1 \mid ADOPT_{it}^1 = 1\} - E\{y^0 \mid ADOPT_{it}^0 = 0\}$$

where the terms y^0 and y^1 represent foreign outsourcing intensities in the pre-switch and post-switch period respectively and $ADOPT^1$ and $ADOPT^0$ represent firms from the treatment and control groups respectively. The last term is needed in order to infer the foreign outsourcing intensities for the Adopters had they not switched (which is, by definition, unobserved). To get this term, we match each Adopter with a derived counterfactual, constructed over the distribution of non-Adopters.

We apply the STATA propensity score routine, *pscore*, based on Rosenbaum and Rubin (1983). Specifically, the first-stage probit captures the likelihood that firms switch to online outsourcing based on observable pre-switching attributes of the firm (firm size and ownership status, the firm's industry sector and lagged levels and intensity of foreign services purchased).[2] Firms from control (non-Adopters) and treatment (Adopters) groups are then assigned to strata according to the propensity score.[3] The selection probit balances firms in the treatment (Adopter) and control (non-Adopters) group on the basis of pre-existing levels of outsourced foreign services in addition to balancing on other covariates. The Adopter and non-Adopters groups are then balanced across several blocks. Figure 3 below illustrates the full continuum of switching probabilities for firms in the Adopter and non-Adopter groups on the basis of the selection probit where the area of common support is seen to be between 2.2 per cent and 26.4 per cent. In this range, the distributions of

[2] Initial levels of outsourced inputs (2002) are used to explain persistence in line with Amiti and Wei (2009). To deal with this, we include total outsourced inputs (levels) for the previous year. The positive connection between a firm's technological ability and its outsourcing intensity is captured in the R&D dummy (e.g., see Bartel *et al.*, 2014). Outsourcing intensity represents foreign factor inputs scaled by total inputs (foreign and domestic). Labour productivity and firm age were used in earlier regressions though their relative inability to explain variations in outsourcing growth led to them being subsequently dropped.

[3] The conditional independence assumption in this instance holds that firms in the control and treatment group demonstrate differing willingness/ability to continue purchasing intermediates in conventional ways versus their willingness to transact with suppliers online based on the employment size and other covariates in the selection equation.

the propensity scores for non-Adopters and Adopters overlap. There are several possible methods to implement propensity score matching. In our final analysis, we settle on three widely-used methods: Kernel Matching, Neighbourhood Matching and Caliper Matching.

The non-parametric matching estimator constructs a match for each firm that starts to outsource online using a weighted average over multiple firms which do not carry out online outsourcing. We can then estimate the growth in foreign outsourcing for firms that have begun to outsource online, and compare it to firms that decided to outsource online, subject to the standard common support assumption. Generally, we expect to see a growth in outsourced services between 2003 and 2004 as suppliers took advantage of improvements in internet speeds and coverage to set up and expand their sales.

IV DATA

4.1 *Services Outsourced over the Internet, the ABSEI and Eurostat (E-Commerce) Surveys*

We start by defining what is meant by services outsourcing. Services outsourcing are services which are supplied by an outside firm. Either the services originate from Irish-based suppliers in the data (domestic services outsourcing) or services are procured from foreign-based suppliers (foreign services outsourcing).[4] The total amount of outsourced services, therefore, corresponds to the sum of domestic and foreign outsourced services. Services could be outsourced in the conventional way, or orders for services from suppliers could be placed using internet-enabled outsourcing tools. We recall that the impact of using the internet for outsourcing on changes in the mix of foreign/domestic services forms the focus of our analysis.

Specifically, we were able to extract information on the adoption of internet-enabled outsourcing from the 2004 Eurostat *E-Commerce Survey*. Eurostat reported that by 2003, 85 per cent of firms had access to the internet. Internet penetration rates in Ireland were even higher. By 2004, 92 per cent of firms had internet access and 34 per cent of firms placed orders over the internet.[5] The Eurostat E-Commerce survey aimed to evaluate how the internet was being used within firms (Eurostat, 2005), under the reasonable

[4] Unfortunately, our measure of foreign outsourcing does not allow us to distinguish between inhouse offshore (i.e., a multinational importing services from an overseas affiliate) and outsourced offshoring.

[5] From UNCTAD aggregate statistics downloaded from the UNCTAD statistics data centre (UNCTADSTAT) at http://unctadstat.unctad.org/wds/ReportFolders/reportFolders.aspx

assumption that the vast majority of firms were already using the internet by the time the survey was launched. The Eurostat E-commerce survey was integrated into the *Irish Annual Business Survey of Economic Impact* (ABSEI) dataset, which we will now go on to describe.

The ABSEI data comprises a panel of Irish and foreign firms which contains, inter alia, rich information on the domestic and foreign outsourcing activities of the firms which are surveyed. The ABSEI data covers the client base of several Irish funding agencies. Client firms with 10 or more employees are captured in the data and the response rate is reasonably strong at around 60 per cent (Forfás, 2010). The ABSEI can be used to estimate the impact of adopting internet-enabled outsourcing on the subsequent growth in foreign outsourced services. The panel data can additionally be used to provide contextual information – e.g., on the economic activity of firms, their employment size and other descriptors of the firm. Specifically, we apply data on firm employment levels, NACE2 sector classification, exports and outsourcing for the period 2000 to 2004.

The E-Commerce survey was administered in the first quarter of 2004 to the IT managers of the firms surveyed (Eurostat, 2002). The reference period was for services outsourced over the internet in 2003. Information on the adoption of internet-enabled outsourcing was also available for 2002 because the ABSEI data integrates consecutive waves of the E-commerce surveys.

We will now expand on the format and sample frame of the E-commerce survey. The Eurostat framework document stipulated that the results from the E-commerce survey should be "representative". However, it gave individual countries that participated in the survey the opportunity to include supplementary questions and exercise their own discretion over the ultimate questionnaire design. Those agencies which delivered the E-commerce questionnaire were obliged to survey firms with at least 50 employees.

It should be immediately clear that the Eurostat E-Commerce survey targeted larger firms (greater than 50 employees) than the ABSEI survey (10 or more employees) and so we expect that by focusing on firms responding to the 2004 Eurostat survey there is a bias towards larger firms. This should be kept in mind when interpreting the results below.

4.2 *Characterising "Adopters", "Non-Adopters" and Data Attrition*

The question which represents the focus of our analysis was a compulsory question in the 2004 E-Commerce survey. Participating firms were asked the following question, "Has the enterprise purchased products/services via the internet?" This question corresponded to C1* in the Eurostat framework document (See Appendix 1 which provides a screen grab for the earlier wave asking the same question).

Based on this question we calculated our measure of internet transactions. Our variable, *Internet Adopters*, indicates whether the firm had used the internet to purchase inputs.

In order to differentiate firms that used the internet for the first time in 2003 to outsource inputs from a foreign or domestic supplier, we checked in the 2004 survey whether these firms had indicated that they had used the internet to outsource inputs in 2002. Firms which did not supply information on their internet purchasing for 2002 were necessarily excluded from the final analysis because only firms providing information for both years could be considered in the analysis. This exclusion was necessary because we focus on Adopters (firms using the internet to outsource inputs for the first time in 2003) and non-Adopters (Firms never using the internet to outsource inputs in the period 2002-2004 inclusive).

Appendix 2 provides a breakdown of the combined ABSEI-Eurostat data. We have information on a total of 3,192 firms for which we had ABSEI data for 2004. In this way, we can measure E-commerce activity for 2003 and relate this to increases/decreases in international outsourcing for 2004, where information on outsourcing is extracted from the ABSEI data.

Looking at the breakdown of the ABSEI/Eurostat data, 2,287 firms were discarded from the final estimation sample because they either (1) contained no information in 2004 on outsourcing patterns nor on internet-outsourcing or (2) these firms did contain information on internet-outsourcing but had been already using the internet to conduct outsourcing since before 2003. A small number of firms (69) were further eliminated from our estimation sample because they belonged in NACE Revision 2 categories with fewer than 15 firms. The latter were excluded from our estimation sample, because due to the considerable variation in firms' outsourcing across the categories of NACE2, it is imperative to control for industry sector. Additionally, the various matching estimation techniques that we later applied perform less well with small group sizes. This is because it is difficult to balance across smaller groups. Overall, therefore, our final estimation sample accounts for around 1 in 4 of all firms in the raw ABSEI data.

We then cleaned the data in the following way. The data was first deflated by applying the Consumer Price Index (CPI) to nominal variables such as *foreign services purchased* which captures the value of foreign services outsourced over the period. Following this, we generated our foreign services intensity measure by calculating the share of foreign services in the firms total spending on external services (foreign services/(foreign services + domestic services)). We also calculated the annual growth in total services outsourced for non-missing values of this variable.

Our key variable for this analysis, *Internet Adopters* was formulated as follows. Firms responding to the 2004 E-commerce survey on internet outsourcing, which had commenced purchasing over the internet by the end of 2003, were characterised as Adopters (*Internet Adopters* = 1). Firms which responded to the survey but which had continued to purchase inputs in the conventional way over the period 2002-2004, were characterised as non-Adopters (*Internet Adopters* = 0). The fact that the E-commerce survey is biased towards larger firms (we shall see this later when we examine the data), implies that any increases in foreign outsourcing for Adopters are likely to represent a lower bound for an overall effect which is likely to be higher. Our reason for making this assumption is based on the premise that smaller firms are in general less prone to outsource inputs abroad due to high costs (Tomiura, 2005) and hence may be more responsive to a positive effect from internet based sourcing.

We now examine the key variables used in our analysis. Table 1 indicates that the median firm was an Irish domestic firm (owner = 1) and non-Adopter (*Internet Adopters* = 0). Firms were indeed large, on average comprising 100

Table 1: *Breakdown of Covariates*

Stats	*Internet Adopters*	*Foreign Firm*		
Mean	0.12	1.29		
Median	0	1		
SD	0.32	0.46		
N	836	836		
Stats	*Employment 2001*	*Employment 2002*	*Employment 2003*	*Employment 2004*
Mean	104	102	101	102
Median	38	36	36	35
SD	227	229	229	239
N	742	836	836	836
Mean	0.13	0.13	0.14	0.14
Median	0.05	0.05	0.05	0.05
SD	0.20	0.21	0.21	0.21
N	742	836	836	836
Stats	*Foreign Services Purchased 2001*	*Foreign Services Purchased 2002*	*Foreign Services Purchased 2003*	*Foreign Services Purchased 2004*
Mean	4,220	4,327	6,136	7,712
Median	14	14	17	21
SD	94,353	101,137	134,269	177,825
N	742	836	836	836

employees. Approximately 13 per cent of all services were outsourced from overseas and this amount remained reasonably constant across the years. The value of foreign services increased over the period although the high standard deviation and the sizeable difference between the average and median values for this variable, *foreign services purchased*, suggests that some firms in the estimation sample were heavy users of foreign services.

In our next section, we begin our econometric analysis by applying a simple OLS regression to the data to reveal whether the start of purchasing services over the internet, was associated with higher levels of foreign outsourced services in the following year.

V ANALYSIS

We begin in Table 2 by regressing the growth in foreign services intensity (change in foreign services/total services), on the firm's employment size, ownership status, lagged foreign services intensity, lagged volume of outsourced services and NACE rev. 2-sector category.[6] For the lagged values we use values for the year 2002. We find that the adoption of the internet for outsourcing was significantly correlated with the growth in the intensity of foreign services in the subsequent year. We also find that firms with lower intensities of foreign to total services are significantly more likely to report higher growth in the intensity of foreign outsourced services. One possibility is that there is some convergence in the optimal amount of foreign services outsourced where firms with *ex ante* rates of foreign outsourced to total outsourced services show reduced growth in this measure the following year.

In estimation (2) we estimate whether the volume of foreign services increases between the two periods. The coefficient on internet adoption is positive but statistically insignificant. We also note that larger firms consume increasing volumes of foreign outsourced services. Generally, therefore, it is harder to show a link between the adoption of internet-based outsourcing and a growth in the overall volume of internationally outsourced services. The adoption of online-outsourcing appears to affect the mix of foreign to domestic outsourcing rather than the total volume of outsourced services.

The simple regression of internet adoption on the changing intensity of foreign outsourced services in the following year reveals a strong and significant association between the two variables. But is this positive

[6] In earlier versions of this paper we included a measure for export growth. This variable added little to the overall model fit, caused considerable attrition in the sample due to firms not reporting their exporting each year and was accordingly dropped from the estimations.

Table 2: *Adoption of Internet-enabled Outsourcing and Foreign Services Outsourced (OLS)*

	(1) *y*: Δ *Foreign Services Intensity*	*(2)* *y*: Δ *Foreign Services Purchased*
Internet Adopter $_{t-1}$	0.033**	0.072
	(0.014)	(0.082)
Employment $_{t-1}$	–0.004	0.039*
	(0.003)	(0.024)
Foreign firm	0.007	–0.027
	(0.007)	(0.039)
Foreign Services Intensity $_{t-1}$	–0.078***	0.095
	(0.020)	(0.107)
Foreign Services Purchased $_{(t-1)}$	0.005**	-0.055
	(0.002)	(0.023)
Sector dummies	yes	yes
Observations	836	833
R^2	0.068	0.045
Adjusted. R^2	0.0406	0.0168
Root mse	0.0940	0.540

Notes: Robust standard errors in parentheses. Employment and foreign services amount logged. ***p<0.01, **p<0.05, *p<0.10. Sector dummies at NACE2 aggregation.

relationship a consequence of selection bias? In the latter case, we would expect that Adopters are *ex ante* different from non-Adopters and that these *ex ante* differences are what drive the perceived relationship. For example, what if those firms which started to use the internet to place orders with suppliers did so because the transaction costs of conventional methods were prohibitive? If this were the case, we might observe that the adoption of internet-based foreign outsourcing was a pattern seen most often in firms with low starting rates of foreign services.

We can check this possibility visually by examining the distribution of foreign outsourced services for internet-Adopters and non-Adopters for 2002 and 2004.

What is evident from comparing Figure 1 and Figure 2 is that firms which adopt the internet for services outsourcing have, on average, lower foreign services intensities (Figure 1) to begin with than firms which never use the internet for outsourcing. Our graphs of the foreign services distributions (kernel density) for the pre- and post-treatment period show that non-Adopters had observationally similar foreign outsourcing intensities in both periods (15.4 per cent versus 15.5 per cent) but for Adopters, the percentage

Figure 1: *Distribution of Foreign Services Outsourcing*

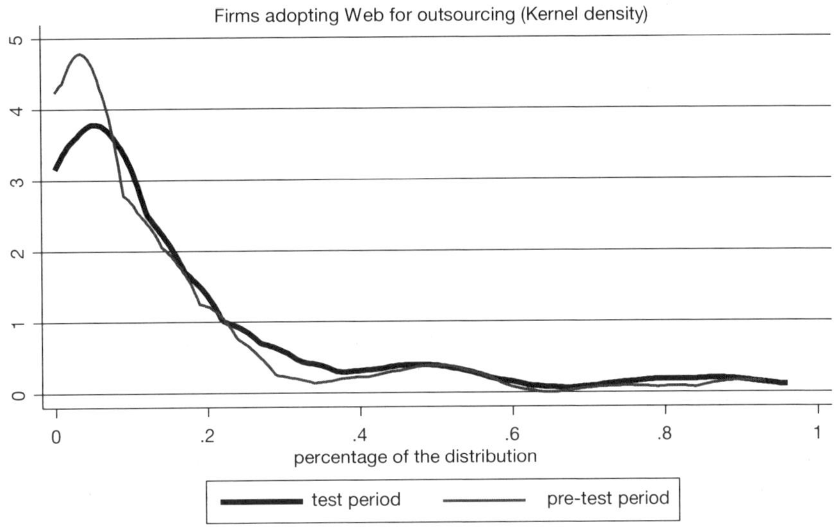

Note: Mean services outsourced pre-test = 11.9 per cent; post-test = 15.2 per cent.

Figure 2: *Distribution of Foreign Services Outsourcing*

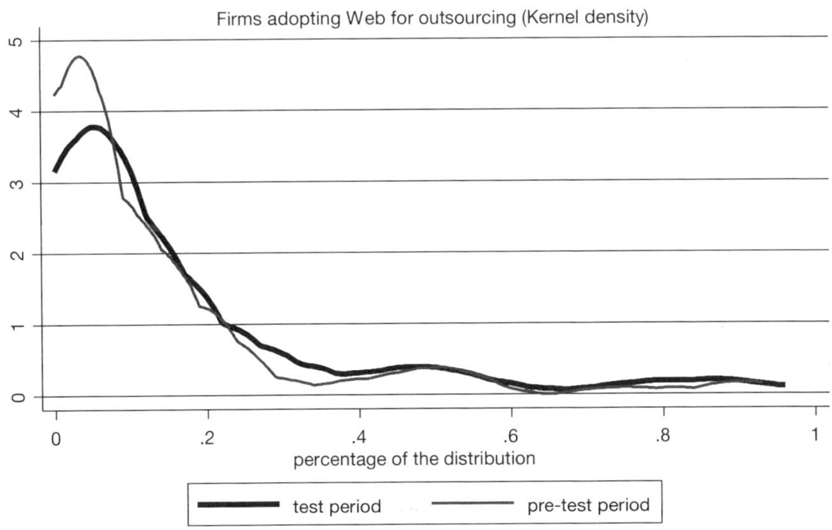

Note: Mean services outsourced pre-test = 15.4 per cent; test = 15.5 per cent.

was seen to rise (11.9 per cent versus 15.2 per cent) between the pre-treatment and post-treatment periods. Therefore, it makes sense to initially model the firm's choice of internet-based outsourcing conditional on the firm's pre-test foreign outsourced services intensity because Adopters and non-Adopters exhibit *ex ante* differences in the ratio of foreign to total outsourced services. This exercise of selecting firms on the basis of their *ex ante* outsourcing behaviour (along with other attributes such as size and sector) leaves us with a more valid basis for comparing any ultimate differences in foreign services outsourcing.

Accordingly, the next step is to estimate a selection Probit regression which estimates the move to adopt the internet to outsource services (*Internet Adopter* = 0 in time t–1 and *Internet Adopter* = 1 in time t). The response variable is conditioned on the lagged share of foreign outsourced to total outsourced services and other variables which are standard in the literature such as firm size and sector. The probit regression in Table 3 shows that there is indeed a significantly negative relationship between the two variables. In other words, firms with a low starting share of foreign outsourced services in their overall basket of outsourced services are significantly more likely to

Table 3: *Decision to Adopt Internet-enabled Outsourcing (Selection Probit)*

	y: Internet Adopter
Foreign Services Intensity $_{t-1}$	–0.87***
	(–2.38)
Employment $_{(t-1)}$	–0.02
	(–0.31)
Foreign firm	–0.10
	(–0.63)
Foreign Services purchased $_{(t-1)}$	–0.018
	(–0.35)
Constant	–0.29
	(–0.41)
Sector dummies	yes
Observations	836
LR $chi^2(23)$	29.94
Prob > chi^2	0.15
Pseudo R^2	0.05
Balanced propensity score[1]	yes

Notes: [1]Full balancing output, including for individual variables available from authors on request. Standard errors in brackets.

become Adopters. The Probit regression generates a propensity score for Adopters and non-Adopters whose distribution we can examine in Figure 3.[7]

Figure 3 illustrates the balanced propensity score for firms which do not adopt internet-based outsourcing and the group of firms which choose to adopt this practice. The area within the graph corresponding to the common support area is for the propensity score within the range 0.022 to 0.264. We subsequently estimate that only 24 firms were excluded on the basis of falling outside the common support region (See also Appendix 2), leaving a total of 812 firms for the estimation sample. We can also visually see the matching process at work in Figure 3. Here we see the largely overlapping distributions for firms which do not adopt the internet to outsource from supplier firms and those that choose to do so. We can also observe the portion of the distribution falling outside of the common support area.

Figure 3: *Distribution of Balanced Propensity Score*

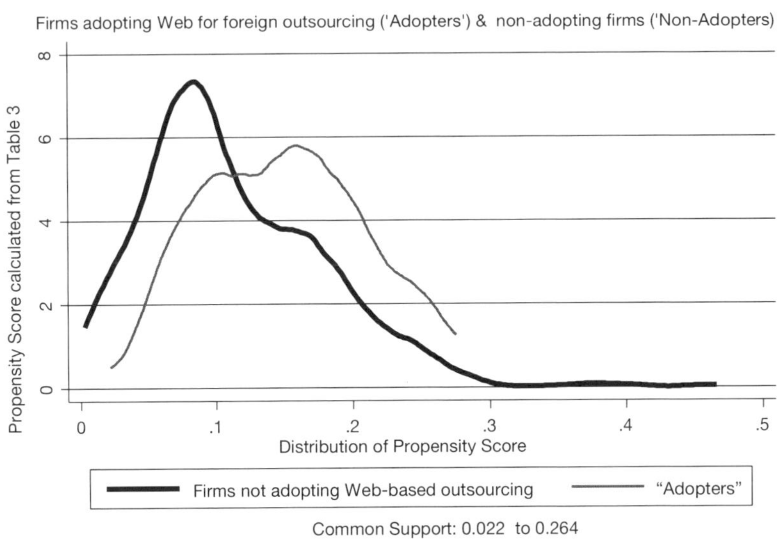

Our next step is to estimate the impact of a firm's adoption of internet-based services outsourcing on the subsequent growth in the firm's share of outsourced foreign services. Table 4 applies the data to this question using a variety of propensity score matching methods. In the first estimation model we

[7] See Appendix 4 on more detail of the balancing. A full description of the balancing tests is available from the authors on request.

use Kernel Matching (KM), followed by Nearest Neighbour Matching (NN) and finally by Caliper Matching (CM). It should be noted that the number of observations in the estimation sample varies according to the method used. KM applies all observations in the estimation sample, weighted by their distance to matched firms along the Gaussian continuum. Nearest Neighbours cuts the sample down to individual Treatment group firms (100 Adopters) and picks the most statistically similar nearest neighbor. Finally, CM uses as its criteria the set of neighbouring firms which fall within a pre-specified radius.

Table 4: *Impact of Internet-Enabled Outsourcing on Foreign Outsourcing*

		Δ Foreign Services Intensity		
	Kernel Matching	*Kernel Matching (Blocks 2-4 only)*	*Nearest Neighbour*	*Caliper Matching*
	(1)	*(2)*	*(3)*	*(4)*
Internet adopter	0.032***	0.034**	0.040***	0.033**
	(2.253)	(1.807)	(2.35)	(2.10)
Observations	812	417	185	836
Firms that adopt (Treatment)	100	72	100	100
Firms that do not adopt (Control)	712	345	85	736

Notes: t-values in brackets. STATA procedure *attk* (Kernel matching) with common support assumption used in estimation (1). Balanced blocks (4) at propensity score cut-offs 0-9 per cent; 10-15 per cent; 15-20 per cent; >20 per cent (See Appendix 4). Common support 2.2-26.4 per cent. STATA procedure *attnd* (Nearest Neighbourhood matching) with common support assumption, random draw and 100 bootstrap repetitions used in (2). Random draw used for NN. 10 neighbours with replacement used in (3) and 50 repetitions.

We can see from Table 4 that the impact of adopting internet-based outsourcing on the subsequent growth in the intensity of foreign services outsourced is 3.2 per cent for Model (1) when we apply Kernel Matching to the full sample across the common support area. These estimates are based on the matched propensity scores that were obtained over 4 blocks (See Appendix 4 for balancing score output). One could argue that the propensity score values for the first block are different, at least at the 5 per cent level of statistical significance. Therefore, Model (2) re-estimates the output for the Kernel Matching method taking only the observations for blocks 2-3 inclusive where the tests for balancing scores pass at the 0.01 level of significance. The estimates for Model (2) reveal that the effects are much the same as before – 3.4 per cent for Model (2) versus 3.2 per cent for Model (1) – although the t-value decreases somewhat. The t-value may have decreased in line with our exclusion of 395 firms from the estimation sample used in Model (2). Because there is such little difference between the results obtained over Models (1) and (2), we continue to estimate Models (3-4) using the full sample for the common support region 2.2 to 26.4 per cent.

The results are reassuringly similar across the different matching methods used. Summarising, the effect is 3.2 to 3.4 per cent for KM, 4.0 per cent for NN respectively and 3.3 per cent for CM. In all cases the effect is statistically significant. A further point worth noting is that the effects documented in Table 4 which are obtained from using a variety of matching methods are relatively similar to the effects obtained when using the straightforward OLS regression (3.3 per cent) method in Table 2.

VI CONCLUSION

What can we conclude from our examination of the adoption of internet-based outsourcing on the intensity of foreign outsourced services? The early years after the Millennium represented a period when firms generally explored new ways of exploiting advances in internet technology to transact with other firms. Even in 2014, the delivery of services to businesses over the internet has improved even further. For example, Blur plc. is a recently floated firm on London's Alternative Investment Market (AIM) which developed a proprietary platform (blur 4.0). This platform allows small businesses to more cost effectively outsource services from suppliers.[8]

It would be interesting, whether the usage of more recent advances in services provision, platforms such as those offered by Blur plc. further increase the competitiveness of foreign services providers versus their domestic competitors. A possible direction for future work is to examine the possible erosion of the domestic services advantage within a cross-country framework taking the size, orientation and importance of the domestic services sector into account. Ideally, data would include information on actual volumes transacted, rather than price amounts, to allow researchers to calculate the changing volumes in the amount outsourced from overseas versus from domestic suppliers.

What our results suggest is that a firm's adoption of internet enabled outsourcing slightly favoured foreign services providers, at least in the sense of increasing their share in the mix of overall outsourced services. This revealed bias towards foreign services providers makes sense if Irish

[8] http://www.ft.com/cms/s/0/6e2a9108-a12f-11e2-990c-00144feabdc0.html#axzz38HLh4kcS

outsourcers faced potentially higher costs when transacting with foreign suppliers and that the use of internet-based outsourcing technologies reduced these transaction costs. If this were the case, the adoption of internet-enabled outsourcing would have disproportionally reduced the marginal cost for outsourcers of transacting with a foreign supplier compared with the cost of transacting with a domestic supplier. In sum, the economic significance of internet-enabled outsourcing for foreign services (3.2-4.0 per cent) is non-trivial and this effect is robust to a variety of estimation methods.

REFERENCES

ABRAMOVSKY, L. and R. GRIFFITH, 2006, "Outsourcing and Offshoring of Business Services: How Important is ICT?", *Journal of the European Economic Association* Vol. 4, No. 23, pp. 594-601.

ABRAMOVSKY, L. and R. GRIFFITH, 2009. *ICT, Corporate Restructuring and Productivity*. No. 09, 10. IFS working papers.

AMITI., M. and S. WEI, 2009. "Service Offshoring and Productivity: Evidence from the US", *The World Economy*, Vol. 32, No. 2, pp 203-220.

BARTEL, A., S. LACH and N. SICHERMAN, 2014, "Technological Change and the Make-or-Buy Decision", *Journal of Law, Economics and Organization*, Vol. 30, pp. 165-192.

EUROSTAT, 2002. "Community Survey on ICT Usage (E-Commerce) of Enterprises 2003", Version of 6.11.2002, final. www.unctad.org/ecommerce/

EUROSTAT, 2005. "Use of the Internet among individuals and enterprises", (available at http://epp.eurostat.ec.europa.eu/cache/ITY_OFFPUB/KS-NP-06-012/EN/KS-NP-06-012-EN.PDF)

EUROSTAT REPORT, 2008. *Information Society: ICT Impact Assesment by Linking Data from Different Sources*, Technical Report, Eurostat.

FORFÁS, 2010. "Annual Business Survey of Economic Impact", (available from http://www.forfas.ie/media/FF08062012-ABSEI-Publication.pdf)

GIRMA, S. and H. GÖRG, 2007. "Evaluating the Foreign Ownership Wage Premium Using a Difference-in-Difference Matching Approach", *Journal of International Economics*, Vol. 72, No. 1, pp. 97-112.

GOLDBERG, P., A. K. KHANDELWAL, N. PAVCNIK and P. TOPALOVA, 2009. "Trade Liberalization and New Imported Inputs", *American Economic Review*, Vol. 99, No. 2, pp. 494-500.

GÖRG, H. and A. HANLEY, 2004. "Does Outsourcing Increase Profitability?", *The Economic and Social Review*, Vol. 35, pp. 267-288.

GÖRG, H. and A. HANLEY, 2011. "Services Outsourcing and Innovation: An Empirical Investigation", *Economic Inquiry*, Vol. 49, No. 2, pp. 321-333.

GÖRG, H., A. HANLEY and E. STROBL, 2008. "Productivity Effects of International Outsourcing: Evidence from Plant Level Data", *Canadian Journal of Economics*, Vol. 41, No. 2, pp. 670-688.

GROSSMAN, G. M. and E. HELPMAN, 2005, "Outsourcing in a Global Economy", *Review of Economic Studies*, Vol. 72, pp. 135-159.

HANLEY, A. and I. OTT, 2012. "What Happened to Foreign Outsourcing when Firms Went Online?", Kiel Working Paper 1774, Kiel Institute for the World Economy.

HECKMAN, J., H. ICHIMURA, J. SMITH and P. TODD, 1997. "Matching as an Econometric Evaluation Estimator: Evidence from Evaluating a Job Training Programme", *Review of Economic Studies*, Vol. 64, pp. 605-654.

HIJZEN, A., T. INUI and Y. TODO, 2010. "Does Offshoring Pay? Firm-Level Evidence from Japan", *Economic Inquiry*, Vol. 48, No. 4, pp. 880-895.

JONES, R. W. and H. KIERZKOWSI, 2001. "A Framework for Fragmentation" in S. Arndt and H. Kierzkowsi (eds.), *Fragmentation: New Production Patterns in the World Economy*, Oxford University Press.

LILEEVA, A. and J. VAN BIESEBROECK, 2013. "Outsourcing When Investments are Specific and Complementary", *Journal of the European Economic Association*, Vol. 11, No. 4, pp. 871-896.

McCANN, F., 2011, "The Heterogeneous Effect of International Outsourcing on Firm Productivity", *Review of World Economics*, Vol. 147, pp. 85-101.

MIROUDOT, S., R. LANZ and A. RAGOUSSIS, 2009. "Trade in Intermediate Goods and Services", OECD Trade Policy Working Paper 93, Paris: OECD.

OECD, 2006, "Working Party on the Information Economy – The Share of Employment Potentially Affected by Offshoring – An Empirical Investigation", Directorate for Science, Technology and Industry Committee for Information, Computer and Communications Policy, 2006

ROSENBAUM, P. and D. RUBIN, 1983. "The Central Role of the Propensity Score in Observational Studies for Causal Effects", *Biometrika*, Vol. 79, No. 1, pp. 41-55.

SAKO, M., 2006. "Outsourcing and Offshoring: Implications for Productivity of Business Services", *Oxford Review of Economic Policy*, Vol. 22, No. 4, pp. 499-512.

SMITH, J. and P. TODD, 2005. "Rejoinder", *Journal of Econometrics*, Vol. 125, pp. 365-375

STATISTICS AUSTRIA, 2005. "Europäischen Erhebung über E-Commerce (2003/2004) in Österreich", Bearbeitungsstand: 14.11.2005

TOMIURA, E., 2005. "Foreign Outsourcing and Firm-Level Characteristics: Evidence from Japanese Manufacturers", *Journal of the Japanese and International Economies*, Vol. 19, pp. 255-271.

UNCTAD, 2004. *World Investment Report: The Shift Towards Services*, New York: United Nations.

APPENDIX 1

Screengrab for the EUROSTAT E-Commerce Survey

The questions are defined in the framework document "EUROSTAT: Community survey on ICT usage (e-commerce)" as follows:

Purchases via Internet				
C1*	Has the enterprise purchased products/services via the internet during 2002 (at least 1 per cent of total purchases)? (Filter question)	Yes?	No ?	Do not know

From EUROSTAT: "Community survey on ICT usage (e-commerce) of enterprises 2003", Version of 6.11.2002, final. www.unctad.org/ecommerce/

APPENDIX 2

Breakdown of the Data

ABSEI Raw Data and Eurostat E-Commerce Survey (2004 wave)		
Total number of firms	3,192	
Exclusions:		
Missing values for outsourcing and internet-usage[1]	2,287	
NACE Revision 2: < 15 firms in industrial group	69	
Estimation sample:		
^{s}"Adopters"	100	
^{sn}"non-Adopters"	712	
Firms outside common support region	24	
Total estimation sample^{s+ns}	812	25.4%

Notes: "Community Survey on ICT usage in enterprises (E-Commerce)", 2004 Wave.
[1] Firms which were contained in the ABSEI survey but not surveyed under the Eurostat criteria. Also firms where we have missing values in the 3-year period 2002-2004.

APPENDIX 3

Variable Definitions

Label	*Description*
Foreign Services Intensity	Total foreign outsourced services/ Total outsourced foreign and domestic services
Internet adopter	Firm adopted internet for purchasing inputs in 2003
Foreign Services purchased	Value of foreign services outsourced
employment	Number of FTE employees in firm
foreign firm	Owner is foreign (coded 2 for foreign; 1 for domestic)
s_*	NACE Revision 2, 2-digit sector dummies (manufacturing)

APPENDIX 4

Propensity Score Balancing

Block #				*Ha: diff ! = 0*	*Block Balances*
1	non-Adopters	372	0.067	0.034	yes
	Adopters	28	0.077		
2	non-Adopters	154	0.122	0.200	yes
	Adopters	19	0.126		
3	non-Adopters	127	0.177	0.753	yes
	Adopters	33	0.178		
4	non-Adopters	83	0.227	0.985	yes
	Adopters	20	0.227		

Chapter I.4

A tale of two literatures: Transaction costs and property rights in innovation outsourcing

Nishaal Gooroochurn, Aoife Hanley *

Industrial Economics Division, Nottingham University Business School, Jubilee Campus, Nottingham, NG8 1BB, England, United Kingdom

Received 2 March 2006; received in revised form 21 June 2007; accepted 3 July 2007
Available online 10 August 2007

Abstract

This paper investigates the relative importance of property rights and transactions cost factors in driving the decision of firms to outsource innovation. Using data for over 8000 firms from the UK Community Innovation Survey, we find that property right factors dominate over transaction cost factors. Transaction cost variables are more important for process innovation, while property rights variables are more significant for firms involved in product innovation. In addition, we find that firms involved in process innovation have a higher probability of outsourcing innovation than firms involved in product innovation.

JEL classification: L2; O3

Keywords: Transaction costs; Property rights; Outsourcing

1. Introduction

Innovation and the outsourcing thereof is a double-edged sword. Using the 'market' for the generation of innovative inputs can confer a cost advantage on a firm. However, the downside is that, specifically in the context of innovation where knowledge can be exclusive to the originating firm, any transfer of knowledge to other firms runs the risk of opportunism by partner firms. Furthermore, reliance on third parties for the production of inputs in general incurs contracting costs, leading to production bottlenecks and quality issues.

This double-edged sword summarising the decision to use the market for the generation of innovation, sits within the transaction cost (TC) and property rights (PR) literatures. However, there is a fuzzy divide between these two literatures defying efforts of 'tidy' economists to attribute predictions to their proper source. One major thrust of this paper is to attempt to do just that: to organise the predictions, even where these agree, for the decision to work together with a partner firm on developing innovative inputs.

The idea that the PR and TC literatures work in tandem in explaining information flows is made clear in a recent paper by Love and Roper (2005). A simple rule of thumb to differentiate between the TC and PR literatures is to locate the theoretical emphasis: does the theory emphasise scale economies as the main way to prevent appropriation of information by the partner firm? If the answer is yes and scale is important, then predictions from this literature should explain how a firm protects itself from opportunism by a partner, on the basis that it is not worth a partner firm's time or effort misap-

* Corresponding author. Tel.: +44 115 84 67420; fax: +44 115 64 66667.
E-mail address: Aoife.Hanley@nottingham.ac.uk (A. Hanley).

0048-7333/$ – see front matter © 2007 Elsevier B.V. All rights reserved.
doi:10.1016/j.respol.2007.07.001

propriating knowledge flows due to the extent of scale economies. Here we think in terms of costly innovation such as redesigning a complete car assembly line, which requires such scale economies to produce cost effectively, and firms will gladly cooperate with each other without fearing opportunistic behaviour from the partner firm. On the other hand, the pure appropriation literature looks formally at appropriation via mechanisms such as patent and copyright (see Levin et al., 1987, for an example). More specifically, Audretsch et al. (1996) discuss this issue of appropriation and in the context of the type of information relayed to the partner. Uncertain, risky outcomes are difficult to appropriate (partners cannot exploit these) and may as well be outsourced to a specialist.

In summary, the TC literature represents an approach predicting cost reductions under certain conditions when the market is used. It has a wide set of applications. The PR literature is more concerned with revenue losses arising from misappropriation by the market. This literature is mostly valid for knowledge transfer and has a narrower set of applications than the TC literature.

Clearly these two literatures are not mutually exclusive but they emphasise different things: costs/benefits in the case of TC and formal protection/appropriation environment in the case of PR. One benefit of using the TC and PR dichotomy is that it may help shed light on how firms manage the procurement of different types of innovation: product and process innovation.[1] The TC literature predicts that large-scale process innovation should enjoy the protection of scale economies, while the PR literature suggests that products may be innovative enough to enjoy patent protection or their returns uncertain enough to make opportunism by partners not viable. It is important to distinguish between the two literatures because we conjecture that the generic TC literature is likely to explain a small part of outsourcing decisions (cost saving aspects), while the PR literature has more to do with revenue maximisation. A further reason to distinguish between the two approaches is that if TC variables dominate, then it follows that innovation outsourcing behaves very much like any other type of outsourcing such as raw materials or janitorial services. On the other hand, if the PR variables take precedence, we can highlight just how different innovation outsourcing is from outsourcing standard inputs where no knowledge transfer takes place.

Accordingly, this paper investigates the relative importance of TC and PR factors in determining the innovation outsourcing decision of firms. Given that firms have three options to undertake their innovation activities (in-house, part-outsourcing and full-outsourcing), their decision is modelled using the multinomial logit (MNL) model. The UK Community Innovation Survey (CIS3) consisting of more than 8000 firms is used. Since not all of the firms are involved in innovation, analysing the innovation outsourcing behaviour of firms based on the sub-sample of innovative firms leads to sample selection bias. Furthermore, since the dependent variable is not continuous, a straight application of the inverse mills ratio (IMR) cannot be used to correct the bias, and instead we use the adjusted IMR proposed by van de Ven and van Praag (1981).

We also analyse whether the relative importance of TC and PR factors differs for firms involved in product and process innovation. The analysis is carried out separately for these two groupings involved in product and process innovation. The coefficients across the two equations are compared using the method proposed by Allison (1999).

We find that there are important differences but also similarities in firms' outsourcing behaviour of innovative products and processes. In general PR rather than TC factors appear to drive the decision to collaborate in innovation. TC factors tend to be more significant for firms involved in process innovation than in product innovation, while PR factors are more significant for firms involved in product innovation. Another important difference arising when firms outsource various types of innovative inputs is that, generally, there is a higher probability for process innovation to be outsourced than product innovation. The common denominator is that, regardless of the innovation type, firms favouring formal and informal ways of protecting their market share will shy away from outsourcing innovative inputs. This finding is in line with a similar result given by Veugelers and Cassiman (1999). What distinguishes our paper from that of Love and Roper (2005) is that where the latter use survey methods to highlight the relevance of strategic over TC factors in innovation outsourcing, we infer similar findings using econometric techniques on over 8000 UK firms.

The remainder of the paper is organised as follows. The next section reviews the literature on TC and PR in a broad as well as an innovation outsourcing context. In Section 3, the data, methodology and variables used in the empirical analysis are described, while the results and implications are explained in Section 4. Finally, the summary conclusions of the paper are set out in Section 5.

[1] An example of a product innovation is where a partner firm helps design a new hybrid engine. Cutting costs by introducing an innovative inventories management system is an example of process innovation.

2. Literature review

At the most basic level, an analysis of the decision to collaborate with a partner firm with a view to producing an innovative input can be based on predictions from two separate but not entirely mutually exclusive literatures. We sketch the literature along the same lines as Veugelers and Cassiman (1999, p. 76) who state that "drawing on transaction costs economics and property rights, the literature stresses the choice between external sourcing and internal development as substitutes, i.e. the classical MAKE or BUY decision." For the sake of discussion, a map of the literature of these two strands is outlined in Table 1.

2.1. Property rights

Property rights are synonymous with appropriation. In other words, can a firm's intellectual inputs survive collaboration with a partner firm or will the knowledge leak out and be exploited by third parties? Property rights represent a subset of the full range of possibilities by which a firm can protect its ideas, through formal mechanisms, e.g. patenting and copyright and informal mechanisms, e.g. product complexity, secrecy and lead time to market (Veugelers and Cassiman, 1999; Cassiman and Veugelers, 2002). A further strand to this literature is the link between opportunistic behaviour and the degree of confidence that an innovation can generate rents (Audretsch et al., 1999). In this view some ideas are not worth protecting because uncertain rents render them immune from opportunism by partner firms (Arrow, 1962).

Table 1 presents a summary of some seminal papers on property rights and innovation, alongside some of the predictions which are testable with our data. Firms rely on different forms of property rights to protect their innovation. Trade and manufacturing secrets and lead time not only complement formal agreements such as patents in helping firms to appropriate returns from R&D activities, they are often considered more important (Cohen et al., 2000). Trade secrets are particularly important for innovations that are difficult and costly to reverse-engineer or discover independently (Lerner, 1994). Peck (1986) argues that lead time is particularly important for high-tech products. To sum up, firms that rely highly on trade secrets, formal agreements such as patents, copyright and trademarks and lead time to protect their innovation are less likely to engage in external innovation and prefer to retain idea generation in-house.

Hypothesis 1. Firms relying heavily on property rights to avoid misappropriation by partner firms are less likely to outsource innovation.

2.2. Transaction cost economics

The role of the TC literature in terms of setting up and policing contracts to manage information flows is well recognised. The standard view advanced by Williamson

Table 1
Taxonomy of property rights and transaction costs in innovation

Study	Key ideas	Predictions
Property rights		
Cassiman and Veugelers (2002)	Appropriation	● Reliance on patents reduces Pr(outsourcing)
Levin et al. (1987)	Appropriation	
Veugelers and Cassiman (1999)	Appropriation	● Need for secrecy reduces Pr(outsourcing)
Love and Roper (1999)	Appropriation (indirect)	
Kamien and Zang (2000)	Appropriation (theory)	● Time to market reduces Pr(outsourcing) and higher concentrated markets show greater sensitivity to time
Grünfeld (2003)	Appropriation/absorptive capacity	
Martin (2002) (theory)	Appropriation/absorptive capacity	
Griliches (1979)	R&D/appropriation (indirect)	
Transaction costs		
Cassiman and Veugelers (2002)	Input specialisation	● R&D specialisation economies mean partner specialises in input production, all things equal, i.e. move is towards outsourcing. Effect moderated by (1) relationship specific assets, (2) absorptive capacity arguments
Veugelers and Cassiman (1999)	Input specialisation	
Kamien and Zang (2000)	Input specialisation	
Martin (2002)	Absorptive capacity	
Audretsch et al. (1996)	Specialisation economies/sector	
Feenstra and Hanson (2005)	Asset ownership	● Capital specialisation economies mean partner specialises in input production, all things equal, i.e. move is towards outsourcing except where moderated by relationship specific assets
Grossman and Hart (1986) and Hart and Moore (1990)	Asset ownership	
Rauch (1999)	Specific investments	
Williamson (1989)	R&D and assets	

(1975, 1989) is that the boundaries of the firm are defined by the degree of asset specificity entering an exchange between firms. Asset specificity invites ex post opportunism and requires costly contracts to safeguard against. The importance of the TC literature in explaining outsourcing patterns is somewhat tarnished by recent evidence of an apparent disconnect between the theoretical predictions and practice.[2]

As outlined by Veugelers and Cassiman (1999, p. 66), "The theoretical framework to explain R&D stresses the advantage of tapping existing often more specialised knowledge if available ... However, technology outsourcing may create considerable transaction costs, ex ante in terms of search and negotiation costs and ex post to execute and enforce the contract". There is thus a consensus that innovation is such a highly specialised activity that firms are better off letting specialised external vendors create the innovation. However, with increasing levels of asset specificity and accordingly a higher probability of hold-up, firms will desist from outsourcing innovation (Rauch, 1999).

From the transaction cost literature, firms that incur heavy sunk costs in capital (Hertog and Thurik, 1993), or R&D expenditure (Love and Roper, 2002; Piga and Vivarelli, 2004) may need to amortize these costs by producing innovation internally. High capital and R&D intensity also signify high potential for scale economies, which favour in-house innovation over outsourcing.

On the other hand, for strategic reasons a firm may choose to conduct R&D to raise its absorptive capacity and hence benefit from collaboration with a partner firm. In this case, outsourcing will be favoured over in-house production. Outsourcing will similarly be favoured if a firm's strategy is to incur heavy immediate R&D sunk costs with eventual amortization over a very long time horizon. In this case, researchers will observe that outsourcing persists in the short term (as we see in survey data) and may even increase despite heavy R&D expenditure.

Hypothesis 2. Firms incurring heavy sunk costs of capital and R&D favour in-house production of innovation. One exception is when R&D is used strategically.

The recent literature has highlighted how property rights more than cost considerations appear to dominate when explaining a firm's approach to outsourcing innovation (Love and Roper, 2005). Accordingly, when examining the outsourcing behaviour of innovative firms, we should see that variables denoting a high aversion towards information leakages (high impacts of the patent, secrecy and lead-time variables) dominate over simple cost considerations (encapsulated in transaction cost variables).

The outsourcing of innovation is a special case. Scale economies may be weak or non-existent. The need to control information leakage may dominate. Accordingly, the need to gain scale economies and reduce costs may be demoted by the stronger necessity to stem knowledge flows and profit maximise, i.e. strategic considerations. Love and Roper (2005) in their investigation of the outsourcing of new product development for approximately 2000 manufacturing firms from three EU countries find that when the transaction cost theory breaks down, the deviations in firms' actions from the theory is systematic. This suggests that firms are motivated by strategic rather than cost considerations. The pre-eminence of controlling leakages in order to maintain market share that we see in the innovation literature leads to the third hypothesis.

Hypothesis 3. Property rights variables are more significant than transaction cost variables in determining firms' behaviour to outsource innovation or not.

2.3. Process and product innovation

Veugelers and Cassiman (1999) note that R&D contracting is more likely to occur for generic, non-firm-specific R&D that allows for specialisation advantages, such as routine tasks like materials testing, and process rather than product innovations. Kamien and Zang (2000) similarly conclude that cooperation can only take place for non-firm-specific inputs. These inputs are analogous to process innovation, and are protected by virtue of their high necessity for scale and specialisation economies. Specifically, the Kamien–Zang model posits that where there is a danger of information leaking to the partner firm (exogenous spillovers), firms opt to play it safe and conduct firm-specific R&D internally within the firm. We can conclude from this that firms are wary of colluding in product innovation since product innovation can be classified as a firm-specific input. Where the danger of information leaking out to and being exploited by a partner firm diminishes, firms are happy to outsource innovation. An example of this is where generic R&D inputs (e.g. process inputs) are readily traded by firms because any information spilled over cannot be used opportunistically (appropriated) by the purchasing firm. In other words, generic process inputs are readily

[2] Love and Roper (2005) report a disconnect between the TC theory (posited by academics) and how outsourcing is carried out by business practitioners.

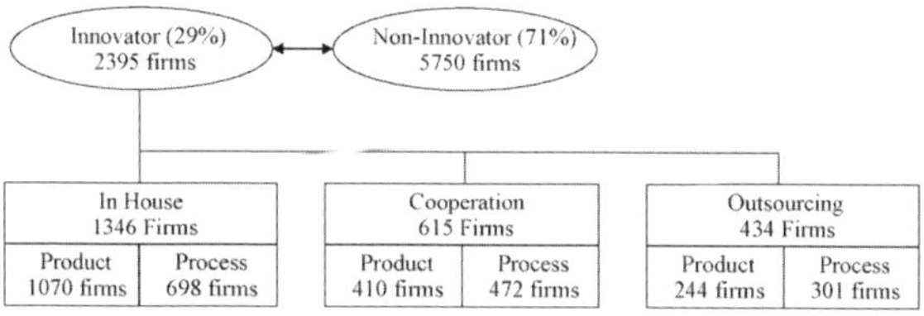

Fig. 1. Structure of data in the UK CIS.

traded due to the additional safeguard against appropriation by partner firms afforded by scale economies. The fourth hypothesis follows from this:

Hypothesis 4. Process innovation is more likely to be outsourced than product innovation.

It seems intuitive that industrial processes (e.g. calibration tools for industrial chemistry), being a generic input used by many potential manufacturers, exhibit strong scale economies. Consequently, the transaction cost literature which accords a role to scale economies fits well with this idea of the importance of scale economies for process innovation. On the other hand, the property rights literature, which places a strong emphasis on such safeguards as patenting laws, can explain leakage prevention strategies where scale economies are less likely to hold. Since scale economies are less likely to arise with the more differentiated product innovations (as opposed to generic in the case of process), firms will rely more on the 'standard toolkit' of patent and copyright protection spelled out in the property rights literature. Hence, the general pattern is that TC considerations are more prevalent for process innovation, while PR concerns are more important for product innovation.

Hypothesis 5. PR and TC variables have a different impact on product and process innovation outsourcing.

3. Data and methodology

The analysis draws on innovation data from the third UK Community Innovation Survey undertaken in 2001, which covers the period 1998–2000. The CIS takes place every 4 years in European countries. It is administered via a postal questionnaire to investigate levels of innovation in businesses on topics such as effects of innovation, factors hampering innovation and innovation-related expenditures. Firms with 10 or more employees, representing small, medium and large businesses in 12 broad sectors across all UK regions, are included. 8172 businesses responded, giving a response rate of approximately 43%. Industry-specific data is obtained from the FAME dataset and the matching is done using the SIC code.

After cleaning the data and dropping firms where data entry cannot be relied upon, the sample consists of 8145 firms, out of which 2395 are actively involved in innovation. 1724 and 1471 of these firms are involved in product and process innovation respectively and of these, 800 firms are involved in both process and product innovation. Innovative firms can either make their own innovation internally (in-house), buy from other institutions such as universities (outsourcing) or a combination of both, that is in collaboration with other institutions (cooperation). The proportion of firms engaged in these options differs across product or process innovation-related firms. Fig. 1 summarises the structure of the dataset.

The primary purpose of our empirical analysis is to investigate the relative importance of transaction cost and property rights factors in determining the innovation outsourcing decision of firms. The response variable is constructed using the question 'How were these innovation developed?', for which there are three possible outcomes (in-house, cooperation or outsourcing).[3] More specifically, questions 4.2 and 5.2 are used for product and process innovation, respectively. The propensity for a given firm i to engage in either of these methods of innovating is measured by the latent variable (OUT_i) representing the three outcomes and is defined

[3] Alternatively, as pointed out by one referee, we could use the proportion of externally acquired R&D expenditure to total R&D expenditure as the response variable in a Tobit framework. However, the external R&D expenditure data in CIS3 is not reliable. For instance, 45% of firms that are involved in external innovation have no external R&D expenditure. On the other hand, 60% of firms that have data for external R&D expenditure are supposed to be conducting their innovation fully in-house.

as

$$\mathrm{OUT}_i = \begin{cases} 0 & \text{if innovation is undertaken in-house} \\ 1 & \text{if innovation is undertaken in conjunction with another firm} \\ 2 & \text{if innovation is fully outsourced} \end{cases}$$

Given that firms have three options to undertake their innovation activities, their decision is modelled using the multinomial logit framework.[4] The basic model is given as

$$\mathrm{OUT}_i = \alpha + \beta X_i^{\mathrm{TC}} + \theta X_i^{\mathrm{PR}} + \delta X_i^{\mathrm{C}} + e_i \qquad (1)$$

where X_i^{TC}, X_i^{PR} and X_i^{C} are vectors of transaction costs, property rights and control variables, respectively, and e_i is the idiosyncratic error term.

For this analysis, we draw on the sub-sample of innovative firms from the dataset. Since the selection is based on the response variable (that is, we can observe the innovation outsourcing behaviour only of firms that are involved in innovation), the selection is not considered as random and standard regression techniques will not produce consistent estimates of the coefficients (Wooldridge, 2002: 551–556). Whether firms will engage in innovation activities or not is a decision that can be modelled using standard logit as follows.

$$\mathrm{INN}_i = \gamma + \phi Z_i + u_i \qquad (2)$$

where INN_i takes the value of one if firm i is innovative or zero otherwise, and Z_i is a vector of explanatory variables. INN_i is constructed from questions 4.1 and 4.2 for process and product innovation, respectively. Firm size is a common variable used in this context. Following the seminal work of Schumpeter (1942), it is hypothesised that the likelihood that a firm will engage in innovative activity rises disproportionately with firm size, although not necessarily linearly. However, it can also be conjectured that larger firms are more likely to engage in in-house innovation than outsourcing, because of their superior resources. With the customary explanatory variables, the error terms in Eqs. (1) and (2) may contain some common omitted variables, leading to a non-zero correlation between e_i and u_i. Hence a sample selection bias arises. The components of vector Z_i are size of firm (*SIZE*), the square of size (*SIZE2*), sectoral dummies (*SEC2-SEC12*), capital intensity (*CAP_INT*), concentration ratio (*CONC*) and types of market—national or international (*MARKET*).[5]

Our concern with sample selection in the behaviour of outsourcing innovation is not unprecedented. Love and Roper (1999) and Piga and Vivarelli (2004) were also concerned with sample selection bias in this context. In our case, we have a case of censored multinomial logit. Our response variable (OUT) has three outcomes, which are observed only if INN_i is equal to one. Because OUT is not a continuous variable, using the inverse mills ratio of Heckman (1979) is not valid. Instead, we use the approach proposed by van de Ven and van Praag (1981). In this approach, the modified IMR (λ_i^*) is calculated as $\lambda_i^* = \lambda_i/\tau_i$, where λ_i is the Heckman's IMR and τ_i is the standard deviation of the error term from model (1) with λ_i as an additional explanatory variable. So the sample selection bias-adjusted MNL model estimated is given as

$$\mathrm{OUT}_i = \alpha + \beta X_i^{\mathrm{TC}} + \theta X_i^{\mathrm{PR}} + \delta X_i^{\mathrm{C}} + \rho\lambda_i^* + e_i' \qquad (3)$$

Since we are also interested in testing whether the relative importance of transaction costs and property rights variables are similar for product and process innovation, the sample is split into two groups, one group consisting of 1724 firms involved in product innovation and the other consisting of 1471 firms involved in process innovation.[6] We estimate model (3) for firms for each sub-sample. However, direct comparison of the coefficients or estimating one equation with an interactive dummy variable for the two groups is not warranted in this case. This is because unlike standard regression, the estimated coefficients in logit models depend on the variance of the error term and there is no reason to assume that the variance will be the same across the different groups. As shown in Hoetker (2004), testing for equality of the coefficients may reveal that the coefficients are different even if they appear to be the same, because the variance of the residual differs across the groups. The solution is to run the logit models without constraining the variance of the error term and then test for equality of the coefficients (Allison, 1999).

[4] Our analysis is based on cross-section data, which show correlations rather than causality. This should be kept in mind while interpreting the results. Potentially, panel data could alleviate this problem as they would allow us to control for unobserved firm-specific (time-invariant) effects and to capture variation over time. Unfortunately, even though there are currently four CIS surveys it is currently not possible to identify individual firms and link surveys over time.

[5] See Love and Roper (1999) for literature reviews on the determinants of innovation.

[6] It is worth noting that there are some firms that are engaged in both process and product innovation, but have different outsourcing policies. For example, they can completely outsource their process innovation and undertake their product innovation in-house. It is hence not possible to estimate one equation for both types of innovation.

Table 2
Definition of variables used in the model

Transaction cost variables (X_i^{TC})	
CAP_INT	Capital intensity (capital expenditure/turnover × 100)
R&D_INT	R&D intensity (internal R&D expenditure/turnover × 100)
Property rights variables (X_i^{PR}) – Likert Scale: '1' not important – '5' very important	
FORMAL	Importance of formal agreement to protect innovation
LEAD	Importance of lead time to protect innovation
SECRET	Importance of secrecy to protect innovation
Firm-specific controlled variables (X_i^C)	
SIZE	Number of employees (000's)
GROUP	Whether firm is part of a group – '1' yes; '0' no
MARKET	Main market – '1' international; '0' national
SKILL	Proportion of employees with a science degree
λ* (IMR)	Adjusted inverse mills ratio
Industry-specific variables (X_i^C)	
CONC	Industry concentration ratio – Herfindahl index
GROWTH	Industry average annual growth rate (1995–2000)
SEC2–SEC 12	Dummy variables for 12 industries classified by 2 digits SIC

A full listing of the variables included in the vectors X_i^{TC}, X_i^{PR} and X_i^C is given in Table 2. As discussed earlier, X_i^{TC} consists of Capital intensity (*CAP_INT*) and R&D intensity (*R&D_INT*). It should be noted that R&D expenditure consists only of internal expenditure, to devise a fairer test of the transaction cost hypothesis. X_i^{PR} includes the importance of trade secrets to protect innovation (*SECRET*), the importance of lead time to protect innovation (*LEAD*) and the importance of formal agreements to protect innovation (*FORMAL*). *FORMAL* is the average of the importance of patents, copyright and trademarks to protect innovation. Based on Hypothesis 1 and 2, it is expected that the coefficients of both PR and TC variables will be negatively correlated with the probability to outsource, and positively related with the probability to innovate in-house. The control variables (X_i^C) are split into firm-specific and industry-specific variables. Kraft (1989) and Acs and Audretsch (1988) posit that firms with skilled labour are more likely to become involved in innovation, especially internal innovation. The proportion of employees with a science degree (*SKILL*) is used as a proxy for skilled labour. Being part of a group of firms (*GROUP*) can also affect the likelihood that a firm will engage in innovation outsourcing. Firms in a group are more likely to be specialised and have more national and international contacts, making it easier to engage in innovation outsourcing. Size of firm, proxied by the number of employees (*SIZE*), is one of the most commonly used variables in the innovation literature. Larger firms are more likely to engage in internal rather than external innovation because the former tends to be more expensive than the latter. Moreover, scale and scope economies in R&D are more likely in larger firms.

Three industry-specific variables are also included in the model. The first is industry growth (*GROWTH*), measured as the average annual growth of the industry turnover over the period 1995–2000 (to coincide with the timing of the survey). Firms in high-growth industries, where no standard product design has yet been developed, tend to be more protective of their innovation ideas and hence prefer internal to external innovation (Audretsch et al., 1996). On the other hand, fast-growing industries can make it difficult for internally innovative firms to keep pace with technology. According to Quinn (2000), with 2 billion 'new minds' coming on the market place between 1995 and 2010, no company acting alone can hope to outperform every competitor and potential competitor in the area of innovation. Technology is moving fast and the only hope of catching-up is by strategically outsourcing innovation.

The second is industry concentration (*CONC*), measured using the Herfindahl index at the 2 SIC digit level. Markets characterised by high levels of concentration are less likely to be associated with innovation outsourcing. Hertog and Thurik (1993) posit that ex ante market power makes it financially less necessary for firms to engage in external innovation, while internal innovation provides firms with the much desired lead time on rivals in order to generate ex post market power. Since lead time is also a determinant in our model, an interactive variable (*CONC_LEAD*) comprising the concentration and lead-time variables is created to investigate the possibility that lead time is more important in a more concentrated market. It should be noted that the marginal effect coefficient of *CONC_LEAD* is not linear in the MNL model (Ai and Norton, 2003). The expected value of OUT is given as:

$$\Phi(\cdot) = \Phi(\beta_1 L + \beta_2 C + \beta_3 \mathrm{CL} + \mathbf{X}\boldsymbol{\beta}) \quad (4)$$

where C is *CONC*, L is *LEAD* and CL is *CONC_LEAD*, $\Phi(\cdot)$ is the logistic distribution and X is a matrix of the other covariates. The marginal effect of *CONC_LEAD* is then given as:

$$\frac{\partial^2 \Phi}{\partial L \partial C} = \beta_3 \Phi'(\cdot) + (\beta_1 + \beta_3 C)(\beta_2 + \beta_3 L)\Phi''(\cdot) \quad (5)$$

as opposed to just β_3 in the linear model. Similarly, the net effect of *LEAD* and *CONC* on the probability are

Table 3
Results for the IIA assumption tests

	Process λ^2 ($P>\lambda^2$)	Product λ^2 ($P>\lambda^2$)
Hausman		
Omitted:out = 2	17.06 (0.846)	1.70 (1.000)
Omitted:out = 3	12.10 (0.955)	−22.63 (1.000)
Small–Hsiao		
Omitted:out = 2	16.32 (0.800)	28.99 (0.145)
Omitted:out = 3	18.68 (0.664)	27.87 (0.180)

H_0: Odds (outcome-*J* vs. outcome-*K*) are independent of other alternatives.

given, respectively, as

$$\frac{\partial \Phi}{\partial L} = (\beta_1 + \beta_3 C)\Phi'(\cdot) \qquad (6)$$

$$\frac{\partial \Phi}{\partial C} = (\beta_2 + \beta_3 L)\Phi'(\cdot) \qquad (7)$$

The marginal effect, the net effect of *LEAD* and *CONC* and their associated standard errors are not readily reported in standard software (using mfx in Stata, for instance), and need to be computed separately using the respective formulae above.

Finally, 11 dummy variables (*SEC2–SEC12*) are included to capture other variations across the 12 sectors in the sample.

A summary of the hypotheses and testable predictions of the paper is tabulated in Table A1 in the Appendix A. Descriptive statistics for the variables to be used in the model, categorised by type of innovation (product and process) and by which party performs the innovation (in-house, cooperation and outsourcing) are given in Table A2 in the Appendix A. It can be seen that firms who outsource innovation tend to be smaller than firms producing innovation in-house. Transaction costs (*R&D_INT*) also tend to be higher for firms that outsource innovation. We can see that the importance of lead time, formal agreement and secrecy to protect innovation, is higher for firms undertaking in-house innovation rather than outsourcing.

Before proceeding with the estimation, we perform some tests for the 'independence of irrelevant alternatives' (IIA) assumption, using the Hausman test (Hausman and McFadden, 1984) and Small–Hsiao test (Small and Hsiao, 1985). The IIA assumption test consists of partitioning the choice set of alternatives into subsets and comparing the coefficients (Hausman test) or the likelihood functions (Small–Hsiao test) of the complete model and the restricted model obtained by leaving out one or more alternatives. The results are given in Table 3 and none of the tests rejects the null hypothesis of IIA. Therefore, the multinomial logit specification seems to be appropriate for modelling the decision to outsource innovation.

4. Results

The MNL model [Eq. (3)] is estimated for the samples of firms involved in process and product innovation and the results are given in Table 4. The results for the selection model, given by Eq. (2), are shown in Table A3 in the Appendix A. Here market growth and types of market are found to be significant determinants of the propensity to innovate for both product and process innovation. We also see that the innovation behaviour of firms is statistically different across sectors.

The results for innovation outsourcing in Table 4 show the marginal effects (d*y*/d*x*) for the extreme cases on the collaboration continuum from in-house manufacture (0) to complete outsourcing (1).[7] Results are given for process and product innovation, estimated separately. It should be noted that the results reported are after removing variables *CAP_INT* and *GROUP*, which were insignificant in all models. The column 'Compare' shows the Chi-square statistics for the Allison test that the coefficients are different between the 'Process 2' and 'Product 2' linear index models.[8] The coefficient of the adjusted IMR (λ^*) is highly significant in all cases. This implies that basing the estimation on the sub-selection of innovative firms does lead to considerable model selection bias. The use of the adjusted IMR to correct for the bias in our case is hence justified.

As stated in Hypothesis 1 and 2, the coefficients of all PR and TC variables are negative for the outsourcing outcome (2) and positive for the fully in-house outcome (0). This holds for both product and process innovation. Comparing the TC and PR variables, it can be seen that PR variables are generally more significant than TC variables, confirming Hypothesis 3 and the assertions of Love and Roper (2005) that firms tend to adopt a more strategic approach to managing their external relationships, while appearing to eschew a purely cost reduction approach (TC). Comparing process and product innovation, it is found that TC variables have a higher impact on process innovation, while PR variables are more significant for product innovation. This supports Hypothesis 5. We first consider the TC variables. Although capital

[7] A brief perusal of the results suggests that the intermediary category does not display much departure from in-house outsourcing.

[8] Stata does not have the capability to run the Allison test on marginal effects.

Table 4
Results for product and process innovation outsourcing model

	Process 0 dy/dx[a]	Process 2 dy/dx[a]	Product 0 dy/dx[a]	Product 2 dy/dx[a]	Compare[b]
Transaction cost variables					
CAP_INT	–	–	–	–	–
R&D_INT	0.0763 (0.042)*	−0.0325 (0.02)*	0.0162 (0.022)	−0.0192 (0.029)	1.61
Property rights variables					
FORMAL	0.006 (0.005)	−0.025 (0.021)	0.013 (0.006)*	−0.032 (0.015)**	2.68*
SECRET	0.0307 (0.018)*	−0.0297 (0.016)*	0.0346 (0.017)**	−0.0332 (0.013)**	5.21**
LEAD	0.0254 (0.021)	−0.0009 (0.014)	0.0267 (0.02)	−0.0064 (0.014)	2.89*
LEAD_N[c]	0.032 (0.031)	−0.041 (0.024)*	0.054 (0.018)**	−0.042 (0.020)**	–
Firm-specific controlled variables					
SIZE	0.0757 (0.038)**	−0.0234 (0.016)	0.0688 (0.035)*	−0.0251 (0.017)	0.23
GROUP	–	–	–	–	–
MARKET	0.0219 (0.052)	0.0134 (0.04)	0.0638 (0.038)*	−0.0476 (0.023)**	4.43**
SKILL	0.0012 (0.001)	−0.0017 (0.001)*	0.0015 (0.001)	−0.0015 (0.001)	0.21
Industry-specific controlled variables					
CONC	−0.0647 (1.092)	0.4332 (0.685)	0.4109 (0.974)	−0.2666 (0.694)	0.46
CONC_N[d]	0.031 (0.022)	−0.703 (0.425)*	−0.083 (0.641)	−0.355 (0.239)	–
GROWTH	−0.0022 (0.003)	0.0025 (0.002)	−0.0031 (0.003)	0.0028 (0.002)*	2.33*
SECTOR[e]	22.61 (0.424)	23.38 (0.280)	18.65 (0.621)	19.31 (0.562)	–
CONC_LEAD	0.001 (0.390)	−0.599 (0.437)	0.009 (0.611)	−0.437 (0.407)	1.01
λ^* (IMR)	−0.0730 (0.029)**	0.0899 (0.037)**	−0.0584 (0.064)**	0.1281 (0.041)***	0.43
Observations	1145	1145	1334	1334	
Chi-square	147.42***	136.55***	210.72***	207.74***	

Standard errors in parentheses.
[a] dy/dx represents the marginal effects.
[b] Chi-square statistics for the difference between the coefficients of linear index model (not marginal effects).
[c] Figures obtained using Eq. (6).
[d] Figures obtained using Eq. (7).
[e] Reported values are Chi-square statistics and p-values in brackets for joint test of the 11 sectoral dummies.
* Significant at 10%.
** Significant at 5%.
*** Significant at 1%.

intensity (*CAP_INT*) is not significant for either product or process innovation, R&D intensity is found to be significant for process innovation. This is not a surprising result given that process innovation tends to be more costly than product innovation and hence involves higher asset specificity in terms of sunk costs. Firms are thus less likely to outsource innovation when they face higher sunk costs. However, there is a positive albeit insignificant effect of R&D intensity on product innovation outsourcing, possibly because capacity absorption is important for the latter. No evidence is found that the coefficient on R&D intensity is different for product and process models using Allison's test.

On the other hand, all the PR variables are significant for both product and process innovation. It should be noted that the coefficient of *LEAD* shows only the direct effect of lead time on the response variable. The net effect (direct and indirect) of lead time is computed using Eq. (6) and is given as *LEAD_N*. As expected, all PR variables have negative coefficients for the fully outsource outcome (2) and positive for internal outcome (0), since firms giving higher importance to property rights issues are more likely to shy away from full innovation outsourcing. It can be seen that lead time has a negative and significant effect on the probability to outsource innovation. This result ties in with survey evidence from the US that entrepreneurs cited production bottlenecks as one of the biggest drawbacks to engaging in outsourcing (Görg and Hanley, 2005). Moreover, since the coefficient of *CONC_LEAD* is also negative for the fully outsourcing case, it implies that the negative effect of lead time on the propensity to outsource is higher in more concentrated industries.

Lead time and formal agreement are more significant for product than for process innovation outsourcing, whereas secrecy is more important for the latter than the former. Allison's test confirms that these differences are significant for all three cases. Given that product innovation is more exposed to competition and to the threat of being copied by rivals, protection in terms of trademarks, copyright and patents (formal agreement) is more important and therefore exerts a higher negative impact on the firms' propensity to outsource than in the case of process innovation. Similarly, since the advantage of lead time in helping to garner a higher market share relates more to product than to process innovation, *LEAD* is more significant for the former than the latter. However, the importance of secrecy is also more important for product innovation, and the difference is considered significant by the Allison test.

Concerning the control variables, firm size has a positive and significant effect on the probability to undertake innovation in-house for both process and product innovation. The variable *SKILL* shows that firms with relatively high endowments of science graduates are more likely to conduct process innovation in-house, perhaps a consequence of their higher self-sufficiency. *SKILL* is significant only for process innovation. Firms whose main market is international as opposed to domestic (*MARKET*) have a lower probability to outsource innovation. This is because these firms are mainly large firms. As expected, *MARKET* is only significant for product innovation. Industry market growth (*GROWTH*) is found to have a significant effect on outsourcing of product innovation, with firms in fast-growing industries tending to engage in external innovation. This is mainly due to the fact that it is difficult to keep up with the pace of innovation when a firm works in isolation. Sectoral dummy variables are found to be insignificant both individually and as a group. The net effect of concentration on OUT is obtained in a similar fashion to *LEAD* using Eq. (7), and is given as *CONC_N*. As expected, firms in highly concentrated markets tend to rely less on outsourcing innovation. For product innovation, although concentration is not significant when evaluated at the mean value of *LEAD*, it becomes significant at higher values of *LEAD*.

Table 5
Probability for each outcome

	Process	Product
P(in-house)	0.52	0.68
P(cooperation)	0.33	0.24
P(outsourcing)	0.15	0.07

The probability of obtaining the possible outcomes of OUT evaluated at the mean value of each explanatory variable is given in Table 5 for both process and product innovation. It can be seen that there is a higher probability of outsourcing innovation for firms involved in process innovation than in product innovation. This confirms Hypothesis 4. The probability of cooperation is also higher for process innovation and as a result there is a lower overall probability of in-house process innovation. This outcome is also driven by the negative impact of PR variables on innovation outsourcing, which is more significant for product innovation.

5. Conclusions

When we look at the differences in how firms outsource product and process innovation, several patterns emerge. Generally, transaction cost factors are more important for process than product innovation,

Table 6
Hypotheses and outcome

Hypotheses	Outcome
Hypothesis 1	
Firms relying on property rights are less likely to outsource	SECRET, FORMAL and LEAD are negatively related to *P*(OUT) – Table 4
Hypothesis 2	
Firms with heavy sunk costs for capital R&D are less likely to outsource	CAP_INT is insignificant but R&D_INT is inversely related to *P*(OUT) – Table 4
Hypothesis 3	
PR is more important than TC in determining innovation	Generally, PR variables are more significant than TC variables – Table 4
Hypothesis 4	
Process innovation is more likely to be outsourced than product	Probability to outsource process innovation is twice as high as product – Table 5
Hypothesis 5	
PR and TC variables have a different impact on product and process innovation	Allison (1999) test is significant for most variables – Table 4

while property rights variables are more important for the latter. This is in line with our expectations. Our strongest finding, one that ties in with Love and Roper (2005), is that taken collectively, property rights variables are best at explaining both product *and* process inputs outsourced from another firm. PR variables dominate over TC variables, in so doing underpinning the high importance given to controlling knowledge flows and maintaining market share for outsourcing innovators. A summary of all the findings in relation to the hypotheses specified in this study is given in Table 6.

An important finding which is in line with expectation is that generally process innovation is more likely to be outsourced from a third party than product innovation. The greater role played by outsourcing for process inputs provides some evidence for the continuing role of scale economies, a consideration for process inputs, in underpinning specialisation and explaining outsourcing. This finding applies to the outsourcing of innovative inputs, traditionally regarded as a field where scale economies are weak. We also found that, on average, the probability of outsourcing is not significantly different across industries classified at the 2 SIC digit level.

In a nutshell, we find that PR rather than TC factors drive the decision to collaborate in innovation where the latter are more significant for firms involved in process rather than product innovation. There are important differences but also similarities in outsourcing innovative products and processes from other firms. Consistent with Veugelers and Cassiman (1999), regardless of the innovation type, all firms shy away from outsourcing when PR factors are high. In line with the TC literature, process inputs are more likely to be outsourced than product inputs. We conclude similarly to Love and Roper (2005) that the TC literature has weaker (although some) relevance for innovation outsourcing.

The policy message from our paper is that economists should not completely dismiss the role of scale economies and hence the TC literature even when investigating the outsourcing of innovative inputs. However, it is fair to say that PR variables dominate over TC variables in explaining the outsourcing of innovation.

Acknowledgements

We would like to thank the generous help of Jim Love, Peter Swann and Holger Görg on an earlier version of this paper. We extend our gratitude to participants at the Leangkollen Workshop on Foreign Ownership, Innovation and Diffusion in Norway 2005 and delegates at the 2005 International Conference on Process Outsourcing and Modelling, Mauritius. We also acknowledge the insightful comments of the referees.

Appendix A

See Tables A1–A3.

Table A1
Hypotheses and testable predictions

SECRET negatively related to *P*(OUT)	Hypothesis 1
FORMAL negatively related to *P*(OUT)	Hypothesis 1
LEAD negatively related to *P*(OUT)	Hypothesis 1
CAP_INT negatively related to *P*(OUT)	Hypothesis 2
R&D_INT negatively related to *P*(OUT) or R&D_INT positively related to *P*(OUT) if innovation is strategic	Hypothesis 2
Greater overall significance of PR variables	Hypothesis 3
$P(\text{OUT})_{\text{process}} > P(\text{OUT})_{\text{product}}$	Hypothesis 4
Comparison of coefficients for PR/TC variables using Allison (1999) test	Hypothesis 5

Table A2
Descriptive statistics for variables used in the model

	Process			Product		
	In-house	Cooperation	Outsourcing	In-house	Cooperation	Outsourcing
CAP_INT	0.169	0.412	0.091	0.386	0.268	0.111
R&D INT	0.079	0.180	0.683	0.347	0.175	0.796
FORMAL	9.305	9.421	7.282	10.410	9.823	7.024
LEAD	2.577	2.472	1.912	2.752	2.482	1.833
SECRET	2.382	2.325	1.702	2.569	2.380	1.670
SIZE	264.284	411.314	257.063	300.606	394.044	195.947
GROUP	0.672	0.748	0.568	0.701	0.734	0.566
MARKET	0.209	0.186	0.116	0.267	0.207	0.086
SKILL	10.139	9.227	5.278	13.292	10.270	8.323
CONC	0.354	0.363	0.364	0.375	0.369	0.326
GROWTH	11.530	12.213	13.303	10.929	12.615	14.777

Table A3
Results for selection model, product and process

	Product	Process
SIZE	0.153 (0.013)***	0.176 (0.014)***
CAP	0.006 (0.005)	0.002 (0.006)
CONC	0.318 (0.446)	−0.524 (0.578)
GROWTH	0.008 (0.003)**	0.01 (0.003)***
MARKET	0.256 (0.021)***	0.14 (0.021)***
SECTOR[a]	−(168.65)***	−(165.73)***
CONSTANT	−2.474 (0.228)***	−2.241 (0.226)***
R-Square	0.15	0.18

Standard errors in parentheses. *Significant at 10%; **significant at 5%; ***significant at 1%.
[a] Chi-square statistics for joint test of 11 sectoral dummies.

References

Acs, Z., Audretsch, D., 1988. Innovation in large and small firms: an empirical analysis. American Economic Review 78, 678–690.

Ai, C., Norton, E., 2003. Interaction terms in logit and probit models. Economics Letters 80, 123–129.

Allison, P.D., 1999. Comparing logit and probit coefficients across groups. Sociological Methods and Research 28, 186–208.

Arrow, K., 1962. Economic welfare and the allocation of resources for invention. In: Nelson, R. (Ed.), The Rate and Direction of Inventive Activity. Princeton University Press, Princeton, NJ, pp. 609–626.

Audretsch, D., Menkveld, A., Thurik, R., 1996. The decision between internal and external R&D. Journal of Institutional and Theoretical Economics 152, 519–530.

Audretsch, D., Santarelli, E., Vivarelli, M., 1999. Start-up size and industrial dynamics: some evidence from Italian manufacturing. International Journal of Industrial Organization 17, 965–983.

Cassiman, B., Veugelers, R., 2002. R&D cooperation and spillovers: some empirical evidence from Belgium. American Economic Review 92, 1169–1184.

Cohen, W., Nelson, R., Walsh, J., 2000. Protecting their intellectual assets: appropriability conditions and why U.S. manufacturing firms patent (or not), NBER Working Paper 7552, Massachusetts.

Feenstra, R., Hanson, G., 2005. Ownership and control in outsourcing to China: estimating the property rights theory of the firm. Quarterly Journal of Economics 20, 729–761.

Görg, H., Hanley, A., 2005. International outsourcing and productivity: evidence from the Irish electronics industry. North American Journal of Economics and Finance 16, 255–269.

Grünfeld, L.A., 2003. Meet me halfway but don't rush - absorptive capacity and strategic R&D investment revisited. International Journal of Industrial Organization 21, 1091–1109.

Hart, O., Moore, J., 1990. Property rights and the nature of the firm. Journal of Political Economy 98, 1119–1158.

Hausman, J., McFadden, D., 1984. Specification tests for the multinomial logit model. Econometrica 52, 1219–1240.

Heckman, J., 1979. Sample selection bias as a specification error. Econometrica 47, 153–161.

Hertog, R.A., Thurik, R., 1993. Determinants of internal and external R&D: some Dutch evidence. De Economist 141, 279–289.

Hoetker, G., 2004. Confounded Coefficients: Accurately Comparing Logit and Probit Coefficients Across Groups. University of Illinois at Urbana-Champaign, Mimeo.

Kamien, M., Zang, I., 2000. Meet me halfway: research joint ventures and absorptive capacity. International Journal of Industrial Organization 18, 995–1012.

Kraft, K., 1989. Market structure, firm characteristic and innovative activity. Journal of Industrial Economics 37, 329–336.

Lerner, J., 1994. The importance of patent scope: an empirical analysis. RAND Journal of Economics 25, 319–333.

Levin, R., et al., 1987. Appropriating the returns from industrial research and development. Brookings Papers on Economic Activity 3, 783–820.

Love, J., Roper, S., 1999. The determinants of innovation: R&D, technology transfer and networking effects. Review of Industrial Organization 15, 43–64.

Love, J., Roper, S., 2002. Internal versus external R&D: a study of R&D choice with sample selection. International Journal of Economics of Business 9, 239–255.

Love, J., Roper, S., 2005. Economists' perceptions versus managers' decisions: an experiment in transaction-cost analysis. Cambridge Journal of Economics 29, 19–36.

Martin, S., 2002. Spillovers, Appropriability and R&D. Journal of Economics (Zeitschrift fur Nationalokonomie) 75, 1–32.

Peck, M.J., 1986. Joint R&D: The case of the Microelectronics and Computer Technology Corporation. Research Policy 15, 219–231.

Piga, C., Vivarelli, M., 2004. Internal and external R&D: a sample selection approach. Oxford Bulletin of Economics and Statistics 66, 457–482.

Quinn, J., 2000. Outsourcing Innovation: The New Engine of Growth. Sloan Management Review, Summer, pp. 13–28.

Rauch, J., 1999. Networks versus markets in international trade. Journal of International Economics 48, 7–35.

Schumpeter, J.A., 1942. Capitalism, Socialism, and Democracy. Harper Collins, New York.

Small, K.A., Hsiao, C., 1985. Multinomial logit specification tests. International Economic Review 22, 619–627.

van de Ven, W., van Praag, B., 1981. The demand for deductibles in private health insurance: a probit model with sample selection. Journal of Econometrics 22, 229–252.

Veugelers, R., Cassiman, B., 1999. Make and buy in innovation strategies: evidence from Belgian manufacturing firms. Research Policy 28, 63–80.

Williamson, O., 1975. Markets and Hierarchies. The Free Press, New York.

Williamson, O., 1989. Transaction cost economics. In: Schmalensee, R., Willig, R. (Eds.), Handbook of Industrial Organization. Elsevier Science Publishing, Amsterdam, pp. 135–182.

Wooldridge, J., 2002. Econometric Analysis of Cross Section and Panel Data. The MIT Press.

Part II

Implications at the Firm Level

Chapter II.1

Outsourcing, Foreign Ownership, and Productivity: Evidence from UK Establishment-level Data

*Sourafel Girma and Holger Görg**

Abstract

The paper presents an empirical analysis of "outsourcing" using establishment-level data for UK manufacturing industries. The authors analyze an establishment's decision to outsource and the subsequent effects of outsourcing on the establishment's productivity. Outsourcing is compared in domestic with foreign-owned establishments. The empirical results suggest that high wages are positively related to outsourcing, suggesting that the cost-saving motive is important. Foreign-owned firms have higher levels of outsourcing than domestic establishments. In the productivity analysis, an establishment's outsourcing intensity is positively related to its labor productivity and total factor productivity growth, and this effect is more pronounced for foreign establishments.

1. Introduction

"Outsourcing" can be loosely defined as the contracting out of activities that were previously performed within a firm, to subcontractors outside the firm.[1] It appears to be becoming more widespread and is attracting increasing attention in the popular business press as well as in the academic literature. For example, the *Financial Times* asserts: "Subcontracting as many non-core activities as possible is a central element of the new economy" (31 July 2001, p. 10). Also, a recent article on car manufacturers in *The Economist* points out: "The whole industry is disintegrating (or becoming less vertical) as vehicle assemblers try to outsource more and more of what they once did for themselves" (23 February 2002, p. 99). There is plenty of anecdotal evidence that this is not limited to the car industry but is also observed in other manufacturing sectors.

Outsourcing (or fragmentation) has also affected the pattern of international trade. For example, Hummels et al. (2001) found that outsourcing (or vertical specialization in their parlance) accounted for 22% of US exports in 1997, and for 30% of the growth in the US export share of merchandise GDP between 1962 and 1997. Görg (2000) reported that, between 1988 and 1994, around 20% of US exports to the EU were for inward processing; that is, they are exported to the EU for processing and subsequent export outside the EU.

Various aspects of the trend to outsourcing have been discussed in the literature. A large literature, starting with the seminal paper by Coase (1937) and including more recent papers by Grossman and Hart (1986), Bolton and Whinston (1993), and

---

*Girma: Department of Economics, University of Leicester, Leicester LE1 7RH, UK. E-mail: sg116@le.ac.uk. Görg: Leverhulme Centre for Research on Globalisation and Economic Policy (GEP), School of Economics, University of Nottingham, Nottingham NG7 2RD, UK, and DIW Berlin, Germany. E-mail: holger.gorg@nottingham.ac.uk. The authors are grateful to the ONS Business Data Linking Project for providing access to the ARD database. Thanks are also due to two anonymous referees, Eric Strobl, and participants at the GEP conference on "Adjusting to Globalisation," in particular Steve Redding, for helpful comments; and to Richard Upward for providing data from the New Earnings Survey. All remaining errors or omissions are, of course, the authors'. Financial support from the Leverhulme Trust (grant F114/BF) is gratefully acknowledged.

Grossman and Helpman (2002a,b), examines theoretically a firm's decision of whether to produce inhouse or to outsource. At the heart of this literature are issues concerned with transaction costs and, in particular, incomplete contracts leading to either vertical integration or specialization. Lyons (1995) provided an empirical application to evaluate the importance of transaction costs theory for firms' outsourcing decisions.

More recently, the trade-related aspects of outsourcing have attracted increasing attention. Trade-theoretic models such as those of Deardorff (2001), Jones and Kierzkowski (2001), and Kohler (2001) examine the effects of trade in "fragmented products" on countries' patterns of specialization and resulting implications for factor prices. On the empirical side, papers by Feenstra and Hanson (1996, 1999) and Hijzen et al. (2004) have analyzed the effect of international outsourcing on relative wages and labor demand using industry-level data for the US and UK, respectively. In line with traditional HOS trade theory, these authors find that international outsourcing (moving low-skill-intensive production to low-skill-abundant countries) leads to increased demand and increases in the wage premium for high-skilled workers in the US and the UK. Egger and Egger (2001) investigated the effect of outsourcing on the productivity of low-skilled labor in the EU using industry-level data. They found that increases in outsourcing have a negative effect on low-skilled labor productivity in the short run, but a positive effect in the long run.

In this paper we are not concerned with the international trade dimension to outsourcing. Rather, we investigate empirically an establishment's decision to outsource and the subsequent effect of outsourcing on productivity of that establishment. We do not distinguish between international and domestic outsourcing since we are interested in the establishment's characteristics that determine outsourcing. We therefore consider it immaterial as to whether the activities are outsourced to firms abroad or in the domestic economy. Also, as we are interested in the subsequent effect on productivity for the outsourcing establishment, it should not matter whether outsourcing takes place internationally or domestically. All we may assume is that the firm will minimize transaction costs when outsourcing activities to any subcontractor.

This paper uses establishment-level data for UK manufacturing industries for the empirical analysis. It contributes in a number of ways. This is, to the best of our knowledge, the first study to analyze the establishment-level determinants of outsourcing using data for the UK.[2] Second, the analysis of the effect of outsourcing on productivity of the establishment is an innovation.[3] Third, we investigate whether there are differences in the determinants of outsourcing, and productivity effects of outsourcing, between domestic establishments and foreign-owned establishments which can be assumed to be part of a larger multinational company.[4]

We focus our analysis on establishments in three broad UK manufacturing sectors: chemicals, mechanical and instrument engineering, and electronics.[5] Foreign-owned firms are important players in all three sectors, accounting for about 12–19% of total employment in the sectors (Griffith and Simpson, 2003, Table 4). We examine these three sectors separately as one may expect at least some heterogeneity in the use of outsourcing and, perhaps more importantly, differences in the impact of outsourcing on productivity across these sectors.

The data used in this paper are available from the Annual Respondents Database (ARD) which is described in more detail in the next section. Section 3 then examines the determinants of outsourcing at the level of the establishment, while section 4 presents the results of our analysis of productivity effects of outsourcing. Section 5 summarizes our main findings and concludes.

2. Data Description and Summary Statistics

For the empirical estimations, this paper draws on the Annual Respondents Database (ARD) provided by the Office for National Statistics. The ARD consists of individual establishments' records that underlie the Annual Census of Production and the data used cover the period 1980 to 1992. As Barnes and Martin (2002) provide a useful introduction to the dataset, we include only a brief discussion of some of the features of the data that are relevant to the present work. For each year the ARD consists of two files. What is known as the "selected file" contains detailed information on a sample of establishments that are sent inquiry forms. The second file comprises the "non-selected" (nonsampled) establishments, and only basic information such as employment, location, industry grouping, and foreign ownership status is recorded. Some 14,000–19,000 establishments are selected each year, based on a stratified sampling scheme. The scheme tends to vary from year to year, but during the period under consideration the sample included all establishments with more than 100 employees plus a selection of smaller ones.

In the ARD, an establishment is defined as the smallest unit that is deemed capable of providing information on the Census questionnaire. Thus a "parent" establishment reports for more than one plant (or "local unit" in the parlance of ARD). For selected multiplant establishments, we have aggregate values only for the constituent plants. Indicative information on the number of plants is available in the "nonselected" file. In the sample period considered in this paper (1980–92), about 95% of the establishments that are present in these industries are single-plant firms. In the actual sample we used for the econometric estimation this figure is around 80%. Hence, most of the data used are actually plant-level data.

The focus of this paper is on outsourcing activities of an establishment. While there has been some empirical research in this area, there does not appear to be a standard definition of what constitutes outsourcing. For example, papers in the empirical trade literature (e.g., Feenstra and Hanson, 1996, 1999; Hijzen et al., 2004) define outsourcing essentially as trade in intermediate products. This appears as a rather wide measure of "outsourcing," especially at the level of the establishment. Abraham and Taylor (1996) define it more narrowly as various activities, namely, contracting out of machine maintenance services, engineering and drafting services, accounting services, computer services, and janitorial services. Our definition includes the first two categories but not the latter three. We define as outsourcing the "cost of industrial services received" by an establishment. This includes activities such as processing of inputs which are then sent back to the establishment for final assembly or sales, maintenance of production machinery, engineering or drafting services, etc. Note that "nonindustrial services" such as accounting, consulting, cleaning, or transportation are not part of that definition.

Outsourcing can be seen as a substitute for inhouse production and may therefore, in the short run, lead to a reduction in the total wage bill. In some sense the cost of outsourcing is therefore equal to the opportunity wage that would have occurred to inhouse employees if the services had not been contracted out. We therefore decided to calculate an indicator of an establishment's propensity to outsource as an outsourcing intensity equal to the cost of industrial services received relative to the total wage bill of the establishment. Some summary statistics for this measure for the three broad manufacturing industries are presented in Table 1. Note that the average outsourcing intensity in the electronics sector is considerably lower than in chemicals and engineering, although the standard deviation is also considerably higher. We also find

Table 1. Mean Outsourcing Intensity by Sector (standard deviation in parentheses)

Sector	*All*	*Foreign*	*Domestic*
Chemicals	0.138	0.161	0.128
	(0.279)	(0.256)	(0.343)
Engineering	0.140	0.161	1.136
	(0.360)	(0.288)	(0.226)
Electronics	0.091	0.097	0.090
	(0.554)	(0.458)	(0.599)

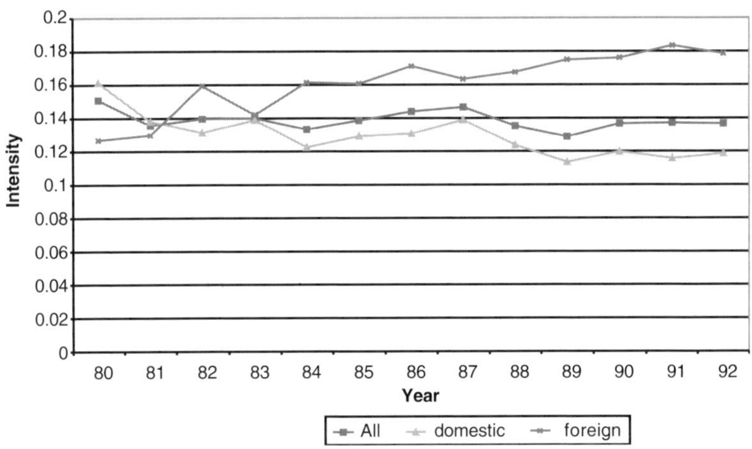

Figure 1. Outsourcing Intensity: Chemicals

that the mean outsourcing intensity for foreign-owned establishments appears to be higher than that for domestic-owned establishments in the same sector.

Figures 1–3 plot the development of outsourcing intensity by sector. Figure 3 in particular indicates that the propensity to outsource in the electronics sector has increased sharply since 1989/90, leaving it at about the same rate as in the other two sectors at the end of the period under consideration. Hence, the lower means in Table 1 can be attributed to the very low levels in the early 1980s. This recovery appears to have been mainly due to domestic establishments where we see a considerable growth in outsourcing since 1989. However, we also find that the outsourcing intensity in foreign-owned establishments has increased over the total period 1980 to 1992, although there has been a slight decrease since 1989.

3. Determinants of Outsourcing

This section investigates what determines firms' use of outsourcing. Abraham and Taylor (1996) postulate that there are three general considerations that may affect

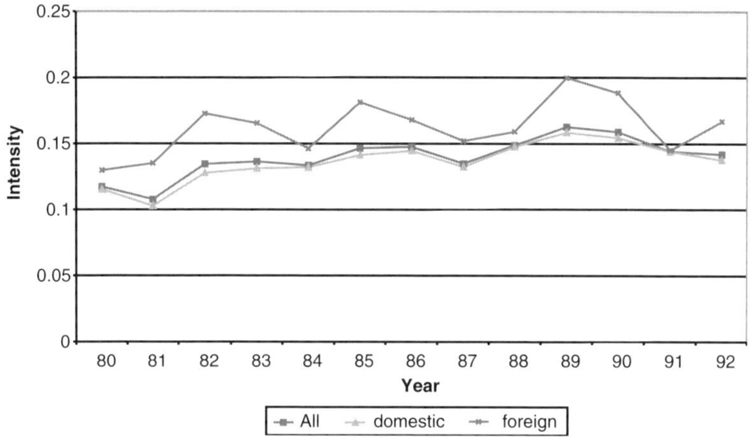

Figure 2. Outsourcing Intensity: Mechanical Engineering

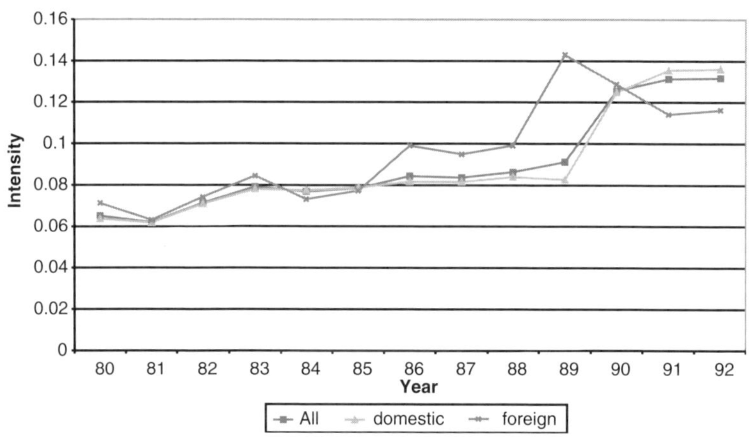

Figure 3. Outsourcing Intensity: Electronics

firms' decisions in that regard, namely, wage costs savings, output cyclicality, and economies of scale.

Firms may try to cut costs by contracting-out activities to firms that operate with lower costs (i.e., offer lower wages to their employees). For outsourcing abroad, this may be the case if market wages are lower in the foreign country due to the abundance of labor. Even if firms outsource in the domestic economy this argument may still hold if, for example, a unionized firm pays wages higher than what it would otherwise choose to pay. Even if a firm is not unionized, a firm may still pay high wages due to paying "efficiency wages" (e.g., Weiss, 1991) to its employees. In this case, while it might be sensible to pay efficiency wages to the firm's "core" workforce, there may be other more peripheral activities for which the extra payments are not justified. These activities could easily be contracted out to low-wage producers.[6,7]

If the firm's output is subject to heavy seasonal or cyclical fluctuations it may revert to outsourcing in order to smooth the workload for the core workforce. Some firms might choose to even the workload by assigning peak-period tasks to outside contractors. Other firms might decide to reduce outsourcing during slow periods by having work performed inhouse that would otherwise have been assigned to outside contractors. Hence, fluctuations in output may affect the use of outsourcing either positively or negatively, depending on the preferences of the firm.

The third reason put forward by Abraham and Taylor for the use of outsourcing is economies of scale for specialized services. It may not be optimal for small or medium-sized enterprises to provide for themselves a full range of support services.

We postulate that one can also expect the nationality of ownership of a firm to matter for its use of outside contractors. Foreign establishments, which are by definition part of a multinational company, can be expected to use higher levels of technology than purely domestic firms, due to their having access to firm-specific assets (e.g., Markusen, 1995). The use of high technology may lead to the contracting-out of activities, in particular low-tech activities. Also, if the foreign establishment is part of a vertical multinational there will be specialization of activities and, by definition, outsourcing of activities to vertically linked plants within the same multinational. Such specialization of activities may be less for purely domestic firms.[8] Furthermore, given that they are embedded in an international production network through their relationship with the parent and other affiliates abroad, they may be expected to have different strategies for dividing inhouse and outsourced production, and may have better access to external providers of services than do purely domestic firms. Hence, we would expect that foreign firms have higher propensities of outsourcing than domestic firms.[9]

In order to test for the importance of these determinants, we estimate empirically variants of the following equation:

$$\begin{aligned} outs_{it} = \beta_0 + \beta_1 w^{s}_{it-1} + \beta_2 w^{us}_{it-1} + \beta_3 un_{jt-1} + \beta_4 size_{it-1} + \beta_5 foreign_{it} + \ldots \\ + D_j + D_t + D_r + dv_{jt} + \varepsilon_{it}, \end{aligned} \tag{1}$$

where *outs* is measured as the log of the cost of industrial services received by establishment i at time t. The regressors w^s and w^{us} are the log of wage rates for skilled and unskilled workers, respectively, while *un* captures the degree of unionization in the four-digit industry j, calculated using data from the *New Earnings Survey*. These variables are included to capture the "cost saving" motive for outsourcing. Given our discussion above, we would expect high-wage firms to do more outsourcing than other firms. Also, firms in highly unionized sectors may prefer outsourcing as union work rules may act to increase costs, even if wages are no different in unionized and non-unionized firms.[10] The *size* variable is the log of establishment size measured in terms of employment and is included to control for the economies-of-scale effect. Based on this reasoning we would expect smaller firms to be more intensive users of outsourcing. However, given that our dependent variable is measured in absolute terms, the size variable controls for the fact that large firms may do more outsourcing (in absolute terms) than smaller firms. *Foreign* is an ownership dummy equal to one if the establishment is foreign owned and zero otherwise. As pointed out above, we would expect this variable to have a positive coefficient if foreign firms are more intensive users of outsourcing. Furthermore, sectoral time dummies (dv_{jt}) are also included to control for

Table 2. Determinants of Outsourcing: OLS Regression in Levels

Dependent variable: log of industrial services received	*(1) chem I*	*(2) chem II*	*(3) engin I*	*(4) engin II*	*(5) electr I*	*(6) electr II*
$size_{t-1}$	1.542	1.587	1.521	1.578	1.754	1.767
	(0.060)***	(0.067)***	(0.047)***	(0.048)***	(0.046)***	(0.050)***
skilled $wage_{t-1}$	0.837	0.814	0.399	0.378	0.392	0.384
	(0.216)***	(0.226)***	(0.163)**	(0.162)**	(0.137)***	(0.138)***
unskilled $wage_{t-1}$	0.028	0.006	0.117	0.148	0.068	0.065
	(0.152)	(0.174)	(0.049)**	(0.057)***	(0.058)	(0.063)
foreign dummy	0.665	0.433	0.612	0.574	0.309	0.144
	(0.139)***	(0.233)*	(0.120)***	(0.140)***	(0.144)**	(0.185)
*foreign** $size_{t-1}$		–0.183		–0.404		–0.097
		(0.119)		(0.147)***		(0.120)
foreign skilled*		0.042		0.330		0.069
$wage_{t-1}$		(0.268)		(0.102)***		(0.129)
foreign unskilled*		0.103		–0.083		0.015
$wage_{t-1}$		(0.270)		(0.055)		(0.114)
union			1.218	1.121		
			(1.368)	(1.363)		
Constant	–5.731	–5.667	–3.999	–4.175	–10.001	–10.041
	(2.510)**	(2.484)**	(1.969)**	(1.948)**	(2.901)***	(2.911)***
Observations	6,917	6,917	23,555	23,555	12,552	12,552
F-test		1.31		3.49**		0.52
R^2	0.32	0.32	0.20	0.21	0.26	0.26

Notes: Heteroskedasticity–autocorrelation consistent standard errors in parentheses. Regressions include four-digit sector, time, region, and sectoral time dummies. Union variable in (1), (2), (5), and (6) is dropped due to multicollinearity with the sectoral time dummies. *F*-test is for joint significance of three interaction terms. ***, **, and *: significant at 1%, 5%, and 10% levels, respectively.

the effect of cyclical or seasonal variations in output in the four-digit industries. Finally, we include four-digit sector (D_j), time (D_t), and region (D_r) dummies in equation (1).

Equation (1) is estimated for each of the three broad sectors separately using ordinary least-squares (OLS) estimation. We allow for heteroskedasticity of the error term, as well as an unspecified correlation between error terms within establishments, but not across establishments. This allows for the possibility that there may be unobserved establishment-specific effects which are correlated with the regressors but which we do not explicitly account for in the empirical model. The estimation results for the three sectors are presented in Table 2.

In line with our prior expectations, we find that high wages are positively correlated with outsourcing, which concurs with the hypothesis that high-wage establishments are more prone to outsource in order to reduce costs. The distinction between skilled and unskilled wages shows that the larger effects seem to stem from the former, rather than the latter part of labor costs. For example, for the engineering sector (column 4) we find that the elasticity of outsourcing with respect to skilled wages is 0.38, while the elasticity for the unskilled wage rate is 0.15. The rate of unionization can be included only for the engineering sector, where the coefficients turn out to be positive, albeit statistically insignificant. Large firms also outsource more than small firms—in all cases, the elasticity is between 1.5 and 1.8. This may reflect a pure size effect—large firms produce higher levels of output and therefore have more activities, in absolute terms, to outsource than do smaller firms.

We now turn to the importance of nationality of ownership for the use of outsourcing. As pointed out above, we would expect foreign firms to be more intensive users of outsourcing. As can be seen from columns 1, 3, and 5, this result is borne out by the data for all three manufacturing sectors. Controlling for size, labor costs, and cyclicity of production, foreign-owned establishments use more outsourcing than domestic establishments.

A reasonable question to ask is whether the determinants of outsourcing are systematically different for the former compared to the latter as well. In other words, do the slope coefficients on the regressors differ between foreign and domestic establishments? To investigate this issue we interact all establishment-level regressors (wage and size variables) with the ownership dummy and rerun the augmented specification of equation (1). The results are reported in columns 2, 4, and 6 of Table 2.

We test for the joint significance of the three interaction terms using an F-test. The test statistics suggest that, for the chemicals and electronics sectors, we cannot reject the hypothesis that the interaction terms are jointly equal to zero. Hence, we do not find systematic differences in the determinants of outsourcing between foreign and domestic establishments in these sectors. It is different in the engineering sector, where the interaction terms are jointly significant. We still find that the ownership dummy is statistically significant and positive, suggesting that foreign firms use more outsourcing. What differs also between the foreign and domestic groups of establishments is the effect of the other regressors included in the equation. The size effect is reduced substantially for foreign establishments, with the elasticities being 1.58 for domestic firms and 1.18 for foreign firms. Also, the elasticity of outsourcing with respect to skilled wages is larger for foreign than domestic establishments (0.71 vs 0.38).

Two criticisms could be directed at equation (1). First, if there are time-invariant establishment-specific effects that are not captured in the explanatory variables but that are correlated with them, then our estimation may produce biased and inconsistent estimates. In other words, if the error term included in equation (1) equals $\varepsilon_{it} = v_i + u_{it}$, then a simple OLS regression is problematic. In order to take this into account, we relate the change in the outsourcing variable to changes in the wage and size variables, thus purging the establishment-specific effect v_i in the levels specification. However, we still include *foreign* and *un* in levels, as we are interested in establishing whether foreign firms or more unionized sectors experience higher growth of outsourcing than others. Second, if there is persistence in the outsourcing decision then we may expect that the decision to outsource in period t is related to the level of outsourcing in the previous period $t - 1$. To allow for such temporal correlation between outsourcing in t and $t - 1$, we include the lagged level of outsourcing also in the equation. Hence, our alternative specification is described by the following equation:

$$\Delta(outs_{it}) = \beta_0 + \beta_1\Delta(w^{s}_{it-1}) + \beta_2\Delta(w^{us}_{it-1}) + \beta_3 un_{jt-1} + \beta_4\Delta(size_{it-1}) + \ldots$$
$$+ \beta_5 foreign_{it} + \beta_6 outs_{it-1} + D_j + D_t + D_r + dv_{jt} + \varepsilon_{it}. \qquad (2)$$

The results of estimations of this equation using data for the three manufacturing sectors separately are presented in Table 3. Note that the lagged level of outsourcing

Table 3. Determinants of Outsourcing: First-differences with Lagged Level of Outsourcing

Dependent variable: log of industrial services received	*(1) chem I*	*(2) chem II*	*(3) engin I*	*(4) engin II*	*(5) electr I*	*(6) electr II*
$outs_{t-1}$	−0.346	−0.345	−0.353	−0.353	−0.327	−0.327
	(0.021)***	(0.021)***	(0.010)***	(0.010)***	(0.012)***	(0.012)***
$\Delta size_{t-1}$	0.211	0.264	−0.131	−0.132	0.156	0.162
	(0.309)	(0.325)	(0.125)	(0.126)	(0.152)	(0.157)
$\Delta skilled\ wage_{t-1}$	0.414	0.344	0.002	−0.005	−0.081	−0.071
	(0.270)	(0.281)	(0.089)	(0.089)	(0.143)	(0.144)
$\Delta unskilled\ wage_{t-1}$	−0.006	0.052	0.151	0.184	−0.050	−0.069
	(0.149)	(0.184)	(0.054)***	(0.064)***	(0.051)	(0.055)
foreign dummy	0.501	0.490	0.581	0.584	0.385	0.390
	(0.083)***	(0.085)***	(0.063)***	(0.065)***	(0.081)***	(0.084)***
$foreign^{*}\ \Delta size_{t-1}$		−0.130		0.015		−0.045
		(0.213)		(0.134)		(0.160)
$foreign^{*}\ \Delta skilled\ wage_{t-1}$		0.266		0.096		−0.113
		(0.247)		(0.103)		(0.118)
$foreign^{*}\ \Delta unskilled\ wage_{t-1}$		−0.185		−0.118		0.145
		(0.239)		(0.074)		(0.072)**
union			−0.796	−0.821		
			(1.524)	(1.527)		
Constant	4.804	3.482	4.120	4.131	5.776	5.788
	(1.090)***	(1.257)***	(0.777)***	(0.778)***	(1.981)***	(1.979)***
Observations	5,707	5,707	18,428	18,428	10,095	10,095
F-test		0.41		0.98		1.41
R^2	0.21	0.21	0.20	0.20	0.18	0.18

Notes: See Table 2.

is highly statistically significant and negative in all cases, suggesting that there is indeed temporal correlation in outsourcing; i.e., present outsourcing is heavily influenced by previous outsourcing. Inclusion of the lagged level leads to most of the explanatory variables being statistically insignificant. However, most importantly from our point of view, the finding that foreign establishments outsource more than domestic ones, *ceteris paribus*, is robust to the inclusion of the lagged level of outsourcing.

4. Productivity Effects of Outsourcing

Having analyzed the determinants of outsourcing, we now turn to investigate whether outsourcing leads to an improvement in establishments' performance. More specifically we analyze whether outsourcing has a positive effect on productivity, measured in terms of labor or total factor productivity (TFP), of the establishment that decides to outsource the activities.

In a recent paper, Ten Raa and Wolff (2001) argued that TFP growth in manufacturing industries is positively related to an increased use of outsourcing, defined as inputs purchased from services industries. Their empirical evidence is based on industry-level data using US input/output tables to calculate the importance of outsourcing. The effects of outsourcing for service industries have also been investigated recently. Fixler and Siegel (1999) argued that outsourcing has played a major role in the growth of the services sector. Their empirical evidence, based on industry-level data for the US, suggests that outsourcing has led to short-run reductions in service sector productivity, but that there have been positive effects in the long run. Our paper is, to the best of our knowledge, the first study to investigate with establishment-level data the effects of outsourcing on productivity in the establishment undertaking the outsourcing.

As argued in the previous section, one of the reasons for outsourcing may be to economize on labor costs. An increase in outsourcing may lead directly to a reduction of employment, while keeping output constant, so having an immediate effect on labor productivity. Our investigation of this issue is based on the following equation of labor productivity augmented by a measure of outsourcing intensity at the level of the establishment:[11]

$$\Delta y/l_{it} = \alpha_0 + \alpha_1 \Delta k/l_{it} + \alpha_2 \Delta m/l_{it} + \alpha_3 outint_{it} + D_t + D_r + \varepsilon_{it}, \tag{3}$$

where y is output, l is labor, k is capital, m is material inputs, D_t and D_r are time and regional dummies, respectively, and ε is an error term. The outsourcing intensity *outint* is calculated as the value of industrial services received divided by total wage costs, as in section 2.[12] In order to see whether there are different productivity effects of outsourcing for foreign and domestic firms, we allow α_3 to vary for the two nationality groups. Outsourcing may affect not only the productivity of labor but also that of other factors of production if it leads to an adjustment of the production process. In order to capture these productivity effects, we also examine whether outsourcing affects TFP growth.[13] Both labor and total factor productivity equations are estimated in levels as well as first-differences.

A major econometric concern with the above equation is that there may be a potential endogeneity problem; i.e., there may be unobserved covariates that are correlated with productivity and outsourcing intensity that may be driving the results. For example, it might be the case that highly productive establishments are more skill-intensive and therefore more likely to use outsourcing to shift the production of low-skill-intensive components outside the firm. In order to take account of this possibility, we instrument for outsourcing intensity with the past level of outsourcing intensity, the growth rates and lagged values of establishment size, skilled and unskilled wages. We use the robust form of Sargan's test of over-identifying restrictions to examine the null hypothesis that the correlation between the instrumental variable candidates and the error terms in the productivity equation is zero—a necessary condition for the validity of the instrumental-variables regression approach. Depending on the particular sector and equation in question (TFP or labor productivity; levels or differences), instruments which are found to be invalid are dropped from the specification.

We are also careful to assess the strength of the relationship between the instruments and the potentially endogenous regressors. It has been noted in the econometric literature (e.g., Staiger and Stock, 1997) that when the partial correlation between the instruments and the endogenous variable is low, instrumental-variables regression is biased in the direction of the OLS estimator. Staiger and Stock recommend that the F-statistics (or equivalently the p-values) from the first-stage regression be routinely reported in applied work. The F-statistic tests the hypothesis that the

Table 4. Labor Productivity and Outsourcing: Instrumental Variables Estimates

	Chemicals sector		*Electronics sector*		*Engineering sector*	
	Levels	*First differences*	*Levels*	*First differences*	*Levels*	*First differences*
Capital intensity	0.020	0.004	−0.049	0.026	0.028	−0.000
	(2.84)***	(0.47)	(1.07)	(1.52)	(2.83)***	(0.01)
Material inputs intensity	0.773	0.732	0.991	0.551	0.587	0.531
	(20.40)***	(13.78)***	(5.63)***	(5.49)***	(15.75)***	(17.16)***
Outsourcing intensity	0.174	0.135	−0.468	−0.410	0.491	0.002
	(6.61)***	(1.28)	(1.13)	(1.63)	(4.63)***	(0.38)
Outsourcing intensity foreigndummy*	0.019	0.009	0.009	0.014	0.076	0.047
	(1.65)*	(0.84)	(0.24)	(0.63)	(2.25)**	(3.34)***
Exogeneity test (*p*-value)	0	1	0.995	1	0.239	0
F (first-stage)	18.71	0.19	2.46	0.51	29.1	51.46
{*p*-value}	(0)	(0.9912)	(0.022)	(0.847)	(0)	(0)
Sargan {*p*-value}	0.377	0.602	0.351	0.237	0.543	0.202
Observations	6,115	6,115	10,882	10,882	18,793	13,245
Number of plants	1,133	1,133	2,184	2,184	4,376	4,376

Notes: Regressions include time and region dummies. Heteroskedasticity-consistent standard errors in parentheses. The test of exogeneity is a Hausman test which examines the null hypothesis that there is no statistically significant difference between the OLS and IV estimates. ***, **, and *: significant at 1%, 5%, and 10% levels, respectively.

instruments should be excluded from the first-stage regressions (i.e., the relevance of the instruments). The idea here is that when the *F*-statistic is small (or the corresponding *p*-value is large), the instrumental variable estimates and the associated confidence interval are unreliable.

Tables 4 and 5 present the empirical estimates from the labor productivity and TFP equations, respectively. Again we estimate the model separately for the three manufacturing sectors. As might be expected, the estimates display some heterogeneity across sectors.

Turning to labor productivity first and focusing on the specification in levels, it can be seen from Table 4 that, for the chemical and engineering sectors, outsourcing is positively related with labor productivity. It does not seem to exert any influence on the productivity path of plants in the electronics sector, however. The elasticity of labor productivity with respect to outsourcing is about three times higher in the engineering than in the chemicals sector. Furthermore, this productivity effect of outsourcing is more pronounced in the sample of foreign-owned establishments as indicated by the positive coefficients on the interaction terms.

The first-difference specification does not yield strong results. Labor productivity and outsourcing growth rates appear to be correlated in foreign establishments within the engineering sector. This lack of robust correlation may be due to the weakness of the instrumental-variable candidates, which are too weak as evidenced by the low

Table 5. TFP and Outsourcing: Instrumental Variables Estimates

	Chemicals sector		*Electronics sector*		*Engineering sector*	
	Levels	*First differences*	*Levels*	*First differences*	*Levels*	*First differences*
Outsourcing intensity	0.087 (4.89)***	0.257 (1.70)*	–0.645 (1.51)	0.054 (0.41)	0.346 (4.63)***	0.158 (2.24)**
Outsourcing intensity foreign dummy*	0.019 (2.22)**	0.026 (1.22)	–0.004 (0.10)	–0.011 (1.63)	0.078 (3.12)***	0.449 (2.60)***
Exogeneity test (*p*-value)	0.01	0.991	1	1	0.499	0.4627
F (first-stage) {*p*-value}	67.25 (0)	1.44 (0.139)	1.83 (0.089)	0.32 (0.924)	34.49 (0)	38.91 (0)
Sargan {*p*-value}	0.155	0.496	0.652	0.133	0.127	0.060
Observations	6,115	5,068	10,882	8,723	18,793	13,245
Number of plants	1,133	896	2,184	1,638	4,376	2,941

Notes: See Table 4.

F-statistics from the first-stage regressions for the chemicals and electronics sectors.[14] In the absence of other instrumental-variable candidates or a "natural experiment" for the outsourcing variable, it does not seem appropriate to draw firm conclusions about the effect of outsourcing on productivity based on the first-differenced specifications.

Table 5 reports the results of the TFP estimations. The level of TFP seems to respond to changes in the outsourcing intensity, again in the chemical and engineering sectors. This is particularly pronounced for foreign establishments. TFP adjusts faster to outsourcing in the engineering sector, particularly in foreign establishments. From the first-differenced estimation there is also evidence of a positive relationship between TFP growth and the changes in the degree of outsourcing for the engineering sector. For the other two sectors, the low *F*-statistics from the first-stage regressions may again indicate the weakness of the instruments used, which may explain the lack of a significant correlation between outsourcing and TFP.

The econometric estimates reported in the above tables give some idea as to the relationship between outsourcing and productivity, and the statistical significance of this association. What, then, is the economic significance of outsourcing in the establishment-level productivity trajectory? As a first attempt towards answering this question, we calculate the implied change in productivity resulting from the change in outsourcing intensity,[15] and relate it to the actual productivity growth observed in the data. Table 6 reports the results from this experiment.

Consistent with the reported point estimates, outsourcing played a more important role in the engineering sector: nearly a quarter of the observed change in *total factor productivity* and almost 15% of the change in *labor productivity* in domestic plants is attributed to the change in outsourcing intensity. The effects on foreign firms' productivity are much smaller—0% and 7%, respectively. Of course, to the extent that the outsourcing variable captures the effect of some omitted variable, the figures in

Table 6. Contribution of Outsourcing to Productivity Growth: Median Values across Establishments

	Chemicals sector		*Engineering sector*	
	Actual yearly growth rate	*Implied % contribution of outsourcing*	*Actual yearly growth rate*	*Implied % contribution of outsourcing*
Labor productivity				
Domestic	2.17%	4.7%	1.6%	14.7%
Foreign	3.06%	2.4%	2.66%	6.8%
TFP				
Domestic	–0.6%	1.1%	–0.1%	24.4%
Foreign	0%	0%	–0.1%	0%

Note: The implied change in productivity due to outsourcing is obtained by multiplying the point estimates of the elasticity of productivity with respect to outsourcing by the actual change in outsourcing intensity in the data. The estimates are obtained from the models in levels.

Table 6 might overstate the importance of outsourcing. Nonetheless these "back-of-envelope" calculations are indicative that the role of outsourcing in enhancing productivity, at least in the engineering sector, is likely to be economically significant.

5. Conclusions

This paper has presented an empirical analysis of "outsourcing" using establishment-level data for UK manufacturing industries. Our results suggest that high wages are positively related to outsourcing, so that the cost-saving motive is important. We also find that foreign-owned firms have higher levels of outsourcing than domestic establishments. In the productivity analysis, we find that an establishment's outsourcing intensity in the chemical and engineering sectors is positively related to its productivity. This relationship appears to be more pronounced in foreign-owned establishments.

Appendix: TFP Estimation

Using log values, we write the production function as $y_{it} \equiv f(l^s_{it}, l^u_{it}, k_{it}, m_{it}, TFP_{it})$, where y is output and there are four factors of production: skilled labor (l^s), unskilled labor (l^u), materials or cost of goods sold (m), and capital stock (k). For estimation purposes we employ a first-order Taylor approximation and write the production function as

$$y_{it} = \beta_0 + \beta_s l^s_{it} + \beta_u l^u_{it} + \beta_k k_{it} + \beta_m m_{it} + TFP_{it}. \quad \text{(A1)}$$

TFP is assumed to follow the following AR(1) process:

$$TFP_{it} = \rho TFP_{it-1} + \delta D_t + f_i + v_{it}, \quad \text{(A2)}$$

where D is a common year-specific shock, f is a time-invariant firm-specific effect, and v a random error term. Note that we do not simply model productivity as a fixed effect, as that would imply that TFP differences are fixed, and there is no role for technology diffusion (convergence).

Recently the fundamental assumption of pooling individual times-series data has been questioned. Pesaran and Smith (1995) demonstrated that standard GMM estimators of dynamic panel models lead to invalid inference if the response parameters are characterized by heterogeneity. They argue that one is better off averaging parameters from individual time-series regressions. This is not feasible here since the individual firm's time-series data are not of adequate length. However, we take some comfort from a recent comparative study by Baltagi and Griffin (1997) which concludes that efficiency gains from pooling are likely to more than offset the biases due to individual heterogeneity. Baltagi and Griffin especially point out the desirable properties of the GLS-AR(1) estimator, and we use this estimator to obtain estimates of the factor elasticities, and derive TFP as a residual term. We estimate equation (4) for each of the four-digit SIC80 industries available in our sample.

References

Abraham, K. G. and S. K. Taylor, "Firms' Use of Outside Contractors: Theory and Evidence," *Journal of Labor Economics* 14 (1996):394–424.
Arndt, S. and H. Kierzkowski (eds.), *Fragmentation: New Production Patterns in the World Economy*, Oxford: Oxford University Press (2001).
Baltagi, B. H. and J. M. Griffin, "Pooled Estimators versus their Heterogeneous Counterparts in the Context of the Dynamic Demand for Gasoline," *Journal of Econometrics* 77 (1997):303–27.
Barnes, M. and R. Martin, "Business Data Linking: an Introduction," *Economic Trends* no. 581 (2002):34–41.
Bolton, P. and M. D. Whinston, "Incomplete Contracts, Vertical Integration, and Supply Assurance," *Review of Economic Studies* 60 (1993):121–48.
Coase, R., "The Nature of the Firm," *Economica* 4 (1937):386–405.
Deardorff, A. V., "Fragmentation in Simple Trade Models," *North American Journal of Economics and Finance* 12 (2001):121–37.
Egger, H. and P. Egger, "International Outsourcing and the Productivity of Low-skilled Labor in the EU," working paper 152/2001, Austrian Institute of Economic Research (WIFO), Vienna (2001).
Feenstra, R. C. and G. H. Hanson, "Globalization, Outsourcing, and Wage Inequality," *American Economic Review Papers and Proceedings* 86 (1996):240–5.
———, "The Impact of Outsourcing and High-technology Capital on Wages: Estimates for the United States, 1979–1990," *Quarterly Journal of Economics* 114 (1999):907–40.
Fixler, D. J. and D. Siegel, "Outsourcing and Productivity Growth in Services," *Structural Change and Economic Dynamics* 10 (1999):177–94.
Görg, H., "Fragmentation and Trade: US Inward Processing Trade in the EU," *Weltwirtschaftliches Archiv* 136 (2000):403–21.
Görg, H. and A. Hanley, "Does Outsourcing Increase Profitability?" working paper 2003/01, Nottingham University Business School (2003).
Görzig, B. and A. Stephan, "Outsourcing and Firm-level Performance," discussion paper 309, DIW Berlin (2002).
Greenhalgh, M., M. Gregory, and A. Ray, "The Changing Structure of UK Production, Trade and Employment: an Analysis using Input–Output Tables," Applied Economics discussion paper 70, University of Oxford (1999).
Griffith, R. and H. Simpson, "Characteristics of Foreign-owned Firms in British Manufacturing," in R. Blundell, D. Card, and R. Freeman (eds.), *Creating a Premier League Economy*, Chicago: Chicago University Press (2003).
Grossman, G. M. and E. Helpman, "Outsourcing in a Global Economy," NBER working paper 8728 (2002a).
———, "Integration versus Outsourcing in Industry Equilibrium," *Quarterly Journal of Economics* 117 (2002b):85–120.

Grossman, S. J. and O. D. Hart, "The Costs and Benefits of Ownership: a Theory of Vertical and Lateral Integration," *Journal of Political Economy* 94 (1986):691–719.
Hijzen, A., H. Görg, and R. C. Hine, "International Outsourcing and the Skill Structure of Labour Demand in the UK," *Economic Journal* (2004): forthcoming.
Holmes, T. J., "Localization of Industry and Vertical Disintegration," *Review of Economics and Statistics* 81 (1999):314–25.
Hummels, D., J. Ishii, and K.-M. Yi, "The Nature and Growth of Vertical Specialization in World Trade," *Journal of International Economics* 54 (2001):75–96.
Jones, R. W. and H. Kierzkowski, "A Framework for Fragmentation," in S. Arndt and H. Kierzkowski (eds.), *Fragmentation: New Production Patterns in the World Economy*, Oxford: Oxford University Press (2001).
Kohler, W., "A Specific Factors View on Outsourcing," *North American Journal of Economics and Finance* 12 (2001):31–53.
Lyons, B. R., "Specific Investment, Economies of Scale, and the Make-or-Buy Decision: a Test of Transaction Cost Theory," *Journal of Economic Behavior and Organization* 26 (1995):431–43.
Markusen, J. R., "The Boundaries of Multinational Enterprises and the Theory of International Trade," *Journal of Economic Perspectives* 9(2) (1995):169–89.
Pesaran, M. H. and R. Smith, "Estimating Long-run Relationships from Dynamic Heterogeneous Panels," *Journal of Econometrics* 68 (1995):79–112.
Staiger, D. and J. H. Stock, "Instrumental Variables Regression with Weak Instruments," *Econometrica* 65 (1997):557–86.
Swenson, D. L., "Firm Outsourcing Decisions: Evidence from US Foreign Trade Zones," *Economic Inquiry* (2000):175–89.
Ten Raa, T. and E. N. Wolff, "Outsourcing of Services and the Productivity Recovery in US Manufacturing in the 1980s and 1990s," *Journal of Productivity Analysis* 16 (2001):149–65.
Turok, I., "Inward Investment and Local Linkages: How Deeply Embedded is 'Silicon Glen'?", *Regional Studies* 27 (1993):401–17.
Weiss, A., *Efficiency Wages*, Princeton, NJ: Princeton University Press (1991).

Notes

1. This phenomenon, which we refer to as outsourcing, may also be termed "make or buy decision" (Grossman and Helpman, 2002b), "vertical disintegration" (Holmes, 1999), "fragmentation" (Arndt and Kierzkowski, 2001), "vertical specialization" (Hummels et al., 2001), to mention but a few synonyms.
2. Greenhalgh et al. (1999) documented that there is an increase in contracting-out of services in the UK. Our approach is closely related to the paper by Abraham and Taylor (1996) who analyze the determinants of outsourcing using plant-level data for the US. However, they do not distinguish between domestic and foreign-owned establishments. A related paper by Swenson (2000) examines the decision to import intermediates for firms located in US foreign-trade zones, paying particular attention to the effect of changes in international prices on imported inputs.
3. There are a few papers that look at the effects of outsourcing on manufacturing (Ten Raa and Wolff, 2001) or service-sector (Fixler and Siegel, 1999) productivity using industry-level data. Also, in related papers, Görzig and Stephan (2002) and Görg and Hanley (2003) look at the relationship between outsourcing and profitability, using film-level data.
4. Note that with the data available we are not able to identify UK multinationals.
5. More precisely, using SIC 1980 classifications, chemicals is SIC 25, mechanical and instrument engineering (hereafter referred to as engineering) includes SIC 32 and SIC 37, and electronics includes SIC 33 (manufacture of office machinery and data processing equipment) and SIC 34 (electrical and electronic engineering).

6. This argument implies that firms cannot pursue different wage strategies, paying high (efficiency) wages to core workers and lower wages to other workers. This may be due to unionization, or to internal equity considerations.
7. Outsourcing may also be undertaken to save on costs other than wages or to provide access to better technology, more favorable regulations, etc. Unfortunately, we cannot from our data measure such other determinants and therefore cannot include them in the empirical analysis.
8. Although it may be similar for domestic establishments which are part of a UK multinational. Unfortunately, we are not able to observe UK multinationals in our dataset.
9. The fact that multinationals have been found to import more of their intermediate inputs than domestic firms (e.g., Turok, 1993) gives some preliminary support for this assumption.
10. On the other hand, as a referee pointed out to us, unions may attempt to prevent outsourcing in order to safeguard jobs, which would have a negative effect on outsourcing.
11. We assume that the intensity of outsourcing shifts the technology parameter of the underlying production.
12. Note that we do not simply measure outsourcing as use of intermediate inputs (m) in the production function.
13. See the Appendix for a description of how TFP is calculated.
14. Notice that these instruments are valid according to the Sargan test, however.
15. The point estimates from the equations in levels are used to this end. We confine our analysis to establishments with more than five years of data.

Chapter II.2

Productivity effects of international outsourcing: evidence from plant-level data

Holger Görg *Kiel Institute of the World Economy and University of Kiel*

Aoife Hanley *Kiel Institute of the World Economy and University of Kiel*

Eric Strobl *École Polytechnique Paris*

Abstract. We investigate the impact of international outsourcing on productivity using plant-level data for Irish manufacturing. Specifically, we distinguish the effect of outsourcing of materials from services inputs. Moreover, we examine whether the impact on productivity is different for plants being more embedded in international markets through exporting or being part of a multinational. Our results show robust evidence for positive effects from outsourcing of services inputs for exporters, either domestic or foreign owned. By contrast, we find no statistically significant evidence of an impact of international outsourcing of services on productivity for firms not operating on the export market. JEL classification: F14, F23, L23

Les effets de productivité de la sous-traitance internationale: résultats à partir de données au niveau des établissements. On examine l'impact de la sous-traitance internationale sur la productivité en utilisant des données sur les établissements irlandais. On distingue la sous-traitance d'intrants qui sont des biens matériels de celle d'intrants de services. On distingue aussi les établissements encastrés dans les marchés internationaux via des liens d'exportations de ceux qui sont parties d'une firme plurinationale. Les résultats montrent des effets importants de la sous-traitance des intrants-services sur la productivité des exportateurs qu'ils soient indépendants ou parties d'une plurinationale. D'autre part, on ne trouve pas de relation statistique significative entre la sous-traitance des intrants-services et la productivité pour les entreprises qui n'opèrent pas sur le marché des exportations.

Görg is also affiliated with GEP Nottingham and CEPR. We are grateful to Carlo Altomonte, Jonathan Eaton, Peter Egger, Keith Head, Saso Polanec, seminar participants at Cardiff University, Nottingham University, DIW Berlin, European Commission in Brussels, and OECD in Paris, and two anonymous referees for helpful comments. Financial support through the Leverhulme Trust (Grant No. F114/BF) is gratefully acknowledged.
Email: holger.goerg@ifw-kiel.de

Canadian Journal of Economics / Revue canadienne d'Economique, Vol. 41, No. 2
May / mai 2008. Printed in Canada / Imprimé au Canada

1. Introduction

International outsourcing has become a growing phenomenon in world trade. Hummels, Ishii, and Yi (2001), for example, provide evidence from data for 10 OECD and four emerging market countries that trade in outsourced components in the vertical chain accounts for 21% of these countries' exports.[1] Moreover, they find that international outsourcing grew approximately 30% between 1970 and 1990. More recently, the attention in many industrialised countries has shifted away from outsourcing of materials to services outsourcing (Amiti and Wei 2005). For instance, much media coverage has been given to the outsourcing of services to developing countries such as India.

Given the considerable growth in outsourcing it is not surprising that a sizeable amount of research has now been devoted to attempting to understand the causes and consequences of this disintegration of production.[2] When investigating the impact of international outsourcing most researchers have focused on the implications for domestic labour markets (see, e.g., Feenstra and Hanson 1999; Head and Ries 2002; Hijzen, Görg, and Hine 2005). Another somewhat neglected, but potentially important, aspect of outsourcing is its impact on productivity.[3] In this regard, standard trade theory tells us that increased specialization following international outsourcing is beneficial for the economy, as it allows reallocation of resources to their best use. A priori, one would also expect the individual plant to be able to benefit from international outsourcing, as it allows the plant to purchase higher-quality intermediates abroad and/or reorganize production to concentrate the most efficient stages in the home country.

The empirical evidence on such a link between international outsourcing and productivity is limited. A few papers that have investigated productivity effects of outsourcing have used aggregate data. Specifically, Egger and Egger (2006) focus on the link between international outsourcing of materials and labour productivity of EU low-skilled labour and conclude that the short-run productivity of low-skilled workers is adversely affected by cross-border fragmentation, while in the long run low-skilled worker productivity rises. Amiti and Wei (2006), using US industry data, find that, in particular, services outsourcing is positively associated with productivity.

1 In the international trade literature, international outsourcing is generally seen to be equivalent to vertical specialisation and is measured in terms of trade in intermediate goods.

2 See, for example, recent special issues on international outsourcing of the *North American Journal of Economics and Finance* (16(1), 2005) and the *International Review of Economics and Finance* (14(2), 2005).

3 The potential importance of this aspect is highlighted by some recent evidence that casts some doubt on the efficacy of outsourcing for boosting company performance. For example, 56% of survey respondents to an IT specialists' journal claimed that outsourced IT work was at least worse than that produced in house. More worryingly, 11% reported that the outsourced work induced a setback in the firm's production; see *Software Development Magazine*, January 2004 issue.

A small number of papers have also looked at the outsourcing/productivity relationship using firm-level data. Tomiura (2005) and Kurz (2006), using data for Japan and the US, respectively, model a firm's decision to outsource and find that more productive firms are more likely to outsource. Neither paper deals specifically with the possibility of endogeneity of the outsourcing decision, though Kurz (2006) concludes that outsourcers are 'outstanding' in that they are larger, more capital intensive, and more productive. The papers by Kasahara and Rodrigue (2005) and Yasar and Morrison Paul (2007) investigate the relationship between firm productivity and firm-level imports of materials in a production function framework using data for Chile and Turkey, respectively. Specifically, Kasahara and Rodrigue find that firms that switch from non-importing to importing status can raise productivity by 3.4% to 22.5%, depending on the estimation technique used.[4]

In the current paper we investigate whether international outsourcing (via imports of intermediate products) affects total factor productivity at the plant level. In contrast to much of the earlier literature focusing on outsourcing, we do so using plant- rather than industry-level data. Furthermore, our work is distinct from Kasahara and Rodrigue (2005) and Yasar and Morrison Paul (2007) in that we look specifically at differences between outsourcing of materials and services inputs. To do so we use current data, which also allows us to capture recent growth in services outsourcing (see, e.g., Amiti and Wei 2005). As far as the authors are aware, ours is the first paper to do this using plant-level data. Recent empirical studies of firm- and plant-level productivity have established that there is large and persistent heterogeneity across firms even within narrowly defined industries (see, e.g., Bartelsman and Doms 2000); hence, accounting for this with the use of micro data is important. Another contribution of our paper is that we allow for potential productivity effects to be different for purely domestic plants, exporters, and foreign-owned affiliates in the host country. This aspect links our paper to the recent theoretical and empirical work on plant/firm heterogeneity and international trade, such as Bernard et al. (2003), Helpman, Melitz, and Yeaple (2004), and Yeaple (2005).

Our analysis, in distinguishing between services and materials outsourcing, is in line with current thinking that recent innovations in communications technology should reduce the search costs for international service partners, as evidenced in the growth of internationally traded services, albeit from a low baseline (Amiti and Wei 2005). That such a categorization may be important has been hinted at by Amiti and Wei (2006), who find stronger productivity benefits from international outsourcing of services than from materials. Similar to the empirical literature using aggregate industry level data (e.g., Feenstra and Hanson 1999), which defines

4 López (2006) also uses similar Chilean data but applies it to a survival analysis; he finds that exporters have higher survival likelihoods but only on the proviso that they are also importers. There is also a somewhat related literature using plant-level data to look at the productivity effects of reductions in tariffs on inputs, for example, Fernandes (2007) and Amiti and Konings (2005).

international outsourcing generally as imported intermediate inputs, we examine input sourcing behaviour at the plant level. Hence, we define international outsourcing as the value of imported intermediates at the level of the plant.

Our empirical analysis utilizes plant-level data for manufacturing industries in the Republic of Ireland. Ireland may be considered an interesting case study, given that Hummels, Ishii, and Yi (2001) argue that a small open economy is most likely to rely heavily on fragmentation of its production processes. Amiti and Wei (2005) point out that Ireland is ranked number one on the list of *industrialized* countries outsourcing business services, characterized by a staggering 15% of Irish GDP comprising internationally outsourced services.[5] Thus, outsourced services are not a trivial component in the Irish economy. Furthermore, over the last few decades Ireland has been an important host country for affiliates of multinational companies, and many plants, both foreign and domestic owned, engage in exporting (see, e.g., Barry and Bradley 1997; Ruane and Sutherland 2002).

Our evidence from econometric estimations controlling for endogeneity of the outsourcing decisions suggests that there are potential positive effects from international outsourcing in particular of services inputs. However, we find that these benefits accrue only to exporters. This suggests that plant-level heterogeneity and, in particular, contacts in foreign markets are important in evaluating the productivity effects of international outsourcing.

The structure of our paper is as follows. In the next section we discuss the theoretical background for our hypothesis that international outsourcing affects productivity. Section 3 sets out the empirical methodology for analyzing the link between outsourcing and total factor productivity at the plant level. Then follows a description of the data along with some descriptive statistics in section 4. We subsequently present the results of our estimations in section 5 before concluding in section 6.

2. International outsourcing and productivity

The theoretical rationale for expecting an effect from international outsourcing on plant-level productivity is fairly straightforward. Assume that goods are produced in a multistage production process, which for each good involves different stages from basic upstream production to the eventual completion of the final good in the downstream stages. In this set-up, one may expect a number of different possible effects. In the short run, the plant engaging in international outsourcing has access to internationally traded inputs, which may be available at higher quality than those available domestically. Hence, increasing use of internationally traded inputs may result in a direct boost in productivity for the plant, shifting its production function outward. This may be particularly important for plants

5 Compare this with 1.03% for the UK and 0.39% for the US.

that are operating far away from the international technological frontier in their industry.[6]

The second type of effect concerns compositional changes induced by international outsourcing, which may have implications for productivity. For example, assuming that a plant carries out multiple production stages in house, it may be beneficial to relocate those parts in which it is relatively inefficient to another country where they can be carried out at lower cost. Home production could then concentrate on those activities that it does more efficiently and import the intermediate good now produced abroad. Hence, it would be able to reallocate resources to the more efficient production stage, expand output, and push its production function outward, thus improving measured total factor productivity.[7]

Given the substantial heterogeneity of units in our plant-level data, it seems reasonable to expect the plant-level productivity effects to differ depending on plant characteristics. We distinguish purely domestic plants from domestic exporters and foreign-owned multinationals. In their theoretical models, Antrás and Helpman (2004) and Grossman and Helpman (2005) make the reasonable argument that international outsourcing involves substantial sunk costs. Firms have to search for foreign suppliers, assess their quality and write contracts. The business literature has also highlighted the fact that there are substantial costs of outsourcing that may potentially cancel out any anticipated costs savings that may to be had from outsourcing. These include, for example, cost of travel, transportation and communication costs, or cost of sending employees to be located in overseas plants (Rasheed and Gilley 2005). One may arguably expect that these types of costs differ between the different types of firms. In particular, we would expect exporters and foreign-owned firms to face lower costs of outsourcing, as they are embedded into international production networks with more foreign contacts than purely domestic firms (e.g., Sjöholm 2003).

Our data provide us with other valuable information that we exploit in the empirical analysis. Namely, we can distinguish international outsourcing of tangible inputs, that is, materials and components, from services inputs (the exact definition of which will be given in the data section below). It is not a priori obvious that we should expect similar productivity effects from the outsourcing of different types of inputs; hence, it seems appropriate to empirically investigate this issue in detail. More specifically, we would expect larger productivity benefits from international outsourcing of services than of materials. For an average manufacturing plant it is likely that services inputs are an activity it performs relatively inefficiently (compared with the other production stages), as the main

6 Of course, international outsourcing may also give plants access to inputs of the same level of quality but at a lower price. However, if the only effect of outsourcing is to provide inputs at lower prices, it is not clear that this should have any sustained effects on measured total factor productivity.

7 Furthermore, there may also be general equilibrium effects associated with the plant-level outsourcing activity, which, through the reallocation of production in the home country may affect relative prices in the economy.

concern of the plant is to produce manufacturing output. Hence, importing the service activity (for example back office accounting or computing operations) may bring higher productivity benefits than outsourcing some tangible intermediate input. In a similar vein, Amiti and Wei (2006) argue that outsourcing of services may be more likely to allow plant restructuring in a way that pushes out the technology frontier than outsourcing of material inputs.

3. Empirical methodology

In order to investigate the effect of international outsourcing on plant-level total factor productivity we estimate production functions that include the effect of international outsourcing. Specifically, we assume a general Cobb-Douglas production function

$$Y_{it} = A_{it}^{\phi}\left(K_{it}^{\alpha}L_{it}^{\beta}M_{it}^{\gamma}S_{it}^{\lambda}\right), \tag{1}$$

where Y is total output, K is capital, L is labour, M and S are materials and services inputs, and A is a technology parameter (or total factor productivity, TFP). Taking logs yields

$$y_{it} = \phi a_{it} + \alpha k_{it} + \beta l_{it} + \gamma m_{it} + \lambda s_{it}, \tag{2}$$

where lower case letters denote natural logs (i.e., $y = \ln Y$) of the variables.

We investigate whether the use of international outsourcing has any effect on total factor productivity by allowing the intensity of international outsourcing to shift the technology parameter a of the underlying production function, $a_{it} = a(outs_{it})$; that is, we assume that international outsourcing leads to a shift of the plant's production function. This is therefore an empirical analysis of the type of effect from international outsourcing on productivity, as discussed in section 2.

The estimation equation is therefore

$$y_{it} = \pi + \delta outs_{it}^{m,s} + \alpha k_{it} + \beta l_{it} + \gamma m_{it} + \lambda s_{it} + \gamma X_{it} + d_t + d_j + \varepsilon_{it}, \tag{3}$$

where $outs^{m,s}$ is the intensity of international outsourcing for either materials m or services s, and X is a vector of other firm characteristics that may impact TFP. The variables d_t and d_j are full sets of time- and industry-specific dummies. The remaining error term ε allows for unspecified heteroscedasticity and correlation of residuals within plants (clustering).

The vector X includes two sets of dummy variables indicating whether a firm is part of a foreign-owned multinational and whether it is an exporter, as it is frequently argued that both types of firms are more productive than purely domestic plants. While the international evidence generally supports this claim (for the US see, e.g., Bernard and Jensen 1999; Doms and Jensen 1998), the evidence for

Ireland is less clear-cut. Girma, Görg, and Strobl (2004) show, using plant-level data, that labour productivity in multinationals is higher than in domestic plants (either exporters or non-exporters), but that there is no significant difference in productivity levels between domestic exporters and non-exporters.[8]

While the standard explanations for these productivity advantages usually focus on firm-specific assets for multinationals and self-selection or learning for exporters (see, e.g., Helpman, Melitz, and Yeaple 2004; Bernard et al. 2003), the possibility that outsourcing enhances productivity can also be advanced. Being part of an international production network, either as an affiliate of an MNE or an exporter, allows firms to reap the advantages of international specialisation of production activities. This arguably allows such establishments to lower the sunk costs of searching for new intermediate-good suppliers from which to outsource inputs. Hence, owing to the lower cost associated with establishing an outsourcing relationship, such firms may reap greater gains from international outsourcing than firms with production facilities and sales only in the domestic market. In the empirical estimations, we relax the assumption that the effect of outsourcing on productivity is the same across different types of plants by allowing for differential productivity effects of international outsourcing by nationality and export status of the plants.

4. Description of the data

In order to investigate the relationship between international outsourcing and productivity we use plant-level data for manufacturing industries in the Republic of Ireland. The data are taken from the *Irish Economy Expenditure Survey*, undertaken annually over the period 1983–98 by Forfás, the government agency with responsibility for enterprise development, science, and technology. This is an annual survey of larger plants in Irish manufacturing with at least 20 employees, although a plant, once it is included, is generally still surveyed even if its employment level falls below the 20-employee cut-off point. The response rate to this survey is generally estimated to be between 60% and 80% of the targeted plant population.[9] Hence, while our data can be regarded as representative of the targeted population of plants, they generally do not include plants with fewer than 20 employees.

8 Ruane and Sutherland (2005) use a different firm-level data set for Ireland and find some evidence that exporters have higher levels of value added per employee, but this is not robust in all econometric specifications they estimate. Greenaway, Gullstrand, and Kneller (2005) also find in a study using Swedish firm-level data that there are no strong productivity differences between domestic exporters and non-exporters. One possible explanation is that, owing to the small domestic market, a much larger percentage of firms are exporters than in, for example, the US or the UK. Hence, not only 'exceptional' firms become exporters, but also those that are 'less exceptional.'

9 Note that the data set does not allow us to distinguish plant exits that are purely due to shut-downs from those that are due simply to non-response. Hence, we cannot correct for the possible relationship between outsourcing and plant exit (López 2006). Our conclusions thus are conditional on continuing plants.

The survey provides plant-level information on, inter alia, output (measured in terms of sales), value added (sales minus intermediate inputs), exports, employment, capital employed, nationality of ownership, as well as details on plants' expenditure on labour, materials, and services inputs.[10] One should note, however, that information on the capital stock is available only from 1990 onward; hence, since we focus on total factor productivity, our sample period consists of the years 1990–98. A plant is defined as foreign owned in the data if at least 50% of its shares are held by foreign owners.[11] Dropping observations with missing values for any of the variables included in equation (3) leaves us with an unbalanced panel consisting of 1,099 plants. Of these, 459 are foreign owned, 534 are exporters, and the remaining 106 are purely domestic.

The main variable of interest is international outsourcing, which is defined as imported inputs at the plant level. This can arguably be seen as a substitute for in-house production and may therefore, at least in the short run, lead to a reduction in the total wage bill. In some sense, the cost of outsourcing is therefore equal to the opportunity wage that may have accrued to in-house employees if the service had not been contracted out. Hence, similar to Girma and Görg (2004), we calculate an indicator of an establishment's propensity to outsource as the expenditure on outsourcing, that is, on either imported services or material inputs, relative to the plant's total wage bill.[12]

An advantage of our data set is that we can break down intermediate inputs into two groups: raw materials and components (referred to as materials) and services inputs, respectively. Additionally, we have information on the proportion of these factors sourced abroad.[13] We can therefore calculate two disaggregated measures of international outsourcing, namely, the ratio of imported materials over total wages and the ratio of imported services inputs over total wages. With regard to the latter measure, services include inputs such as consultancy, maintenance, security, cleaning, and catering. They do not include other indirect costs such as rent, interest payments, and depreciation.

To illustrate the development of international outsourcing over the nine-year time period studied, figure 1 plots the aggregate totals for the materials and services outsourcing ratios by year. Two points are worthy of note. Firstly, international outsourcing of materials has consistently been more important than outsourcing of services in terms of aggregate values. Secondly, both types of

10 All nominal values are deflated using a standard consumer price index, as there are no official sector-level price deflators available for Ireland.

11 While this may leave out plants with minority foreign ownership it has been the case in Ireland, certainly over the period covered, that most FDI was in the form of new fully foreign-owned greenfield investment (see, e.g., Barry and Bradley 1997).

12 Another option may be to calculate outsourcing relative to total inputs; we explore this alternative in a robustness check in the econometric analysis below.

13 One should note that materials and services not sourced abroad may have been purchased from foreign affiliates of multinationals located in Ireland rather than just from purely domestic firms. Unfortunately, the data set does not allow us to distinguish these two sources for domestically purchased inputs. Also, the data set does not provide information on the source country of the inputs.

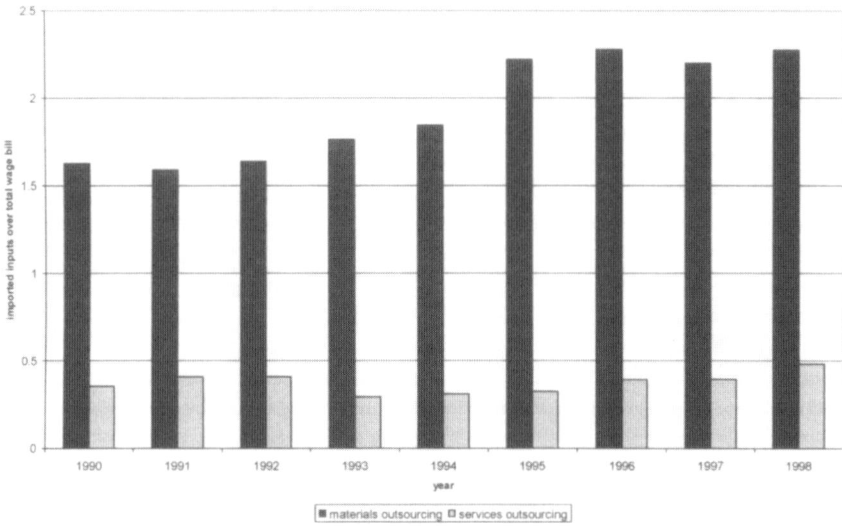

FIGURE 1 Development of international outsourcing
NOTE: Outsourcing is measured as imported services or material inputs over total wage bill.

outsourcing increased, on average, between 1990 and 1998, reflecting the general notion that international outsourcing has become more important over the 1990s.

Table 1 presents some summary statistics on some of the variables of interest. We find that foreign-owned plants as well as domestic exporters are larger (in terms of employment) and more productive (in terms of value added per worker) than purely domestic oriented local plants. We also find that foreign-owned plants have the highest intensities of international outsourcing for both services and materials, while there is no strong difference in the average outsourcing intensities between domestic exporters and non-exporters.

In order to get a preliminary idea of the relationship between international outsourcing and productivity (in terms of value added per employee), we decompose the latter variable in two groups: low (below median) and high (above median) labour productivity, respectively. Table 2 then describes average outsourcing intensities for these low- and high-productivity establishments. One can see that high-productivity plants exhibit higher average outsourcing intensities of both materials and services. We also find that a greater proportion of foreign-owned establishments are located in the higher-productivity category.

5. Econometric analysis

While the summary statistics give some insight into the potential relationship between productivity and outsourcing, they do not, of course, allow us to take adequately into account other covariates that may impact on plant-level produc-

TABLE 1
Summary statistics

	Domestic non-exporters	Domestic exporters	Foreign
Employment	64.7	102.74	184.14
	(127.94)	(227.51)	(244.92)
Labour productivity	0.202	0.214	0.530
	(0.193)	(0.178)	(1.366)
Services o/s intensity (outs^s)	0.255	0.238	0.332
	(0.443)	(0.450)	(2.188)
Materials o/s intensity (outs^m)	1.579	1.368	2.213
	(2.903)	(1.866)	(3.363)
Observations	2,117	7,358	6,358

NOTES: Table reports means and standard deviations in parentheses. Labour productivity is value added per employee. Outsourcing intensities are imported services (materials) over total wage bill.

TABLE 2
Summary statistics for low and high-productivity plants

	Low labour productivity		High labour productivity	
	Mean	Std. Deviation	Mean	Std. Deviation
Materials o/s intensity (outs^m)	1.36	1.88	2.29	3.56
Services o/s intensity (outs^s)	0.26	1.79	0.30	3.56
Share of foreign plants	0.29	0.45	0.57	0.49

NOTES: 'High labour productivity' is a plant with value added per employee > median plant.

tivity and may be correlated with outsourcing, or to say anything about directions of causality. In order to deal with these issues we now turn to estimating the production function described in equation (3). The results of the estimation of the baseline specification of equation (3) using OLS are reported in column (1) of table 3.[14] An examination, first, of the coefficients on the standard production factors k, l, s, and m shows that these return coefficients that are statistically significant and positive as expected. The coefficient on capital is arguably lower than is generally found in manufacturing industries; see, for example, Hall and Mairesse (1995) or Wakelin (2001), who find capital coefficients around 0.15 to 0.20. In our case, this smaller coefficient is due to the inclusion of services inputs.[15] However, a comparison of our estimates with those of Amiti and Wei

14 In order to have a comparable set of observations across the different econometric specifications we use observations only for those firms for which we also have data on instruments used in subsequent regressions. Hence, the number of observations is the same in all regressions.

15 In fact, in unreported regressions excluding services inputs we find that the size of the capital coefficient is larger.

(2006), who also include k, l, s, and m in the production function, shows that our coefficient on k does not appear to be much out of line.

In terms of the other variables, we find that foreign-owned plants are more productive than domestic ones, as is generally found in the literature. However, we do not find any statistically significant productivity premium for exporters.[16] As pointed out above, this is not unexpected, as there is, as far as we are aware, no clear-cut evidence for Ireland, substantiating that exporters are more productive than non-exporters. We are, of course, mostly interested in the effect of international outsourcing. Examination of these results shows that international outsourcing of services appears to have a negative effect on plant-level productivity, while the impact of materials is positive.

However, there are a number of econometric problems with this estimation. First, factor inputs should be considered potentially endogenous in the estimation of the production function. This is the case because the contemporaneous level of TFP may affect the current choice of variable input factors, in which case inputs would be correlated with the error term (e.g., Levinsohn and Petrin 2003). Second, the relationship between outsourcing and productivity may be endogenous if there are unobserved variables that are potentially correlated with outsourcing and the error term. For example, plants with high- or low-productivity levels may be more likely to engage in outsourcing than other plants. This may explain the negative coefficient on services outsourcing in column (1) if, for example, low-productivity firms use outsourcing as a defensive strategy out of desperation.

There are various ways of dealing with these problems, and we employ a number of alternatives here. Our first approach is based on the assumption that the part of the error term that is correlated with either the input choices or the outsourcing variables is time invariant. This can be the case either if, for example, the simultaneity of input choice and TFP is due to a particular manager in a plant who was in charge over the whole time the plant spends in our sample, or if plants that are consistently of low productivity always make particular outsourcing decisions. Under this assumption of a time-invariant plant-specific effect the model can be estimated using a fixed-effects (within transformation) estimator. The results are reported in column (2). It is notable that the point estimates change slightly, but all coefficients are similar to OLS in terms of sign and statistical significance.[17] Of course, assuming the observed component to be a fixed effect is not a reasonable assumption in a long panel.

16 While the focus of this paper is not on exporting per se, we dug a little deeper into the data in order to try to understand why we fail to find a productivity premium for exporters in this regression. In unreported regressions we find that if we do not include services inputs in the production function (as is commonly done in many studies), then we also find a productivity premium for exporters. However, as shown in columns (2) and (3) once we use a fixed-effects estimator, we are able to find a positive productivity effect for exporters. As regards further regressions, our experimentation indicated that once we use the TFP measure based on the Levinsohn and Petrin (2003) methodology, then the exporting premium again disappears.

17 Note that the nationality dummy cannot be estimated, as it is time invariant; the nationality status reported in the data refers to the last year in which the plant was in the sample. Arguably, this does not allow for changes in ownership due to, for example, acquisitions of domestic firms

Before we continue dealing with the simultaneity problem, we face another potential issue with regressions thus far: since we do not allow coefficients on inputs to vary by sector, we are assuming that sectors use the same technology. This is a very restrictive assumption. In order to deal with this, as a first step we estimate a production function regressing output on only the factor inputs, using a fixed-effects estimator; to take account of sectoral heterogeneity, production functions are estimated separately for 2-digit industries. We then retrieve total factor productivity as the residual. TFP is then regressed on the other explanatory variables included in the model, which are assumed to be exogenous, using OLS. The results of this are reported in column (3). We now unearth important differences to the previous estimates. In particular, we find that international outsourcing of services has a positive and statistically significant effect on productivity, while the coefficient on materials outsourcing is still positive and statistically significant. This indicates that taking account of sectoral heterogeneity in the estimation of the production function is important for our conclusions.

In column (4) we deal more appropriately with the endogeneity of inputs choices by implementing the approach of estimating TFP due to Levinsohn and Petrin (2003). They suggest overcoming the simultaneity problem in production function estimations by essentially using inputs as a proxy for the unobserved productivity component. We implement their methodology, using plant-level energy consumption as proxy. Accordingly, we now estimate production functions separately for 2-digit industries using their approach and then generate total factor productivity as the residual from that regression. The second-stage TFP is performed using OLS.

Results reported in column (4) still show that international services outsourcing has a positive and statistically significant effect on productivity, although the point estimate is much lower than in the regression in column (3). The coefficient on materials outsourcing, though still positive, is also much lower than previously estimated. This model, while improving on the earlier estimations, still has one major flaw, namely, the assumption that international outsourcing is exogenous to plant-level productivity.[18]

In order to take account of this potential endogeneity problem, we implement an instrumental variables (IV) regressor in column (5). This treats the two outsourcing variables as endogenous. We use services and materials outsourcing in period $t-2$ as instruments, as well as a plant's total expenditure on trans-

by foreign owners. However, this may not be a problem for our particular study, as foreign acquisitions in Ireland were virtually zero in the 1980s and 1990s, and by far the vast majority of foreign firms were established through greenfield investment (Barry and Bradley 1997).

18 A potential concern is that our results are driven by outliers. While an inspection of the data does not show any obvious outliers, we investigate this problem by re-estimating the equation reported in column (4) using outlier robust regression (e.g., Rousseeuw and Leroy 1987) to mitigate the influence of the extreme observations. Results, which are not reported here to save space, produce very similar point estimates and standard errors to those produced in column (4), which suggests that outliers are not responsible for our results.

port costs. The latter seems a reasonable instrument, as it is likely to be correlated with international outsourcing but can be assumed orthogonal to the error term.

We are careful to assess the validity of the instruments using a Sargan type (Hansen) test, as well as the instrument relevance, examining the strength of the relationship between the instruments and the potentially endogenous regressors. It has been noted by, for example, Staiger and Stock (1997) that, when the partial correlation between the instruments and the endogenous variable is low, instrumental variables regression is biased in the direction of the OLS estimator. Staiger and Stock (1997) recommend that the F-statistics (or equivalently the p-values) from the first-stage regression be routinely reported in applied work.[19] These tests, as reported in column (5), indicate that instruments are both valid and relevant.

Turning to the coefficients, and in particular the outsourcing variables, we find that the result for services outsourcing is qualitatively similar to the one reported in column (4): services outsourcing positively affects plant-level productivity. However, we now find that there is no statistically significant relationship between productivity and international outsourcing of materials.

The last column in table 3 reports results of an estimation using the Generalized Methods of Moments (GMM) estimator as implemented by Baum, Schaffer, and Stillman (2003). This estimator is more efficient in the presence of heteroscedasticity than the standard IV estimator. We use the same instrument set as used for the estimations in column (5). Results are, reassuringly, much in line with the IV results. Looking at the point estimate, our results suggest that a 10 percentage point increase in the measure of international services outsourcing leads to an increase in plant-level productivity by approximately 0.8% to 0.9%.[20]

The estimations reported in table 3 constrain the effect of international outsourcing to be the same across different types of plants. As hinted at in section 3, this may not be a reasonable assumption. In particular, in line with the recent literature stressing firm-level heterogeneity in international trade theory, an important aspect of differences in plants is their level of international involvement:

19 The F-statistic tests the hypothesis that the instruments should be excluded from the first-stage regressions (i.e., the relevance of the instruments). The idea here is that when the F-statistic is small (or the corresponding p-value is large), the instrumental variable estimates and the associated confidence interval are unreliable.

20 A potential question is whether the effects of outsourcing are related to the intensity of outsourcing (as assumed in the estimations thus far) or just related to the outsourcing status of the plant. In order to investigate this, we first checked the persistence of outsourcing activity at the plant level (see the appendix). Table A1 shows that only 11% of firms that do not outsource services switch into outsourcing, while the equivalent number for materials outsourcing is 8%. Hence, outsourcing appears a relatively persistent activity in our data. In a further analysis we also re-estimated our equation using two dummy variables for whether a plant outsources services or materials, respectively. These estimations do not produce any statistically significant results, which suggests that it is indeed the intensity rather than the discrete status that matters (as would be expected from the results in table A1). To save space results are not reported.

TABLE 3
Regression results for various specifications

Dependent variable	(1) *Log output* OLS	(2) *Log output* FE	(3) *Log TFP (FE)* OLS	(4) *Log TFP (LP)* OLS-LP	(5) *Log TFP (LP)* IV-LP	(6) *Log TFP (LP)* GMM-LP
Log capital	0.069	0.024				
	(0.014)*	(0.004)*				
Log labour	0.190	0.265				
	(0.030)*	(0.011)*				
Log services	0.478	0.501				
	(0.020)*	(0.007)*				
Log materials	0.289	0.149				
	(0.020)*	(0.006)*				
Export dummy	0.021	0.039	0.438	0.010	0.008	0.007
	(0.026)	(0.015)*	(0.107)*	(0.015)	(0.015)	(0.015)
Foreign dummy	0.078		0.718	0.019	0.018	0.016
	(0.019)*		(0.072)*	(0.012)	(0.012)	(0.012)
Services	−0.051	−0.037	0.253	0.040	0.090	0.076
outsourcing	(0.016)*	(0.007)*	(0.069)*	(0.009)*	(0.026)*	(0.022)*
Materials	0.013	0.008	0.090	0.004	0.002	0.003
outsourcing	(0.004)*	(0.002)*	(0.013)*	(0.002)*	(0.003)	(0.003)
Observations	5,337	5,337	5,337	5,337	5,337	5,337
R-squared	0.96	0.84	0.34	0.64	0.63	0.64
F-test (s2) p-value					0.00	0.00
F-test (m2) p-value					0.00	0.00
Hansen J p-value					0.31	0.31

NOTES: Robust standard errors are in parentheses. *Significant at 5%. Constant term and full set of time and 2-digit industry dummies are included. TFP in (3) is calculated from fixed effects regressions for each 2-digit industry. TFP in (4) to (6) is calculated using the Levinsohn and Petrin (2003) technique for each 2-digit industry.

are plants part of a foreign multinational, are they domestic firms that export, or are they purely domestic firms? This distinction can have implications for their ability to benefit from international outsourcing. As highlighted in recent theoretical work (e.g., Antrás and Helpman 2004) international outsourcing involves sunk costs of searching for partners overseas. The potentially high costs of international outsourcing have also been pointed out in the business literature (Rasheed and Gilley 2005). Arguably, these costs of international outsourcing may be much higher for firms without any previous international contacts, that is, purely domestic firms, than for those with such contacts through either exporting or being a multinational.

In order to allow for these potential differences in the effects of international outsourcing, we generate interaction terms of the two outsourcing variables with dummy variables for exporters and foreign-owned plants. Column (1) of table 4 reports results for estimations including only the first set of interaction terms, that is, allowing the effect of outsourcing to differ for exporters

TABLE 4
Regression results with heterogeneous outsourcing effects

Dependent variable	(1) *Log TFP (LP)* GMM-LP	(2) *Log TFP (LP)* GMM-LP	(3) *Log TFP (LP)* GMM-LP
Export dummy	−0.035	−0.023	0.005
	(0.025)	(0.023)	(0.032)
Foreign ownership dummy	0.016	−0.008	0.065
	(0.012)	(0.017)	(0.031)*
Services outsourcing	−0.146	−0.144	−0.125
	(0.090)	(0.082)	(0.080)
Materials outsourcing	−0.001	−0.005	0.023
	(0.004)	(0.004)	(0.051)
Services outsourcing ∗ export dummy	0.230	0.180	0.187
	(0.094)*	(0.083)*	(0.086)*
Materials outsourcing ∗ export dummy	0.004	0.001	−0.061
	(0.005)	(0.004)	(0.054)
Services outsourcing ∗ foreign dummy		0.054	0.011
		(0.040)	(0.049)
Materials outsourcing ∗ foreign dummy		0.010	−0.069
		(0.004)*	(0.036)
Observations	5,337	5,337	5,332
R-squared	0.63	0.64	0.64
F-test (s2) p-value	0.00	0.00	0.00
F-test (m2) p-value	0.00	0.00	0.00
F-test (exp_s2) p-value	0.00	0.00	0.00
F-test (exp_m2) p-value	0.00	0.00	0.00
F-test (for_s2) p-value		0.00	0.00
F-test (for_m2) p-value		0.00	0.00
Hansen J p-value	0.37	0.45	0.12

NOTES: Robust standard errors are in parentheses. **Significant at 5%; ***significant at 1%. Constant term and full set of time and 2-digit industry dummies are included. TFP is calculated using the Levinsohn and Petrin (2003) technique for each 2-digit industry. Column (3) is based on alternative outsourcing measures: outsourcing relative to total services or material inputs, respectively.

and non-exporters regardless of their nationality. The results show that we now find a negative yet statistically insignificant effect of international services outsourcing on the productivity of non-exporting plants. For exporters, the results turn positive, with a coefficient of 0.23. This suggests that the search for partners with which to outsource production indeed involves costs and that these may outweigh any benefits of this outsourcing, at least in the short run, for firms that are not already established on international markets through exporting.

Column (2) includes interaction terms for both exporters and foreign-owned plants. Results show statistically significantly positive effects of services outsourcing for exporters. However, there is no further advantage to exporters that are foreign-owned, as indicated by the statistically insignificant (though positive) interaction term. It is noteworthy also that even when including the interaction terms we do not find any strong evidence to suggest that there are significant benefits associated with the international outsourcing of materials inputs.[21]

One potential criticism with our results so far concerns the measurement of international outsourcing, which reflects the value of imported inputs (services or materials) relative to the total wage bill in the plant. While we have argued in section 4 that this is potentially an appropriate measure of international outsourcing intensities, alternative measures are, of course, possible. We therefore construct a different measure of international outsourcing as imported services (materials) relative to total services (materials) inputs and use this in the estimation of the model. The results of this exercise are reported in column (3) of table 4. Note that the conclusions on the effects of international outsourcing on plant-level productivity do not change. International outsourcing of services is associated with higher productivity in exporting plants, but not in domestic-oriented plants. Also, we do not find any effects associated with increases in international outsourcing of materials.

6. Conclusions

This paper analyzes the effect of international outsourcing of services and materials inputs at the plant level on productivity of the plant. We use various techniques to account for potential endogeneity of international outsourcing in the productivity estimation. Our results show robust evidence for positive effects from outsourcing of services inputs. However, these results hold only for exporters, either domestic or foreign owned. By contrast, we find no statistically significant evidence of an impact of international outsourcing of services on productivity for firms not operating on the export market. A possible reason for this is that firms that are members of international production networks possess extensive knowledge on where to procure competitively priced inputs and, hence, face lower costs of outsourcing, in particular searching for potential suppliers abroad.

Overall, our results suggest that plant-level heterogeneity is important in evaluating the productivity effects of international outsourcing. It also indicates that further research into this area, either theoretical or empirical, would be very fruitful.

21 Using industry-level data for the US, Amiti and Wei (2006) also find much stronger evidence for beneficial effects of international outsourcing of services than materials.

Appendix

TABLE A1
Persistence of materials and services outsourcing

	Percentage
Services outsourcing	
Firms with services outsourcing (ever outsourcing)	84
Non-service outsourcing firms that switch to services outsourcing	11
Service outsourcing firms that discontinue to outsource	4
Materials outsourcing	
Firms with materials outsourcing (ever outsourcing)	94
Non-materials outsourcing firms that switch to materials outsourcing	8
Materials outsourcing firms that discontinue to outsource	0

NOTES: Row one suggests that 84% of plants outsource services at some stage during the sampling period. Of those plants that initially do not outsource services, 11% start outsourcing in the sampling period. Of those plants that initially do outsource, 4% stop at some stage.

References

Amiti, Mary, and Jozef Konings (2005) 'Trade liberalization, intermediate inputs and productivity: evidence from Indonesia,' CEPR Discussion Paper 5104

Amiti, Mary, and Shang-Jin Wei (2005) 'Fear of service outsourcing: is it justified?' *Economic Policy* 20, 308–47

— (2006) 'Service offshoring and productivity: evidence from the United States,' NBER Working Paper No. 11926

Antrás, Pol, and Elhanan Helpman (2004) 'Global sourcing,' *Journal of Political Economy* 112, 552–80

Barry, Frank, and John Bradley (1997) 'FDI and trade: the Irish host-country experience,' *Economic Journal* 107, 1798–811

Bartelsman, Eric J., and Mark Doms (2000) 'Understanding productivity: lessons from longitudinal microdata,' *Journal of Economic Literature* 38, 569–95

Baum, Christopher F., Mark E. Schaffer, and Steven Stillman (2003) 'Instrumental variables and GMM: estimation and testing,' Working Paper No. 545, Boston College

Bernard, Andrew B., and J. Bradford Jensen (1999) 'Exceptional exporter performance: cause, effect, or both?' *Journal of International Economics* 47, 1–25

Bernard Andrew B., Jonathan Eaton, Bradford Jensen, and Samuel S. Kortum (2003) 'Plants and productivity in international trade,' *American Economic Review* 93, 1268–90

Doms, Mark E., and J. Bradford Jensen (1998) 'Comparing wages, skills, and productivity between domestically and foreign-owned manufacturing establishments in the United States,' in *Geography and Ownership as Bases for Economic Accounting*, ed. Robert Baldwin, Robert Lipsey, and David Richardson (Chicago: Chicago University Press)

Egger, Hartmut, and Peter Egger (2006) 'International outsourcing and the productivity of low-skilled labor in the EU,' *Economic Inquiry* 44, 98–108

Feenstra, Robert C., and Gordon H. Hanson (1999) 'The impact of outsourcing and high-technology capital on wages: estimates for the United States, 1979–1990,' *Quarterly Journal of Economics* 114, 907–41

— (2001) 'Global production sharing and rising inequality: a survey of trade and wages,' NBER Working Paper 8372

Fernandes, Ana M. (2007) 'Trade policy, trade volumes and plant level productivity in Colombian manufacturing industries,' *Journal of International Economics* 71, 52–71

Girma, Sourafel, and Holger Görg (2004) 'Outsourcing, foreign ownership and productivity: evidence from UK establishment level data,' *Review of International Economics* 12, 817–32

Girma, Sourafel, Holger Görg, and Eric Strobl (2004) 'Exports, international investment, and plant performance: evidence from a non-parametric test,' *Economics Letters* 83, 317–24

Greenaway, David, Joakim Gullstrand, and Richard Kneller (2005) 'Exporting does not always boost productivity,' *Review of World Economics* 141, 561–84

Grossman, Gene M., and Elhanan Helpman (2005) 'Outsourcing in a global economy,' *Review of Economic Studies* 72, 135–59

Hall, Bronwyn H., and Jacques Mairesse (1995) 'Exploring the relationship between R&D and productivity in French manufacturing firms,' *Journal of Econometrics* 65, 263–93

Head, Keith, and John Ries (2002) 'Offshore production and skill upgrading by Japanese manufacturing firms,' *Journal of International Economics* 58, 81–105

Helpman, Elhanan, Marc J. Melitz, and Stephen R. Yeaple (2004) 'Export versus FDI with heterogeneous firms,' *American Economic Review* 94, 300–16

Hijzen, Alexander, Holger Görg, and Robert C. Hine (2005) 'International outsourcing and the skill structure of labour demand in the United Kingdom,' *Economic Journal* 115, 861–79

Hummels, David, Jun Ishii, and Kei-Mu Yi (2001) 'The nature and growth of vertical specialization in world trade,' *Journal of International Economics* 54, 75–96

Kasahara, Hiroyuki, and Joel Rodrigue (2005) 'Does the use of imported intermediates increase productivity? Plant-level evidence,' mimeo, Queen's University, Kingston

Kurz, Christopher J. (2006) 'Outstanding outsourcers: a firm and plant level analysis of production sharing,' Working Paper, Federal Reserve Board, Washington DC

Levinsohn, James, and Amil Petrin (2003) 'Estimating production functions using inputs to control for unobservables,' *Review of Economic Studies* 70, 317–42

López, Ricardo A. (2006) 'Imports of intermediate inputs and plant survival,' *Economics Letters* 92, 58–62

Rasheed, Abdul A., and K. Matthew Gilley (2005) 'Outsourcing: national- and firm-level implications,' *Thunderbird International Business Review* 47, 513–28

Rousseeuw, Peter J., and Annick M. Leroy (1987) *Robust Regression and Outlier Detection* (New York: John Wiley)

Ruane, Frances, and Julie Sutherland (2002) 'Globalization, Europeanization and trade in the 1990s: export responses of foreign and indigenous manufacturing companies,' in *Europe and Globalization*, ed. Henryk Kierzkowski (London: Palgrave Macmillan)

— (2005) 'Export performance and destination characteristics of Irish manufacturing industry,' *Review of World Economics* 141, 442–59

Sjöholm, Fredrik (2003) 'Which Indonesian firms export? The importance of foreign networks,' *Papers in Regional Science* 82, 333–50

Staiger, Douglas, and James H. Stock (1997) 'Instrumental variables regression with weak instruments,' *Econometrica* 65, 557–86

Tomiura, Eiichi (2005) 'Foreign outsourcing and firm-level characteristics: evidence from Japanese manufacturers,' *Journal of the Japanese and International Economies* 19, 255–71

Wakelin, Katharine (2001) 'Productivity growth and R&D expenditure in UK manufacturing firms,' *Research Policy* 30, 1079–90

Yasar, Mahmut, and Catherine J. Morrison Paul (2007) 'International linkages and productivity at the plant level: foreign direct investment, exports, imports and licensing,' *Journal of International Economics* 71, 373–88

Yeaple, Stephen (2005) 'A simple model of firm heterogeneity, international trade and wages,' *Journal of International Economics* 65, 1–20

Chapter II.3

OFFSHORING AND PRODUCTIVITY: THE CASE OF IRELAND, SWEDEN AND THE UNITED KINGDOM

Chiara Criscuolo
Centre for Economic Perfomance, London School of Economics

Eva Hagsten
Statistics Sweden

Aoife Hanley
Nottingham University Business School

Patrik Karpaty
Swedish Business School, Orebro University

Stefan Svanberg
Statistics Sweden

This paper analyses the relationship between offshoring of services and total factor productivity across three different OECD countries: Ireland, Sweden and the United Kingdom. Offshoring activity is widely believed to play an important role for firm productivity due to the fragmentation of the production process across countries when there are differences in the relative endowments of skilled and unskilled labour and of technology. The paper firstly shows that offshoring firms tend to be more labour productive, are larger, pay higher wages and are more likely to be multinational and foreign-owned. Secondly, there appears to be some suggestive evidence of a positive relationship between offshoring and firm productivity although the statistical and/or economic significance of this relationship is not very strong across the three countries. One possible explanation is the small time horizon over which our analysis span.

This chapter is a revised version of a paper presented at the Statistical Working Party of the OECD Industry Committee at its November 2006 meeting.

Introduction

In recent years, thanks to trade liberalisation and progress in information and communication technology (ICT), an increasing number of firms are trading a wide variety of services with both developed and emerging economies. Before the ICT revolution most services (call-centres, IT consultancy, accounting services, etc.) were non–tradable. This makes services trade, in particular the importing or "offshoring" of services (from low wage countries), a relatively new phenomenon, whose consequences are the subject of much debate among policy makers and the public opinion.

Attention has focused on the possibility that offshoring of services might lead to the migration of jobs to countries, such as India, where firms can pay qualified workers much less than in their home countries. In general, the discussion has concentrated on the negative effects of offshoring. However, offshoring is likely to bring benefits to developed economies through lower costs of services, restructuring and increased specialisation. Moreover, the largest exporters of services in absolute terms remain developed countries, such as the United States and United Kingdom. An increase in services trade implies for these countries not only an increase in imports but also a potential increase in exports and therefore a larger market where domestic firms can offer their services. This may also yield gains to firms in developed economies.

This paper aims to describe these trends and compare the experience of three OECD countries that are quite different in terms of industrial structures and labour market regulations -- Ireland, Sweden and the UK -- using previously unavailable detailed official data.

Most of the existing evidence reports the experience of single countries as it cannot compare responses across different countries because of confidentiality constraints associated with the use of official firm-level data. Given these constraints our approach is to conduct a similar type of analysis over the same time frame across the three countries using similar detailed micro-level data so that the results are as comparable as possible and differences are not driven by methodology or the time frame considered.

In each of the three countries analysed, Ireland, Sweden and the UK, the available data gives information on firm performance, domestically and internationally outsourced services and foreign ownership. With these datasets we document a series of facts about offshoring and related measures (characteristics of firms that offshore; amount of trade; differences in patterns between manufacturing and services sectors; association of services offshoring with productivity).

The paper is organised as follows. In the next section we give a brief overview of the data in the three countries and we describe broad patterns related to offshoring in the data. In Section 3 we move on to describe the empirical approach used in the analysis; we then present the results of this analysis in Section 4. Section 5 concludes. In Annex 7.A we describe in more detail each of the data sources used.

Data description

We are using firm level data that cover manufacturing and services. The data comes from the Statistical offices in Sweden (Statistics Sweden); the UK (Office for National Statistics, ONS) and from Forfás, Ireland's national policy and advisory board for enterprise, trade, science, technology and innovation. Table 7.1 summarises the characteristics of the data used; such as the sampling frame and the variables available in each countries. The data covers the period 2000-2003 for the UK; 2000 to 2002 for Sweden and 1999 to 2002 for Ireland. To make the analysis comparable in all three countries we use data for the period 2000 to 2002. In all three countries the data contains information on output (gross output and value added); inputs; foreign ownership. Most importantly we have data on imports and exports of intermediate services (UK; Sweden and Ireland) and intermediate goods (Sweden and Ireland) at the firm level. The table also reports information on other variables available in the data such as skills and R&D in Sweden; or training expenditure in Ireland. A detailed description of the data sources can be found in the Annex 7.A.

Table 7.1. Description of data across countries

	Ireland	Sweden	United Kingdom
Source	Forfás	Statistics Sweden	Office for National Statistics
Sample	Census 60- 80% response rate of targeted plant population	Census of firms with at least 20 employees	Stratified sample: selects all the largest businesses (>249) with a reducing fraction of smaller businesses
Sectors covered	Manufacturing (and services)	Manufacturing and services	Manufacturing and services
Time period covered	1999- 2002	2000- 2002	2000-2003
Output variables	Gross output; value added; net value added and gross value added	Gross output and value added	Gross output and value added
Input variables	Materials and services	Materials and services*	Materials and services
Import of intermediate goods	Yes	Yes	No
Export of goods	Yes	Yes	No
Imports of intermediate services	Yes	Yes	Yes
Export of services	No	Yes	Yes
Other relevant variables	Wages; capital R&D; training	Wages; capital; R&D; skills	Wages; capital
Ownership variables	Domestic and foreign;	Domestic single firm; part of a group; domestic MNE; foreign owned	Domestic single firm; part of a group UK MNE; foreign owned

*The data for Sweden have time series break in 2002 that prevents the construction of a continuous time series.

Note: Data on total purchases of services are imputed from sector level data. For Ireland, coverage of service sector is very limited.

Descriptive evidence

The aim of this section is to present some initial evidence on how firms that do offshore differ from firms who don't. The question we want to answer is who the firms are that offshore in each of the countries analysed. Are these firms similar or do we observe stark differences across countries?

The first figures we are going to present look at the overall presence of offshoring firms in the three economies in a particular year (2000). As the UK is not a census but is a stratified sample, we present for this country both weighted[60] and unweighted figures. This has two aims: we want to make the UK sample representative of the population of UK businesses; and we present unweighted figures to look for differences in the samples analysed. Also we present the figures separately for manufacturing and services. This highlights that for Ireland data for services is very limited (*i.e.* only 172 firms).

Table 7.2. Offshoring intensity in each country, 2000

	Actual number of firms in the sample		Share offshorers (%)[a]		
Year 2000	Non-offshorers	Offshorers	Firms	Employment	Value added
			Manufacturing		
Ireland	361	721	67	84	68
Sweden	4096	1177	22	58	68
UK	8824	1874	17	29	33
UK weighted				22	27
			Services sector		
Ireland	62	110	64	79	66
Sweden	5332	1580	23	54	57
UK	24011	1725	7	19	20.5
UK weighted				13	15

Notes:

Numbers and shares reported refer to 2000 and only relate to outsourcing of international service intermediates.

For the UK, shares reported are weighted using probability weights.

As is evident from the statistics reported, Ireland is the country where offshoring is most widespread: more than half of the sample offshore international services. This might reflect the higher reliance of Ireland on foreign intermediate trade relative to Sweden and the UK, but also differences in the industrial structure and in the presence of foreign multinationals. About a fifth of Swedish firms offshore, while their activities in terms of value added is at least twice the size (even more than so for manufacturers), indicating that the group of offshorers consist of many large firms. We also note for Ireland that although service offshorers contribute proportionally more to employment, their contribution to value added is in line with that of their non-offshoring counterparts. We will investigate this below. To help compare values for the three countries, we report only the

60. To weight the figures presented we use inverse probability weights provided by the Office for National Statistics.

international outsourced service intermediates although data is also available for materials intermediates for Sweden and Ireland.

How much do differences in the presence of offshorers reflect differences in industrial composition across the three countries? Table 7.3 answers this question. We find that across all of the sectors analysed and independently of measure used (number of firms, share of value added or employment) Ireland has a much larger presence of offshorers and the UK a smaller one, with Sweden somewhere in between. This is especially so when we look at the weighted figures for the UK in which we account for the fact that large firms that are more likely to offshore are over-sampled in the ARD data.

Table 7.3. Distribution of offshoring firms by sector (2000)

	Ireland		Sweden		UK		Ireland	Sweden	UK	UK weighted
Sector	Non-OFF	OFF	Non-OFF	OFF	Non-OFF	OFF	Percentage offshorers			
15-16	65	115	240	66	967	128	64%	22	12%	6%
17-19	17	47	78	35	716	126	73%	31	15%	4%
20	11	20	260	69	265	19	65%	21	7%	1%
21-22	36	36	365	132	1230	184	50%	27	13%	4%
23-25	40	136	265	134	960	349	77%	34	27%	11%
26	14	16	65	28	350	93	53%	30	20.9%	21.3%
27-28	52	85	717	144	1509	240	62%	17	14%	4%
29-33	82	191	715	363	1765	516	70%	34	23%	8%
34-35	15	26	187	75	471	126	63%	29	21%	9%
36-37	29	49	192	33	591	93	63%	15	14%	5%
50-52	9	2	2372	463	11619	775	18%	16	6%	3%
55	0	1	557	48	2563	71	100%	8	3%	1%
60-63	n/a	n/a	721	207	1822	211	n/a	22	10%	5%
64	1	4	40	60	225	25	80%	60	10%	2%
70-74	51	97	1642	802	7782	643	66%	33	8%	3%

Note: Authors' calculation from ARD; Forfás and SBS data. The sectors considered are: 15-16 Food and beverages and tobacco; 17-19 Textile; Wearing apparel and Leather; 20 Wood and wood products; 21-22 Pulp, paper and paper products; Publishing, printing and reproduction of recorded media; 23-25 fuel Chemicals and chemical products; Rubber and plastic products; 26 Other non-metallic mineral products; 27-28 Basic and fabricated metals; 29-33 Machinery and equipment not elsewhere classified (nec); Office machinery and computers; Electrical machinery and apparatus nec; Radio, television and communication equipment and apparatus; Medical, precision and optical instruments, watches and clocks; 34-35 Motor vehicles, trailers and semi-trailers; Other transport equipment; 36-37 Furniture, manufacturing nec and Recycling. 50-52 wholesale and retail trade; repair of motor vehicle, motorcycles and personal and household goods; 55 Hotels and Restaurants; 60-63 transport and storage; 64 post and telecommunications; 70-74 real estate; renting and business activities.

We know from the existing literature that within industry heterogeneity exists. Table 7.3 looks at the characteristics of firms that offshore relative to those who do not. One issue that arises when conducting cross-country analysis is how to overcome the fact that these countries use different currencies. The way we have solved the issue here is to express all of the variables considered as log deviation from the average non-offshoring firm in the three-digit industry of firm i at time t. Therefore in the table we present for each country the following mean:

$$\Sigma_{i \in OFF}(\ln X_i - E(\ln X)^{NON\text{-}OFF})/N^{OFF}$$

For example, column 1, row 1 shows that in Ireland offshorers are on average 35% more labour productive than the average non-offshoring firm in the same industry; where we define labour productivity as value added per employee. In the UK and Sweden the difference in labour productivity is smaller at 21% for both countries.

Table 7.4. Characteristics of offshoring firms relative to non offshorers (year 2000)

	Advantage of offshorers vs. non-offshorers	Ireland	Sweden	UK
(1)	Value added per employee	0.35***	0.21***	0.21***
		(0.89)	(0.01)	(0.77)
(2)	Gross output per employee	0.32***	0.35***	0.35***
		(0.94)	(0.01)	(0.78) ***
(3)	Employment	0.73***	0.74***	1.02***
		(1.21)	(0.02)	(1.67)
(4	Purchased materials per employee	0.24**	0.48***	0.42***
		(1.36)	(0.02)	(1.23)
(5)	Purchased services per employee	0.24***		0.65***
		(1.05)		(1.04)
(6)	Capital per employee	0.30***	0.25***	0.50***
		(1.29)	(0.02)	(1.01)
(7)	Average wages	0.14***	0.51***	0.30***
		(0.49)	(0.02)	(0.61)
	Observations	1,259	12,185	36,434

Note: Figures reported are log deviation from the average non-offshoring firm and represent differences in means for services offshorers and non-services offshorers respectively. Standard deviations in brackets.

One clear pattern emerges from this table. In all three countries we observe that offshoring firms are more labour productive; larger; more intermediates- and capital-intensive and pay higher wages than the average non-offshoring firm.

From previous country level evidence we know that offshoring firms are mainly globally engaged firms and that this helped explain at least partly the observed differences between offshoring and non-offshoring firms. Is this the case in all three countries? Table 7.5 attempts to answer this question. We do find that in all three countries the proportion of foreign multinationals is larger among offshorers. In the UK and Sweden where the data is available this is true also for the proportion of domestic multinationals. Concerning differences across countries note that the proportion of foreign owned affiliates is much higher in Ireland and that they make up about two-fifths of offshorers in Ireland, while only a third in Sweden and a quarter in the UK.

Table 7.5. Offshoring and other dimensions of global engagement (% of sample)

	Ireland		Sweden		UK	
	Non-offshorers	Offshorers	Non-offshorers	Offshorers	Non-offshorers	Offshorers
Proportion of domestic firms (%)	83	59	73	31	90	65
Proportion of domestic MNEs (%)	n/a	n/a	17	34	4.5	11
Proportion of foreign MNEs (%)	17	41	10	35	5.5	24

Note: For the Irish data we cannot distinguish for domestic multinationals.

The econometric framework

To estimate the importance of offshoring for firms' productivity, we estimate a production function augmented by measures of import intensities and a set of control variables assumed to affect total factor productivity.

Assuming that firms produce according to a linear homogenous general differentiable production function:

$$Y_{it} = A_{it} F(X_{it}) \qquad (1)$$

where Y_{it} is gross output, A_{it} is the firm specific productivity factor, and X_{it} is a vector of inputs (labour, capital, intermediate goods and intermediate services), in the *i*:th firm in period *t*. Following Klette (1999), we express the production function in terms of logarithmic deviations from the median firm in the industry of firm *i* at time t, which we use as our point of reference so that we can rewrite equation (1) as:

$$\tilde{y}_{it} = \tilde{a}_{it} + \alpha_K \tilde{k}_{it} + \alpha_M \tilde{m}_{it} + \alpha_S \tilde{s}_{it} + \alpha_L \tilde{l}_{it} \qquad (2)$$

where the small letters with tildes denote the transformed variable and we now write each of the inputs separately.

We assume that the TFP of the *i*:th firm relative to the "representative firm" in the industry at period t ($\tilde{a}_{it}$) might be affected by offshoring of services. Finally, we allow for the fact that multinational firms (MNE) -- both foreign and domestic -- have higher TFP than non-MNEs, as suggested by existing evidence.[61]

One question we will investigate is whether MNEs may be better able to gain from offshoring since they are already active within an international network or whether for firms with a history of high levels of exposure to international markets the possibilities for positive effects may have been exhausted in a way that they have not for other firms. Another indicator of being active within an international network that we use is whether the firm is exporting or not. We also control for firm age and age squared in order to control for heterogeneity among firms. Substituting out $\tilde{a}_{it}$ and adding industry, λ_i, time,

61. Criscuolo and Martin (2004) for the UK and Karpaty (2006) for Sweden show that multinational firms, both domestic and foreign are more productive than domestic firms.

λ_t, and region λ_r, gives:

$$\begin{aligned}\widetilde{y}_{it} &= \beta_O + \beta_1 Off_{it} + \beta_2 DomMNE + \beta_3 USMNE + \beta_4 ForeignMNE + \beta_5 Exporter \\ &+ \beta_6 \widetilde{k}_{it} + \beta_7 \widetilde{m}_{it} + \beta_8 \widetilde{s}_{it} + \beta_9 \widetilde{l} + \beta_{10} age + \beta_{11} age^2 + \lambda_i + \lambda_t + \lambda_r + \varepsilon_{it}\end{aligned} \quad (3)$$

We start by estimating equation 3 using OLS. This approach presents several limitations.

Firstly, we impose the same production function across all firms; in particular we have imposed that the offshoring effects on productivity are the same. It is, however, possible that offshoring effects on productivity may be different depending on the characteristics of the firm, its nationality and whether it has previous experience of international trade through export, (Görg *et al.*, 2005). We will investigate these differences in the three countries.

Secondly, OLS regressions report correlations. However, if we are in search of a causal relationship between offshoring and productivity, OLS estimates are not likely to give us the right answer as the error term and the explanatory variables, in particular choices on the production inputs and on offshoring, are likely to be correlated. We assume that we can divide the productivity shocks in two components: a firm specific time invariant component and an idiosyncratic time varying productivity shock. If inputs choices were only correlated with the time invariant establishment specific effect, taking first differences or estimating a fixed effect model would solve the endogeneity problem.[62]

Finally, we choose a static specification. This choice is driven by the loss of observations that we would incur if we were to have a dynamic specification for the UK data and by the short time period available to us for the comparative study (just three years from 2000 to 2003). In country level studies for Sweden and Ireland for which where there is a census of firms for every year, the authors have relaxed this assumption and controlled for the possible correlation between production inputs and offshoring intensity with the time varying productivity shock using the GMM estimator suggested by Blundell and Bond (1998).[63] We will discuss the results obtained at the country level in more detail below.

62. We prefer fixed effects to first differences estimation not only because of the structure of the data, but also because first differencing can exacerbate measurement error problems (Griliches and Hausman, 1986). For the UK, given the nature of the data, the difference between fixed effects and first differences over the three year period is very marginal. The fixed effect estimator (FE) is more efficient than the first differencing (FD) under the assumption of no serial correlation in the idiosyncratic errors µit. However if µit follow a random walk the FD estimator is more efficient (Woolridge, 2002, p.284).

63. The differenced GMM estimator uses time differenced variables in order to remove permanent unobserved heterogeneity, Arellano & Bond (1991). When there is relatively little persistence in the series the lagged levels may be valid instruments for endogenous variables. However, when time series are short or when there is persistence in the time series over time, the Arellano and Bond GMM estimator suffers from poor precision (Blundell et al 2000). Blundell and Bond (2000) propose an improved GMM for shorter panels and when there is persistence in the series. The model suggests that lagged time differenced regressors should be used as instruments for the endogenous variables.

Results

We now answer the question: are the offshoring firms more productive, even after controlling for differences in capital intensity; intermediate usage; multinationality and industry distribution shown above in Tables 7.3, 7.4 and 7.5?

Table 7.6 shows the regression parameters, estimated by OLS, of equation 3. The estimations have been performed for both manufacturing and service sectors together, and for manufacturing and services separately. Note that in all regressions, a polynomial in age and industry, time and region dummy variables are included, as specified in equation 4 but not reported in the tables.[64]

The offshoring variable is defined as the ratio of imported services over total services purchased. We start by looking at both the manufacturing and services sector: the first two rows of panel 1 report the coefficients and the robust standard errors of the OLS estimates. When comparing the coefficient across the three countries we observe that in Ireland the coefficient is not significant; in Sweden it is strongly significant but economically small at a level similar to that of the UK, which in turn is significant at the 10% level.

If we look separately at manufacturing and services sector we find that the order of magnitude of the coefficient looks much more similar across the three countries, with Sweden having the largest and most significant estimate of 0.076[65] for the manufacturers. The coefficient for Ireland remains insignificant and the one for the UK significant only at the 10% level. The last panel reports estimates for the services sector, we could not estimate this for Ireland as the number of observations is too small. Now the offshoring coefficient becomes insignificant for the UK and economically smaller for Sweden.

The rest of the table confirms existing evidence; the MNE variables are positive and strongly significant in all three countries. For Ireland we can only identify Foreign MNEs, *i.e.* we cannot identify domestic Irish MNEs, but we separate out British Multinationals by including a dummy for UK MNEs but report it in the table in the domestic MNE column. The association of global engagement in terms of exporting activity with productivity differ between sectors, with the exporters' advantage being stronger in the services sector for both the UK and Sweden. For the UK, one note of caution here relates to the fact that "exporters" both in the manufacturing and services sectors are firms that export services; this implies that in the manufacturing sector we cannot identify firms that export goods but not services. This might imply that we are identifying a very specific group of manufacturing firms who actually export both manufacturing and services (*e.g.* machinery and equipment manufacturers who also export the engineering and maintenance services) and might therefore be a lower bound estimate of the actual exporters' advantage for the UK.

The above regressions found some suggestive evidence of a positive relation between offshoring intensity and productivity mainly in the UK and Swedish manufacturing sectors. It is however important to address a number of econometric problems. We expect that the presence of unobserved influences, *e.g.* firm-specific fixed effects such as different quality of labour and capital between firms may affect the results. The fixed

64. Note that in the UK we also included a dummy to account for the fact that the age of the firm is only known if the firm is established after 1980 in the manufacturing sector and after 1997 in the services sector.

65. Note that this coefficient is a semi-elasticity.

effects estimates reported in Table 7.7 try to get at this. However, given the short time period available for the analysis, the results must be taken with some caution.

Table 7.6. Effects of offshoring on productivity performance in manufacturing and service, 2000-2002, OLS estimations

	Both sectors			Manufacturing			Services	
	Ireland	Sweden	UK	Ireland	Sweden	UK	Ireland	UK
Offshoring	0.074	0.025	0.027	0.062	0.076	0.030	0.022	0.021
	(0.060)	(0.003)***	(0.016)*	(0.057)	(0.011)***	(0.018)*	(0.003)***	(0.024)
Ln(EMP)	0.406	0.005	-0.009	0.433	0.015	0.008	-0.001	-0.015
	(0.020)**	(0.003)*	(0.001)***	(0.020)**	(0.004)***	(0.002)***	(0.004)	(0.001)***
Ln(K/EMP)	0.065	0.083	0.211	0.049	0.072	0.136	0.089	0.229
	(0.010)**	(0.002)***	(0.004)***	(0.010)**	(0.003)***	(0.006)***	(0.003)***	(0.004)***
Ln(M/EMP)	0.369	0.178	0.228	0.402	0.177	0.270	0.176	0.218
	(0.011)**	(0.003)***	(0.003)***	(0.011)**	(0.005)***	(0.008) ***	(0.004)***	(0.003)***
Ln(S/EMP)	0.226		0.198	0.181		0.258		0.184
	(0.013)**		(0.003)***	(0.013)**		(0.007)***		(0.003)***
Domestic MNEs	0.112	0.053	0.077	0.144	0.025	0.028	0.075	0.130
	(0.062)	(0.007)***	(0.008)***	(0.058)*	(0.009)***	(0.007)***	(0.01)***	(0.014)***
Foreign US MNEs		0.117	0.145		0.04	0.092	0.15	0.184
		(0.014)***	(0.011)***		(0.022)*	(0.011)***	(0.018)***	(0.021)***
Foreign other MNEs	0.219	0.055	0.120	0.154	0.035	0.048	0.065	0.169
	(0.03)**	(0.008)***	(0.008)***	(0.028)**	(0.011)***	(0.008)***	(0.011)***	(0.013)***
Exporter	0.032	0.021	0.040	0.025	-0.016	0.013	0.037	0.054
	(0.034)	(0.006)***	(0.006)***	(0.032)	(0.009)*	(0.007)*	(0.009)***	(0.008) ***
Observations	2526	36367	95143	2179	15602	22856	20751	72287

Note: For Ireland ,domestic MNEs are UK MNEs. OLS estimations heteroskedasticity-consistent standard errors in parenthesis, ***, **, *, significant at the 1%, 5% and 10% level respectively. Unreported time, region and four-digit industry dummies are always included. The estimations consist of an unbalanced panel including all firms with at least 20 employees. Offshoring defined as services offshored divided by total purchases of service intermediates.

Comparing Tables 7.6 and 7.7 we find some interesting features of the results: the loss of significance of the ownership and offshoring variables for the UK while the Swedish estimates remain significant and similar to those reported from the pure OLS estimation. The exception to this general similarity in the Swedish findings is with respect to the ownership variables which are now smaller than in Table 7.6. These results are partly at odds with those obtained in the single countries (*e.g.* Criscuolo and Leaver, 2004; Hagsten *et al.*, 2007). In fact, the results from the UK show that looking over the period 2000 to 2003, the positive association between offshoring and productivity is robust to controlling for fixed effects. We have investigated the source of this discrepancy in more detail. This analysis (unreported but available upon request) shows that the difference is due to the short time horizon analysed. For the UK, when the analysis is extended to include later years the significance of the services offshoring variables is resumed. In the Swedish case, the discrepancies in the results between the single country studies and this comparative one seem to be driven by differences in specification of the models and variables used.

Table 7.7. Effects of offshoring on productivity performance in manufacturing and service, 2000-2002, fixed effects estimations

	Both sectors			Manufacturing			Service	
	IRL	SWE	UK	IRL	SWE	UK	SWE	UK
Offshoring	0.032	0.025	0.012	0.125	0.074	-0.006	0.022	0.024
	(0.121)	(0.003)***	(0.017)	(0.120)	(0.011)***	(0.019)	(0.003)***	(0.030)
Ln(EMP)	0.302	0.012	-0.106***	0.277	0.018	-0.025**	0.01	-0.102***
	(0.038)**	(0.003)***	(0.008)	(0.039)**	(0.004)***	(0.010)	(0.004)**	(0.013)
Ln(K/EMP)	0.025	0.081	0.241***	0.014	0.069	0.244***	0.087	0.303***
	(0.031)	(0.002)***	(0.009)	(0.032)	(0.003)***	(0.017)	(0.003)***	(0.015)
Ln(M/EMP)	0.194	0.182	0.137***	0.240	0.176	0.222***	0.183	0.105***
	(0.022)**	(0.003)***	(0.006)	(0.022)**	(0.005)***	(0.013)	(0.004)***	(0.007)
Ln(S/EMP)	0.117		0.143***	0.117		0.169***		0.127***
	(0.021)**		(0.006)	(0.020)**		(0.008)		(0.008)
Domestic MNEs		0.03	-0.003		0.021	0.000	0.036	-0.001
		(0.006)***	(0.008)		(0.008)***	(0.008)	(0.009)***	(0.015)
Foreign US MNEs		0.081	-0.013		0.035	-0.008	0.1	-0.023
		(0.013)***	(0.014)		(0.02)*	(0.012)	(0.018)***	(0.032)
Foreign other MNEs		0.025	0.000		0.025	0.004	0.021	-0.000
		(0.007)***	(0.010)		(0.01)***	(0.010)	(0.01)**	(0.019)
Exporter		-0.002	-0.008	0.014	-0.016	0.004	-0.002	-0.010
		(0.005)	(0.006)	(0.064)	(0.007)**	(0.007)	(0.007)	(0.009)
Observations	2526	36733	73428	1104	11703	22856	12048	72287

Note: For Ireland Domestic MNEs are UK MNEs. OLS estimations heteroskedasticity-consistent standard errors in parenthesis, ***, **, * significant at the 1%, 5% and 10% level respectively. Unreported time, region and four-digit industry dummies are always included. The estimations consist of an unbalanced panel including all firms with at least 20 employees. Offshoring is defined as services offshored divided by total purchases of service intermediates.

Offshoring and international experience

Up to this point, we have dealt with the issue of offshoring assuming that the association between offshoring and productivity is the same across domestic and foreign firms and across exporters and non-exporters. It is, however, possible that potential effects from offshoring on productivity may be different depending on the global engagement of the firm. First, we ran a regression on domestic firms only; then on foreign-owned, and for Sweden and the UK we performed the same regression for domestic multinational firms. As argued the correlation between offshoring intensity might be either larger or smaller for firms with global engagement than pure local firms. However, the results shown in Table 7.8 and 7.10 for Sweden and the UK do not seem in line with the hypothesis that firms with global engagement having a more positive offshoring-productivity relationship (explained for example by smaller transaction cost and lower search costs): the offshoring coefficient estimates seem to suggest a weaker correlation for the globally engaged firms, exporters and MNEs (domestic and foreign).[66] One possible explanation is that this might be due to difficulties in measurement due to transfer pricing issues.

66. Column 2: the offshoring coefficient for the Swedish domestic exporters is not significant., while all 21 781 exporters, not included in the table above, are positively significant at the one per cent level with the estimate 0.022 and standard deviation 0.003.

Table 7.8. Offshoring and previous international experience: Sweden

Sweden	Domestic non-exporter	Domestic exporter	Domestic MNE	Foreign MNE	Domestic non-exporter Manufacturing sector
	(1)	(2)	(3)	(4)	(5)
Offshoring*	0.224	0.023	0.027	0.022	0.274
	(0.058)***	(0.016)	(0.005)***	(0.004)***	(0.076)***
Ln(EMP)	-0.001	0.006	0.007	0.019	-0.002
	(0.007)	(0.006)	(0.006)	(0.006)***	(0.008)
Ln(K/EMP)	0.083	0.073	0.097	0.071	0.094
	(0.003)***	(0.003)***	(0.005)***	(0.006)***	(0.003)***
Ln(M/EMP)	0.187	0.165	0.195	0.16	0.2
	(0.005)***	(0.006)***	(0.009)***	(0.008)***	(0.006)***
Observations	12350	9915	7191	6100	3855

Note: OLS estimations. Robust standard errors in parenthesis, ***, **, * significant at the 1%, 5% and 10% level respectively. Unreported time, region and four-digit industry dummies are included. The estimations consist of an unbalanced panel including all firms with at least 20 employees. Offshoring is defined as imports of services over total purchases of services intermediates.

Table 7.9. Offshoring and previous international experience: Irish manufacturing firms

Ireland	Domestic firms	Foreign MNEs	Exporters
Offshoring	-0.199	0.268	0.098
	(0.075)**	(0.096)**	(0.063)
Ln(EMP)	0.486	0.320	0.427
	(0.023)**	(0.035)**	(0.022)**
Ln(K/EMP)	0.039	0.068	0.056
	(0.011)**	(0.017)**	(0.011)**
Ln(M/EMP)	0.336	0.511	0.398
	(0.013)**	(0.021)**	(0.013)**
Ln(S/EMP)	0.174	0.175	0.188
	(0.016)**	(0.024)**	(0.015)**
Firm is an exporter	0.065	-0.066	
	(0.032)*	(0.098)	
UK MNE			0.140
			(0.066)*
Foreign			0.147
			(0.030)**
Observations	1452	727	1866

Note: OLS estimations heteroskedasticity-consistent standard errors in parenthesis, ***, **, * significant at the 1%, 5% and 10% level respectively. Unreported time, region and four-digit industry dummies are always included. The estimations consist of an unbalanced panel including all firms with at least 20 employees. Offshoring is defined as services imported divided by total purchases of service intermediates. For Ireland we cannot discriminate between domestic firms and domestic MNEs and so report results for all domestic firms.

Table 7.10. Offshoring and previous international experience: United Kingdom

UK	Domestic non-exporter	Domestic exporter	Domestic MNE	Foreign MNE	Domestic non-exporter Manufacturing sector
	(1)	(2)	(3)	(4)	(5)
Offshoring	0.035	-0.002	0.036	0.040	**0.076***
	(0.029)	(0.027)	(0.053)	(0.036)	**(0.039)**
Ln(EMP)	-0.010***	0.004	0.003	-0.012***	0.006**
	(0.001)	(0.004)	(0.006)	(0.004)	(0.003)
Ln(K/EMP)	0.200***	0.214***	0.234***	0.259***	0.129***
	(0.004)	(0.012)	(0.017)	(0.012)	(0.008)
Ln(M/EMP)	0.243***	0.140***	0.179***	0.241***	0.265***
	(0.003)	(0.008)	(0.010)	(0.009)	(0.010)
Ln(S/EMP)	0.183***	0.284***	0.284***	0.259***	0.249***
	(0.003)	(0.012)	(0.014)	(0.012)	(0.009)
Observations	75613	7006	5029	7495	13808

Note: OLS estimations heteroskedasticity-consistent standard errors in parenthesis, ***, **, * significant at the 1%, 5% and 10% level respectively. Unreported time, region and four-digit industry dummies are always included. Offshoring is defined as services imported divided by total purchases of service intermediates.

On the other hand, the results for Ireland, as shown in Table 7.9, show a negative offshoring coefficient for domestic firms; an insignificant one for exporters and a significant one in both economic and statistical terms, at 26.8%, for foreign owned firms based in Ireland.[67] In a nutshell, our Irish results show us that international services outsourcing and TFP are positively and significantly correlated only for globally engaged firms (foreign MNEs). How does this result fit in with previous evidence on Irish firms?

Our finding ties in with existing work for an earlier time period (1990-1998) by Görg *et al.* (2006) who use data from the Forfás Irish Economy Expenditure Survey. Görg *et al.* similarly find that foreign MNEs benefit most from international services outsourcing (as well as materials outsourcing), most likely through use of their extensive foreign distribution networks or pecuniary scale economies when dealing with suppliers.

67. In unreported results we have checked the robustness of the Irish and Swedish results to the presence of endogeneity of factor inputs and the offshoring decision allowing for an autoregressive error term using the system GMM first suggested by Blundell and Bond 1998. The results show that the offshoring coefficient remains significant in the overall sample for Sweden, but this significance is driven by the estimates in the services sector. In Ireland the estimates becomes strongly significant. However, we believe that given the very short time period of the analysis these results might not be reliable.

Conclusions

Offshoring activity is widely believed to play an important role for firms due to the fragmentation of the production process across countries when there are differences in the relative endowments of skilled and unskilled labour and of technology. The question is, however, if it is possible to prove empirically the existence of offshoring effects.

In this paper, we have looked at the relationship between offshoring of services and total factor productivity across three different OECD countries: Ireland, Sweden and the United Kingdom.

The three countries are similar in that all three are open economies, but they are very different in terms of industrial structures and labour regulation.

The first question the paper answer is which firms offshore in the three countries? Is there a clear pattern of characteristics across these countries? Are there striking differences?

The answer is that in all three countries offshoring firms are more labour productive, are larger, pay higher wages and are more likely to be multinational and foreign-owned. This latter feature is particularly evident in the Irish data.

Concerning the association between multifactor productivity and services offshoring we find some suggestive evidence of a positive relationship although the statistical and/or economic significance of this relationship is not very strong across the three countries. One possible explanation is the small time horizon over which our analysis span. Moreover, firms that already are globally engaged do not benefit more from offshoring than pure local firms in the UK, while foreign owned firms are the only ones to have a positive services offshoring coefficient in Ireland. In Sweden the domestic non-exporters benefit more from offshoring than globally engaged firms. This bonus is somewhat stronger than in Hagsten *et al.* (2007) but is considered to arise from differences in the specifications of the equations and the exclusion here of the smallest firms. However, the direction of the results is in line with the pure Swedish study.

ANNEX 7.A. DATA DESCRIPTION

Ireland

The data for Ireland comprises plant level data for manufacturing industries in the Republic of Ireland. The data are taken from the *Irish Economy Expenditure Survey*, undertaken annually since 1983 by Forfás, the government agency with responsibility for enterprise development, science and technology. This is an annual survey of larger plants in Irish manufacturing with at least 20 employees, although a plant, once it is included, is generally still surveyed even if its employment level falls below the 20 employee cut-off point. The response rate to this survey is generally estimated to be between 60 and 80 per cent of the targeted plant population. The survey provides plant level information on, inter alia, output, value added, exports, employment, capital employed, nationality of ownership, as well as details on plants' expenditure on labour, materials, and services inputs.

One should note, however, that information on the capital stock is only available from 1990 onwards. In this study we only use the period 2000-2002 for comparability with Sweden and the UK. A plant is defined as foreign owned in the data if at least 50 percent of its shares are held by foreign owners.

Sweden

The data used in this analysis originate from the International Trade Statistics, The Structural Business Statistics (SBS) and The Swedish Register of Education as well as from the National Accounts. The Riksbank (Sveriges Riksbank, Swedish Central Bank) is the authority responsible for the trade statistics, and did formerly even produce them. However, as from 2003, Statistics Sweden produces these series. When the responsibility for producing the import of services series changed, also the methods of data collections were altered. This led to irreparable breaks in the disaggregated series. For a more detailed description of the data sources we refer to Hertzman et al (2006) and Fors and Jansson (2006) or to Hagsten *et al.* (2007).

The SBS consists of information on profit and loss accounts, investments and employment and rely heavily on administrative data from the Tax Authority. All firms operating in Sweden are included in the register and are reported by their unique identification number.

Until the last quarter of 2002 the settlement system was used which registered collated bank transactions between Sweden and other countries when the transactions amounted to more than SEK 150 000. This threshold value meant that most firms were included, but many lesser transactions were lost. As from 2003, when Statistics Sweden started to produce the series on imports and exports of services, the representative sample amounts to slightly more than 10% of the population of international traders, which in turn corresponds to 41 000 firms.

The Swedish Register of Education consists of data on graduation and educational background from the 1990 and 1970 censuses, each year updated with graduation and examination data from regular educational institutions such as primary and secondary schools, universities et cetera. The register comprises the population 16-74 years old registered as residents in Sweden. Each person is registered by their unique identification number.

United Kingdom

The Office of National Statistics (ONS) Annual Respondents Database (ARD) is described in detail in Criscuolo, Haskel and Martin (2003), so only a brief description is included here. Since 1997 The ARD consists of the replies to the mandatory *Annual Business Inquiry* (ABI).

The ABI is the major source of establishment level data in the UK and underlies the construction of aggregate output and investment in the national accounts. The ABI forms request information on inputs and outputs: gross output,[68] value added, employment, investment, intermediates and wage costs. Information is also collected on establishments' industry, region, and nationality of ownership. Each unit that replies is assigned a unique identification number, which allows units to be linked over time. The ONS also assigns a second identification number corresponding to the entity that owns the unit so units under common ownership share the same firm identifier.

The ABI asks firms on their purchases of goods, materials and services. Since 2000 the ABI forms include a question which asks firms to report the amounts of services traded with other countries (imports and exports of services). The question explicitly excludes the value of imported and exported goods. The values reported should include, according to the notes of the surveys, "*all transactions with individuals, enterprises and other organisations domiciled in a country rather than the UK*". This definition includes subsidiaries and parents that are operating abroad. This means that the value of imported/exported services reported includes both inter- and intra-firm trade. These services include industrial and non-industrial services. Industrial services include repair of construction equipment and computers; non industrial services include among others: consultancy services (market research, advertising, accountancy and R&D); telecommunications services; computer services (excluding hardware).

The ARD provides information on investment but does not contain information on firms' capital stock. We use capital stock built using the information on investment from the ABI using a perpetual inventory method, details of which can be found in Martin (2000).

The Inter Departmental Business Register (IDBR), the register from which the ABI sample is drawn, identifies foreign owned firms. The main source of information is Dun and Bradstreet's Who owns Whom database. To obtain information on which UK firms are outward direct investors we need to match into the dataset information from the AFDI register. Details of the AFDI register data and the procedure followed to merge the AFDI and the ARD can be found in Criscuolo and Martin (2004).

This study uses ARD data from 2000 to 2002, and covers both manufacturing and services sectors.

68. The ABI contains gross output at current values. The ONS provides PPI deflators with base year 2000 for the manufacturing sector (MM17). For a limited number of service sector industries the ONS provides a set of experimental deflators. For all the other industries in the service sector a common service sector deflator is used.

References

Blundell, Richard and Bond, Stephen (1998), "Initial conditions and moment restrictions in dynamic panel data models", *Journal of Econometrics* 87: pages 115-43

Criscuolo, Chiara and Leaver, Mark (2006) "Offshore outsourcing and productivity", OECD and Office of national Statistics

Criscuolo, C. and Martin, R. (2004). "Multinationals and US productivity leadership: evidence from Great Britain", *STI Working Paper 2004/5*, OECD, Paris.

Criscuolo, Chiara; Haskel, Jonathan and Martin, Ralf (2003) 'Building the evidence base for productivity policy using business data linking', *Economic Trends* 600 November2003,39-51, available at www.statistics.gov.uk/articles/economic trends/ETNov03Haskel.pdf.

Fors, Martin and Jansson, Ronnie (2006), "Trade in goods and services", Statistics Sweden, internal background memorandum

Görg, Holger, Hanley, Aoife and Strobl, Eric (2005) "Productivity effects of international outsourcing: Evidence from plant level data"

Hagsten, Eva; Karpaty, Patrik and Svanberg, Stefan (2007) "Effects on productivity from Swedish offshoring", Statistics Sweden, mimeo.

Hertzman, Cecilia, Johansson, Marcus and Berg, Stefan (2006), "Developing and implementing a new SBS at Statistics Sweden", paper prepared for the European Conference on Quality in Survey Statistics, Cardiff, May 2006

Karpaty, Patrik (2006) Does multinationality matter? Evidence from Swedish firm data, *Applied Economics Quarterly* 52/2 (2006).

Klette, Tor, Jakob (1999). "Market Power, Scale Economies and Productivity: Estimates from a Panel of Establishment Data", *Journal of Industrial Economics*, 47(4), 451-76, December.

Wooldridge, J.M. (2002) Econometric Analysis of cross section and Panel Data. (Cambridge: MIT Press).

Chapter II.4

SERVICES OUTSOURCING AND INNOVATION: AN EMPIRICAL INVESTIGATION

HOLGER GÖRG and AOIFE HANLEY*

We provide a comprehensive empirical analysis of the links between international services outsourcing, domestic outsourcing, profits, and innovation using plant-level data. We find a positive effect of international outsourcing of services on innovative activity at the plant level. Such a positive effect can also be observed for domestic outsourcing, but the magnitude is smaller. We also find that international services outsourcing has a positive effect on profitability, as predicted by theory, whereas this is not true for domestic sourcing. The results are robust to various specifications and an instrumental variables analysis. (*JEL* F19, O31)

I. INTRODUCTION

The practice of sourcing services inputs from abroad has increased substantially over the last decades. For example, Amiti and Wei (2006) document that in the U.S. international outsourcing of services by manufacturing firms has grown at an annual rate of around 6% over the period 1992 to 2000. If anything, this growth is probably to have accelerated in more recent years. This trend has given rise to public debates and policy concerns about the possible impact of this increasingly global division of labor.[1] Trade economists have also got involved in this debate, generally using a response based on intuition derived from simple trade theory: International outsourcing of production allows firms to access cheaper inputs abroad, foster gains from international specialization, and will hence lead to the restructuring of production in the industrialized countries toward more "skill-intensive" or "innovative" activities.[2]

In a standard Heckscher-Ohlin model, this is an argument made at the level of the economy: There will be restructuring out of low skill–intensive sectors and into high skill–intensive sectors in the skill-abundant-industrialized country. This will imply adjustment costs for workers laid off in the outsourced sectors who may or may not be able to move into employment in the other sector (e.g., Davidson and Matusz 2000). A related yet slightly different question is what will happen in the firm that does the outsourcing? Here, models with homogeneous firms (such as Glass and Saggi 2001)

*We are very grateful to Forfás for the provision of the data and to Sourafel Girma, Catia Montagna, Frances Ruane, Vincenzo Quadrini, seminar participants at Aarhus School of Business, Queen Mary University of London, University of Göttingen, University of Munich, ESRI Dublin, CEPII Paris, IfW Kiel, and anonymous referees for helpful comments. In addition, financial support from Nottingham University through grant number NLF A2 RBL6 and the Tuborg Foundation is gratefully acknowledged.

Görg: Professor of International Economics, Kiel Institute for the World Economy and University of Kiel, Kiel, Germany. Phone +49 431 8814 258, Fax +49 431 880 1618, E-mail holger.goerg@ifw-kiel.de. He is also affiliated with GEP Nottingham and CEPR.

Hanley: Associate Professor, Kiel Institute for the World Economy and University of Kiel, Kiel, Germany. Phone +49 431 8814 339, Fax +49 431 85853, E-mail aoife.hanley@ifw-kiel.de

1. Preceding the rise of services outsourcing, the outsourcing of materials attracted considerable attention. A sizeable amount of research has been devoted to attempting to understand the causes and consequences of this type of disintegration of production. For example, Swenson (2000, 2004) and Görg (2000) examine empirically the determinants of international outsourcing of materials. Feenstra and Hanson (1999), Head and Ries (2002) and Geishecker and Görg (2008) consider the implications for domestic labor markets.

2. See, for example, Blinder (2006) for a good discussion. Blinder not only points out the "textbook" gains but also argues that the current wave of offshoring brings with it additional challenges, as basically speaking all manufacturing and services activities that do not require face-to-face contact are potentially outsourceable from the industrialized countries. Eaton and Kortum (2006) provide a recent theoretical model dealing with the relationship between trade and innovation.

ABBREVIATIONS

3SLS: Three-Stage Least Squares
GDP: Gross Domestic Product
IV: Instrumental Variables
OLS: Ordinary Least Squares
R&D: Research and Development
RHS: Right Hand Side

Economic Inquiry
(ISSN 0095-2583)
Vol. 49, No. 2, April 2011, 321–333

doi:10.1111/j.1465-7295.2010.00299.x
Online Early publication June 20, 2010

or heterogeneous firms (e.g., Antrás and Helpman 2004) illustrate a similar process. Firms outsource part of the production and concentrate home production on what may be termed their "core activity."

Recently, a small but growing literature using firm- or plant-level data has established empirically that international outsourcing, in particular of services inputs, is associated with higher productivity in the outsourcing plant, in line with such theory (e.g., Hijzen, Inui, and Todo 2009; Görg, Hanley, and Strobl 2008; Tomiura 2007). However, these papers are largely silent on the *mechanisms* as to how international outsourcing may affect productivity at the level of the firm or plant. Our goal is to contribute to this literature by examining directly how international outsourcing of services activities impacts on innovative activity in the outsourcing establishment. We ask the specific question of whether a firm that sources some of its service activities abroad consequently increases its rate of innovation—which is what the theoretical argument would suggest. As far as we are aware, this paper is the first to address explicitly the link between international outsourcing and innovative activity empirically.[3]

We expand on this seemingly straightforward relationship by addressing a number of related questions. A theoretical model by Glass and Saggi (2001) predicts that firms outsource activities due to lower factor costs abroad. Hence, outsourcing leads to higher profits, which are then reinvested in higher R&D expenditure. First, we check explicitly whether we can observe this "outsourcing-profit" channel, and its relationship with innovation, in our data. Second, we also consider domestic outsourcing and contrast the effects domestic and international outsourcing have on profits and innovation. In that respect, we provide some evidence that relates to a recent paper by Leahy and Montagna (2008) which shows that domestic outsourcing may lead to reductions in operating profits by the outsourcing firms, due to a strategic motive for outsourcing. We discuss these theoretical ideas in Section II.

To investigate the link between outsourcing of services, profits, and innovation at the level of the establishment empirically, we use plant-level data for the Republic of Ireland. This is an economy where international services outsourcing appears to be much more important than in the United States. In our data, the average ratio of internationally outsourced services to sales is around 4% over the period 2002 to 2004. Although not perfectly comparable, these mean values appear higher than those found by Amiti and Wei (2006) for the United States. They report that between 1992 and 2000, services outsourcing (calculated similarly as imported services over total production in a sector) increased from 0.2% to 0.3%.[4] Our data run up to the year 2004 and hence capture much of the very recent activity in international outsourcing.

The data set provides a unique source to study these links. Unlike many data sets that have been used in the past, it does not only provide us with plant-level information on international outsourcing of services and R&D expenditure (as a proxy for innovation) but also contains information on domestic outsourcing. Hence, we are able to compare and contrast the effects of *international* and *domestic* outsourcing on innovation. This is important as, a priori, it is not clear that the two modes of outsourcing should have the same effects on innovation or profits. Furthermore, the data also allow us to pay particular attention to the possible endogeneity of the outsourcing decision using instrumental variables techniques. We have available a number of establishment level variables that we consider to be good instrumental variables candidates for outsourcing activities of plants. These are discussed in detail in the empirical analysis below.

Previewing our results briefly, we find that there are indeed positive effects of international services outsourcing on innovation, in line with expectations. These effects appear stronger than those of domestic outsourcing of services. Furthermore, we establish that international outsourcing of services has a positive effect on

3. Tomiura (2009) investigates whether there is a difference in the propensity to outsource depending on a firm's technology intensity, measured in terms of research and development (R&D) intensities, but does not look at how outsourcing affects firms' innovation activity. A related literature has looked at correlation between firms' export activity, foreign ownership and innovation; see, for example, Criscuolo, Haskel, and Slaughter (2005) for a recent paper for the United Kingdom.

4. When we apply the median values, we get a picture more consistent with the U.S. data although still higher. The median ratio of internationally outsourced service inputs to sales is around 0.8% in our data. From our data, we can also calculate the measure of international services outsourcing for the full sample in 2000. This shows that the mean of this ratio stands at roughly 3% (with the median at 0.6%). Hence, it is unlikely that the higher values of international services outsourcing are merely due to our sample covering more recent years.

profitability in the plant, whereas this is not true for domestic outsourcing.[5] These results are robust to various specifications which among other things also control for outsourcing of materials and also hold in an instrumental variables approach.

The remainder of the paper is structured as follows. Section II discusses the expected link between outsourcing, innovation, and profits. Section III describes the methodology used in the empirical analysis. This is followed by an overview of the data and some summary statistics in Section IV. Section V presents the results of our analysis and Section VI concludes.

II. OUTSOURCING, INNOVATION, AND PROFITS

We use the theoretical analysis by Glass and Saggi (2001) as a starting point for our empirical analysis. They develop a model, based on Ricardian technology differences between an industrialized northern and a less advanced southern country, to explain the effect of outsourcing on wages and innovation in the north. In their model, potential wage savings will prompt the north to outsource those processes from the south which are relatively low in technological complexity and retain those other processes which are more truly original, innovative or relatively near the technological frontier. The predicted result is that the wage rate (relative to the south) in the north falls due to outsourcing.

Although this result is not new, the innovation in Glass and Saggi (2001) is to set this into a dynamic setting, which shows additional positive effects of outsourcing. As cost savings are realized (due to the reduction in the wage in the north) firms' profits rise. These additional profits get reinvested (fully or partially) in northern innovation through increasing R&D expenditure. Hence, the profits accruing to the firm from wage savings can be plowed back into R&D to shift the technological frontier in the north further outward. As such the predicted effect of international outsourcing on innovation is unequivocal in the model: Increased proportions of international outsourcing lead to higher innovation rates in the outsourcing establishment.[6] Hence, we would expect to be able to identify two effects of international services outsourcing in our data. First, it should lead to increased profits and second, it should raise innovative activity in the outsourcer. Note that the latter effect, strictly speaking, works through the profit channel; outsourcing raises profits and, as a result, increases innovation.

However, outsourcing may, over and above the "profit channel," have a more direct effect on innovation. Outsourcing allows a plant to restructure activities toward more skill-intensive (innovative) activity. This may happen immediately, which only as a result of the innovation leads to increases in profitability. Although this would be observationally similar to the "outsourcing-affecting-profits" hypothesis, it would be different in the chain of events, as outsourcing first affects innovation which in turn impacts on profits. Hence, in the empirical analysis, this would imply that we may find an effect of outsourcing on innovation even when controlling for contemporaneous profits. Unfortunately, however, we cannot investigate this hypothesis fully empirically, due to the short time dimension of our data. There are, of course, also other data-related issues for why we may find both outsourcing and profits affecting innovation in an empirical model. These are discussed below in the empirical part.

The Glass and Saggi (2001) model only covers international outsourcing and does not consider domestic outsourcing. In the empirical analysis, we distinguish these two types. International outsourcing is probably to be strongly driven by international factor cost differences, as in the theoretical model. Domestic outsourcing may of course also be driven by some factor cost differences between regions, but these are unlikely to be as important as the potentially much larger international factor cost differences are for international outsourcing. Domestic outsourcing is more probably to reflect mainly efforts by the firm to respond to competitive pressure through restructuring activities and gains from specializing in core activities.

In this regard, Leahy and Montagna (2008) develop a model of final good producing firms' choice to outsource domestically. Their setup is a two-firm oligopoly where firms compete in Cournot competition. Outsourcing implies that the supplier undertakes some relationship-specific investments (which determines the

5. The latter finding may reflect firms' choosing to outsource domestically due to strategic reasons as in Leahy and Montagna (2008).

6. We should qualify this by saying that positive benefits from international outsourcing are expected to tail off after a certain point. As ever more activities closer to the technical frontier are outsourced abroad, so too does the ease at which foreign manufacturers pose a competitive threat to the north.

quality of the intermediate) after it has been chosen as supplier. Because of the impossibility of agreeing on the level of this investment ex ante, there is the possibility that the supplier provides lower quality inputs, which may lead to the production costs of the final good producer increasing relative to a scenario where it chooses no outsourcing. However, outsourcing may still be preferred by the firm because of its strategic motive. Given that the competitor knows that the firm will face higher production costs if it outsources, the rival will also invest less in quality—it is less aggressive. Hence, through outsourcing, the firm induces in the competitor an incentive to invest less in quality, which in turn affects positively its total output. Hence, Leahy and Montagna (2008) show that firms' outsourcing decision may lead to higher costs, and lower profits as a result. Although their model focuses on domestic outsourcing, it is of course also plausible that this strategic motive matters for international outsourcing. However, the cost reduction motive, which unambiguously always leads to higher profits associated with outsourcing, is probably to be stronger for international outsourcing than domestic outsourcing.

The analysis in our paper provides empirical evidence related to these theoretical hypotheses. We study in detail the relationship between innovation (measured as R&D activity) and outsourcing. Although we start with international outsourcing, we also consider domestic outsourcing and compare the effects both types have on innovation. Furthermore, we explicitly consider the relationship between profits and innovation. In particular, we check whether the effect of outsourcing on innovation can be fully explained by the profit variable or whether, for some reason, outsourcing has an effect on innovation even when controlling for contemporaneous profits. Moreover, we investigate what the relationship is between outsourcing and profits—does outsourcing increase profits (as in Glass and Saggi 2001) or is there evidence in line with the strategic motive of outsourcing highlighted by Leahy and Montagna (2008) which may lead to outsourcing implying a reduction in operating profits?

III. METHODOLOGY

We start the empirical investigation by examining the hypothesis that international outsourcing of services can impact on plants' innovation activity. To do so, we formulate the following empirical model:

$$(1)\quad (\mathrm{R\,\&\,D}/Y)_{\mathrm{it}} = \beta_1 int\_\mathrm{outs}_{it-1} + \beta_2 \mathrm{dom\_outs}_{it-1} + \beta_3 \mathrm{profitratio}_{it-1} + \beta_4 X_{it-1} + d_t + d_j + \mu_i + \varepsilon_{it}$$

where the measure of innovation activity employed is the R&D intensity, defined as R&D expenditure over total sales, for plant i at time t. On the right-hand side, int_outs is a measure of international outsourcing of services (defined as imported services inputs relative to sales) at the level of the plant.[7]

The vector X considers a number of other plant characteristics that have been identified in the literature as affecting R&D activity. We include logged employment as a proxy of firm size, as well as dummy variables indicating whether a firm invests in in-house training or is an exporter. The latter controls for the possibility that export-active firms may also be more R&D and innovation intensive (e.g., Criscuolo, Haskel, and Slaughter 2005; Salomon and Shaver 2005). Training activity is included as a rough measure of investment in skills (e.g., Van Dijk et al. 1997). From theory, the expected relationship between this variable and R&D intensity is ambiguous, as investment in skills and R&D can be either complements or substitutes (e.g., Redding 1996). Finally, Acs and Audretsch (1991) and Kohn and Scott (1982), among others, show that plant size is an important determinant of R&D and innovation activity. Hence, we control for this variable in the estimation.[8]

In order to properly identify the effect of international services outsourcing on R&D, we also consider two further variables. As the theoretical model by Glass and Saggi (2001) shows, international outsourcing has an effect on innovation because it increases profits, which can then be reinvested in R&D. Hence, we control for profitability to examine whether it captures

7. This measure is, thus, somewhat in line with the definitions used by Feenstra and Hanson (1999) and Amiti and Wei (2006) for aggregate data.

8. Note that it would also be important to control for nationality of ownership, given that foreign-owned firms in Ireland are generally found to be less R&D active than domestic firms (e.g., Cassidy, Görg, and Strobl 2005). The nationality of ownership information in our data is time invariant, however, which implies that this is captured by the plant-specific effect included in the model.

all of the (potential) effect of outsourcing on innovation. It is probable that international services outsourcing has an effect on R&D even when we control for profitability for a number of reasons. From an empirical point of view, outsourcing may not impact immediately on profits but this may take some time. Including first lags of both services, outsourcing and profitability in the model would therefore not capture these more long-term effects. Second, it is difficult to measure economic profitability accurately and our variable may not be a perfect proxy for profits. Third, outsourcing may have a more direct effect on innovation. It may allow the plant to immediately restructure activities toward innovation, which only as a result of the innovation leads to increases in profitability.

As an additional variable, we also include domestic outsourcing of services in our model. The main aim here is to see whether domestic and international outsourcing has similar effects on innovation. A priori it is not clear that they should, as international outsourcing is more probably to be strongly driven by factor cost differences, whereas domestic outsourcing may reflect strategic and other motives. In additional robustness checks, we also control for the levels of international and domestic outsourcing of materials. Although this is not the main focus of our paper, it may be important to control for these as services and material outsourcing may be correlated and, hence, not controlling for this would lead to biased estimates of the effects of services outsourcing.

Finally, the equation also includes a full set of three-digit industry dummies and a full set of time dummies to control for any sector-specific time-varying effects that are unobserved in this econometric specification. The final error term is composed of a plant-specific time invariant effect μ_i and a remaining white noise error term ε. Note that in the econometric specification, all plant-level control variables are included as 1-yr lags not only to minimize potential endogeneity problems but also to allow for time lags in the effect.[9] For example, services outsourcing in time t may only affect R&D activity in later periods. Although it would be ideal to allow for longer lags, this is not possible given the short-time dimension in our panel.

Glass and Saggi (2001) show that international outsourcing allows firms to increase profits (due to international factor cost differences) which in turn allows them to spend more on R&D. In order to investigate explicitly the relationship between services outsourcing and profits, we also estimate a second equation

$$\text{profitratio}_{it} = \gamma_1 int\_\text{outs}_{it-1} + \gamma_2\,\text{dom\_outs}_{it-1} + \gamma_3 Z_{it-1} + d_t + d_j + \nu_i + \phi_{it} \qquad (2)$$

where Z is a vector of plant and industry characteristics including log employment as a measure of size, a plant's market share (in terms of sales) in the three-digit industry and two (potentially time varying) dummies for plants that are exporters or provide in-house training. The latter two variables capture the fact that exporters and skill-intensive firms can be expected to be more productive and profitable. At the industry level, we include the growth rate of three-digit industry sales. This variable, together with the market share variable, proxy levels of competition in the industry and the plant's relative standing in it. This is an important determinant of profitability (Shepherd 1972). Also, in addition to international outsourcing, we again include domestic services outsourcing in the equation. If the factor cost saving motivation for international outsourcing is dominant, we would expect the coefficient γ_1 to be positive in the estimation. The coefficient on γ_2 may be positive or negative, depending on how important the strategic motive, which may lead to reductions in operating profits, is for domestic outsourcing.

In the first instance, we estimate the two equations separately using a fixed effects panel estimator treating lagged outsourcing (international and domestic) as exogenous. We relax this assumption subsequently using instrumental variables for the outsourcing variables in both equations (which are within transformed to purge the plant-specific fixed effect). The details of this are discussed in Section IV. Furthermore, it may be the case that profits are endogenous in Equation (1), and moreover that the two error terms ε and ϕ are correlated. In order to allow for these possibilities, we also estimate within transformed versions of the two equations jointly using a three-stage least square estimator also treating lagged international and domestic outsourcing as endogenous.

IV. DATA DESCRIPTION AND PRELIMINARY ANALYSIS

For the econometric part of our paper, we use recent microdata from the Republic of

9. We also deal with endogeneity more appropriately using an instrumental variables approach, see details below.

Ireland. This is plant-level information collected by Forfás, the Irish policy and advisory board with responsibility for enterprise, trade, science, and technology in Ireland. Specifically, our data source is the *Annual Business Survey of Economic Impact (ABSEI)*, covering the period from 2000 to 2004. This is an annual survey of plants in Irish manufacturing with at least ten employees, although a plant, once it is included, is generally still surveyed even if its employment level falls below the ten-employee cut-off point. The survey was started in 2000 and the response rate is estimated by Forfás to be around 55% to 60% of the targeted population per year. This data set provides information on services purchases, distinguishing imported and domestically procured services, as well as total R&D expenditure at the plant level. Further data available from this source that is relevant to the current paper are total sales (as a measure of output), employment, expenditure on wages and total purchases, exports (distinguishing exports to the United Kingdom, European Union, and the rest of the world), expenditure on in-house training, nationality of ownership, and three-digit sector of production.[10,11]

In 2002, the survey also started collecting information on whether a plant uses the internet for their purchases of intermediates, and if so, how much as a percentage of sales. As we use this variable as an instrument for outsourcing in our econometric estimation, this necessarily restricts the time period of our econometric analysis to 2002 to 2004. Fortunately, this is the most up-to-date data available from the survey which covers recent activity in international outsourcing of services.

In order to have a first look at the data and the possible relationship between R&D and outsourcing of services, Table 1 shows the means, medians, and standard deviations for these variables from our plant-level data, based on the sample that is also used in the regression analysis below.

10. Forfás defines foreign plants as plants that are majority-owned by foreign shareholders, that is, where there is at least 50% foreign ownership. Although, arguably, plants with lower foreign ownership should still possibly be considered to be foreign owned, this is not necessarily a problem for the case of Ireland because most inward foreign direct investment has been greenfield rather than acquisitions of local firms. Note that our data only provide a dummy based on this definition rather than a percentage of ownership, and that this dummy relates to nationality of the plant in 2004, that is, is fixed over time.

11. All nominal variables are deflated using the consumer price index.

TABLE 1

Summary Statistics: R&D and Outsourcing

		2002	2003	2004
International services outsourcing	*M*	0.042	0.036	0.047
	Median	0.008	0.008	0.008
	SD	0.325	0.108	0.325
	Obs.	1596	1596	1701
R&D intensity	*M*	0.080	0.105	0.097
	Median	0.003	0.004	0.003
	SD	0.771	0.961	0.826
	Obs.	1596	1596	1701
Domestic services outsourcing	*M*	0.201	0.206	0.226
	Median	0.119	0.120	0.121
	SD	0.794	0.802	1.067
	Obs.	1596	1596	1701

Notes: Domestic services outsourcing, domestic services inputs/sales; international services outsourcing, imported services inputs/sales; R&D intensity, expenditure on R&D/sales.

The average ratio of internationally outsourced services to sales is around 4% over the period 2002 to 2004. There has been some increase in the arithmetic mean of this variable between 2003 and 2004, but it is difficult to judge whether this is persistent as no post-2004 years are available. We are also able to observe the extent of domestic outsourcing of services in our data. This is defined as the value of domestically procured services inputs relative to sales. The mean of this variable, shown in Table 1, represents around 20% to 22% in the period analyzed. In the econometric analysis below, one important question is whether the effect of international and domestic outsourcing of services on innovation is similar or not.

As concerns the average R&D intensity, the table indicates that the mean has fluctuated around 8% to 10% of sales, although the medians are far lower at around 0.3%. It is important to consider in this context that Ireland generally registers a relatively low level of R&D intensity, a fact noted by the OECD (1998). Total business expenditure on R&D in total amounted to only 0.8% of gross domestic product (GDP) which leaves Ireland closer to Mediterranean countries which in general are characterized by low-technology output than the northern European countries which tend to have higher technological intensities and higher R&D expenditures.

Because we are investigating the relationship between international services outsourcing and the intensity of R&D, it is illuminating to

TABLE 2
Summary Statistics by Outsourcing Activity

		R&D Intensity	Profit Ratio	Employment	Training Intensity	Export Intensity
No international services outsourcing	Median	0.001	0.058	31	0.002	0.200
	SD	0.948	6.742	228	0.034	0.396
	Obs.	1517				
International services outsourcing	Median	0.006	0.055	44	0.002	0.72
	SD	0.845	5.481	312	0.056	0.390
	Obs.	1780				

Notes: Employment, number of employees; export intensity, exports/sales; profit ratio, (sales—wages—total purchases)/sales; R&D intensity, expenditure on R&D/sales; training intensity, expenditure on in-house training/sales.

format the same information across the group of firms which do not procure any internationally outsourced services at all and those which do. We see from Table 2 that firms reporting at least some internationally outsourced services have, on average, higher R&D intensities. They are also larger in terms of employee numbers and export more, on average, than their counterparts which do not report any internationally outsourced services. There is no obvious difference, however, in terms of profitability and investment in skills in the raw data. Of course, this simple look at the data does not allow controlling for the potential impact of any other variable, and this is something we will turn to in the next section.

Before moving on to the results from our regressions, however, it is worthwhile looking briefly at which sectors are most actively engaged in international outsourcing of services. To do so, Table 3 reports the percentage of plants in each broad sector that outsource at least some services internationally. The first impression we get is that there is considerable sectoral variation in international outsourcing. Within the services sector, transport and storage, real estate & business services, and community & personal services register the highest levels of internationally outsourced services. However, according to Forfás, the coverage of our data is not as exhaustive for services sectors as it is for manufacturing and, hence, is somewhat biased toward the latter. Within the set of manufacturing plants, at 67%, the textiles sector has the highest proportion of firms purchasing service inputs on foreign markets. However, chemicals, machinery, and transport equipment are also in close range with percentages well close to 60.

TABLE 3
Percentage of Plants in Sector Outsourcing At Least Some Services

STAN Code	Description	Number of Plants	Percentage of Total Sector
1	Food, beverages, and tobacco	216	49.8
2	Textiles, leather, and footwear	80	66.7
3	Wood and wood products	53	52.5
4	Pulp, paper, printing, and publishing	52	38.5
5	Chemicals, rubber, and plastics	221	62.1
6	Nonmetallic mineral products	45	50.6
7	Basic and fabricated metal products	106	39.1
8	Machinery and equipment	393	58.5
9	Transport equipment	40	58.8
10	Other manufacturing and recycling	91	50.5
11	Wholesale and retail trade	19	45.2
12	Hotels and restaurants	2	40.0
13	Transport and storage	11	57.9
14	Post and telecommunications	7	53.9
15	Financial intermediation	12	42.9
16	Real estate, renting, and business services	376	56.9
17	Community, social, and personal services	50	63.3
	Total	1774	54.2

TABLE 4
R&D Equation

	1 OLS	2 FE	3 FE	4 FE	5 IV
International services outsourcing	0.302	0.164	0.873	0.389	2.481
	(0.158)*	(0.075)**	(0.111)***	(0.153)**	(0.136)***
Domestic services outsourcing				0.178	0.176
				(0.040)***	(0.020)***
International material outsourcing				−0.003	0.110
				(0.360)	(0.054)**
Domestic material outsourcing				0.913	0.165
				(0.330)***	(0.103)
Profit ratio			0.100	0.122	0.300
			(0.012)***	(0.013)***	(0.011)***
Training	0.031	0.335	0.304	0.274	0.036
	(0.062)	(0.116)***	(0.113)***	(0.112)**	(0.099)
Export dummy	−0.209	0.065	0.137	0.114	−0.268
	(0.115)*	(0.170)	(0.165)	(0.164)	(0.128)**
Employment	−0.048	−0.047	−0.002	0.034	−0.094
	(0.010)***	(0.119)	(0.116)	(0.115)	(0.106)
Observations	3297	3297	3297	3297	3297
Plants	1929	1929	1929	1929	1929
F-test international service outsourcing					1469.31
F-test domestic service outsourcing					423.87
F-test international material outsourcing					455.26
F-test domestic material outsourcing					451.64
Sargan test (*p*-value)					0.23
R-squared	0.06	0.01	0.06	0.08	0.23

Notes: Dependent variable: R&D intensity as defined in notes to Table 1. Column 5 is an IV regression on within transformed variables. Instrumented variables are international and domestic outsourcing of services and materials. Instruments used are twice lagged growth of outsourcing variables, dummy for exporting to the United Kingdom, export intensity to United Kingdom, dummy for purchases of inputs via the web. Regression includes constant and full sets of three-digit industry and time dummies. All right hand side (RHS) variables are lagged one period standard errors in parentheses.

*Significant at 10%; **significant at 5%; ***significant at 1%. FE: fixed effects; OLS: ordinary least squares; IV: instrumental variables.

V. ECONOMETRIC RESULTS

In order to investigate the relationship between international outsourcing of services and R&D activity more formally, we now turn to the estimation of Equations (1) and (2). The results for various specifications of Equation (1) are reported in Table 4. Column 1 reports the simplest specification of the model, only including international outsourcing, which is estimated using ordinary least squares (OLS) to establish a benchmark. In this estimation, we find that there is a positive and statistically significant association between international services outsourcing and R&D activity, in line with expectations. This estimation does not of course control for unobserved plant-level heterogeneity. In order to do so we estimate Equation (1) using a (within transformation) fixed effects estimator in column 2. Hence, the coefficients are identified using the within-plant variation (deviations from the mean) in variables.[12] This does not

12. Specifically, this implies for the coefficient on international services outsourcing that it reflects the effect of within plant *changes* in outsourcing on changes in R&D activity, as suggested by the theoretical model.

change the positive coefficient on the outsourcing variable, although the coefficient size is now somewhat reduced from 0.30 to 0.17.

The theoretical idea behind the empirical analysis is that outsourcing affects profits, which in turn enhances a firm's ability to invest in R&D. In order to investigate whether our data is fully in line with this explanation we include an empirical measure of plant profitability in the model. As column 3 shows, the coefficient on this variable is positive and statistically significant as expected. However, it does not reduce the impact of the outsourcing variable, which is still positive and statistically significant.[13] As pointed out in Section III, there are various explanations for why our empirical estimation may not fully capture the true impact of profits in this model: first, due to measurement problems, second, because including outsourcing and profits measured in the same period does not allow for a more long- or medium-term impact of outsourcing on profits. Furthermore, outsourcing may indeed have a direct effect on innovation that is not mediated through profits, if it leads directly to restructuring in the firm toward more R&D. This would only as a result affect profitability and, hence, would not be captured by the profits variable (which is measured in the same period as outsourcing) in the empirical estimation.

The model thus far may be misspecified as it does not consider domestic outsourcing. From an empirical point of view, if domestic and international outsourcing decisions are correlated, then not controlling for the former in the estimation would lead to a biased coefficient on the latter. Furthermore, firms may also outsource materials and, if these decisions are correlated with services sourcing and are not controlled for this may lead to biased coefficients. Column 4, therefore, presents estimation results that include a measure of domestic outsourcing of services, as well as outsourcing of materials. Domestic services sourcing returns a statistically significantly positive coefficient, as does domestic sourcing of materials. It can also be noted that the coefficient size on the international outsourcing variable is now reduced, suggesting that in the model in column 3 the effect of domestic and international outsourcing of services and materials is confounded. Although it appears from a casual look that the coefficient on international outsourcing of services is higher than that of domestic services sourcing (which may be expected, as it provides more opportunities for exploiting international factor cost differences), a simple F-test does not allow us to reject the hypothesis that the two are statistically equal (probability value 0.19). However, as we show below, once endogeneity of the outsourcing variables is taken adequately into account, the effects of the two types of outsourcing become statistically different.

The assumption in the analysis thus far that international and domestic services outsourcing are treated as exogenous is arguably problematic.[14] Although the lagged variable is intended to address this problem, this may not be sufficient. In order to deal with this more appropriately, we therefore now proceed to treat international and domestic outsourcing of services and materials explicitly as endogenous in the estimation. The challenge is to find instrumental variables candidates that are highly correlated with outsourcing but not with the error term in Equation (1).

We use the following instruments for outsourcing: First, twice lagged *growth rates* of international and domestic outsourcing of services and materials intensities, as these are expected to be highly correlated with lagged *levels* of outsourcing but a priori are not obviously correlated with the error term. Second, we use a dummy indicating whether a plant exports to the United Kingdom, as well as the share of exports relative to sales by a plant that are directed to the United Kingdom rather than other export markets. The choice of these variables is inspired by Ruane and Sutherland (2005) who find that there is little evidence that Irish firms that export to the United Kingdom have performance premia compared with nonexporters. However, they find that Irish exporters compared with the rest of the world are clearly more productive, technology intensive, and pay higher wages. Hence, although exporting to the United Kingdom clearly indicates cross-border engagement, which may also help to find partners for international outsourcing, this variable

13. Inspection shows that the coefficient is now larger than in column 2. This may be due to a strong negative correlation in the raw data between international outsourcing and profitability. This negative unconditional correlation does not hold when controlling for other variables, as shown below in the estimation of Equation (2).

14. For example, Bartel, Lach, and Sicherman (2005) argue that technological change is partly responsible for the increase in outsourcing and if general technological change is correlated with plant-level R&D expenditure then this may cause an endogeneity problem.

should be less correlated with R&D activity. Furthermore, we use the percentage of inputs purchased over the web as an additional instrument. Again, this should be correlated with services outsourcing but is likely to be orthogonal to R&D. As a matter of course, we test for the validity and relevance of the instruments in the estimations.

Column 5 presents the estimation result. Note that the instruments used for services and materials outsourcing are valid as indicated by the Sargan test for overidentifying restrictions, which cannot reject the hypothesis of instrument validity. Furthermore, we ascertain that the instruments used are relevant in that they exhibit sufficiently strong correlation with the instrumented variable. We report the F-statistic for the excluded instruments (and associated p-value) from the first-stage regression.[15] When the F-statistic is small (or the corresponding p-value is large), the instrumental variable estimates and confidence intervals would be unreliable. We find that our instruments are appropriate on this criterion.

The regression results confirm the importance of international outsourcing of services for R&D activity. Taking the point estimate at face value suggests that an increase in the ratio of internationally outsourced services to sales by 1% point increases the R&D ratio by 2.5% points. This is an economically important effect. The instrumental variables (IV) regression also shows that the coefficient on international services outsourcing is higher than that on domestic outsourcing, the magnitude of which remains unchanged. This difference is confirmed in an F-test, which rejects the equality of the two coefficients (p-value 0.00).

To sum up, our analysis thus far suggests an important role for international services outsourcing for plants' innovative activity. This effect is not fully captured by profits in the same period. Furthermore, international outsourcing is more important than the impact of domestic outsourcing of services.[16]

Theory posits that international services outsourcing allows firms to increase profits, as they have access to cheaper intermediate inputs abroad. As shown above, this mechanism is not fully captured in our data, as inclusion of the profit variable does not negate the impact of the outsourcing measure in the R&D equation. Still, it is of interest as to whether there is any positive relationship between international services outsourcing and profits, and we now turn to investigate this link with our data by estimating different specifications of Equation (2). The results are reported in Table 5. Column 1 presents a specification which is based on a (within transformation) fixed effects estimator and only includes the two services outsourcing variables. Column 2 shows coefficients obtained from a fixed effects estimation including materials outsourcing and sectoral variables. Column 3 shows an equivalent IV regression on within transformed variables, and column 3 also presents a similar IV regression but including more plant-level controls.[17]

All estimations show that international services outsourcing has a positive effect on profitability, as expected. The point estimate in column 3 indicates that a 1% point increase in the international services outsourcing intensity increases the profit ratio by roughly 0.4% points. However, we also find a consistently negative effect on profits from domestic outsourcing of services. This even holds in the IV estimations which treat the variable as endogenous using suitable and valid instruments.

The analysis thus far treats Equations (1) and (2) as unrelated and, hence, they are estimated separately. However, it is arguable that the profit variable is endogenous in Equation (1) and, furthermore, that the error terms in both equations may be correlated as the dependent variable in Equation (2), as well as other covariates are also included as exogenous variables in Equation (1). If this is the case, then estimating the two equations jointly improves efficiency of the estimates. Hence, we now proceed to treat Equations (1) and (2) as a system of equations and estimate them jointly using three-stage least squares (3SLS) techniques. We also treat services outsourcing as endogenous using the same set of instruments as employed previously. The results are reported in Table 6.

In the R&D equation in column 1, we see that the signs, significance, and magnitude

15. The F-statistic tests the hypothesis that the instruments should be excluded from the first-stage regressions.

16. In terms of the control variables we find in column 5 that employment is negatively correlated, a result in line with, for example, Acs and Audretsch (1991) who argue that small firms may not be able to bear the costs of the high expenditure on setting up and running R&D facilities. The coefficients on the export and training dummy variables are not statistically significant.

17. International and domestic outsourcing intensities are treated as endogeneous, using the same instruments as in the estimation of Equation (1). The tests again support the validity and relevance of the chosen instruments.

TABLE 5
Profit Equation

	1 FE	2 FE	3 IV	4 IV
International services outsourcing	0.491	0.516	0.413	0.413
	(0.417)	(0.419)*	(0.215)*	(0.215)*
Domestic services outsourcing	−0.299	−0.305	−0.441	−0.440
	(0.100)***	(0.101)***	(0.035)***	(0.036)***
International material sourcing		1.386	0.035	0.034
		(0.691)**	(0.096)	(0.096)
Domestic material sourcing		0.138	0.396	0.399
		(0.210)	(0.182)**	(0.183)**
Industry sales		0.288	0.087	0.090
		(0.448)	(0.253)	(0.254)
Market share		−0.000	−0.000	−0.000
		(0.000)	(0.000)	(0.000)
Training dummy				−0.074
				(0.177)
Export dummy				0.053
				(0.229)
Employment				−0.011
				(0.190)
Observations	3297	3297	3297	3297
Plants	1929	1929	1929	1929
F-test international service outsourcing			2128.52	2114.67
F-test domestic service outsourcing			488.67	474.90
F-test international material outsourcing			455.68	455.27
F-test domestic material outsourcing			458.02	454.56
Sargan test (p-value)			0.15	0.14
R-squared	0.04	0.02	0.03	0.03

Notes: Dependent variable: profit ratio as defined in notes to Table 2. Columns 3 and 4 are IV regressions on within transformed variables. Instrumented variables are international and domestic outsourcing of services and materials. Instruments used are twice lagged growth of outsourcing variables, dummy for exporting to the United Kingdom, export intensity to United Kingdom, dummy for purchases of inputs via the web. Regression includes constant and full sets of three-digit industry and time dummies. All RHS variables are lagged one period. Standard errors in parentheses.

*Significant at 10%; **significant at 5%; ***significant at 1%.

of the coefficients are very similar to those reported in the IV regression in Table 4. In the profit equation, we still find a negative and statistically significant coefficient on domestic outsourcing, although the coefficients size is somewhat smaller than in the IV regressions in Table 5. The coefficient on international services outsourcing is still positive and statistically significant but has doubled in size: The point estimate now suggests that a 1% point increase in international services outsourcing increases profitability by almost 0.9% points.

VI. CONCLUSIONS

Recent breakthroughs in information technology and the wholesale adoption of purchasing media such as the internet have provided scope for an explosion in the proportions of services that are outsourced internationally.

TABLE 6
Simultaneous Estimation

	1 R&D Intensity	2 Profit Ratio
International services outsourcing	2.506	0.897
	(0.116)***	(0.193)***
Domestic services outsourcing	0.145	−0.311
	(0.014)***	(0.025)***
International material outsourcing	0.135	0.035
	(0.038)***	(0.068)
Domestic material outsourcing	0.103	0.074
	(0.072)	(0.128)
Profit ratio	0.259	
	(0.008)***	
Training	0.053	−0.072
	(0.098)	(0.175)
Export dummy	−0.286	0.159
	(0.126)**	(0.225)
Employment	−0.065	−0.175
	(0.104)	(0.186)
Industry sales		0.170
		(0.199)
Market share		0.000
		(0.000)
Observations	3297	3297
R-squared	0.24	0.05

Notes: 3SLS regression on within transformed variables. International and domestic outsourcing variables assumed endogenous, instruments as before. Standard errors in parentheses.

*Significant at 10%; **significant at 5%; ***significant at 1%.

Theory has something to say about the predicted effect of internationally outsourced inputs on the ability of a firm to sustain growth through its growth in innovative activity. Starting from these theoretical predictions we provide, to the best of our knowledge for the first time, a comprehensive empirical analysis of the link between international outsourcing, domestic sourcing, profits and innovation using plant-level data covering the recent period 2002 to 2004.

Consistent with the predictions of theory (e.g., Glass and Saggi 2001), we observe a positive relationship between international outsourcing of services and innovative activity, measured in terms of R&D, at the plant level. Such a positive effect can also be observed for domestic outsourcing of services, but the magnitude is smaller. This makes intuitive sense, as international outsourcing allows more scope for exploiting international factor price differentials, therefore giving the establishment higher profits and more scope to restructure production activities toward innovation. We also find, again in line with theory, that international outsourcing has a positive effect on profitability, although this does not appear to be the case for domestic outsourcing.[18] Overall, the outsourcing of international services is seen in our analysis as a force for the good: A firm's innovation rates rise, hence allowing plants to continue to shift their technological frontier further outwards and, hence, sustaining their competitive position.

A recent fear even among proponents of international outsourcing is that developed countries started with outsourcing unskilled-intensive (manufacturing) production but have now moved to skilled-intensive (including services) activities also. If this process continues, it may lead to a "hollowing out" of production in the industrialized countries.[19] However, if international services outsourcing indeed promotes innovation, as our analysis suggests, then there is a case to be made for its continuance. If involvement in international outsourcing causes the technology frontier to shift through further innovation, the technological gap between industrialized and industrializing countries remains and outsourcing is then a persistent strategy. Thus, understanding the impact of international outsourcing on innovation is key to understanding whether we can expect it to continue in the future.

REFERENCES

Acs, Z., and D. Audretsch. "Innovation and the Size at the Firm Level." *Southern Economic Journal*, 57, 1991, 739–44.

Amiti, M., and S. J. Wei. "Service Outsourcing, Productivity and Employment: Evidence from the US." CEPR Discussion Paper 5475, 2006.

Antràs, P., and E. Helpman. "Global Sourcing." *Journal of Political Economy*, 112, 2004, 552–80.

Bartel, A., S. Lach, and N. Sicherman. "Outsourcing and Technological Change." NBER Working Paper 11158, 2005.

Blinder, A. S. "Offshoring: The Next Industrial Revolution?" *Foreign Affairs*, 85(2), 2006, 113–18.

Cassidy, M., H. Görg, and E. Strobl. "Knowledge Accumulation and Productivity: Evidence from Plant Level Data for Ireland." *Scottish Journal of Political Economy*, 52, 2005, 344–58.

18. This result can be explained by recent models such as Leahy and Montagna (2008) which show that outsourcing can lead reductions in profits.

19. See Sinn (2006) for an argument along those lines made for the particular example of Germany.

Criscuolo, C., J. E. Haskel, and M. J. Slaughter. "Global Engagement and the Innovation Activities of Firms." NBER Working Paper 11479, 2005.

Davidson, C., and S. Matusz. "Globalization and Labor Market Adjustment: How Fast and at What Cost?" *Oxford Review of Economic Policy*, 16(3), 2000, 42–56.

Eaton, J., and S. Kortum. "Innovation, Diffusion, and Trade." NBER Working Paper 12385, 2006.

Feenstra, R. C., and G. H. Hanson. "The Impact of Outsourcing and High-Technology Capital on Wages: Estimates for the United States, 1979-1990." *Quarterly Journal of Economics*, 114, 1999, 907–41.

Geishecker, I., and H. Görg. "Winners and Losers: A Micro-Level Analysis of International Outsourcing and Wages." *Canadian Journal of Economics*, 41, 2008, 243–70.

Glass, A., and K. Saggi. "Innovation and Wage Effects of International Outsourcing." *European Economic Review*, 45, 2001, 67–86.

Görg, H. "Fragmentation and Trade: US Inward Processing Trade in the EU." *Review of World Economics*, 136, 2000, 403–22.

Görg, H., A. Hanley, and E. Strobl. "Productivity Effects of International Outsourcing: Evidence from Plant Level Data." *Canadian Journal of Economics*, 41, 2008, 670–88.

Head, K., and J. Ries. "Offshore Production and Skill Upgrading by Japanese Manufacturing Firms." *Journal of International Economics* 58, 2002, 81–105.

Hijzen, A., T. Inui, and Y. Todo. "Does Offshoring Pay? Firm-Level Evidence from Japan." *Economic Inquiry*, 2008. Forthcoming. DOI:10.1111/j.1465-7295.2008.00175.x

Kohn, M., and J. T. Scott. "Scale Economies in Research and Development: The Schumpeterian Hypothesis." *Journal of Industrial Economics*, 30, 1982, 239–49.

Leahy, D., and C. Montagna. "Make or Buy in International Oligopoly and the Role of Competitive Pressure." GEP Research Paper, University of Nottingham, 2008.

OECD. *Internationalisation of Industrial R&D: Patterns and Trends*. Paris: OECD, 1998.

Redding, S. "The Low-skill, Low-quality Trap: Strategic Complementarities between Human Capital and R & D." *Economic Journal*, 106, 1996, 458–70.

Ruane, F., and J. Sutherland. "Export Performance and Destination Characteristics of Irish Manufacturing Industry." *Review of World Economics*, 141, 2005, 442–459.

Salomon, R. M., and J. M. Shaver. "Learning by Exporting: New Insights from Examining Firm Innovation." *Journal of Economics and Management Strategy*, 14, 2005, 431–60.

Shepherd, W. G. "The Elements of Market Structure." *Review of Economics and Statistics*, 54, 1972, 25–37.

Sinn, H. W. "The Pathological Export Boom and the Bazaar Effect. How to Solve the German Puzzle." CESifo Working Paper No. 1708, 2006.

Swenson, D. "Firm Outsourcing Decisions: Evidence from U.S. Foreign Trade Zones." *Economic Inquiry*, 38, 2000, 175–89.

———. "Entry Costs and Outsourcing Decisions: Evidence from the U.S. Overseas Assembly Provision." *North American Journal of Economics and Finance*, 15(3), 2004, 267–86.

Tomiura, E. "Foreign Outsourcing, Exporting, and FDI: A Productivity Comparison at the Firm Level." *Journal of International Economics*, 72, 2007, 113–27.

———. "Foreign Versus Domestic Outsourcing: Firm-Level Evidence on the Role of Technology." *International Review of Economics and Finance*, 18, 2009, 219–226.

Van Dijk, B., R. den Hertog, B. Menkveld, and R. Thurik. "Some New Evidence of the Determinants of Large- and Small-firm Innovation." *Small Business Economics*, 9, 1997, 335–43.

Chapter II.5

Outsourcing, Importing and Innovation: Evidence from Firm-level Data for Emerging Economies

*Ursula Fritsch and Holger Görg**

Abstract

This paper investigates two sourcing strategies of firms, outsourcing and importing, and links these to innovation activities. The authors examine this empirically using firm-level data for 28 emerging market economies and find robust evidence that outsourcing increases the likelihood to spend on R&D and via this channel raises innovation output, whereas importing increases innovation output, but not R&D. The results hold when implementing an instrumental variables approach. It is found that results crucially depend on the institutional environment in the economy, e.g. property rights and intellectual property rights protection. The results suggest that better institutions magnify the gains from importing, but not from outsourcing. EU countries also reap additional positive innovation effects from importing compared with non-EU countries.

1. Introduction

In this paper we look empirically at the implications of outsourcing and importing for innovation activities in the outsourcing and/or importing firm. We differentiate between outsourcing and importing as the former involves a realignment of the boundaries of the firm, whereas the latter provides access to a larger variety of goods and services. We investigate these relationships using firm-level data for emerging economies in Central and Eastern Europe, and Central Asia. Our focus on innovation as a measure of firm performance reflects the importance of innovations as a driver of productivity growth.

Outsourcing can be loosely defined as the contracting out of activities that were previously performed within a firm, to subcontractors outside the firm. Since firms are assumed to outsource parts of the production process that are not at the core of their activities, it allows the firm to save on factor costs and restructure operations towards higher value-added activities, such as R&D and innovation (e.g. Glass and Saggi, 2001; Girma and Görg, 2004).[1]

If outsourcing crosses borders it also leads to importing of intermediate inputs. However, importing may also occur without outsourcing if, e.g. a firm merely switches

---

* Fritsch: Kiel Institute for the World Economy, Kiellinie 66, 24105 Kiel, Germany. Tel: +49-431-8814468; E-Mail: ursula.fritsch@ifw-kiel.de. Also affiliated to: Christian-Albrechts-University of Kiel. Görg: Kiel Institute for the World Economy, Kiellinie 66, 24105 Kiel, Germany. Also affiliated to: Christian-Albrechts-University of Kiel and Tuborg Research Centre for Globalisation and Firms at Aarhus University. The authors would like to thank Laszlo Halpern and two anonymous referees for very helpful comments. They are also grateful to Robert Gold, Aoife Hanley, Wan-Hsin Liu and Iulia Siedschlag for insightful discussions on earlier drafts and seminar participants at the Kiel Institute, University of Kiel, EBRD, ZEW Mannheim, the 2013 FIW conference in Vienna and the 2013 GEP Postgraduate conference in Nottingham. Part of the work for this paper was carried out while Holger Görg was visiting IIIS at Trinity College Dublin. The hospitality is gratefully acknowledged, as is financial support through the Fritz Thyssen Foundation and the European Commission 7th Framework Programme, Grant Agreement no: 244 552 (SERVICEGAP).

from a domestic to a foreign supplier or imports goods that it never used to make itself. The use of imported inputs—our second sourcing variable—in particular, from industrialized countries, is likely to provide strong learning effects for firms in emerging economies, which affect their technology level and productivity (e.g. Amiti and Konings, 2007; Kasahara and Rodrigue, 2008; Goldberg et al., 2010; Halpern et al., 2005; Topalova and Khandelwal, 2011; Bas, 2012). This allows the firm to learn new technologies and push outwards its technology frontier. Chen and Ma (2012) look at this from a welfare perspective and estimate that the welfare gain as a result of newly imported varieties amounts to 6.2% of Chinese GDP for the period 1997–2008.

Both outsourcing and importing of intermediates are highly relevant activities for firms in emerging economies. About a sixth of the firms in our sample report that they have outsourced activities in the last 3 years to another firm (either domestic or abroad). 58 per cent of the firms import intermediates. Miroudot et al. (2009) present some stylized facts on trade in intermediates. They show that, while exports of intermediates were about double the level of imports of intermediates for the Commonwealth of Independent States (CIS) countries in 2006, imports of intermediate goods amounted to about US$100 billion. Imports of intermediate services account for an additional US$30 billion. They also show that there is no discernible difference in the growth rate of trade in intermediates between Organisation for Economic Co-operation and Development (OECD) economies and emerging market economies. Furthermore, a growing literature has recently focused on global value chain participation highlighting that transition countries are heavily integrated into global production networks (Koopman et al., 2014). This involves importing intermediates and most likely, outsourcing.

Hence, it is relevant to investigate the implications of these two activities for firms in emerging economies. We are, to the best of our knowledge, the first to differentiate the effects of outsourcing and importing on innovation. We choose to do so as outsourcing is likely to reflect benefits from reorganizing production while importing captures the ability to access larger input varieties or higher quality inputs. Distinguishing these two effects is not possible when just considering imports that also include, to some extent, benefits from outsourcing-related restructuring (see most empirical studies on firm-level effects of importing as cited above).

Another contribution of our paper is to consider the importance of the institutional environment for these effects. Since we have firm-level data covering a number of countries we can consider differences in property rights, intellectual property rights protection, labour market flexibility and supplier availability in different countries.

We use firm-level data from the Business Environment and Enterprise Performance Survey (BEEPS), provided by the European Bank for Reconstruction and Development (EBRD)–World Bank, for 28 transition countries. Specifically, the dataset covers companies located in Eastern and Central European, and Central Asian countries.

The papers by Gorodnichenko et al. (2010), Correa et al. (2010), Crinò (2012) and Seker (2012) also use BEEPS data to investigate various aspects of innovation activity in emerging countries. The main difference in our paper is that we consider firm-level information on outsourcing, which is not being done in the other studies. Hence, we are able to distinguish outsourcing-related restructuring from importing-related variety effects. Gorodnichenko et al. (2010) consider the effects of foreign competition, exports and imports on innovation. Seker (2012) differentiates exporters, importers and firms doing both and relates these to innovation. Correa et al. (2010) investigate determinants of technology absorption. Crinò (2012) also focuses on the effects of imported intermediates as a transmission channel for technology upgrading. He finds positive effects on skill upgrading. Imports also boost various innovation activities given that firms are engaged in high-skill intensive activities. He suggests that these effects might be related. The paper by Crinò (2012) is closest in terms of analysis as he also looks at causal effects of importing (though not outsourcing). We use, however, a different identification strategy and—in contrast to the other studies—data from 2001, 2004 and 2007.[2]

We find evidence that outsourcing is associated with a greater probability to spend on research and development and—via the R&D channel—to introduce new products and to upgrade existing products. Importing is as well associated with the latter two innovation measures but not with spending on research and development. This suggests that outsourcing leads to restructuring of activities towards more complex activities (such as R&D) while importing of larger input varieties or higher quality inputs has direct effects on innovation (but not R&D). We address endogeneity concerns by implementing instrumental variable estimations.

We also show that the results crucially depend on the institutional environment in the economy. In particular, property rights and intellectual property protection, and to a smaller extent the availability of local suppliers, impact positively on the effect of importing on innovation. This is not true for outsourcing, however, which does not appear to depend on such institutional characteristics. This suggests that importing is more complex than outsourcing, as it involves partners in countries with different institutional setups. Furthermore, being located in an EU member state is associated with higher gains from importing. We attribute these findings to better overall institutions and lower trade barriers within the EU.

The remainder of the paper is structured as follows. Section 2 presents the dataset, section 3 the methodology and section 4 discusses the empirical results. In section 5, we summarize the main findings and present conclusions.

2. Data Description

We use the BEEPS dataset to analyze the impact of outsourcing and importing on innovation.[3] The dataset comprises companies with at least five full-time employees in 28 countries in Central and Eastern Europe, the Baltic, the CIS and Central Asia (including Turkey) (see Table 1). The BEEPS survey provides a wide range of information on companies in the manufacturing and service sector. The survey was conducted roughly every 3 years (1999, 2002, 2005 and 2009). We skip, however, observations for 1999 as variables are only consistently defined for the following three waves of the survey. The 2009, 2005 and 2002 surveys provide information relating to 2007, 2004 and 2001, respectively. The data is exploited in the cross-sectional dimension.

The data enable us to measure two aspects of sourcing strategies: outsourcing, i.e. the realignment of the boundaries of the firm, and importing. The first measurement is based on the explicit question whether firms have "contracted with other companies (outsourced) activities previously performed in-house". Firms are also asked to declare their "foreign material inputs as a proportion of all material inputs".

The dataset also provides alternative measures of innovation at the firm-level. It has information on whether "the establishment invested in R&D (in-house or outsourced) in the last 3 years", which reflects well the effort that the firm undertakes to generate innovation output. The survey offers two questions with respect to innovation output, namely whether or not firms have, over the last 3 years, "newly introduced

Table 1. Country Coverage (Number of Firms)

Country	*Number*	*Country*	*Number*
Albania	130	Lithuania	254
Armenia	373	Moldova	223
Azerbaijan	116	Montenegro	30
Belarus	152	Poland	769
Bosnia	164	Romania	481
Bulgaria	226	Russia	843
Croatia	189	Serbia	247
Czech Republic	346	Slovakia	181
Estonia	220	Slovenia	249
FYROM	179	Tajikistan	204
Georgia	190	Turkey	631
Hungary	422	Ukraine	632
Kazakhstan	382	Uzbekistan	207
Kyrgyz Republic	182		
Latvia	189	*Total*	8411

products and services", or "upgraded products and services". We use these three measures for 2007, 2004 and 2001 to generate dummy variables for whether or not firms spend on R&D, introduced new products, or upgraded products, respectively. Thus, we differentiate between a measure that proxies an input factor (R&D spending) into the innovation process and the latter two output measures. We view the introduction of new products as a stronger measure of innovation compared with upgrading, as this concerns the development of completely new products.[4] Tables 2 and 3 present descriptive statistics for outsourcing vs non-outsourcing firms and importing vs non-importing firms. (The variables are discussed in more detail in section 3—Table 4 shows the definitions.) We document that there are strong selection effects into outsourcing and importing presumably because of sunk costs associated with these activities, as suggested by Antràs and Helpman (2004), Bernard et al. (2007) and Kasahara and Lapham (2013). Observations for 8,879 firms are available for the analysis. Of those, 1,556 (18%) outsource production and 5,044 (59%) import.

Outsourcers differ from non-outsourcers with respect to all innovation measures. They are also more likely to be importers or exporters. Additionally, outsourcers are on average larger and older than non-outsourcers. Ownership structures also differ between outsourcing and non-outsourcing firms. Firms that are part of a partnership or limited partnership are less likely to outsource and so are firms in which the government holds a stake. On the contrary, foreign-owned firms are associated with a higher likelihood to outsource. Outsourcers are less financially constrained and perceive domestic competition less of a pressure that induces them to innovate. Outsourcers and non-outsourcers are not different with respect to the percentage of people holding a university degree. Hence, there are significant differences between the two groups of firms.

A similar pattern emerges for importing and non-importing firms. The table also shows that the propensity to outsource is higher for importers than non-importers. The raw correlation between outsourcing and an importer dummy is at 0.14 positive but not very high. Table 5 also shows that only a small share of firms import and outsource simultaneously (1,113 firms equalling 13% of firms). This suggests that we can differentiate outsourcing from importing activities.

Table 2. Descriptives: Outsourcing vs Non-outsourcing Firms

Outsourcing	*Yes*	*No*	*Difference*
Newproduct	0.675	0.454	0.220***
	(0.469)	(0.498)	(0.013)
Upgrading	0.835	0.627	0.208***
	(0.372)	(0.484)	(0.011)
R&D	0.466	0.28	0.186***
	(0.499)	(0.449)	(0.014)
Imports	39.025	30.384	8.641***
	(36.678)	(37.147)	(1.042)
Partnership	0.131	0.216	–0.084***
	(0.338)	(0.411)	(0.010)
Foreign Owners	11.922	8.645	3.277***
	(29.915)	(25.685)	(0.818)
Gov	4.797	5.94	–1.143**
	(19.364)	(22.316)	(0.557)
Exports	24.77	13.647	11.123***
	(34.485)	(27.576)	(0.932)
Age	18.211	15.359	2.853***
	(20.364)	(17.98)	(0.557)
Finance	0.096	0.128	–0.033***
	(0.294)	(0.335)	(0.008)
University	25.745	24.69	1.055
	(25.747)	(26.234)	(0.721)
Dom. Competition	2.742	2.837	–0.095***
	(1.041)	(1.027)	(0.029)
Size	2.116	1.785	0.331***
	(0.785)	(0.79)	(0.022)
Observations	1556	7323	8879

Notes: Mean values in columns (1) and (2). Standard deviation in parentheses for columns (1) and (2) and standard error in parentheses for column (3). *Outsourcing* is a dummy variable taking on the value of 1 if the establishment outsourced activities previously done in-house in the last three years and 0 otherwise. For other definitions, see Table 4.

3. Econometric Methodology

In order to investigate whether outsourcing and importing have an impact on innovation activity at the firm-level we estimate variants of the following model

$$Prob(Innov_{it}) = \alpha + \beta \times Out_{it} + \gamma \times Imports_{it} + \lambda \times X_{it} + \kappa_1 \times D_c + \kappa_2 \times D_i + \kappa_3 \times D_y + \varepsilon_{it} \quad (1)$$

where *Innov* is alternatively defined as a dummy if the firm conducted R&D in t (= 2007, 2004 or 2001), or if the firm introduced new products in t (= 2007, 2004 or 2001) or the previous 3 years, or if it upgraded a product over the same period. *Out* captures outsourcing activities of a firm over the last 3 years, as defined in section 2. *Imports* captures the share of intermediate inputs that is sourced from abroad in a given fiscal year. D_c, D_i and D_y are full sets of country, industry and year dummies. The error term ε_{it} is robust to heteroskedasticity. It is important to note that R&D

Table 3. Descriptives: Importing vs Non-importing Firms

Importing	*Yes*	*No*	*Difference*
Newproduct	0.582	0.369	0.214***
	(0.493)	(0.483)	(0.011)
Upgrading	0.736	0.556	0.180***
	(0.441)	(0.497)	(0.010)
RD	0.392	0.200	0.192***
	(0.488)	(0.4)	(0.010)
Outsourcing	0.221	0.111	0.110***
	(0.415)	(0.314)	(0.008)
Partnership	0.200	0.203	–0.003
	(0.4)	(0.403)	(0.009)
Foreign Owners	12.881	4.074	8.807***
	(30.788)	(17.62)	(0.525)
Gov	5.247	6.212	–0.965**
	(20.755)	(22.867)	(0.482)
Exports	20.926	7.877	13.049***
	(32.285)	(21.75)	(0.582)
Age	16.714	14.800	1.914***
	(19.703)	(16.728)	(0.394)
Finance	0.100	0.157	–0.056***
	(0.3)	(0.363)	(0.007)
University	25.965	22.888	3.077***
	(25.995)	(25.876)	(0.567)
Dom. Competition	2.813	2.834	–0.021
	(1.034)	(1.023)	(0.022)
Size	1.976	1.664	0.312***
	(0.813)	(0.744)	(0.017)
Observations	5044	3576	8620

Notes: *Importing* is a dummy variable taking on the value of 1 if the establishment imported material inputs and supplies in the last fiscal year and 0 otherwise. For other definitions, see Table 4

also includes outsourced R&D, which is by definition correlated with outsourcing. We report results for R&D but are careful to point out that the measure might overestimate the effect on in-house R&D.

The model also includes a number of control variables that are collected in the vector X. We include in the baseline estimation a number of control variables that are standard in the literature. First, we include the share of sales that the firm directly or indirectly exports. This variable controls for the fact that firms that are internationally engaged in exporting tend to be more productive (e.g. Melitz, 2003; Muûls and Pisu, 2009; Siedschlag et al., 2011) and, hence, may also be more active in innovation, even in the absence of any outsourcing. Furthermore, we include a dummy equal to one if a firm reports any R&D expenditure (in-house or outsourced) over the last 3 years. R&D, of course, is an important input into the knowledge creation process, see, for example, Criscuolo et al. (2010) and Correa et al. (2010).[5] We further control for firm age, which has been identified to be an impediment to innovation (Lin et al., 2010). We look at the innovation potential of the firm acknowledging that high-skilled labor,

Table 4. Variable Definitions

Variable	*Variable definition*
Newproduct	Has this establishment introduced new products or services in the last 3 years?*
Upgrading	Has this establishment upgraded an existing product line or service in the last 3 years?*
R&D	Has this establishment invested in R&D (in-house or outsourced) in the last 3 years?*
Outsourcing	Has this establishment outsourced activities previously done in-house in the last three years?*
Imports	Percentage of material inputs and supplies of foreign origin in the last fiscal year
Partnership	Is this establishment's current legal status a partnership or limited partnership?*
Foreign owner	Share of the establishment that is owned by private foreign individuals, companies or organizations****
Government	Share of the establishment that is owned by the government/state****
Exports	In fiscal year xxxx, what percentage of this establishment's sales were indirect and direct exports?
University	Percentage of employees at the end of 2007 with a university degree
Age	Number of years in operation since establishment
Finance	Dummy variable taking on the value of 1 if the establishment reports that it did not apply for a loan and checks any of the following answers: the application procedures are complex, interest rates are not favorable, collateral requirements are too high, the size of the loan is insufficient, it is necessary to make an informal payment, the establishment did not think it would be approved and other. It takes on the value of 0 if the establishment applied for a loan or if there was not a need for a load as the establishment reported to have sufficient capital.
Size	Small (5–19 employees), medium (20–99) and large (100 and more)
Dom. Competition	How important is pressure from domestic competitors in affecting decisions to develop new products or services and markets?**
Concentration ratio	Sum over the four largest market shares of firms for the respective country–industry-year
HHI	Herfindahl–Hirschman Index for the respective country–industry-year
Instruments	
Dom. Compet. IV	How important is pressure from domestic competitors in affecting decisions with respect to reducing the production costs of existing products or services?**
For. Compet. IV	How important is pressure from foreign competitors in affecting decisions with respect to reducing the production costs of existing products or services?**
Customers Compet. IV	How important is pressure from customers in affecting decisions with respect to reducing the production costs of existing products or services?**
Institutional variables	
Property rights	How would you rate the protection of property rights, including financial assets, in your country? (1 = very weak; 7 = very strong)
Intellectual property protection	How would you rate intellectual property protection, including anti-counterfeiting measures, in your country? (1 = very weak; 7 = very strong)
Hiring and firing practices	How would you characterize the hiring and firing of workers in your country? (1 = impeded by regulations; 7 = flexibly determined by employers)
Local supplier quantity	How numerous are local suppliers in your country? (1 = largely nonexistent; 7 = very numerous)
Local supplier quality	How would you assess the quality of local suppliers in your country? (1 = very poor; 7 = very good)

Note: *1 = yes and 0 = no; ** Scaled 1–4 (1 being the least important); *** If very severe or major obstacle, we set a dummy equal to 1, otherwise 0; **** Defined between 0 and 100.

Table 5. Descriptives: Outsourcing and Importing Activities of Firms

		Importing		
		No	Yes	Total
Outsourcing	No	3180	3931	7111
Outsourcing	Yes	396	1113	1509
	Total	3576	5044	8620

Note: The table depicts information on the number of importing/non-importing firms vs outsourcing/non-outsourcing firms.

measured as the share of employees with a university degree, is a prerequisite for innovation (Gorodnichenko et al., 2010). We also control for the degree of domestic competition that makes firms innovate (a point similarly made by Correa et al. (2010)). Furthermore, we include size as a proxy for productivity, as we are not able to compute an accurate productivity measure from the data without losing a large number of observations.[6]

Finally, we take the financial situation in a firm into account. This may be important as innovation is likely to be affected by financial constraints in a firm (Hall, 2002). We do not consider self-reported financial constraints as firms might be reluctant to state openly whether they are financially constrained or not. Instead, we rely on a measure whether firms did not apply for a loan although they *did not* have sufficient own capital. They give a number of reasons that are related to inefficient financial markets, for instance, "the application procedures are complex" or "it is necessary to make informal payments to get bank loans".

In an extended specification, ownership controls are added to the vector X. Partnership and limited partnership is supposed to reflect pressure from private equity owners or a joint partner of the firm. We believe that these firms are better run than other firms that are less exposed to ownership control. This may, however, come at the cost that these firms do not experience the necessary flexibility to innovate or are specialized in medium-skilled tasks in the production chain. We also control for the share of foreign owners. This reflects the prior that foreign capital may be an important source of finance for firms, in particular for financing innovative activities (Girma et al., 2008). However, it may also control for the fact that multinationals are more likely to undertake R&D and innovate in the headquarters in the home country (UNCTAD, 2005). We hypothesize that the effect might not be linear. It is, for instance, likely that affiliates that are 100% owned by the headquarter are specialized in assembling rather than innovation activities. By contrast, a 5% stake in a foreign company is likely to be a capital investment that might stimulate innovation activities of the domestic firm. Finally, we also control for government ownership.

Two econometric issues arise in the estimation of equation (1). First, we have a binary dependent variable. In order to deal with this, we estimate probit models and linear probability models (LPM). Secondly, outsourcing and importing are likely to be endogenous because of unobserved firm effects. For example, well-performing firms may both be likely to innovate but may also have high propensities to outsource and import as they are able to overcome the sunk costs associated with these activities

(Antràs and Helpman, 2004; Kasahara and Lapham, 2013). While the inclusion of our control variables should mitigate this problem—in particular the inclusion of exporting and importing, which is also related to sunk costs—we nevertheless also implement instrumental variable techniques.

The challenge is, of course, to find instruments that are both relevant (i.e. correlated with the potentially endogenous variables) and valid (i.e. uncorrelated with innovation conditional on exogenous regressors in the model). Specifically, we use three variables for two endogenous variables: (i) the average share of imports reported by other firms operating in the same industry and country in the same year, (ii) the average propensity to outsource reported by other firms operating in the same industry and country in the same year and (iii) an average assessment of the firm on whether cost reduction is important for its operations. That latter variable is computed using information on the firm's assessment of whether pressure from domestic companies, foreign companies and customers induces the firm to reduce production costs. To do so we standardize (mean = 0 and std. dev. = 1) three questions on the importance of (a) domestic competitors, (b) foreign competitors and (c) customers in affecting decisions with respect to reducing the production costs of existing products or services. We compute an average over these variables.

The rationale for the choice of these variables is as follows. The average assessment of other firms' propensity to import and outsource should be a good proxy for the outsourcing/importing behavior of the individual firm. Average assessments of other firms operating in the same industry and the same country reflect a multitude of factors that affect the outsourcing/importing decision such as trade barriers or transportation obstacles. These barriers differ on the country–industry level. This should be strongly correlated with the individual firm decision to outsource and import. These averages should, most importantly, not be correlated with firm-specific effects and can, hence, be considered to be exogenous instruments.[7]

The average assessment of the importance of cost reduction is our third instrument. Minimizing production costs is one of the main arguments for outsourcing put forth in the literature (e.g. Glass and Saggi, 2001; Antràs and Helpman, 2004; Rodríguez-Clare, 2010). Egger and Egger (2003) instrument outsourcing of Austrian firms with unit labor costs in Eastern Europe. They show that cost reduction is a significant driver of outsourcing. Similarly, Girma and Görg (2004) document that firms with higher wages outsource more. Hence, our instrument should be positively correlated with outsourcing and importing.

Given the definition of our cost reduction variable it is possible that it is correlated with competition in general, and competition has been shown to impact innovation (Aghion et al., 2004, 2005; Gorodnichenko et al., 2010; Bloom et al., forthcoming). If this were the case then our instrument would be correlated with the error term in equation (1) and, hence, be invalid. We believe, however, that our instrument can be differentiated from competition that may impact on innovation as we control for the importance of pressure from domestic competitors to develop new products or services in equation (1). The question on which this variable is based precedes the questions on the reduction of production costs in the survey questionnaire. We may therefore argue that our instrument picks up a distinct effect and that firms can distinguish these effects. We come back to this issue in the discussion of our empirical results.

Furthermore, we test for instrument relevance and validity of over-identification restrictions in the empirical analysis using the standard tests.

4. Econometric Results

Baseline Model and IV Estimation

Table 6 presents the baseline estimates from equation (1) using alternative dependent variables: new product development (columns 1–3), product upgrading (columns 4–6) and R&D (columns 7–9). Columns (1), (4) and (7) show the baseline estimation including only outsourcing and control variables. Columns (2), (5) and (8) also include importing. Columns (3), (6) and (9) furthermore include a set of ownership controls. We report marginal effects from Probit regressions. Linear probability model (LPM) estimations are not presented here to save space, as they produce very similar results. They are available from the authors upon request.[8]

We find evidence for a positive association between outsourcing, importing and the innovation variables. The magnitude and the significance of the results are robust and not affected by the inclusion of further control variables. They are fully in line with the predictions that outsourcing and importing (a) increase productivity and this increases innovation activities within the firm and (b) there is a direct learning effect because of superior products that have been outsourced/imported. It is also important to note that we pick up two distinct effects of sourcing strategies as the estimated coefficient of outsourcing barely changes with the inclusion of the importing variable.

As for our control variables, results show that the probability of generating innovation output is statistically significantly related to a firm's own R&D activity and its skill potential, as found by Gorodnichenko et al. (2010), Correa et al. (2010) and Crinò (2012). This suggests that the firm's own input into the innovation process is very important, in line with the literature (Criscuolo et al., 2010). Exporting is no longer positively associated with innovation after controlling for importing. We find negative effects of age, similar to Lin et al. (2010) corroborating the hypothesis that young firms tend to be more innovative than older firms. Older firms are, however, more likely to spend on R&D. Size, the proxy for productivity, is highly significant and shows that larger firms tend to be more innovative. The finance variable depicts the expected sign and is very robust throughout all specifications. Additionally, we find that domestic competition fosters innovation.

In the final step, we include a set of ownership control variables. Partnership turns out to significantly negatively affect innovation, probably because partners like private equity companies in transition countries rely on medium-skilled labor and not on highly innovative work. We find an inverted-U-shaped effect of foreign ownership on R&D. This relates most likely to the idea that foreign owners that hold small shares in companies do not interfere with the innovation activities of firms. In contrast, if we look at an affiliated company of a foreign-owned company, R&D is most likely located at the headquarters. Government ownership has no effect on R&D spending but affects negatively innovation output. This is a plausible result as governments may not be as effective as private companies in terms of generating innovation output.

The assumption in the estimations thus far is that outsourcing and importing are exogenous in the model, i.e. not correlated with the error term in equation (1). If this assumption were violated, our estimates would be biased. We therefore now proceed to testing this assumption explicitly, using instrumental variable estimations. The regression estimates for the instrumental variable estimations (LPM and Probit) are shown in Table 7. Detailed first stage results for the LPM model appear in Table 8.

Table 6. Exogenous Outsourcing and Importing

	Newprod.	*Newprod.*	*Newprod.*	*Upgrading*	*Upgrading*	*Upgrading*	*R&D*	*R&D*	*R&D*
Sourcing strategy									
Outsourcing	0.106***	0.100***	0.100***	0.122***	0.118***	0.119***	0.109***	0.105***	0.104***
	(0.014)	(0.014)	(0.014)	(0.014)	(0.014)	(0.014)	(0.010)	(0.010)	(0.010)
Imports		0.001***	0.001***		0.001***	0.001***		0.001***	0.001***
		(0.000)	(0.000)		(0.000)	(0.000)		(0.000)	(0.000)
Ownership structure									
Partnership			−0.005			−0.033***			−0.032***
			(0.014)			(0.013)			(0.012)
Foreign Owners			0.002			−0.001			0.002**
			(0.001)			(0.001)			(0.001)
For. Own. squared			−0.000			0.000			−0.000**
			(0.000)			(0.000)			(0.000)
Gov			−0.001**			−0.001***			0.000
			(0.000)			(0.000)			(0.000)
Other control variables									
Exports	0.000**	0.000	0.000	0.000**	0.000	0.000	0.000	0.000	0.000
	(0.000)	(0.000)	(0.000)	(0.000)	(0.000)	(0.000)	(0.000)	(0.000)	(0.000)
Age	−0.001**	−0.001**	−0.000	−0.001**	−0.001**	−0.000	0.000**	0.001**	0.000**
	(0.000)	(0.000)	(0.000)	(0.000)	(0.000)	(0.000)	(0.000)	(0.000)	(0.000)
R&D	0.227***	0.216***	0.216***	0.177***	0.170***	0.169***			
	(0.012)	(0.013)	(0.013)	(0.013)	(0.013)	(0.013)			
Finance	−0.091***	−0.087***	−0.088***	−0.075***	−0.079***	−0.079***	−0.034**	−0.037***	−0.036***
	(0.016)	(0.016)	(0.016)	(0.014)	(0.014)	(0.014)	(0.014)	(0.014)	(0.014)
University	0.001***	0.001***	0.001***	0.001***	0.001***	0.001***	0.001***	0.001***	0.001***
	(0.000)	(0.000)	(0.000)	(0.000)	(0.000)	(0.000)	(0.000)	(0.000)	(0.000)
Dom. Competition	0.017***	0.018***	0.016***	0.024***	0.024***	0.022***	0.005	0.005	0.005
	(0.005)	(0.005)	(0.005)	(0.005)	(0.005)	(0.005)	(0.004)	(0.004)	(0.004)
Size medium	0.071***	0.069***	0.070***	0.076***	0.075***	0.081***	0.117***	0.118***	0.119***
	(0.012)	(0.012)	(0.012)	(0.011)	(0.011)	(0.012)	(0.010)	(0.010)	(0.010)
Size large	0.071***	0.067***	0.067***	0.069***	0.067***	0.076***	0.215***	0.212***	0.214***
	(0.015)	(0.015)	(0.015)	(0.014)	(0.015)	(0.015)	(0.011)	(0.011)	(0.012)
Observations	8874	8616	8579	8859	8601	8564	8879	8620	8583

Notes: Reported coefficients are marginal effects from Probit estimations. Robust standard errors are in parentheses. Industry, country and time dummies included. *, **, *** Denote significance at 10%, 5% and 1%, respectively. Coefficients from standard ordinary least squares (OLS)-regressions are quantitatively similar.

Table 7. Endogenous Outsourcing and Importing

	Newproduct LPM	*Newproduct Probit*	*Upgrading LPM*	*Upgrading Probit*	*R&D LPM*	*R&D Probit*
Sourcing strategy						
Outsourcing	0.497**	0.512***	0.341*	0.316***	0.735**	0.742***
	(0.218)	(0.132)	(0.196)	(0.114)	(0.290)	(0.174)
Imports	0.004***	0.004***	0.004***	0.004***	−0.000	0.000
	(0.001)	(0.001)	(0.001)	(0.001)	(0.001)	(0.001)
Ownership structure						
Partnership	−0.003	−0.004	−0.032**	−0.035**	−0.018	−0.033*
	(0.015)	(0.018)	(0.015)	(0.016)	(0.013)	(0.018)
Foreign Owners	0.001	0.001	−0.002	−0.002	0.002*	0.003**
	(0.001)	(0.001)	(0.001)	(0.001)	(0.001)	(0.001)
For. Own. squared	−0.000	−0.000	0.000	0.000	−0.000*	−0.000**
	(0.000)	(0.000)	(0.000)	(0.000)	(0.000)	(0.000)
Gov	−0.001*	−0.001*	−0.001***	−0.001***	−0.000	−0.000
	(0.000)	(0.000)	(0.000)	(0.000)	(0.000)	(0.000)
Other control variables						
Exports	−0.000*	−0.001*	−0.000	−0.000	−0.000	−0.000
	(0.000)	(0.000)	(0.000)	(0.000)	(0.000)	(0.000)
Age	−0.000	−0.000	−0.000	−0.000	0.000	0.000
	(0.000)	(0.000)	(0.000)	(0.000)	(0.000)	(0.000)
R&D	0.153***	0.170***	0.101***	0.129***		
	(0.028)	(0.031)	(0.025)	(0.027)		
Finance	−0.059***	−0.068***	−0.071***	−0.080***	−0.008	−0.021
	(0.019)	(0.023)	(0.018)	(0.022)	(0.020)	(0.025)
University	0.000	0.001	−0.000	−0.000	0.001*	0.001**
	(0.000)	(0.000)	(0.000)	(0.000)	(0.000)	(0.000)
Dom. Competition	0.015**	0.017**	0.022***	0.025***	0.001	0.002
	(0.006)	(0.007)	(0.006)	(0.006)	(0.005)	(0.007)
Size medium	0.057***	0.062***	0.080***	0.080***	0.087***	0.145***
	(0.016)	(0.018)	(0.014)	(0.015)	(0.018)	(0.022)
Size large	0.040**	0.043*	0.057***	0.058***	0.188***	0.267***
	(0.020)	(0.023)	(0.019)	(0.020)	(0.028)	(0.034)
F-test Outsourcing	13.83		14.08		8.38	
F-test Imports	80.67		81.05		100.11	
Underidentification (p-value)	0.0000		0.0000		0.0000	
Hansen J test (p-value)	0.4731		0.6669			
Exogeneity test (p-value)	0.0000	0.0000	0.0000	0.0000	0.0332	0.0720
Observations	8233	8233	8217	8217	8529	8529

Notes: We report marginal effects for Probit estimations. Robust standard errors are in parentheses. Industry, country and time dummies included. Instruments used for *Newproduct* and *Upgrading*: the average share of imports reported by other firms operating in the same industry, country and year, the average propensity to outsource reported by other firms operating in the same industry, country and year and an assessment of the firm on the variable whether pressure from domestic companies, foreign companies and customers induce the firms to reduce production costs. Instruments used for R&D: the average share of imports reported by other firms operating in the same industry, country and year and the average propensity to outsource reported by other firms operating in the same industry, country and year. *, **, *** Denote signficance at 10%, 5% and 1%, respectively.

Table 8. First Stage Regression Results for Excluded Instruments from Linear Probability Model

	New product Outsourcing	*New product Importing*	*Upgrading Outsourcing*	*Upgrading Importing*	*R&D Outsourcing*	*R&D Importing*
Average pressure to reduce costs	0.028***	3.361***	0.028***	3.375***		
	(0.005)	(0.503)	(0.005)	(0.503)		
IV Imports	0.000	0.463***	0.000	0.465***	0.000	0.463***
	(0.000)	(0.033)	(0.000)	(0.033)	(0.000)	(0.033)
IV Outsourcing	0.164***	−3.954	0.168***	−3.830	0.179***	−1.507
	(0.045)	(3.700)	(0.045)	(3.712)	(0.045)	(3.675)
F-test joint significance	13.83	80.67	14.08	81.05	8.38	100.11
Observations	8233	8233	8217	8217	8529	8529

Notes: Robust standard errors are in parentheses. Industry, country and time dummies included. *, **, *** Denote signficance at 10%, 5% and 1%, respectively.

First note that we use all three instruments in the *Newproduct* and *Upgrading* equations while we do not use the cost reduction instrument in the R&D equation. The reason is that R&D includes R&D outsourced to other companies. This could be correlated with cost reduction motives. Therefore, only two instruments are used in the R&D equation. When considering instrument relevance, note that the first stage F-tests are statistically significant, suggesting that the excluded instruments are jointly relevant. The reported F-statistics are well above 10 (except for outsourcing in the R&D specification), the critical value usually considered as "safe" for instrument relevance. We also report an under-identification test, which allows us to reject the assumption of under-identification. We show in Table 8 that the excluded instruments are individually statistically significant predictors of outsourcing and importing.[9] In terms of instrument validity, tests of over-identification restrictions do not reject the assumption of instrument validity. Based on these instruments, we can reject the assumption of exogeneity of the two regressors for all innovation variables. Note also that we report marginal effects from a Probit model and a LPM to show that our estimates are robust to different model specifications.

Looking at the estimates in Table 7 we find that the significance of the control variables broadly reflects previous findings in Table 6. A difference is that age and education are no longer statistically significant in most specifications. The coefficients on the finance variable are significant for new product development and product upgrading but not for the R&D regression. Also, the coefficient for size in the new product regression appears somewhat smaller than in Table 6.[10]

Our results for outsourcing and importing are similar to previous findings. This suggests that our results are robust to specifications that address endogeneity concerns. We have discussed potential drawbacks of the instruments in section 3 and are careful to point out that our results rely on the assumption of instrument exogeneity. Comparing our results with the previous literature, we can confirm a positive link between importing and innovation output (e.g. Gorodnichenko et al., 2010; Goldberg et al., 2010; Crinò, 2012). We add to this literature that importing does not increase the propensity to spend on R&D so that the ability to engage in novel innovation might not be increased by importing. We can also differentiate the importing effect from an outsourcing effect. Outsourcing depicts complementarity with conducting own R&D, which is a positive effect that the literature on outsourcing has neglected thus far.

Robustness Checks

In this section we consider a number of robustness checks. The first issue that one may be concerned with is that we may have a relatively low number of firms with which to calculate the instruments based on the averages of importing or outsourcing in the same country, industry and year. If that were the case we might be likely observing a limited number of firms in each cell, potentially implying that our innovation variable is based on a strategic competitive response to the outsourcing or importing activity of other firms. This could then invalidate our instruments.

To counter such criticisms we show in Tables 1 and 9, as well as in Figures 1 and 2, the number of firms per country and industry and the distribution of the actual number of firms used to calculate the instrument, respectively. The figures show that for most cases we have a fairly large number of firms.[11] In order to check the robustness of our results we report estimations where we drop those observations for which the instrument is based on less than nine observations (lowest 10% of the

Table 9. Industry Coverage (Number of Firms)

Country	*No.*	*Country*	*No.*
Other manufacturing	906	Electronics	78
Food	1600	Construction	536
Textiles	282	Other services	706
Garments	727	Wholesale	512
Chemicals	296	Retail	474
Plastics & rubber	166	Hotel and restaurants	233
Non metallic mineral products	284	Transport	310
Basic metals	73	IT	37
Fabricate metal products	644		
Machinery and equipment	547	*Total*	8411

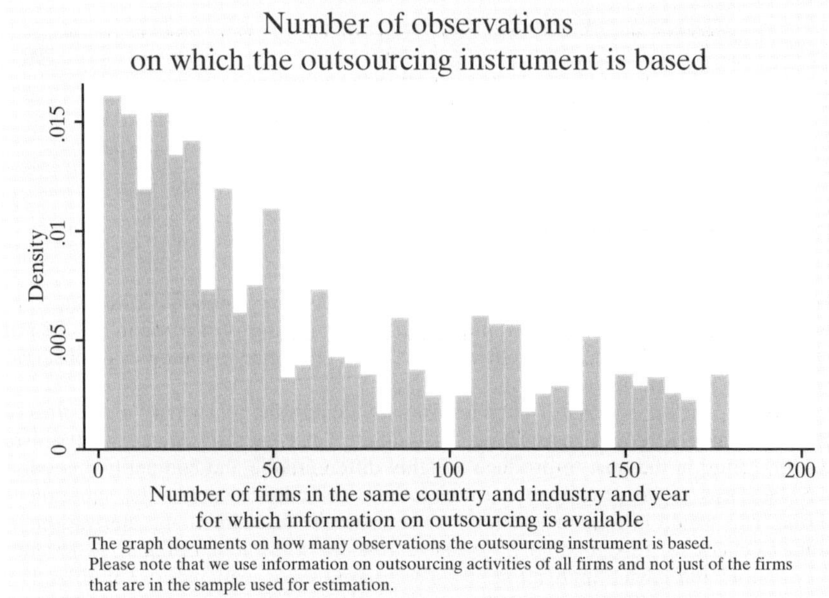

Figure 1. Validity of Instrumental Variable: Outsourcing

distribution). Results are very similar to those obtained earlier, see Table 10, with one difference being the coefficients on outsourcing in the R&D equation that are lower than before.

To control for the possibility of a strategic effect we also run an estimation where we control additionally for the concentration ratio of the top four firms with the largest market shares or the Hirschman–Herfindahl index of concentration, respectively. The results are in Table 11. The inclusion of these variables again does not change results strongly. Market concentration does not emerge as a robust and significant control in the model, which might be partly because we already control for

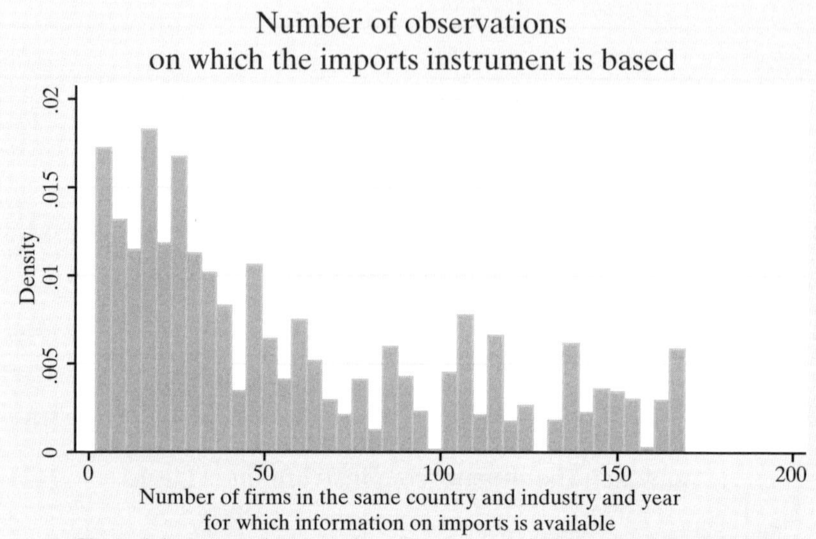

The graph documents on how many observations the imports instrument is based.
Please note that we use information on importing activities of all firms and not just of the firms that are in the sample used for estimation.

Figure 2. Validity of Instrumental Variable: Imports

domestic competition. As the concentration variables are calculated using sales per firms, for which we have a substantial number of missing observations we do not include these variables in what follows in order to maximize the number of observations in our estimations.

Another concern is with our third instrument, namely, the assessment of the firm of the importance to reduce costs. Here, a potential reverse causality may exist. If a firm has innovated in the past to produce a highly differentiable and competitive good, it may face less or no pressure from competition to reduce costs in the subsequent period. This would introduce a correlation between the instrument and innovation. In order to check for this possibility, we ran regressions with the instrument as dependent variable and lagged innovation and R&D variables as explanatory variables. For this purpose, we exploit the panel dimension of the data. The innovation variables are in all cases statistically insignificant, suggesting that reverse causality is not an issue. Results appear in Table 12.

A further potential problem with this instrument is that it may be correlated with competition in general, which might drive firms to outsource. In order to alleviate such concerns, we can refer back to the above robustness check, where we included measures of the Herfindahl index and concentration ratios. Furthermore, equation (1) includes the firm's assessment of pressure from domestic competition to developing new products (i.e. innovate) as explanatory variable. However, if pressure to reduce costs and pressure to innovation were highly correlated, then this might introduce a problem as the instrument may then be correlated with innovation activity. In order to consider this issue, we first check the raw correlation of the two variables, which at 0.57 is indeed high (see Table 13). However, what matters is not

Table 10. Robustness of Construction of Instrumental Variables

	Newprod. *Test outsourcing-IV*	*Newprod.* *Test imports-IV*	*Upgrading* *Test outsourcing-IV*	*Upgrading* *Test imports-IV*	*R&D* *Test outsourcing-IV*	*R&D* *Test imports-IV*
Sourcing strategy						
Outsourcing	0.427**	0.472**	0.385**	0.338*	0.449**	0.448**
	(0.184)	(0.191)	(0.168)	(0.173)	(0.176)	(0.191)
Imports	0.005***	0.004***	0.003***	0.004***	0.000	0.000
	(0.001)	(0.001)	(0.001)	(0.001)	(0.001)	(0.001)
Ownership structure						
Partnership	−0.011	−0.010	−0.033**	−0.035**	−0.020	−0.019
	(0.016)	(0.016)	(0.016)	(0.016)	(0.012)	(0.012)
Foreign Owners	−0.000	−0.000	−0.002*	−0.002**	0.002*	0.002*
	(0.001)	(0.001)	(0.001)	(0.001)	(0.001)	(0.001)
For. Ow. squared	−0.000	−0.000	0.000	0.000	−0.000*	−0.000**
	(0.000)	(0.000)	(0.000)	(0.000)	(0.000)	(0.000)
Gov	−0.001*	−0.001**	−0.001***	−0.001***	−0.000	−0.000
	(0.000)	(0.000)	(0.000)	(0.000)	(0.000)	(0.000)
Other control variables						
Exports	−0.000	−0.000	−0.000	−0.000	−0.000	−0.000
	(0.000)	(0.000)	(0.000)	(0.000)	(0.000)	(0.000)
Age	0.000	0.000	0.000	0.000	0.000	0.000
	(0.000)	(0.000)	(0.000)	(0.000)	(0.000)	(0.000)
R&D	0.158***	0.155***	0.109***	0.111***		
	(0.026)	(0.027)	(0.023)	(0.024)		
Finance	−0.065***	−0.063***	−0.072***	−0.073***	−0.019	−0.018
	(0.019)	(0.020)	(0.019)	(0.019)	(0.016)	(0.016)
University	0.000	0.000	−0.000	−0.000	0.001**	0.001**
	(0.000)	(0.000)	(0.000)	(0.000)	(0.000)	(0.000)
Dom. Competition	0.017***	0.018***	0.023***	0.023***	0.003	0.003
	(0.006)	(0.006)	(0.006)	(0.006)	(0.005)	(0.005)
Size medium	0.057***	0.058***	0.075***	0.077***	0.098***	0.099***
	(0.016)	(0.016)	(0.015)	(0.015)	(0.014)	(0.015)
Size large	0.035*	0.036*	0.045**	0.051***	0.205***	0.204***
	(0.021)	(0.021)	(0.019)	(0.020)	(0.022)	(0.023)
F-test Outsourcing	18.33	16.50	18.41	16.55	18.76	15.52
F-test Imports	76.13	79.76	76.16	79.78	98.55	104.54
Underidentification (p-value)	0.0000	0.0000	0.0000	0.0000	0.0000	0.0000
Hansen J test (p-value)	0.2769	0.2712	0.5241	0.4252		
Exogeneity test (p-value)	0.0000	0.0000	0.0001	0.0001	0.1344	0.1589
Observations	7307	7304	7293	7290	7572	7569

Notes: Reported coefficients are from LPMs using instrumental variables as in Table 7. We drop all observations for which the number of observations used to construct the outsourcing (importing) instrument is in the lowest 10% of observations, i.e. it is based on less than nine (9) observations. We report these results in columns *Test outsourcing IV* (*Test imports IV*). Robust standard errors are in parentheses. Industry, country and time dummies included. Instruments used for *Newproduct* and *Upgrading*: the average share of imports reported by other firms operating in the same industry, country and year, the average propensity to outsource reported by other firms operating in the same industry, country and year and an assessment of the firm on the variable whether pressure from domestic companies, foreign companies and customers induce the firms to reduce production costs. Instruments used for *R&D*: the average share of imports reported by other firms operating in the same industry, country and year and the average propensity to outsource reported by other firms operating in the same industry, country and year. *, **, *** Denote significance at 10%, 5% and 1% respectively.

Table 11. Controlling for Market Concentration

	Newproduct	*Newproduct*	*Upgrading*	*Upgrading*	*R&D*	*R&D*
Sourcing strategy						
Outsourcing	0.591***	0.560**	0.397**	0.377*	0.733***	0.754***
	(0.226)	(0.221)	(0.201)	(0.197)	(0.274)	(0.272)
Imports	0.004***	0.004***	0.004***	0.004***	−0.001	−0.001
	(0.001)	(0.001)	(0.001)	(0.001)	(0.001)	(0.001)
Market concentration						
Concentration ratio	0.081**		−0.003		−0.045	
	(0.039)		(0.035)		(0.034)	
HHI		0.032		−0.060*		−0.005
		(0.036)		(0.033)		(0.032)
Ownership structure						
Partnership	−0.008	−0.007	−0.031**	−0.030**	−0.020	−0.020
	(0.016)	(0.016)	(0.015)	(0.015)	(0.014)	(0.014)
Foreign Owners	0.001	0.001	−0.002*	−0.002*	0.002**	0.002**
	(0.001)	(0.001)	(0.001)	(0.001)	(0.001)	(0.001)
For. Ow. squared	−0.000	−0.000	0.000	0.000	−0.000**	−0.000**
	(0.000)	(0.000)	(0.000)	(0.000)	(0.000)	(0.000)
Gov	−0.001*	−0.001*	−0.001***	−0.001***	−0.000	−0.000
	(0.000)	(0.000)	(0.000)	(0.000)	(0.000)	(0.000)
Other control variables						
Exports	−0.000*	−0.000*	−0.000*	−0.000*	−0.000	−0.000
	(0.000)	(0.000)	(0.000)	(0.000)	(0.000)	(0.000)
Age	−0.000	−0.000	−0.000	−0.000	0.001	0.001
	(0.000)	(0.000)	(0.000)	(0.000)	(0.000)	(0.000)
R&D	0.140***	0.142***	0.098***	0.100***		
	(0.028)	(0.028)	(0.025)	(0.024)		
Finance	−0.062***	−0.063***	−0.073***	−0.074***	−0.005	−0.004
	(0.021)	(0.020)	(0.019)	(0.019)	(0.020)	(0.020)
University	0.001*	0.001*	−0.000	−0.000	0.001**	0.001**
	(0.000)	(0.000)	(0.000)	(0.000)	(0.000)	(0.000)
Dom. Competition	0.014**	0.014**	0.022***	0.022***	−0.002	−0.002
	(0.006)	(0.006)	(0.006)	(0.006)	(0.006)	(0.006)
Size medium	0.057***	0.058***	0.079***	0.079***	0.086***	0.085***
	(0.016)	(0.016)	(0.015)	(0.015)	(0.017)	(0.017)
Size large	0.035	0.037*	0.060***	0.061***	0.198***	0.196***
	(0.021)	(0.021)	(0.020)	(0.019)	(0.028)	(0.028)
F-test Outsourcing	14.55	14.76	18.41	14.85	9.89	10.11
F-test Imports	77.41	77.69	76.16	77.84	93.12	93.84
Underidentification (p-value)	0.0000	0.0000	0.0000	0.0000	0.0000	0.0000
Hansen J test (p-value)	0.4574	0.4541	0.8158	0.7989		
Exogeneity test (p-value)	0.0000	0.0000	0.0001	0.0000	0.0205	0.0121
Observations	7703	7703	7689	7689	7967	7967

Notes: Reported coefficients are based on instrumental variables estimation of a LPM as in Table 7. Robust standard errors are in parentheses. Industry, country and time dummies included. Instruments used for *Newproduct* and *Upgrading*: the average share of imports reported by other firms operating in the same industry, country and year, the average propensity to outsource reported by other firms operating in the same industry, country and year and an assessment of the firm on the variable whether pressure from domestic companies, foreign companies and customers induce the firms to reduce production costs. Instruments used for *R&D*: the average share of imports reported by other firms operating in the same industry, country and year and the average propensity to outsource reported by other firms operating in the same industry, country and year. *, **, *** Denote significance at 10%, 5% and 1% respectively.

this raw correlation but the correlation conditional on other variables included in the model. As our results thus far show, this does not seem to be problematic, as we are able to identify a statistically significant coefficient on the "exogenous" pressure to innovate variable as well as on the excluded instrument in the first step regression (see Table 7 and Table 8). A test for multicollinearity is also reassuring, returning a VIF test of 1.70 and 1.65 for the instrument and the domestic competition control. Still, we do acknowledge that even when controlling for these variables, we may not be able to capture all aspects of competition that may potentially be driving outsourcing, importing and innovation activities. This should be kept in mind when interpreting our results.[12]

Table 12. Robustness Check: Testing Reverse Causality

	Average pressure to reduce costs	*Average pressure to reduce costs*	*Average pressure to reduce costs*
Innovation activities			
Newproduct lagged	0.023		
	(0.033)		
Upgrading lagged		0.039	
		(0.033)	
RD lagged			0.021
			(0.069)
Other control variables			
Partnership	−0.018	−0.015	0.030
	(0.047)	(0.047)	(0.066)
Foreign Owners	0.001	0.001	−0.002
	(0.003)	(0.003)	(0.005)
For. Ow. squared	−0.000	−0.000	0.000
	(0.000)	(0.000)	(0.000)
Gov	−0.003***	−0.003***	0.000
	(0.001)	(0.001)	(0.001)
Exports	0.004***	0.004***	0.005***
	(0.001)	(0.001)	(0.001)
Age	0.003***	0.003***	0.003**
	(0.001)	(0.001)	(0.001)
R&D	0.080**	0.080**	
	(0.040)	(0.040)	
Finance	0.049	0.047	0.016
	(0.042)	(0.042)	(0.058)
University	0.000	0.000	0.001
	(0.001)	(0.001)	(0.001)
Dom. Competition	0.507***	0.507***	0.504***
	(0.017)	(0.017)	(0.024)
Size medium	0.022	0.021	−0.007
	(0.038)	(0.038)	(0.053)
Size large	0.022	0.021	0.039
	(0.051)	(0.051)	(0.072)
Observations	2653	2654	1328
R^2	0.40	0.40	0.42

Notes: Reported coefficients are from LPMs. Robust standard errors are in parentheses. Industry, country and time dummies included. *, **, *** Denote significance at 10%, 5% and 1% respectively.

Another robustness issue concerns the R&D variable, which is treated as exogenous in the innovation equations. In the results in Table 14 we treat R&D instead as endogenous, using an instrument based on the average **propensity to spend on R&D reported by other** firms in the same industry, country and year. The results show that this has no impact on the import variable, however, it does render the outsourcing variable statistically insignificant. This suggests that in the previous tables the positive coefficient on outsourcing is driven by the effect that outsourcing has on R&D and that this is not properly controlled for. Once this is taken into account, there is no direct impact of outsourcing on innovation. This suggests that outsourcing affects

Table 13. Correlation Table: Instruments and Endogenous Variables

Variables	*Average pressure to reduce costs*	*New products: dom. competition*	*Outsourcing*	*Imports*
Average pressure to reduce costs	1.000			
New products: dom. competition	0.566*	1.000		
Outsourcing	0.056*	−0.029*	1.000	
Imports	0.085*	−0.045*	0.087*	1.000

Note: * Denotes significance at 1%.

R&D and through this R&D effect also impacts on innovation. However, there is no direct impact on innovation from outsourcing, in contrast to importing.

To summarize our results for different innovation variables, we find that only outsourcing leads to a reorganization of the production process towards R&D activities. This is in line with productivity enhancements either owing to cost savings or because of superior inputs. Once R&D is controlled for, we observe a direct positive effect of importing (though not outsourcing) on innovation activities. We do not observe this effect explicitly for importing in the R&D estimations, but the firm could nevertheless undertake efforts in the production process to improve existing products or respond to changing preferences of customers. The summary statistics show, for instance, that 30% of all firms spend on R&D but that about half of all firms introduce new products or services and two thirds of all firms upgrade existing products and services. Hence, firms that change their product line do not necessarily report to have spent on R&D. Many firms might also not have their own R&D laboratory but they have measures in place that ensure quality control. We, therefore, conclude that foreign inputs as a result of, for instance, larger product variety and outsourcing involve the sourcing of specific inputs that, likely in combination with own R&D improvements, lead to higher innovation output.[13]

Model Extensions

We now turn to exploiting an important aspect of heterogeneity as an extension to our baseline model, namely different institutional variables. We consider the quality of property rights, the strength of intellectual property rights (IPR), hiring and firing practices as well as the quantity and the quality of local suppliers of the country in which the firm is located. There is great variation in these variables among the countries in our sample. We use the *Global Competitiveness Report* to group our countries into two groups with favorable and less favorable institutions.[14] We then estimate equation (1) with two additional interaction effects, namely interacting outsourcing and importing with the different institutional proxies, respectively. We treat outsourcing and importing, as well as the interaction terms as endogenous. Additional instruments are the instruments used before interacted with the institutional variables.[15] We estimate a LPM for all innovation models.

Results in Table 15 show that institutions such as property rights and intellectual property rights protection matter, in particular for importing. This is intuitively reasonable as importing involves complicated transactions and partners in more than one country. Clear property rights may therefore be important for the trade partner abroad in order to facilitate trade.

Table 14. Endogenous Outsourcing, Importing and Spending on R&D

	Newproduct LPM	*Newproduct Probit*	*Upgrading LPM*	*Upgrading Probit*
Sourcing strategy				
Outsourcing	0.159	0.226	0.053	0.116
	(0.230)	(0.241)	(0.215)	(0.212)
Imports	0.004***	0.004***	0.004***	0.005***
	(0.001)	(0.001)	(0.001)	(0.001)
Spending on R&D				
R&D	0.513***	0.524***	0.382***	0.358***
	(0.094)	(0.075)	(0.089)	(0.068)
Ownership structure				
Partnership	−0.000	−0.000	−0.030*	−0.032**
	(0.016)	(0.018)	(0.015)	(0.016)
Foreign Owners	0.001	0.001	−0.002**	−0.002**
	(0.001)	(0.001)	(0.001)	(0.001)
For. Ow. squared	−0.000	−0.000	0.000	0.000
	(0.000)	(0.000)	(0.000)	(0.000)
Gov	−0.000*	−0.001*	−0.001***	−0.001***
	(0.000)	(0.000)	(0.000)	(0.000)
Other control variables				
Exports	−0.000	−0.000	−0.000	−0.000
	(0.000)	(0.000)	(0.000)	(0.000)
Age	−0.000	−0.001	−0.000	−0.000
	(0.000)	(0.000)	(0.000)	(0.000)
Finance	−0.062***	−0.072***	−0.073***	−0.082***
	(0.019)	(0.022)	(0.018)	(0.022)
University	0.000	0.000	−0.000	−0.000
	(0.000)	(0.000)	(0.000)	(0.000)
Dom. Competition	0.015**	0.017**	0.021***	0.024***
	(0.006)	(0.007)	(0.006)	(0.006)
Size medium	0.030*	0.031	0.059***	0.060***
	(0.017)	(0.019)	(0.016)	(0.017)
Size large	−0.023	−0.029	0.011	0.012
	(0.026)	(0.029)	(0.024)	(0.027)
F-test Outsourcing	13.51		13.73	
F-test Imports	62.64		62.93	
F-test R&D	61.59		61.51	
Underidentification (p-value)	0.0000		0.0000	
Hansen J test (p-value)	0.6860		0.4194	
Exogeneity test (p-value)	0.0012	0.0000	0.0000	0.0000
Observations	8200	8200	8184	8184

Notes: We report marginal effects for Probit estimations. Robust standard errors are in parentheses. Industry, country and time dummies included. Instruments used for *Newproduct* and *Upgrading*: the average share of imports reported by other firms operating in the same industry, country and year, the average propensity to \outsource reported by other firms operating in the same industry, country and year, the average propensity to spend on R&D reported by other firms operating in the same industry, country and year and an assessment of the firm on the variable whether pressure from domestic companies, foreign companies and customers induce the firms to reduce production costs. *, **, *** Denote significance at 10%, 5% and 1% respectively.

Table 15. Extension 1: Institutions

	Newprod.	*Upgrad.*	*R&D*	*Newprod.*	*Upgrad.*	*R&D*	*Newprod.*	*Upgrad.*	*R&D*	*Newprod.*	*Upgrad.*	*R&D*	*Newprod.*	*Upgrad.*	*R&D*
Imports	0.006***	0.003***	–0.003***	0.005***	0.003***	–0.002*	0.007***	0.004***	–0.003**	0.005***	0.003***	–0.003**	0.005***	0.003***	–0.003**
	(0.001)	(0.001)	(0.001)	(0.001)	(0.001)	(0.001)	(0.001)	(0.001)	(0.001)	(0.001)	(0.001)	(0.001)	(0.001)	(0.001)	(0.001)
Outsourcing	0.129	0.109	0.027	0.135	0.169	0.127	0.166	0.194	0.114	0.329**	0.018	0.210*	0.369**	0.104	0.207
	(0.135)	(0.118)	(0.109)	(0.147)	(0.128)	(0.114)	(0.145)	(0.129)	(0.113)	(0.157)	(0.133)	(0.127)	(0.159)	(0.135)	(0.135)
Imports × Prop. rights	0.002*	0.002**	0.003***												
	(0.001)	(0.001)	(0.001)												
Outsourcing × Prop. rights	0.047	0.126	0.054												
	(0.137)	(0.123)	(0.107)												
Imports × Intell. prop. rights				0.003**	0.002***	0.000									
				(0.001)	(0.001)	(0.001)									
Outsourcing × Intell. prop. rights				–0.056	–0.112	–0.108									
				(0.138)	(0.123)	(0.107)									
Imports × Hiring firing							–0.001	–0.000	0.001*						
							(0.001)	(0.001)	(0.001)						
Outsourcing × Hiring firing							–0.035	–0.094	–0.046						
							(0.137)	(0.122)	(0.112)						
Imports × Supplier Quantity										0.001	0.002**	0.001			
										(0.001)	(0.001)	(0.001)			
Outsourcing × Supplier Quantity										0.001	0.122	–0.232*			
										(0.151)	(0.131)	(0.122)			
Imports × Supplier Quality													0.002	0.001	0.001
													(0.001)	(0.001)	(0.001)
Outsourcing × Supplier Quality													–0.062	0.031	–0.188
													(0.140)	(0.120)	(0.115)
Observations	6861	6846	7095	6861	6846	7095	6861	6846	7095	6307	6294	6525	6307	6294	6525

Notes: Reported coefficients are from LPMs using instrumental variables. Robust standard errors are in parentheses. Industry, country and time dummies included. Instruments used for *Newproduct* and *Upgrading*: the average share of imports reported by other firms operating in the same industry, country and year, a dummy for whether the propensity to outsource reported by other firms operating in the same industry, country and year is high (=1) or low (=0), an assessment of the firm on the variable whether pressure from domestic companies, foreign companies and customers induce the firms to reduce production costs and interaction terms of these three instruments with the respective institutional variables. Instruments used for *R&D*: the average share of imports reported by other firms operating in the same industry, country and year, a dummy for whether the propensity to outsource reported by other firms operating in the same industry, country and year is high (= 1) or low (= 0) and interaction terms of these two instruments with the respective institutional variables. *, **, *** Denote significance at 10%, 5% and 1% respectively.

Also, IPR might be important as firms may only engage in upgrading technology if they are ensured that they can reap the gains of such investments, i.e. if their output can be sufficiently protected. This relationship does not hold for R&D though, implying that direct complementarily between imports and innovation is IPR-sensitive. It is nevertheless a reassuring result because firms are ultimately concerned with protecting their innovation output and not R&D spending. Hiring and firing captures the flexibility of national labor markets. This institutional aspect only matters for the relationship between importing and R&D in our estimation. This may indicate that flexible labour markets are important for hiring the best talent for R&D.

Local supplier quantity and quality may be important as they facilitate importing in the first place. Importing requires a sufficient quantity of local suppliers that provide auxiliary services to importing. We find that the quantity of suppliers matters for the relationship between importing and innovation, though this is statistically significant only for product upgrading. Supplier quality does not appear to matter, which may perhaps indicate poor measurement of actual quality in the country level index we use.

Note that the interactions of institutional variables with outsourcing are generally statistically insignificant, as are the coefficients on the outsourcing variable on its own. This suggests that the specification without interactions is more appropriate for the outsourcing–innovation link. It is likely that we cannot identify more detailed results for outsourcing as we cannot quantify the amount of outsourcing and this is more likely to be reflected in the importing measure. Institutions may also be more relevant for importing as this involves partners abroad with potentially different institutional set-ups, while this is not the case for outsourcing within the same country. Lastly, it is interesting to find a negative coefficient for importing and R&D. This could suggest that imports substitute for domestic R&D in countries that are far away from the technological frontier and that institutions play a crucial role in stimulating or hampering R&D in domestic firms.

In a further extension, we distinguish firms in EU countries from firms in non-EU countries, see Table 16. The results comparing EU with non-EU countries show that the benefits in terms of innovation from importing are higher in EU than in non-EU countries, while this is not the case for outsourcing. This may indicate that complex sourcing strategies involving foreign partners, such as importing, are easier to implement within the EU because of lower trade barriers and fewer institutional impediments.[16]

5. Conclusion

This paper looks at the link between outsourcing, importing and various innovation measures using rich firm-level data for *emerging economies*. We add to a literature on gains from outsourcing that has mostly focused on industrialized countries. We also consider importing as an important channel to access goods of different variety and quality. Arguably, gaining access to foreign technology as a result og quality and variety effects may be an important motive for importing in transition economies (Crinò, 2012).

Using firm-level data for 28 transition countries from the BEEPS dataset, we find evidence that outsourcing is associated with a greater probability to spend on research and development and, through this R&D channel, to introduce new products and to upgrade existing products. Importing is as well associated with the latter two innovation measures but not with spending on research and development. This suggests that

24 *Ursula Fritsch and Holger Görg*

Table 16. Extension 2: EU vs non-EU Countries

	Newproduct	*Upgrading*	*R&D*
Sourcing strategy			
Imports	0.004***	0.004***	−0.000
	(0.001)	(0.001)	(0.001)
Outsourcing	0.069	0.058	0.131
	(0.116)	(0.109)	(0.090)
Imports × EU	0.003**	0.003**	0.001
	(0.001)	(0.001)	(0.001)
Outsourcing × EU	0.184	0.114	−0.002
	(0.123)	(0.115)	(0.096)
Ownership structure			
Partnership	−0.010	−0.037**	−0.030***
	(0.015)	(0.015)	(0.011)
Foreign Owners	0.001	−0.001	0.002*
	(0.001)	(0.001)	(0.001)
For. Ow. squared	−0.000*	0.000	−0.000**
	(0.000)	(0.000)	(0.000)
Gov	−0.001*	−0.001***	−0.000
	(0.000)	(0.000)	(0.000)
Other control variables			
Exports	−0.000*	−0.000*	0.000
	(0.000)	(0.000)	(0.000)
Age	−0.000	−0.000	0.001**
	(0.000)	(0.000)	(0.000)
R&D	0.193***	0.127***	
	(0.019)	(0.017)	
Finance	−0.077***	−0.083***	−0.039***
	(0.017)	(0.017)	(0.013)
University	0.001**	0.000	0.001***
	(0.000)	(0.000)	(0.000)
Dom. Competition	0.017***	0.023***	0.005
	(0.005)	(0.005)	(0.004)
Size medium	0.070***	0.089***	0.115***
	(0.014)	(0.013)	(0.011)
Size large	0.063***	0.074***	0.238***
	(0.018)	(0.017)	(0.015)
Observations	8233	8217	8529

Notes: Reported coefficients are from LPMs using instrumental variables. Robust standard errors are in parentheses. Industry, country and time dummies included. Instruments used for *Newproduct* and *Upgrading*: the average share of imports reported by other firms operating in the same industry, country and year, a dummy for whether the propensity to outsource reported by other firms operating in the same industry, country and year is high (=1) or low (=0), an assessment of the firm on the variable whether pressure from domestic companies, foreign companies and customers induce the firms to reduce production costs and interaction terms of these three instruments with the EU dummy. Instruments used for *R&D*: the average share of imports reported by other firms operating in the same industry, country and year, a dummy for whether the propensity to outsource reported by other firms operating in the same industry, country and year is high (=1) or low (=0) and interaction terms of these two instruments with the EU dummy. *, **, *** Denote significance at 10%, 5% and 1% respectively.

outsourcing leads to restructuring of activities towards higher value-added activities (such as R&D) while importing of better varieties/qualities of intermediate inputs has direct effects on innovation (but not R&D). We implement an instrumental variable strategy to address endogeneity concerns.

We also show that the results crucially depend on institutional characteristics. Outsourcing leads to more R&D and thus innovation activities irrespective of the institutional environment. However, institutional characteristics influence the effects of importing. Good institutions related to property rights, intellectual property rights protection and quantity of suppliers increase the benefits that firms may reap from importing. This may not be too surprising, as good institutions facilitate trade. We also show that there are pronounced differences between EU and non-EU member states. Our findings suggest that being an EU-member increases the positive effects of importing on innovation. Complex sourcing strategies, such as importing, should be easier to implement within the EU owing to lower trade barriers and fewer institutional impediments. These are important findings for policy makers.

References

Abramovsky, Laura and Rachel Griffith, "Outsourcing and Offshoring of Business Services: How Important is ICT?" *Journal of the European Economic Association* 4 (2006):594–601.

Aghion, Philippe, Nick Bloom, Richard Blundell, Rachel Griffith, and Peter Howitt, "Competition and Innovation: An Inverted-U Relationship," *The Quarterly Journal of Economics* 120 (2005):701–28.

Aghion, Philippe, Richard Blundell, Rachel Griffith, Peter Howitt, and Susanne Prantl, "Entry and Productivity Growth: Evidence from Microlevel Panel Data," *Journal of the European Economic Association* 2 (2004):265–76.

Amiti, Mary and Jozef Konings, "Trade Liberalization, Intermediate Inputs, and Productivity: Evidence from Indonesia," *American Economic Review* 97 (2007):1611–38.

Antràs, Pol and Elhanan Helpman, "Global Sourcing," *Journal of Political Economy* 112 (2004):552–80.

Arvanitis, Spyros and Euripidis N. Loukis, "Outsourcing and Firm Performance—A Comparative Study of Swiss and Greek Firms," *Industrial and Corporate Change* 22 (2013):771–806.

Bas, Maria, "Input-trade Liberalization and Firm Export Decisions: Evidence from Argentina," *Journal of Development Economics* 97 (2012):481–93.

Bernard, Andrew B., J. Bradford Jensen, Stephen J. Redding, and Peter K. Schott, "Firms in International Trade," *Journal of Economic Perspectives* 21 (2007):105–30.

Bloom, Nicholas, Mirko Draca, and John Van Reenen, "Trade Induced Technical Change: The Impact of Chinese Imports on Innovation, Diffusion and Productivity," *Review of Economic Studies*, forthcoming.

Chen, Bo and Hong Ma, "Import Variety and Welfare Gain in China," *Review of International Economics* 20 (2012):807–820.

Correa, Paulo G., Ana M. Fernandes, and Chris J. Uregian, "Technology Adoption and the Investment Climate: Firm-level Evidence for Eastern Europe and Central Asia," *World Bank Economic Review* 24 (2010):121–47.

Crinò, Rosario, "Imported Inputs and Skill Upgrading," *Labour Economics* 19 (2012):957–69.

Criscuolo, Chiara, Jonathan E. Haskel, and Matthew J. Slaughter, "Global Engagement and the Innovation Activities of Firms," *International Journal of Industrial Organization* 28 (2010):191–202.

Cusmano, Lucia, Maria Luisa Mancusi, and Andrea Morrison, "Innovation and the Geographical and Functional Dimensions of Outsourcing: Evidence from Italian Firm-level Data," *Structural Change and Economic Dynamics* 20 (2009):183–95.

26 *Ursula Fritsch and Holger Görg*

Egger, Hartmut and Peter Egger, "Outsourcing and Skill-specific Employment in a Small Open Economy: Austria after the Fall of the Iron Curtain," *Oxford Economic Papers* 55 (2003): 625–43.

Fisman, Raymond and Jakob Svensson, "Are Corruption and Taxation Really Harmful to Growth? Firm Level Evidence," *Journal of Development Economics* 83 (2007):63–75.

Girma, Sourafel and Holger Görg, "Outsourcing, Foreign Ownership, and Productivity: Evidence from UK Establishment-level Data," *Review of International Economics* 12 (2004):817–32.

Girma, Sourafel, Yundan Gong, and Holger Görg, "Foreign Direct Investment, Access to Finance, and Innovation Activity in Chinese Enterprises," *World Bank Economic Review* 22 (2008):367–82.

Glass, Amy Jocelyn and Kamal Saggi, "Innovation and Wage Effects of International Outsourcing," *European Economic Review* 45 (2001):67–86.

Goldberg, Pinelopi Koujianou, Amit Kumar Khandelwal, Nina Pavcnik, and Petia Topalova, "Imported Intermediate Inputs and Domestic Product Growth: Evidence from India," *The Quarterly Journal of Economics* 125 (2010):1727–67.

Görg, Holger and Aoife Hanley, "Services Outsourcing and Innovation: An Empirical Investigation," *Economic Inquiry* 49 (2011):321–33.

Gorodnichenko, Yuriy, Jan Svejnar, and Katherine Terrell, "Globalization and Innovation in Emerging Markets," *American Economic Journal: Macroeconomics* 2 (2010):194–226.

Hall, Bronwyn H., "The Financing of Research and Development," *Oxford Review of Economic Policy* 18 (2002):35–51.

Halpern, László, Miklós Koren, and Adam Szeidl, "Imports and Productivity," CEPR discussion papers 5139, London (2005).

Hoskisson, Robert E., Richard A. Johnson, Laszlo Tihanyi, and Robert E. White, "Diversified Business Groups and Corporate Refocusing in Emerging Economies," *Journal of Management* 31 (2005):941–65.

Kasahara, Hiroyuki and Beverly Lapham, "Productivity and the Decision to Import and Export: Theory and Evidence," *Journal of International Economics* 89 (2013):297–316.

Kasahara, Hiroyuki and Joel Rodrigue, "Does the Use of Imported Intermediates Increase Productivity? Plant-level Evidence," *Journal of Development Economics* 87 (2008):106–18.

Koopman, Robert, Zhi Wang, and Shang-Jin Wei, "Tracing Value-added and Double Counting in Gross Exports," *American Economic Review* 104 (2014):459–94.

Lin, Chen, Ping Lin, and Frank Song, "Property Rights Protection and Corporate R&D: Evidence from China," *Journal of Development Economics* 93 (2010):49–62.

Lin, Chen, Ping Lin, Frank M. Song, and Chuntao Li, "Managerial Incentives, CEO Characteristics and Corporate Innovation in China's Private Sector," *Journal of Comparative Economics* 39 (2011):176–90.

Marjit, Sugata and Arijit Mukherjee, "International Outsourcing and R&D: Long-run Implications for Consumers," *Review of International Economics* 16 (2008):1010–22

Melitz, Marc J., "The Impact of Trade on Intra-industry Reallocations and Aggregate Industry Productivity," *Econometrica* 71 (2003):1695–725.

Miroudot, Sébastien, Rainer Lanz, and Alexandros Ragoussis, "Trade in Intermediate Goods and Services," OECD Trade Policy working papers 93, Paris (2009).

Muûls, Mirabelle and Mauro Pisu, "Imports and Exports at the Level of the Firm: Evidence from Belgium," *The World Economy* 32 (2009):692–734.

Rodríguez-Clare, Andrés, "Offshoring in a Ricardian World," *American Economic Journal: Macroeconomics* 2 (2010):227–58.

Seker, Murat, "Importing, Exporting, and Innovation in Developing Countries," *Review of International Economics* 20 (2012):299–314.

Siedschlag, Iulia, Neill Killeen, Donal Smith, and Catriona O'Brien, "Internationalisation and the Innovation Activities of Services Firms," ESRI Series 406, Economic and Social Research Institute, Dublin (2011).

Topalova, Petia and Amit Khandelwal, "Trade Liberalization and Firm Productivity: The Case of India," *The Review of Economics and Statistics* 93 (2011):995–1009.

UNCTAD, "World Investment Report 2005: Transnational Corporations and the Internationalization of R&D," United Nations, Geneva (2005).

Notes

1. Note that Marjit and Mukherjee (2008) model outsourcing and R&D as either substitutes or complements. Hence, the effect is *a priori* unclear.

2. Our paper also relates and contributes to other studies that look specifically at the link between innovation and outsourcing—e.g. Görg and Hanley (2011) for Ireland and Cusmano et al. (2009) for Italy. Bloom et al. (forthcoming) have a related paper that looks at the impact of Chinese imports on productivity and innovation in 12 advanced European countries. Arvanitis and Loukis (2013) relate various forms of outsourcing to product and process innovation. Abramovsky and Griffith (2006) use British data to investigate the link between ICT investment and outsourcing.

3. The EBRD–World Bank Business Environment and Enterprise Performance Survey (BEEPS) is carried out by the European Bank for Reconstruction and Development (EBRD) and the World Bank. For detailed information on the BEEPS dataset, for instance the questionnaires and the report on sampling and implementation, see http://www.ebrd.com/pages/research/analysis/surveys/beeps.shtml.

4. Our innovation measures are different from innovation measures previously deployed in studies that use BEEPS data. This is because these studies use data from 2005 and 2002 only and because different waves of the survey offer different innovation measures (e.g. Correa et al., 2010; Gorodnichenko et al., 2010; Crinò, 2012).

5. We only control for R&D when considering innovation measured as the introduction of a new product or product upgrading.

6. We included lagged productivity for $t - 3$ computed as log(*sales*/*workers* + 1) in the baseline regression. The results show that lagged productivity matters for R&D, but is highly insignificant for the other innovation measures. Including lagged productivity does not qualitatively change the results but is, in our view, a flawed measure as it is not defined in terms of value added. Results are available from the authors upon request.

7. A number of papers use similar instrumentation strategies, see, e.g. Fisman and Svensson (2007) for industry–location averages of bribes, Lin et al. (2010) for industry–location averages of contract enforcement and government expropriation, Gorodnichenko et al. (2010) for industry–location averages of foreign competition, Lin et al. (2011) for industry–location averages of chief executive officer (CEO) incentive measures.

8. We also estimated an alternative specification with country–industry dummies instead of separate sets of country and industry dummies. This does not change the results. Results are not reported here to save space.

9. Note that, if weak instruments were a problem, this would lead to the estimates being biased towards the OLS estimates. However, as we show, the IV estimates differ significantly from the OLS estimates.

10. One possible explanation for the weaker result on finance in the IV regression is that finance negatively correlates with both innovation and outsourcing/importing. The latter result is evident from the unreported first stage results, which show a robust and strong negative coefficient for finance. If our proposed instruments are correlated with confounding factors such as economic development/institutions, then this variation is captured in the second stage of the IV estimation by offshoring/importing and this reduces the impact of the finance variable. We are confident that these effects are not too strong though as the estimated coefficients on finance in the second stage are only slightly reduced for innovation output.

11. We construct the instrument based on all available observations, not just the observations that are part of the final sample.

28 *Ursula Fritsch and Holger Görg*

12. We also test whether our results are sensitive to the inclusion of the cost reduction instrument. Results using only two instruments in the *Newproduct* and *Upgrading* specifications are broadly similar to results using all three instruments. Results can be obtained upon request.
13. It is noteworthy that foreign technology can affect innovation patterns through multiple channels and importing is just one channel. It may, for example, also happen through sourcing inputs from foreign multinationals located in the countries, or from firms being part of large diversified business groups. Unfortunately, we do not have information on individual sourcing behavior and therefore cannot test this hypothesis directly. However, research in the management literature (Hoskisson et al., 2005) discuss the importance of such "business groups" in emerging economies and highlight the role played by firms with foreign ownership within such groups. In our data, such local sourcing would be picked up by our outsourcing variable.
14. The *Global Competitiveness Report* presents country rankings based on hard data and survey data carried out in 2001, 2004 and 2007. We compute the median value over all country–year observations for which data is available and use the median as cut off. This means that countries can switch classification between years. A list of country groupings is available from the authors upon request.
15. We use a slightly different instrument for outsourcing: a dummy for whether the propensity to outsource reported by other firms operating in the same industry, country and year is high (=1) or low (=0). We split the sample, for this purpose, at the median value of all country–industry–year observations. We subsequently interact this dummy with the institutional variables. The instruments pass the usual tests for instrument relevance and validity. We do not report these in the table to save space but they can be obtained upon request.
16. Note that this does not hold for R&D. This highlights that the differentiation between R&D and innovation output is crucial. It also suggests that R&D might not cover all innovation activities that firms engage in.

Chapter II.6

Does Outsourcing Increase Profitability?*

HOLGER GÖRG
University of Nottingham and DIW Berlin

AOIFE HANLEY
University of Nottingham

Abstract: We investigate the relationship between outsourcing and profitability paying particular attention to the endogeneity of outsourcing. The empirical analysis uses unique plant level data for the electronics sector in Ireland. A particular feature of the data is that it records detailed information for 12 electronics sub-sectors covering both manufacturing and services activities. We distinguish outsourcing of materials from outsourcing of services inputs. We find that plants that are substantially larger than the mean employment size benefit from outsourcing materials while this does not appear to be the case for small plants. Results for outsourcing of services are not as clear-cut, however.

I INTRODUCTION

Both the popular press and academic literature have recently covered the growth of outsourcing or contracting out, of business activities and its economic implications. While Heshmati (2003) in his recent survey points out that there is no general definition or measurement of outsourcing, he broadly describes it as *...different kinds of corporate action related to all subcontracting relationships between firms and the hiring of workers in non-traditional jobs* (p. 99). Outsourcing may provide a viable strategy if firms aim to save on labour costs (Abraham and Taylor, 1996), exploit production differentials both within the services sector and between services and manufacturing (Fixler and Siegel, 1999), or take advantage of globalisation

Paper presented at the Eighteenth Annual Conference of the Irish Economic Association, Belfast, 2004.

*We are grateful to Forfás for the provision of the data and to David Paton, Don Siegel and participants at the IEA 2004 conference, in particular John Sutton, and an anonymous referee for very helpful comments. The usual disclaimer applies. Holger Görg acknowledges financial support from the Leverhulme Trust (Programme Grant F114/BF).

(Feenstra and Hanson, 1999). According to an article in the *Financial Times, Subcontracting as many non-core activities as possible is a central element of the new economy.*[1]

A fundamental question to ask is whether outsourcing is value enhancing and, in particular, whether the firm that undertakes outsourcing shows higher profitability as a result. Essentially this question renders down to the transactions cost question regularly posed to university undergraduates: should a firm manufacture its own inputs by some form of vertical merger or should it seek to obtain possibly more competitively priced inputs on the open market? While the viability of vertical mergers as a determinant of profitability is comparatively well researched, less work has been undertaken on the viability of pursuing a less integrated strategy, namely of outsourcing inputs.[2]

Recent evidence from practitioners casts some doubt on the benefits to outsourcing. A UK survey by Manpower focusing on the benefits accruing to firms from offshoring services, found that 68 per cent of firms outsource at least some services, the main motivation being cost reduction.[3] However, in a recent survey, 56 per cent of IT specialists claimed that outsourced IT work was at least inferior to that produced in-house. More worryingly, 11 per cent reported that the outsourced work actually induced a setback to the firm's production.[4] Accordingly, in the popular press one appears to have arrived at a point where experts begin to question the validity of outsourcing as a long-term strategy or even short term as a cost reduction exercise.

To the best of our knowledge, there is only a very limited number of more rigorous statistical or econometric studies looking at this issue. The evidence that has been produced in such papers, however, suggests that the value-enhancing link between outsourcing and profitability is not clearly established. Specifically, Kimura (2002) does not find any evidence that subcontracting leads to higher profits in Japanese manufacturing firms. Differentiating between outsourcing of services and non-services inputs, Görzig and Stephan (2002) find that outsourcing of materials is positively correlated with profits, while there is a negative relationship between profitability and outsourced services for a sample of German manufacturing firms.

[1] *Financial Times*, 31 July 2001, p. 10. Feenstra (1998) provides an excellent overview of the increase in outsourcing activities worldwide.

[2] See Bhuyan (2002) for a recent analysis of whether vertical mergers induce higher profits or Knarvik and Steen (2002) for an investigation of whether vertical mergers induce other positive externalities through agglomeration effects.

[3] http://www.manpower.co.uk/news/OutsourcingSurvey.pdf

[4] *Software Development Magazine,* January 2004 issue.

Motivated by the benefits to outsourcing claimed by some practitioners and the corresponding lack of any direct evidence as to the truth behind these assertions, we aim to establish whether outsourcing does indeed raise profitability.[5] We use unique plant level panel data for the electronics sector in the Republic of Ireland. Ireland represents an interesting case study for outsourcing as noted by Ruane and Görg (2001), who document the increasing growth in outsourcing in the electronics sector for the Irish economy.[6] The novelty of our data stems from the fact that we can distinguish 12 electronics sub-sectors which cover both manufacturing and services activities. Also, we have detailed information on outsourcing activities at the plant level. Furthermore, in comparison to the study by Görzig and Stephan (2002) which is the one most closely related to ours, we pay particular attention to the possible endogeneity of outsourcing and profitability. We attempt to circumvent this problem by using an instrumental variable approach, implemented using a General Method of Moments (GMM) estimator.

The remainder of the paper is structured as follows. The following section briefly discusses recent literature on firms' decisions to outsource, in order to provide the context for our subsequent empirical analysis. The data are described in Section III. Section IV outlines the econometric methodology and discusses the results. Finally, Section V presents some conclusions.

II OUTSOURCING AND PROFITABILITY

Essentially outsourcing addresses the issue as to whether a firm should make or buy intermediate inputs; an issue that has a long tradition in economics, dating back to the seminal work by Coase (1937) on the boundaries of a firm. Since then, a large body of literature has been concerned with analysing the determinants of this "make-or-buy decision", focusing on the role of incomplete contracts, specific assets and transactions costs (e.g., Williamson, 1975; Grossman and Hart, 1986; Bolton and Whinston, 1993). In a nutshell, firms would prefer to "buy" as opposed to "make" as long as the cost of outsourcing is lower than in-house production. Hence, outsourcing can be used to economise on production cost, in particular labour cost (Abraham and

[5] Note that, in this paper, we do not distinguish domestic from international outsourcing, but concern ourselves with outsourcing in general. In a related paper, Görg *et al.* (2004) investigate whether international outsourcing (imported intermediates) is associated with higher productivity in the outsourcing plant, using data for manufacturing plants in Ireland.

[6] This growth was revealed using plant level data on input purchasing behaviour of computer manufacturers where the ratio of bought-in materials to total sales has risen significantly over the past decade, a sign that firms revert increasingly to outsourcing their inputs rather than opting to produce them in-house.

Taylor, 1996) by substituting in-house production with the buying-in of components. The cost of outsourcing is not only determined by the price of the bought-in components, but also by transaction costs due to transport and incomplete contracting costs, and the possible implications of asset specificity for supplier and/or customer.

In a recent paper, Grossman and Helpman (2002) provide a comprehensive theoretical analysis of firms' outsourcing decisions. In their model, firms decide whether to be vertically integrated or to outsource production of components to specialised producers. This involves a search process, whereby final good producers search for subcontractors and vice versa. There is incomplete information – subcontractors cannot easily signal their quality – and therefore a potential for a hold-up problem arises. *Inter alia*, Grossman and Helpman (2002) show that the viability of outsourcing is determined by the distribution of bargaining power between the two parties involved, the degree of competition in the market, and the number of potential partners in the market.

Taking this as a theoretical background, one may expect that the benefits from outsourcing are not always the same, but in particular depend on the characteristics of the firm and industry in question. Large firms may be in a better position to achieve high bargaining power *vis-à-vis* suppliers and may hence be better able to benefit from outsourcing. Also, large firms may face lower search costs as they may be better established in the market and have better knowledge of competitors and suppliers than small establishments.

In terms of industry characteristics, if there are more potential subcontractors in the industry, if the bargaining power is tilted towards the final good producers, or if the level of competition is high among subcontractors, final good producers are more likely to find outsourcing a viable strategy. While this is difficult to address in formal empirical work (as opposed to case studies) due to data constraints, our data set possesses one advantageous characteristic that allows us to have at least a first cut at this question.

From our data set, we can distinguish outsourcing of tangible materials and components from outsourcing of services activities. For the latter, one may expect that many of the services are non-traded and therefore localised with possibly only a small number of potential suppliers and low degrees of competition. Hence, one may expect the benefits (if any) from services outsourcing to be lower than the outsourcing of tangible (and tradable) components. This theoretical prior is corroborated by Görzig and Stephan (2002) who use German data for a sample of large companies to examine the benefits of outsourcing. They find that firms that engage in materials outsourcing experience benefits, in terms of increased returns per employee, while services outsourcing induces a negative effect on measured returns. This, they infer, is due to the non-transparent way in which outsourced services are priced *vis-à-vis* more tangible inputs. They conclude that while the markets for intermediate products appear to function, outsourced services may be subject to certain inefficiencies.[7]

In related work, Kimura (2002) discovers that poorly performing firms (low surplus to sales and low value added to sales) are more likely to use subcontractors, in an analysis of the Japanese machinery manufacturing industry. He concludes that profits are highest for those firms that do not get involved in any type of subcontracting, whether as a supplier or as an outsourcer. These results, accordingly, are in line with the findings for Germany by Görzig and Stephan (2002).

III DATA

In order to investigate the relationship between outsourcing and profits we use plant level data for the electronics industry in Ireland. This industry has undergone rapid growth in the Irish economy, in particular in the 1990s. As Ruane and Görg (2001) document, employment in the sector has increased threefold between 1984 and 1997, from roughly 7,300 to 22,700. Most of this growth arose during the mid-1990s; in 1994, total industry employment was only approximately 11,700. One striking feature is that the majority of firms operating in this industry are subsidiaries of foreign owned multinationals; they accounted for over 85 per cent of employment in 1997. The importance of multinationals in this sector is not least due to policies directed towards foreign firms. Ruane and Görg (2001) note that the Irish Development Authority (IDA Ireland) identified the electronics industry as a potential source of growth for the Irish economy as far back as the mid-1970s. This judgement was in part based on the perceived potential for outsourcing activities in that sector. Such outsourcing potential was expected to raise the scope for domestic Irish, as well as foreign companies to supply to final goods producers, thereby allowing the location of various stages of the production

[7] Interestingly, they draw attention to the need to focus on profitability rather than efficiency alone. Higher wages, while inducing higher efficiency (output per worker) lowered overall profitability. This result was arrived at because the net effect of higher wages was to increase the cost of labour inputs to an extent that diminished overall profitability. Hence efficiency, as noted by Grossman and Helpman (2002), is not always the most appropriate indicator of how a firm is performing. Girma and Görg (2004) provide a firm level analysis of the effect of outsourcing on efficiency (i.e., productivity) in the UK.

process in the country.[8] Currently, electronics firms located in Ireland include such high-profile names as IBM, Microsoft, Intel etc.

The data used in this analysis are taken from the *Irish Economy Expenditure Survey*, undertaken annually by Forfás, the government agency with responsibility for enterprise development, science and technology. The survey provides anonymised plant level information on output, employment, profitability, nationality of ownership and industry, as well as details on plants' expenditure on labour, materials, and service inputs.[9,10]

The survey is sent out to all plants with thirty or more employees based in Ireland in either the manufacturing or internationally traded services sectors. Response rates are generally good; plants responding to the survey account for around 60-80 per cent of employment of the target population each year (O'Malley, 1995). The exclusion of small plants with less than 30 employees from the sample, precludes us from investigating how outsourcing affects small firms in particular, and this factor has to be kept in mind for the subsequent interpretation of our results.

While the survey has been undertaken by Forfás since 1982, an examination of the data showed that for our purposes, information on outsourcing and profitability has only been available since 1990. Accordingly, we use electronics sector data for the period 1990 to 1995. These data are classified into 12 sub-sectors of electronics, which cover both manufacturing and service activities, making the dataset quite unique. These sub-sectors are: Computers; Consumer Electronics; Electronic Components; Instrumentation; Networking & Data Communication; Printed Circuit Board Assembly (PCBA); Peripherals & Media; Semiconductors; Software Development; Software Production; Telecommunications and IT Services.[11] The inclusion of both manufacturing and services sub-sectors makes the dataset particularly interesting for our analysis.[12] All in all, there are 215 plants included in the sample, although the structure of the panel is highly unbalanced.

[8] See also White (2000) for an excellent insiders-view on Irish industrial policy towards multinationals.

[9] Unfortunately, the nature of our data does not allow us to distinguish between inputs sourced from other plants within the same firm, and inputs sourced from other sources.

[10] All nominal variables are deflated using an output price deflator available from the Irish Central Statistics Office.

[11] IT Services include IT related services not included in the other sub-sectors, such as Systems Integration, IT Consulting and training and education.

[12] The availability of data for this six year period is of course limiting, as fragmentation activities can be expected to have expanded considerably over the last two decades. However, our data still cover a period over which there has been variation in outsourcing activities, which we pick up in our data. Also, this is the period over which there was a rapid growth of the electronics industry, as discussed by Ruane and Görg (2001).

The main variables of interest are outsourcing and profitability at the level of the plant. The former is measured as the ratio of externally sourced inputs to value added in the plant, thus giving us a measure of the importance of bought-in intermediates in the production process. Specifically, we calculate three measures of outsourcing. Total outsourcing is defined as the ratio of total bought-in inputs over value added. As alluded to earlier, another advantage of our data is that we can distinguish intermediate inputs into raw materials and components (referred to as materials) and services inputs. We can therefore calculate two more disaggregated measures of outsourcing, namely, the ratio of bought-in tangible materials and components over value added, and the ratio of bought-in services inputs over value added. With regard to the latter measure, services inputs are comprised of other direct and indirect costs, excluding materials, wages, rent, interest payments and depreciation. This includes contracted out services, such as consultancy, maintenance, security, cleaning, catering etc. An increase in these outsourcing ratios indicates an increasing importance of outsourcing for production in the plant, as more inputs are purchased for further processing.

The measure of profitability is calculated as the ratio of net profits (i.e., total sales – total costs) over total output. Total costs includes all direct and indirect costs accruing to the plant. Table 1 shows some summary statistics on outsourcing of intermediary and materials inputs (*O1*) and services inputs (*O2*) respectively. *O1* is noted for its higher ratio of inputs to value added compared to *O2*. It is possible that the higher ratios registered for *O1* inputs, are due to a higher degree of vertical integration in materials inputs *vis-à-vis* services inputs. Overall, the median value of the *O1* ratio just exceeds unity (1.18) and the overall average ratio is 2.28, indicating that values in the upper tail of the distribution are driving the average value up. The corresponding values for *O2* inputs are 0.40 and 0.97 respectively. We would expect services inputs to exhibit lower values given their invariably ancillary function in industry.[13] However, firms with strong affiliations to suppliers in a value chain, to the extent that they are fully integrated, should be expected to register high values for the *O1* ratio where components are purchased from an intermediary.[14]

We are unable to disclose detailed summary statistics for the profitability measure due to confidentiality reasons. The raw correlations between profits

[13] Abraham and Taylor (1996) outline types of business services received and include supportive services such as accounting, auditing and bookkeeping and services to buildings in addition to more direct inputs such as personnel supply services.

[14] In Table A1 in the Appendix we present further summary statistics for the two outsourcing measures, disaggregated by the electronics sub-sector. The figures show that there is a wide variability in the extent of outsourcing across electronics sub-sectors.

Table 1: *Breakdown of Outsourcing to Value Added Ratios for O1 and O2*

Year	*Mean*	*Std. Dev.*	*Variance*	*Median*	*Obs*
	O1 Materials and Intermediate Product Inputs				
1990	2.04	5.28	27.88	1.07	82
1991	2.01	6.55	42.95	1.11	111
1992	1.81	2.22	4.94	1.12	120
1993	3.43	10.96	120.2	1.2	114
1994	1.96	2.63	6.92	1.19	116
1995	2.44	3.96	15.69	1.29	114
	O2 Services Inputs				
1990	0.77	2.03	4.14	0.4	82
1991	0.90	2.83	8	0.38	131
1992	1.20	5.87	34.41	0.36	122
1993	1.28	4.27	18.23	0.4	131
1994	0.81	1.25	1.55	0.44	131
1995	0.88	1.42	2.01	0.42	131

Source: Own calculations based on *Irish Economy Expenditure Survey* data.

and *O1* and profits and *O2* are –0.13 and –0.16 respectively, and the correlation between *O1* and *O2* is 0.21 (all statistically significant at the 1 per cent level).

In Table 2 we present further summary statistics for the outsourcing variables, as well as for average employment and the capital-sales ratio (which are covariates included in the empirical model below). We distinguish the overall means, as well as means for 'high profitability' and 'low profitability' plants in order to highlight differences between these two groups of plants. For illustrative purposes, the former category is simply defined as plants demonstrating at least median profitability levels, while low profitability establishments are those with less than median profitability. As we can see, highly profitable firms tend to use more outsourcing in general. A simple t-test for the equality of means for the two groups of plants can be rejected. Note, however, that low profitability plants are on average larger (in terms of employment levels) than the other group of plants.

The differences in outsourcing usage between these two groups of plants are further highlighted in Figures 1 to 3. These graphs chart the distribution of outsourcing intensities of plants in high and low profitability categories for total, materials and services outsourcing respectively. The accompanying table containing the actual proportions used to generate these cross-sections is contained in Table A2 in the Appendix.

If low and high profitability plants demonstrated no difference in

Table 2: *Comparison of Outsourcing Intensity and Other Control Variables Across High and Low Profit Plants*

	Low Profitability Mean Std.	*High Profitability Mean Std.*	*Overall Mean Mean Std.*	*p-value for t-test that* $\bar{x}_{highprofit} = \bar{x}_{lowprofit}$ *(unequal variance assumed)*	*No. Obs*
Materials outsourcing (outs1)	1.49	3.19	2.29	*(0.0007)*	657
	1.718	*8.534*	*6.040*		
Services outsourcing (outs2)	0.58	1.42	0.98	*(0.0011)*	728
	1.065	*4.715*	*3.40*		
Total outsourcing (outs3)	1.96	4.20	3.05	*(0.0007)*	728
	2.203	*12.136*	*8.675*		
Capital-sales ratio	0.49	0.47	0.48	*(0.5380)*	632
	0.395	*0.424*	*0.410*		
Employment	214.88	83.46	150.96	*(0.0000)*	728
	272	*136*	*227*		

Source: Own calculations based on *Irish Economy Expenditure Survey* data.

outsourcing intensity, they would both register equal proportions (i.e. 50 per cent) across all intensity quartiles. However, we see that certain biases emerge depending on (a) the nature of the outsourcing and (b) the level of the outsourcing intensity. Accordingly, we see in Figure 1 that of those establishments engaged in high level outsourcing (4th quartile), a disproportionate number (62 per cent) belong to the low profit group. Overall therefore, outsourcing appears to be an activity in which low profit plants are particularly active.

Moving to Figures 2 and 3, we now examine the composition of establishments according to the *nature* of outsourcing i.e. whether we are dealing with materials or services outsourcing respectively. Consistent with what we have seen in Figure 1, a disproportionate percentage of plants in the highest intensity category (4th quartile) belong to the low profit category. This proportion is 60 and 68 per cent for materials and services outsourcing respectively. Accordingly, the nature of the outsourcing activity does matter. It appears that of plants actively engaged in high level outsourcing, disproportionately more exhibit low profitability.

This profits discrepancy is more striking when non-tangible as opposed to tangible inputs are outsourced, a fact we infer from the disproportionate percentage of low profits plants engaged in services outsourcing. Staying with the issue of services outsourcing, accompanying the disproportionate activity of low profit plants in the fourth quartile, is a relatively weak showing in the lowest outsourcing intensity category (1st quartile). Here we see that a mere 23 per cent of establishments belong to the low profit group while a disproportionate proportion (77 per cent) belong to the high profit category.

Figure 1: *Net Profits by Total Outsourcing Intensity*

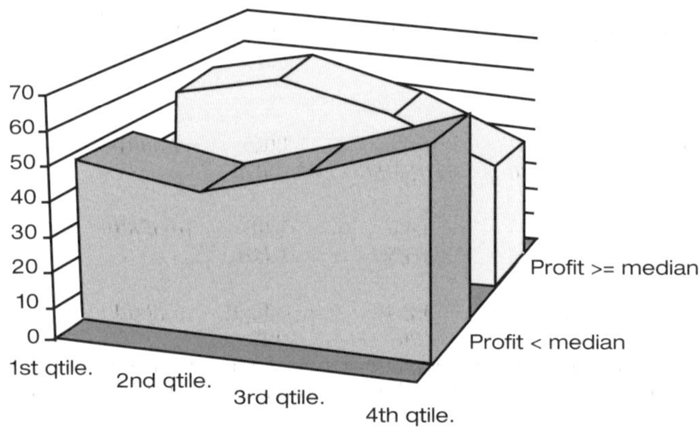

Figure 2: *Net Profits by Materials Outsourcing Intensity*

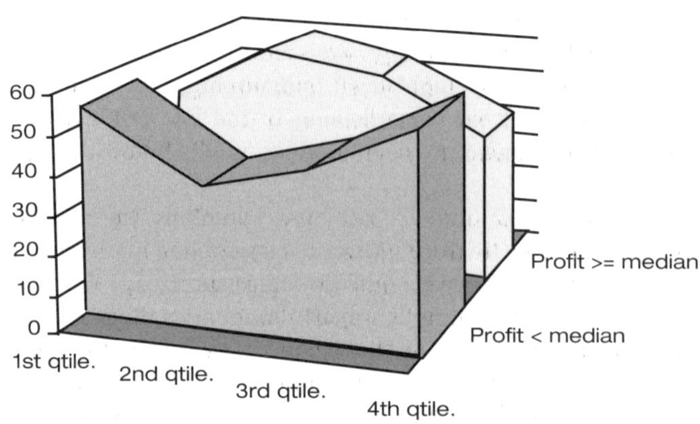

Figure 3: *Net Profits by Services Outsourcing Intensity*

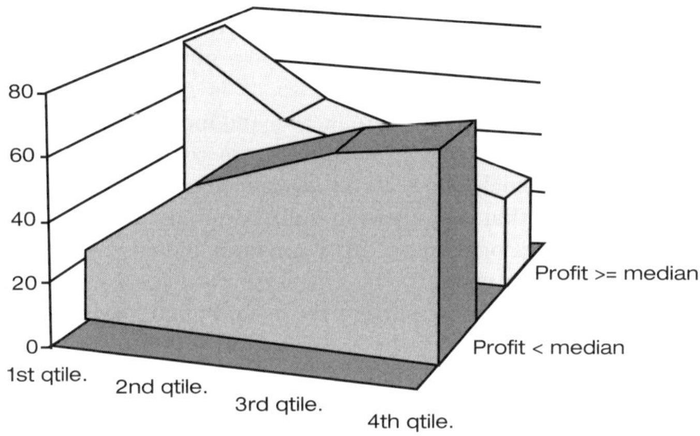

IV ECONOMETRIC ANALYSIS

The analysis of simple summary statistics does, of course, not allow us to isolate the possible effects on profitability of other covariates. In order to disentangle the effect of outsourcing and other factors on plant profitability, we turn to an econometric analysis. We start off with a profit function which we formulate in levels in order to explain profitability in plant i at time t, Π_{it}

$$\ln \Pi_{it} = \beta_1 + \beta_1 O_{it} + \beta_2 \ln ksr_{it} + \beta_3 \ln employ_{it} + \beta_3 \ln netgr_{jt} + \alpha_j + v_t + \mu_i + \varepsilon_{it} \quad (1)$$

where O_{it} is one of the measures of outsourcing as defined above, ksr_{it} is the capital-to-sales ratio (where capital is measured as capital employed, i.e., working capital), $employ_{it}$ is establishment size measured in terms of employment, and $netgr_{jt}$ is the net annual growth rate (measured in terms of employment) of the electronics sub-sector j. Furthermore, α_j and v_t are full sets of sector and time dummies, μ_i is a plant specific time invariant effect, and ε_{it} is the remaining error term which allows for heteroskedasticity as well as an unspecified correlation within but not across establishments.[15]

It is important to point out that the specification in (1) is not based on any particular theoretical framework. It is thus of a purely descriptive nature and

[15] The plant specific effect captures, *inter alia*, the nationality of the plant in order to allow for the possible profitability advantage of foreign-owned plants (e.g., Kumar, 1990).

meant to give some indication as to what attributes impact on plant profitability. Profits, of course, depend on barriers to entry (e.g, Shepherd, 1972, Domowitz *et al.*, 1987). The capital-to-sales ratio is, therefore, included in the model in order to control for differences in profits across plants that are due to differences in capital intensity. Also, it is frequently found in the literature that large firms are more productive and more profitable than small establishments (e.g., Audretsch, 1995), hence, we control for establishment size in the empirical model. The sectoral net growth rate is included in order to account for the fact that fast growing industries may allow plants to reap higher profits, as additional entry in a growing industry may not affect incumbents' profits negatively.

In order to purge the time invariant sector and plant specific effects from the estimation we first difference the equation and obtain

$$\Delta \ln \Pi_{it} = \lambda_1 \Delta O_{it} + \lambda_2 \Delta \ln ksr_{it} + \lambda_3 \Delta \ln employ_{it} + \lambda_4 \Delta \; netgr_{it} + v_t + u_{it} \qquad (2)$$

From the discussion in Section II we would not expect the coefficient λ_1 to be equal across different establishment types. In particular, we may expect differences in the returns to outsourcing for small and large plants. In particular, large establishments may be in a better bargaining position than small establishments *vis-à-vis* their suppliers and, hence, may be better able to reap benefits from outsourcing. In order to allow for this difference we interact ΔO with log employment size in the empirical implementation of the model. One further point to note is that by estimating Equation (2) on our six year panel we can only capture short-run effects of outsourcing on profitability. This should be kept in mind for the interpretation of results.

The results of simple OLS regressions of Equation (2) including the interaction term are presented in columns (1) to (4) in Table 3. Column (1) shows the results for estimating Equation (2) including total outsourcing, whereas columns (2) and (3) distinguish outsourcing of materials and intermediate components from outsourcing of services activities, as defined in Section III. Column (4) presents results including both materials and services outsourcing jointly.

Examining, firstly, the coefficients on the explanatory variables, we find that employment size of the plant shows the expected positive signs, although the coefficients are statistically insignificant. The sectoral growth rate also returns statistically insignificant coefficients. Surprisingly, the capital-to-sales ratio returns a statistically significant negative result. This is contrary to expectations, if *ksr* is taken as a proxy for barriers to entry. However, much of the entry by foreign firms into Irish manufacturing has been in capital and technology intensive industries (see Barry and Bradley, 1997); this entry which would lead to reductions in profit margins could be reflected in our findings.[16]

Turning to the results on the effect of outsourcing on profits, we observe a negative effect from total outsourcing. However, the positive and statistically significant coefficient on the outsourcing and (log) employment size interaction term shows that for larger plants increased outsourcing is associated with higher profits. This also holds when distinguishing materials and services outsourcing, see the results in columns (2) and (3). However, when including both materials and services outsourcing jointly in the estimation, then the signs on services outsourcing switch, while materials outsourcing still returns the same result (column 4).[17] This indicates that there are important interactions between services and materials outsourcing. When controlling for materials outsourcing, there are no benefits from services outsourcing for large firms.

Before interpreting these results further we need to address an econometric concern. Specifically, one potential problem with the estimations in Table 3 is that there may be a potential endogeneity problem in the profitability-outsourcing relationship that is not accounted for. For example, it may be the case that badly performing plants decide to outsource part of the production process in order to boost profits further, or that further unobserved variables drive the outsourcing-profitability relationship. In order to deal with this issue we instrument for the outsourcing intensity variable O using its first and second lags. The equation is estimated using a Generalised Method of Moments (GMM) estimator.

The results for estimating (2) using the GMM estimator are reported in Table 4 for total, materials and services outsourcing respectively. We report the Hansen J statistic to examine the null hypothesis that the correlation between the instrumental variable candidates and the error terms in Equation (2) is zero; a necessary condition for the validity of the instrumental variables approach. We are also careful to assess the strength of the relationship between the instruments and the potentially endogenous regressors. It has been noted in the econometric literature that when the partial correlation between the instruments and the endogenous variable is low, instrumental variables regression is biased in the direction of the OLS estimator. Staiger and Stock (1997) recommend that the F-statistics from the first stage

[16] Unfortunately, with the data at hand we are not able to investigate this issue further. However, the negative coefficient on *ksr* is persistent and striking in our results.

[17] One possible explanation may be that this is driven by the fact that there are 28 observations less in column (4) than column (3). To address this point we re-estimated the model in column (3) using the 340 observations only. This does not change the results and, hence, cannot explain this switch in signs.

Table 3: *Results from First Differenced OLS Regressions*

	(1)	*(2)*	*(3)*	*(4)*
Total outsourcing	–0.027 (0.008)***			
Total outsourcing * employment	0.004 (0.001)***			
Materials outsourcing		–0.039 (0.009)***		–0.084 (0.019)***
Materials outsourcing * employment		0.006 (0.002)***		0.015 (0.004)***
Services outsourcing			–0.077 (0.038)**	0.118 (0.050)**
Services outsourcing * employment			0.012 (0.007)*	–0.025 (0.009)***
Capital-sales ratio	–0.044 (0.015)***	–0.048 (0.016)***	–0.047 (0.015)***	–0.047 (0.015)***
Employment	0.014 (0.020)	0.015 (0.022)	0.008 (0.021)	0.022 (0.021)
Sector growth	–0.001 (0.003)	0.000 (0.004)	–0.001 (0.003)	–0.001 (0.004)
Observations	368	340	368	340
R-squared	0.58	0.62	0.51	0.65

Notes: Response variable is profitability (first differenced).
Regression includes time dummies and constant term.
Clustered standard errors in parentheses
* significant at 10 per cent; ** significant at 5 per cent; *** significant at 1 per cent.

regression be routinely reported in applied work. The F-statistic tests the hypothesis that the instruments should be excluded from the first-stage regressions (i.e., the relevance of the instruments). The idea here is that when the F-statistic is small, the instrumental variable estimates and the associated confidence intervals are unreliable.

The Hansen test does not allow us to reject the null hypothesis of instrument validity, while the F tests also indicate that the instruments are relevant. We note, however, that the F-tests are only marginal in the case of services outsourcing in column (3), hence we are cautious in interpreting those results. Overall, however, we can be reasonably confident that our results are valid. Furthermore, the Hausman test, which examines the null hypothesis that there is no statistically significant difference between the OLS and IV estimates, suggests that the GMM estimates are only preferred in the case of total outsourcing in column (1) and when jointly including materials and services outsourcing in column (4).

Turning to the coefficients we find similar results in columns (1) to (3) to the first differenced OLS regressions discussed earlier. However, the coefficients are in all cases somewhat larger. However, as pointed out above, for the analysis of materials and services outsourcing we prefer the OLS estimates in columns (2) and (3) to the GMM estimates. From column (4) we now find that once we control for materials outsourcing, there are no statistically significant profitability enhancing effects from services outsourcing. Materials outsourcing still benefits large plants, however. Note that this finding is in line with Görzig and Stephan's (2002) study which finds from German micro data that materials outsourcing benefits firm performance, while there is no such evidence from services outsourcing. Taking the coefficients at face value, column (4) suggests that establishments start to benefit from materials outsourcing once they reach a size of 262 employees. Recalling that the mean employment level is around 150 (Table 2), this suggests that only plants considerably larger than the mean size are able to benefit from outsourcing.

Taken together, our results suggest that only large plants are able to improve their performance in terms of profitability following increasing use of outsourcing of material inputs. In the framework of the Grossman-Helpman (2002) model discussed in Section II, this may indicate that these large establishments have more bargaining power *vis-à-vis* their suppliers and are therefore able to extract rents. This appears to be not the case for smaller plants in the electronics industry. Another possible explanation is that large firms face lower search costs for potential suppliers since they may be better established on the market, and hence be in a better position to benefit from outsourcing. Unfortunately, with the data at hand, we are not able to investigate these issues further. The results for services outsourcing are less clear-cut, however. When looking at services outsourcing we find benefits for large plants, similar to materials outsourcing. However, once controlling for materials outsourcing, there are no such benefits evident. One important caveat to keep in mind is that we investigate the short-run effects of outsourcing on profitability. Given the potential obstacles for small plants they

Table 4: *Results from GMM Regressions*

	(1)	*(2)*	*(3)*	*(4)*
Total outsourcing	–0.138			
	(0.048)***			
Total outsourcing * employment	0.023			
	(0.009)***			
Materials outsourcing		–0.184		–0.206
		(0.072)**		(0.068)***
Materials outsourcing * employment		0.031		0.037
		(0.012)**		(0.017)**
Services outsourcing			–0.516	0.088
			(0.290)*	(0.206)
Services outsourcing * employment			0.127	_0.030
			(0.073)*	(0.062)
Capital-sales ratio	–0.052	–0.054	–0.043	–0.056
	(0.018)***	(0.017)***	(0.016)***	(0.019)***
Employment	0.030	0.034	0.006	0.036
	(0.020)	(0.021)	(0.028)	(0.020)*
Sector growth	0.002	0.004	–0.007	0.006
	(0.005)	(0.006)	(0.008)	(0.006)
Observations	282	268	282	268
F first stage (p-value)				
Total outsourcing	0.001			
*Total outsourcing * employment*	0.000			
Materials outsourcing		0.000		0.00
*Materials outsourcing *employment*		0.000		0.00
Services outsourcing			0.12	0.03
*Services outsourcing *employment*			0.15	0.01
Hansen J (p-value)	0.34	0.44	0.64	0.22
Hausman (p-value)	0.01	0.70	0.34	0.00

Notes: Response variable is profitability (first differenced).
Regression includes time dummies and constant term.
Instruments used are first and second lags of the outsourcing variable in levels.
Clustered standard errors in parentheses.
* significant at 10 per cent; ** significant at 5 per cent; *** significant at 1 per cent.

may only be able to benefit in the medium to long run, while large plants may be better able to reap the benefits in the short run.

V CONCLUSIONS

We analyse empirically the relationship between outsourcing and profitability at the level of the plant, using data for the electronics sector in the Republic of Ireland. Our results suggest that the profit/outsourcing relationship depends on characteristics of the plant, in particular its size. We find that plants that are substantially larger than the mean employment size benefit from outsourcing materials inputs, while this does not appear to be the case for small plants. Within our empirical analysis we are not able to explain this size disadvantage, although we can speculate on the basis of the theoretical work by Grossman and Helpman (2002) that this reflects higher transaction costs for small plants. In particular, they may face lower bargaining power *vis-à-vis* suppliers and/or higher costs in searching for adequate suppliers. The benefits from services outsourcing are less clear-cut, however. When interpreting these results one needs to keep in mind that our empirical methodology implies that we are essentially analysing short-run effects. Due to the relatively short period of data covered we are unable to examine the long-run effects of outsourcing on profitability.

REFERENCES

ABRAHAM, KATHARINE G. and SUSAN K. TAYLOR, 1996. "Firms' Use of Outside Contractors: Theory and Evidence", *Journal of Labor Economics*, Vol. 14, pp. 394-424.

AUDRETSCH, DAVID B., 1995. *Innovation and Industry Evolution*, Cambridge: MIT Press.

BARRY, FRANK, and JOHN BRADLEY, 1997. "FDI and Trade: The Irish Host-Country Experience", *Economic Journal*, Vol. 107, pp. 1798-1811.

BHUYAN, SANJIB, 2002. "Impact of vertical mergers on industry profitability: an empirical evaluation", *Review of Industrial Organization*, Vol.20, pp. 61-79.

BOLTON, PATRICK and MICHAEL D. WHINSTON, 1993. "Incomplete contracts, vertical integration, and supply assurance", *Review of Economic Studies*, Vol. 60, pp. 121-148.

COASE, RONALD, 1937. "The nature of the firm", *Economica*, Vol. 4, pp. 386-405.

DOMOWITZ, IAN, R. GLENN HUBBARD and BRUCE C. PETERSEN, 1987. "Oligopoly supergames: Some empirical evidence on prices and margins", *Journal of Industrial Economics*, Vol. 35, pp. 379-398.

DOMS, MICHAEL E. and J. BRADFORD JENSEN, 1998. "Comparing Wages, Skills, and Productivity between Domestically and Foreign-Owned Manufacturing

Establishments in the United States", in R.E. Baldwin, R.E. Lipsey and J.D. Richardson (eds.), *Geography and ownership as bases for economic accounting*, Chicago: University of Chicago Press, pp. 235-255.

FEENSTRA, ROBERT C., 1998. "Integration of Trade and Disintegration of Production in the Global Economy", *Journal of Economic Perspectives*, Vol. 12, pp. 31-50.

FEENSTRA, ROBERT C. and GORDON H. HANSON, 1999. "The impact of outsourcing and high-technology capital on wages: Estimates for the United States", *Quarterly Journal of Economics*, Vol. 114, pp. 907-940.

FIXLER, DENNIS and DONALD SIEGEL, 1999. "Outsourcing and productivity growth in services", *Structural Change and Economic Dynamics*, Vol. 10, pp. 177-194.

GIRMA, SOURAFEL and HOLGER GÖRG, 2004. "Outsourcing, foreign ownership and productivity: Evidence from UK establishment level data", *Review of International Economics*, Vol. 12, pp. 817-832.

GÖRG, HOLGER, AOIFE HANLEY and ERIC STROBL, 2004. "Outsourcing, foreign ownership, exporting and productivity: An empirical investigation with plant level data", GEP Research Paper 04/08, University of Nottingham.

GÖRZIG BERND and ANDREAS STEPHAN, 2002. "Outsourcing and firm-level performance", Discussion Paper No. 309, DIW Berlin.

GROSSMAN, GENE M. and ELHANAN HELPMAN, 2002. "Integration versus Outsourcing in Industry Equilibrium", *Quarterly Journal of Economics*, Vol. 117, pp.85-120.

GROSSMAN, SANFORD J. and OLIVER HART, 1986. "The costs and benefits of ownership: A theory of vertical and lateral integration", *Journal of Political Economy*, Vol. 94, pp. 691-719.

HESHMATI, ALMAS, 2003. "Productivity growth, efficiency and outsourcing in manufacturing and service industries", *Journal of Economic Surveys*, Vol. 17, pp. 79-112.

KIMURA, FUKUNARI, 2002. "Subcontracting and the performance of small and medium firms in Japan", *Small Business Economics*, Vol. 18, pp. 163-175.

KNARVIK MIDELFART, KAREN and FRODE STEEN, 2002. "Vertical industry linkages: sources of productivity gains and cumulative causation?" *Review of Industrial Organization*, Vol. 21, pp. 3-20.

KUMAR, NAGESH, 1990. "Mobility barriers and profitability of multinational and local enterprises in Indian manufacturing", *Journal of Industrial Economics*, Vol. 38, pp. 449-463.

O'MALLEY, EOIN, 1995. *An Analysis of Secondary Employment Associated with Manufacturing Industry*, General Research Series No. 167, Dublin: The Economic and Social Research Institute.

RUANE, FRANCES and HOLGER GÖRG, 2001. "Globalisation and Fragmentation: Evidence for the Electronics Industry in Ireland", in S. Arndt and H. Kierzkowski (eds.), *Fragmentation: New Production Patterns in the World Economy*. Oxford: Oxford University Press, pp. 144-164.

SHEPHERD, WILLIAM G., 1972. "The elements of market structure", *Review of Economics and Statistics*, Vol. 54, pp. 25-37.

STAIGER, DOUGLAS and JAMES H. STOCK, 1997. "Instrumental variables regression with weak instruments", *Econometrica*, Vol. 65, pp. 557-586.

WHITE, PADRAIC A., 2000. "The Muscles of the Celtic Tiger: The IDA's Winning Sectors" in R. MacSharry and P.A. White (eds.), *The Making of the Celtic Tiger: The Inside Story of Ireland's Boom Economy*, Cork: Mercier Press, pp. 272-308.

WILLIAMSON, OLIVER E., 1975. *Markets and hierarchies: Analysis and antitrust implications*, New York: Free Press.

APPENDICES

Table A1: *Summary Statistics for O1 and O2 by Sub-sector*

	1990	*1995*
O1		
Components	1.53 (0.46)	2.59 (2.11)
Computers	1.67 (1.67)	2.51 (2.77)
Consumer Electronics	1.74 (0.78)	2.34 (1.78)
Instrumentation	3.18 (5.72)	2.08 (1.42)
Networking/Data Com	2.57 (0.09)	1.97 (1.22)
PCBA	10.36 (23.86)	2.83 (2.35)
Peripherals & Media	2.42 (0.87)	5.00 (5.53)
Semiconductors	2.85 (2.16)	6.87 (7.39)
IT Services	1.62 (1.08)	0.72 (0.58)
Software Development	–	1.67 (2.61)
Software Production	–	6.15 (11.54)
Telecommunications	2.26 (1.91)	4.48 (5.49)
O2		
Components	0.70 (0.41)	1.28 (0.21)
Computers	0.86 (0.52)	1.96 (2.17)
Consumer Electronics	0.96 (0.32)	0.99 (0.44)
Instrumentation	0.89 (0.45)	1.23 (0.86)
Networking/Data Com	1.76 (0.68)	0.91 (0.16)
PCBA	0.89 (0.78)	1.46 (0.96)
Peripherals & Media	1.26 (0.56)	1.61 (2.15)
Semiconductors	1.23 (0.01)	3.82 (4.33)
IT Services	0.43 (0.52)	0.48 (0.41)
Software Development	–	0.29 (0.41)
Software Production	–	1.31 (1.78)
Telecommunications	1.03 (0.62)	1.61 (1.05)

Note: Means (Standard deviation in parentheses).
Source: own calculations based on *Irish Economy Expenditure Survey* data.

Table A2: *Breakdown by Quartile for Low and High Profit Plants*

Outsourcing Intensity	*Low profit*	*High Profit*	*Total*
	Total O/S Intensity (proportion of plants)		
1st quartile	47	53	100
2nd quartile	41	59	100
3rd quartile	50	50	100
4th quartile	62	38	100
	Materials O/S Intensity (proportion of plants)		
1st quartile	54	46	100
2nd quartile	40	60	100
3rd quartile	46	54	100
4th quartile	60	40	100
	Services O/S Intensity (proportion of plants)		
1st quartile	23	77	100
2nd quartile	48	52	100
3rd quartile	61	39	100
4th quartile	68	32	100

Chapter II.7

Labour demand effects of international outsourcing: Evidence from plant-level data

Holger Görg[a,b,*], Aoife Hanley[a]

[a]*University of Nottingham, United Kingdom*
[b]*DIW Berlin, Germany*

Accepted 15 December 2004
Available online 21 January 2005

Abstract

We examine empirically the effect of international outsourcing on labour demand at the level of the individual plant. We do so by estimating a dynamic model of plant-level labour demand, using a Generalised Method of Moments estimator. We use plant-level data for the Irish Electronics sector, an industry that has expanded rapidly over the last decade and that has witnessed significant offshoring activity. Our results suggest that, in the short-run, there are significant reductions in plant-level labour demand, which we attribute to the use of international outsourcing. There appears to be stronger negative effects from outsourcing of materials than from services outsourcing.

JEL classification: F14; J23; L23
Keywords: International outsourcing; Offshoring; Labour demand; Electronics industry

1. Introduction

The term international outsourcing, or more specifically the location of production processes abroad and the subsequent imports of intermediates, has been a widely discussed topic in the U.S. and European

* Corresponding author. School of Economics, University of Nottingham, University Park, Nottingham NG7 2RD, United Kingdom.
E-mail address: holger.gorg@nottingham.ac.uk (H. Görg).

1059-0560/$ - see front matter
doi:10.1016/j.iref.2004.12.007

media recently.[1] It appears to arouse either concern with unions that home jobs will be lost to workers abroad without commensurate job gains in other sectors, resulting in net job losses. Alternatively, employers can argue that productivity gains outweigh job losses especially in the lower skilled sectors and may be accompanied by increases in high skilled jobs. Kohler (2001) appropriately summarises the argument as "the perennial tension between efficiency and distributional concerns" (p. 49).

The media in the Republic of Ireland, the country for which we analyse data in this paper, fears employment losses as a consequence of offshoring, particularly with respect to financial services being relocated to India. This, it is argued, contributes to the growing competitiveness of these developing countries, despite Ireland's traditional strength in financial service provision. However, it is acknowledged that there may also be opportunities to be garnered from relocating the production of certain more routine inputs to partner countries, on condition that Ireland retains certain other high value added activities.[2] Ireland's island neighbour, Britain has recently highlighted the effects of outsourcing on competitiveness and employment in a recent UK Government White paper.[3] A recent Financial Times article reports findings from an independent consultant that a 'two-speed Europe is emerging', with the UK and Ireland reporting the highest levels of worker replacement.[4] The article estimates, for example, that 100,000 UK jobs will have relocated abroad by 2005 as a direct consequence of international outsourcing. The corresponding estimates for Germany and France are 11,000 and 7000, respectively. Accordingly, offshoring is a particularly burning issue in the island economies of Ireland and the UK.

The purpose of this paper is to examine empirically the effect of international outsourcing on demand for labour at the level of the individual plant. As pointed out above, workers' concerns about possible job losses are often countered with the argument that offshoring can increase employment in the country. It is, however, usually not made clear whether these new jobs occur in the same plant in the short-run, or whether jobs are lost in one plant and at some stage in the future other jobs are created in a completely separate plant.

In this paper, we focus on short-run employment effects in the outsourcing plants. We do so by estimating a dynamic model of plant-level labour demand, using a generalised method of moments estimator. We use plant-level data for the Irish Electronics sector, an industry that has expanded rapidly over the last decade and that has witnessed significant offshoring activity (Ruane & Görg, 2001). Our results suggest that, in the short-run, there are significant reductions in plant-level labour demand, which we attribute to the use of international outsourcing. There appear to be stronger negative effects from outsourcing of materials than from services outsourcing.

Our paper contributes to an existing and growing literature on the employment effects of international outsourcing. The issue that has attracted most attention thus far is whether offshoring has contributed to a shift in labour demand for different types of workers and consequently a change in the wage differential between high and low skill wages (e.g., Egger & Egger, 2003; Feenstra & Hanson, 1999; Hijzen, Görg, & Hine, in press). These analyses use industry-level data for their empirical estimations. However, there appears to be a lack of micro-level analyses in this area. An extension of this research is provided by Head and Ries (2002) who use Japanese firm-level data to look at the effect of international outsourcing

[1] Much of the media and policy-making community now refers to this as "offshoring", partly in order to distinguish it from domestic as opposed to international outsourcing. In the trade theoretic literature it is usually referred to as "fragmentation".

[2] Irish Times, "Outsourcing may see services sector 'decline'", 30/12/2003. "'Offshoring' to boost financial services—report", 09/12/2003.

[3] UK Government White Paper on Trade and Investment, "Making Globalisation a Force for Good", July 2004, CM6278, DTI.

[4] Financial Times, Monday 16th August, "Europe set to move 1 m jobs abroad in a decade" (World News).

on relative labour demand at the level of the plant.[5] Furthermore, some researchers have also used individual-level data to focus on intra-sectoral worker flows that arise as a consequence of outsourcing domestic production (Egger, Pfaffermayr, & Weber, 2003; Kletzer, 2000). However, no paper that we are aware of has looked specifically at the net effects of international outsourcing on labour demand using plant-level data.[6]

Our analysis adopts the following format. Section 2 outlines the relevant literature and our hypotheses. Section 3 presents the model used and outlines the estimation technique. Section 4 describes the data which relate to a 6-year micro-level panel of Irish electronics plants. Section 5 reports and discusses our results, while Section 6 concludes.

2. Background

The existing literature investigating labour responses to outsourcing contains several strands. One common theme running through the standard trade theoretic models based on Heckscher–Ohlin or specific factors assumptions, is an investigation of how international outsourcing (fragmentation) is predicted to change the composition of skilled and unskilled labour in a country (Arndt, 1997; Deardoff, 2001; Egger & Egger, 2003; Jones & Kierkowski, 2001; Kohler, 2001). In these models, international outsourcing mainly emerges in order to exploit differences in factor costs across countries. Since most models, to our knowledge, work on the premise that the home country is more developed than the country to which production is outsourced, broadly speaking the consensus is that fragmentation of production should induce a developed country to focus on higher skilled activities. This shift in skill configuration has implications for relative demand and wages for high and low skilled workers. In fact, the fragmentation of production and trade in intermediates is expected to affect employment and wages far more profoundly than the trade in final goods (Krugman, 1995).

Feenstra and Hanson (1996, 1999) provide probably the most prominent examples of empirical work on this issue. They investigate the impact of international outsourcing on relative demand and wage differentials between workers of different skill levels using industry-level data for the United States. They note that the two most widely cited explanations for rises in wage inequalities are skill-biased change and trade with low-wage countries. The latter is conductive to outsourcing in the vertical chain of production. They conclude that their results give credence to these two explanations for wage inequalities, where technical change in the form of capital expenditures is responsible for the lion's share of the wage premium enjoyed by non-production workers. Nevertheless, outsourcing remains a major and significant driver of the wage differential. Following Feenstra and Hanson's work, similar evidence has been produced for a number of European countries, e.g., Hijzen et al. (in press) for the United

[5] Geishecker and Görg (2004) look at the wage effects of international outsourcing, using individual worker data.

[6] Greenaway, Hine, and Wright (1999) and Konings and Vandenbussche (1995) provide somewhat related papers where they look at the effects of total trade on labour demand. Apart from using overall trade rather than focussing on outsourcing, the analyses are different in other ways. Greenaway et al. use industry level data for the UK, while Konings and Vandenbussche use UK firm-level data. The latter also do only specify a static model of labour demand. Another strand of related literature looks at the employment effects of outward foreign direct investment (e.g., Konings & Murphy, 2001). However, those papers do not distinguish horizontal from vertical FDI (with the latter being more akin to offshoring).

Kingdom, Geishecker (2002) for Germany, Strauss-Kahn (2003) for France and Egger and Egger (2003) for Austria.

This literature that sticks closely to standard trade theoretic models is, however, silent on whether the reallocation of resources due to international outsourcing takes place within a given firm or between firms in the same or different sectors. This is not a trivial question, as one may assume that the adjustment costs for workers increase if they have to move to another firm or even another sector (cf., Davidson & Matusz, 2001). In other words, the implications of outsourcing for the individual worker may be easiest if it just means that the individual has to perform a different sort of task within the same firm. It becomes more complicated if the worker is made redundant in the initial firm and then has to move to a different firm in the same or another sector to find alternative employment. In order to address questions like this, micro-level data are necessary.

An example of the use of firm-level data in looking at the impact of offshoring on the relative demand for skilled labour, is provided by Head and Ries (2002). They find that Japanese firms increasing employment in foreign affiliates in low-income countries raise the skill intensity of employment in their headquarters. No such effect is apparent for offshore production in high-income countries, however.

Egger et al. (2003) use individual-level panel data from Austria to examine in more detail the consequences for workers of increased international outsourcing. As they point out, complete labour adjustment in response to outsourcing may be a long-run aspiration but the immediate effects of outsourcing may bring unemployment in its wake because people who are laid off by their current employer, cannot immediately switch into alternative employment. This persistence of unemployment makes it more appropriate to investigate short-run transition probabilities where individuals can move into and out of unemployment and between different sectors.

Accordingly, they examine the impact of trade on employment using a worker flow framework similar to that pioneered by Kletzer (2000) which takes on board short-run employment changes. They explore the impact of several drivers on individual transition probabilities between size and different states of employment and unemployment. These drivers include growth changes in imported goods, exports, outsourcing, and technical change. They are able to model transition probabilities between different employment stages owing to the longitudinal and highly disaggregated nature of the data. They find that outsourcing reduces worker flow to the sectors in which the economy has a comparative disadvantage (CDA). However, net changes to the comparative advantage sectors (CA) of the economy remain unchanged. This overall finding suggests net unemployment increases, on the basis that a reduction in the likelihood that workers switch to the CDA sector is not matched by a proportionate inflow of workers to the CA sector. To put this result in context, Kletzer (2000) also finds that US outsourcing leads to net job losses.

We can see from our brief review of the literature, that while there is broad agreement from theory and aggregate empirical work on the direction of movement between sectors, lack of available micro-level data has made it difficult to capture the net employment effect of outsourcing at the level of the individual or the plant/firm. This is what we set out to provide in this paper—a detailed analysis of the short-run impact of international outsourcing on labour demand at the level of the plant. As far as we are aware, this is the first study to do so.

Of course, we would expect net employment effects to be relatively country specific. This expectation is shaped by country specific factors such as relative factor endowments and comparative advantage. Given the need to isolate overall effects of outsourcing, we set out to quantify how outsourcing affects net employment within the Irish Electronics sector. Within this sector are grouped activities as diverse or inter-related as software and chip production (see Appendix for a list of subsectors).

Moreover, existing research has not differentiated between outsourced services and materials, thereby creating a gap in our understanding of how the nature of outsourced inputs affects the overall labour situation. The evolution of the banking and health sectors shows increasingly high volumes of service intermediates being offshored to locations such as India. More specifically in the Electronics sector, 'high abstraction' or intellectual activities once integral to production in a developed country, are being offshored.[7] This highlights the growing centrality of outsourced services in the production chain where they perform less of an ancillary and increasingly more of a core role. Accordingly, we distinguish between outsourced materials and service inputs in our empirical work.

3. Modelling and estimating labour demand

In modelling the net employment impact of international outsourcing we consider a plant-level dynamic employment equation of the form

$$n_{it} = \alpha_1 n_{it-1} + \alpha_2 w_{it-s} + \alpha_3 y_{jt-s} + \alpha_4 o_{jt-s} + \lambda_t + \mu_i + v_{it} \quad (1)$$

where n is log employment in plant i at time t and w is the log of the average wage in plant i. The log of total output in sector j is included to control for industry demand shocks (see, e.g., Arellano & Bond, 1991; Nickell, 1986) while common demand shocks are controlled for using a time trend (λ_t). The error term is made up of a plant specific component (μ_i) as well as a remaining white noise term (v_{it}).[8] The lagged dependent variable allows for the presence of adjustment costs, which imply that the level of employment may deviate from its steady state as adjustment to equilibrium takes place.

In this dynamic employment equation, we include a measure of (the log of) an industry's propensity to utilise internationally outsourced components (o_j). The coefficient α_4 captures the short-run effect of international outsourcing on labour demand in this specification. This approach, which is similar to the modelling of the effects of total trade on employment by Greenaway et al., (1999) and Konings and Vandenbussche (1995) implicitly assumes that international outsourcing increases technical efficiency in the underlying production function.[9] These changes in technical efficiency or total factor productivity can have implications for use of factors of production, which is what we examine in this equation.

For estimation purposes, we first-difference Eq. (1) in order to purge the plant specific component μ_i. As is by now well known, first differencing this dynamic panel equation induces bias in the coefficient on the lagged dependent variable due to correlation between this variable and the error term. Hence, an instrumental variable approach has to be adopted for the estimation. Specifically, we apply the

[7] See http://www.manpower.co.uk/news/OutsourcingSurvey.pdf for a discussion of this recent phenomenon.

[8] Note that we do not include a plant specific measure of the cost of capital in this equation. We assume that the effect of cost of capital is controlled for by either or both of these two variables: the time trend (assuming that cost of capital varies over time but not over plants in the electronics industry) or the plant-specific effect (assuming that cost of capital does not vary over time).

[9] Görg, Hanley and Strobl (2004) examine in more detail the effect of international outsourcing on plant level total factor productivity.

generalised method of moments (GMM) technique introduced by Arellano and Bond (1991), which essentially uses lagged levels of the endogenous variables dated $t-2$ and earlier as instruments. This estimation technique also allows to treat some of the covariates as endogenous, again using lagged levels of the variables as instruments.

The first-differenced version of Eq. (1) produces unbiased and consistent estimates under the assumption that there is no second order serial correlation of the error term. We test for this, as well as for instrument validity in all estimations. In the estimation we furthermore allow for unspecified heteroskedasticity of the error term.

4. Data and descriptive statistics

Eq. (1) is estimated using plant-level data for the Irish Electronics industry for the period 1990 to 1995. The data derive from the *Irish Economy Expenditure Survey*, undertaken annually by *Forfás*, the government agency responsible for Enterprise Development, Science and Technology in Ireland. This comprises an annual survey of plants in Irish manufacturing with at least 20 employees, although a plant, once it is included, is generally still surveyed even if its employment level falls below the 20-employee cut-off point. The response rate to this survey is generally estimated to be between 60 and 80 per cent of the targeted population of plants. The data provided include plant-level information on, inter alia, output, employment, total wage bill, as well as details on plants' expenditure on materials and services inputs. Quite uniquely, we are able to distinguish materials and services purchased abroad from those bought at home. Unfortunately, however, the data set does not provide information on different skill categories of labour, hence we are forced to consider labour as homogeneous.

Our variable of interest, o_j, represents international outsourcing in terms of imported intermediates. Such measures of outsourcing have been predominant in the literature using aggregate industry-level data to examine the implications of outsourcing for workers (e.g., Feenstra & Hanson, 1999; Hijzen et al., in press). We expect outsourced intermediates, at least in the short-run, to reduce a plant's wage bill by eliminating potentially inefficient in-house production on products or services requiring otherwise longer production runs or a broader market. It follows that the cost of outsourcing is analogous to the opportunity wage that may have accrued to in-house employees, had the service not been contracted out. Accordingly, in line with Girma and Görg (2004) and Görg et al., (2004), we calculate an indicator of an establishment's propensity to outsource as the expenditure on outsourcing, i.e., on either services or material inputs, relative to the plant's total wage bill.

As alluded to earlier, an advantage of our data set is that we can break down intermediate inputs into raw materials and components (referred to as materials) and services inputs, and the proportion of these factors offshored.[10] We can therefore calculate two disaggregated outsourcing variables, namely, the ratio of imported materials and the ratio of imported services inputs over total wages, respectively. With regard to the latter measure, services inputs are defined as other direct and indirect costs, excluding

[10] One should note that materials and services not sourced abroad may have been purchased from foreign affiliates of multinationals located in Ireland rather than just from purely domestic firms. Unfortunately, the data set does not allow us to distinguish these two sources for domestically purchased inputs.

materials, wages, rent, interest payments, and depreciation. This includes contracted out services, such as consultancy, maintenance, security, cleaning, catering, etc.

Table 1 contains some descriptive statistics for the main variables of interest. We see that the first year of the study, 1990, only around half the plants were captured but the data set includes a higher number of

Table 1
Descriptive statistics

	1990	1991	1992	1993	1994	1995
Average number of employees						
Mean	174	136	124	137	153	180
Median	106	61	61	76	73	78
S.D.	183	170	149	160	233	308
N	54	109	120	121	123	125
Average annual wage (IRP 000)						
Mean	14.0	15.58	16.69	18.03	18.49	19.00
Median	13.79	15.49	16.40	16.54	16.76	17.00
S.D.	4.59	5.71	6.05	7.25	8.46	8.25
N	54	109	120	121	123	125
Average total outsourcing ratio (o_j)						
Mean	3.1	2.9	3.1	2.9	4	3.9
Median	2	1.3	1.4	1.3	1.2	1.4
S.D.	3.1	4.8	5	6	10.9	8.3
N	54	109	120	121	123	125
Average total inputs (inputs)						
Mean	17,718	15,195	14,812	16,678	20,291	38,316
Median	6473	2635	2790	3613	3419	4236
S.D.	49,432	43,412	39,905	48,757	55,099	122,381
N	54	109	120	121	123	125
Average outsourced inputs (for1)						
Mean	12,970	9716	9160	11,962	13,154	23,761
Median	3840	1286	1333	1782	1640	1718
S.D.	40,135	31,756	26,060	36,010	39,586	76,623
N	54	109	120	121	123	125
Average outsourced material inputs (for2)						
Mean	11,976	9238	8658	12,384	12,031	23,463
Median	3250	1409	1180	1926	1661	1731
S.D.	38,312	30,950	24,769	33,385	37,709	78,161
N	53	99	110	106	108	108
Average outsourced service inputs (for3)						
Mean	1077	1257	1224	1113	2590	3488
Median	112	38	57	70	61	60
S.D.	2921	5130	6209	5783	11,399	19,050
N	53	108	120	121	123	125

All wages and input prices inflation adjusted (consumer price index base year 1990=100).

firms over the 5 years that follow. As such, the 1990 values occasionally appear at variance with those of the following 5 years. This anomaly is most likely due to sample composition.[11]

The most noticeable change across the years, arises between 1994 and 1995, when average total inputs increased from 20.3 K to 38.3 K (35 percent), total outsourced inputs rising by 13.2 K to 23.8 K (36 percent). Service inputs experience the highest proportional rise, albeit from a low initial level. They increase from an average of 2.6 K to 3.5 K, an increase of 43 percent. Interestingly, the outsourcing ratio (i.e., total outsourced inputs over the wage bill) increased substantially between 1993 and 1994 but does not rise further with the increasing use of intermediates in the year that follows. This is due to a simultaneous increase in the average wage and the average total wage bill between 1994 and 1995, which implies that our outsourcing measure remains constant. However, it should be noted that the average wage also increased significantly in the earlier years since 1990. Has the increased use of international outsourcing been a reaction at the plant level to the rising wage bill? While we do not address this question directly in this paper, our analysis goes into that direction as it allows us to determine whether outsourcing leads to reductions in labour demand.

5. Analysis

In the estimation of Eq. (1) we can opt to treat our covariates as fully exogenous, in which case we employ a standard GMM specification comprising a fully exogenous dynamic panel model with appropriate tests for autocorrelation. Alternatively, it can be argued that the interrelationships among the determinants of employment (in particular wages and international outsourcing) are more complex and accordingly pre-determined. This assumption is reasonable because we can argue that errors in predicting employment at time $t+1$, based on values of outsourcing and wages at time t, are themselves predictive of employment at time $t+2$. In this latter instance, the GMM framework is modified to allow this relaxation of strict exogeneity. The predetermined variables (outsourcing and wages) are now instrumented, using lagged levels as instruments as described in Arellano and Bond (1991).

We first estimate the changes to employment levels when outsourcing and wages are treated as fully exogenous, see column (1) of Table 2.[12] As expected, there is a strong element of persistence in employment, where higher employment levels in the previous year are associated with higher contemporaneous employment levels. As we would expect, higher contemporaneous as well as lagged industry demand, induce higher employment levels. Moreover, increases in a firm's average wage, lead to staff reductions. Most interesting from our point of view, higher levels of outsourcing are associated with reduced employment, as evidenced by a negative coefficient for the variable o_j, ceteris paribus, although the coefficient is not statistically significant in this specification.

In the second estimation in column (2), wages and outsourcing are formulated as pre-determined variables; an arguably reasonable assumption in the estimation of labour demand equations (see Arellano & Bond, 1991). On this occasion, the main difference between equations in columns (1) and (2) is that in the latter, international outsourcing is statistically significant and negative. The point estimate (i.e., the

[11] Note that this should not cause a problem in the econometric analysis below, where we follow each individual plant over the time period, hence the composition of the total sector does not matter.

[12] Nickell (1986) argues that additional lags beyond $t-1$ may be necessary to capture adequately adjustment costs. We experimented with including higher order lags in the estimations, the coefficients on these higher lags beyond lag two are generally, however, statistically insignificant.

Table 2
Impact of total outsourcing (O/S) on employment

	(1)	(2)	(3)	(4)
n_{it-1}	0.616 (2.62)***	0.548 (2.63)***	0.648 (2.73)***	0.454 (2.48)***
n_{it-2}	0.074 (0.59)	0.136 (1.17)	0.058 (0.45)	0.123 (1.11)
y_{it}	0.089 (1.88)*	0.092 (2.18)**	0.089 (1.88)*	0.106 (2.56)***
y_{it-1}	0.036 (0.76)	0.064 (1.25)	0.031 (0.65)	0.080 (1.91)*
w_{it}	−0.520 (3.32)***	−0.621 (3.11)***	−0.537 (3.33)***	−0.766 (2.57)***
w_{it-1}	0.029 (0.16)	−0.078 (0.47)	0.055 (0.31)	−0.080 (0.41)
Total outsourcing (o_j)	−0.048 (0.76)	−0.277 (1.93)**		
ΔTotal outsourcing (Δo_j)			−0.046 (1.03)	−0.093 (2.22)**
Time trend	0.020 (0.99)	0.032 (1.50)	0.018 (0.87)	0.028 (1.49)
Wald χ^2	135.25	127.67	144.77	117.59
Arellano-Bond (order 2)[a]	0.15	0.12	0.15	0.11
Sargan test[b]	0.82	0.69	0.80	0.78
Observations	173	173	172	172
Number of plants	80	80	79	79

Dynamic panel equation with robust standard errors, t-statistics in parentheses.
*, **, *** signify statistical significance at 10, 5 and 1 percent, respectively.
[a] H_0: no autocorrelation ($P>z$).
[b] Overidentifying restrictions where H_0: overidentified ($P>\chi^2$). χ^2 from 2-step estimates columns (1) and (3): apart from lagged employment, all covariates treated as exogenous columns (2) and (4): outsourcing and wages treated as pre-determined.

elasticity of labour with respect to outsourcing) suggests that a 1 percent increase in the outsourcing ratio reduces employment by 0.27 percent.

As a consequence of estimating our model with robust standard errors (i.e., allowing for heteroskedasticity), we are obliged to use the Sargan test statistic as calculated for the two-step model in line with guidance issued by Arellano and Bond (1991). We apply the second-step estimates because the one-step Sargan test over-rejects in the presence of heteroskedasticity. We cannot reject the null in the Sargan test in either specification. This null tests the overall validity of the instruments by analysing the sample analog of the moment conditions used during estimation. Failure to reject the hypothesis, i.e. lower χ^2 test values or higher p-values, lend support to the model. The other diagnostic examined is the null hypothesis of no second-order serial autocorrelation. If the test rejects the null, we must conclude that the original error term is serially correlated. Fortunately, we are unable to reject the null of no second order serial autocorrelation in both specifications at conventional levels of statistical significance.

Having looked at how the levels of bought in intermediates change the demand for labour, it is also reasonable to argue that changes in demand for these intermediates could also influence labour demand. Accordingly, we estimate the effects of changes in offshoring (i.e., Δo_j) on labour demand. Again, we distinguish estimations, which treat outsourcing and wages as exogenous (column 3) or pre-determined (column 4). From column (4) we find that international outsourcing negatively affects labour demand, although the elasticity is somewhat lower than in the "levels estimation" in column (2).

As noted earlier, no analysis to our knowledge has yet examined the potential effect of materials and service intermediates on labour demand despite the prima facie case for treating service intermediates separately. We therefore document the individual effects of materials and

Table 3
Impact of material and service O/S on employment

	(1)	(2)
n_{it-1}	0.474 (2.54)**	0.176 (1.03)
n_{it-2}	0.159 (1.40)	0.224 (2.55)**
y_{it}	0.107 (2.47)**	0.045 (1.31)
y_{it-1}	0.075 (1.58)	0.040 (0.82)
w_{it}	−0.558 (2.26)**	−1.157 (4.49)***
w_{it-1}	−0.074 (0.43)	−0.249 (1.40)
Materials outsourcing (o_j)	−0.192 (2.22)**	
Services outsourcing (o_j)		−0.149 (2.31)**
Time trend	0.025 (1.06)	0.066 (2.52)**
Wald χ^2	115.96	59.30
Arellano-Bond (order 2)[a]	0.13	0.22
Sargan test[b]	0.54	0.92
Observations	170	143
Number of plants	78	70

Dynamic panel equation with robust standard errors, t-statistics in parentheses.
*, **, *** signify statistical significance at 10, 5 and 1 percent, respectively.
[a] H_0: no autocorrelation ($P>z$).
[b] Overidentifying restrictions where H_0: overidentified ($P>\chi^2$). χ^2 from 2-step estimates outsourcing and wages treated as pre-determined.

services outsourcing (in terms of levels) on employment in Table 3. We only report estimations treating outsourcing and wages as pre-determined.

The elasticity of employment with respect to materials outsourcing is negative, indicating that higher levels of the latter are associated with lower employment levels. A similarly negatively signed coefficient is registered for services offshoring, although the point estimate is somewhat smaller than for materials outsourcing. Hence, negative employment effects appear to be due to both types of international outsourcing, with somewhat stronger effects from materials outsourcing. As in the case of all analyses thus far, we find that second order serial autocorrelation does not appear to be a problem. Also, the failure to reject the Sargan test indicates instrument validity.

6. Conclusions

In this, to our knowledge, first analysis on the net or overall effects of international fragmentation of production on labour demand at the plant level, we find that outsourcing in the Irish Electronics sector, significantly decreases labour demand in the short-run. This finding is robust to changes in different specifications of wages and the outsourcing ratio to accommodate possible pre-determination of these variables.

We should qualify our findings by emphasising that they pertain to offshoring for the Electronics sector. Nevertheless, our data captures firms from many subsectors within Electronics, including manufacturing and services activities, which are potentially upstream or downstream processes in the production chain. Accordingly, the negative relationship between offshoring and employment evidenced in our data, is arrived at despite arguably some potential for employment switching among subsectors. If every offshored input occasioned an intra-sectoral employment switch, the net impact of offshoring on employment would be zero. Of course, our analysis fails to pick up overall economy-wide employment gains because it merely captures employment losses *within* this one sector. Accordingly, there may be extra-sectoral employment leakages, e.g. between Electronics and Pharmaceuticals, occasioned by offshoring and hence our results may over-exaggerate net employment losses.

In addition, we are cautious to point out that our estimations merely capture the short-run effects of international outsourcing in the plant. In the medium or longer run, plants may increase labour demand due to increased competitiveness following international outsourcing. Unfortunately, our relatively short panel does not allow us to examine long-run effects in any detail.

Our findings appear largely in line with the conclusions of Egger et al. (2003) that unemployment arises as a short-run consequence of offshoring. Intuitively, we argue that the movement into a new job is a medium or even long-run phenomenon and that offshoring shocks are expected to induce net job losses at the level of the plant in the short-run. However, in order to judge the overall economy-wide net employment effects as well as the long-run implications of outsourcing at the level of the plant, further research is needed using micro and macro-level data.

Acknowledgements

We are grateful to Forfás for the provision of the data. Financial support through the Leverhulme Trust (Grant No. F114/BF) is gratefully acknowledged. We would like to thank David Paton for helpful comments on an earlier version of the manuscript. All errors and omissions are our own.

Appendix A. Number of firms by sub-sector

Electronics sector (Republic of Ireland)	Frequency	%
Components	112	17
Computers	23	4
Consumer Electronics	67	10
Instrumentation	66	10
Networking/Data Communications	18	3
Peripherals and Media	72	11
Printed Circuit board Assembly (PCBA)	53	8
Semiconductors	23	4
Services	39	6
Software Development	96	15
Software Production	33	5
Telecommunications	50	8
Total	652	100

References

Arellano, M., & Bond, S. (1991). Some tests of specification for panel data: Monte Carlo evidence and application to employment equations. *Review of Economic Studies*, *58*, 277–297.

Arndt, S. (1997). Globalisation and the open economy. *North American Journal of Economics and Finance*, *8*, 71–79.

Davidson, C., & Matusz, S., 2001, On adjustment costs, GEP Research Paper 2001/24, University of Nottingham.

Deardoff, A. (2001). Fragmentation in simple trade models. *North American Journal of Economics and Finance*, *12*, 121–137.

Egger, H., & Egger, P. (2003). Outsourcing and skill-specific employment in a small economy: Austria after the fall of the iron curtain. *Oxford Economic Papers*, *55*, 625–643.

Egger, P., Pfaffermayr, M., & Weber, A., 2003. Sectoral adjustment of employment: The impact of outsourcing and trade at the micro level, IZA Discussion Paper No. 921, IZA Bonn.

Feenstra, R., & Hanson, G. (1999). The impact of outsourcing and high-technology capital on wages: Estimates for the United States, 1979–1990. *Quarterly Journal of Economics*, *114*, 907–940.

Feenstra, R., & Hanson, G. (1996). Globalization, outsourcing, and wage inequality. *American Economic Review*, *86*, 240–245.

Geishecker, I., 2002. Outsourcing and the demand for low-skilled labour in German manufacturing: New evidence, Discussion Paper 313, DIW Berlin.

Geishecker, I., & Görg, H., 2004. International outsourcing and wages: Winners and losers, mimeo, University of Nottingham.

Girma, S., & Görg, H. (2004). Outsourcing, foreign ownership and productivity: Evidence from UK establishment level data. *Review of International Economics*, *12*, 817–832.

Görg, H., Hanley, A., & Strobl, E., 2004, Outsourcing, foreign ownership, exporting and productivity: An empirical investigation with plant level data, GEP Research Paper 2004/08, University of Nottingham.

Greenaway, D., Hine, R. C., & Wright, P. (1999). An empirical assessment of the impact of trade on employment in the United Kingdom. *European Journal of Political Economy*, *15*, 485–500.

Head, K., & Ries, J. (2002). Offshore production and skill upgrading by Japanese manufacturing firms. *Journal of International Economics*, *58*, 81–105.

Hijzen, A., Görg H., Hine, R.C., in press. International outsourcing and the skill structure of labour demand in the United Kingdom. *Economic Journal*.

Jones, R., & Kierkowski, H. (2001). Globalization and the consequences of international fragmentation. In R. Dornbusch, G. Calvo, & M. Obstfield (Eds.), *Festschrift in honour of Robert Mundell*. Cambridge, MA: MIT Press.

Kletzer, L. (2000). Trade and job loss in U.S. Manufacturing, 1979–1994. In R. Feestra (Ed.), *The impact of international trade on wages*. Chicago: Chicago University Press.

Kohler, W. (2001). A specific-factors view on outsourcing. *North American Journal of Economics and Finance*, *12*, 31–53.

Konings, J., & Murphy, A. (2001). Do multinational enterprises substitute parent jobs for foreign ones? Evidence from European firm level panel data. *CEPR Discussion Paper*, *2972*. CEPR, London.

Konings, J., & Vandenbussche, H. (1995). The effect of foreign competition on UK employment and wages: Evidence from firm-level panel data. *Weltwirtschaftliches Archiv*, *131*, 655–671.

Krugman, P. (1995). Growing world trade: Causes and consequences. *Brookings Papers on Economic Activity*, *I*, 327–377.

Nickell, S. (1986). Dynamic models of labour demand. In O. Ashenfelter, & R. Layard (Eds.), *Handbook of Labour Economics*, *vol. 1*. Amsterdam: North Holland.

Ruane, F., & Görg, H. (2001). Globalization and fragmentation: Evidence for the electronics industry in Ireland. In S. Arndt, & H. Kierzkowski (Eds.), *Fragmentation: New production patters in the world economy*. Oxford: Oxford University Press.

Strauss-Kahn, V., (2003). The role of globalization in the within-industry shift away from unskilled workers in France, NBER Working Paper 9716.

Part III

Labour Market Consequences at the Worker Level

Chapter III.1

INTERNATIONAL OUTSOURCING AND THE SKILL STRUCTURE OF LABOUR DEMAND IN THE UNITED KINGDOM*

Alexander Hijzen, Holger Görg and Robert C. Hine

This article investigates empirically the link between international outsourcing and the skill structure of labour demand in the UK. It is the first detailed study of this issue for the UK. Outsourcing is calculated using import-use matrices of input-output tables for manufacturing industries for the period 1982 to 1996. Estimating a system of variable factor demands, our main results show that international outsourcing has had a strong negative impact on the demand for unskilled labour. Hence, international outsourcing is an important component in explanations of the changing skill structure of manufacturing industries in the UK.

One of the main consequences of globalisation is the increasing use of international outsourcing of production, i.e., the contracting out of activities that were previously performed within a production unit to foreign subcontractors.[1] This activity has attracted increasing attention in the popular business press as well as in the academic literature. For example, the *Financial Times* asserts that: 'Subcontracting as many non-core activities as possible is a central element of the new economy' (31 July 2001, p. 10).

The establishment of international production networks associated with international outsourcing generates trade in intermediates. Some recent studies have provided evidence of the growing importance of trade in intermediates (Campa and Goldberg, 1997; Hummels *et al.*, 2001; Yeats, 2001). From the data for the UK used in this article it follows that total international outsourcing in terms of value-added increased from 33% in 1984 to 40% in 1995, while outsourcing within the same industry increased from 11% to 16% over the same period.

Outsourcing not only affects the composition of international trade but may also change the pattern of trade. In the international trade literature one of the main driving forces behind outsourcing is the existence of differences in factor prices across national borders (Feenstra and Hanson, 1996; Kohler, 2004). Unskilled labour-intensive stages of production tend to be shifted to unskilled labour-abundant developing countries, while more technologically advanced stages remain in skilled labour-abundant developed countries. As a result the increasing use of international outsourcing enhances the integration of developing countries into the world economy. Indeed for the UK the share of imports from developing

* The authors thank Richard Upward for the provision of the NES data by industry and skill category and Sourafel Girma for help with the Census of Production data. Thanks are also due to David Greenaway, Sébastien Jean, Doug Nelson, Peter Wright and an anonymous referee for very helpful comments and suggestions. All remaining errors are, of course, the authors'. Financial support from the European Commission Fifth Framework Programme (Contract No. HPSE-CT-1999-00017) and the Leverhulme Trust (Programme Grant F114/BF) is gratefully acknowledged.

[1] Many terms are used to describe the same phenomenon. These are amongst others, vertical specialisation (Hummels *et al.*, 2001), delocalisation (Leamer, 1998), fragmentation (Jones and Kierzkowski, 2001). Throughout this article we use the term 'outsourcing'.

countries over total imports increased from 18% to 22% over the period 1982–96 indicating increased competition from low-wage countries.

Many have expressed the fear in developed countries that outsourcing will tend to reduce the demand for relatively unskilled workers resulting in either falling relative wages for, or increased unemployment of, unskilled labour. Some recent examples are the discussions following the decisions by a number of UK manufacturing firms to relocate production to Asia ('Dyson, champion of British industry, switches production to Far East. Surprise decision to shed 800 jobs angers unions and shocks ministers', *The Guardian*, 6 February 2002; 'Speedo Shifts Production from Britain to China', *Daily Mail*, 30 January 2003). However, from the theoretical literature it is by no means clear that this is always necessarily the case in a general equilibrium setting (Jones and Kierzkowski, 2001; Kohler, 2004). Moreover, even if a certain theoretical framework suggests an adverse effect on labour markets it is an empirical question whether outsourcing is a sufficiently large phenomenon in order to account for any economically significant labour market effects. It is, therefore, worth analysing the impact of international outsourcing of production on domestic labour markets and in particular on the skill structure of labour demand.

The purpose of this article is to examine the effects of international outsourcing on the demand for skilled labour in the UK. While related issues have been examined for a number of developed countries (Feenstra and Hanson, 1996, for the US; Falk and Koebel, 2001 for Germany; Strauss-Kahn, 2004 for France) there does not appear to be any in-depth analysis for the UK.[2] This is surprising given that the country experienced rising wage inequality since the 1980s, even though the causes of this trend are still subject to debate.

Outsourcing differs importantly from import penetration in final goods in the sense that it explicitly takes into account the extent to which firms move production activities abroad. Moreover, labour demand is not only affected in import-competing industries but in all industries that use foreign inputs. Hence, the impact of outsourcing may not be limited to changing labour demands between industries, but also affects the relative demand for labour within industries.

This article applies and extends the approach of estimating relative demand functions for skilled workers derived from a translog cost function, which is used frequently in the literature (Feenstra and Hanson, 1996; Strauss-Kahn, 2004). The estimation uses input-output data for 50 manufacturing industries for the period 1982–96. Our main extension to this approach is to go beyond single equation estimates of relative demand for skilled labour by simultaneously estimating a system of four variable factor demands using panel data techniques.

We calculate a detailed measure of international outsourcing from the import-use matrices of the UK input-output tables. This is considered superior to the use of

[2] Anderton and Brenton (1999) examine the effect of outsourcing on relative wages, but do so by considering all imports from developing countries as outsourcing. Hence, strictly speaking, they do not explicitly measure outsourcing but total imports. Machin and Reenen (1998), Haskel and Heden (1999) and Haskel and Slaughter (2001) aim at explaining the increase in UK wage inequality but do not consider the role of international outsourcing. In a related paper Hijzen (2005) looks explicitly at outsourcing but concentrates on the price and productivity effects of outsourcing on wages using the mandated wage methodology.

total imports from a particular source country, as used by Anderton and Brenton, (1999), or the calculation of imported intermediate purchases used by Feenstra and Hanson (1996). The inclusion of the 1990s in the analysis is also a crucial part of the contribution of this article, as international fragmentation seems to be particularly a phenomenon of the last decade. Finally, labour market data obtained from the New Earnings Survey (NES) allow us to define skill groups on the basis of the Standard Occupational Classification (SOC) instead of the crude distinction between manual and non-manual workers used mostly in the literature.

The remainder of the article is structured as follows. Section 1 presents the data used and charts the trends in the labour market and in international outsourcing. Section 2 describes the econometric methodology employed. Section 3 presents and discusses the results of the estimation, while Section 4 gives a short summary and conclusions.

1. Trends in Labour Markets and International Outsourcing

This Section presents a preliminary review of the relationship between the relative demand for skilled labour and international outsourcing by discussing the data sources and some summary statistics; subsequent Sections report and discuss the econometric results.

Labour market data are obtained from the New Earnings Survey Panel Data Set (NESPD). This data set, which is described in more detail in Appendix I, allows one to construct a more accurate measure of skill than the one based on manual/non-manual workers generally used in the literature (Feenstra and Hanson, 1996; Machin and Reenen, 1998) by using employee information on occupations in accordance with the Standard Occupational Classification (SOC). The SOC distinguishes 9 Major Groups, which rank occupations according to qualifications, training, skills and experience. The SOC Major Group codes thus provide a natural way to measure skill by relating job types to skill requirements. Following the approach taken by Gregory *et al.* (2001) we distinguish three skill groups, namely skilled, semi-skilled and unskilled (see Appendix II).

Data on sales, value added, capital stock as well as prices and quantities of material purchases are obtained from the Census of Production and are described in more detail in Appendix I. Tables 1 and 2 report some summary statistics for the labour market and production data. Table 1 shows the average cost shares of high skilled, semi-skilled and unskilled workers (S_H, S_S, S_U respectively) and

Table 1

Average Cost Shares, 1982–96

	Obs	Mean	Std. Dev.	Min	Max
S_H	750	0.0745	0.0648	0.0025	0.3559
S_S	750	0.0713	0.0521	0.0000	0.2867
S_U	750	0.0702	0.0586	0.0002	0.5255
S_M	750	0.7840	0.0990	0.3227	0.9628

Subscripts refer to high skilled labour, semi-skilled labour, unskilled labour and materials respectively.

Table 2

Annual Percentage Change, 1982–96

	Obs	Mean	Std. Dev.	Min	Max
Cost shares					
S_H	50	0.0023	0.0056	−0.0126	0.0198
S_S	50	0.0000	0.0044	−0.0173	0.0115
S_U	50	0.0010	0.0045	−0.0106	0.0139
S_M	50	−0.0033	0.0052	−0.0160	0.0080
Input quantities					
L_H	50	−0.0189	0.0535	−0.2252	0.0776
L_S	50	−0.0371	0.0913	−0.3098	0.1774
L_U	50	−0.0367	0.1066	−0.2844	0.2644
M	50	0.0218	0.0468	−0.1064	0.1638
Flexible factor prices					
W_H	50	0.0654	0.0169	0.0164	0.1166
W_S	50	0.0583	0.0132	0.0178	0.1032
W_U	50	0.0583	0.0173	0.0134	0.0970
P_M	50	0.0330	0.0203	−0.0162	0.1029
Fixed input and output quantities					
K	50	0.0050	0.0361	−0.0640	0.1136
Y	50	0.0130	0.0452	−0.1173	0.1190

Subscripts refer to high skilled labour, semi-skilled labour, unskilled labour and materials respectively.

materials (S_M) at the level of the industry (50 industries). It is apparent that the average variable cost shares of labour amount to about 7% of total variable costs for all three labour types. Materials constitute the lion's share of the variable costs accounting for almost 80% of total variable costs.[3]

Table 2 reports average annual changes for the production data for the period 1982–96. The Table shows that average variable cost shares have been very stable over the sample period, which is in line with the data presented by Haskel and Slaughter (2001) for the UK.

The data on the changes in input quantities and prices, however, imply that there has been a substantial increase in labour market inequality over the period in question. Specifically, while the data show that the absolute quantities for all three types of labour decreased, the reductions in quantities of semi-skilled and unskilled labour have been stronger than the reduction for skilled workers. Hence, we note a relative employment increase by an annual average of about 1.8% in favour of skilled workers. The ratio between unskilled and semi-skilled workers remained stable. The absolute wage of skilled workers also rose faster than that for the two other skill categories, implying an increase in the relative wage of skilled workers by about 0.6% per annum.

The key issue addressed in this article is whether or not any of this trend towards the use of more skilled labour in manufacturing can be explained by industries engaging in international outsourcing of production. Recently, several studies have attempted to shed light on the development of trade in intermediates world-wide using diverse data sources. Broadly speaking three main sources have been used to document the trend in trade in intermediate inputs: data on outward processing trade, trade statistics on trade in intermediate goods, and input-output tables.

[3] Note that these data refer to the industry level. At the country level the labour requirements of domestically supplied materials would also be taken into account.

Outward processing trade in the EU or the Offshore Assembly Program in the US refers to the customs arrangement in which complete tariff exemptions or partial levy reductions are granted in accordance to the domestic input content of imported goods. These data have been used by, for example, Görg (2000) and Egger and Egger (2001) for the EU and Feenstra *et al.* (2000) for the US. In some cases the classification of trade statistics can be used to infer whether trade in some particular industry is trade in intermediate or final goods, as for example in the papers by Yeats (2001) and Hummels *et al.* (2001).

For the present purposes input-output tables are considered the most appropriate source as they allow one to analyse developments across industries and time simultaneously. Comparisons over time on the basis of outward processing trade data can be problematic when trade arrangements change. Think for example of the Europe Agreements, which make outward processing trade arrangements increasingly redundant. Comparisons across industries on the basis of the classification of trade statistics seem to be difficult to justify given the different levels of aggregation for different industries.

Input-output tables, however, are also subject to a number of shortcomings. There seem to be two main drawbacks of using input-output tables to analyse outsourcing. First, when focusing on trade in intermediates one necessarily ignores the possibility of outsourcing of the final production stage such as assembly (Ng and Yeats, 1999). Second, the data do not capture outsourcing when products are not re-imported, but exported to third markets.

Data on imported intermediate imports are obtained directly from the UK Input-Output Analytical Tables (I-O ATs), which are compiled approximately every five years by the Office for National Statistics (ONS). The I-O ATs distinguish between intermediate purchases from domestic suppliers ('domestic use matrix') and imported intermediate purchases ('import use matrix'). The present study uses input-output tables for 1984, 1990 and 1995. In addition, from 1992 onwards combined-use matrices are available annually. For more details on the Input-Output data see Appendix I.

Generally, international outsourcing has been defined on the basis of the foreign content of domestic production by taking into account the share of imported intermediate inputs in production. Consequently, the measure has typically been used to asses to what extent workers at home have been substituted by workers abroad, i.e. to evaluate the elasticity of substitution of domestic value-added with respect to imported intermediate inputs. Thus the measure captures the essence of international outsourcing, i.e. a firm's decision to substitute domestic value-added by foreign production.[4]

We use a narrow definition of international outsourcing which only considers imported intermediates in a given industry from the same industry (which corresponds to diagonal terms of the import-use matrix), i.e.,

[4] Campa and Goldberg (1997) using this measure observe that the ratio of imported intermediates to sales in manufacturing rose from 4% in 1974 to 8% in 1993 in the US, from 16% to 20% in Canada and from 13% to 22% in the UK.

$$S_O^N = \frac{O_{i=j,t}}{VA_{jt}} \tag{1}$$

where *O* is imported intermediates in industry *j* only, and *VA* is value added in the industry.

Feenstra and Hanson (1999) refer to this as *narrow outsourcing*. They prefer this measure to *broad outsourcing*, i.e. imported inputs from all industries, as it is thought to come closer to the essence of fragmentation which necessarily takes place within the industry. The narrow measure of outsourcing seems particularly appropriate at relatively high levels of aggregation.[5] The motivation to limit oneself to the narrow measure is slightly different here. As we show below we extend the standard translog cost framework only by measures of factor-biased technological change (FBTC), namely outsourcing and innovation activity. It has been widely documented that the increase in the relative demand for skilled labour occurred largely within industries. Consequently, in order to analyse the sources of wage inequality one should concentrate on factors that change relative factor demand within industries. This is exactly what the narrow definition of outsourcing does, while it is not obscured by shifts between domestic and foreign suppliers.

We calculate our outsourcing measure directly from the import-use matrices of the input-output tables. By contrast, Feenstra and Hanson (1996, 1999) use combined-use matrices in combination with total import penetration ratios calculated from the trade data. Our direct measure may be considered superior to this as it has the advantage that outsourcing is no longer driven by increased import penetration of all goods. After all, increased import penetration refers both to trade in intermediate and trade in final goods. A measure of outsourcing defined as trade in intermediates may therefore be biased when final goods are included, i.e. the significance of outsourcing may be underestimated when trade in intermediates grows faster than trade in final goods.

Table 3 shows descriptive statistics for international outsourcing for the years for which the data are available. In addition to the narrow measure of outsourcing the table also contains information on *broad outsourcing* and *differential outsourcing*, i.e. the difference between the broad and narrow definition. Narrow outsourcing was more or less constant during the 1980s around 14–15% of value-added, but increased during the first half of the 1990s to 19% of value-added. Differential outsourcing remained fairly stable over the whole period 1984 to 1995, while broad outsourcing, the sum of narrow and differential outsourcing, also increased from 46% in 1984 to 49% in 1995 (reflecting the increase in outsourcing within the same industry).

[5] The distinction between narrow and broad outsourcing as introduced by Feenstra and Hanson (1999) may not be without problems as it is entirely based on the way industries are classified. From a fragmentation perspective it can well be the case that industries are classified on an unequal level of disaggregation. Compare for example the two following industries: 'motor vehicles and parts' and 'textiles'. Both industries are classical examples where fragmentation occurs. However, 'automobiles and parts' is represented in the input-output tables for the UK as one single industry, whereas textiles are made up of 10 different industries. As a result the narrow measure of outsourcing will not pick up much of the outsourcing in textiles. The broad measure on the other hand will be distorted through the inclusion of packaging and raw materials.

Table 3

International Outsourcing in 1984, 1990 *and* 1995

	Total	Unskilled-intensive	Skilled-intensive
Narrow			
1984	0.152	0.173	0.122
1990	0.135	0.152	0.112
1995	0.186	0.177	0.200
Differential			
1984	0.308	0.288	0.335
1990	0.317	0.322	0.310
1995	0.302	0.295	0.311
Broad			
1984	0.459	0.461	0.457
1990	0.452	0.474	0.422
1995	0.488	0.472	0.511

Based on unweighted averages.

An interesting question is whether outsourcing is related to the skill-intensity of the purchasing industry. Traditional trade theory generally emphasises the role of sector-biased structural change, which refers to the cost-saving effect of outsourcing. Only when it is cost-saving will it be consistent with profit-maximising behaviour. Assuming that the effectiveness of outsourcing is homogeneous across industries, the change in outsourcing will be proportional to productivity growth. To the extent that outsourcing contributes to the sector bias of TFP outsourcing is a plausible source of the increase in domestic wage inequality.

In a specific-factors model (as implicitly assumed in the econometric analysis below given that capital is assumed to be quasi-fixed) the factor bias of outsourcing could also affect relative wages. If one assumes that all imported intermediates are unskilled-intensive the factor bias of outsourcing will on average exert a downward pressure on the relative wage of unskilled workers. This reasoning holds irrespective of the skill-intensity of the purchasing (outsourcing) industry. Thus from a general equilibrium perspective tabulating outsourcing against skill-intensity can only reveal something about its sector bias, not its factor bias.

The last two columns of Table 3 present outsourcing by skill-intensity where skill-intensity is defined on the basis of the cost share of skilled labour in the wage bill in 1989. Narrow outsourcing remained more or less constant in importance in the unskilled intensive industries and almost doubled in the skill-intensive industries. One cannot observe a clear pattern for differential outsourcing. Clearly, narrow outsourcing has been subject to a strong sector bias towards the more skill-intensive activities. Unfortunately, no information with regards to the factor bias of outsourcing is available.

2. Econometric Methodology

In order to investigate the relationship between international outsourcing and the skill structure of labour demand econometrically we start off from the by now standard approach to analysing the relative demand for skilled labour based on the estimation of a translog cost function, introduced by Berman *et al.* (1994). This approach has been used widely in the literature on the effects of outsourcing on the skilled-unskilled wage differential (Feenstra and Hanson, 1996; Strauss-Kahn, 2004). However, our methodology departs in two important ways from the standard labour demand regressions *à la* Berman *et al.* (1994).

First, rather than estimating a single cost share equation we estimate a system of demand equations for all variable factors.[6] We estimate this system simultaneously, which yields more efficient results than single equation estimation when the disturbances are correlated across equations. Given that the right-hand side is identical across equations and that there are cross-equation restrictions this is bound to be the case (Berndt, 1991). In addition, estimating a system of variable factor demands provides more detailed information on the impact of structural change on industry level factor demands. The variable factors are skilled, semi-skilled, unskilled labour, and materials. As in Berman *et al.* (1994) capital is assumed to be quasi-fixed so that both output and capital can be treated as exogenous in the short run.

Second, while most studies take first differences in order to purge industry-specific time-invariant effects, we apply a fixed-effects (within) estimator to estimate the model. The within estimator emphasises the short run dimension of the data which is consistent with the specification of the restricted or short run cost function. Also it is well known that first-differencing can exacerbate potential problems of measurement error in the data (Griliches and Hausman, 1986), hence we prefer the fixed effects technique.

We extend the standard translog cost framework to analyse explicitly the impact of factor-biased technological change (FBTC) on relative labour demand, and the sources of FBTC. Two measures of FBTC are used: first, international outsourcing as described above. Second, to ensure that the international outsourcing variable does not just pick up the effects of technical change in the industry *per se*, we include the industry's R&D intensity. This proxy is intended to pick up technological change in working practices due to the adoption of more sophisticated technologies. Machin and Reenen (1998) also include this variable to capture the impact of changes in technology on relative labour demand. Alternative measures of technological change could be computer intensity (Haskel and Heden, 1998) or actual measures of technology adoption (Doms *et al.*, 1997). However, such data are unfortunately not available to us.

As in Berndt (1991) and Berman *et al.* (1994) it is assumed that the industry cost functions can be approximated by a translog function, which is twice differentiable, linearly homogenous and concave in factor prices. In general notation, the translog variable (or restricted) cost function can be represented as follows:

$$\begin{aligned}\ln C_i(w, x, z) &= \alpha_0 + \sum_{j=1}^{J} \alpha_j \ln w_{ij} + \sum_{k=1}^{K} \beta_k \ln x_{ik} + \sum_{r=1}^{R} \gamma_r z_{ir} \\ &+ \frac{1}{2}\sum_{j=1}^{J}\sum_{s=1}^{J} \alpha_{ij} \ln w_{ij} \ln w_{is} + \frac{1}{2}\sum_{k=1}^{K}\sum_{l=1}^{K} \beta_{kl} \ln x_{ik} \ln x_{il} + + \frac{1}{2}\sum_{r=1}^{R}\sum_{t=1}^{R} \gamma_{rt} z_{ir} z_{it} \qquad (2) \\ &+ \frac{1}{2}\sum_{j=1}^{J}\sum_{k=1}^{K} \delta_{jk} \ln w_{ij} \ln x_{ik} + \frac{1}{2}\sum_{j=1}^{J}\sum_{r=1}^{R} \delta_{jr} \ln w_{ij} z_{ir} + \frac{1}{2}\sum_{k=1}^{K}\sum_{r=1}^{R} \delta_{kr} \ln x_{ik} z_{ir}\end{aligned}$$

[6] See Berndt (1991) for an overview of the methodology.

where C_i represents total variable cost in industry $i = 1, \ldots, N$, and is a function of factor prices w_{ij} for factor $j = 1, \ldots, J$, and industry $i = 1, \ldots, N$; fixed inputs and outputs x_{ik} for fixed input or output $k = 1, \ldots, K$ in industry $i = 1, \ldots, N$; and technological change z_{ir} for proxy $r = r, \ldots, R$ in industry $i = 1, \ldots, N$.[7] Time subscripts are omitted throughout for ease of presentation. A full set of time dummies is included in order to capture economy-wide technological change over time.

Constant returns to scale requires that the variable cost function is linearly homogenous in variable factor prices.

$$\sum_{j=1}^{J} \alpha_j = 1 \text{ and} \sum_{j=1}^{J} \alpha_{js} = \sum_{s=1}^{J} \alpha_{sj} = \sum_{j=1}^{J} \delta_{jk} = \sum_{j=1}^{J} \delta_{jr} = 0. \tag{3}$$

Without loss of generality symmetry implies that $\alpha_{js} = \alpha_{sj}$.[8] Differentiating the translog cost function with respect to factor prices yields the cost share of factor j in total variable costs.

$$S_{ij} = \alpha_j + \sum_{s=1}^{J} \alpha_{js} \ln w_{ij} + \sum_{k=1}^{K} \delta_{jk} \ln x_{ik} + \sum_{r=1}^{R} \delta_{jr} z_{ir}, j = 1, .., s, .., J \tag{4}$$

where $S_{ij} = \partial \ln C_i / \partial \ln w_{ij} = (w_{ij}/C_i)(\partial C_i / \partial w_{ij}) = w_{ij} x_{ij} / C_i$ and $\sum_{j=1}^{J} S_{ij} = 1$.

The complete system of share equations is estimated using Zellner's method for seemingly unrelated regression equations (SUR). Due to the adding up condition of the variable cost shares the disturbance covariance matrix of the system will be singular and one equation therefore needs to be dropped. The SUR estimates will normally not be invariant to the equation deleted. Fortunately, invariance can be obtained by iterating Zellner's method (ISUR) so that the parameter estimates and residual covariance matrix converge (Berndt and Wood, 1975).[9] We combine the SUR estimator with panel data estimation techniques to estimate the system given by (4) whilst controlling for time-invariant industry-specific effects.

In addition to reporting the results obtained from estimating the variable cost function the elasticities of factor demand will be represented. The elasticity of factor demand j with respect to a change in factor prices is given by:

$$\varepsilon_{js} = \frac{\partial \ln v_j}{\partial \ln w_s} = \frac{\alpha_{js}}{s_j} + s_s - \phi_{js}, \quad \sum_{j=1}^{N} \varepsilon_{js} = 0 \tag{5}$$

where $\phi = 1$ if $j = s$. The elasticity of factor demand j with respect to a change in the capital stock or output is given by:

$$\varepsilon_{jk} = \frac{\partial \ln v_j}{\partial \ln x_k} = \frac{\delta_{jk}}{s_j}, \quad \sum_{l=1}^{M} \varepsilon_{jk} = 1. \tag{6}$$

The elasticity of factor demand with respect to factor-biased technological change due to international outsourcing or R&D is given by:

[7] Note that z_{ir} does not enter the function in log form as they are already in percentages.
[8] A Wald-test for the validity of symmetry restrictions could not be rejected.
[9] However, convergence might not always be possible.

$$\varepsilon_{jr} = \frac{\partial \ln v_j}{\partial z_r} = \frac{\delta_{jr}}{s_r}, \quad \sum_{k=1}^{M} \varepsilon_{jr} = 1. \tag{7}$$

The command ANALYZ in TSP can used to obtain approximate standard errors (Kohli, 1991).[10]

3. Results

Table 4 reports the results of estimating the system of equations using two alternative econometric techniques. Specification 1 uses the pooled iterative Zellner or seemingly unrelated regression estimator (pooled ISUR). Specification 2 accounts

Table 4

Regression Results, 1982–96

	Pooled SUR			Fixed effects SUR		
		(a)	(b)		(a)	(b)
α_H	0.163	(0.035)**	(0.038)**	0.001	(0.006)	(0.006)
α_S	0.195	(0.028)**	(0.031)**	0.009	(0.006)	(0.008)
α_U	0.114	(0.030)**	(0.029)**	0.017	(0.006)**	(0.009)*
α_{HH}	0.002	(0.014)	(0.014)	0.038	(0.010)**	(0.011)**
α_{HS}	−0.037	(0.009)**	(0.012)**	−0.014	(0.007)	(0.009)
α_{HU}	−0.017	(0.009)*	(0.010)	−0.022	(0.007)**	(0.009)*
α_{SS}	0.034	(0.011)**	(0.012)**	0.046	(0.009)**	(0.012)**
α_{SU}	−0.022	(0.008)**	(0.010)*	−0.024	(0.007)**	(0.009)**
α_{UU}	0.069	(0.011)**	(0.012)**	0.064	(0.010)**	(0.012)**
δ_{HK}	0.020	(0.005)**	(0.004)**	0.040	(0.008)**	(0.009)**
δ_{HY}	−0.008	(0.005)	(0.004)*	−0.018	(0.005)**	(0.004)**
δ_{HT}	0.014	(0.008)	(0.007)*	0.015	(0.007)*	(0.007)*
δ_{HO}	−0.034	(0.009)**	(0.007)**	−0.010	(0.013)	(0.013)
δ_{SK}	0.020	(0.004)**	(0.004)**	0.002	(0.008)	(0.008)
δ_{SY}	−0.024	(0.004)**	(0.004)**	−0.011	(0.005)*	(0.007)
δ_{ST}	−0.030	(0.007)**	(0.007)**	−0.002	(0.007)	(0.009)
δ_{SO}	−0.040	(0.007)**	(0.005)**	−0.016	(0.013)	(0.011)
δ_{UK}	0.019	(0.004)**	(0.004)**	0.004	(0.009)	(0.008)
δ_{UY}	−0.030	(0.004)**	(0.004)**	−0.013	(0.006)*	(0.004)**
δ_{UT}	−0.031	(0.007)**	(0.010)**	−0.014	(0.008)	(0.011)
δ_{UO}	−0.044	(0.008)**	(0.006)**	−0.045	(0.015)**	(0.011)**
Groups		50			50	
Years		15			15	
N		748			748	
$\tilde{R}^2$		0.407			0.534	

Notes.
Unweighted regressions, standard errors in parentheses, **, *, refer to 5% and 1% significance levels.
Subscripts refer to high skilled labour (*H*), semi-skilled labour (*S*), unskilled labour (*U*), materials (*M*), capital (*K*), output (*Y*), R&D (*T*) and narrow outsourcing (*O*) respectively.
In column (a) standard errors are computed from the quadratic form of analytic first derivatives (Gauss).
In column (b) standard errors are computed from a heteroscedastic-consistent matrix (Robust-White).

[10] The command ANALYZ computes the values along with the estimated covariance matrix for *a set of nonlinear functions of the parameters.* The method involves linearising the non-linear functions around the estimated parameter values. Subsequently, the standard formulas for the variance and covariance in the context of linear functions of random variables are used (TSP International, 1999)

for industry fixed effects (fixed effects ISUR). In line with theory, the capital stock is included rather than capital-intensity as is the case in most single-equation studies. The regressions include a full set of time dummies. The R^2 measure for the goodness of fit reported by most statistical packages applies only to single equation regressions. In a system the R^2 is no longer constrained between zero and one as system estimators do not share the same objective function (min $\mathbf{e}'\mathbf{e}$). This article therefore presents the generalised R^2 as suggested by Berndt (1991). All estimations are performed in TSP.

The interpretation of the results is not straightforward since the right-hand side variables are in natural logarithms (except for the technological change variables) whereas the dependent variables are not. Results will therefore be discussed on the basis of the estimated price and quantity elasticities. A Hausman test on the performance of the pooled ISUR versus fixed effects ISUR estimator indicates that fixed effects ISUR estimator should be preferred ($\chi^2(7) \sim 13.575$, Upper tail area: 0.000).

The cost functions are well behaved if they are concave in factor prices. If curvature conditions are not satisfied the results are inconsistent with economic theory. Concavity implies that the matrix of second-order derivatives with respect to factor prices is negative semi-definite. A sufficient condition for negative semi-definiteness is that all the principal minors are negative. The translog cost function does not satisfy these properties globally. One should therefore check whether the curvature conditions are satisfied at each observation (Diewert and Wales, 1987). With 750 observations this is not only cumbersome but it is also unlikely that curvature conditions will be satisfied at all points. Instead we require that curvature conditions are satisfied on average. The elasticities are therefore evaluated on the basis of the simple average cost shares across industries (consistent with unweighted regression).

Table 5 reports the price elasticities of factor demand. A necessary but not sufficient condition for concavity in factor prices is that all the own price elasticities are negative (italic in the Table). Inspection of the signs reveals that elasticities are

Table 5

Factor Demand Elasticities, 1982–96

	Pooled SUR				Fixed effects SUR			
	w_H	w_S	w_U	p_M	w_H	w_S	w_U	p_M
L_H	*−0.903*	−0.427	−0.165	1.494	*−0.421*	−0.120	−0.220	0.760
	(0.184)**	(0.154)**	(0.134)	(0.215)**	(0.153)**	(0.118)	(0.123)	(0.109)
L_S	−0.446	*−0.458*	−0.237	1.141	−0.125	*−0.284*	−0.266	0.675
	(0.161)**	(0.162)**	(0.135)	(0.177)**	(0.124)	(0.173)	(0.121)*	(0.102)**
L_U	−0.175	−0.241	***0.046***	0.369	−0.234	−0.270	*−0.011*	0.515
	(0.142)	(0.137)	(0.174)	(0.159)**	(0.130)	(0.123)*	(0.165)	(0.095)**
M	0.142	0.104	0.033	*−0.278*	0.072	0.061	0.046	*−0.180*
	(0.020)**	(0.016)**	(0.014)*	(0.033)**	(0.010)**	(0.009)**	(0.009)**	(0.014)**

Notes. The elasticities correspond to the regression results reported in Table 4. Standard errors in parentheses, **, *, refer to 5% and 1% significance levels. The standard errors of the elasticities are computed with the command ANALYZ in TSP using the Gaussian standard errors. Italic elements refer to the own price elasticities of factor demand. The bold italic elements highlight the own price elasticities that are inconsistent with economic theory.

negative except for the price elasticity of the demand for unskilled labour in the pooled estimation, which is statistically insignificant. The qualitative pattern of the factor demand elasticities is identical for the two sets of results, although quantitatively the elasticities that are obtained from the fixed effects estimates are smaller.

Note that materials are substitutes for all three types of labour. A relatively small reduction in the price of materials can lead to fairly large reductions in the demand for labour. Conversely, a change in wages only has a fairly small impact on the demand for materials. The different types of labour appear to be complements. The results suggest that make-or-buy decisions tend to outweigh substitution effects between variable primary factors. Once the decision has been taken to produce a component in-house the mix of primary inputs is relatively stable.

Table 6 reports the remainder of the elasticities that can be obtained from the estimates presented in Table 4. Here, we are particularly interested in the elasticities for outsourcing and R&D intensity. The latter measure of factor-biased technological change has a positive and significant effect on the demand for skilled workers and a negative effect on the demand for semi-skilled and unskilled workers (although the negative effect is only statistically significant in the pooled regressions); findings that are in line with the results in Machin and Reenen (1998) and Haskel and Heden (1999).

Narrow outsourcing has a negative effect on the demand for all types of labour and a positive effect on the demand for materials. Importantly, the impact of international outsourcing is stronger the lower the level of skills. When controlling for industry fixed effects only the elasticity with respect to the demand for unskilled labour is statistically significant. Hence, when analysing the impact of international outsourcing on labour demand it seems important to distinguish between semi-skilled and unskilled workers. Indeed, the most unskilled-intensive activities seem to be most suitable for outsourcing because the potential cost-saving effect is likely to be highest and the need for monitoring and quality control lowest.[11]

Table 6

Other Elasticities, 1982–96

	Pooled SUR				Fixed SUR			
	K	*Y*	*RND*	*OUT*	*K*	*Y*	*RND*	*OUT*
L_H	0.272	−0.110	0.186	−0.453	0.538	−0.239	0.207	−0.135
	(0.050)**	(0.051)*	(0.092)*	(0.090)**	(0.125)**	(0.056)**	(0.094)*	(0.168)
L_S	0.280	−0.340	−0.426	−0.557	0.027	−0.153	−0.029	−0.222
	(0.056)**	(0.061)**	(0.097)**	(0.076)**	(0.116)	(0.098)	(0.122)	(0.154)
L_U	0.271	−0.428	−0.436	−0.623	0.055	−0.180	−0.205	−0.639
	(0.055)**	(0.061)**	(0.136)**	(0.083)**	(0.117)	(0.063)**	(0.163)	(0.158)**
M	−0.076	0.080	0.060	0.149	−0.059	0.053	0.001	0.090
	(0.009)**	(0.010)**	(0.015)**	(0.013)**	(0.014)**	(0.010)**	(0.007)	(0.021)**

Notes. The elasticities correspond to the regression results reported in Table 4. Standard errors in parentheses, **, *, refer to 5% and 1% significance levels. The standard errors of the elasticities are computed with the command ANALYZ in TSP using the Gaussian standard errors.

[11] Replacing narrow with broad outsourcing did not produce statistically significant results.

A brief examination of the other elasticities shows that capital accumulation has a positive effect on all types of workers, while it has a negative impact on the purchases of materials. Only when accounting for industry fixed effects does capital accumulation disproportionately favour the demand for skilled workers as predicted by the capital-skill complementarity hypothesis. The impact of output on factor demand mirrors qualitatively and to some extent also quantitatively that of capital.[12]

In order to comment on the robustness of these results we present two alternative sets of estimations. First, we use the employment shares instead of cost shares as dependent variables. It has become common practice in single equation factor demand studies to run an additional set of regressions in which the cost shares are replaced by the employment shares in order to highlight the labour market outcome in the presence of labour market rigidities (Machin and Reenen, 1998; Anderton and Brenton, 1999; Strauss-Kahn, 2004).

The factor demand approach is neutral with respect to the channel of adjustment. With perfectly inelastic labour supply, labour markets adjust in response to a labour demand shock by a combination of changes in wages and changes in the output mix. In rigid labour markets, wages and outputs do not adjust to the full extent to clear the labour market. Instead, a relative labour demand shock will be reflected by an increase in unemployment of the factor whose relative demand falls. In practice, one does not observe labour demand shocks but instead one only observes the change in relative labour demand after wages *and* employment have adjusted.

Given that when using a translog cost function the dependent variable of the labour demand equation is both a function of wages and employment it is not surprising that an increase in the relative demand for skilled labour has been interpreted as an increase in wage inequality in economies with flexible labour markets such as the US and the UK. Using employment shares instead of cost shares will give the impact of a labour demand shock on factor demand net of wage effects. This specification is therefore only justified when wage adjustment is negligible as may be the case in rigid labour markets.[13]

Table 7 reports the elasticities for the cost and employment share regressions. This system now excludes materials since employment shares can only be constructed for the three types of labour as materials cannot be expressed in comparable units. An interesting consequence of excluding materials is that the different types of labour now act as substitutes rather than complements. This is consistent with the above explanation that make-or-buy decisions drive the pattern of the elasticities above. Furthermore, we now find from the elasticities based on the cost share estimates that outsourcing only affects low skilled workers, while the elasticities on R&D remain qualitatively and quantitatively similar to those reported in Table 6.

[12] In principle this seems to suggest that constant returns to scale might be a reasonable approximation for the technology. However, the restriction of constant returns to scale was rejected in all cases.

[13] Put differently, as long as the elasticity of substitution between production and non-production workers exceeds unity changes in cost shares provide a better measure of changes in relative demand than changes in employment shares (Berman *et al.*, 1994).

Table 7

Elasticities Based on Cost and Employment Share Regressions, 1982–96

	Cost shares with fixed SUR				Employment shares with fixed SUR			
	w_H	w_S	w_U		w_H	w_S	w_U	
L_H	*−0.267*	0.261	0.007		*−0.787*	0.494	0.293	
	(0.128)*	(0.106)*	(0.097)		(0.165)**	(0.150)**	(0.124)*	
L_S	0.263	*−0.230*	−0.032		0.347	*−0.501*	0.153	
	(0.106)*	(0.130)	(0.097)		(0.105)**	(0.133)**	(0.098)	
L_U	0.007	−0.032	***0.026***		0.193	0.144	*−0.337*	
	(0.098)	(0.097)	(0.121)		(0.082)*	(0.092)	(0.110)**	
	K	*Y*	*RND*	*OUT*	*K*	*Y*	*RND*	*OUT*
L_H	0.108	0.080	0.265	0.241	0.127	0.078	0.317	0.285
	(0.092)	(0.070)	(0.099)**	(0.141)	(0.107)	(0.083)	(0.120)**	(0.165)
L_S	−0.129	−0.017	−0.185	0.199	−0.110	−0.004	−0.145	0.186
	(0.096)	(0.064)	(0.149)	(0.150)	(0.094)	(0.063)	(0.143)	(0.156)
L_U	0.020	−0.063	−0.082	−0.441	0.020	−0.048	−0.073	−0.362
	(0.098)	(0.079)	(0.148)	(0.176)*	(0.092)	(0.071)	(0.136)	(0.161)*

Notes. Based on unweighted regressions. Standard errors in parentheses, **, *, refer to 5% and 1% significance levels. The standard errors of the elasticities are computed with the command ANALYZ in TSP using the Gaussian standard errors. Italic elements refer to the own price elasticities of factor demand. The bold italic elements highlight the own price elasticities that are inconsistent with economic theory. Materials are excluded.

There does not seem to be a significant difference between the cost and employment share regressions in Table 7. If anything, our results show that the price elasticities of factor demand in the cost share regression tend to be smaller than in the employment regressions. This might indicate that the estimated elasticities obtained with the cost share regression are biased upwards due to simultaneity bias between the labour cost shares and wages. The negative impact of outsourcing on the demand for unskilled workers is smaller in the employment share regressions than in the cost share regressions. This is consistent with findings in previous studies.

A second alternative set of regressions replaces the industry level wages by country level wages. Berman *et al.* (1994) argue that the cross-industry variation of wages reflects only differences in the quality of workers and thus assume that quality-adjusted wages will be constant across industries. They, therefore, suggest that the wage terms can be dropped from the right-hand side of (4) above. In the present case we are dealing with a panel rather than a cross-section. Instead of dropping wages altogether in the last set of results, industry-level wages are replaced by country-level wages.

The motivation for doing so is twofold. Firstly, country-level wages are consistent with the standard version of the specific-factors model.[14] The specifications estimated above could be considered to reflect the perspective of a labour economist. While capital is fixed in the short-run, the different types of labour can adjust instantaneously. However, in contrast to the specific-factors model, labour markets

[14] The prices of materials will also be equalised across industries. However, the data used for the price of materials are indices which take into account the composition of material purchases. The price indices are therefore allowed to change across industries.

continue to be segmented between industries (as reflected by industry level wages). The specific-factors model relaxes the assumption of segmented labour markets but instead assumes that labour is perfectly mobile across sectors. Consequently, wages will be equalised across industries. By replacing industry-level wages by country-level wages we thus effectively implement a framework based on the specific-factors model. Secondly, country-level wages are unlikely to be endogenous as no single industry is likely to be large enough to exert a substantial effect on country-level wages. Thus, one would expect the own price elasticities of labour demand to be more negative.

Table 8 represents the elasticities obtained from the cost share regressions with country-level wages using both pooled and fixed effects SUR. Due to multicollinearity between country level wages and time dummies the latter cannot be estimated separately and, hence, comparisons of the estimations with previous results are more difficult. The results change in two directions. First, the own price elasticities of labour demand tend to be more negative, as anticipated. Second, while materials continue to act as substitutes for all three types of labour, the pattern of elasticities of substitution between the different types of labour changes. In the fixed effects regression, skilled and semi-skilled labour appear to act as substitutes as do semi-skilled and unskilled workers. However, unskilled and skilled workers are apparently so different that they act as each other's complements. The elasticities on outsourcing and R&D are similar in sign and magnitude to those reported in Table 6.

Table 8

Elasticities Specific-factors Model (with labour mobility), 1982–96

	Pooled SUR				Fixed SUR			
	w_H	w_S	w_U	p_M	w_H	w_S	w_U	p_M
L_H	***0.271***	−0.117	−0.505	0.350	*−0.528*	0.745	−0.368	0.151
	(0.577)	(0.675)	(0.619)	(0.180)	(0.450)	(0.599)	(0.528)	(0.140)
L_S	−0.122	*−3.348*	3.563	−0.094	0.779	*−4.776*	3.525	0.472
	(0.705)	(2.341)	(1.871)	(0.189)	(0.626)	(2.008)*	(1.604)*	(0.163)**
L_U	−0.536	3.619	*−2.977*	−0.106	−0.391	3.580	*−3.431*	0.241
	(0.657)	(1.901)	(1.636)	(0.217)	(0.560)	(1.630)*	(1.435)*	(0.205)
M	0.033	−0.009	−0.010	*−0.015*	0.014	0.043	0.022	*−0.079*
	(0.017)	(0.017)	(0.019)	(0.022)	(0.013)	(0.015)**	(0.018)	(0.013)**
	K	*Y*	*RND*	*OUT*	*K*	*Y*	*RND*	*OUT*
L_H	0.255	−0.141	0.154	−0.482	0.549	−0.220	0.416	−0.181
	(0.057)**	(0.064)*	(0.106)	(0.089)**	(0.124)**	(0.098)*	(0.093)**	(0.139)
L_S	0.352	−0.420	−0.377	−0.626	0.170	−0.244	−0.048	−0.112
	(0.050)**	(0.053)**	(0.090)**	(0.075)**	(0.104)	(0.089)**	(0.171)	(0.142)
L_U	0.282	−0.435	−0.562	−0.663	0.211	−0.220	−0.107	−0.589
	(0.054)**	(0.062)**	(0.110)**	(0.089)**	(0.138)	(0.132)	(0.145)	(0.157)**
M	−0.082	0.090	0.070	0.162	−0.087	0.063	−0.026	0.080
	(0.009)**	(0.009)**	(0.011)**	(0.012)**	(0.015)**	(0.014)**	(0.011)*	(0.018)**

Notes: Based on unweighted regressions. Standard errors in parentheses, **, *, refer to 5% and 1% significance levels. The standard errors of the elasticities are computed with the command ANALYZ in TSP using the Gaussian standard errors. Italic elements refer to the own price elasticities of factor demand. The bold italic elements highlight the own price elasticities that are inconsistent with economic theory. No time dummies included.

4. Conclusion

In this article international outsourcing is related to the debate on trade and wages. Although both the sector and the factor bias of outsourcing are likely to affect relative wages this study focuses exclusively on the factor bias by incorporating outsourcing as a proxy for factor-biased technological change in the factor demand equations. In order to emphasise the factor bias of outsourcing the measure of international outsourcing was constructed on the basis of the diagonal elements of the import-use matrices of the input-output tables. Only imported intermediate purchases from the same manufacturing industry are included as such changes induce factor-biased technological change.

Estimating a system of equations for variable cost factors, our main results show that international outsourcing has had a strong negative impact on the demand for unskilled labour in the UK. R&D activity, on the other hand, appears to have increased the demand for skilled labour, as has also been found in other studies. Hence, both international outsourcing and technological change induced through R&D are important components in explanations of the changing skill structure of manufacturing industries in the UK. The main results are robust to alternative specifications of the econometric model.

University of Nottingham

Submitted: 7 August 2002
Accepted: 26 July 2004

Appendix I: Data

A1 *Description of the New Earnings Survey Panel Data Set*

The NESPD is based on a series of surveys carried out by the Office for National Statistics that covers approximately 1% of the working population. The survey is directed to employers who complete it on the basis of payroll records for the employee for a specific week in April. As the employer and employee are linked via an employee's income tax records the NESPD tends to under-represent employees whose income falls below the income tax threshold. The present study only takes into account male workers aged between 18–65 who work full time and are not self-employed.

A2 *Description of Input-Output Data*

Data on imported intermediate imports are obtained directly from the UK Input-Output Analytical Tables (I-O ATs), which are compiled approximately every five years by the Office for National Statistics (ONS). The I-O ATs are derived from the Input-Output Supply and Use Tables (I-O SUTs) which were compiled approximately every five years until 1991 and annually from 1992 onwards. The I-O tables are consistent with National Accounts. The I-O SUTs provide detailed information on the supply and demand for product in terms of industries. Consequently, the I-O SUTs constitute a source of rich information on the interdependence between industries and institutional sectors. The

I-O ATs distinguish between intermediate purchases from domestic suppliers ('domestic use matrix') and imported intermediate purchases ('import use matrix'). I-O ATs are symmetric by construction showing the interdependence between either products and products or industries and industries. The present study uses product by product tables, which are recommended as the industry by industry tables are associated with certain conceptual problems that are encountered in the product by product tables. The product by product tables are also less vulnerable to structural change resulting from mergers and acquisitions or fragmentation of production (ONS, 2002). The present study uses input-output tables for 1984, 1990 and 1995. In addition, from 1992 onwards combined-use matrices are available annually. The outsourcing variable is constructed using the following procedure. Imported intermediate purchases are therefore extrapolated using total intermediate purchasing where possible. The remaining gaps are filled up with linear extrapolation.

A3 *Description of Variables*

Data on sales, value added and capital expenditure are obtained from the Census of Production. Capital stock data are estimated from capital expenditures using the Perpetual Inventory Method (PIM). At least two difficulties arise when estimating the capital stock. First, economic depreciation consists of two elements: physical deterioration due to usage or ageing, and obsolescence, which refers to the reduction of efficiency relative to new assets. Second, different types of capital are subject to different rates of depreciation. Oulton and O'Mahony (1994) provide estimates for the total rate of economic depreciation for five different types of capital. In addition, they present estimates of the proportion of capital expenditure on each capital type for various years over the period 1968–84 for 10 industries. Combining this information it is possible to generate industry-specific depreciation rates. Applying PIM with a pattern of geometric decay gives the following formula:

$$K_{it} = \sum\nolimits_{t-q}^{t} \left(1 - \sum\nolimits_{1}^{k} S_k\delta_k\right)^{q-1} I_{i,t-q} + \left(1 - \sum\nolimits_{1}^{k} S_k\delta_k\right)^{t-1979} K_{i,1979}.$$

The capital stock for industry i at time t equals the sum of expenditure on asset k at time $t - q$ depreciated by the asset-specific economic depreciation rate δ_k plus the depreciated benchmark capital stock. Both the proportion of capital expenditure on each asset, S_k, and the depreciation rate are assumed constant over time. This way annual capital stock estimates are generated.

Disaggregated data on expenditure on R&D are only available for the period 1982–90. For the missing years R&D is extrapolated using sales. Trade data are obtained from the OECD Trade Database. The trade data are classified according to SITC Rev2 and Rev3. The industry data on sales, value added and capital are classified according to SIC(80) and SIC(92) respectively. Based on product descriptions and industry size a 'best guess' for each SIC(92) industry was obtained. Consequently, industries were regrouped in order to make the classification compatible to the level of aggregation in the I-O tables. The correspondence table thus obtained distinguished 53 SIC manufacturing industries. The table should be fairly reliable in both ways.[16]

Import penetration is measured as the value of imports over industry value added. Developed countries include: US, Canada, EU15 (excl. UK), Switzerland, Norway, Japan, Australia and New Zealand. The remaining countries are included in the category developing countries.

[16] The most detailed mapping publicly made available by the CSO, allows just a maximum of 28 industries. This clearly shows that there is a cost of having a larger sample size (Gregory *et al.*, 2001).

Appendix II: Standard Occupational Classification

	Major Groups	Sub-Major Groups
Skilled	1 Managers and Administrators	1 Corporate Managers and Administrators
		2 Managers/Proprietors in Agriculture and Services
	2 Professional Occupations	3 Science and Engineering Professionals
		4 Health Professionals
		5 Teaching Professionals
		6 Other Professional Occupations
Semi-skilled	3 Associate Professional and Technical Occupations	7 Science and Engineering Associate Professionals
		8 Health Associate Professionals
		9 Other Associate Professional Occupations
	4 Clerical and Secretarial Occupations	10 Clerical Occupations
		11 Secretarial Occupations
	5 Craft and Related Occupations	12 Skilled Construction Trades
		13 Skilled Engineering Trades
		14 Other Skilled Trades
	6 Personal and Protective Service Occupations	15 Protective Service Occupations
		16 Personal Service Occupations
	7 Sales Occupations	17 Buyers, Brokers and Sales Representatives
		18 Other Sales Occupations
Unskilled	8 Plant and Machine Occupations	19 Industrial Plants and Machine Operators, Assemblers
		20 Drivers and Mobile Machine Operators
	9 Other Occupations	21 Other Occupations in Agriculture, Forestry & Fishing
		22 Other Elementary Occupations

References

Anderton, B. and Brenton, P. (1999). 'Outsourcing and low-skilled workers in the UK', *Bulletin of Economic Research*, vol. 51, pp. 267–85.

Berman, E., Bound, J. and Griliches, Z. (1994). 'Changes in the demand for skilled labor within U.S. manufacturing: evidence from the Annual Survey of Manufacturers', *Quarterly Journal of Economics*, vol. 109, pp. 367–97.

Berndt, E.R. (1991). *The Practice of Econometrics*, Reading, MA: Addison-Wesley.

Berndt, E.R. and Wood, D.O. (1975). 'Technology, prices, and the derived demand for energy', *Review of Economics and Statistics*, vol. 57, pp. 259–68.

Campa, J. and Goldberg, L.S. (1997). 'The evolving external orientation of manufacturing industries: evidence from four countries', *Federal Reserve Bank of New York Economic Policy Review*, vol. 3, pp. 53–81.

Diewert, W.E. and Wales, T.J. (1987). 'Flexible functional forms and global curvature conditions', *Econometrica*, vol. 55, pp. 43–68.

Doms, M., Dunne, T. and Troske, K.R. (1997). 'Workers, wages and technology', *Quarterly Journal of Economics*, vol. 112, pp. 253–90.

Egger, H. and Egger, P. (2001). 'Cross-border sourcing and outward processing in EU manufacturing', *North American Journal of Economics and Finance*, vol. 12, pp. 243–56.

Falk, M. and Koebel, B.M. (2001). 'Outsourcing, imports and labour demand', *Scandinavian Journal of Economics*, vol. 104, pp. 567–86.

Feenstra, R.C. and Hanson, G.H. (1996). 'Globalization, outsourcing, and wage inequality', *American Economic Review*, vol. 86, pp. 240–5.

Feenstra, R.C. and Hanson, G.H. (1999). 'The impact of outsourcing and high-technology capital on wages: estimates for the United States, 1979–1990', *Quarterly Journal of Economics*, vol. 114, pp. 907–41.

Feenstra, R.C., Hanson, G.H. and Swenson, D.L. (2000). 'Offshore assembly from the United States: production characteristics of the 9802 program', in (R.C. Feenstra, ed.) *The Impact of International Trade on Wages*, Chicago: University of Chicago Press.

Gregory, M., Zissimos, B. and Greenhalgh, C. (2001). 'Jobs for the skilled: how technology, trade, and domestic demand changed the structure of UK employment, 1979–1990', *Oxford Economic Papers*, vol. 53, pp. 20–41.

Griliches, Z. and Hausman, J. (1986). 'Errors in variables in panel data', *Journal of Econometrics*, vol. 31, pp. 93–118.

Görg, H. (2000). 'Fragmentation and trade: US inward processing trade in the EU', *Review of World Economics/Weltwirtschaftliches Archiv*, vol. 136, pp. 403–21.

Haskel, J.E. and Heden, Y. (1999). 'Computers and the demand for skilled labour: industry- and establishment-level panel evidence for the UK', *Economic Journal*, vol. 109, pp. 68–79.

Haskel, J.E. and Slaughter, M. (2001). 'Trade, technology, and UK wage inequality', ECONOMIC JOURNAL, vol. 111, pp. 163–87.

Hijzen, A. (2005). 'Fragmentation, productivity and relative wages in the UK: a mandated wage approach', *Review of International Economics*, forthcoming.

Hummels, D., Ishii, J. and Yi, K. (2001). 'The nature and growth of vertical specialisation in world trade', *Journal of International Economics*, vol. 54, pp. 75–96.

Jones, R.W. and Kierzkowski (2001). 'A framework for fragmentation', in (S.W. Arndt and H. Kierzkowski, eds), *Fragmentation: New Production Patterns in the World Economy*, Oxford: Oxford University Press.

Kohler, W. (2004). 'International outsourcing and factor prices with multistage production', ECONOMIC JOURNAL, vol. 114, pp. C166–85.

Kohli, U. (1991). *Technology, Duality and Foreign Trade: The GNP Function Approach to Modelling Imports and Exports*, Hemel Hempstead: Harvester Wheatsheaf.

Leamer, E. (1998). 'In search of Stolper-Samuelson linkages between international trade and lower wages', in (S.M. Collins, ed.), *Imports, Exports, and the American Worker*, pp. 143–203, Washington DC: Brookings Institution.

Machin, S. and van Reenen, J. (1998). 'Technology and changes in skill structure: evidence form seven OECD countries', *Quarterly Journal of Economics*, vol. 113, pp. 1215–44.

Ng, F. and Yeats, A. (1999). 'Production sharing in East Asia: who does what for whom and why?', World Bank Working Paper No. 2197.

Office of National Statistics (2002). *United Kingdom Input-Output Analytical Tables, 1995*, London: HMSO.

Oulton, N. and O'Mahony, M. (1994). *Productivity and Growth: A study of British Industry, 1954–1986*, NIESR Occasional Paper 46, Cambridge: Cambridge University Press.

Strauss-Kahn, V. (2004). 'The role of globalization in the within-industry shift away from unskilled workers in France', in (R. Baldwin and A. Winters, eds), *Challenges to Globalization*, Chicago: University of Chicago Press.

TSP International (1999). *Reference Manual*, Version 4.5.

Yeats, A.J. (2001). 'Just how big is global production sharing?', in (S.W. Arndt and H. Kierzkowski, eds). *Fragmentation: New Production Patterns in the World Economy*, Oxford: Oxford University Press.

Chapter III.2

Winners and losers: a micro-level analysis of international outsourcing and wages

Ingo Geishecker *Department of Economics, Georg-August-Universität Göttingen*

Holger Görg *Institut für Weltwirtschaf and Christian-Albrechts Universität Kiel*

Abstract. Our paper investigates the link between international outsourcing and wages utilizing a large household panel and combining it with industry-level information on industries' outsourcing activities from input-output tables. This approach avoids problems such as aggregation bias, potential endogeneity bias, and poor skill definitions that commonly hamper industry-level studies. We find that outsourcing has had a marked impact on wages. Applying two alternative skill classifications, we find evidence that a 1 percentage point increase in outsourcing reduced the wage for workers in the lowest skill categories by up to 1.5%, while it increased wages for high-skilled workers by up to 2.6%. This result is robust to a number of different specifications. JEL classification: F16, J31

Gagnants et perdants : une analyse micro-économique de la sous-traitance internationale et des salaires. Ce mémoire étudie le lien entre la sous-traitance internationale et les salaires à l'aide de données d'un grand panel de ménages qu'on combine avec des données au niveau des industries sur les activités de sous-traitance de celles qui en font obtenues des tableaux interindustriels. Cette approche évite les problèmes qui habituellement polluent les études au niveau de l'industrie (biais d'agrégation, biais d'endogénéité potentielle, mauvaises définitions des habiletés). On découvre que la sous-traitance a un effet sur les salaires. A l'aide de différentes formes de classification des habiletés, il appert qu'un point de pourcentage d'augmentation dans la sous-traitance réduit les salaires des travailleurs dans les catégories d'habileté les plus basses de 1.5% alors qu'il accroît les salaires de travailleurs spécialisés de 2.6%. Ce résultat est robuste et avéré même quand on utilise diverses spécifications.

Görg is also affiliated with GEP, Nottingham. Earlier versions of the paper were presented at a workshop at Claremont McKenna College, the annual GSOEP user conference, the Annual Congress of the European Economic association and seminars at Berlin, Birmingham, and Zurich. The authors are particularly grateful to Mitsuyo Ando, Alan Deardorff, Josef Falkinger, Edward Leamer, Matt Slaughter, Andreas Stephan, Eric Strobl, Rainer Winkelmann, and two anonymous referees for helpful comments. The authors gratefully acknowledge financial support from the Leverhulme Trust (Grant No. F114/BF) and the German Science Foundation (Project: Labour market effects of international outsourcing: a comparative analysis with micro-data). Email: ingo.geishecker@ wiwi.uni-goettingen.de

Canadian Journal of Economics / Revue canadienne d'Economique, Vol. 41, No. 1
February / février 2008. Printed in Canada / Imprimé au Canada

1. Introduction

International outsourcing is a growing phenomenon in world trade and has sparked a lot of interest in the recent academic literature and business press.[1] Hummels, Ishii, and Yi (2001) provide evidence for the worldwide importance of outsourcing from data collected for 10 OECD and four emerging-market countries. They find that trade in outsourced components in the vertical production chain accounts for around 21% of these countries' exports. Moreover, international outsourcing grew very strongly by approximately 30% between 1970 and 1990.[2]

Given that the increase in international outsourcing coincided with deteriorating relative wages and employment chances for low-skilled workers in many developed countries, much research has been devoted to assessing the impact of this disintegration of production on domestic labour markets. Most of these studies, as reviewed by Feenstra and Hanson (2001), investigate the impact of international outsourcing by estimating the relative demand for skilled labour derived from a cost function or mandated wage regressions using aggregate industry-level data. However, outsourcing has implications for micro units (firms or workers), which should arguably be studied using micro-level data in order to take into account individual heterogeneity.[3]

Our paper pays particular attention to the role of individual heterogeneity for the impact of international outsourcing on workers. In particular, we investigate the link between outsourcing and wages, utilizing a large household panel and combining it with industry level information on industries' outsourcing activities measured as imported material inputs constructed from input-output tables.[4] Hence, we directly assess the effects of international outsourcing on wages at the level of the individual, controlling for observable and unobservable worker characteristics. In particular, our attention focuses on the role of individual skill levels for the effect of outsourcing on wages. To the best of our knowledge this is the first study to do so using micro-level data.

One of the main contributions of our study is that the use of micro-level data enables us to identify winners and losers from international outsourcing among workers with different skills in absolute terms. This is a highly policy-relevant issue, which cannot be addressed by merely analysing relative demand changes, as

1 For example, Jones and Kierzkowski (2001) provide examples from IT, car manufacturing, sport shoe manufacturing, etc.

2 See Chen, Kondratowicz and Yi (2005) for further discussions of the growth of international outsourcing.

3 There are a few exceptions in the literature that have used micro level data. See, for example, Head and Ries (2002) and Görg and Hanley (2005), using firm-level data for Japan and Ireland, respectively, to investigate the impact of outsourcing on labour demand in a firm and Egger, Pfaffermayr, and Weber (2007) and Geishecker (2007) analysing the impact of industry-level international outsourcing on individual employment transitions.

4 A related issue is outsourcing of services which has attracted some interest in the case of the U.S. and the U.K. but which is beyond the scope of our study. Interested readers are referred to Amiti and Wei (2005).

Winners and losers: a micro-level analysis 245

in, for example, Feenstra and Hanson (1996b,1999). Also, we extend the literature by employing more accurate definitions of workers' skill levels than the commonly used production vs. non-production workers differentiation (see, e.g., Feenstra and Hanson 1996b; Berman, Bound, and Machin 1998). In addition, we can overcome the potential aggregation bias inherent in industry-level studies by directly controlling for individual observed and unobserved heterogeneity.[5]

Our empirical analysis uses data from the large German Socio-Economic Panel Study (GSOEP), which is described in some detail below, combined with industry-level data for the period 1991 to 2000.[6] Germany is an interesting case to analyse, as there is a general consensus that relative wages of high- vs. low-skilled workers have remained virtually unchanged since the 1980s, even though outsourcing of activities has increased substantially during the 1990s, probably aided by the opening up of low-wage Eastern and Central European markets, which provided potential for outsourcing (see, e.g., Geishecker 2006). Still, Germany is a highly regulated labour market, in terms both of price of labour (through unionization) and quantity (through high levels of employment protection) and therefore adjustment may go through either, both, or no channel. However, international outsourcing may give particular rise to wage moderation in bargaining between firms and unions if, for example, it corresponds to improved outside options for employers. This may be especially true for Germany, where employment is highly protected. Thus, even if wages are relatively rigid in Germany, they may still adjust if faced with increasing outsourcing pressure.

Against the background of nearly constant relative wages on aggregate, we find from our individual-level data that international outsourcing has nevertheless had a marked impact on wages. Distinguishing three skill categories that comply with the International Standard Classification of Education (ISCED) we find evidence that outsourcing reduced the real wage for workers in the lowest skill categories; the results are similar in terms of magnitude and statistical significance, when instead we apply a skill grouping that is based on required on-the-job skills rather than educational attainment. Furthermore, we find evidence that high-skilled workers experienced increased wages, owing due to international outsourcing.

The remainder of the paper is structured as follows. Section 2 reviews briefly the theoretical and empirical literature on international outsourcing and labour markets. Section 3 highlights recent labour market trends and motivates our empirical study. Section 4 introduces the empirical model, and section 5 discusses the data set. Section 6 presents the empirical findings, and section 7 considers

5 Furthermore, combining individual-level and industry-level data arguably also helps to reduce the potential endogeneity of the outsourcing measure as the assumption that individual heterogeneous wages are unlikely to affect industry-level aggregates is less heroic than the assumption necessary in the literature using aggregate data that industry level relative wages are not affecting industry-level outsourcing measures.

6 See, for example, Hunt (2001) and Krueger and Pischke (1995) for analyses using this data set in different contexts.

some robustness checks. Section 8 evaluates the economic significance of our estimates, and section 9 concludes.

2. International outsourcing and wages

The causes and consequences of international outsourcing have attracted considerable interest in the theoretical literature. While papers like Feenstra and Hanson (1996b) and Kohler (2004b) stress the importance of international differences in relative prices as the driving force of outsourcing, Jones and Kierzkowski (2001) and Harris (2001), for example, focus on the role of exogenous reductions in general services and telecommunications costs for allowing outsourcing to occur. However, the consequences of outsourcing for local labour markets are not clear-cut in theory. For example, Feenstra and Hanson (1996a) formulate a model of international outsourcing that is a specific form of a Heckscher-Ohlin-type model with only one final good and two countries, North and South. By changing relative unit costs of production, for instance, through Hicks-neutral technological progress in the South, production fragments with lower skill intensity are shifted from the North to the South, thereby raising the average skill intensity of production in both countries. As a results, relative demand for skilled labour increases in both the North and the South. By contrast, Arndt (1997, 1999), develops a model of international outsourcing that is also based on an HO framework but makes less restrictive assumptions. In particular, he considers trade between a small price-taking economy and the rest of the world, allowing for two factors of production and two final goods. In this model, if the low-skill-intensive industry shifts some fragments of production abroad, this results in a productivity improvement in the low-skill-intensive industry and, with given world prices, ultimately in higher relative wages for unskilled workers. Hence, depending on the models and assumptions chosen, outsourcing of the low-skill-intensive part of production can lead to decreases or increases in the wage of (unskilled) labour in the outsourcing economy (see also Jones and Kierkowski 2001 and Kohler 2004a for other theoretical papers). Whether workers in practice gain or lose from international outsourcing is, therefore, essentially an empirical question.

One of the first systematic empirical studies on the labour market impact of international outsourcing is Feenstra and Hanson (1996a). In their study for the United States they estimate a factor share equation for an industry panel of more than 400 industries. In the model international outsourcing, approximated by the industries' import penetration ratios, is implemented as a shift parameter similar to technological progress. Following this procedure, the authors report that approximately 15% to 33% of the increase in the cost share of non-production labour over the period 1979–87 can be explained by international outsourcing. An extension to this study is Feenstra and Hanson (1996b), which uses a more precise outsourcing definition based on imported intermediate inputs and calculates that approximately 31% to 51% of the increase of the cost share of non-production labour over the same period can be explained by international outsourcing. In a follow-up study Feenstra and Hanson (1999) apply a narrower definition of international outsourcing by focusing on imported intermediate inputs of an industry from the same industry abroad. According to this study, international outsourcing can explain between 11% and 15% of the observed decline in the cost share of production labour in U.S. manufacturing between 1979 and 1990. Morrison-Paul and Siegel (2001) extend the above studies by simultaneously incorporating several trade- and technology-related measures that can shift relative labour demand in a system of factor demand equations. Their results suggest that international outsourcing as well as trade and technological change significantly lowered relative demand for low-skilled labour.

Falk and Koebel (2002) present an analysis of the effect of outsourcing on wages using industry-level data for Germany. They use a Box-Cox cost function, which nests the normalized quadratic as well as the translog functional form, and estimate elasticities of substitution from a system of input-output equations. International outsourcing is implemented in the model as a flexible choice variable captured by relative prices for imported intermediate goods and purchased services. Their findings suggest that between 1978 and 1990 neither imported material inputs nor purchased services substituted for unskilled labour in German manufacturing industries.[7]

Our approach differs significantly from the previous empirical studies and may be considered suitable to overcome some of the shortcomings associated with using industry-level data. Utilizing a large household panel, we incorporate the industry's international outsourcing activity as a shift parameter in a Mincerian (Mincer 1974) wage model. This approach has substantial advantages over an industry-level analysis, as it allows controlling for individual observed and unobserved heterogeneity, thereby avoiding aggregation bias. In addition, changes in relative earnings can now be decomposed into wage gains and losses for different skill groups. Furthermore, since the industry's outsourcing activities may be considered largely exogenous to the individual, endogeneity bias due to simultaneous determination of labour demand and international outsourcing at the industry level arguably may be to some extent reduced.

Given the nature of our econometric estimation our results should be interpreted as the short-run effects of international outsourcing on wages of individuals within industries. Hence, we can think of our approach as essentially partial equilibrium, in line with the theoretical one-sector setting of, for example, Feenstra and Hanson (1996a). This is consistent with a short-run view of the economy

7 Their approach can be criticized, since the impact of international outsourcing is captured only by relative price changes for imported intermediate inputs. However, intensified international outsourcing is consistent with unchanging or even increasing observed relative prices for imported intermediate inputs. Factors such as trade liberalization, the opening up of former communist states, or new advances in communication technologies reduce the costs of outsourcing. These developments are not necessarily reflected in relative prices for intermediate goods if outsourcing costs previously were prohibitive.

TABLE 1
Inter-industry mobility between 1991 and 2000

	Number in percent of total sample		
Respondents who left manufacturing	253	1.66	15235
Respondents who stayed in manufacturing but changed industry	207	2.84	7294

NOTE: Sample is constrained according to the criteria discussed in section 5.

such that labour is immobile between industries. Many previous industry-level studies implicitly or explicitly make the same assumption (e.g., Feenstra and Hanson 1996a; Morrison-Paul and Siegel 2001; Hsieh and Woo 2005). Clearly, this assumption is plausible only in the short run. To get an idea of how restrictive this assumption is we calculated the number of respondents in our sample that indeed moved between industries; these are reported in table 1. As is apparent, the number of switchers is low. Between 1991 and 2000 only 253 individuals left manufacturing, and of those respondents who stayed in manufacturing only 207 changed industry. Thus, even for a period of 10 years the short-run assumption arguably is not too problematic.

Similar to Feenstra and Hanson (1996b) and Feenstra and Hanson (1999), we construct outsourcing on the basis of input-output data. Specifically, we apply a narrow and a wide definition such that

$$OUT_{jt}^{narrow} = \frac{IMP_{jt}}{Y_{jt}} \tag{1}$$

$$OUT_{jt}^{wide} = \frac{\sum_{j=1}^{J} IMP_{jt}}{Y_{jt}}, \tag{2}$$

with j denoting the respective 2-digit manufacturing industry ($j \in J$), IMP the value of imported intermediate inputs from a foreign industry, and Y the industry's output value. Hence, narrowly defined outsourcing captures only an industry's imported intermediate inputs from the same industry abroad, while broadly defined outsourcing incorporates all imported intermediate manufacturing goods of an industry.

In comparison with Feenstra and Hanson, we can directly differentiate between imported and domestic inputs in the German input-output tables rather than having to rely on aggregated input-use data. However, this advantage of our data also comes with a disadvantage. We are able to calculate this measure for only 21 2-digit industries, while Feenstra and Hanson identify intermediate inputs for over 400 4-digit industries, albeit not differentiating between domestic and imported inputs. It is, important however, to stress that our more aggregated data do not result in a different concept of narrow and wide outsourcing, as

Winners and losers: a micro-level analysis 249

in Feenstra and Hanson (1999) such differentiation also takes place only at the 2-digit level.[8]

A further difference between our approach and that of Feenstra and Hanson (1996b) and Feenstra and Hanson (1999) refers to the denominator in equations (1) and (2). While Feenstra and Hanson express industry-level intermediate imports as a share of total non-energy input purchases, we normalize by industry-level output instead. Thus, in addition to non-energy input purchases, our denominator includes value added and energy purchases. Our main motivation is to separate domestic and international outsourcing. A trend towards domestic outsourcing, that is, increased purchases of intermediate goods from domestic suppliers, ceteris paribus, lowers the international outsourcing intensity in the formulae employed by Feenstra and Hanson (1996b) and Feenstra and Hanson (1999). Our measures are better suited to correct for this problem, as, abstracting from overall efficiency gains, increasing industry-level domestic purchases are countered by decreasing industry-level value added.

3. Recent labour market trends and international outsourcing

It is well established that relative earnings of low-skilled workers have decreased in most OECD countries during the last two decades. However, wage trends are far from uniform across countries, since the U.S. and Great Britain have experienced very strong increases in the wage dispersion, and countries such as Australia, Canada, Japan, and Spain experienced only modest decreases in the relative earnings of low-skilled workers (see Freeman and Katz 1995 and OECD 1994 for a detailed discussion).

In this study we focus on the German labour market, which is an interesting case, since it is not only the largest economy in Europe, but it is also far more open to international trade than, for instance, the U.S. and has a fairly rigid labour market. Furthermore, political and economic transition in the former communist Central and Eastern European countries (CEECs) during the 1990s now allows for intensive production sharing with these economies at Germany's doorstep, with potentially large implications for the German labour market. Nonetheless, considering the wage distribution in Germany, abundant empirical evidence suggests that relative wages of the low skilled have virtually not changed or have even increased since the 1980s (see Fitzenberger 1999; Prasad 2004; Beaudry and Green 2003).

Our own analysis on the basis of our sample from the German Socio-Economic Panel (which will be discussed in more detail in section 5) for the years 1991–2000 also fails to identify significant changes in the earnings distribution between different skill groups, which is in line with the literature. Figure 1 shows median

8 Recent studies by Hsieh and Woo (2005) and Hijzen, Görg, and Hine (2005) also use outsourcing measures calculated at levels of aggregation similar to ours.

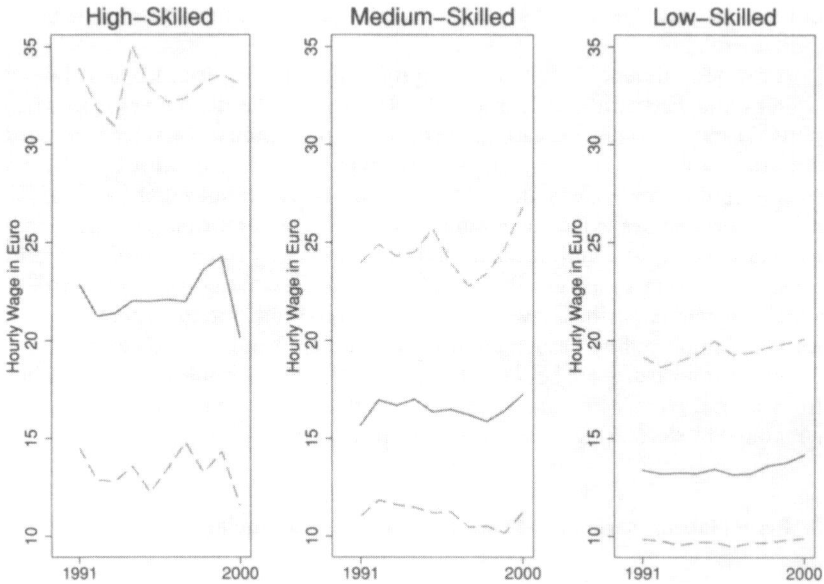

FIGURE 1 Median, top, and bottom decile wages by skill

wages and wages of the 10th and 90th percentile for low-, medium-, and high-skill workers. As becomes apparent, there is considerable variation in wages across the three skill categories. In addition, while we observe some wage variation within skill groups over time, there is no general upward or downward trend.

Against this background, international outsourcing in German manufacturing has grown substantially. Figure 2 shows the development of international outsourcing during the 1990s for the manufacturing industry as a whole. As can be seen, narrowly defined international outsourcing (as in equation (1)) increased by around 60% between 1991 and 2000, while broadly defined outsourcing grew somewhat slower by 45% over the same period. Table 2 shows the differences in levels and growth rates of international outsourcing by 2-digit NACE industries. Even though international outsourcing is of very different importance for the separate industries and the dynamic patterns vary considerably, almost every industry shows significant growth in the outsourcing activity.

Thus, constant relative earnings for low-skilled workers coincide with pronounced increases in international outsourcing, which at first sight casts doubt on a connection between relative earnings and outsourcing. However, relative earnings can be determined by a range of demand and supply factors that might cancel each other out. A thorough analysis of the impact of international outsourcing on the wage distribution therefore requires simultaneous controlling for other important determinants of the wage structure.

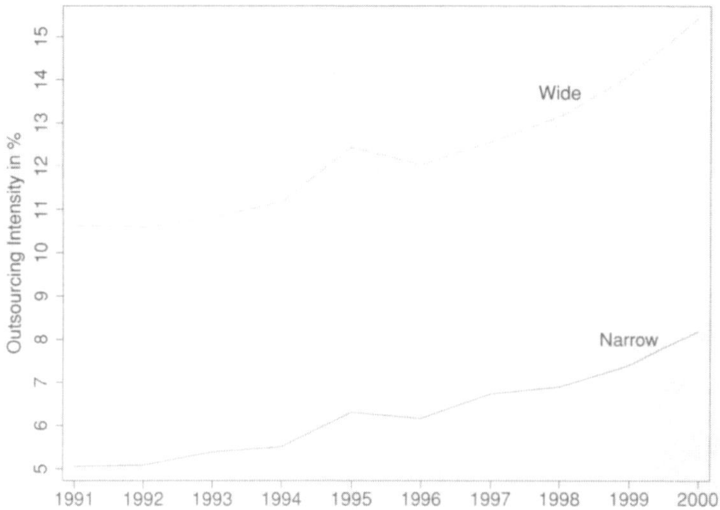

FIGURE 2 Outsourcing in German manufacturing industry

4. The empirical model

In order to analyse more rigorously the impact of international outsourcing on wages we estimate variants of the following log wage equation:

$$\ln WAGE_{ijt} = \alpha + \beta DEMOG_{it} + \gamma WORK_{it} + \delta EDUC_{it} + \theta IND_{jt} + \lambda OUT_{jt} + \tau_j + \mu_t + \iota_i + \epsilon_{it}, \quad (3)$$

where $WAGE_{ijt}$ denotes individual i's hourly wages in industry j, which are defined in the next section.

We apply control variables that are standard in such wage regressions (see, e.g., Mincer 1974; Brown and Medoff 1989; Schmidt and Zimmerman 1991). *DEMOG* denotes the demographic control variables for age, marital status, and geographic region. The second set of control variables (*WORK*) contains characteristics related to the workplace, such as size and ownership of the firm and tenure. A third set of control variables (*EDUC*) contains educational dummies for high education (*ISCED* : *high*) and medium education (*ISCED* : *med*); low education (*ISCED* : *low*) is the omitted category. We also control for time-changing industry characteristics (*IND*) by including the size of the industry (measured in terms of output) and two types of capital (plant and equipment).

We subsequently incorporate a narrow and a wide definition of international outsourcing (*OUT*) as in equations (1) and (2). The error term is decomposed into general industry-specific effects (τ_j) and general time-specific effects (μ_t), which

TABLE 2
Outsourcing intensity and growth rate in percent

	Narrow			Wide		
Industry	1991	2000	Growth	1991	2000	Growth
(15,16) Food, beverages	2.73	3.40	24.26	4.28	5.47	28.00
(17) Textiles	4.82	9.51	97.14	12.50	20.40	63.19
(18) Clothing	9.23	23.27	152.06	20.38	39.14	92.05
(19) Leather	10.47	25.75	145.90	16.79	32.16	91.60
(20) Wood	4.21	4.66	10.62	7.24	8.72	20.50
(21) Pulp, paper	7.65	10.48	36.93	17.66	22.32	26.42
(22) Printing, publish	0.16	0.13	−21.71	6.42	7.52	17.10
(23) Coke, petroleum	5.21	4.98	−4.26	7.52	5.73	−23.77
(24) Chemicals	7.07	12.94	82.94	12.47	19.42	55.73
(25) Rubber, plastic	0.45	0.95	114.16	14.78	19.52	32.10
(26) Non-metal, minerals	2.01	2.27	12.95	3.94	4.66	18.29
(27) Basic metals	10.78	16.33	51.45	14.14	21.15	49.51
(28) Metal products	1.04	1.53	48.10	7.77	10.03	29.06
(29) Machinery, equ.	4.48	5.83	30.21	10.21	13.31	30.42
(30) Computers	8.61	23.28	170.58	17.37	34.87	100.70
(31) Electr. machinery	3.67	6.59	79.66	7.34	12.06	64.23
(32) Radio, TV	13.01	21.42	64.69	17.82	26.87	50.73
(33) Instruments	3.51	4.22	20.47	8.30	11.37	36.93
(34) Motor vehicles	6.76	9.79	44.88	13.56	19.17	41.35
(35) Transport equip.	18.91	37.34	97.47	23.33	41.50	77.84
(36) Furniture, n.e.c.	4.72	8.54	80.84	14.02	19.02	35.66
Total manufacturing	5.05	8.19	62.02	10.63	15.43	45.21

we estimate with a full set of industry dummies, and time dummies, respectively. This also enables us to control extensively for time invariant industry-level wage determinants other than those captured by our outsourcing variable (OUT) and the additional time-varying industry variables.

One key challenge for our analysis is to distinguish the effects of international outsourcing from the effects of technological change. In addition to the general time dummies that capture manufacturing-wide technological progress and business cycles, we make full use of the three data dimensions and include a full set of industry-specific time trend variables that capture industry level technological changes that depart from manufacturing wide trends.

Furthermore, we allow for individual fixed effects (ι_i) that take account of unchanging observable and unobservable individual characteristics.[9] The remaining error term (ϵ_{it}) is assumed to be normally distributed. All regressions are weighted using the standard GSOEP cross-sectional sampling weights to adjust for different individual sampling probabilities.[10]

9 Random effects were rejected in a Hausman specification test.

10 A detailed description of the rather complex construction of the GSOEP sampling weights is provided in Haisken-DeNew and Frick (2003). However, person-related characteristics that are

Combining individual- and industry-level data could give rise to contemporaneous correlation that results in distorted standard errors as discussed in Moulton (1990). As has become standard in the literature, we therefore adjust the standard errors to allow for an unspecified correlation of error terms across individuals within the same industry. One further potential problem casting doubt on the validity of our results could arise from sample selection. We expect outsourcing to affect not only wages but also employment. As workers become unemployed, we cannot observe their wages; thus, our sample potentially is incidentally truncated. Within the context of our fixed-effects estimation, sample selection bias should, however, be a problem only if selection and the idiosyncratic errors are correlated. We apply a sample selection test that is suggested by Wooldridge (1995) and extends Heckman (1976) to the fixed-effects context. As a first step, we estimate a reduced-form selection equation by pooled weighted probit, including all explanatory variables plus the mean of the respective explanatory variables. In a second step we estimate the fixed-effects wage equation, including the inverted Mills ratio from the selection equation. Selection bias is only an issue if the inverse Mills ratio is statistically significant. However, we can reject this in all model specifications, as the t-statistics in tables 5–7 indicate. Accordingly, we do not have to correct for selection bias and all specifications reported in tables 5–9 exclude the inverted Mills ratio.

In addition, the estimated coefficients could be biased if wages and international outsourcing were determined simultaneously. Particularly for industry-level studies this is a common concern. However, for our analysis we utilize micro-level data. While it is true that in Germany wages are generally collectively bargained, collective bargaining merely sets a wage floor. Individual earnings can differ significantly from these *minimum wages*. As a result, there is substantial variation of hourly earnings at the individual level. Arguably, the industry-level outsourcing intensity can therefore be considered as largely exogenous to the individual wage. Nevertheless, we formally test for the exogeneity of outsourcing using lagged values of outsourcing as instruments. As becomes apparent from table 5, while our instruments prove to be valid, a C-test cannot reject the exogeneity of international outsourcing within reasonable confidence bounds.

5. Data

The analysis is based on data from Sample A, B, C, D, and E from the German Socio Economic Panel (GSOEP) for the years 1991 to 2000.[11] We exclude

used to construct the GSOEP sampling weights can be considered exogenous to our analysis and include gender and age of the household head and the individual as well as individual marital status and occupational placement. Weights for the foreigner sample (Sample B), in addition, are based on nationality of the household head and the individual, while weights for the East German sample (Sample C) involve only individual gender and age.

11 See Haisken-DeNew and Frick, 2003 for a detailed description of the panel. The data used in this paper were extracted from the 2003 GSOEP Database provided by the DIW Berlin (http://

respondents who report to work in East Germany, as wages in the East are to a large extent shaped by the dramatic structural change of the economy that has been taking place since the fall of the wall and that most likely dominates the impact of other changing structural factors such as outsourcing.

We restrict our sample to prime age (18 to 65 years) male blue- and white- collar workers in full-time employment over the whole period in the manufacturing industry (NACE 15-36). As is well known, female workers have substantially different labour market outcomes than males and, hence, as is common in the literature, we focus exclusively on males.

In order to maximize the number of observations, we choose an unbalanced design of the sample. The sample therefore covers 1,754 individuals, yielding a total of 7,624 observations. In order to avoid selection bias with respect to item non-response that might be not completely at random, each explanatory variable was supplemented with a dummy for missing values. Subsequently, missing values were recoded to zero, and the generated dummies for missing values also act as regressors in the model.[12]

Wages are defined as average hourly gross labour earnings, including bonuses, premiums, and other extra payments over the year preceding the respective interview month. Gross yearly wages and yearly working hours are derived from the cross-national equivalent files (CNEF). Observations with missing wage information were excluded from the sample; hence, we disregard observations with imputed wage information in the subsequent analysis.[13]

We apply two different skill definitions, which only partly overlap. A description of the alternative skill groupings can be found in table 3. First, we utilize internationally comparable information following the International Standard Classification of Education (ISCED) (see UNESCO 1997). Secondly, we apply an alternative skill grouping based on the respondents' information on the qualification that their current job actually requires. Applying this alternative skill grouping is an interesting extension, since it takes account of the actually demanded qualification by employers as opposed to the supplied qualification by employees.

Table 4 shows the skill structure, based on the ISCED classification, within each manufacturing industry and the employment share of the respective industry.

www.diw.de/soep) using the Add-On package SOEPMENU for Stata(TM). SOEPMENU was written by Dr John P. Haisken-DeNew (Haisken-DeNew 2005) and is now available in an updated version at http://www.panelwhiz.eu. The SOEPMENU-generated DO file to retrieve the GSOEP data used here is available from us upon request. Any data or computational errors in this paper are our own.

12 These coefficients are reported only if they are statistically significant. As a robustness check we also run regressions dropping observations with item non-responses. Overall, we drop 176 observations. However, the results, which are not reported here to save space, are robust to this amendment.

13 Frick and Grabka (2003) describe the imputation procedure for missing wage information. Since the procedure does not use industry-level information, heterogeneity in the wage distribution with respect to industry-level variables, particularly outsourcing, is reduced, thus preventing the use of imputed data for our analysis.

TABLE 3
Alternative skill classifications

1. International Standard Classification of Education (ISCED)	
Low skill	Lower secondary education, Second stage of basic education
Medium skill	Upper secondary education, Post-secondary non-tertiary education, first stage of tertiary education
High skill	Second stage of tertiary education
2. Required qualification	
Low skill	Work requires less than technical college or university degree
High skill	Work requires technical college or university degree

TABLE 4
Employment shares and skill * structure of industries in percentage

	Employment share of industry	High-skilled	Medium-skilled within industry	Low-skilled
Food products, beverages, tobacco	6.08	10.61	21.22	68.16
Textiles	2.53	2.94	11.76	85.29
Wearing apparel	0.22	0.00	27.78	72.22
Tanning,dressing of leather	0.47	21.05	0.00	78.95
Wood products, except furniture	1.87	0.00	7.28	92.72
Pulp, paper and paper products	1.84	6.08	7.43	86.49
Publishing, printing and reproduction	2.69	18.89	13.82	67.28
Coke, refined petroleum	0.55	15.91	4.55	79.55
Chemicals and chemical products	11.31	20.75	14.16	65.09
Rubber and plastic products	3.84	3.24	10.03	86.73
Other non-metallic mineral products	3.41	0.36	15.64	84.00
Basic metals	3.49	9.61	9.61	80.78
Fabricated metal products	21.54	7.72	12.62	79.65
Machinery and equipment	11.67	20.96	16.70	62.34
Office machinery and computer	0.19	60.00	0.00	40.00
Electrical machinery and apparatus	7.80	29.14	22.45	48.41
Radio, television and communication	1.40	30.97	23.89	45.13
Medical, precision and optical instruments	3.09	18.07	31.73	50.20
Motor vehicles, trailers	12.46	16.63	13.45	69.92
Other transport equipment	1.68	22.96	15.56	61.48
Furniture; manufacturing n.e.c.	1.87	5.96	7.95	86.09

*applying the first skill definition from table 3.

Industry-level data on international outsourcing were obtained from imported input use tables provided by the German Federal Statistical Office. Intermediate inputs corresponding to narrowly defined international outsourcing are represented by the main diagonal of the input-matrix for imports. Intermediate inputs corresponding to the wide definition are represented by the column sum of imported intermediate inputs from manufacturing industries. Data on industry output and plant and equipment were obtained from the German Federal Statistical Office.

6. Results

The results of estimating different specifications of equation (3) using a fixed-effects estimator to allow for time-invariant individual specific effects and applying the ISCED skill definition are reported in tables 5 and 6. The regressions include full sets of industry and time dummies.

Table 5 presents the results from pooled estimations over all individuals. The coefficients on the individual-and firm-level control variables generally have the expected sign but only age (in a non-linear fashion) and education are found to be significant. One potential explanation for the lack of significant coefficients is that there are differences in the effects across different types of workers.[14] Another is that the individual fixed effects wipe out most of the variation in variables. This may, for example, explain the statistically insignificant result on tenure, which for most individuals in our sample is just a linear trend.

The variable of interest to us is, of course, the measure of international outsourcing, while all other variables are merely included to control for individual heterogeneity. Column (a) in table 5 reports results for the narrow measure of outsourcing as defined in equation (1), while column (d) does so for the wide measure as in equation (2). As can be seen, in these regressions we find statistically significant negative effects of international outsourcing on wages. However, when allowing for different coefficients across skill groups by interacting outsourcing and education, we find a small but statistically significant negative effect of outsourcing on wages for medium- (at the 10% level) and low-skilled workers, while for high-skilled workers the effect is rendered insignificant (columns (b) and (e)).

In a further specification we test the robustness of these findings by more thoroughly controlling for time-changing industry characteristics, such as technological change. Arguably, technological change is an important determinant of labour demand, but it is difficult to control for empirically, since measures such as research and development expenditure constitute only crude proxies. In the specifications reported in columns (c) and (f) we make use of all panel dimensions and include industry-specific time trends in an effort to allow for industry-specific technological change that departs from the common pattern, as captured by the set of time dummies. Both time dummies and industry-specific time trends are jointly significant in all specifications. With respect to international outsourcing, we now find a statistically significant effect for low-skilled workers only when applying the wide definition of international outsourcing (see column (f)).

We now relax the assumption of equal coefficients on all covariates across different skill groups by estimating the model separately for each skill group. Hence, we allow for differences in the wage determination for different skill groups as well as skill-specific unobserved industry characteristics.

14 In fact, as we show in table 6, this seems to be the case. When we allow coefficients to differ across skill groups, more variables are statistically significant.

TABLE 5
Fixed-effects log wage regression

	Narrow outsourcing			Wide outsourcing		
	(a)	(b)	(c)	(d)	(e)	(f)
Age: 18–24	0.027	0.025	0.031	0.027	0.023	0.028
	[0.46]	[0.42]	[0.52]	[0.46]	[0.38]	[0.47]
Age: 25–34	0.051	0.051	0.053	0.052	0.051	0.053
	[1.15]	[1.12]	[1.19]	[1.16]	[1.12]	[1.18]
Age: 35–44	0.054	0.054	0.056	0.054	0.054	0.055
	[1.55]	[1.52]	[1.56]	[1.55]	[1.52]	[1.54]
Age: 45–54	0.035	0.035	0.039	0.035	0.035	0.039
	[2.05]*	[2.10]**	[2.46]**	[2.06]*	[2.14]**	[2.50]**
Married	0.019	0.018	0.008	0.019	0.017	0.008
	[0.75]	[0.72]	[0.35]	[0.74]	[0.68]	[0.34]
Dummy: Respondent	0.012	0.012	0.014	0.012	0.011	0.014
has children	[1.06]	[1.02]	[1.39]	[1.05]	[0.99]	[1.35]
Firm size: <20	−0.065	−0.065	−0.065	−0.063	−0.064	−0.064
	[1.60]	[1.63]	[1.67]	[1.58]	[1.62]	[1.67]
Firm size: <200	−0.018	−0.018	−0.015	−0.017	−0.016	−0.015
	[0.59]	[0.59]	[0.53]	[0.55]	[0.54]	[0.52]
Firm size: <2000	−0.009	−0.009	−0.010	−0.009	−0.009	−0.010
	[0.52]	[0.54]	[0.61]	[0.51]	[0.53]	[0.61]
Firm: Public owner	0.018	0.019	0.023	0.018	0.019	0.024
	[0.64]	[0.69]	[0.89]	[0.65]	[0.72]	[0.92]
Tenure	0.000	0.000	0.000	0.000	0.000	0.000
	[0.05]	[0.04]	[0.23]	[0.07]	[0.06]	[0.23]
ISCED: high	0.035	−0.016	−0.013	0.035	−0.092	−0.083
	[1.73]*	[0.46]	[0.38]	[1.75]*	[1.55]	[1.43]
ISCED: medium	0.001	−0.017	−0.010	0.001	−0.053	−0.037
	[0.03]	[0.29]	[0.17]	[0.04]	[0.68]	[0.48]
Industry: *Equipment/Y*	0.154	0.145	−0.326	0.088	0.073	−0.344
	[0.45]	[0.43]	[0.87]	[0.27]	[0.23]	[0.93]
Industry: *Plant/Y*	−0.895	−0.827	0.336	−0.731	−0.643	0.428
	[1.28]	[1.17]	[0.77]	[1.13]	[1.00]	[1.03]
Industry: Output	−0.098	−0.098	−0.037	−0.091	−0.093	−0.034
Y (in 100 billion)	[1.69]	[1.71]	[0.60]	[1.63]	[1.69]	[0.60]
Out	−0.009			−0.009		
	[2.53]**			[2.86]***		
Out ∗ ISCED:high		−0.003	−0.002		−0.002	−0.001
		[0.99]	[0.30]		[0.76]	[0.19]
Out ∗ ISCED:middle		−0.008	−0.007		−0.007	−0.007
		[1.76]*	[0.95]		[1.88]*	[1.06]
Out ∗ ISCED:low		−0.011	−0.010		−0.012	−0.010
		[2.66]**	[1.46]		[3.16]***	[1.80]*
Constant	2.964	2.880	−84.848	3.067	3.133	−82.320
	[20.81]***	[18.76]***	[3.42]***	[19.43]***	[18.10]***	[3.79]***
Year dummies	YES	YES	YES	YES	YES	YES
Industry dummies	YES	YES	YES	YES	YES	YES
Industry specific time trends	NO	NO	YES	NO	NO	YES
Individual fixed effects	YES	YES	YES	YES	YES	YES
Region dummies	YES	YES	YES	YES	YES	YES
Observations	7294	7294	7294	7294	7294	7294
R^2	0.82	0.82	0.82	0.82	0.82	0.82

(*continued*)

TABLE 5 (*Continued*)

	Narrow outsourcing			Wide outsourcing		
	(a)	(b)	(c)	(d)	(e)	(f)
Exogeneity test for *OUT*						
Shea-partial R^2	0.281			0.309		
Hansen J statistic:	1.076			0.652		
p-val =	0.584			0.722		
Hansen J statistic for unrestricted equation:	0.540			0.238		
p-val =	0.462			0.626		
C statistic for exogeneity test	0.536			0.414		
p-val =	0.464			0.520		
Excluded instruments	OUT_{t-1}^{NARROW}, OUT_{t-2}^{NARROW}			OUT_{t-1}^{WIDE}, OUT_{t-2}^{WIDE}		
Inverted Mills-ratio from selection test (separate regression)	−0.219 [1.28]	−0.210 [1.36]	−0.229 [1.70]	−0.228 [1.30]	−0.208 [1.29]	−0.226 [1.65]

NOTES: t-statistics are in parentheses.* significant at 10%,** at 5%,*** at1%. Not reported: full set of federal state dummies. Default categories: Age:>54. Firm size:>2000; ISCED:Low.

Again, we incorporate a full set of year and industry dummies and also include industry-specific time trends. Table 6 depicts the estimation results with narrowly and broadly defined outsourcing for each skill group. Notably, the coefficients on the individual-and firm-level variables differ significantly between the estimations for the different skill groups. Constraining the coefficients to be uniform across skill groups therefore indeed seems inappropriate.[15]

With regard to the impact of outsourcing the coefficients also differ substantially from the previous specification (compare table 5 and table 6). For high-skilled workers the coefficient of narrowly defined outsourcing is now found to be statistically significant and positive with a 1 percentage point increase in the outsourcing intensity, ceteris paribus, yielding a positive wage premium of about 2.6%. For broadly defined outsourcing the effect is somewhat smaller but still statistically significant (see table 6, columns (a) and (d)). Hence, international outsourcing appears to raise the wage for high-skilled workers, a finding that is in line with the idea that firms outsource the low-skill-intensive parts of production and, hence, increase the relative demand for skilled workers. For medium- and low-skilled workers we find negative coefficients on the outsourcing intensity, which is also in line with this reasoning. However, these coefficients are only statistically significant for low-skilled workers. A 1 percentage point increase in the industries' outsourcing intensity lowers wages for

15 This is also confirmed more formally by an F-test that rejects the parameter constraints.

TABLE 6
Fixed-effects log wage regression by ISCED skill groups

	Narrow outsourcing			Wide outsourcing		
	High (a)	Medium (b)	Low (c)	High (d)	Medium (e)	Low (f)
Age: 18–24	0.164	0.032	0.022	0.168	0.034	0.021
	[1.08]	[0.26]	[0.28]	[1.09]	[0.28]	[0.26]
Age: 25–34	0.140	0.025	0.042	0.139	0.026	0.041
	[1.08]	[0.24]	[0.70]	[1.06]	[0.25]	[0.69]
Age: 35–44	0.124	0.047	0.053	0.121	0.048	0.052
	[1.09]	[0.45]	[1.06]	[1.05]	[0.46]	[1.04]
Age: 45–54	0.074	0.041	0.044	0.073	0.041	0.043
	[0.79]	[0.42]	[1.50]	[0.78]	[0.43]	[1.47]
Married	0.011	−0.114	0.021	0.010	−0.114	0.021
	[0.44]	[3.19]***	[0.70]	[0.42]	[3.19]***	[0.73]
Dummy: Respondent has children	0.037	0.054	0.006	0.038	0.054	0.006
	[1.77]*	[3.81]***	[0.58]	[1.82]*	[3.82]***	[0.54]
Firm size: <20	−0.351	0.010	−0.067	−0.353	0.011	−0.067
	[3.22]***	[0.16]	[1.33]	[3.29]***	[0.17]	[1.34]
Firm size: <200	−0.024	−0.044	−0.022	−0.024	−0.044	−0.022
	[0.61]	[0.59]	[0.67]	[0.63]	[0.58]	[0.67]
Firm size: <2000	0.037	−0.021	−0.017	0.039	−0.020	−0.017
	[2.02]*	[0.58]	[0.76]	[2.18]**	[0.57]	[0.77]
Firm: Public owner	0.068	0.044	0.025	0.070	0.046	0.025
	[0.41]	[1.18]	[0.71]	[0.42]	[1.25]	[0.71]
Tenure	0.000	0.000	−0.002	0.000	0.000	−0.002
	[0.07]	[0.08]	[0.97]	[0.09]	[0.09]	[0.95]
Industry: *Equipment/Y*	−1.802	−1.463	0.102	−1.604	−1.438	0.061
	[1.12]	[1.52]	[0.22]	[1.03]	[1.51]	[0.14]
Industry: *Plant/Y*	3.834	2.255	−0.496	3.109	2.282	−0.334
	[1.37]	[2.18]**	[0.80]	[1.18]	[2.39]**	[0.52]
Industry: Output *Y* (in 100 billion)	0.093	−0.057	−0.067	0.024	−0.069	−0.050
	[0.48]	[0.45]	[0.81]	[0.12]	[0.68]	[0.61]
Out	0.026	−0.007	−0.015	0.019	−0.010	−0.013
	[2.15]**	[0.42]	[2.25]**	[2.22]**	[0.77]	[2.03]*
Constant	4.013	−199.050	−48.608	−8.450	−198.570	−57.096
	[0.04]	[4.59]***	[1.18]	[0.09]	[4.60]***	[1.25]
Year dummies	YES	YES	YES	YES	YES	YES
Industry dummies	YES	YES	YES	YES	YES	YES
Industry specific time trends	YES	YES	YES	YES	YES	YES
Individual fixed effects	YES	YES	YES	YES	YES	YES
Region dummies	YES	YES	YES	YES	YES	YES
Observations	1021	1085	5188	1021	1085	5188
R^2	0.84	0.84	0.74	0.84	0.84	0.74
Inverted Mills ratio from selection test (separate regression)	0.028	−0.100	−0.063	0.014	−0.102	−0.067
	[0.18]	[1.03]	[0.76]	[0.09]	[1.07]	[0.77]

NOTES: t-statistics are in parentheses. *significant at 10%,** at 5%,*** at 1%. Not reported: full set of federal state dummies. Default categories: Age:>54. Firm size:>2000.

low-skilled workers by 1.5% and 1.3% for narrowly and broadly defined outsourcing respectively.[16]

7. Robustness checks

This section briefly considers some extensions of the empirical model in order to check the robustness of our results.

First, in order to check how robust our results thus far are to different skill definitions, we apply an alternative skill measure based on self-reported required qualifications for the respondent's current job (See section 5 and table 3) and estimate the impact of narrow and wide outsourcing for each skill group.

The results for this skill definition support our findings. International outsourcing, both narrow and wide, has a statistically significant positive impact on workers who report that their job requires a college or technical school training. For example, a 1 percentage point increase in the narrow outsourcing intensity, ceteris paribus, raises wages by about 2%. For workers with lower required qualifications we find a statistically significant negative effect of outsourcing, with a 1 percentage point increase in narrow outsourcing, yielding a wage loss of around 1.2%, all other things being equal (see table 7).

Secondly, we consider the impact of domestic outsourcing as well as international outsourcing in our model context. However, we construct a measure of narrow domestic outsourcing similar to the international outsourcing variable in equations (1) instead using domestic intermediate inputs from input-output use tables:

$$DOMOUT_{jt}^{narrow} = \frac{DOM_{jt}}{Y_{jt}}, \tag{4}$$

with j again denoting the respective 2-digit manufacturing industry ($j \in J$), DOM the value of domestic intermediate inputs and Y the industry's output value.

We then proceed to estimate two specifications of the model, one with domestic outsourcing only and one controlling for domestic and international outsourcing simultaneously. For this analysis we use the ISCED skill classification. The results are reported in table 8.

As is apparent, domestic outsourcing is always rendered insignificant for all skill groups. Furthermore, in the model controlling for domestic and international outsourcing simultaneously, the point estimates on the coefficient on

16 As a means of comparison, we have also estimated our model including industries' import penetration calculated as imports from OECD countries and imports from non-OECD countries over gross production. As Anderton and Brenton (1999) state, import penetration from non-OECD countries in particular may be considered as measuring the outsourcing of low-skill intensive production to low-wage locations. However, in our regressions the coefficients of import penetration are always statistically insignificant, thus casting doubt on this assertion. Results are available from the authors.

TABLE 7
Fixed-effects log wage regression by required skill

	Narrow outsourcing		Wide outsourcing	
	High (a)	Low (b)	High (c)	Low (d)
Age: 18–24	–	0.038	–	0.036
	–	[0.59]	–	[0.57]
Age: 25–34	0.020	0.051	0.022	0.051
	[0.33]	[1.09]	[0.36]	[1.08]
Age: 35–44	0.041	0.050	0.042	0.050
	[0.67]	[1.19]	[0.67]	[1.18]
Age: 45–54	0.003	0.041	0.004	0.041
	[0.10]	[1.88]*	[0.11]	[1.86]*
Married	0.011	−0.012	0.010	−0.011
	[0.31]	[0.47]	[0.30]	[0.46]
Dummy: Respondent	0.009	0.019	0.010	0.018
has children	[0.47]	[1.89]*	[0.49]	[1.84]*
Firm size: <20	−0.390	−0.053	−0.390	−0.053
	[3.13]***	[1.18]	[3.16]***	[1.17]
Firm size: <200	−0.030	−0.022	−0.029	−0.022
	[0.64]	[0.71]	[0.62]	[0.71]
Firm size: <2000	0.064	−0.017	0.067	−0.017
	[2.12]**	[0.75]	[2.15]**	[0.74]
Firm: Public owner	0.102	−0.009	0.103	−0.009
	[0.68]	[0.26]	[0.68]	[0.26]
Tenure	−0.002	0.000	−0.002	0.000
	[0.56]	[0.02]	[0.59]	[0.02]
Industry: *Equipment/Y*	−0.901	−0.426	−0.808	−0.437
	[0.60]	[1.00]	[0.55]	[1.05]
Industry: *Plant/Y*	2.173	0.671	1.625	0.790
	[0.71]	[0.68]	[0.56]	[0.83]
Industry: Output	−0.135	−0.073	−0.175	−0.066
Y (in 100 billion)	[0.52]	[1.01]	[0.64]	[1.00]
Out	0.020	−0.012	0.017	−0.012
	[2.02]*	[1.82]*	[2.07]*	[2.12]**
Constant	−19.472	−37.015	−34.195	−34.074
	[0.33]	[1.46]	[0.53]	[1.42]
Year dummies	YES	YES	YES	YES
Industry dummies	YES	YES	YES	YES
Industry specific time trends	YES	YES	YES	YES
Individual fixed effects	YES	YES	YES	YES
Region dummies	YES	YES	YES	YES
Observations	900	6799	900	6799
R^2	0.82	0.76	0.82	0.76
Inverted Mills ratio	−0.008	−0.105	−0.021	−0.107
from selection test	[0.12]	[1.07]	[0.30]	[1.07]
(separate regression)				

NOTES: t-statistics are in parentheses.* significant at 10%,** at 5%,*** at1%. Not reported: full set of federal state dummies. Default categories: *Age*: > 54. Firm size:>2000

TABLE 8
Fixed-effects log wage regression by ISCED skill groups for domestic and international outsourcing

	Only domestic			Domestic and international		
	High (a)	Medium (b)	Low (c)	High (d)	Medium (e)	Low (f)
Age: 18–24	0.178	0.010	0.017	0.173	0.025	0.018
	[1.08]	[0.09]	[0.22]	[1.08]	[0.21]	[0.23]
Age: 25–34	0.144	0.011	0.035	0.145	0.019	0.034
	[0.99]	[0.10]	[0.62]	[1.02]	[0.17]	[0.62]
Age: 35–44	0.118	0.043	0.048	0.125	0.048	0.048
	[0.93]	[0.43]	[0.98]	[1.02]	[0.48]	[0.99]
Age: 45–54	0.079	0.033	0.040	0.079	0.035	0.039
	[0.77]	[0.35]	[1.48]	[0.79]	[0.37]	[1.47]
Married	0.004	−0.089	0.017	0.009	−0.090	0.020
	[0.19]	[2.75]**	[0.59]	[0.40]	[2.77]**	[0.72]
Dummy: Respondent has children	0.034	0.040	0.004	0.036	0.041	0.003
	[1.61]	[2.10]**	[0.39]	[1.62]	[2.16]**	[0.28]
Firm size: < 20	−0.339	0.027	−0.069	−0.346	0.024	−0.067
	[3.43]***	[0.35]	[1.32]	[3.49]***	[0.30]	[1.29]
Firm size: < 200	−0.017	−0.035	−0.021	−0.014	−0.039	−0.019
	[0.51]	[0.51]	[0.63]	[0.41]	[0.54]	[0.57]
Firm size: < 2000	0.030	−0.017	−0.015	0.025	−0.018	−0.012
	[1.59]	[0.44]	[0.67]	[1.23]	[0.47]	[0.57]
Firm: Public owner	0.090	0.058	0.029	0.079	0.062	0.030
	[0.55]	[1.58]	[0.85]	[0.47]	[1.67]	[0.87]
Tenure	−0.001	0.000	−0.001	−0.001	0.000	−0.002
	[0.38]	[0.06]	[0.89]	[0.43]	[0.07]	[0.97]
Industry: *Equipment/Y*	−102.340	−109.850	−15.425	−132.840	−110.010	3.509
	[1.04]	[1.62]	[0.37]	[1.21]	[1.69]	[0.11]
Industry: *Plant/Y*	162.010	195.870	4.052	275.100	171.000	−46.436
	[0.96]	[2.73]**	[0.07]	[1.34]	[2.04]*	[0.88]
Industry: Output *Y* (in 100 billion)	−0.053	0.020	−0.007	0.057	−0.002	−0.040
	[0.49]	[0.28]	[0.24]	[0.23]	[0.07]	[0.65]
Out – Domestic	0.001	−0.005	0.002	0.015	−0.013	−0.008
	[0.04]	[0.39]	[0.15]	[0.59]	[0.94]	[0.61]
Out – International				0.028	−0.015	−0.019
				[1.44]	[0.78]	[2.22]**
Constant	−123.110	−141.400	−21.067	−62.489	−134.060	−48.903
	[0.73]	[3.03]***	[0.49]	[0.34]	[2.95]***	[1.19]
Year dummies	YES	YES	YES	YES	YES	YES
Industry dummies	YES	YES	YES	YES	YES	YES
Industry specific time trends	YES	YES	YES	YES	YES	YES
Individual fixed effects	YES	YES	YES	YES	YES	YES
Region dummies	YES	YES	YES	YES	YES	YES
Observations	1021	1085	5188	1021	1085	5188
R^2	0.850	0.850	0.740	0.850	0.850	0.740

NOTES: t-statistics are in parentheses. *significant at 10%,** at 5%,*** at1%. Not reported: full set of federal state dummies. Default categories: Age:>54. Firm size:>2000.

international outsourcing are not significantly altered, which supports our findings reported above. However, for high-skilled workers the formerly weakly statistically significant coefficient on international outsourcing is now insignificant, which points to a multicollinearity issue.

A last robustness check considers the impact of technological change on our estimates. As pointed out above, we are confident that the inclusion of time and year dummies as well as industry-specific time trends provide comprehensive controls to capture technological change. Still, as a robustness check we also include industry-level research and development spending in order to capture non-linear industry-specific technological change.

Before we report the results of this exercise, it is important to mention that data on research and development expenditure for German industries are notoriously sketchy. The OECD publishes annual R&D data at the 2-digit industry level, starting in 1995. However, research and development data for Germany are collected only biannually by the *Stifterverband für die deutsche Wissenschaft*. Thus, the published yearly OECD data already involve some imputations.[17] Clearly, this is already somewhat unsatisfactory and casts doubt on whether much is gained by including R&D intensity as an additional control variable to our model with industry-specific time trends.

Nevertheless, columns (a) to (c) of table 9 report the estimated coefficients for high, medium-, and low-skilled workers in the augmented model. R&D intensity, measured as industry research and development expenditure over industry output, is always rendered statistically insignificant. Furthermore, although the outsourcing coefficients are somewhat smaller (particularly for high-skilled workers) than before, our general findings still hold: high skilled workers experience significant wage gains, while low-skilled workers suffer wage losses owing to outsourcing.

In a further model specification, reported in columns (d) to (f), we re-estimate the augmented model but exclude industry-specific time trends. Again, R&D intensity is always rendered insignificant, indicating the weak predictive power of the variable. Hence, the inclusion of this variable does not improve our estimates – possibly because of the low quality of the data – and hence we prefer our previous estimations, which capture manufacturing wide technological progress in a non-linear fashion via time dummies and industry-specific technological progress at least in a linear way.[18]

17 To estimate our model with R&D intensity we further impute missing information for the years 1991 to 1995 with an – industry-specific trend.

18 In a final robustness check we also estimate our empirical model excluding industry output. In a sense this regression is less restrictive, as it allows for wage effects of outsourcing through output effects. Our results show, however, that this does not alter our general findings. To save space, the estimations are not reported here.

264 I. Geishecker and H. Görg

TABLE 9
Fixed-effects log wage regression by ISCED skill groups with R&D intensity

	Narrow outsourcing			Wide outsourcing		
	High (a)	Medium (b)	Low (c)	High (d)	Medium (e)	Low (f)
Age: 18–24	0.167	0.030	0.020	0.076	−0.041	0.027
	[1.11]	[0.24]	[0.24]	[0.48]	[0.31]	[0.33]
Age: 25–34	0.142	0.024	0.039	0.068	−0.062	0.054
	[1.10]	[0.23]	[0.66]	[0.53]	[0.53]	[0.91]
Age: 35–44	0.126	0.047	0.051	0.066	−0.013	0.063
	[1.11]	[0.45]	[1.01]	[0.63]	[0.12]	[1.26]
Age: 45–54	0.076	0.040	0.043	0.034	0.000	0.045
	[0.81]	[0.42]	[1.47]	[0.45]	[0.00]	[1.58]
Married	0.007	−0.115	0.021	0.035	−0.093	0.035
	[0.30]	[3.26]***	[0.70]	[1.03]	[2.24]**	[1.11]
Dummy: Respondent has children	0.037	0.053	0.006	−0.016	0.048	0.005
	[1.76]*	[3.81]***	[0.57]	[0.30]	[2.76]**	[0.41]
Firm size: < 20	−0.352	0.012	−0.067	−0.352	0.032	−0.064
	[3.23]***	[0.18]	[1.33]	[3.01]***	[0.44]	[1.19]
Firm size: < 200	−0.024	−0.044	−0.021	−0.018	−0.041	−0.023
	[0.61]	[0.58]	[0.65]	[0.53]	[0.54]	[0.65]
Firm size: < 2000	0.036	−0.020	−0.017	0.044	−0.007	−0.018
	[2.00]*	[0.56]	[0.74]	[2.88]**	[0.21]	[0.75]
Firm: Public owner	0.069	0.042	0.025	0.084	0.046	0.022
	[0.42]	[1.07]	[0.71]	[0.53]	[1.27]	[0.61]
Tenure	0.000	0.000	−0.002	−0.003	0.003	−0.001
	[0.02]	[0.08]	[0.97]	[1.17]	[0.49]	[0.42]
Industry: *Equipment/Y*	−1.735	−1.469	0.152	−0.790	0.802	0.117
	[1.12]	[1.54]	[0.32]	[0.65]	[1.07]	[0.26]
Industry: *Plant/Y*	3.977	2.315	−0.662	0.979	−1.666	−0.809
	[1.41]	[2.33]**	[1.07]	[0.70]	[1.03]	[0.91]
Industry: Output *Y* (in 100 billion)	0.042	−0.080	−0.003	−0.117	−0.194	−0.105
	[0.24]	[0.52]	[0.03]	[0.66]	[2.01]*	[1.57]
Out	0.023	−0.008	−0.014	0.005	−0.021	−0.012
	[2.18]**	[0.45]	[2.14]**	[0.58]	[1.35]	[3.02]***
R&D/Y	−1.742	−0.770	1.881	−0.433	−0.862	−0.489
	[0.91]	[0.47]	[1.03]	[0.51]	[0.67]	[0.70]
Constant	18.035	−129.240	35.772	3.234	3.121	3.294
	[0.18]	[3.05]***	[0.87]	[9.79]***	[11.45]***	[15.94]***
Year dummies	YES	YES	YES	YES	YES	YES
Industry dummies	YES	YES	YES	YES	YES	YES
Industry specific time trends	YES	YES	YES	NO	NO	NO
Individual fixed effects	YES	YES	YES	YES	YES	YES
Region dummies	YES	YES	YES	YES	YES	YES
Observations	1021	1085	5188	1021	1085	5188
R^2	0.85	0.84	0.74	0.83	0.83	0.73

NOTES: t-statistics are in parentheses. *significant at 10%,** at 5%,*** at 1%. Not reported: full set of federal state dummies. Default categories: Age:>54. Firm size:>2000.

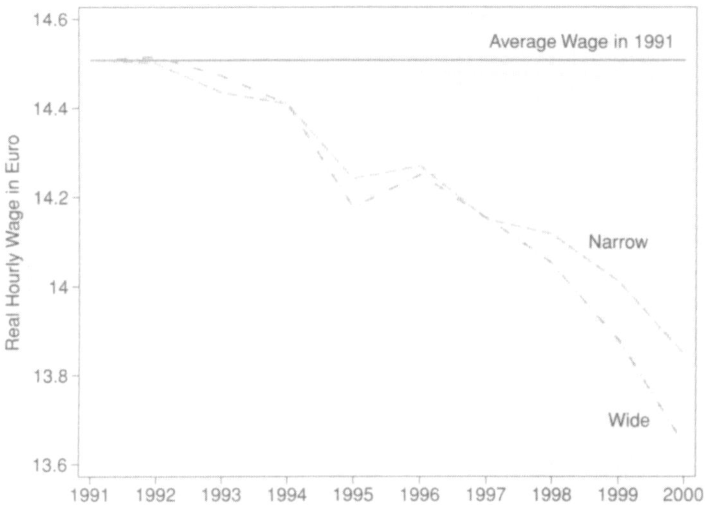

FIGURE 3 Cumulated marginal effects of outsourcing for ISCED low-skilled workers

8. Economic significance

In order to get a better idea of the true impact of international outsourcing we calculate cumulative marginal effects based on the statistically significant results in table 6 and the change in the intensity of international outsourcing over the years 1991 to 2000. Basically this amounts to multiplying the percentage point change in the outsourcing intensity, starting from the basis year 1991, with the point estimate of the outsourcing variable from the wage regression and the average wage for each respective skill group in 1991. Overall the narrowly defined outsourcing intensity increased by 3 percentage points between 1991 and 2000. When we apply the wide outsourcing definition, the increase was about 5 percentage points.[19]

Applying the ISCED definition, for low-skilled workers, we calculate that between 1991 and 2000 increased outsourcing, accounts for a reduction in hourly earnings by 0.66 Euro and 0.86 Euro for narrowly and broadly defined outsourcing, respectively. For an average low-skilled worker with, for instance, 1,600 working hours per year, this amounts to an earnings loss of, respectively, 1,055 Euro and 1,376 Euro, owing to increased outsourcing (see figure 3).

On the other hand, high-skilled workers significantly gained from increased outsourcing. On average, their hourly wages increased by about 1.98 Euro

19 Accordingly, using the point estimates from table 6, our calculations indicate that the average hourly wage for low-skilled workers decreased by 4.5% and 6.5%, respectively, between 1991 and 2000. The same calculations can be made for each year between 1991 and 2000 and are plotted in figures 3 to 6.

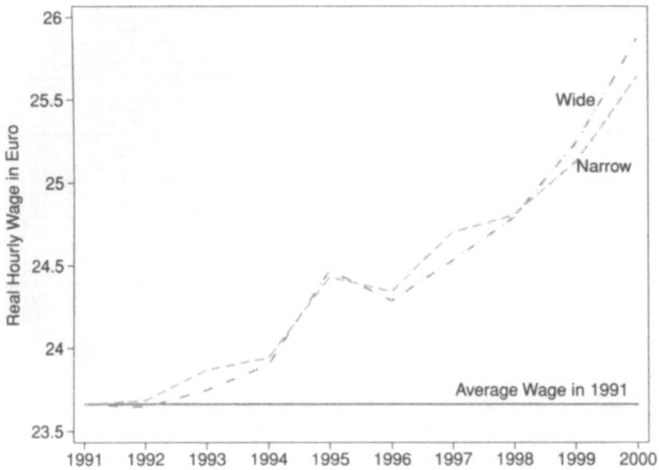

FIGURE 4 Cumulated marginal effects of outsourcing for ISCED high-skilled workers

FIGURE 5 Cumulated marginal effects of outsourcing for workers with low skill requirements

and 2.21 Euro in 2000, compared with 1991, owing to outsourcing. Again, with assumed 1,600 working hours per year, this amounts to an earnings gain of 3,168 Euro and 3,536 Euro for narrow and wide outsourcing, respectively (figure 4).

Figures 5 and 6 show similar calculations for our alternative skill definition based on actual on the job skill requirements. Again, a comparison of hourly wages of low-skilled workers in 1991 and 2000 shows increased international outsourcing accounts for an hourly wage reduction of 0.57 Euro and 0.86 Euro.

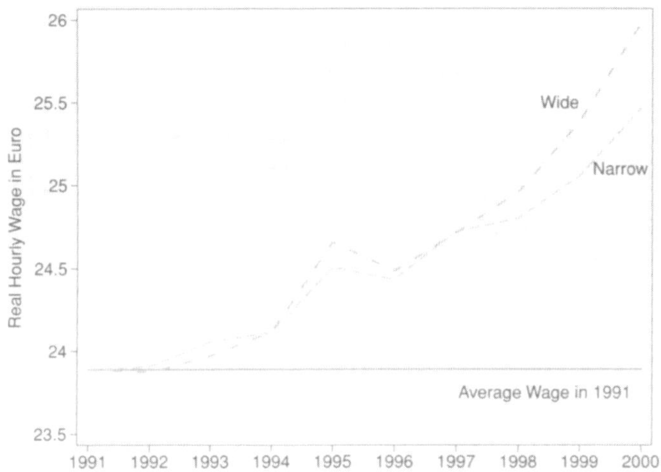

FIGURE 6 Cumulated marginal effects of outsourcing for workers with high skill requirements

High-skilled workers, however, significantly gained, with increased outsourcing raising hourly wages by 1.58 Euro to 2.1 Euro.

9. Conclusion

This paper adds to the literature on the implications of outsourcing for labour markets by investigating the effect of international outsourcing, measured in terms of imports of intermediates, on wages for different skill groups. To the best of our knowledge, this is the first paper to look at this issue by using individual-level data, which makes it possible to control for compositional changes of the workforce and to estimate the gains and losses for accurately defined skill groups in absolute terms.

Our results show that outsourcing has a marked impact on wages. We find evidence of a negative effect of outsourcing on the real wage for low-skilled workers. We also find evidence that high-skilled workers gain from outsourcing in terms of receiving higher wages. These results are robust to a number of different specifications and definitions of outsourcing.

This suggests that low-skilled workers are the losers from this form of globalization of production, while high-skilled workers are, on average, the group that may be able to gain. This may have implications for policy makers, who need to debate whether losers should be compensated or in any other way be the focus of policies aimed at easing the adjustment cost of globalization.[20]

20 However, our estimates relate to the immediate short-run effects of international outsourcing. With regard to the long-run effects of international outsourcing, the theoretical literature is not conclusive (see section 2). At what point long-run effects materialize, however, essentially

Our results, of course, raise the question of how the relative wages of skilled to unskilled workers could have remained relatively unchanged if outsourcing has had this opposing effect? While a thorough investigation of this issue is beyond the scope of this paper, recent research has brought up two possible explanations. First, Krueger and Pischke (1997) find that the returns to skills in Germany fell during the 1980s, and this would have had a mediating effect on increases in wages for skilled workers. Secondly, Beaudry and Green (2003) argue that Germany has been able to avoid increases in wage inequality by following a path of balanced growth in the ratio of physical to human capital, as opposed to the U.S., where the accumulation of physical capital was too slow. Evaluating these explanations in the context of our findings is a priority for further research.

References

Amiti, Mary, and Shang-Jin Wei (2005) 'Fear of service outsourcing – is it justified?' *Economic Policy* 20, 307–47

Anderton, Bob, and Paul Brenton (1999) 'Outsourcing and low-skilled workers in the UK,' *Bulletin of Economic Research* 51, 267–85

Arndt, Sven W. (1997) 'Globalization and the open economy,' *North American Journal of Economics and Finance* 8, 71–9

— (1999) 'Globalization and economic development,' *Journal of International Trade and Economic Development* 8, 309–18

Beaudry, Paul, and David A. Green (2003) 'Wages and employment in the United States and Germany: what explains the differences?' *American Economic Review* 93, 573–602

Berman, Eli, John Bound, and Stephen Machin (1998) 'Implications of skill-biased technological change: international evidence,' *Quarterly Journal of Economics* 113, 1245–80

Brown, Charles, and James Medoff (1989) 'The employer size-wage effect,' *Journal of Political Economy* 97, 1027–59

Chen, Hogan, Matthew Kondratowicz, and Kei-Mu Yi (2005) 'Vertical specialisation and three facts about U.S. international trade,' *North American journal of Economics and Finance* 16, 35–59

Egger, Peter, Michael Pfaffermayr, and Andrea Weber (2007) 'Sectoral adjustment of employment to shifts in outsourcing and trade: evidence from a dynamic fixed effects multinominal logit model,' *Journal of Applied Econometrics* 22, 559–80

Falk, Martin, and Bertrand M. Koebel (2002) 'Outsourcing, imports and labour demand,' *Scandinavian Journal of Economics* 104, 567–86

Feenstra, Robert C., and Gordon H. Hanson (1996a) 'Foreign direct investment, outsourcing and relative wages,' in *The Political Economy of Trade Policy: Papers in Honor of Jagdish Bhagwati,* ed. Robert C. Feenstra, Gene M. Grossman, and D.A. Irwin (Cambridge, MA: MIT Press)

— (1996b) 'Globalization, outsourcing, and wage inequality,' *American Economic Review* 86, 240–5

— (1999) 'The impact of outsourcing and high-technology capital on wages: estimates for the United States, 1979-1990,' *Quarterly Journal of Economics* 114, 907–40

— (2001) 'Global production sharing and rising inequality: a survey of trade and wages,' NBER Working Paper No. 8372

depends on the inter-industry mobility of labour which, arguably, is in itself a function of labour market policies.

Winners and losers: a micro-level analysis 269

Fitzenberger, Bernd (1999) 'International trade and the skill structure of wages and employment in West Germany,' *Jahrbücher für Nationalökonomie und Statistik* 219, 67–89
Freeman, Richard B., and Lawrence F. Katz (1995) 'Introduction and summery,' in *Differences and Changes in Wage Structures,* ed. Richard B. Freeman and Lawrence F. Katz (Chicago and London: University of Chicago Press)
Frick, Joachim R., and Markus M. Grabka (2003) 'Imputation of item-non-response on income questions in the SOEP 1984 to 2002,' Research Notes 29, DIW
Geishecker, Ingo (2006) 'Does outsourcing to Central and Eastern Europe really threaten manual workers' jobs in Germany?' *World Economy* 29, 559–83
— (2007) 'The impact of international outsourcing on individual employment security: a micro-level analysis,' forthcoming in *Labour Economics*
Görg, Holger, and Aoife Hanley (2005) 'Labour demand effects of international outsourcing: evidence from plant level data,' *International Review of Economics and Finance* 14, 365–76
Haisken-DeNew, John P. (2005) 'SOEPMENU: a menu-driven Stata/SE interface for accessing the German Socio-Economic Panel,' mimeo, updated program version available at http://www.panelwhiz.eu
Haisken-DeNew, John P., and Joachim R. Frick (2003) 'Desktop companion to the German Socio-Economic Panel,' manual, available at http://www.diw.de/deutsch/sop/service/dtc/dtc.pdf, DIW Berlin
Harris, Richard G. (2001) 'A communication-based model of global production fragmentation,' in *Fragmentation: New Production Patterns in the World Economy,* ed. Sven W. Arndt and Henryk Kierzkowski (Oxford: Oxford University Press)
Head, Keith, and John Ries (2002) 'Offshore production and skill upgrading by Japanese manufacturing firms,' *Journal of International Economics* 58, 81–105
Hijzen, Alexander, Holger Görg, and Robert C. Hine (2005) 'Outsourcing and the skill structure of labour demand in the United Kingdom,' *Economic Journal* 115, 861–79
Hsieh, Chang-Tai, and Keong T. Woo (2005) 'The impact of outsourcing to China on Hong Kong's labour market,' *American Economic Review* 95, 1673–87
Hummels, David, Jun Ishii, and Kei-Mu Yi (2001) 'The nature and growth of vertical specialization in world trade,' *Journal of International Economics* 54, 75–96
Hunt, Jennifer (2001) 'Post-unification wage growth in East Germany,' *Review of Economics and Statistics* 83, 190–5
Jones, Ronald W., and Henryk Kierzkowski (2001) 'A framework for fragmentation,' in *Fragmentation: New Production Patterns in the World Economy,* ed. Sven W. Arndt and Henryk Kierzkowski (Oxford: Oxford University Press)
Kohler, Wilhelm (2004a) 'Aspects of international fragmentation,' *Review of International Economics* 12, 793–816
— (2004b) 'International outsourcing and factor prices with multistage production,' *Economic Journal* 114, C166–85
Krueger, Alan B., and Jörn-Steffen Pischke (1995) 'A comparative analysis of East and West German labour markets: before and after unification,' in *Differences and Changes in Wage Structures,* ed. Richard Freeman and Lawrence Katz (Chicago and London: University of Chicago Press)
Krueger, Alan B., and Jörn Steffen Pischke (1997) 'Observations and conjectures on the US employment miracle,' NBER Working Paper No. 6146.
Mincer, Jacob (1974) *Schooling, Experience and Earnings* (New York: National Bureau of Economic Research)
Morrison-Paul, Catherine J., and Donald S. Siegel (2001) 'The impacts of technology, trade and outsourcing on employment and labour composition,' *Scandinavian Journal of Economics* 103, 241–64
Moulton, Brent R. (1990) 'An illustration of the pitfall in estimating the effects of aggregate variables in micro units,' *Review of Economics and Statistics* 72, 334–8

OECD (1994) *Job Study, Part 1* (Paris: OECD)
Prasad, Eswar S. (2004) 'The unbearable stability of the German wage structure: evidence and interpretation,' *IMF Staff Papers* 51, 354–86
Schmidt, Christoph M., and Klaus F. Zimmermann (1991) 'Work characteristics, firm size and wages,' *Review of Economics and Statistics* 73, 705–10
UNESCO (1997) 'International standard classification of education,' Technical Report, UNESCO
Wooldridge, Jeffrey M. (1995) 'Selection corrections for panel data models under conditional mean independence assumptions,' *Journal of Econometrics* 68, 115–32

Chapter III.3

Do labour market institutions matter? Micro-level wage effects of international outsourcing in three European countries

**Ingo Geishecker · Holger Görg ·
Jakob Roland Munch**

Published online: 19 January 2010

Abstract This paper studies the impact of outsourcing on individual wages in three European countries with markedly different labour market institutions: Germany, the UK and Denmark. To do so we use individual-level data sets for the three countries and construct comparable measures of outsourcing at the industry level, distinguishing outsourcing by broad region. We discuss some possible intuitive reasons for why there may be differences in the impact of outsourcing across the three countries, based on labour market institutions.

Keywords International outsourcing · Individual wages · Labour market institutions

JEL Classification F16 · J31 · C23

1 Introduction

Over the last years globalisation and its alleged negative effects for the distribution of income, unemployment, poverty and social cohesion has caused immense public

---

I. Geishecker
Georg-August-Universität Göttingen, Germany, and Aarhus School of Business, Aarhus, Denmark

H. Görg
Kiel Institute for the World Economy, Christian-Albrechts-Universität Kiel, Germany, and CEPR, London, UK

J. R. Munch
University of Copenhagen and EPRU, Copenhagen, Denmark

I. Geishecker (✉)
Faculty of Economic Sciences, Platz der Göttinger Sieben 3, 37073 Göttingen, Germany
e-mail: ingo.geishecker@wiwi.uni-goettingen.de

anxiety in Europe, particularly against the backdrop of eastern enlargement of the European Union. Indeed, globalisation in the form of intensified international trade and, in particular, international outsourcing of production, has a deep structural impact fostering the specialisation of open economies in industries where they possess a comparative advantage. Other, less competitive industries on the other hand shrink. Following standard trade theory, international specialisation is expected to yield significant efficiency gains improving the welfare of open economies.[1]

However, even if there are overall welfare gains there will inevitably be distributional consequences leading to winners and losers of the globalisation process in the economy. This paper concerns itself with one aspect of globalisation, namely the practice of outsourcing of production around the globe. A key feature of today's globalisation process is the ever increasing international fragmentation of production resulting in outsourcing, that manifests itself in a fast growing share of trade with intermediate goods. What we witness now is a dramatically intensified international division of labour which does not only take place between industries but is prevalent within each manufacturing industry and increasingly within business services.

Trade liberalisation and technological progress have substantially lowered transaction costs which increasingly enables firms to outsource and relocate production to those locations where production costs are lowest. Analogue to conventional trade this outsourcing potentially yields large efficiency gains that materialise in the form of increased competitiveness and thus higher growth and employment.[2] However, it is also clear that this process generates winners and losers. Particularly low-skilled workers in industrialised countries are arguably at risk to suffer higher economic insecurity, income losses, unemployment and social exclusion.

The aim of the paper is, hence, to try and identify winners and losers from international outsourcing in European economies. Specifically, we investigate the impact of outsourcing on wages of individual workers. A further aim of the paper is to establish whether the impact of international outsourcing differs across countries with different types of welfare states and, in particular, labour market institutions. In other words, we try to address the question as to what role labour market institutions may play in shaping the wage effect of international outsourcing on workers.

This makes our paper of particular relevance in the European context and highlights the importance of institutional characteristics of the labour market that affect the wage setting. Welfare states face the challenge of mitigating adverse effects of the globalisation process while at the same time the institutional characteristics of the welfare system directly shape the potential welfare gains and

[1] Slightly newer trade models, however, have shown that the paradigm of universal welfare gains through international trade is heavily based on the assumptions of perfect competition and flexible factor prices. For example, Krugman (1995) shows that with rigid relative factor prices imports from low-wage countries cannot be met by a sufficient specialisation in export oriented activities. As a result, trade with low-wage countries can dramatically lower aggregate domestic production and employment.

[2] See, e.g., Amiti and Wei (2009) and Görg et al. (2008).

losses from international outsourcing. In the public but also academic debate one often refers to the European Social Model or the European Welfare System partly to contrast the American Social Model. However, institutional characteristics of the welfare system starkly differ within Europe. Somewhat simplifying, one can identify three types of social models within the European Union: the Anglo-Saxon, the Central European and the Scandinavian. All three substantially differ in terms of institutions and legislation particularly with respect to employment protection, unemployment benefits, minimum wages or the role of unions. The literature lacks detailed theories on how labour market institutions affect the impact of outsourcing on wages, so it is an open question that will be addressed empirically in this paper which social model is best suited to cope with the challenges of globalisation through outsourcing of production.

Empirical evidence so far suggests that low-skilled workers are the losers from international outsourcing of production in many countries.[3] However, the existing empirical studies generally use fairly aggregated data which prevents an in-depth analysis of the social impact of this phenomenon. Namely, existing studies do not allow to separate changes in the composite demand for various skill groups in wage and employment effects. Furthermore, using aggregated data does not allow differentiating absolute gains and losses from relative ones. However, when designing policies it clearly matters whether the task is for instance to tackle increased income inequality that comes through absolute wage gains for highly educated workers or through absolute wage losses of low-skilled workers.

This paper provides a detailed disaggregated estimation of the impact of international outsourcing on individual wages for various population groups. We will identify winners and losers from the globalisation process and assess to what extent education and, thus, skills determine the individually experienced impact of globalisation. Although wages at the aggregate level are central determinants of social cohesion our micro level approach allows us to also look at other important factors. It is now not only possible to look at aggregated wage effects but also to assess the role of globalisation for individual economic security that manifests itself in annual income fluctuations.

The analysis is carried out for three countries: the United Kingdom, Germany and Denmark, that exemplary stand for the three different social models in Europe and significantly differ in terms of the institutional setting. Comparing the social impact of relocation across these three countries can provide interesting new insights into the role of institutions and social policies for shaping and mitigating the impact of globalisation.

Section 2 discusses briefly the theoretical background and the expected impact of labour market institutions on the relationship between international outsourcing and wages. Section 3 describes the empirical approach, measurement of outsourcing and micro data for the three countries. Estimation results are reported in Sect. 4. The final section offers a brief conclusion.

---

[3] See for example Feenstra and Hanson (1996) on the US, Hijzen et al. (2005) on the UK and Geishecker (2006) on Germany.

2 International outsourcing, labour market institutions and wages

In theory the consequences of outsourcing for workers of different skill types are not clear cut. For example, Feenstra and Hanson (1996) formulate a model of international outsourcing that is a specific form of a Heckscher–Ohlin (HO) type model with only one final good and two countries, North and South. By changing relative unit costs of production, for instance through Hicks-neutral technological progress in the South, production fragments with lower skill intensity are shifted from the North to the South, thereby raising the average skill intensity of production in both countries. As a result, relative demand for skilled labour increases in both the North and the South. By contrast, Arndt (1997, 1999) develops a model of international outsourcing that is also based on a HO framework but makes less restrictive assumptions. In particular, he considers trade between a small price-taking economy and the rest of the world, allowing for two factors of production and two final goods. In this model, if the low-skill intensive industry shifts some fragments of production abroad, this results in a productivity improvement in the low-skill intensive industry and with given world prices, ultimately in higher relative wages for unskilled workers. Hence, depending on the models and assumptions chosen, outsourcing of the low-skill intensive part of production can lead to decreases or increases in the wage of (unskilled) labour in the outsourcing economy.[4] Whether workers in practice gain or lose from fragmentation and relocation is, therefore, largely an empirical question.

These theoretical models assume that wages are flexible and that there is no unemployment. Furthermore, the two sector models assume that labour is mobile between industries. Clearly, these assumptions are generally violated in the real world, at least in the short run. This is where the role of labour market institutions comes into play. Many countries have, in some form or other, collective wage bargaining or coordination of wage bargaining, as well as some form of employment protection and unemployment benefits. This, on the one hand, leads to rigidities in the labour market but is also designed to safeguard workers against adverse shocks in the economy. However, to our knowledge there is a gap in the theoretical literature about what role labour market institutions play in shaping the effects of outsourcing on wages, so to provide some knowledge about the relationship we will as a first step assess empirically how outsourcing affects wages in the three countries under consideration. Nevertheless, based on a description of how labour market institutions work in United Kingdom, Germany and Denmark we will try to outline some plausible relationships and predictions.

Of the three countries considered, Germany has arguably the least flexible labour market institutions. In terms of employment protection, Germany has an elaborate system of legal rules and contracts that stipulate conditions for dismissal, providing fairly secure employment prospects for workers, but making hiring and firing of workers difficult for firms. In fact, as Nickell et al. (2005) show, Germany has one of the highest levels of employment protection among OECD countries. Furthermore, the German labour market is characterised by the importance of unions in

[4] See also Jones and Kierzkowski (2001) and Kohler (2004) for other related theoretical papers.

wage bargaining. While the actual level of unionisation is only about 30 percent of employees, the percentage of employees who are covered by wage bargaining is around 90 percent (Nickell et al. 2005). Collective bargaining generally takes place annually between unions and employer federations and can be at either industry and/or regional level.[5] It is important to note, however, that in collective bargaining only *minimum* wages are determined, while many workers are paid wages above that floor rate.

Compared to Germany, the UK represents the other, more flexible, end of the spectrum in terms of European labour market institutions. The level of employment protection is one of the lowest among OECD countries (with only the US and Canada being more flexible) and it also has substantially lower levels of union density and coverage than most other continental European countries (Nickell et al. 2005). Indeed, wage setting is generally decentralised and is relatively free of regulations, as discussed in some detail by Borland et al. (2002). The UK has adopted a system of a national minimum wage in 1999.

Turning to Denmark, an important characteristic of the labour market is that it is heavily unionised and although a process of decentralisation of wage formation has been ongoing since the late 1980's the wage structure is still relatively compressed even by European standards. Compared to other continental European labour markets the Danish labour market is often described as being very flexible as employment protection is relatively weak, while at the same time replacement rates of unemployment insurance (UI) benefits are high. A third distinguishing characteristic of the Danish labour market is that large sums are spent on active labour market policies. Together these ingredients form what by some has been dubbed the 'flexicurity' model. The idea behind this model is that Danish firms relatively easily may adjust employment according to demand. As compensation for high job turnover workers receive relatively generous UI benefits when unemployed, but incentives to search for jobs during unemployment are reinforced by a strict 'activation' regulation.

This labour market model has led to turnover rates and an average tenure which are in line with those of the Anglo-Saxon countries. In 1995 the average tenure in the Danish labour market was the lowest in continental Europe with 7.9 years just exceeding the number for the UK (7.8 years) while average tenure in the German labour market was 9.7 years (OECD 1997). Motivated by the fact that unemployment in Denmark is very low, OECD (2005) has recently recommended Germany to learn from the Danish 'flexicurity' model in its attempt to combat unemployment.

Table 1 summarises some important characteristics for the labour markets in (West) Germany, the UK and Denmark, which are taken from Nickell et al. (2005). The wage setting processes are clearly important to our analysis, and they are evidently following different mechanisms in the three countries. Wage formation in the UK is very flexible as union density, collective bargaining coverage and union co-ordination are lowest in the UK. In contrast, unions play a much more important role in the German and Danish labour markets—union density is highest in

[5] See also Bender et al. (2002) for a good description of labour market institutions in Germany.

Table 1 Labour market characteristics, 1994–1999

	Germany (W)	UK	Denmark
Union density (%, 1996–1998)	27	35	76
Collective bargaining coverage (%, 1994)	92	40	69
Co-ordination index (1995–1999)	2.5	1.0	2.0
Employment protection index (1998)	1.30	0.35	0.70
UI replacement ratio (1999)	0.37	0.17	0.66
Expenditure on ALMP (% of GDP, 1998)	1.26	0.34	1.66

Source: Nickell et al. (2005)

Denmark while the coverage rate is highest in Germany, and wage bargaining in both countries is highly coordinated. Thus based on these observations we should expect that wages are most sensitive to changes in international outsourcing at the industry level in the UK.

However, this is not the complete picture since adjustments may go through employment changes instead. Coupled with the average tenures cited above it is clear that employment protection stands out as the most restrictive in Germany. Therefore the German labour market may be seen as the least flexible as wages are relatively rigid and employment is protected. The UK in contrast is the most flexible of the three economies with very little regulation of employment and wages, while Denmark is in between with rigid wage formation and low employment protection.

A possible expectation concerning the differential impact of outsourcing in the three countries is that wages should be least affected in Denmark, since with rigid wages adjustments are likely to go through employment changes instead. International outsourcing may give rise to wage moderation in bargaining between firms and unions if, for example, it corresponds to improved outside options for employers. This may be especially true for labour markets such as the German where employment is highly protected and thus cannot easily adjust. Thus even if wages are relatively rigid in Germany they may still adjust if faced with increasing outsourcing pressure. Furthermore, it is important to recall that centralised bargaining only determines the minimum level of wage, while most workers are paid above that level. Hence, wages may adjust by moving towards the minimum. In the UK both wages and employment may adjust so it is not entirely clear which dimension any adjustment may follow. Thus one may expect wages to be relatively insensitive to international outsourcing in Denmark, while they are more likely to adjust in Germany and the UK. In the following sections we address this question empirically in order to get a first impression of what the data tell us.

3 Methodology

To assess the impact of outsourcing on individual wages we follow the approach in Geishecker and Görg (2008) and Munch and Skaksen (2009) and estimate simple Mincer human capital wage equations of the form

$$\log w_{ijt} = \alpha + \beta X_{it} + \gamma Y_{jt} + \lambda \mathrm{OUT}_{jt-1} + \mu_t + \alpha_i + \iota_j + \epsilon_{ijt}, \tag{1}$$

where w_{ijt} is the hourly wage of worker i in industry j at time t. X_{it} is a vector of standard demographic and human capital variables which includes age, age squared, dummies for the presence of children and being married, job tenure, tenure squared, an indicator variable for high education, dummies for occupation using the nine main categories of the ISCO code, dummies for firm size and regional dummies. Year effects, μ_t, and individual specific fixed effects, α_i, are also controlled for. In addition we include industry dummies ι_j, and to control for time varying industry characteristics and industry-specific technological progress we also enter industry output, Y_{jt}, and industry research and development intensity, R&D/Y, in the model. The main explanatory variable of interest, of course, is the outsourcing variable, OUT_{jt-1}, which we describe in more detail below. Industry level variables such as outsourcing are likely exogenous to the individual worker, but if there are industry components in individual wages (e.g. through collective bargaining) there may still be some endogeneity. We use the lagged value of outsourcing as a simple approach to alleviate any such problems.

All the regressions are weighted using the standard sampling weights from the respective data sets to adjust for different individual sampling probabilities. Finally a methodological point should be mentioned. In the wage Eq. 1 we estimate the effect of an aggregate variable (i.e. outsourcing at the industry level) on wages of individual workers, so the standard errors of the estimated coefficients may be biased downwards as indicated in Moulton (1990). Accordingly, we adjust standard errors allowing for contemporaneous correlation as has become standard in the literature.

3.1 Measurement of international outsourcing

Anecdotal evidence on firms shifting production stages abroad by subcontracting legally independent suppliers or establishing foreign production sites is manifold. However, systematically measuring the process of international outsourcing presents a challenge. Ideally one would want firm-level measures of outsourcing, but such information is rarely available and this is also the case for the three countries under consideration here. Instead we follow most of the literature and construct outsourcing measures at the industry level.

Most authors rely on trade statistics, exploiting the close relation between international outsourcing and trade in intermediate goods. Authors such as Yeats (2001) seek to measure international outsourcing or, as he calls it, *production sharing*, by directly quantifying trade in intermediate goods, assessing the intermediate character of the traded goods on the basis of disaggregated goods classifications. However, such calculations most likely are upward-biased, as imported parts and components (of machinery and transport equipment) are assumed to be intermediate goods imports of the respective broader industry that produces such parts and components itself (machinery and transport equipment industry). This abstracts from the possibility that parts and components from one industry can be also used by other manufacturing and service industries or by final consumers. Having said that, at the country level, differentiating trade in intermediate goods arguably is a valid way to derive a broad picture of the overall outsourcing intensity. However, in order to generate industry-level outsourcing measures, one needs to find ways to appropriately allocate imports of parts and components to those industries that actually use them.

Authors such as Feenstra and Hanson (1999) or Campa and Goldberg (1997) quantify international outsourcing by combining input coefficients that can be found in input-output tables and trade data. The estimated value of imported intermediate inputs of an industry thereby largely depends on whether one applies a narrow or wide definition of international outsourcing.

Campa and Goldberg (1997) assume that the total sum of imported intermediate goods in each industry as a share of the respective industry's production value represents a reasonable indicator for international outsourcing. However, according to Feenstra and Hanson (1999) the above definition might be too broad if one understands international outsourcing to be the result of a make-or-buy decision. Following this approach, it is not the total sum of imported intermediate inputs but only the part that could be produced within the respective domestic industry that actually constitutes international outsourcing. However, depending on the aggregational level, the range of products that an industry can produce varies. Accordingly, the more highly aggregated the industries are, the broader the definition of international outsourcing becomes.

For the present analysis we loosely follow the concept proposed in Feenstra and Hanson (1999) and measure narrow international outsourcing as the shift of a two-digit industry's *core activities* abroad, represented by the value of the industry's imported intermediate inputs from the same industry abroad as a share of the domestic industry's production value. The challenge is now to measure the respective industry's imports of intermediate goods. A simple procedure would be to assume that all imports from a certain foreign industry i^* are directed towards the respective domestic industry i and nowhere else. Essentially, this would amount to the construction of industry-level import penetration ratios, which are however rather poor measures of industries' outsourcing activities. Instead, input-output data that are available from national Statistic Offices are utilised in order to allocate imports according to their usage as input factors across industries. The use of input-output tables renders obsolete the differentiation of intermediate goods on the basis of disaggregated goods classifications. Imports are always counted as intermediate goods imports if they are used in manufacturing.

Formally, outsourcing is constructed as:

$$\mathrm{OUTS}_{it} = \frac{IMP_{i^*t} \times \Omega_{ii^*t}}{Y_{it}} \tag{2}$$

with IMP_{i^*t} denoting imported intermediate inputs from industry i^* and Y_{it} the production value of industry i at time t. Ω_{ii^*t} denotes the share of imports from a foreign industry i^* that is consumed by the respective domestic industry i in t with $\sum_{i=1}^{I} \Omega_{ii^*t} \times IMP_{i^*t} =$ total imports from industry i^* which are not only used in manufacturing but also in agriculture, services, private and public consumption, investment and exports in t.

Table 2 Availability of input–output data

Country	Separate I–O tables for imports	
United Kingdom	Not available	Instead aggregated yearly tables 1992–2004
Denmark	Available	1990–2002
Germany	Available	1991–2000

Accordingly, we construct industry-level outsourcing measures for each country. In doing so we are, however, constrained by different availability of input-output tables for the different countries. While for Denmark use tables for imported inputs are available from 1990 to 2002, for Germany comparable tables are only available for 1991 until 2000.[6]

For the UK data availability is even more limited as input–output data differentiating between imports and domestic production is only available for 1995.[7] Accordingly we use available yearly input-output tables from UK National Statistics which, however, do not differentiate between imports and domestic supplies. Table 2 summarises these constraints. In order to estimate our empirical model for a common period with as many years as possible we select the years 1991 until 2000 as joint sample period and for the UK use 1992 values of Ω for the missing year 1991.

Table 3 presents international outsourcing as weighted averages over all manufacturing industries in the UK, Denmark and Germany as well as corresponding growth rates. Generally speaking, the level of international outsourcing is roughly comparable across the three countries ranging from six to seven percent in 1999. In terms of total growth of international outsourcing, which is of course more meaningful than the sheer level, the UK stands out. Here outsourcing grew by about 49% over the years 1991 to 1999. In comparison growth rates in Germany and Denmark are somewhat lower, but with 30% and 25% still substantial.

By differentiating imports by their origin while assuming Ω_{ii^*t} to be constant across import origins we can in a next step construct outsourcing measures for different geographic regions. Against the backdrop of dramatic political and economic change we are particularly interested in outsourcing towards Central and Eastern European Countries (CEEC) but also towards low-wage countries in Asia.

Equation 2 can then be separated geographically:

$$\mathrm{OUTS}_{it} = \frac{\sum_{c=1}^{C} IMP_{i^*ct} \times \Omega_{ii^*t}}{Y_{it}} \tag{3}$$

[6] In 2007 the German Federal Statistical Office released a major update of input–output tables, however only for the years from 1995 onwards. The present analysis is restricted to the 1990s. We therefore only utilize the initial release for the years 1991–2000.

[7] Input-output data for the UK in this respect are similar to that for the US which also do differentiate between imports and domestic production.

Table 3 Outsourcing intensity (per cent)

Year	World	CEEC	LwAsia	HwOECD	RoW
Germany					
1991	5.25	0.10	0.31	4.45	0.39
1992	5.40	0.13	0.31	4.59	0.37
1993	5.13	0.23	0.36	4.26	0.28
1994	5.35	0.28	0.40	4.35	0.32
1995	5.93	0.38	0.44	4.74	0.37
1996	5.71	0.38	0.44	4.56	0.33
1997	6.31	0.47	0.47	5.00	0.37
1998	6.69	0.56	0.47	5.26	0.40
1999	6.84	0.63	0.51	4.90	0.80
Growth rate	30.33	546.21	64.26	10.11	104.54
United Kingdom					
1991	4.10	0.02	0.22	3.49	0.38
1992	4.45	0.02	0.25	3.71	0.47
1993	4.71	0.04	0.33	3.69	0.64
1994	5.08	0.06	0.36	4.15	0.51
1995	5.23	0.07	0.39	4.27	0.50
1996	5.49	0.07	0.47	4.30	0.65
1997	5.79	0.08	0.56	4.82	0.32
1998	6.31	0.09	0.66	5.19	0.37
1999	6.11	0.09	0.63	4.67	0.72
Growth rate	48.92	430.85	193.91	33.76	89.94
Denmark					
1991	4.94	0.09	0.26	3.22	1.37
1992	4.90	0.10	0.25	3.14	1.42
1993	4.43	0.08	0.20	2.91	1.23
1994	4.97	0.11	0.20	3.23	1.44
1995	5.67	0.12	0.18	3.98	1.39
1996	6.27	0.12	0.20	4.40	1.54
1997	6.57	0.12	0.20	4.82	1.43
1998	6.50	0.11	0.21	4.76	1.41
1999	6.18	0.13	0.17	4.41	1.47
Growth rate	25.07	34.68	−33.55	37.11	7.36

with IMP_{i^*ct} denoting imported inputs from industry i^* in the country of origin c and Y_{it} the production value of industry i at time t.

To account for potentially heterogenous effects we differentiate between outsourcing towards four economic regions: CEEC, low-wage Asia (LwAsia), high-wage OECD (HwOECD) and all other countries in the rest of the World

(RoW).[8] The respective figures are reported in Table 3. As becomes apparent, the intensity of outsourcing towards CEEC significantly differs between the three countries with Germany's outsourcing intensity towards CEEC in 1999 being more than four times higher than that of Denmark and the UK. Also in terms of growth rates, Germany is leading with a total growth rate of 546%, swiftly followed by the UK with total growth of 431%. Clearly, such figures are impressive; one has, however, to bear in mind, that outsourcing almost started from zero in 1991.

With respect to outsourcing towards low-wage countries in Asia, the UK shows the highest intensity closely followed by Germany and in some distance Denmark. Also in terms of growth of outsourcing towards low-wage Asia the UK is with a total growth rate of 194% most dynamic, followed by Germany while Danish firms substantially reduced their respective outsourcing intensity.

3.2 Individual-level data

We measure wages and worker characteristics using individual-level data for the three countries. The nature of data sets we use differs to some extent as data for the UK and Germany are based on surveys while data for Denmark come from administrative registers. However, in all cases we look at individual panel data for the period 1991–2000, and we restrict the samples to include only 18–65 year old male manufacturing workers. Special attention has been paid to construction of the explanatory variables in a consistent way across countries. For example, the education variable 'High education' is defined as the two highest categories in the International Standard Classification of Education (ISCED), which corresponds to the individual having tertiary education.

For Germany, the analysis is based on individual-level data from the German Socio Economic Panel (GSOEP). Specifically, the analysis is based on data from Sample A, B, C, D and E.[9] We exclude respondents who report to work in East Germany as wages in the East are to a large extent shaped by the dramatic structural change of the economy that has been taking place since the fall of the wall and that dominates the impact of other changing structural factors such as outsourcing. Wages are defined as average hourly gross labour earnings including bonuses, premia and other extra payments over the year preceding the respective interview month.

For the UK, data come from the Britsh Household Panel Survey (BHPS), a household survey that follows the same representative sample of individuals over time. Again, as for Germany wages are defined as average hourly gross labour

[8] CEEC are: Bulgaria, Czech Republic, Estonia, Hungary, Latvia, Lithuania, Poland, Romania, Slovak Republic, Slovenia. LwAsia comprises: Bangladesh, Cambodia, China, India, Indonesia, Korea, Laos, Malaysia, Philippines, Taiwan, Thailand, Vietnam but also Hong Kong and Singapur as they are important trade intermediaries. HwOECD countries are all OECD countries except CEEC, Korea, Mexico and Turkey.

[9] See Haisken-DeNew and Frick (2003) for a detailed description of the panel. The GSOEP data used in this paper were extracted using the Add-On package PanelWhiz for Stata. PanelWhiz (http://www.PanelWhiz.eu) was written by Dr. John P. Haisken-DeNew (john@PanelWhiz.eu). See Haisken-DeNew and Hahn (2006) for details. The PanelWhiz generated DO file to retrieve the data used here is available on request. Any data or computational errors in this paper are our own.

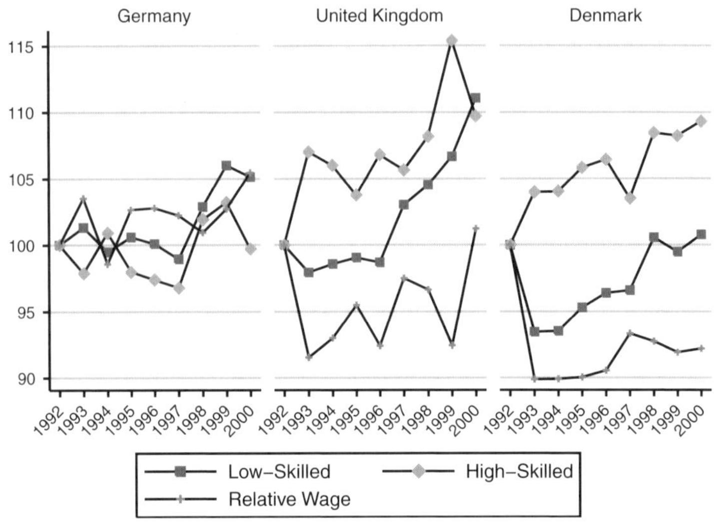

Fig. 1 Median wages by country

earnings including bonuses, premia and other extra payments over the year preceding the respective interview month.

For Denmark, the analysis relies on a large data set which is extracted from the Integrated Database for Labour Market Research (IDA) and the Income Registers in Statistics Denmark. There is information about individual characteristics for a 10% sample of workers in Danish manufacturing industries, and since the data is based on administrative registers its reliability is highly regarded. The hourly wage rate is calculated as total labour income divided by the total number of hours worked in any given year.

Figure 1 charts the development of median wages for high- and low-skilled workers, as well as the relative wage of unskilled workers to skilled workers, for the three countries over the period of analysis. The wages are expressed as indices with the levels in 1992 corresponding to 100. What is notable is that for the UK and Denmark we see increases in the wage for skilled workers outstripping that for low-skilled workers. For Germany there is no such clear picture. Of course, these aggregate tables hide a lot of variation at the micro level. In order to examine the link between outsourcing and individual wages we, therefore, turn to econometric estimations of variants of Eq. 1 for the three countries under consideration.

4 Estimation results

In this section we present the results from estimating Eq. 1 for all three countries. Columns (1), (3) and (5) in Table 4 report the baseline results for Germany, the UK and Denmark, respectively. Focussing on the coefficient on international outsourcing we find that there is a small negative and weakly statistically significant effect

Table 4 Estimation results

	Germany		UK		Denmark	
	(1)	(2)	(3)	(4)	(5)	(6)
Age: 25–39	−0.0073 (0.20)	−0.0068 (0.18)	0.0688 (1.75)*	0.0706 (1.78)*	0.1244 (9.49)***	0.1248 (9.57)***
Age: 40–54	−0.0041 (0.11)	−0.0027 (0.07)	0.0548 (1.29)	0.0572 (1.31)	0.0938 (7.51)***	0.0940 (7.55)***
Age: 55–65	−0.0224 (0.51)	−0.0221 (0.50)	0.0227 (0.37)	0.0269 (0.43)	0.0366 (2.84)***	0.0368 (2.86)***
Married: dummy	0.0605 (2.29)**	0.0600 (2.28)**	0.0133 (0.39)	0.0110 (0.32)	−0.0027 (0.58)	−0.0028 (0.61)
Children: dummy	−0.0080 (0.51)	−0.0078 (0.50)	0.0059 (0.37)	0.0063 (0.40)	0.0249 (10.91)***	0.0248 (10.90)***
Tenure	0.0071 (1.44)	0.0071 (1.44)	0.0008 (1.82)*	0.0008 (1.80)*	0.0063 (13.13)***	0.0063 (12.91)***
Tenure^2	−0.0003 (2.01)*	−0.0003 (2.02)*	0.0000 (1.38)	0.0000 (1.37)	−0.0006 (12.85)***	−0.0006 (12.74)***
FirmSize: small	−0.0625 (1.44)	−0.0620 (1.42)	−0.0538 (1.26)	−0.0541 (1.27)	−0.0251 (0.92)	−0.0253 (0.93)
FirmSize: medium	−0.0062 (0.20)	−0.0056 (0.18)	−0.0348 (1.03)	−0.0352 (1.04)	0.0142 (0.54)	0.0140 (0.54)
FirmSize: large	−0.0136 (0.60)	−0.0130 (0.58)	0.0013 (0.04)	0.0007 (0.02)	0.0243 (0.98)	0.0241 (0.97)
Firm: public ownership dummy	0.0354 (1.11)	0.0352 (1.10)	0.0537 (0.51)	0.0481 (0.46)		
Educ: high-skilled	−0.0102 (0.40)	−0.0093 (0.21)	−0.0334 (1.37)	−0.0614 (1.77)*	0.2279 (5.78)***	0.2076 (5.33)***
Industry output value	0.0001 (0.18)	0.0001 (0.19)	0.0000 (0.39)	0.0000 (0.42)	0.0019 (1.86)*	0.0019 (1.84)*
R&D/Y	−0.3737 (0.73)		0.0064 (0.88)		0.1256 (1.12)	
R&D/Y × Educ: high-skilled		−1.0942 (1.97)*		0.0076 (1.04)		0.2136 (1.63)
R&D/Y × Educ: low-skilled		−0.0129 (0.02)		0.0043 (0.56)		0.0989 (0.75)
OUT	−0.0160 (1.98)*		0.0132 (1.95)*		0.0021 (1.34)	
OUT × Educ: high-skilled		−0.0123 (0.94)		0.0156 (2.20)**		0.0039 (2.14]**
OUT × Educ: low-skilled		−0.0172 (2.40)**		0.0112 (1.65)		0.0017 (1.06]
Constant	2.6960 (15.76)***	2.6899 (14.43)***	1.8165 (8.55)***	1.8319 (8.59)***	5.0269 (37.59)***	5.0328 (37.82)***
Observations	6,858	6,858	4,568	4,568	23,0164	23,0164
R^2	0.82	0.82	0.85	0.85	0.84	0.84
Individual fixed effects	Yes	Yes	Yes	Yes	Yes	Yes

Table 4 continued

	Germany		UK		Denmark	
	(1)	(2)	(3)	(4)	(5)	(6)
Occupation dummies	Yes	Yes	Yes	Yes	Yes	Yes
Industry dummies	Yes	Yes	Yes	Yes	Yes	Yes
Region dummies	Yes	Yes	Yes	Yes	Yes	Yes
Year dummies	Yes	Yes	Yes	Yes	Yes	Yes

t-statistics in parentheses *, **, *** denote significance at the level of 10, 5 and 1%, respectively

on wages for Germany. An one percentage point increase in German outsourcing intensity lowers average German manufacturing wages by about 1.6 percent. Thus, the overall demand effect of outsourcing is very small, which also becomes apparent when looking at the cumulative wage effect of outsourcing between 1991 and 1999. From Table 3 we know that over the sample period average outsourcing increased by 1.6 percentage. Hence outsourcing cumulatively reduced wages by about 2.5 percent.

For the UK aggregated outsourcing appears to have the opposite effect. An one percentage point increase in outsourcing ceteris paribus raises UK wages by on average 1.3 percent. Over the sample period outsourcing in the UK increase by 2 percentage points. Accordingly, the cumulative effect of UK outsourcing over the sample period is a 2.7 percent increase in average wages. For Denmark we fail to find any statistically significant coefficient.

While this regression controls for the skill level of the worker, it does not allow the effect of outsourcing to differ according to skills. However, from theory we may expect different effects: if countries outsource mainly low-skill production activities then in partial equilibrium the demand for low-skilled workers falls, bringing with it a reduction in the wage for these types of workers.

In order to allow for differential effects we interact the outsourcing variable with dummy variables for high- and low-skilled workers, respectively. These results are reported in Columns (2), (4) and (6) in Table 4.

We find that the negative effect found in the previous estimation for Germany only accrues to low-skilled workers. There is no statistically significant effect of outsourcing on high-skilled workers in Germany. Hence, this suggests that in Germany wages for low-skilled workers adjust downward in response to increased international outsourcing. Accordingly, in Germany on average an one percentage point increase in the outsourcing intensity lowers wages for low-skilled workers by a little more than one percent.[10]

In the UK, however, our results indicate that the previously identified positive wage effect of outsourcing is limited to high-skilled workers. Cumulatively outsourcing leads to high-skilled wage increases of on average three percent. For low-skilled UK workers we cannot identify an outsourcing effect with sufficient precision.

Similarly, when differentiating between different skill groups in Denmark we find that outsourcing raises high-skilled workers wages while the coefficient for low-skilled workers is statistically insignificant. The positive wage effect is, however, very small. An one percentage point increase in outsourcing raises high-skilled wages by 0.4 percent. Cumulatively this amounts to a 0.5 percent wage increase for high-skilled workers due to aggregate outsourcing.

In the estimations thus far we treat outsourcing across regions as one homogeneous activity. Clearly, this is not the case. In order to allow for some

[10] The result of a negative effect for low-skilled workers is in line with Geishecker and Görg (2008). However, they also find a positive effect of outsourcing for high-skilled workers. This is likely to be due to their using more control variables and a finer skill classification, distinguishing three skill types, in the empirical model. This was not possible in our case in order to ensure that we estimate the same model for all three countries.

Table 5 Estimation results—geographic differentiation

	Germany		UK		Denmark	
	(1)	(2)	(3)	(4)	(5)	(6)
Age: 25–39	−0.0088 (0.24)	−0.0109 (0.29)	0.0672 (1.70)	0.0708 (1.74)	0.1245 (9.48)***	0.1255 (9.59)***
Age: 40–54	−0.0042 (0.11)	−0.0024 (0.06)	0.0525 (1.22)	0.0566 (1.27)	0.0938 (7.50)***	0.0946 (7.54)***
Age: 55–65	−0.0240 (0.55)	−0.0213 (0.47)	0.0188 (0.31)	0.0237 (0.37)	0.0364 (2.82)**	0.0371 (2.87)***
Married: dummy	0.0594 (2.30)**	0.0597 (2.30)**	0.0110 (0.32)	0.0078 (0.22)	−0.0027 (0.59)	−0.0030 (0.67)
Children: dummy	−0.0088 (0.54)	−0.0088 (0.55)	0.0051 (0.32)	0.0047 (0.30)	0.0248 (10.81)***	0.0246 (10.67)***
Tenure	0.0069 (1.41)	0.0072 (1.45)	0.0008 (1.83)*	0.0008 (1.85)*	0.0063 (13.01)***	0.0063 (12.70)***
Tenure^2	−0.0003 (1.95)*	−0.0003 (2.01)*	0.0000 (1.40)	0.0000 (1.40)	−0.0006 (12.80)***	−0.0006 (12.64)***
FirmSize: small	−0.0635 (1.46)	−0.0643 (1.49)	−0.0551 (1.32)	−0.0549 (1.30)	−0.0249 (0.90)	−0.0243 (0.89)
FirmSize: medium	−0.0055 (0.17)	−0.0062 (0.20)	−0.0363 (1.08)	−0.0361 (1.07)	0.0142 (0.54)	0.0149 (0.57)
FirmSize: Large	−0.0157 (0.69)	−0.0159 (0.70)	−0.0004 (0.01)	−0.0010 (0.03)	0.0243 (0.97)	0.0247 (1.00)
Firm: public ownership dummy	0.0359 (1.14)	0.0315 (0.99)	0.0505 (0.48)	0.0457 (0.44)		
Educ: high-skilled	−0.0123 (0.48)	−0.0240 (0.50)	−0.0360 (1.48)	−0.0665 (1.85)*	0.2277 (5.78)***	0.2018 (5.07)***
Industry output value	0.0003 (0.47)	0.0004 (0.57)	0.0000 (0.06)	0.0000 (0.20)	0.0019 (1.90)*	0.0019 (1.82)*
R&D/Y	−0.2448 (0.49)		0.0068 (1.01)		0.1173 (1.04)	
R&D/Y × Educ: high-skilled		−0.9308 (1.14)		0.0097 (1.30)		0.2619 (2.12)**
R&D/Y × Educ: low-skilled		−0.0193 (0.03)		0.0040 (0.50)		0.0694 (0.53)
$\text{OUT}_{\text{LwAsia}}$	−0.0315 (0.63)		0.0465 (1.48)		0.0112 (0.99)	
$\text{OUT}_{\text{LwAsia}}$ × Educ: high-skilled		−0.0879 (0.90)		0.0639 (1.67)		0.0036 (0.40)
$\text{OUT}_{\text{LwAsia}}$ × Educ: low-skilled		−0.0155 (0.37)		0.0257 (0.87)		0.0120 (0.98)
OUT_{CEEC}	−0.0228 (0.59)		−0.3879 (2.90)**		−0.0434 (2.41)**	
OUT_{CEEC} × Educ: high-skilled		−0.0554 (0.75)		−0.2040 (0.95)		0.0489 (1.93)*
OUT_{CEEC} × Educ: low-skilled		−0.0106 (0.24)		−0.4573 (2.69)**		−0.0552 (3.14)***
$\text{OUT}_{\text{HwOECD}}$	−0.0086 (1.34)		0.0145 (1.84)*		0.0031 (1.88)*	

Table 5 continued

	Germany		UK		Denmark	
	(1)	(2)	(3)	(4)	(5)	(6)
OUT_{HwOECD} × Educ: high-skilled		0.0048 (0.84)		0.0135 (1.60)		0.0030 (1.57)
OUT_{HwOECD} × Educ: low-skilled		−0.0140 (1.61)		0.0156 (1.74)		0.0030 (1.69)
OUT_{RoW}	−0.0574 (1.29)		0.0051 (0.69)		−0.0051 (0.35)	
OUT_{RoW} × Educ: high-skilled		−0.0678 (0.83)		−0.0041 (0.42)		−0.0047 (0.26)
OUT_{RoW} × Educ: low-skilled		−0.0554 (1.55)		0.0098 (1.19)		−0.0067 (0.46)
Constant	2.8165 (14.01)***	2.5299 (15.20)***	1.6955 (8.05)***	1.7190 (8.28)***	4.8789 (40.25)***	5.0454 (36.18)***
Observations	6,858	6,858	4,568	4,568	23,0164	23,0164
R^2	0.82	0.82	0.85	0.85	0.84	0.84
Individual fixed effects	Yes	Yes	Yes	Yes	Yes	Yes
Occupation dummies	Yes	Yes	Yes	Yes	Yes	Yes
Industry dummies	Yes	Yes	Yes	Yes	Yes	Yes
Region dummies	Yes	Yes	Yes	Yes	Yes	Yes
Year dummies	Yes	Yes	Yes	Yes	Yes	Yes

t-statistics in parentheses *, **, *** denote significance at the level of 10, 5 and 1%, respectively

heterogeneity in the activities that are outsourced we distinguish outsourcing to CEEC from outsourcing to low-wage Asia (LwAsia), high-wage OECD (HwOECD) countries and some remaining RoW category. While outsourcing to CEEC and LwAsia is likely to include outsourcing of many low-skilled manufacturing activities the latter group of countries contains outsourcing mainly to other developed countries and, therefore, the type of outsourcing should be considered different. Table 5 presents regression results where we split up the outsourcing variable by broad region, and also allow for differential effects according to skill levels.

Results for Germany (column 1) show that when decomposing outsourcing by region the wage effects of outsourcing cannot be identified with sufficient precision. For the UK (Table 5, column 3) we now, however, find a sizable negative and statistically significant wage effect of outsourcing to CEEC. An one percentage point increase in the average intensity of outsourcing to CEEC ceteris paribus lowers UK manufacturing wages by about 38 percent. To put this into perspective, according to Table 3 UK outsourcing to CEEC increased by 0.07 percentage points. Thus the cumulative effect of outsourcing to CEEC is very modest wage reduction of 2.7 percent. In comparison, outsourcing to high-wage OECD countries is found to yield weakly statistically significant positive wage effects. According to Table 3 UK outsourcing to high-wage OECD countries increased by 1.2 percentage points. Thus, UK manufacturing wages are cumulatively raised by modest 2.6 percent. Furthermore, outsourcing to LwAsia and RoW also appears to raise average UK wages. However, the effects can only be estimated with insufficient precision.

For Denmark we also find a statistically significant negative wage effect of outsourcing to CEEC (Table 5, column 5). According to Table 3 Danish outsourcing to CEEC increased by 0.04 percentage points. Thus, the cumulative wage effect of of outsourcing to CEEC is only −0.2 percent and economically negligible.

Nevertheless, simply looking at homogenous outsourcing masks important differences in effects depending on individual skills. In a next step we therefore interact geographically decomposed outsourcing with educational attainment to capture potentially different effects across skill groups. The respective results are reported in columns (2), (4) and (6) in Table 5.

For Germany, although the coefficients of outsourcing partly are sizable (see column 2) we cannot reject their insignificance within reasonable confidence bounds suggesting that the demand effects of outsourcing are fairly heterogenous across individuals irrespective of the outsourcing region.

For the UK, however, we find low-skilled workers to experience statistically significant wage cuts due to outsourcing to CEEC (see Table 5, column 4). The 0.07 percentage point increase of UK outsourcing towards CEEC lowers wages of low-skilled workers by about 3 percent. At the same time there is some evidence that also high-skilled workers experience wage cuts due to outsourcing to CEEC, the effect, however, cannot be identified with sufficient precision.

Finally, for Denmark (column 6) we find a negative statistically significant effect of outsourcing to CEEC on low-skilled workers wages and a positive statistically significant wage effect for high-skilled workers. Cumulatively, increased outsourcing towards CEEC lowered low-skilled wages by only 0.2 percent while the respective cumulative effect for high-skilled workers is a 0.2 percent wage increase. Albeit statistically significant coefficients, both effects are negligible in an economic sense. Other types of outsourcing do not appear to have any statistically significant effect on either skilled or unskilled workers.

Recall that one possible expectation concerning the mediating impact of labour market institutions on outsourcing was that wages should be least sensitive to outsourcing in Denmark, since wages are set in negotiations between unions and firms, while employment protection is low so that any adjustments are more likely to go through job separations. By contrast we argued that wages in Germany and the UK could be more responsive to outsourcing.

First of all, we find that low-skilled workers in all three countries are likely to suffer negative wage effects, in the case of the UK and Denmark particularly from outsourcing to CEEC. In line with our intuition wage effects of outsourcing in Denmark are significantly lower (if not negligible) than those in Germany and the UK. However, wage cuts due to outsourcing are very small even in the UK and Germany. One interesting result is that we find a positive, small but not negligible wage effect of outsourcing for high-skilled workers in the UK which, arguably, is in line with the idea of more flexibel wage setting institutions in the UK. However, overall we conclude that our results only lend weak support for simple intuition regarding the mitigating impact of labour market institutions.

5 Conclusion

This paper studies the impact of international outsourcing on individual wages in Germany, the UK and Denmark. To do so we use individual-level wage data for the three countries and construct comparable measures of outsourcing at the industry level, distinguishing outsourcing to Central and Eastern Europe from other countries. While our discussion of labour market institutions may suggest an intuitive predication that there should be differences in effects across countries, our empirical analysis, based on estimating the same specification for the three countries, shows that the effects are, actually, quite similar and fairly small. Low-skilled workers experience reductions in real wages, in the UK particular through outsourcing to Central and Eastern European Countries. There is also some evidence that high-skilled workers benefit through higher wages at least in the UK. This suggests that the relationship between labour market institutions, outsourcing and wages is more complex than our simple intuitive discussion. More theoretical work is needed to pin down the exact nature of the relationship, in order to get a better understanding of the effects of outsourcing on wages under different institutional settings.

Acknowledgments Financial support from the Economic Policy Research Network and the Leverhulme Trust (Grant No. F114/BF) is gratefully acknowledged. We would like to thank participants at the 2007 Zeuthen Workshop, University of Copenhagen for valuable comments. Holger Görg is also affiliated with GlobID, Aarhus School of Business/University of Aarhus.

References

Amiti, M. & Wei S. J. (2009). Service offshoring and productivity: Evidence from the US. *The World Economy, 32*(2), 203–220.

Arndt, S. W. (1997). Globalization and the open economy. *North American Journal of Economics and Finance, 8*(1), 71–79.

Arndt, S. W. (1999). Globalization and economic development. *The Journal of International Trade and Economic Development, 8*(3), 309–318.

Bender, S., Dustmann, C., Margolis, D., & Meghir, C. (2002). Worker displacement in France and Germany. In P. J. Kuhn (Ed.), *Losing work, moving on: International perspectives on worker displacement*. W.E. Upjohn Institute for Employment Research.

Borland, J., Gregg, P., Knight, G., & Wadsworth, J. (2002). They get knocked down. Do they get up again? In P. J. Kuhn (Ed.), *Losing work, moving on: International perspectives on worker displacement*. W.E. Upjohn Institute for Employment Research.

Campa, J., & Goldberg, L. S. (1997). The evolving external orientation of manufacturing industries: Evidence from four countries. *Federal Reserve Bank of New York Economic Policy Review, 3*, 53–81.

Feenstra, R. C., & Hanson, G. H. (1996). Globalization, outsourcing, and wage inequality. *American Economic Review, 86*(2), 240–245.

Feenstra, R. C., & Hanson, G. H. (1999). The impact of outsourcing and high-technology capital on wages: Estimates for the United States, 1979–1990. *Quarterly Journal of Economics, 114*(3), 907–941.

Geishecker, I. (2006). Does outsourcing to Central and Eastern Europe really threaten manual workers' jobs in Germany? *The World Economy, 29*, 559–583.

Geishecker, I., & Görg, H. (2008). Winners and losers: A micro-level analysis of international outsourcing and wages. *Canadian Journal of Economics, 41*, 243–270.

Görg, H., Hanley, A., & Strobl, E. (2008). Productivity effects of international outsourcing: Evidence from plant level data. *Canadian Journal of Economics, 41*, 670–688.

Haisken-DeNew, J. P., & Frick, J. R. (2003). Desktop companion to the German Socio-Economic Panel. DIW Berlin, manual (http://www.diw.de/deutsch/sop/service/dtc/dtc.pdf).

Haisken-DeNew, J. P., & Hahn, M. (2006). PanelWhiz: A flexible modularized stata interface for accessing large scale panel data sets. Mimeo (http://www.PanelWhiz.eu).

Hijzen, A., Görg, H., & Hine, R. C. (2005). International outsourcing and the skill structure of labour demand in the United Kingdom. *Economic Journal, 115*(506), 861–879.

Jones, R. W., & Kierzkowski, H. (2001). A framework for fragmentation. In S. W. Arndt, & H. Kierzkowski (Eds.), *Fragmentation: New production patterns in the world economy*. Oxford: Oxford University Press.

Krugman, P. (1995). Growing world trade: Causes and consequences. *Brookings Papers on Economic Activity, 1*, 327–377.

Kohler, W. (2004). International outsourcing and factor prices with multistage production. *Economic Journal, 114*, C166–C185.

Moulton, B. (1990). An illustration of the pittfall in estimating the effects of aggregate variables in micro units. *Review of Economics and Statistics, 72*, 334–338.

Munch, J. R., & Skaksen, J. R. (2009). Specialization, outsourcing and wages. *Review of World Economics/Weltwirtschaftliches Archiv, 145*(1), 57–73.

Nickell, S., Nunziata, L., Ochel, W. (2005). Unemployment in the OECD since the 1960s. What do we know? *Economic Journal, 115*, 1–27.

OECD (1997). *OECD employment outlook 1997*. Paris: OECD.

OECD (2005). *OECD employment outlook 2005*. Paris: OECD.

Yeats, A. J. (2001). Just how big is global production sharing? In S. W. Arndt, & H. Kierzkowski (Eds.), *Fragmentation: New production patterns in the world economy*. Oxford: Oxford University Press.

Chapter III.4

Services offshoring and wages: evidence from micro data

By Ingo Geishecker* and Holger Görg†

*Department of Economics, Georg-August-Universität Göttingen, 37073 Göttingen, Germany; e-mail: ingo.geishecker@wiwi.uni-goettingen.de
†Kiel Institute for the World Economy, University of Kiel, 24100 Kiel, Germany; e-mail: holger.goerg@ifw-kiel.de

This paper investigates the effects of services offshoring on wages using individual-level data combined with industry information on offshoring for the United Kingdom. Our results show that services offshoring affects the real wage of low- and medium-skilled individuals negatively. By contrast, skilled workers may benefit from services offshoring in terms of higher real wages. Hence, offshoring has contributed to a widening of the wage gap between skilled and less skilled workers. This result is obtained while controlling for individual and sectoral observed and unobserved heterogeneity. In particular, our empirical model also controls for the impact of technological change and offshoring of materials.

JEL classifications: F16, J31, C23.

1. Introduction

Offshoring from industrialized countries has been a topical issue, both in academic discourse and public debate for a number of years. Inititally, the concern was with offshoring of manufacturing activities and the implications for domestic labour markets, in particular as regards shifts in the demand for skilled labour (see Feenstra and Hanson, 1999, for the US and Hijzen *et al.*, 2005, for the UK). More recently, the attention has turned towards offshoring of services activities. In a much cited paper, Amiti and Wei (2005) show that services offshoring is still at relatively low levels compared to materials offshoring. However, its growth rates are much higher. In order to examine the implications of offshoring for domestic labour they estimate labour demand equations which incorporate services and materials offshoring. Using sector level data for the UK they find that employment growth is not negatively related to services offshoring.[1] Using highly disaggregated firm-level data on job creation and destruction, and firm-level data on trade in services, Hijzen *et al.* (2007) also fail to find any negative effects of services offshoring (measured as services imports). By contrast, they find that, on average, firms that start offshoring services experience faster employment growth than other comparable firms. Hence, the conclusion that may be drawn from the work so far is that there is little to worry about for domestic workers. However, the papers by Amiti and Wei (2005) and Hijzen *et al.* (2007) focus on one aspect of labour adjustment only, namely, the quantity of labour. However, an adjustment in the labour market to offshoring can go through either quantity or the price of labour, or both. In this case, concluding on the benevolent (or otherwise) effects of offshoring purely on the basis of an analysis of the quantity of labour can be misleading. Especially in a country with flexible labour markets (such as the UK) a full labour market picture of the effects of offshoring of services needs to look at the price of work as well. This is the gap we fill in this paper.

We investigate the effect of offshoring of services activities on UK wages. To do so, we use household-level panel data from the British Household Panel Survey (BHPS) and combine these with industry-level measures of offshoring of services inputs over the period 1992 to 2004. Hence, our approach allows us to estimate the effect of increasing offshoring activities in an industry on individual wages of workers in the affected industry. The idea of assessing the labour market impact of offshoring by utilizing individual-level data has already been applied in a small number of studies, e.g., Egger *et al.* (2007), Geishecker and Görg (2008), Geishecker (2008), or Munch and Skaksen (2009) for Europe and most recently, building on this body of literature, Ebenstein *et al.* (2009) for the US. However, these studies only look at offshoring of materials, not services. An exception is Liu and Trefler (2008), who, however, limit themselves to investigating the impact of services offshoring to China and India using US data.

The present paper is the first analysis we are aware of that looks at the wage effects of services offshoring in general using individual-level data, while controlling for technological progress and materials offshoring.[2] This is a highly policy relevant issue and deserves of detailed inspection. In our analysis we are careful to assess the economic significance of our estimates, and compare and constrast the effects of services and materials offshoring.

The main advantage of using individual-level data is that they allow to control for observed and unobserved heterogeneity while avoiding aggregation bias that may hamper more aggregate studies. Also, utilizing micro-level data allow to clearly identify the winners and losers from offshoring. Furthermore, the combination of

[1] In a companion paper Amiti and Wei (2007) provide evidence for the US which also shows little evidence of reductions in employment following increased levels of services offshoring.

[2] These variables have been shown to affect the relative wages of skilled workers; see, e.g., Feenstra and Hanson (1999), Hijzen *et al.* (2005).

household-level data for wages and industry-level data for services offshoring mitigates concerns about the possible endogeneity of offshoring.[3]

We use two strategies to identify a link between offshoring and wages. The first follows the standard approach in the literature looking at the impact of within-industry changes in offshoring intensities on wage changes of individuals in the same industry.[4] The second strategy is based on the idea that offshoring may not only affect wages of workers with a given skill level in the industry in which the offshoring takes place, but also in industries that use workers with the same skill levels. This approach implicitly allows for movement of workers of a given skill level across industries.

Our results show that services offshoring affects the real wage of low- and medium-skilled individuals in the same industry negatively. By contrast, skilled workers benefit from services offshoring in their industry in terms of higher real wages. When allowing for movement of workers across industries, we find statistically significant evidence that offshoring of services in industries that use the same skills reduces wages for low- and medium-skilled workers. We cannot identify with any precision any wage effect for high-skilled workers, however. These results are obtained while controlling for individual and sectoral observed and unobserved heterogeneity. In particular, our empirical model also controls for the impact of technological change and offshoring of materials. The remainder of the paper is structured as follows. Section 2 provides a brief theoretical background to motivate the empirical analysis. Section 3 introduces the data on offshoring of both services and materials, while Section 4 discusses the empirical methodology. Section 5 presents the results of the estimation based on within-industry changes; Section 6 presents the alternative empirical strategy. Some concluding remarks are in Section 7.

2. Theoretical background

Before we proceed to the empirical analysis, which forms the core of this paper, it is useful to discuss briefly the theoretical framework which we use to motivate our empirics. This framework is provided by the recent theoretical model by Grossman and Rossi-Hansberg (2008) (GRH). In their model, a firm produces output using a continuum of production stages (which they refer to as tasks). Some of these stages are performed by low-skilled workers, while others require more skills and can only be carried out by high-skilled workers. Firms can perform these production stages either at home or abroad. Offshoring is costly, and these costs apply economy-wide but differ across tasks.[5] Carrying out production stages abroad may be

[3] However, we also explicitly test for the exogeneity of our services offshoring variable.

[4] This is the approach of Feenstra and Hanson (1999) and is also followed in the micro level studies cited above.

[5] Kohler (2008) provides an interesting theoretical discussion which shows how results may differ if costs are assumed to be industry-specific rather than economy-wide.

advantageous due to factor cost differences, but these potential savings have to be weighed against the costs of offshoring.

GRH focus on the offshoring of tasks performed by low-skilled workers. In their setup, there are three types of effects on wages if offshoring costs for this set of tasks decline, that is, if offshoring of production stages carried out by low-skilled workers increases. First, increased offshoring raises the productivity of low-skilled workers, and thereby generates a real wage increase for this factor. Second, there is a labour supply effect. The excess workers who have been freed up through offshoring have to be re-absorbed in the economy, which leads to a fall in the real wage for low-skilled workers. Third, in general equilibrium there is a relative price effect, whereby the price of the final good that uses offshoring declines. This will, via the familiar Stolper-Samuelson effect, also negatively affect low-skilled workers' wages. In sum, the model predicts an ambiguous effect of increased offshoring for low-skilled workers' wages, depending on the relative strength of the positive productivity and negative factor supply and relative price effects. By contrast, a fall in offshoring costs for low-skill tasks has unequivocal positive wage effects for high-skilled workers. First of all, the aforementioned labour supply effect of offshoring lowers the proportion of high-skilled workers in the remaining activities, increasing their marginal product. Second, in general equilibrium the relative price effect implies wage increases for high-skilled workers through the usual Stolper-Samuelson mechanism. One reason why services offshoring has attracted such attention is that it may lead to the relocation abroad of production stages that are performed by high-skilled, not low-skilled workers. GRH cite examples of software development, radiology or preparing tax forms that has been offshored from the US to India. Hence, they expand their model to study the offshoring of such high-skilled production stages. Similar to the offshoring of low-skilled tasks, they show that there is a productivity enhancing effect which benefits high-skilled workers. There can also be relative price and factor supply effects, however, that harm high-skilled labour. Furthermore and along the lines of the previous discussion, offshoring of such high-skill production stages generates wage increases for low-skilled workers. The implication for empirical research is that the model does not predict unambiguous effects. For both low- and high-skilled workers there is the possibility of positive productivity effects as well as adverse relative price and factor supply effects. The extent to which offshoring, on balance, harms or benefits workers' wages therefore depends on the relative strength of these effects and on whether offshored activities are low-skill or high-skill intensive.

3. Service offshoring in the UK

Before we can investigate the impact of offshoring, we need to have a good measure of the phenomenon. This is not straightforward, neither for services nor for materials. Measurement is greatly limited by data availability of coherent and comparable (across sectors and/or countries) information on such activities.

Hence, trade economists usually revert to measuring trade in intermediates as a proxy. We follow this approach here. However, data on trade in intermediates are also difficult to come by. Amiti and Wei (2005) measure the importance of intermediates in a sector using data from input-output tables and combine it with data on imports (which do not distinguish final and intermediate goods) from official trade statistics.[6] They cannot observe the actual proportion of imported inputs. The implicit assumption in this definition is that imports are used as inputs in the same proportion as domestic inputs. On the one hand this approach could be problematic if, e.g., an industry uses different types of inputs from domestic and foreign sources. On the other hand the approach allows to differentiate service imports that are more likely to be associated with offshoring, e.g., telecommunication services and other business services, from overall aggregated services imports. In the present study we apply two different measures of service offshoring, a broad measure utilising aggregate intermediate service import data and a narrow one including only intermediate imports of telecommunication, computer, and other business services. The construction of narrowly defined service offshoring is similar to the method employed in Amiti and Wei (2005) and combines input output data from UK National Statistics supply and use tables with sectoral data on service imports. More specifically, we allocate overall imports of telecommunication, computer, and other business services (SIC92 industries 64, 72, and 74) according to their typical use in manufacturing industries and set them in relation to the respective industry's output:

$$OSS_{jt}^{narrow} = \frac{\frac{BS_{jt}}{TBS_t} \times TBS_t^{Imp}}{Y_{jt}}, \tag{1}$$

where BS_{jt}/TBS_t denotes telecommunication, computer, and other business services purchases of industry j as a share of the total supply of such services at time t and is constructed using UK National Statistics' supply and use tables.[7] TBS_t^{Imp} denotes all imports of telecommunication, computer, and other business services at t and is derived from Eurostat's balance of payment statistics. Y_{jt} represents output of industry j in t and is directly observable in the supply and use tables.[8] Our second measure of service offshoring is a more direct measure of imported services inputs but is also more broadly defined. Specifically, we obtain directly data on imported services inputs from national accounts' input-output supply tables provided by UK National Statistics for the years 1992 to 2004.[9]

[6] This follows the definition of materials offshoring used by Feenstra and Hanson (1999).

[7] UK National Statistics, Input-Output, Supply, and Use Tables, August 2006.

[8] Note that our denominator is industry output. Thus, it does not only consist of intermediate input purchases as in Amiti and Wei (2005) but also contains value added. This approach has the advantage that domestic outsourcing does not change the calculated offshoring measures as any corresponding increase in intermediate input purchases is mirrored by decreasing value added.

[9] UK National Statistics, Input-Output, Supply, and Use Tables, August 2006. It would be interesting to investigate to which countries services are offshored. However, this is not possible to determine with the data from the supply and use tables.

Formally, broad service offshoring is defined as:

$$OSS_{jt}^{broad} = \frac{TS_{jt}}{Y_{jt}}, \tag{2}$$

with TS_{jt} denoting all imported services from the foreign service sector of industry j. Y_{jt} represents the production value of the domestic industry j in period t. For materials offshoring we have to draw again on international trade data as the available detailed input-output use tables do not differentiate between imported and domestically supplied materials.[10] Thus, we look at aggregate imports of manufactured goods and allocate them according to their use share in domestic industries based on aggregate input-output use tables. Conceptionally, we follow Feenstra and Hanson (1999) and calculate two measures of material offshoring, which to some extent mirrors our distinction of services offshoring. The first is defined as narrow materials offshoring, which is calculated as:

$$OSM_{jt}^{narrow} = \frac{IMP_{j^*t} \times \Omega_{jj^*t}}{Y_{jt}}, \tag{3}$$

with IMP_{j^*t} denoting imported intermediate inputs from the same respective foreign industry j^*. Ω_{jj^*t} denotes the share of domestic and foreign inputs from industry j that are consumed in industry j.[11] Hence, this measure only considers offshoring of activities from the same industry, which may be most likely to capture what is generally meant by offshoring of manufacturing activity.

The second measure, broad materials offshoring, also considers intermediate imports from other industries and is calculated as:

$$OSM_{jt}^{broad} = \frac{\sum_{k=1}^{K} IMP_{k^*t} \times \Omega_{jk^*t}}{Y_{jt}}, \tag{4}$$

where k represents all industries from which industry j sources inputs (including its own). This, hence, captures all imported manufactured intermediate materials that are used in industry j. Table 1 looks at the development of the various offshoring measures, aggregated for the whole manufacturing sector over time. A few points are noteworthy. Firstly, narrowly defined services offshoring is still very low at 0.29% of industry output in 2004. By contrast, broad services offshoring is more than ten times more important. Compared to materials offshoring, however, both types of services offshoring are still at very low levels. Services do, however, have the highest growth rates over the period 1992 to 2004.

[10] This is a common problem, e.g. US input output tables suffer from the same shortcoming. Industry-level import data was generated drawing on Eurostat's COMEXT commodity trade data base.

[11] Note that $\sum_{j=1}^{J} \Omega_{jj^*t} = 1$ only if industries J contain agriculture, services, private and public consumption, inventories, capital formation, and exports.

Table 1 Service and material offshoring intensity in %

Year	OSS^{narrow}	OSM^{narrow}	OSS^{broad}	OSM^{broad}
1992	0.17	4.10	2.35	9.38
1993	0.21	4.28	2.42	9.41
1994	0.19	4.60	2.41	10.11
1995	0.18	4.74	2.34	10.76
1996	0.23	4.95	2.27	11.43
1997	0.21	5.24	2.37	11.95
1998	0.25	5.65	2.72	13.11
1999	0.27	5.48	3.12	12.76
2000	0.28	5.74	3.39	13.61
2001	0.28	5.70	3.55	13.55
2002	0.29	5.92	3.80	13.83
2003	0.28	6.05	3.93	14.05
2004	0.29	6.33	3.92	14.20
Absolute change	0.12	2.23	1.57	4.81
Growth rate in %	69.78	54.35	66.58	51.32

Notes: Authors' calculations.

4. Methodology and data

Based on these measures of offshoring we now want to assess how individual level wages are affected by offshoring activity in an industry. To do so, we estimate simple Mincerian wage equations of the form

$$\log w_{ijt} = \alpha + \beta X_{it} + \gamma Y_{jt} + \delta(R\&D/Y)_{jt} + \lambda_S OSS_{jt} + \lambda_M OSM_{jt} + T_{jt} + \mu_t + \alpha_i + \iota_j + \epsilon_{ijt}, \quad (5)$$

where w_{ijt} is the hourly wage of worker i in industry j at time t, defined as average hourly gross labour earnings including bonuses, premia, and other extra payments over the year preceding the respective interview month.[12] X_{it} is a vector of standard demographic and human capital variables which includes age, age squared, dummies for the presence of children and being married, job tenure, tenure squared, indicator variables for educational attainment, dummies for occupation using the nine main categories of the ISCO code, dummies for firm size, and regional dummies. Year effects, μ_t, and individual-specific fixed effects, α_i, are also controlled for. In addition we include industry dummies ι_j, and to control for time varying industry characteristics we also enter industry output, Y_{jt}, the ratio of industry-level R&D to output, and industry-specific time trends T_j in the model. The inclusion of R&D and industry-specific time trends controls for

[12] Labour earnings above the 99.5th percentile were top coded to clean up implausibly high income information. Our results are robust to this exercise.

industry-specific technological progress. The main explanatory variables of interest are the variables for services and material offshoring, OSS_{jt} and OSM_{jt}. In the econometric estimation these are measured alternatively as narrow or broad offshoring as described above. In our main model the wage effect of offshoring is estimated conditional on individual as well as industry fixed effects. Accordingly, the parameters are identified through within-industry changes in the respective offshoring variables. Sudden changes in offshoring intensities that would result from individuals changing between industries are controlled for by the inclusion of industry fixed effects. Since in the main model only within-industry changes of offshoring are considered the empirical model corresponds to the partial equilibrium setting discussed in Grossmann and Rossi-Hansberg (2008) in which labour is immobile between industries. In Section 6 we also estimate a model where we allow for cross industry effects of offshoring.

All the regressions are weighted using the standard sampling weights from the household data to adjust for individual sampling probabilities. In the wage equation (5), we estimate the effect of an aggregate variable (i.e. offshoring at the industry level) on wages of individual workers, so the standard errors of the estimated coefficients may be biased downwards. Accordingly, we adjust standard errors allowing for serial error correlation within individuals and contemporaneous correlation within two digit industries applying the two-way cluster robust method suggested in Cameron *et al.* (2011).[13] Furthermore, to account for the small number of industries we follow Cameron *et al.* (2008) and make some asymptotic refinement by calculating cluster bootstrapped-t statistics. We measure wages and worker characteristics using individual-level data from the British household panel survey (BHPS) for the period 1992–2004. The annual survey, which started in 1991, is based on a nationally representative sample of households. Individuals are followed over time. The database provides data on wages and education levels, as well as many individual characteristics which are included in our empirical model to control for observed individual-level heterogeneity. Table 2 provides descriptive statistics for our explanatory variables. In the estimation, we restrict our sample to male prime age individuals (i.e., 18–65 years old) working in manufacturing. Our unbalanced sample covers 997 individuals yielding 5775 observations. In order to avoid selection bias with respect to item non-response that might be non-random each explanatory variable was supplemented with a dummy for missing values. Subsequently, missing values where recoded to zero and the generated dummies for missing values also act as regressors in the model. A particular focus of our analysis lies on skill-specific effects of offshoring. We follow the International Standard Classification of Education (ISCED) and differentiate between high-skilled workers (*ED*: *high*), medium-skilled workers (*ED*: *med*), and low-skilled workers (*ED*: *low*) according to the grouping presented in Table 3. To estimate skill-specific effects we

[13] Note that in the presence of industry switchers individuals are not nested within industries.

Table 2 Summary statistics

	Mean	Standard deviation
Hourly wage	9.0566	4.5981
Age: 18–25	0.1118	0.3152
Age: 26–35	0.2564	0.4367
Age: 36–50	0.4257	0.4945
Married: dummy	0.6473	0.4779
Children: dummy	0.4452	0.4970
Tenure	214.9854	107.5176
Tenure^2	57776.74	54080.26
Tenure: noresponse	0.0978	0.2971
ISCED: high	0.0267	0.1612
ISCED: med	0.7402	0.4386
FirmSize: < 25	0.1824	0.3862
FirmSize: 25–100	0.2235	0.4166
FirmSize: 100–1000	0.4714	0.4992
Firm: public	0.0042	0.0648
Firm: unknownowner	0.0002	0.0123
Industry: output	29.1356	16.6245
Industry: R&D/Y	2.1599	2.4851
Observations	5775	

interact the offshoring variables with dummies for the three skill categories. Figure 1 provides some evidence on the development of the median wage rate and the 10th and 90th percentile for the three different skill groups between 1992 to 2004. Note that wages for all three groups increased over time. The trends for all three skill groups have been fairly consistent over time. There are, however, a couple of spikes in the trend for the 90th percentile for high-skilled workers in the late 1990s and 2002-3 probably reflecting the small number of observations for high-skilled workers. In order to investigate whether some part of the wage developments may be attributed to offshoring, we now turn to econometric analysis in the next section.

5. Estimation results

We start off with considering the effect on individual wages of offshoring of services and materials narrowly defined. The results of estimating eq. (5) with the narrow offshoring measures are reported in Table 4. We report cluster bootstrap t-tests for each regression specification, following the approach described in Cameron *et al.* (2008). Column I presents a benchmark model estimated using simple OLS. Column II estimates the same model using individual fixed effects. In the OLS model services offshoring has no statistically discernible effect on individual wages. In the fixed effects model, service offshoring is negative and weakly statistically

Table 3 Skill grouping

Skill-group	Description	Years of schooling
High-skilled	Second stage of tertiary education (Masters degree and higher)	approx. 16 ⩽ years
Medium-skilled	Upper-secondary education Post-secondary but non-tertiary education First stage of tertiary education	approx. 11 ⩽ years < 16
Low-skilled	Pre-primary education Primary education Lower-secondary education	approx. years < 11

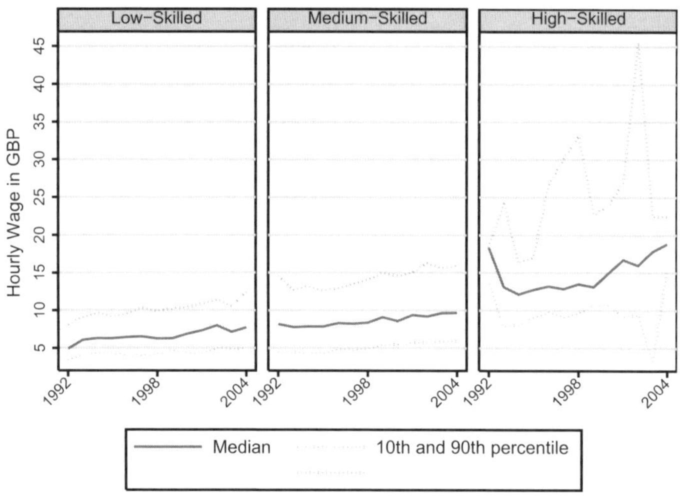

Fig. 1 Wages by skill
Note: Authors' calculations.

significant when considering the cluster bootstrapped t-statistics.[14,15] Column III shows results which also include the intensity of material offshoring in the industry. This is included for two reasons. First, it allows us to see whether the estimated

[14] One noteworthy difference between the OLS and FE results concerns the individual level controls. These are highly statistically significant in the OLS estimation, but many are insignificant in the FE model. In particular, the coefficients on the education dummies are positive and statistically significant in the OLS regression, but less significant in the FE estimation. This reflects the fact that in the FE estimation, coefficients are identified using the variation within individuals, which is low for most of the variables.

[15] Another noteworthy point regarding the control variables is R&D where we find statistically insignificant but negative effects in most cases in Tables 4 and 5. It is important to point out that R&D is not our only variable to capture technological progress. We also include industry-specific time trends to also control for industry-specific technology shocks. Furthermore, general time dummies also capture economy wide technological progress. Jointly, all technology related control variables exert a positive wage effect in all specifications.

Table 4 Narrow offshoring regression results

	I OLS	II FE	cluster boot-t	III FE	cluster boot-t	IV FE	cluster boot-t
Age: 18–25	−0.2701	−0.0496		−0.0485		−0.0454	
	[6.78]***	[1.28]	*	[1.25]	*	[1.16]	
Age: 26–35	−0.0689	0.0397		0.0401		0.0411	
	[2.81]***	[1.24]		[1.25]		[1.29]	
Age: 36–50	−0.0286	0.0521		0.0523		0.0524	
	[1.12]	[2.09]**	*	[2.10]**	*	[2.10]**	*
Married: dummy	0.1093	0.0234		0.0238		0.0235	
	[5.29]***	[1.00]		[1.02]		[1.02]	
Children: dummy	0.0627	0.0244		0.0245		0.0254	
	[4.46]***	[1.88]*	**	[1.89]*	**	[1.95]*	**
Tenure	0.0008	0.0008		0.0008		0.0008	
	[2.41]**	[2.91]***	***	[2.93]***	***	[2.75]***	***
Tenure^2	−0.0001	−0.0001		−0.0001		−0.0001	
	[2.78]***	[2.31]**	***	[2.35]**	***	[2.21]**	***
Tenure: noresponse	0.1511	0.1264		0.1270		0.1222	
	[2.39]**	[3.06]***	***	[3.07]***	***	[2.92]***	***
ISCED: high	0.4492	0.1317		0.1356		−0.2793	
	[8.27]***	[2.75]***	**	[2.80]***	**	[1.88]*	**
ISCED: med	0.1533	−0.0178		−0.0179		−0.1095	
	[7.34]***	[0.55]		[0.55]		[2.00]**	**
FirmSize: < 25	−0.2272	−0.0746		−0.0748		−0.0756	
	[7.52]***	[2.61]***	***	[2.65]***	***	[2.71]***	***
FirmSize: 25–100	−0.2055	−0.0377		−0.0379		−0.0366	
	[7.48]***	[1.70]*	**	[1.74]*	**	[1.67]*	**
FirmSize: 100–1000	−0.1028	−0.0033		−0.0033		−0.0034	
	[4.52]***	[0.15]		[0.15]		[0.16]	
Firm: public	−0.1770	0.0730		0.0743		0.0685	
	[1.98]**	[0.89]		[0.90]		[0.80]	
Firm: unknownowner	0.1971	−0.1561		−0.1597		−0.1648	
	[6.09]***	[7.82]***	***	[7.76]***	***	[7.88]***	***
Industry: output	0.0123	0.0130		0.0176		0.0159	
	[0.80]	[1.38]		[1.83]*	*	[1.72]*	*
Industry: R&D/Y	−0.0020	−0.0073		−0.0126		−0.0136	
	[0.12]	[0.89]		[1.50]		[1.63]	**
OSS	−0.1437	−0.1510		−0.0886			
	[0.47]	[0.95]	*	[0.60]			
OSS × ISCED: high						0.5188	
						[2.24]**	**
OSS × ISCED: med						−0.0469	
						[0.30]	
OSS × ISCED: low						−0.3014	
						[1.91]*	***
OSM				−0.0080			
				[1.87]*	*		
OSM × ISCED: high						0.0053	
						[0.75]	
OSM × ISCED: med						−0.0078	
						[1.81]*	
OSM × ISCED: low						−0.0162	
						[2.99]***	***
Constant	1.4834						
	[5.95]***						
Observations	5775		5775		5775		5775
R^2	0.49		0.83		0.83		0.83

Note: t-statistics in brackets, *** significant at 1%, ** at 5%, * at 10%. Default categories: Age: >50, ISCED: low, FirmSize: >1000. Occupation, region, industry dummies, and industry time trends included. Cluster bootstrapped t-test with 500 repetitions.

coefficient is biased in that it just reflects an industry's propensity to offshore in general. Second, it also enables us to distinguish the relative magnitude of services and material offshoring for wage changes. The results show that, firstly, the magnitude of the coefficient on services offshoring is reduced and now becomes statistically insignificant. By contrast, material offshoring has a weakly statistically significant and negative impact on wages. A one percentage point increase in material offshoring is associated with decreases in real wages of less than 1%. The estimations thus far assume that the effect of offshoring on wages is the same across education groups. This is unlikely to be a reasonable assumption. If, for example, industries offshore mainly low-skilled services and material activities abroad, then we may expect negative effects on unskilled workers if the positive productivity effect identified by Grossman and Rossi-Hansberg (2008) is dominated by the negative factor supply effects. By contrast, high-skilled workers should always benefit in this case. In order to investigate this, we report in Column IV results of an estimation in which we interact the two offshoring variables with dummy variables for individuals in three different skill groups, namely, low, medium and high-skilled. As the results show, we now find negative coefficients of services offshoring for low- and medium-skilled workers. The coefficient for medium-skilled workers is statistically insignificant, however. High-skilled workers benefit from offshoring of services, as the statistically significant and positive coefficient indicates. For material offshoring, we also find that wages for low- and medium-skilled workers are negatively affected, although the effect is statistically insignificant for medium-skilled workers. For high-skilled workers we find a positive, albeit statistically insignificant coefficient. While the narrow definition of offshoring arguably best captures the phenomenon of relocating production stages abroad that are close to an industry's core activities, it leaves out many additional types of intermediate goods or services that are used in production. We now investigate how broadly defined offshoring (defined as all intermediate inputs, including narrow offshoring) affects wages by estimating the same model but now using our broad offshoring measures on the right hand side. The results are reported in Table 5. The coefficients on the offshoring variables have the same signs as before, but there are some differences in statistical significance and magnitude of the point estimates. Looking at Column IV, which allows for different effects depending on educational status, shows that we find a statistically significant positive effect of services offshoring and a positive albeit insignificant effect of materials offshoring for high-skilled workers. A one percentage point increase in services offshoring implies a wage increase by about 2.5%. Low- and medium-skilled workers are now both statistically significantly negatively affected by services offshoring. In fact, we cannot reject the hypothesis that the two coefficients are equal, hence, reductions in wages due to services offshoring are the same for low- and medium-skilled workers. We also estimate negative coefficients for material offshoring for both types of workers, though the coefficient for medium skilled workers is not estimated with precision. To sum up, our results thus far are consistent with a partial equilibrium view along the lines of

Table 5 Broad offshoring regression results

	I	II	cluster	III	cluster	IV	cluster
	OLS	FE	boot-t	FE	boot-t	FE	boot-t
Age: 18–25	−0.2701	−0.0492		−0.0484		−0.0467	
	[6.77]***	[1.28]	**	[1.25]	*	[1.16]	*
Age: 26–35	−0.0690	0.0396		0.0402		0.0417	
	[2.82]***	[1.23]		[1.25]		[1.27]	
Age: 36–50	−0.0285	0.0519		0.0518		0.0525	
	[1.12]	[2.06]**		[2.07]**		[2.10]**	
Married: dummy	0.1095	0.0232		0.0233		0.0221	
	[5.30]***	[0.99]		[1.00]		[0.95]	
Children: dummy	0.0627	0.0248		0.0247		0.0241	
	[4.46]***	[1.90]*	**	[1.90]*	**	[1.86]*	**
Tenure	0.0008	0.0008		0.0008		0.0008	
	[2.41]**	[2.90]***	***	[2.88]***	***	[2.70]***	***
Tenure^2	−0.0001	−0.0001		−0.0001		−0.0001	
	[2.79]***	[2.29]**	***	[2.29]**	***	[2.15]**	**
Tenure: noresponse	0.1507	0.1248		0.1243		0.1204	
	[2.39]**	[3.04]***	***	[3.03]***	***	[2.87]***	***
ISCED: high	0.4495	0.1316		0.1347		−0.1642	
	[8.27]***	[2.74]***	**	[2.85]***	***	[1.49]	
ISCED: med	0.1533	−0.0162		−0.0161		−0.0885	
	[7.34]***	[0.50]		[0.50]		[1.45]	*
FirmSize: < 25	−0.2272	−0.0744		−0.0747		−0.0758	
	[7.49]***	[2.62]***	***	[2.64]***	***	[2.69]***	***
FirmSize: 25–100	−0.2053	−0.0376		−0.0378		−0.0391	
	[7.45]***	[1.70]*	**	[1.72]*	**	[1.78]*	**
FirmSize: 100–1000	−0.1027	−0.0029		−0.0030		−0.0044	
	[4.49]***	[0.13]		[0.14]		[0.21]	
Firm: public	−0.1771	0.0719		0.0729		0.0710	
	[1.97]**	[0.87]		[0.88]		[0.86]	
Firm: unknownowner	0.1906	−0.1141		−0.1105		−0.1275	
	[5.28]***	[4.64]***	***	[4.99]***	***	[5.47]***	***
Industry: output	0.0141	0.0093		0.0118		0.0119	
	[0.84]	[0.87]		[1.12]		[1.14]	
Industry: R&D/Y	−0.0013	−0.0072		−0.0101		−0.0109	
	[0.08]	[0.78]		[1.18]		[1.27]	*
OSS	0.0028	−0.0082		−0.0100			
	[0.37]	[1.91]*	*	[2.47]**	**		
OSS × ISCED: high						0.0257	
						[3.15]***	**
OSS × ISCED: med						−0.0115	
						[2.78]***	**
OSS × ISCED: low						−0.0144	
						[2.65]***	***
OSM				−0.0034			
				[0.81]			
OSM × ISCED: high						0.0043	
						[1.46]	
OSM × ISCED: med						−0.0036	
						[0.89]	
OSM × ISCED: low						−0.0096	
						[1.84]*	*
Constant	1.4427						
	[6.32]***						
Observations	5775	5775		5775		5775	
R^2	0.49	0.83		0.83		0.83	

Note: t-statistics in brackets, *** significant at 1%, ** at 5%, * at 10%. Default categories: Age: >50, ISCED: low, FirmSize:> 1000. Occupation, region, industry dummies and industry time trends included. Cluster bootstrapped t-test with 500 repetitions.

Grossman and Rossi-Hansberg (2008) in which low-skill activities in services and materials production are offshored and the resulting negative labour supply effect dominates the positive productivity effect for low-skilled workers while raising wages for high-skilled workers. There is much evidence that indicates that offshoring of materials production is indeed the relocation of low-skilled activities abroad. For example, Hijzen *et al.* (2005) cite examples of the British firms Speedo and Dyson, both of which relocated production activities (which are mainly low skill activities) abroad. For services activities, the evidence is not as straightforward. The literature, including Grossman and Rossi-Hansberg (2008) as discussed above, presents many anecdotes of offshoring of high-skill intensive activities, such as software development or radiology. However, while there is undoubtedly offshoring of such services, many low-skilled service activities are also relocated abroad. Ellram *et al.* (2008) present a study of eight Fortune 500 companies and their offshoring decisions.[16] The study shows that all eight firms offshore some low skill service activities, such as call centres, IT help desks, back office operations, or dealing with travel reimbursements. This is in line with Blinder's (2007) classification of occupations, where he lists telemarketers, telephone operators, customer service representatives, and travel clerks, alongside high-skilled occupations such as computer programmers and mathematicians, among the 20 occupations with the highest risk of being offshored. While we do not know of any in-depths study that examines exactly what type of activity is offshored by a firm, our results are consistent with the idea that the offshoring of low skill services is an important component of offshoring activity in the UK. An important assumption implicit in our estimation thus far is that of exogeneity of regressors. This may be questionable in particular with respect to the offshoring variables. These may be endogenous due to reverse causality—industries with unskill intensive production (and low wages for unskilled workers) may also be those that are more likely to offshore. In this case our conclusions based on the estimations thus far would be problematic. We have three responses to this concern. First, given that there is substantial heterogeneity in individual wages the described scenario, that variation in individual wages causes industry-level offshoring, is unlikely. Second, we control for industry-level fixed effects which would control for time invariant characteristics, such as production technology, of the different industries. Third, we explicitly test the assumption of exogeneity of the offshoring variables using a C-test, based on a re-estimation of the equations in Columns I and II using an instrumental variable GMM approach. Finding valid instruments for testing the exogeneity of the offshoring variables presents a challenge. One needs variables that are important determinants of the respective industry's offshoring activities but do not impact on industry's wages. The literature points to advances in trade liberalization, lowering of transport and

[16] The firms operate in manufacturing and services, specifically financial services (two firms), software, computer manufacturing, packaging, transport, manufacturing of consumer products, and manufacturing of PC hardware.

communication costs as well as technological progress as important drivers of increased offshoring (see Amiti and Wei, 2005, Bartel *et al.*, 2005). However, these factors are difficult to measure at the industry level and, thus, cannot be differentiated from common macro economic effects that impact on wages. We therefore apply a different strategy. Instead of directly including determining factors of an industry's offshoring activities as excluded instruments we use information on offshoring activities of the same industry in a different country, namely Germany. Arguably, offshoring activities of the same industry in different countries are driven by the same global factors. This should be particularly true if countries share the same trade policy and have a similar industrial structure. We thus expect a close correlation between offshoring activities in the UK and Germany within any given manufacturing industry. At the same time, conditional on fluctuations in industry output offshoring activities of German industries are unlikely to have a direct impact on wages at the worker level in the UK. Hence, German offshoring activities should be relevant as well as valid instruments. The test statistics reported in Table 6 support our reasoning. Based on the first step F-test we find that the instruments have a high explanatory power. Also, we can clearly reject underidentification and weak identification, suggesting that our instruments are indeed relevant. We cannot reject orthogonality of our excluded instruments within reasonable confidence bands based on the Hansen J statistic, supporting our assumption of instrument validity. Furthermore, the C-test indicates that we cannot reject exogeneity of services and materials offshoring. Accordingly, the efficiency loss associated with instrumenting for services and materials offshoring cannot be justified and the fixed effects coefficients reported in Tables 4 and 5 can be considered consistent estimates of the true parameters.[17]

Thus far we have focussed on statistical significance. The point estimates and standard errors of the coefficients allow us to examine the direction and significance of the effects, but do not tell us much about their actual importance. To judge the economic significance of our estimates we engage in a thought experiment of implied wage changes. We do this separately for our estimates in Table 4 and Table 5. Table 7 reports the median hourly wages in British pounds (£) for the three skill groups in 1992, the beginning of our sample period. We also report the coefficients from the estimation of the preferred specification in Column IV of Tables 4 and 5.

Consider the effect of narrow offshoring first. Over the full sample period, narrowly defined services offshoring increased by 0.12 percentage points, while the increase for narrow materials offshoring was 2.23 percentage points. For a high-skilled worker with an average number of working hours (1,732 per year for the UK; see OECD, 2008) this implies that the cumulative increase in wages due to services offshoring was roughly GBP 2,000. Materials offshoring has no statistically significant impact on high-skilled workers wages. Accordingly, the

[17] All estimations and corresponding tests are carried out using the Stata add-ons ivreg2 and xtivreg2 provided by Baum *et al.* (2003, 2007).

Table 6 Exogeneity tests of offshoring

Instrumented	OSS^{narrow}	OSS^{narrow} OSM^{narrow}	OSS^{broad}	OSS^{broad} OSM^{broad}
Instruments	$OSS^{narrow}_{Germany,t}$ $OSS^{broad}_{Germany,t}$	$OSS^{narrow,broad}_{Germany,t}$ $OSM^{narrow}_{Germany,t,t-1}$	$OSS^{broad}_{Germany,t}$ $OSS^{broad}_{Germany,t-1}$	$OSS^{broad,narrow}_{Germany,t-1}$ $OSM^{broad}_{Germany,t,t-1}$
First stage F-test				
	F=45.03 p=0.00	F=30.57/F=32.72 p=0.00/p=0.00	F=28.56 p=0.00	F=31.60/F=53.47 p=0.00/p=0.00
Underidentification test				
Kleibergen-Paap rk LM statistic	$\chi^2(2) = 132.88$ p=0.00	$\chi^2(3) = 121.02$ p=0.00	$\chi^2(2) = 64.20$ p=0.00	$\chi^2(3) = 80.49$ p=0.00
Weak identification test				
Kleibergen-Paap rk Wald F statistic	F=70.31	F=33.69	F=28.56	F=22.43
Stock-Yogo critical values for wrong rejection rate of 10%				
	19.93	16.87	19.93	16.87
Overidentification test of all instruments				
Hansen J statistic	$\chi^2(1) = 1.65$ p=0.20	$\chi^2(2) = 3.54$ p=0.17	$\chi^2(1) = 0.04$ p=0.84	$\chi^2(2) = 1.52$ p=0.47
Exogeneity of regressors				
C-Test	$\chi^2(1) = 0.17$ p=0.68	$\chi^2(2) = 0.09$ p=0.95	$\chi^2(1) = 0.05$ p=0.83	$\chi^2(2) = 1.85$ p=0.40
Observations	5775	5775	5775	5775

Table 7 Cumulated wage effects of increased offshoring, at 1992 median wages

	High-skilled	Medium-skilled	Low-skilled
Median hourly wage (1992)	18.37	8.19	4.92
Narrow definition of offshoring, coefficients, Table 4, Column IV			
OSS	0.519	–	−0.3014
OSM	–	–	−0.0162
Percentage point change, 1992-2004: $\triangle OSS = 0.12$, $\triangle OSM = 2.23$			
Cumulated yearly wage change in GBP (1732 work hours)			
OSS	1999.74	–	−310.86
OSM	–	–	−308.36
Broad definition of offshoring, coefficients, Table 5, Column IV			
OSS	0.026	−0.0115	−0.0144
OSM		–	−0.0096
Percentage point change, 1992-2004: $\triangle OSS = 1.57$, $\triangle OSM = 4.81$			
Cumulated yearly wage change in GBP (1732 work hours)			
OSS	1278.70	−256.02	−191.83
OSM	–	–	−393.73

Note: Assumed 1732 annual work hours in 1992 according to OECD (2008, Factbook)

cumulative increase in wages due to materials offshoring is nil. For low-skilled workers, we observe a corresponding cumulative reduction in wages by GBP 619, GBP 311 of which were due to services offshoring and the remainder due to materials offshoring. The effects of offshoring for medium-skilled workers were not identified precisely enough to rule out that they are nil. The corresponding calculations for broadly defined offshoring are reported in the bottom panel of Table 7. The results are similar to those obtained from narrow offshoring, indicating wage gains for high-skilled workers of about GBP 1,278 due to services offshoring, and wage losses for medium- and low-skilled workers of about GBP 256–584 over the period 1992 to 2004. Given that these are effects of cumulative changes of offshoring over a 12-year period these numbers are small, but not so small as to be neglected. The economic significance calculation also shows that, even though services offshoring, especially when defined narrowly, is still at low levels it has important economic implications for workers' wages.[18]

[18] A potential question regarding our estimations is how robust this is to the definition of skills we use. As an alternative, we use a skill definition based on the Standard Occupational Classification (SOC) of individuals, information on which is in the BHPS. We classify individuals into high (SOC=1 to 3), medium (SOC=4 to 5), and low-skilled (SOC=6 to 9) occupations. For broad services offshoring and narrow materials offshoring the coefficients based on this approach are comparable to the estimates reported here in terms of signs, statistical significance, and magnitude for low- and medium-skilled workers. One notable difference is that we now do not find any statistically significant effect of services or material offshoring on high-skilled workers. Furthermore, narrow service offshoring and broad material offshoring are always rendered insignificant in this approach. Accordingly, there is some evidence that medium- and low-skilled workers are more negatively affected by offshoring than high-skilled workers. However, results are indeed sensitive to the definition of skills and offshoring. Results are not reported here to save space, but can be obtained upon request.

6. Alternative approach

Thus far we have investigated how offshoring within an industry affects wages of workers in the same industry. Thus, the empirical approach corresponds to a partial equilibrium short-run view of the economy outlined in, e.g., Grossman and Rossi-Hansberg (2008) where employees are immobile between industries. In that case, what matters is how important offshoring is in the own industry, what happens in other industries is irrelevant. However, in the long run it is more realistic that employees can potentially move between industries. Accordingly, labour market effects of offshoring in one industry can also impact on other industries. One approach that has been used in the literature to analyse empirically such long-run effects of offshoring is the estimation of mandated wage regressions (see e.g., Feenstra and Hanson, 1999, for the US and Hijzen, 2007, for the UK). This approach is based on fairly aggregated sectoral data for long time series. Our disaggregated individual-level panel data lends itself to another approach. Instead of analysing wage effects of within-industry changes of offshoring we can construct education-specific offshoring measures and regress them on individual wages. Accordingly, we allow for cross-industry spillovers of labour demand effects of offshoring by assuming that workers are unable to change their educational attainment once they entered employment but can potentially move between industries.[19] This assumption is born out by our data: while we count 1,093 occurrences of industry changes we have only 63 cases where individuals move between skill groups. To construct education-specific offshoring measures, we re-weight industry-level offshoring measures (cf. eqs (1)–(4) with respect to industry employment within a given educational group (s = high-, medium-, low-skilled) as a share in total employment L within educational group s in 1991 (pre-sample):

$$OSS^z_{st} = \sum_{j=1}^{J} \frac{L_{sj}}{L_s} OSS^z_{jt} \tag{6}$$

$$OSM^z_{st} = \sum_{j=1}^{J} \frac{L_{sj}}{L_s} OSM^z_{jt}, \tag{7}$$

with z = *narrow*, *broad*. Similarly, we construct education-specific output (Y_{st}) to account for education-specific time varying industry characteristics.

[19] Our approach is similar to Ebenstein *et al.* (2009) and Baumgarten *et al.* (2010) who construct occupation-specific offshoring measures to allow for cross-industry effects of offshoring. However, in the context of the UK we find it more realistic to assume that individuals potentially can change their occupation while changing their educational attainment is more difficult.

We then re-estimate our empirical model in eq. (5) substituting Y_{st}, OSS_{st} and OSM_{st} for Y_{jt}, OSS_{jt} and OSM_{jt}, yielding

$$\log w_{ist} = \alpha + \beta X_{it} + \gamma Y_{st} + \delta (R\&D/Y)_{st} + \lambda_S OSS^z_{st} + \lambda_M OSM^z_{st} + T_t + \mu_t + \alpha_i + \iota_k + \epsilon_{ist}. \quad (8)$$

When estimating the model we allow for clustered standard errors within educational groups s at time t yielding 39 clusters.[20] The results are reported in Table 8, where, for the sake of brevity, we only report coefficients and t-statistics for the offshoring variables interacted with education dummies.[21]

One striking point is particularly noteworthy. In the full specifications reported in Columns I and V, eight out of 12 offshoring coefficients in the two specifications are statistically insignificant. This reflects the substantially reduced variation in the offshoring variable compared to the earlier offshoring measures used above, as offshoring only varies over three education categories and time. Furthermore, when comparing the coefficients in Columns II to III and VI to VII, where we respectively excluded materials and services offshoring from the model, statistical significance of our services and materials offshoring variables changes drastically indicating multicollinearity of the two. As a consequence it is doubtful whether one can indeed separate the effects of services and materials offshoring. To reflect this we also estimate model specifications where only the sum of education-specific services and materials offshoring enters. The respective coefficients are reported in Columns IV and VIII of Table 8.

When applying our narrow definitions of offshoring, services and material offshoring taken together exert statistically significant negative wage effects on medium- and low-skilled workers while the effect is rendered insignificant for high-skilled workers. When applying the broad offshoring definitions, high-skilled workers are found to gain from services and materials offshoring while low-skilled workers lose. For medium-skilled workers the effect of broad offshoring is rendered statistically insignificant. Similar to the within-industry discussion, our results are consistent with the wage effects postulated in Grossman and Rossi-Hansberg (2008) for offshoring of low-skill intensive activities. Accordingly, low-skilled workers experience wage cuts due to the dominance of the negative labour supply effect and, if one prescribes to the long run general equilibrium view, the negative Stolper-Samuelson type relative price effect. High-skilled workers, however, experience wage increases due to this type of offshoring, as both the labour supply as well as the relative price effect work in their favour. The implied economic significance of the estimates is, in a similar manner to Table 7 calculated in Table 9. Concentrating on the statistically significant coefficients reported in Columns IV and VIII of Table 8 we find a joint cumulated wage loss

[20] Note that since in our data individuals do not change education within a given year, individuals are nested within the education-year clusters.

[21] Results for the other variables included in the model are similar to those reported above. They can be obtained from the authors upon request.

Table 8 Education-specific offshoring — regression results

	Narrow				Broad			
	I	II	III	IV	V	VI	VII	VIII
OSS × ISCED: high	−1.8381	−0.5163			−0.0132		−0.0011	
	[1.05]	[0.35]			[0.37]		[0.05]	
OSS × ISCED: med	−1.7730	−2.3101			−0.0319		−0.0530	
	[1.07]	[1.81]*			[0.78]		[1.59]	
OSS × ISCED: low	−2.0036	−2.8231			−0.0561		−0.0844	
	[1.39]	[2.46]**			[1.04]		[2.23]**	
OSM × ISCED: high	−0.0331		0.0011		−0.4067	−0.5388		
	[0.49]		[0.02]		[1.60]	[3.32]***		
OSM × ISCED: med	−0.1883		−0.1455		−0.2599	−0.3696		
	[2.73]***		[1.98]*		[1.92]*	[5.34]***		
OSM × ISCED: low	−0.2387		−0.2184		−0.1609	−0.2506		
	[3.04]***		[2.91]***		[2.03]**	[6.10]***		
(OSS + OSM) × ISCED: high				−0.0059				0.0260
				[0.09]				[1.81]*
(OSS + OSM) × ISCED: med				−0.1468				−0.0201
				[2.03]**				[1.03]
(OSS + OSM) × ISCED: low				−0.2160				−0.0345
				[2.95]***				[1.95]*
Observations	5775	5775	5775	5775	5775	5775	5775	5775
R-squared	0.83	0.83	0.83	0.83	0.83	0.83	0.83	0.83

Note: t-statistics in brackets, *** significant at 1%, ** at 5%, * at 10%. Complete set of control variables included. t-tests on the basis of clustered standard errors by education and year.

Table 9 Cumulated wage effects of increased offshoring, at 1992 median wages: education-specific offshoring

	High-skilled	Medium-skilled	Low-skilled
Median hourly wage (1992)	18.37	8.19	4.92
Narrow definition of offshoring, coefficient, Table 8, Column IV			
OSS+OSM	–	−0.1468	−0.2160
Percentage point change, 1992-2004: $\Delta(OSS + OSM) = 2.35$			
Cumulated yearly wage change in GBP (1732 work hours)			
OSS+OSM	–	−4893.08	−4323.73
Broad definition of offshoring, coefficient, Table 8, Column VIII			
OSS+OSM	0.0260	–	−0.0345
Percentage point change, 1992-2004: $\Delta(OSS + OSM) = 6.38$			
Cumulated yearly wage change in GBP (1732 work hours)			
OSS+OSM	5282.85	–	−1872.82

Note: assumed 1732 annual work hours in 1992 according to OECD (2008, Factbook)

due to narrowly defined services and materials offshoring of GBP 4893 and GBP 4323 for medium- and low-skilled workers respectively. The cumulated wage loss of broadly defined services and materials offshoring is GBP 1873 for low-skilled workers while high-skilled workers gain GBP 5283. The wage effects of our education-specific offshoring variable thus follow a similar pattern as in the industry-specific partial equilibrium analysis carried out in Section 5. However, the magnitude of the effects is much higher. This may reflect that the labour supply effect highlighted by Grossman and Rossi-Hansberg (2008) is now allowed to operate across industries. If offshoring sets free workers of a given skill type, this will, *ceteris paribus*, depress the wage paid to those workers in all industries. Furthermore, the negative wage effects due to relative price changes predicted by Grossman and Rossi-Hansberg (2008) are not present in a within-industry partial equilibrium setting but may be present here.

7. Conclusion

This paper investigates the relationship between offshoring of services and individual workers' wages, using household-level panel data from the British Household Panel Survey (BHPS) combined with industry-level measures of offshoring of services activities and materials offshoring over the period 1992–2004. We use two different estimation strategies. One uses only within-industry changes in offshoring, while the other also considers offshoring effects across industries. Our results show that services offshoring in an industry affects the real wage of low- and medium-skilled individuals in the same industry negatively. By contrast, there is evidence that skilled workers in the industry benefit from such services offshoring in terms of higher real wages. This is consistent with the partial equilibrium view in Grossman and Rossi-Hansberg

(2008) if one assumes that mainly low- and medium skilled services activities are offshored. This has positive effects for high-skilled workers but may affect low skilled workers negatively, if the negative labour supply effect is not outweighed by a positive productivity effect. Once allowing for the fact that offshoring in one particular industry potentially also affects labour demand in other industries, then we cannot separately identify effects of services and materials offshoring. However, our results show some evidence for a statistically significant positive effect on high-skilled wages and negative effects for low- and medium-skilled workers for services and materials offshoring taken together.

In sum, our results suggest that offshoring of services has contributed to a widening of the wage gap between skilled and less skilled workers. However, looking at the magnitude of these effects we find that they are rather small, but not so small as to be negligible. Hence, we have identified winners and losers in terms of wage gains from services offshoring. The policy relevant question is now whether the losers should be compensated and, if this is answered in the affirmative, what form such a compensation should have. Another policy implication is that skill upgrading needs to be continued in order to allow unskilled workers to move into the 'winning' category of skilled work.

Acknowledgements

Ingo Geishecker and Holger Görg are also affiliated with GlobID at Aarhus School of Business, Aarhus University, Denmark. The authors are grateful to anonymous referees for helpful comments on an earlier draft.

Funding

European Commission, FP7 SERVICEGAP Project (Grant Agreement no: 244 552).

References

Amiti, M. and Wei, S.J. (2005) Fear of service outsourcing: is it justified? *Economic Policy*, **20**, 308–47.

Amiti, M. and Wei, S.J. (2007) Service offshoring, productivity and employment: evidence from the US, Discussion Paper 5475, CEPR, London.

Bartel, A., Lach, S., and Sicherman, N. (2005) Outsourcing and technological change, Working Paper 11158, NBER, Boston, MA.

Baum, C.F., Schaffer, M.E., and Stillman, S. (2003) Instrumental variables and GMM: estimation and testing, *Stata Journal*, **3**, 1–31.

Baum, C.F., Schaffer, M.E., and Stillman, S. (2007) Enhanced routines for instrumental variables/GMM estimation and testing, Economics Working Paper 667, Boston College, Boston, MA.

Baumgarten, D., Geishecker, I., and Görg, H. (2010) Offshoring, tasks, and the skill-wage pattern, Discussion Paper 7756, CEPR, London.

Blinder, A. (2007) *How many US jobs might be offshorable?* CEPS Working Paper 142, Princeton University, Princeton, NJ.

Cameron, C.A., Gelbach, J.B., and Miller, D.L. (2008) Bootstrap-based improvements for inference with clustered errors, *Review of Economics and Statistics*, **90**, 414–27.

Cameron, C.A., Gelbach, J.B., and Miller, D.L. (2011) Robust inference with multi-way clustering, *Journal of Business and Economic Statistics*, **29**, 238–49.

Ebenstein, A., Harrison, A., McMillan, S., and Phillips, S. (2009) Estimating the impact of trade and offshoring on American workers using the current population surveys, Working Paper 15107, NBER, Boston, MA.

Egger, P., Pfaffermayr, M., and Weber, A. (2007) Sectoral adjustment of employment to shifts in outsourcing and trade: evidence from a dynamic fixed effects multinominal logit model, *Journal of Applied Econometrics*, **22**, 559–80.

Ellram, L.M., Tate, W.L., and Billington, C. (2008) Offshore outsourcing of professional services: a transaction cost economics perspective, *Journal of Operations Management*, **26**, 148–63.

Feenstra, R.C. and Hanson, G.H. (1999) The impact of outsourcing and high-technology capital on wages: estimates for the United States, 1979-1990, *Quarterly Journal of Economics*, **114**, 907–41.

Geishecker, I. (2008) The impact of international outsourcing on individual employment security: a micro-level analysis, *Labour Economics*, **15**, 291–314.

Geishecker, I. and Görg, H. (2008) Winners and losers: a micro-level analysis of international outsourcing and wages, *Canadian Journal of Economics*, **41**, 243–70.

Grossman, G.M. and Rossi-Hansberg, E. (2008) Trading tasks: a simple theory of offshoring, *American Economic Review*, **98**, 1978–97.

Hijzen, A. (2007) International outsourcing, technological change, and wage inequality, *Review of International Economics*, **15**, 188–205.

Hijzen, A., Görg, H., and Hine, R.C. (2005) International outsourcing and the skill structure of labour demand in the United Kingdom, *Economic Journal*, **115**, 860–78.

Hijzen, A., Pisu, M., Upward, R., and Wright, P. (2007) Employment, job turnover, and the trade in producer services: firm-level evidence, GEP Research Paper 2007/37, University of Nottingham, Nottingham.

Kohler, W. (2008) Outsourcing: why do stories differ? Working Paper 2231 CESIfo, Munich.

Liu, R. and Trefler, D. (2008) Much ado about nothing: American jobs and the rise of service outsourcing to China and India, Working Paper 14061, NBER, Boston, MA.

Munch, J.R. and Skaksen, J.R. (2009) Specialization, outsourcing and wages, *Review of World Economics*, **145**, 57–73.

Chapter III.5

Offshoring, wages and job security of temporary workers

Holger Görg[1,2,3] **· Dennis Görlich**[1]

Published online: 20 May 2015

Abstract Temporary contracts have become an important mode of employment in many countries. We investigate the impact of offshoring on individual level wages and unemployment probabilities and pay particular attention to the question if workers with temporary contracts are affected differently than workers with permanent contracts. Data are taken from the German Socio-Economic Panel, linked with industry level data on offshoring. We do not find systematic differences between temporary and permanent workers with respect to the effects of offshoring for wages. We find, however, that offshoring increases the unemployment risk of low-skilled workers, and more so for temporary than permanent workers. Also, offshoring reduces the unemployment risk for all high- and medium-skilled workers.

Keywords Offshoring · Imported value added · Temporary contracts · Wages · Job security

JEL Classification F14 · F16 · J31

1 Introduction

An important facet of today's world economy is that trade is no longer mostly in final goods. Instead, the recent wave of globalization is characterized by the strong emergence of vertical specialization and the offshoring of parts of the production

✉ Dennis Görlich
dennis.goerlich@ifw-kiel.de

1 Kiel Institute for the World Economy, Kiel, Germany

2 University of Kiel, Kiel, Germany

3 Tuborg Research Centre for Globalisation and Firms, Aarhus University, Århus, Denmark

(see Yi 2003). The labour market consequences of this offshoring of production are debated in the media as well as among policy makers and academic economists.

At least since Feenstra and Hanson (1999) trade economists have concerned themselves with investigating the impact of offshoring on labour markets. While Feenstra and Hanson (1999) and many papers since investigate this issue using industry or country level data (e.g. Foster-McGregor et al. 2013), recent research tends to use individual level data in order to examine whether offshoring has any impact on an individual's job security or wage. Using micro data has the advantage that it allows to focus on the level of the individual where one can control for observable and unobservable characteristics that may play a role for transitions in employment status or wages, but that cannot be controlled for in firm or industry data (e.g. age, tenure or marital status of a worker). It also provides information on the various aspects of skills of an individual, which can be exploited in the estimations. Moreover, unobserved time-invariant characteristics can be controlled for by using panel data methods.

A number of recent studies have investigated the effects of offshoring using individual level data. Baumgarten et al. (2013), Ebenstein et al. (2014), Liu and Trefler (2008) and Geishecker and Görg (2008, 2013) use individual level data for the United States, Germany and the United Kingdom, respectively, to study the impact of offshoring on individual wages. Liu and Trefler (2008), Geishecker (2008), Bachmann and Braun (2011) and Pfaffermayr et al. (2007) also use individual level data for the US, Germany and Austria, respectively, to investigate whether offshoring has any implications for job security, measured in terms of whether an individual switches jobs or moves into unemployment. Overall, it seems from this literature that, in general, offshoring may have some effects on employment and wages in line with expectations, where low-skilled workers may be more likely to lose and high-skilled workers more likely to benefit in terms of job security and wages.

What has, to the best of our knowledge, been neglected in this literature thus far is the question as to how workers with different types of contracts fare in this wave of offshoring. This is the focus of this paper, where we particularly consider whether workers on temporary contracts experience different labour market effects of offshoring than their peers on permanent contracts. This is an important issue, given that temporary contracts are an important mode of employment today (see Table 1).

Table 1 Incidence of temporary contracts, by country, 15–64 year old persons

	1999	2000	2001	2002	2003	2004	2005	2006	2007
European Union	13.3	13.6	13.5	13.2	13.1	13.5	14.5	15.1	14.6
Germany	13.1	12.8	12.4	12.0	12.2	12.5	14.2	14.5	14.6
Denmark	10.1	10.2	9.4	8.9	9.5	9.8	9.8	8.9	8.6
Spain	32.8	32.4	32.1	32.1	31.8	32.1	33.4	34.1	31.7
France	13.9	15.4	14.9	14.1	13.4	13.0	14.1	14.9	15.2
Italy	9.8	10.1	9.6	9.9	9.5	11.9	12.3	13.1	13.2
United Kingdom	6.7	6.6	6.6	6.0	5.7	5.6	5.7	5.7	5.7
United States	4.5	–	4.0	–	–	–	4.2	–	–

Source: Eurostat (LFS), OECD Employment and Labour Market Statistics (for US)

European Union refers to EU15 until 2004, EU25 until 2006, and EU27 thereafter

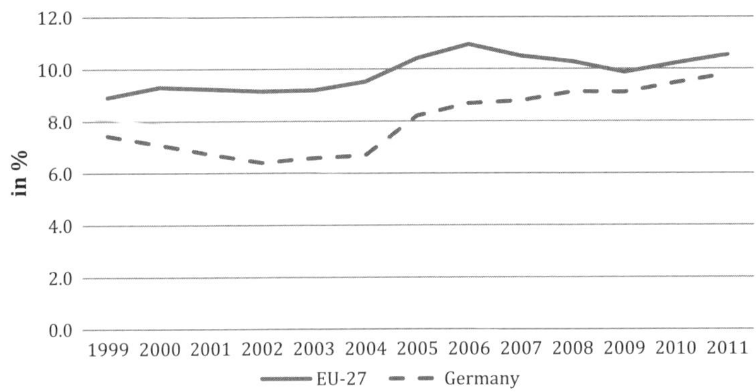

Fig. 1 Share of workers holding a temporary contract in total employment. *Source* Eurostat

Table 2 Incidence of temporary contracts by educational attainment, Germany, 15–64 year old persons

	1999	2000	2001	2002	2003	2004	2005	2006	2007
Primary	26.8	27.5	27.8	27.9	29.2	29.8	30.4	30.4	31.9
Secondary	8.6	8.4	8.0	7.9	7.9	8.0	9.7	10.0	10.2
Tertiary	7.9	7.4	7.2	6.5	6.9	7.0	7.8	8.2	8.0

Source: Eurostat (LFS)

Primary education refers to ISCED levels 0–2, secondary refers to ISCED levels 3–4, tertiary refers to ISCED level 5–6

In Germany, the country studied in this paper, the share of temporary contracts in the group of workers aged 25–49 years increased slightly from 7.4 % in 1999 to 9.8 % in 2011 (according to Eurostat statistics, not shown).[1] Having been well below the European average, Germany has now almost caught up with the European average (see Fig. 1).

The share of temporary contracts is particularly high among younger workers and low-skilled workers (see Table 2). According to Eurostat data in Table 2, almost one-third of workers with primary education hold a temporary contract in 2007 (up from one-fourth in 1999). Among workers with secondary or tertiary education, only 10 or 8 % hold a temporary contract, respectively.

Negative economic shocks such as a recession with many jobs being shed, can cause high levels of unemployment among groups with a high prevalence of temporary contracts (cf. Blanchard and Landier 2002; Cahuc and Postel-Vinay 2002; Boeri and Garibaldi 2007). Yet, the possibility to use temporary contracts should also increase overall employment as employers may be more willing to create jobs given the lower cost of eliminating jobs. Moreover, the use of temporary

[1] Note, however, that this increase may be overstated due to a change in the statistical methodology in 2004.

contracts by employers also enhances employment stability for regular core employees who hold permanent contracts (Gramm and Schnell 2001).

While, in principle, all workers in an industry are equally likely to be affected by the pressures on labour brought about by offshoring, there are several reasons to believe that workers on temporary contracts are affected differently than workers on permanent contracts. Booth et al. (2002a) characterize temporary labour under fixed-term contracts as "a buffer stock that allows firms to adjust to changes in the business environment due to seasonal or other transitory causes" (p. F182). Accordingly, if firms and industries adjust to offshoring, this may lead to a stronger adjustment among temporary workers; both positively and negatively.

In terms of wages, temporary workers might be particularly affected because they supposedly have a weaker bargaining position than permanent workers. They might also be represented less well in collective wage bargaining processes. Moreover, they have possibly obtained less on-the-job training or job-specific human capital, making their bargaining position even weaker. Hence, they might incur stronger wage reductions in case employers adjust to globalization pressure at the intensive margin.

In terms of job security, temporary workers might, on the one hand, have a stronger propensity to lose their job due to international competition because their contracts have a natural termination date after which employers might not renew it. Moreover, they have typically obtained less firm-specific human capital, making them less attractive for employers to keep them. On the other hand, when firms expand due to offshoring-induced cost savings or productivity improvements, temporary workers might benefit from renewed contracts or conversion to a permanent contract. Indeed, there is some evidence that temporary contracts can serve as a stepping-stone to regular employment (e.g. Holmlund and Storrie 2002; Booth et al. 2002b).

We address the question of whether employees on temporary contracts are differently affected by offshoring by looking at individual wages and the risk of becoming unemployed. The sample consists of male workers between 18 and 64 years in manufacturing industries between 1999 and 2007. Data are taken from the German Socio-Economic Panel (SOEP), an annual, representative, and widely used individual level panel data set for Germany (see Wagner et al. 2007, for a description of the SOEP). In order to integrate offshoring into the data, we link the SOEP with industry level data on offshoring, specifically the share of imported value added in industry production, which we calculate from the world input–output database (WIOD). In the regressions, we interact offshoring intensities with contract type and can thus infer the potentially differential impact of offshoring on permanent and temporary workers.

The remainder of the paper is structured as follows. Section 2 describes our measure for offshoring and gives an overview about the evolution of offshoring. Section 3 introduces the other data and presents our methodological approach. In Sect. 4 we discuss our empirical results. Section 5 concludes.

2 Measuring offshoring

Empirical work in international trade generally gauges the importance of offshoring by looking at imports of intermediate goods from the respective industry abroad. Following Feenstra and Hanson (1999), many studies use input–output tables to estimate the importance of intermediate goods trade for certain industries. In this study, we measure offshoring by the share of foreign value added contained in domestic production. Similar indicators have been derived by Hummels et al. (2001), Daudin et al. (2011), Johnson and Noguera (2012) and Koopman et al. (2014), and have been calculated with various data sets. Our offshoring measure is calculated using the WIOD.[2]

The WIOD contains detailed information about the production structure, imports and exports of 40 countries, which jointly represent 85 % of world GDP. Moreover, the WIOD distinguished 35 industries, of which 14 are manufacturing industries. A list of industries in the WIOD and their NACE equivalents can be found in "Appendix 1". Note that the industries textiles and leather had to be aggregated because of some missing values in the WIOD. The world input–output tables are available on an annual basis between 1995 and 2009, and they are comparable across countries and time.

We employ the concept of narrow offshoring here. Narrow offshoring describes the share of imported value added, which the worker's industry imports from the same industry abroad. Changes in narrow offshoring are expected to affect the worker's wage and job loss probability because the measure captures imported tasks, which could as well be carried out by the domestic worker. For example, an increase in narrow offshoring could be due to the relocation of production steps which were previously carried out domestically. The formal derivation of our offshoring measure can be found in "Appendix 2". We are using the expressions offshoring and imported value added interchangeably throughout the text.

Figure 2 shows the evolution of narrow offshoring, i.e. the share of imported own-industry value added, across German manufacturing industries between 1999 and 2007. It is clear that there are differences in the *level* of imported value added, with the food/beverage industry showing a ratio of material imports to output of between 0.5 and 1 %, while industries such as basic and fabricated metals import between 5 and 10 % of value added. However, in most industries there is also a clear and upward trend over time.

Table 3 shows that the share of imported value added increased by a bit more than 1 percentage point between 1999 and 2007 in manufacturing industries. This increase is mostly driven by an increase in offshoring to low-wage countries, which include Central and Eastern European countries.

[2] The WIOD is available at http://www.wiod.org/database/index.htm. See Timmer (2012) for a detailed description of the construction of the world input–output tables.

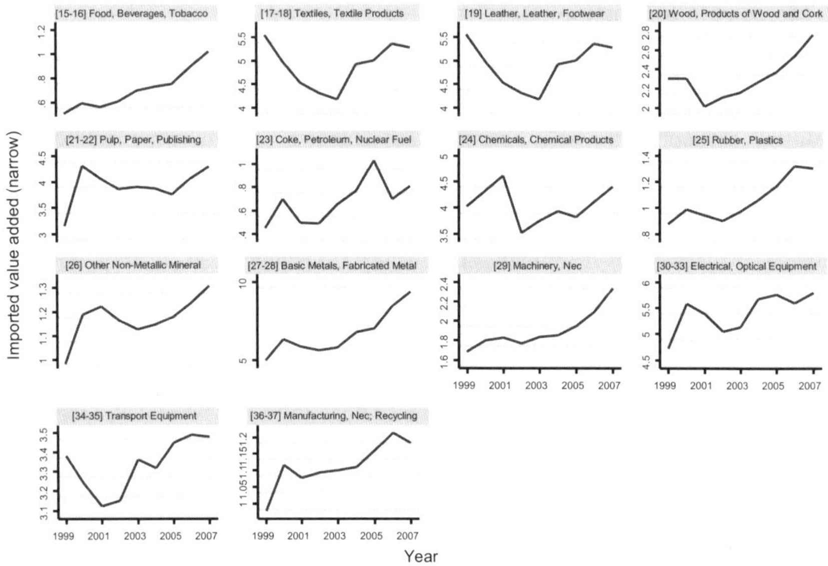

Fig. 2 Offshoring, 1999 and 2007, by manufacturing industry, in percent of output. *Source* WIOD, own calculations

Table 3 Average share of imported value added (offshoring) in total production, manufacturing industries

Years	Imported value added		
	Total	From high-wage countries	From low-wage countries
1999	3.60	2.70	0.91
2000	3.95	2.78	1.17
2001	3.83	2.68	1.14
2002	3.64	2.53	1.11
2003	3.77	2.53	1.23
2004	4.04	2.65	1.39
2005	4.12	2.69	1.43
2006	4.44	2.78	1.66
2007	4.79	2.92	1.87
Change 1999–2007	1.19	0.23	0.96

The WIOD countries are allocated as follows. High-wage countries include OECD countries (except Mexico, Turkey, and Middle and Eastern countries), as well as Taiwan. Low-wage countries include non-OECD countries (except Taiwan), Mexico, Turkey, Middle and Eastern European countries

3 Other data and methodology

The aim of our analysis is to investigate the effect of offshoring on individual wages and unemployment probabilities and to see whether temporary work arrangements affect these outcomes. Such labour market effects may strongly depend on individual level characteristics, such as education, age, employment duration with the employer etc. In order to be able to abstract from such confounding effects we therefore turn to an econometric analysis where we use individual level data combined with the industry level measures for imported value added (i.e., offshoring).

The analysis relies on individual level data from Samples A to E, as well as Samples H and I of the German Socio-Economic Panel (SOEP; see Tables 6, 7 in "Appendix 3" for variable descriptions and summary statistics of the individual level variables). Using the industry identifier we combine the individual level data with the industry level data on offshoring described in Sect. 2. Our sample includes all regular full-time employees as well as employees with atypical employment relationships, which include temporary contracts, part-time employment, marginal or irregular employment, and employment by temporary work agencies. We restrict our sample to male workers that are between 18 and 64 years old and that are employed in manufacturing industries (NACE 15–36) in West Germany.[3] Moreover, we exclude apprentices and self-employed from our estimation sample. Apprentices have a rather specific and special status on the German labour market because of the German dual apprenticeship system. In particular, they hold temporary contracts but, due to their special status, they cannot be regarded as regular labour market participants. The analysis spans the period 1999 to 2007. The starting date of our time period is set because information about the workers' contract types is only available since 1999. We concentrate on the period up to 2007 only in order to avoid results, which are driven by the financial crisis.

The first part of the analysis looks at wages. To investigate the relationship between offshoring and individuals' wages, we estimate variants of the following Mincerian wage regression[4]:

$$\ln WAGE_{ijt} = \beta X_{it} + \gamma_1 OFF_{jt} + \gamma_2 TEMP_{it} + \gamma_3 (OFF_{jt} \times TEMP_{it}) + Y_{jt} + d_j + d_t + d_i + v_{it}, \tag{1}$$

where *WAGE* is the hourly gross wage for individual *I* in industry *j* in year *t*. Wage data are derived from the SOEP cross-national equivalent file (CNEF) and include

[3] We exclude workers from East Germany, as wages in the East are to a large extent shaped by the structural change of the economy that has been taking place since the fall of the wall and that most likely dominates the impact of other changing structural factors. We also exclude female workers since, as is well known, female workers have substantially different labour market outcomes than males. Hence, our sample is similar to that used in Geishecker and Görg (2008), though we have a more up-to-date time period.

[4] This approach is similar to Geishecker and Görg (2008, 2013) and Liu and Trefler (2008). However, these papers do not allow for differential effects depending on the type of employment contract and use a different offshoring measure.

bonuses, premia, and other extra payments. Hourly wages are calculated by dividing gross yearly labour earnings by yearly working hours.[5]

Explanatory variables include individual-specific characteristics, which are represented by X (and include marital status, employment duration with the employer, work experience, education, size of the firm where the individual works, and a dummy for individuals living in East Germany, in addition to gender and age in case of the unemployment risk regressions).[6] Dummies d for industry j, time t and individual fixed effects d_i control for unobserved effects at these levels. Y represents measures of industry level R&D (relative to the output of industry j) in order to control for technical change that is specific to an industry, and of industry level production in order to control for activity. Industry level R&D data are taken from the ANBERD database provided by the OECD. Production data are taken from the WIOD.

The main variables of interest are the vector *OFF* which is our measure of narrow offshoring as described in Sect. 3 and *TEMP*, which is an indicator variable equal to one if the individual holds a temporary contract and zero if the contract is permanent. The interaction term $OFF \times TEMP$ captures the differential effect (if any) of offshoring on wages for workers with temporary contracts.

The incidence of temporary contracts differs by the educational attainment of the worker (see Table 2 above): low-skilled workers are more likely to hold a temporary contract than the other skill groups. Hence, estimates may partly capture the effects of education. Therefore, we split the sample by educational group, in order to derive within group estimates of the differential offshoring effects of temporary contracts and atypical employment relationships.

An important assumption implicit in our estimation is that of exogeneity of regressors. This may be questionable in particular with respect to the offshoring variables. These may be endogenous due to reverse causality—e.g. industries with many unskilled, low-wage workers may also be those that are more likely to offshore. However, given that there is substantial heterogeneity in individual wages it is unlikely that reverse causality is an issue. Also, we control for industry-level fixed effects, which would control for time-invariant characteristics, such as production technology at the industry level. Another potential source of correlation between the offshoring variable and the error term is measurement error, which is, however, hard to correct as alternative measures are not available.

The second part of the analysis looks at employment probabilities. To investigate the link between an individual's probability of losing her job and offshoring we estimate the probability of job loss conditional on individual and industry characteristics:

$$\Pr(job\ loss)_{ijt} = \beta X_{it} + \lambda_1 OFF_{jt} + \lambda_2 TEMP_{it} + \lambda_3 (OFF_{jt} \times TEMP_{it}) + Y_{jt} + d_j + d_t + d_i + e_{it} \tag{2}$$

where *job loss* is defined as a dummy variable equal to one in period t if the individual

[5] Imputed wages are dropped throughout the analysis. See Frick et al. (2007) for a documentation of the CNEF.

[6] A definition of the explanatory variables is given in "Appendix 3".

I moves from full-time employment in period t into unemployment in period $t+1$, and zero otherwise.[7] The explanatory variables are identical to those in Eq. (1), except that we add age and, in a separate regression, replace the linear measure of employment duration (tenure) by several dummies for relevant groups of employment duration in order to limit potential collinearity between the temp contract indicator and employment duration. Given the binary nature of the dependent variable the model is estimated using probit techniques.[8] Since a fixed effects estimation of the unemployment risk equation would require dropping a large number of observations, we revert to random effects estimations. It is assumed that the individual specific effect d_i is uncorrelated with the other independent variables.

4 Results

This section discusses the results of our econometric estimations. We first discuss the impact of offshoring on wages and then the impact on the probability to become unemployed.

4.1 Wage effects

The results of the wage regressions are shown in Table 4. The coefficients on the control variables have generally the expected signs but are mostly statistically insignificant. This is not too surprising as the equation includes individual fixed effects and, hence, only exploits the within variation in the data.

The full sample regression (column 1 in Table 4) shows that there is no statistically significant relationship between offshoring and wages. The interaction of offshoring with the dummy for temporary contracts is also not statistically significant.

In columns 2, 3, and 4, we split the sample by educational attainment in order to obtain within-group estimates. Column 2 shows the result for the sample of low-skilled workers, i.e. unqualified workers without vocational or tertiary education (ISCED 1 and 2). Column 3 shows results for medium-skilled workers with vocational education and Abitur (A-levels; ISCED 3 and 4), and column 4 for high-skilled workers with tertiary education (ISCED 5 and 6). Distinguishing the effects by educational attainment may be important as the coefficients for holding a temporary contract may mask an education effect in the full sample as less-skilled workers are more likely to hold temp contracts (32 % among low-skilled versus 10 and 6 % among medium- and high-skilled, respectively).

However, we still do not find any strong statistically significant effects in the estimations. The coefficients on the offshoring variable return a negative coefficient

[7] There are, of course, also other possibilities of employment exits in our data, e.g. workers may move into maternity leave, non-participation or new jobs. These options are not considered here. Moves into maternity leave or non-participation are set to missing (right-censored) while moves into new jobs are considered as stayers.

[8] This approach is similar to Geishecker (2008) and Bachmann and Braun (2011) who, however, only consider the period 1991–2000. Also, they do not distinguish temporary and permanent work arrangements.

Table 4 Fixed effects regression on log hourly wage, 1999–2007

	(1) Total	(2) Low-skilled	(3) Medium-skilled	(4) High-skilled
Offshoring	0.00909	−0.0128	0.00889	0.0130
	(0.0104)	(0.0196)	(0.0121)	(0.0266)
Temp contract	0.00166	−0.143	0.0141	−0.0381
	(0.0477)	(0.106)	(0.0531)	(0.0920)
Offshoring × Temp.	−0.0157	0.0349	−0.0206*	−0.00648
	(0.0100)	(0.0234)	(0.0113)	(0.0158)
Educational attainment				
Medium-skilled	−0.00321			
	(0.0237)			
High-skilled	0.0728			
	(0.0446)			
Married	0.0303	0.0793	−0.0341	0.117***
	(0.0316)	(0.0625)	(0.0362)	(0.0350)
Employment duration	−0.00118	0.00685	0.000142	−0.00548
	(0.00253)	(0.00796)	(0.00315)	(0.00444)
Public employer	0.0459	0.121	0.0217	−0.168**
	(0.0417)	(0.0860)	(0.0290)	(0.0655)
Firm size				
20–199 employees	0.0169	−0.0319	0.0188	−0.0128
	(0.0408)	(0.0793)	(0.0495)	(0.0616)
200–1999 employees	0.0724	0.00768	0.0979*	−0.00984
	(0.0447)	(0.0831)	(0.0576)	(0.0683)
>2000 employees	0.0681	−0.00735	0.130**	−0.0307
	(0.0490)	(0.0899)	(0.0567)	(0.0807)
Work experience	0.113***	0.122***	0.0710*	0.207***
	(0.0263)	(0.0379)	(0.0419)	(0.0549)
Work experience^2	−0.000454***	−0.000298	−0.000255**	−0.00102**
	(0.000122)	(0.000183)	(0.000127)	(0.000416)
Industry output	1.94e−07	4.59e−07	3.46e−07	−3.63e−07
	(2.45e−07)	(5.61e−07)	(3.53e−07)	(5.09e−07)
R&D expenditure	4.16e−06	−9.58e−06	−8.20e−06	2.52e−05
	(1.30e−05)	(3.02e−05)	(2.00e−05)	(1.97e−05)
Average fixed effect	0.717	0.262	1.365*	0.329
	(0.452)	(0.732)	(0.707)	(0.866)
No. of observations	6074	1012	3547	1515
No. of groups	1515	295	962	416
R^2 within	0.116	0.190	0.0921	0.202

All specifications include industry and year dummies. Offshoring (narrow) is measured by the share of imported value-added from the same industry abroad. Robust standard errors in parentheses

* $p < 0.10$; ** $p < 0.05$; *** $p < 0.01$

for low-skilled and positive coefficients for medium- and high-skilled workers, though these are statistically insignificant at standard levels of confidence. Still, these coefficients are in line with Geishecker and Görg (2008) and suggest that low-skilled workers tend to lose from offshoring, while high and medium skilled workers are more likely to gain in terms of wages. The interactions of offshoring and temporary contracts are also statistically significant, though the signs suggest that the negative effect for low-skilled and positive for high- and medium-skilled are somewhat dampened for temporary workers.

Overall, our results suggest that there is no strong evidence for systematic differences between temporary and permanent workers with respect to the effects of offshoring on wages. Given that we only observe workers who *remain* in manufacturing after any effects of offshoring played out, these results may not be too surprising as the remaining workers are likely to be more productive than workers who drop out of manufacturing employment (Autor et al. 2013). In order to gain more insights on the relationship between offshoring and employment, we now turn to look at effects on the extensive margin.

4.2 Unemployment risk

This section reports results for the estimations of the risk to become unemployed. A priori, it is not clear what to expect. On the one hand, it is likely that workers holding temporary contracts are the first to be shed when firms adjust to offshoring on the extensive margin. After all, their contracts have a natural termination date, employment protection is weaker, and the workers have probably built up less firm-specific human capital. On the other hand, offshoring may make firms more productive, leading to increased production and, thus, a higher demand for labour. This may play out to the benefit of workers with temporary contracts whose contracts may be extended or converted into permanent ones.

We estimate the model of unemployment risk in Eq. (2) using a random-effects probit regression. As this is a non-linear estimator, interaction terms are inherently difficult to interpret. Hence, we report here the marginal effects of offshoring for workers with temporary and permanent contracts (Table 5) while the full regression results are relegated to "Appendix 4". In the estimations presented in Table 8 in "Appendix 4",

Table 5 Marginal effects after random effects probit estimation, regression coefficient in Table 9 in "Appendix 4"

Contract type	(1) Total	(2) Low-skilled	(3) Medium-skilled	(4) High-skilled
Permanent	−0.00276***	0.000696***	−0.00365***	−0.0147***
	(0.0000466)	(0.000125)	(0.0000650)	(0.000195)
Temporary	−0.00284***	0.00124***	−0.00322***	−0.0305***
	(0.000129)	(0.000115)	(0.000234)	(0.000658)
N	7534	1008	4314	1473

Average marginal effects, standard errors in parentheses

*** $p < 0.01$

duration dependence is modeled through the variable "employment duration", which is a continuous variable including the years of current tenure with the employer. In Table 9 in "Appendix 4", we use a more flexible modeling approach where we define dummy variables for different stages of employment duration. The definition of these dummies follows Geishecker (2008). The regression results are very similar. The marginal effects presented in Table 5 are based on the regressions in Table 9.

The full sample regression in column (1) shows that offshoring is negatively associated with the probability of job loss for permanent contracts, i.e. the risk to become unemployed in the next period is reduced as the share of imported value added rises. This is in line with an earlier study by Bachmann and Braun (2011) who, however, use different data and another time period. Workers with a temporary contract also face a lower risk to become unemployed as offshoring rises, and the effect appears to be of a similar magnitude as that for permanent workers. The finding of a lower unemployment risk is in line with the following argument: As offshoring makes firms more productive (see e.g. Grossman and Rossi-Hansberg 2008), labour demand increases and existing workers may keep their jobs, despite potential pressure from abroad. However, the aggregate picture hides some important heterogeneity between education groups.

In the group of low-skilled workers (column 2), an increase in offshoring is associated with an increase in the unemployment risk for both types of workers. The effect appears much stronger for workers holding a temporary contract, however. For those workers, a 1 percentage point increase in offshoring is associated with a 0.12 % increase in the unemployment risk. Given that our offshoring measure rose by 1.2 percentage point over our sample period (1999 and 2007), the implied effect is that the unemployment risk for low-skilled temporary workers would have been 0.148 % lower in the absence of offshoring.[9] Hence, low-skilled workers, especially those with temporary contract, may be more likely to be driven into unemployment as offshoring increases.

In the groups of medium-skilled and high-skilled workers, offshoring is associated with a *decrease* in the unemployment risk for both permanent and temporary contracts. For medium-skilled workers there appears to be no difference between temporary and permanent workers. However, for high-skilled workers the marginal effect is significantly higher for workers with temporary contracts compared to their peers on permanent contracts. The marginal effect suggests that the rise in offshoring over our sample period reduced the risk of unemployment by 3.66 % for high-skilled workers on temporary contracts.[10] Hence, offshoring may, through reallocation of activities lead to more employment opportunities for high-skilled workers and in particular benefit workers on temporary contracts.

[9] Calculated as the rise in offshoring (1.2 %) multiplied with the marginal effect for low-skilled temporary workers (0.00124). The average overall risk of being unemployed in period $t + 1$ was 3.46 % for low-skilled workers.

[10] The average overall risk of being unemployed in period $t + 1$ is 0.96 % for high-skilled workers.

5 Conclusions

In our empirical analysis based on individual level data for Germany, we do not find systematic differences between temporary and permanent workers with respect to the effects of offshoring for wages. In other words, the contract type does not appear to matter for wage effects of offshoring. We also find that, on the one hand, offshoring is associated with an *increase* in the unemployment risk for all low-skilled workers, and more so for those with temporary contracts than for permanent workers. On the other hand, offshoring is associated with a *decrease* in the unemployment risk for high-skilled workers with both temporary and permanent contracts, as well as for all medium-skilled workers.

The results for offshoring effects on unemployment risk fit well into the literature. Autor et al. (2013) argue that only the most productive workers remain in a firm while the less productive leave. If low-skilled workers may be considered less productive than high-skilled workers, this is in line with our finding of different effects on unemployment risk of for these two skill groups. We add to the literature by also estimating different effects for workers with temporary and permanent contracts, however.

Our findings provide some evidence for the policy debate on whether globalization and employment insecurity are linked (cf. Rodrik 1998; Scheve and Slaughter 2004) by investigating whether the nature of employment contracts matters. While a full answer to this issue would clearly need further research, we take our paper as providing a first step in this direction.

Acknowledgments The authors are very grateful to an anonymous referee, Bernhard Boockmann, and conference participants at the ILRR Conference on job quality at Cornell University and the Aarhus-Kiel Workshop for very helpful comments on an earlier draft. Thanks are also due to Tillmann Schwörer for help with the WIOD data. Fares Al-Hussami provided excellent research assistance. The authors gratefully acknowledge financial support through the European Commission as part of the 7th Framework Programme, Grant Agreement No. 244 552 (SERVICEGAP). Financial support from the Fritz-Thyssen Stiftung is gratefully acknowledged.

Appendix 1: List of manufacturing industries contained in the WIOD

No.	NACE	Description
1	15–16	Food, beverages and tobacco
2	17–18	Textiles and textile products
	19	Leather, leather and footwear
3	20	Wood and products of wood and cork
4	21–22	Pulp, paper, paper, printing and publishing
5	23	Coke, refined petroleum and nuclear fuel
6	24	Chemicals and chemical products
7	25	Rubber and plastics
8	26	Other non-metallic mineral

No.	NACE	Description
9	27–28	Basic metals and fabricated metal
10	29	Machinery, nec
11	30–33	Electrical and optical equipment
12	34–35	Transport equipment
13	36–37	Manufacturing, nec; recycling

Textiles (17–18) and leather (19) had to be combined for calculation of imported value added

Appendix 2: Derivation of offshoring measure: share of imported value added

Our indicator for offshoring should describe the value of imported value added, i.e. value added purchased abroad, relative to the total value of industry's production. The difference between one and the indicator's value should thus be the share of value which is added domestically. The indicator should also account for the cases in which imported intermediate goods (e.g. German motor imports from the Czech Republic) contain parts which were previously produced domestically (e.g. the crankshaft produced in Germany). These parts should be classified as domestic and not as foreign value added.

The indicator is derived from the WIOD. The WIOD assumes that each industry ($s, r = 1, \ldots, S$) in each country ($i, j, k = 1, \ldots, L$) produces a single, homogenous good, which is different from the same industry's goods produced in other countries. Hence, there are *LS* different goods produced in the world.

The input–output tables of the WIOD consist of four components. (i) The intermediate inputs matrix, **W**, of dimension ($LS \times LS$), describes the values of bilateral trade in intermediate goods between all countries of the world. The element in row *is* and column *jr* describes the value of intermediate goods which industry *r* in country *j* purchases from industry *s* in country *i*. (ii) The final use matrix, **C**, of dimension ($LS \times L$), describes the value of all *LS* goods sold to final users (private households, investors, the government, and changes in inventories) in all *L* countries. (iii) The vector $\mathbf{y}$ of dimension ($1 \times LS$) describes the value added input of each industry, and (iv) the ($1 \times LS$) vector of total production, **p**, describes the total output of each industry.

An industry's total production (**p**) can be formally described as

$$p_{is} = \sum_{j=1}^{L} \sum_{r=1}^{S} w_{is,jr} + \sum_{j=1}^{L} c_{is,j}, \tag{3}$$

where p_{is} is the sum of a product's intermediate use and final use. Note that a matrix' cell is denoted by a small letter here. Alternatively, total production can be written as

$$p_{is} = \sum_{j=1}^{L}\sum_{r=1}^{S} w_{jr,is} + y_{is}, \tag{4}$$

where p_{is} is the sum of intermediate inputs and the industry's value added.

Equations (3) and (4) can be combined using matrix notation:

$$\mathbf{p} = \mathbf{Ap} + \mathbf{CI_L} \tag{5}$$

$$= \mathbf{W}'\mathbf{I_{LS}} + \mathbf{y}. \tag{6}$$

where $\mathbf{p} = (p_{11}, \ldots, p_{1S}, p_{21}, \ldots, p_{2s}, \ldots, p_{L1}, \ldots, p_{LS})$ is the $(LS \times 1)$ vector of all production values and $\mathbf{y} = (y_{11}, \ldots, y_{1S}, y_{21}, \ldots, y_{2s}, \ldots, y_{L1}, \ldots, y_{LS})$ is the $(LS \times 1)$ vector of value added in all industries. In Eq. (5), matrix $\mathbf{C}$ is multiplied by the identity vector $\mathbf{I_L}$ in order to aggregate across all countries that consume the respective good. The $(LS \times LS)$ matrix of input coefficients, $\mathbf{A}$, is constructed by dividing each element of the $\mathbf{W}$ matrix along the vertical by the total output of that industry:

$$A = \mathbf{W} \times \mathrm{diag}(\mathbf{p}^{-1}), \tag{7}$$

Its elements $a_{is,jr} = w_{is,jr}/p_{jr}$ denote how many cents industry r in country j purchases from country i in order to produce one unit of output.

Matrix $\mathbf{A}$ contains input coefficients for a representative step in production. However, the production of many goods requires more than one production step, so that we have attribute the value added contributions of all intermediate inputs to their countries of origin as well. Ultimately, we would like to derive how many cents of value added each industry in each country contributes to one dollar of each final good. To that end, Eqs. (3) and (4) are rewritten so that the relationships between output and final use, and between output and value added can be used to derive a direct relationship between final use and value added:

$$\mathbf{p} = (\mathbf{I_{LS}} - \mathbf{A})^{-1} \times \mathbf{C} \times \mathbf{I_L}, \tag{8}$$

$$\mathbf{y} = [\mathrm{diag}(\mathbf{I_{LS}} - \mathbf{A}' \times \mathbf{I_L})] \times \mathbf{p}, \tag{9}$$

$$\mathbf{y} = \mathbf{V} \times \mathbf{p}, \tag{10}$$

where $\mathbf{V} = \mathrm{diag}(\mathbf{I_{LS}} - \mathbf{A}' \times \mathbf{I_{LS}})$.

Equation (8) describes the relationship between final use and output. Matrix $\mathbf{B} = (\mathbf{I_{LS}} - \mathbf{A})^{-1}$ is the Leontief inverse; its elements $b_{is,jr}$ describe by how much of the output of industry s in country i contributes to each dollar of the final good of industry r from country j.

Equation (9), which is presented in a simplified way in Eq. (10), describes the relationship between value added and output. The diagonal elements of the $(LS \times LS)$ matrix $\mathbf{V}$, $v_{ir} = y_{ir}/p_{ir}$, denote the fraction of value added in total output of industry jr.[11] Substituting Eq. (8) into Eq. (10) results in:

[11] In Eq. (9), this is expresses as 1 minus the share of intermediates in total output. It can be shown that $\mathbf{W}'\mathbf{I_{LS}} = \mathrm{diag}(\mathbf{A}'\ \mathbf{I_{LS}})\mathbf{p}$.

$$\mathbf{y} = [\mathbf{V} \times (\mathbf{I}_{\mathbf{LS}} - \mathbf{A})^{-1}] \times \mathbf{C} \times \mathbf{I}_{\mathbf{L}}, \tag{11}$$

$$\mathbf{y} = \mathbf{M} \times \mathbf{C} \times \mathbf{I}_{\mathbf{L}}, \tag{12}$$

Matrix $\mathbf{M} = \mathbf{V} \times (\mathbf{I}_{\mathrm{LS}} - \mathbf{A})^{-1}$ contains all the information needed for the estimations. It describes the contribution of value added by all industries in all countries to one dollar of final good production. Its elements $m_{is,jr}$ denote how many cents industry *is* contributes to each dollar of the final good produced by industry *jr*.

For our estimations, we calculate a measure of narrow offshoring, *OFF*, for each German industry, i.e. the share of value added in industry production, which is imported from the same industry in all other countries. Specifically, we sum over the relevant elements of **M**:

$$OFF = \sum_{i \neq j} m_{is,js},$$

where s is the respective industry, i is the country where the imported value added stems from, and j denotes Germany.

Appendix 3: Variable definitions and summary statistics

The econometric analysis is based on the German Socio-Economic Panel (SOEP), waves 1999–2007. We use all SOEP samples for the analysis. Yearly industry level information about trade and offshoring is merged with the SOEP on basis of industry classification provided in the SOEP (NACE 1.1). Variables are defined as follows (SOEP variable names are mentioned in parentheses).

See Tables 6 and 7.

Table 6 Variable definitions

Variable	SOEP variable and modifications
Log hourly wage	The log hourly wage is calculated using two variables from the SOEP Cross-national equivalent file: annual individual labour earnings (i11110$$) and annual work hours of the individual (e11101$$)
	Annual labour earnings include wages and salary from all employment including training, primary and secondary jobs, and self-employment, plus income from bonuses, overtime, and profit-sharing
	Annual work hours are constructed using information on employment status in the survey year, average number of hours worked per week, and the number of months worked (see Grabka 2011, p. 24 for details)
	Imputed incomes and hours are *not* used
Job loss	Dummy for job loss is set to 1 in period t if person is unemployed in t (LFS$) and was working full time in $t-1$ (EMPLST$). For unemployed persons, no industry information is provided in period t. We replace the missing value in t by the values in $t-1$
Female	Dummy = 1 if person is female
Age	Age at time of survey

Table 6 continued

Variable	SOEP variable and modifications
Married	Dummy = 1 if person is married ($FAMSTD)
Employment duration (1)	Number of years with employer ($ERWZEIT)
Employment duration (2)	Derived from employment biography 1. 1–6 months 2. 6–12 months 3. 13–36 months 4. 37–96 months 5. more than 96 months
Public ownership	Dummy = 1 if employer is public service (OEFFD$)
	(Continued on next page)
Variable	SOEP variable and modifications
Firm size	Firm size categories (ALLBET$) 1. Less than 20 employees (omitted category) 2. Greater/equal 20 and less than 200 employees 3. Greater/equal 200 and less than 2000 employees 4. Greater/equal 2000 employees
Education	Highest educational level obtained (ISCED$) 1. Unqualified labour, up to secondary education (ISCED 1 and 2) 2. Skilled labour, apprenticeship, vocational education (ISCED 3 and 4) 3. High-skilled labour, tertiary education (ISCED 5 and 6)
Experience	Years of work experience; 1 year of full-time work (EXPFT$) counts as 1 year, 1 year of part-time work (EXPPT$) counts as 0.5 year.
East Germany	Dummy for Eastern federal state (BULA$)
Industry production	Taken from WIOD supply and use tables. See discussion of offshoring measures
R&D expenditure	Taken from the Analytical Business Enterprise Research and Development (ANBERD) database provided by the OECD. Series runs until 2008. Values for 2009 are extrapolated

Table 7 Summary statistics

Variable	Obs.	Mean	SD	Min	Max
Real hourly wage	6074	17.858	6.504	1.514	37.603
Job loss between t and $t+1$	6074	0.0201		0	1
Educational attainment					
Low-skilled	6074	0.167		0	1
Medium-skilled	6074	0.584		0	1
High-skilled	6074	0.249		0	1
Age	6074	40.848	9.644	18	64
Married	6074	0.743		0	1
Employment duration	6074	12.092	9.545	0	46.4

Table 7 continued

Variable	Obs.	Mean	SD	Min	Max
Employment duration (months)					
1–6	6074	0.044		0	1
7–12	6074	0.037		0	1
13–36	6074	0.114		0	1
37–96	6074	0.229		0	1
>96	6074	0.576		0	1
Public employer	6074	0.0092		0	1
Firm size (employees)					
<20	6074	0.105		0	1
20–199	6074	0.269		0	1
200–1999	6074	0.325		0	1
>2000	6074	0.301		0	1
Work experience	6074	18.935	10.301	0	48
Work experience^2	6074	464.642	437.556	0	2304
Industry output	6074	177886.5	90995.5	3260.3	480661.7
R&D expenditure	6074	4547.48	4754.93	3.4	15609.9

Full sample used in wage regressions

Appendix 4: Results of the random effects probit models

See Tables 8 and 9.

Table 8 Random effects probit regression on dummy for unemployment in next period, 1999–2007, linear measure for employment duration

	(1) Total[a]	(2) Low-skilled[b]	(3) Medium-skilled[c]	(4) High-skilled[d]
Offshoring	−0.118***	0.0800***	−0.140***	−0.656***
	(0.00186)	(0.00988)	(0.00226)	(0.00824)
Temp contract	0.393***	−0.501***	0.475***	−0.220***
	(0.00479)	(0.0271)	(0.00629)	(0.0136)
Offshoring × Temp.	0.0665***	0.0453***	0.0995***	0.229***
	(0.000963)	(0.00593)	(0.00124)	(0.00296)
Educational attainment				
Medium-skilled	−0.113***			
	(0.00197)			
High-skilled	−0.665***			
	(0.00277)			
Age	0.0355***	−0.0130***	0.0532***	0.0313***
	(0.000211)	(0.00127)	(0.000267)	(0.000532)

Table 8 continued

	(1) Total[a]	(2) Low-skilled[b]	(3) Medium-skilled[c]	(4) High-skilled[d]
Married	−0.135***	1.478***	−0.395***	0.187***
	(0.00181)	(0.0161)	(0.00238)	(0.00583)
Employment duration	−0.00812***	−0.00815***	−0.00125***	−0.0446***
	(0.0000927)	(0.000521)	(0.000119)	(0.000256)
Public employer	−0.0550***		−0.323***	
	(0.00753)		(0.00842)	
Firm size (employees)				
20–199	−0.00276	0.204***	0.0186***	0.191***
	(0.00231)	(0.0132)	(0.00290)	(0.00600)
200–1999	−0.185***	−0.0624***	−0.217***	0.180***
	(0.00242)	(0.0129)	(0.00305)	(0.00639)
>2000	−0.333***	−1.169***	−0.150***	−0.302***
	(0.00275)	(0.0154)	(0.00331)	(0.00738)
Work experience	−0.0559***	−0.302***	−0.0458***	0.00775***
	(0.000330)	(0.00308)	(0.000407)	(0.000953)
Work experience^2	0.000942***	0.00656***	0.000389***	2.10e−06
	(5.52e−06)	(6.04e−05)	(6.85e−06)	(1.78e−05)
Industry output	1.24e−06***	−9.07e−06***	4.04e−06***	−1.34e−06***
	(4.86e−08)	(2.68e−07)	(5.99e−08)	(1.96e−07)
R&D expenditure	−6.67e−06**	0.000568***	−0.000186***	0.000110***
	(2.94e−06)	(1.66e−05)	(3.72e−06)	(1.02e−05)
Constant	−2.967***	0.451***	−3.999***	−3.341***
	(0.0175)	(0.0447)	(0.0207)	(0.0306)
No. of observations	7534	1008	4314	1473
No. of groups	1796	309	1156	384
Log likelihood	−2541379.3	−399688.3	−1656374.0	−295365.9

All specifications include industry and year dummies. Offshoring (narrow) is measured by the share of imported value added from the same industry abroad. Standard errors in parentheses

** $p < 0.05$; *** $p < 0.01$

[a] Industries NACE 19 and 23 are excluded as they predict failure perfectly (16 and 15 obs.)

[b] Public employer is excluded as it predicts failure perfectly (18 obs.). Industry NACE 20 is excluded as it predicts failure perfectly (17 obs.). Year 2000 is excluded as it predicts failure perfectly (168 obs.)

[c] Industries NACE 19 and 23 are excluded as they predict failure perfectly (14 and 14 obs.)

[d] Public employer is excluded as it predicts failure perfectly (2 obs.). Industries NACE 19, 20, 21, 23, 25, 26, 34, and 36 are excluded as they predict failure perfectly (2, 5, 99, 1, 32, 43, 334, and 13 obs.)

Table 9 Random effects probit regression on dummy for unemployment in next period, 1999–2007, dummies for groups of employment duration

	(1) Total[a]	(2) Low-skilled[b]	(3) Medium-skilled[c]	(4) High-skilled[d]
Offshoring	−0.109***	0.0720***	−0.125***	−0.687***
	(0.00180)	(0.0129)	(0.00217)	(0.00884)
Temp contract	0.246***	−0.599***	0.299***	−0.278***
	(0.00469)	(0.0393)	(0.00602)	(0.0146)
Offshoring × Temp.	0.0667***	0.0944***	0.0921***	0.220***
	(0.000924)	(0.00856)	(0.00117)	(0.00310)
Educational attainment				
Medium-skilled	−0.0991***			
	(0.00185)			
High-skilled	−0.647***			
	(0.00260)			
Age	0.0352***	−0.0270***	0.0512***	0.0422***
	(0.000201)	(0.00181)	(0.000249)	(0.000535)
Married	−0.138***	1.899***	−0.371***	0.109***
	(0.00170)	(0.0218)	(0.00218)	(0.00596)
Employment duration (months)				
7–12	0.333***	1.708***	0.357***	0.188***
	(0.00350)	(0.0247)	(0.00449)	(0.00904)
13–36	0.0976***	0.604***	0.0813***	0.108***
	(0.00320)	(0.0224)	(0.00404)	(0.00702)
37–96	−0.169***	1.613***	−0.227***	−0.252***
	(0.00323)	(0.0284)	(0.00413)	(0.00661)
>96	−0.388***	0.737***	−0.358***	−0.714***
	(0.00326)	(0.0283)	(0.00412)	(0.00684)
Public employer	−0.0494***		−0.315***	
	(0.00717)		(0.00795)	
Firm size (employees)				
20–199	0.00443**	0.625***	0.0294***	0.202***
	(0.00220)	(0.0190)	(0.00271)	(0.00609)
200–1999	−0.137***	0.192***	−0.168***	0.197***
	(0.00231)	(0.0174)	(0.00287)	(0.00648)
>2000	−0.260***	−1.365***	−0.0728***	−0.397***
	(0.00257)	(0.0203)	(0.00307)	(0.00744)
Work experience	−0.0412***	−0.419***	−0.0308***	0.00572***
	(0.000314)	(0.00439)	(0.000383)	(0.000939)
Work experience^2	0.000673***	0.00938***	0.000191***	−0.000286***
	(5.20e−06)	(8.42e−05)	(6.38e−06)	(1.74e−05)
Industry output	1.46e−06***	−1.44e−05***	4.01e−06***	−3.50e−06***
	(4.71e−08)	(3.48e−07)	(5.76e−08)	(1.94e−07)

Table 9 continued

	(1) Total[a]	(2) Low-skilled[b]	(3) Medium-skilled[c]	(4) High-skilled[d]
R&D expenditure	−7.01e−06**	0.000832***	−0.000174***	0.000131***
	(2.86e−06)	(2.12e−05)	(3.59e−06)	(1.02e−05)
Constant	−2.943***	−0.287***	−3.802***	−3.335***
	(0.0169)	(0.0641)	(0.0199)	(0.0305)
No. of observations	7534	1008	4314	1473
No. of groups	1796	309	1156	384
Log likelihood	−2511469.9	−393186.6	−1636256.6	−299265.1

All specifications include industry and year dummies. Offshoring (narrow) is measured by the share of imported value added from the same industry abroad. Standard errors in parentheses

** $p < 0.05$; *** $p < 0.01$

[a] Industries NACE 19 and 23 are excluded as they predict failure perfectly (16 and 15 obs.)

[b] Public employer is excluded as it predicts failure perfectly (18 obs.). Industry NACE 20 is excluded as it predicts failure perfectly (17 obs.). Year 2000 is excluded as it predicts failure perfectly (168 obs.)

[c] Industries NACE 19 and 23 are excluded as they predict failure perfectly (14 and 14 obs.)

[d] Public employer is excluded as it predicts failure perfectly (2 obs.). Industries NACE 19, 20, 21, 23, 25, 26, 34, and 36 are excluded as they predict failure perfectly (2, 5, 99, 1, 32, 43, 334, and 13 obs.)

References

Autor, D. H., Dorn, D., & Hanson, G. H. (2013). The China syndrome: Local labor market effects of import competition in the United States. *American Economic Review, 103*(6), 2121–2168.

Bachmann, R., & Braun, S. (2011). The impact of international outsourcing on labour market dynamics in Germany. *Scottish Journal of Political Economy, 58*(1), 1–28.

Baumgarten, D., Geishecker, I., & Görg, H. (2013). Offshoring, tasks, and the skill-wage pattern. *European Economic Review, 61*(C), 132–152.

Blanchard, O., & Landier, A. (2002). The perverse effects of partial labour market reform: Fixed-term contracts in France. *Economic Journal, 112*(480), F214–F244.

Boeri, T., & Garibaldi, P. (2007). Two tier reforms of employment protection: A honeymoon effect? *Economic Journal, 117*(521), F357–F385.

Booth, A. L., Dolado, J. J., & Frank, J. (2002a). Symposium on temporary work: Introduction. *Economic Journal, 112*(480), F181–F188.

Booth, A. L., Francesconi, M., & Frank, J. (2002b). Temporary jobs: Stepping stones or dead ends? *Economic Journal, 112*(480), F189–F213.

Cahuc, P., & Postel-Vinay, F. (2002). Temporary jobs, employment protection and labor market performance. *Labour Economics, 9*(1), 63–91.

Daudin, G., Rifflart, C., & Schweisguth, D. (2011). Who produces for whom in the world economy? *Canadian Journal of Economics/Revue canadienne d'économique, 44*(4), 1403–1437.

Ebenstein, A., Harrison, A., McMillan, M., & Phillips, S. (2014). Estimating the impact of trade and offshoring on American workers using the current population survey. *Review of Economics and Statistics, 96*(4), 581–595.

Feenstra, R. C., & Hanson, G. H. (1999). The impact of outsourcing and high-technology capital on wages: Estimates for the United States, 1979–1990. *Quarterly Journal of Economics, 114*(3), 907–941.

Foster-McGregor, N., Stehrer, R., & de Vries, G. J. (2013). Offshoring and the skill structure of labour demand. *Review of World Economics/Weltwirtschaftliches Archiv, 149*(4), 631–662.

Frick, J. R., Jenkins, S. P., Lillard, D. R., Lipps, O., & Wooden, M. (2007). The cross-national equivalent file (CNEF) and its member country household panel studies. *Schmollers Jahrbuch, 127*(4), 626–654.

Geishecker, I. (2008). The impact of international outsourcing on individual employment security: A micro-level analysis. *Labour Economics, 15*(3), 291–314.

Geishecker, I., & Görg, H. (2008). Winners and losers: A micro-level analysis of international outsourcing and wages. *Canadian Journal of Economics, 41*(1), 243–270.

Geishecker, I., & Görg, H. (2013). Services offshoring and wages: Evidence from micro data. *Oxford Economic Papers, 65*(1), 124–146.

Grabka, M. M. (2011). *Codebook for the $PEQUIV file* 1984–2010: *CNEF variables with extended income information for the SOEP*. Berlin: Deutsches Institut für Wirtschaftsforschung. http://www.diw.de/documents/publikationen/73/diw_01.c.377728.de/diw_datadoc_2011-057.pdf

Gramm, L., & Schnell, F. (2001). The Use of flexible staffing arrangements in core production jobs. *Industrial and Labor Relations Review, 54*(2), 245–258.

Grossman, G., & Rossi-Hansberg, E. (2008). Trading tasks: A simple theory of offshoring. *American Economic Review, 98*(5), 1978–1997.

Holmlund, B., & Storrie, D. (2002). Temporary work in turbulent times: The Swedish experience. *The Economic Journal, 112*(480), F245–F269.

Hummels, D., Ishii, J., & Yi, K. (2001). The nature and growth of vertical specialization in world trade. *Journal of International Economics, 54*(1), 75–96.

Johnson, R. C., & Noguera, G. (2012). Accounting for intermediates: Production sharing and trade in value added. *Journal of International Economics, 86*(2), 224–236.

Koopman, R., Wang, Z., & Wei, S.-J. (2014). Tracing value-added and double counting in gross exports. *American Economic Review, 104*(2), 459–494.

Liu, R., & Trefler, D. (2008). *Much Ado About Nothing: American jobs and the rise of service outsourcing to China and India* (NBER Working Paper 14061).

Pfaffermayr, M., Egger, P., & Weber, A. (2007). Sectoral adjustment of employment to shifts in outsourcing and trade: Evidence from a dynamic fixed effects multinomial logit model. *Journal of Applied Econometrics, 22*(3), 559–580.

Rodrik, D. (1998). Has globalization gone too far? *Challenge, 41*(2), 81–94.

Scheve, K., & Slaughter, M. J. (2004). Economic insecurity and the globalization of production. *American Journal of Political Science, 48*(4), 662–674.

Timmer, M. (2012). *The world input-output database (WIOD): Contents, sources and methods* (WIOD Working Paper 10).

Wagner, G., Frick, J. R., & Schupp, J. (2007). The German Socio-Economic Panel study (SOEP)—scope, evolution and enhancements. *Schmollers Jahrbuch, 127*(1), 139–169.

Yi, K. M. (2003). Can vertical specialization explain the growth of world trade? *Journal of Political Economy, 111*(1), 52–102.

Chapter 6

Offshoring, Tasks, and the Skill-Wage Pattern

Daniel Baumgarten[a,*], Ingo Geishecker[b,1], Holger Görg[c,1]

[a] *Rheinisch-Westfälisches Institut für Wirtschaftsforschung (RWI), Berlin Office, Hessische Str. 10, D-10115 Berlin, Germany*
[b] *European University Viadrina — Frankfurt (Oder), Germany*
[c] *Kiel Institute for the World Economy and Christian-Albrechts-University of Kiel, Germany and CEPR, UK*

Received 27 April 2011
Accepted 27 March 2013
Available online 6 April 2013

The paper investigates the relationship between offshoring, wages, and the occupational task profile using rich individual-level panel data. Our main results suggest that, when only considering within-industry changes in offshoring, we identify a moderate wage reduction due to offshoring for low-skilled workers, though wage effects in relation to the task profile of occupations are not estimated with sufficient precision. However, when allowing for cross-industry effects of offshoring, i.e. allowing for labor mobility across industries, negative wage effects of offshoring are quite substantial and depend strongly on the task profile of workers' occupations. A higher degree of interactivity and, in particular, non-routine content effectively shields workers against the negative wage impact of offshoring.

Keywords: Tasks, Offshoring, Outsourcing, Skills, Wages

JEL classification: F1, F2, J3

*Corresponding author. Tel.: +49 30 202159811; fax: +49 30 202159819.
E-mail address: daniel.baumgarten@rwi-essen.de (D. Baumgarten).
[1] Tuborg Research Centre for Globalisation and Firms at Aarhus University.

http://dx.doi.org/10.1016/j.euroecorev.2013.03.007

1. Introduction

Research on job tasks has become increasingly popular in recent years. This is reflected in the labor economics literature by, for example, Autor *et al.* (2003), Spitz-Oener (2006), and Gathmann and Schönberg (2010). In the international trade literature, the concept of tasks has also entered into the debate on international outsourcing or offshoring. For example, Blinder (2006) argues that certain tasks that are interactive, i.e., require face-to-face contact are unlikely to be offshored (e.g., hairdressers, lawyers) while tasks without these characteristics may easily be moved abroad irrespective of their skill requirements (e.g., computer programmers). Levy and Murnane (2004) and Leamer and Storper (2001) also highlight the differences between what may be called routine and non-routine tasks, with the latter being less likely to be moved abroad.

What is clear from the earlier literature and also from the empirical work presented in this paper is that "tasks" are not synonymous with "skills". While there may be some overlap, non-routine or more interactive tasks (which according to the literature should make jobs less offshorable) are not necessarily identical with higher educational attainment. Blinder and Krueger (forthcoming), for example, find that the proportion of "offshorable jobs" appears to be higher among workers with a college degree compared to those without. But all educational groups show significant percentages of jobs that may be offshorable. Jensen and Kletzer (2010) come to a similar conclusion — there is a positive correlation between skills and tasks (that define offshorability), but this is far from perfect. By contrast, Blinder (2006) finds no clear correlation between skills and "offshorability". Our data description also shows substantial heterogeneity between skills and tasks, although there is a tendency that high-skilled workers are more likely to hold jobs that use tasks that are less offshorable.

Traditionally, the literature has concluded that offshoring from newly industrialized countries has led to a shift in labor demand towards more skilled workers, implying that unskilled workers lose while skilled workers gain from this form of globalization (e.g., Feenstra and Hanson, 2001; Biscourp and Kramarz, 2007). However, when considering tasks as well as skills, the conclusions may be more subtle. This is what we investigate in this paper.

By using rich individual-level panel data, we are able to measure in detail wages, skills, and occupations of individuals. Importantly, we are able to construct various measures of the task content of occupations which we can link to the individual data via the occupational code. The individual-level data is combined with data on offshoring activities at the level of the industry.[2] The use of individual-level data allows us also to control in our empirical analysis for a host of observable and unobservable characteristics at the individual level avoiding aggregation and selection bias.

We use these data to model empirically the impact of offshoring on wages and focus on how offshoring affects individuals with particular skill levels and task characteristics differently. More specifically, we study the interaction between skill levels and tasks and investigate whether within skill groups, the nature of tasks carried out by an individual matters for the effect of offshoring on wages. Our working hypothesis is that, in the absence of a one-to-one relationship between tasks and skills, taking account of tasks as an aspect of individual heterogeneity matters. Our empirical results support this hypothesis.[3]

Why should task content matter in addition to skills? As we show below, tasks and skills are not synonymous concepts, hence allowing for task differences in the wage effect captures one additional aspect of individual heterogeneity. This is an important aspect in this context, as a number of papers have established that there is a strong correlation between tasks and offshorability — jobs or occupations with certain task profiles are more easily offshorable than others. With regards to our empirical analysis, we should reiterate Blinder and Krueger's (forthcoming) important point that "offshorability" is a different concept than offshoring. The first is a job or occupation characteristic, the second is the observable action of relocating production abroad. One difficulty when measuring offshoring is that data are fairly aggregate, that is, in general there is no direct information on the concrete skill requirement or task content of offshored

[2]We measure offshoring as imported intermediates, both from foreign subsidiaries and independent suppliers. This approach dates back to Feenstra and Hanson (1999). More recent applications are Liu and Trefler (2008) or Geishecker and Görg (2008).

[3]The model by Grossman and Rossi-Hansberg (2008) is frequently alluded to in discussions of tasks and offshoring. Another theoretical model focusing on offshoring and tasks is Kohler and Wrona (2010). While we recognize these papers, we do not test the models explicitly. The main reason for this is that in the models, offshoring costs are task-specific, while our data do not allow us to measure task-specific offshoring, or offshoring costs. Rather, as in Becker *et al.* (2013) and Hummels *et al.* (2011), we are able to measure the task content of occupations and see whether this matters, in conjunction with skills, for the link between offshoring and individual wages. Our analysis therefore relates particularly to the recent empirical work by Blinder and Krueger (forthcoming), who not only describe task content (i.e., offshorability) but also the implications of differences in tasks for labor market outcomes of individuals.

activities. However, when looking at aggregate offshoring activities, they may constitute a stronger threat for offshorable occupations than for non-offshorable occupations. Hence, actual measured aggregate offshoring may be expected to have larger negative wage effects on workers carrying out easily offshorable tasks.

Summarizing the literature on offshoring and tasks (as we do in Section 2), it is yet an open question whether there are indeed occupational task-specific offshoring effects that go beyond any already established education-related heterogeneity. The main contribution of the paper is to shed some light on this issue.

We use two strategies for identifying a link between offshoring and wages. The first is to use within-industry changes in offshoring intensity and wages. The assumption is that only offshoring activity in the same industry affects individual wages, while any wage effects that occur indirectly through offshoring in other industries are ruled out.[4] This is a very limiting assumption. In order to relax this, we propose a second identification strategy based on the idea that individual i's wage is determined not only by offshoring activity in the industry in which i is employed, but also by offshoring and associated demand effects in other industries. Specifically, the wages of i holding occupation k will depend on offshoring activities affecting occupation k in any industry. Take, for example, electrical engineers working in the automobile and machinery industries. Offshoring an engineer's tasks in automobiles affects not only engineers in this industry, but also in the machinery industry, as engineers may move from automobiles into machinery and vice versa.[5]

An important challenge in this literature (including our paper) is to isolate fully the effect of offshoring. This is not an easy task, as other unobserved variables may be confounding the effects and, hence, lead to endogeneity of the offshoring measure. One example would be reverse causality: offshoring decisions may be related to the wage level in the industry, with high-wage industries being more likely to offshore. To investigate and deal with the potential endogeneity of offshoring, we

[4]This essentially confines the analysis to the short run, assuming that labor is immobile between industries. This is a common assumption in the literature. It is, for example, implicit in the studies examining the relationship between relative labor demand and offshoring using aggregate industry-level data (Feenstra and Hanson, 2001). Studies using individual-level data such as Geishecker and Görg (2008) or Liu and Trefler (2008) are based on the same assumption.

[5]Note that actual movement of workers is not required to generate these cross-industry effects: the potential for movement is sufficient.

implement instrumental variables regressions, where we predict industry- or occupational-level offshoring in the first-stage regressions using various trade cost measures and world export supply as instruments. In the choice of instruments, we follow the recent paper by Hummels *et al.* (2011). We discuss and test for instrument relevance and validity, and we present tests of the hypothesis that our offshoring measures are exogenous in the individual-level wage regressions.

To further aid identification, we — depending on the identification strategy — also include industry or occupation fixed effects or even industry-specific time effects to capture unobserved time (in)variant industry or occupation characteristics that may be related to the offshoring decision. Furthermore, we also include a host of observable industry or occupation characteristics that may determine both wages and the offshoring decision.

Based on these identification strategies, we find pure industry-level offshoring to have a very moderate effect on wages. However, when allowing for cross-industry effects, our empirical results show that wage effects of offshoring are substantial and very heterogeneous within skill groups, strongly depending on the degree of interactivity or non-routine content of the respective tasks of workers. Thus, offshorability of tasks matters over and above skills and the more traditional dichotomy between high-skilled and low-skilled workers may need to be revised, taking the nature of tasks into account.

In the next section, we provide a brief review of the related literature that motivates our empirical analysis. We then give a detailed account of our data and the classification of tasks according to their degree of interactivity and non-routine content. Section 4 explains the empirical model and addresses potential caveats. Our within-industry results are presented in Section 5, while Section 6 shows our estimates when allowing for cross-industry wage effects of offshoring. Section 7 discusses robustness checks, while Section 8 concludes the analysis.

2. Related literature

In the growing literature on offshoring and tasks our paper mainly relates to and expands on Becker *et al.* (2013), Ebenstein *et al.* (forthcoming), and Hummels *et al.* (2011).[6]

[6]Other studies analyzing task-specific offshoring effects include Crinò (2010) who uses aggregate data to look at the impact of services offshoring on demand for skilled workers while differentiating between "tradable" and "non-tradable" occupations and

Becker *et al.* (2013) analyze the link between tasks, skills, offshoring by multinationals, and relative labor demand using German plant-level panel data. They estimate wage-bill share equations for skills and tasks, respectively, applying the translog cost function framework of Feenstra and Hanson (1996) and Head and Ries (2002). Their results indicate that offshore employment within multinational enterprises in manufacturing and service industries alike is related to onshore skill-upgrading. Moreover, offshore employment is related to demand shifts away from routine and non-interactive job tasks, suggesting that indeed offshorability is inversely related to the non-routine content and interactivity of job tasks. Our paper differs from Becker *et al.* (2013) in three main respects. First, while they look at plant-level wage-bill shares, thus mixing employment and wages, we focus on task-specific absolute wage gains and losses associated with offshoring. Second, by using individual-level data, we are able to control for individual-level observed and unobserved heterogeneity. Moreover, we take into account cross-plant effects of offshoring. Third, while Becker *et al.* (2013) consider the skill-upgrading effect of offshoring conditional on plant's changing task composition, we conversely investigate to what extent the task-specific effects of offshoring on labor demand go beyond any potential education-related heterogeneity in the offshoring effect.

Ebenstein *et al.* (forthcoming) employ cross-sectional data from the US Current Population Surveys to assess the wage and employment effects of offshoring depending on the non-routine content of job tasks. Approximating offshoring by affiliate employment, similar to Becker *et al.* (2013), the authors find that individual wages are positively affected by offshoring towards high-income and negatively by offshoring towards low-income locations. However, both, positive and negative wage effects of offshoring are concentrated in occupations which are classified as the most routine. They argue that these tasks are most easily offshorable and, hence, should be the most affected by actual offshoring activity. What, furthermore, separates the paper of Ebenstein *et al.* (forthcoming) from earlier micro-level studies (e.g., Liu and Trefler, 2008; Geishecker and Görg, 2008) is that they allow for cross-industry effects of offshoring, resulting in considerably larger wage effects of offshoring than in pure within-industry studies. Ebenstein *et al.* (forthcoming), however, do not analyze the interaction of job tasks and educational attainment, that is,

Baumgarten (2009) who uses similar data to ours to investigate the relationship between offshoring, tasks, and employment stability.

occupational task-specific effects of offshoring and education-specific effects are potentially confounded. Furthermore, due to data limitations, Ebenstein *et al.* (forthcoming) cannot control for unobserved individual heterogeneity and the associated selection of individuals into specific industries.

Another related paper is by Hummels *et al.* (2011) who use matched employer–employee data for Denmark to investigate wage effects of offshoring in individual firms. They measure offshoring as imported intermediate inputs at the firm level. While they focus on effects by different skill levels, they, in an extension, also look at the interaction of skills and occupational task measures, similar to our approach. They find, as we do, that such an interaction is important. A limitation of their approach is the measure of offshoring at the level of the firm, as in Becker *et al.* (2013). While this provides important new information, it does assume that the relevant labor market is firm-specific. Hence workers are affected only by their own firm's offshoring activities, not by others in the same industry or occupation. We expand on this by assuming either industry- or occupation-specific labor markets taking into account these important between-firm effects.

3. Data and methodology

The empirical strategy in this paper rests on combining individual-level data on wages and worker characteristics with more aggregate data on offshoring activity and other observable industry characteristics. Specifically, we use data from the German Socio-Economic Panel (SOEP), a representative longitudinal survey of private households in Germany, for the years 1991–2006.[7] We restrict our unbalanced sample to prime-age (18–65 years) employees in the manufacturing sector (NACE/ISIC 15–36). To abstract from gender-specific labor market outcomes (see, e.g., Prasad, 2004; Beaudry and Green, 2003), we focus exclusively on males. In our empirical model, we utilize retrospectively collected yearly individual labor earnings and yearly individual work hours from the Cross-National Equivalent Files (CNEF), which are part of the standard SOEP data

[7]Specifically, we use sample A–F of SOEP. Wagner *et al.* (2007) provide a detailed description of the SOEP. Our data was extracted using the add-on package PanelWhiz for Stata. Panelwhiz (http://www.PanelWhiz.eu) was written by Dr. John P. Haisken DeNew (john@PanelWhiz.eu). See Haisken-DeNew and Hahn (2006) for details. The do-file generated by PanelWhiz to retrieve the data in the present paper is available from the authors upon request. Any data or computational errors in the paper are our own.

package. Gross wages include payments from bonuses, overtime, and profit-sharing. Annual work hours in the CNEF are constructed by combining information on average number of hours per week and calendar information on employment status, full- and part-time work.[8] Excluding observations with missing or imputed wage information, this yields 13,695 observations for 2129 individuals.[9,10]

In order to obtain measures of the task content of occupations, we employ occupational information following the classification of the German Federal Statistical Office (*Klassifizierung der Berufe — KldB92*) that has only recently become available in the SOEP. On the basis of this disaggregated occupational coding, we can map associated task contents, which are calculated using yet another micro-level data set, the German Qualification and Career Survey 1998/99. The main part of our analysis is based on the mapping procedure used by Becker *et al.* (2013).[11]

To make the German Qualification and Career Survey sample comparable to the one used in our wage regression, we restrict the sample to males aged 18–65, which leaves us with some 19,000 individuals (out of about 34,000). Our occupational grouping is based on the two-digit level of the KldB92, which is available in both data sets. Only in cases where occupational cells become too small do we switch to the next-highest level of aggregation.[12]

[8] A detailed description of the CNEF files is provided in Grabka (2012).

[9] According to Frick and Grabka (2003), the imputation procedure disregards industry-level information such as offshoring. As a result, the imputation of missing wage information compresses the wage distribution with respect to the industry-level variables that are of most interest for our analysis and is therefore not suitable for this application. Accordingly, individuals with imputed wage data are excluded from the analysis.

[10] In principle, it would also be possible to conduct the analysis relying on the IAB Employment Sample (IABS), a considerably larger micro data set based on administrative social security records. For the question at hand, we prefer the SOEP for several reasons. First, wages are not top-coded as in the IABS. Second, in contrast to the IABS the SOEP contains information on the hours of work. Third, the IABS follows the NACE industry classification — which enables us to merge offshoring information from input–output only from 1999 onwards whereas it is available in the SOEP as early as 1991. Fourth, in the SOEP information on educational attainment is more complete and precise.

[11] We also use a different mapping based on Spitz-Oener (2006), which we describe below, as a robustness check. The German Qualification and Career Survey was previously used, for example, by DiNardo and Pischke (1997). Like Becker *et al.* (2013), we rely on the most recent wave as it follows a comparable occupational classification (KldB92).

[12] The classification contains five levels of aggregation. The two-digit level is the third-highest and distinguishes 88 occupational groups. The next-highest consists

The distinct advantage of this survey is that respondents not only state their occupation but also give a detailed account of the tasks they perform on the job and the associated work tools they use to do so. Using this detailed information, Becker *et al.* (2013) propose a mapping of tasks into occupations.

In the first step, each of the 81 tools identified in the survey is connected with a task, which is classified as (i) routine or non-routine and (ii) interactive or non-interactive, where the first grouping refers to non-repetitive tasks and the second to tasks requiring interpersonal contact. For illustration, the use of an overhead projector or beamer is coded as both non-routine and interactive, whereas the opposite holds for computer-controlled machinery. Simple means of transport are an example of tools denoting an interactive but routine task, whereas precision-mechanical tools are coded as non-routine and non-interactive (see Table A1 in Appendix A for the list of tools and their respective classifications).[13]

In a next step, we calculate the average number of non-routine and interactive tasks for each occupation. A higher number implies a more intensive use of the associated task category.

Finally, for every occupation, a continuous task intensity measure in the range of 0 to 1 — where 1 denotes maximum intensity — is derived by normalizing the figures by the maximum sum of non-routine and interactive tasks in any occupation. Thus, in compact form, the formula reads as follows:

$$TASK_{zk} = \frac{\text{Average number of } z - \text{tasks in occupation } k}{\text{Maximum number of } z - \text{tasks in any occupation}}, \quad (1)$$

where k denotes the occupation and $z \in \{\text{non}-\text{routine, interactive}\}$ the task category.

On the basis of these mappings, occupations are classified according to their non-routine or interactive task contents, irrespective of the associated educational attainment of workers. Accordingly, it is in principle possible to observe, for example, some highly non-routine (interactive) tasks to be performed by low-skilled workers, and vice versa.

of 33 occupational sections while the highest level differentiates between six broad occupational areas (Statistisches Bundesamt, 1992).

[13]We use the authors' preferred strict classification, where only a few tasks are coded as interactive (non-routine). As a robustness check, we also use the authors' lenient classification instead. The results stay virtually the same. These results are not reported here but can be obtained upon request.

For the definition of skill groups we utilize the International Standard Classification of Education (ISCED) and rely on the highest degree attained taking into account general schooling, vocational, and university education. Low-skilled workers are workers without any degree, a lower secondary degree (Elementary School), basic vocational training, or a higher secondary degree (High School) without any vocational training (OECD, 1999: ISCED-1997, 1–3). High-skilled workers have basic vocational training combined with a higher secondary degree, higher vocational training, or a university degree (OECD, 1999: ISCED-1997, 4–6).

To what extent non-routine and interactive tasks and skills, measured in terms of educational attainment, are related is summarized in Table 1.[14] As becomes apparent in the mean comparison tests, high-skilled workers on average have occupations with a significantly higher content of interactive as well as non-routine tasks. These are tasks that should make a job less offshorable (Blinder and Krueger, forthcoming). However, from Figs. 1 and 2, it also becomes clear that there is a significant heterogeneity within skill groups.

This finding is somewhat in contrast to the results by Blinder and Krueger (forthcoming) and Jensen and Kletzer (2010). Using data for the US, both of these studies find that there is a positive correlation between skills and offshorability of tasks, although they also show that low skilled workers have a significant share of offshorable tasks. Our evidence suggests that, in our German data, low-skilled workers are those who, on balance, tend to have occupations with a task profile that makes them easier to offshore.

Still, while higher skills and non-routine or more interactive tasks, respectively, seem to be correlated, we can nevertheless identify low-skilled manufacturing workers that occupy positions that are highly interactive or non-routine and vice versa. Hence, the task profile may add an important aspect of worker heterogeneity in a wage regression.

Among the low-skilled, a typical occupation characterized by low non-routine content is "storekeeper, warehouse keeper", while "assemblers" is an example of an occupation with low interactivity. "Metalworkers," the largest occupational group among low-skilled workers, score low in our interactivity index but are in the medium range of our non-routine indicator. On the other hand, "truck drivers" display a low intensity of

[14]Table 1 also reports on alternative task measures which are used for later robustness tests.

Table 1. Description of task indices.

TASK	All	Low-skilled	High-skilled
Interactivity index based on Becker *et al.* (2013)			
Mean μ	0.358	0.319	0.445
Standard deviation	0.146	0.137	0.125
Mean comparison test		$H_0 : \mu_{Low\text{-}skilled} = \mu_{High\text{-}skilled}$ $p = 0.000$	
Non-routine index based on Becker *et al.* (2013)			
Mean μ	0.492	0.407	0.682
Standard deviation	0.237	0.186	0.229
Mean comparison test		$H_0 : \mu_{Low\text{-}skilled} = \mu_{High\text{-}skilled}$ $p = 0.000$	
Interactivity index based on Spitz-Oener (2006)			
Mean μ	0.343	0.268	0.512
Standard deviation	0.230	0.189	0.224
Mean comparison test		$H_0 : \mu_{Low\text{-}skilled} = \mu_{High\text{-}skilled}$ $p = 0.000$	
Non-routine index based on Spitz-Oener (2006)			
Mean μ	0.428	0.345	0.612
Standard deviation	0.239	0.198	0.129
Mean comparison test		$H_0 : \mu_{Low\text{-}skilled} = \mu_{High\text{-}skilled}$ $p = 0.000$	
Modified interactivity index			
Mean μ	0.095	0.092	0.101
Standard deviation	0.041	0.045	0.030
Mean comparison test		$H_0 : \mu_{Low\text{-}skilled} = \mu_{High\text{-}skilled}$ $p = 0.000$	
Modified non-routine index			
Mean μ	0.215	0.189	0.275
Standard deviation	0.076	0.061	0.072
Mean comparison test		$H_0 : \mu_{Low\text{-}skilled} = \mu_{High\text{-}skilled}$ $p = 0.000$	
Observation	13,695	9458	4237

non-routine tasks but have frequent interactions with co-workers or third parties.

"Engineers" are the most frequently encountered occupational group among the very high-skilled, followed by "technicians". Both occupations are characterized by high degrees of non-routine and interactive tasks. However, there is still heterogeneity. For example, "computer scientists" are characterized by a high non-routine content but are less intensive in interactive tasks.

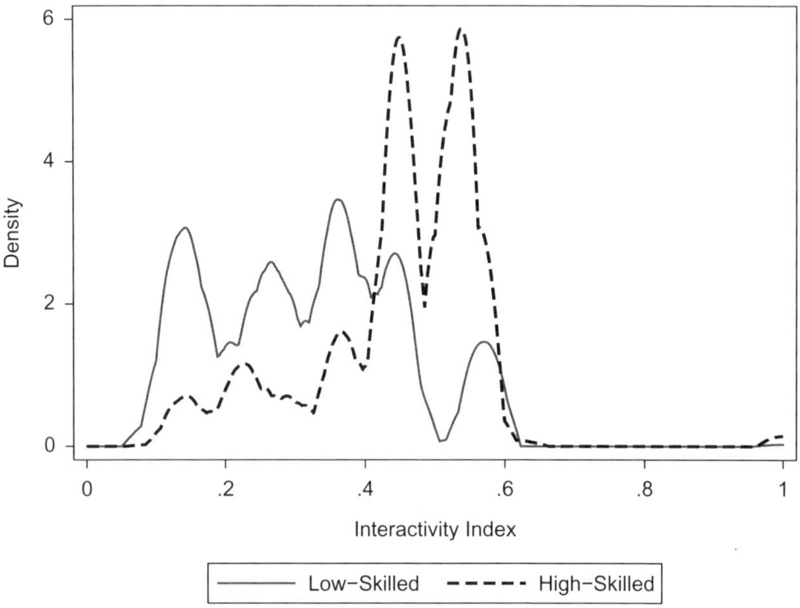

Fig. 1. Distribution of interactivity index by skill (based on Becker *et al.*, 2013).

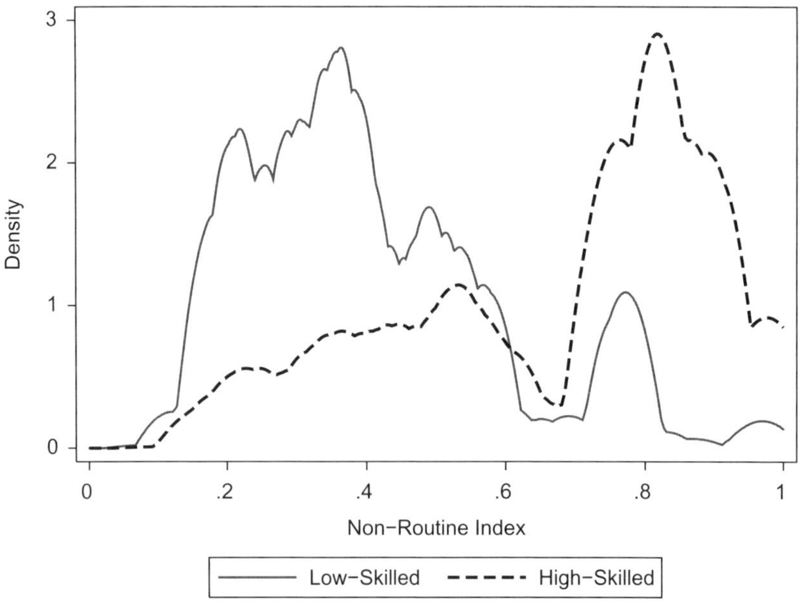

Fig. 2. Distribution of non-routine index by skill (based on Becker *et al.*, 2013).

4. Empirical approach: Baseline analysis of within-industry offshoring

The challenge for the econometric analysis is to establish whether workers with highly interactive or non-routine occupations are indeed differently affected by increased offshoring than their counterparts with occupations that have low interactivity and are fairly routine. In addition to that, it is challenging to determine whether the occupational task content matters (i) over and above the level of education and (ii) differently for workers with different levels of education. To investigate these issues, we first proceed by assuming that workers' wages are affected by offshoring activity in the industry in which the worker is employed. In Section 6 we relax this assumption and consider cross-industry effects of offshoring.

In order to implement the first strategy, we merge our individual-level data with industry-level offshoring measures. Offshoring is constructed by utilizing input–output tables provided by the German Federal Statistical Office that report imported intermediate inputs separately industry by industry.[15] We follow a narrow concept of materials offshoring by focusing on imported intermediate inputs that correspond to a make-or-buy decision, that is, inputs that in principle could be produced by the importing industry itself (see Feenstra and Hanson, 1999). Accordingly, we focus on the main diagonal of our input–output table for imports. We consider this offshoring measure to be more accurate than relying solely on affiliate employment (as in, e.g., Ebenstein *et al.*, forthcoming) since (i) affiliate employment also reflects horizontal MNE activities and (ii) not all offshoring takes place through foreign direct investment.[16]

Formally we can denote offshoring as

$$OS_{jt} = \frac{IMP_{jjt}}{Y_{jt}} \tag{2}$$

with IMP_{jjt} denoting intermediate inputs used in industry j that are imported from the same industry abroad. Imports are reported in input–output tables. Y_{jt} is the production value of industry j at time t.

---

[15]See e.g., Statistisches Bundesamt (2009), Table 2.

[16]On the other hand, we acknowledge that our offshoring measure might omit potentially unobserved service trade flows that are not tied to observed merchandize trade but reflected in foreign capital holdings or employment within multinationals. Also, we acknowledge that not all imported intermediates (even if they are from the same industry) necessarily substitute for domestic production.

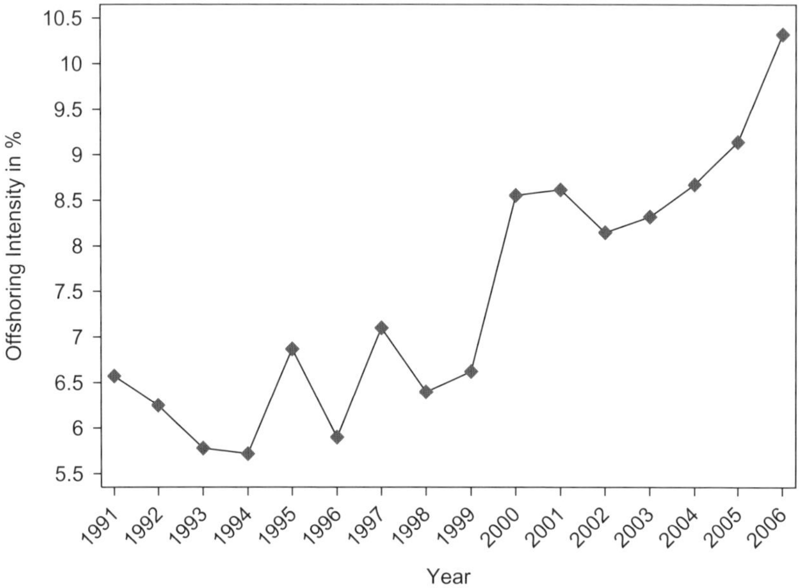

Fig. 3. Offshoring in manufacturing. Note: $\Delta OS_{1991-2006} = 3.75\% - pts.$

Fig. 3 depicts the weighted average offshoring intensity in manufacturing for the years 1991–2006. The average offshoring intensity grew substantially during our sample period: between 1991 and 2006 it increased from 6.6% to 10.3%.

As pointed out above, data for the costs or the level of offshoring are not separately available for different skill-groups, let alone for different occupational tasks. We therefore look at the differential wage impact of overall industry-level offshoring across occupational tasks. This reflects differential changes in the true offshoring exposure, which generates heterogeneous wage pressure for (still non-offshored) workers.[17] Accordingly, we assess whether the wage effects of offshoring are indeed in line with hypothesized differences in the offshorability of tasks as predicted in e.g., Blinder and Krueger (forthcoming).

To do so, while conditioning on observed and unobserved heterogeneity, we estimate variants of the following Mincer wage equation separately for

[17]Note that we cannot rule out that even a uniform across-the-board change in offshoring of a particular industry could have differential task-specific wage effects if it is associated with a differential (future) relocation threat for workers carrying out different tasks.

low- and high-skilled workers:[18]

$$\begin{aligned}\ln\ WAGE_{ijkt} &= \alpha + \beta DEMOG_{it} + \gamma WORK_{it} \\ &\quad + \delta TASK_k + \lambda OS_{jt} + \nu OS_{jt} \times TASK_k \\ &\quad + \theta IND_{jt} + \rho R\&D/Y_{jt} + \tau_j + \mu_t + \iota_i + \epsilon_{ijkt} \qquad (3)\end{aligned}$$

where $WAGE_{ijkt}$ denotes individual i's hourly wage at time t in industry j and occupation k.[19]

Our controls include the standard variables in such wage regressions, see, for example, Mincer (1974), Brown and Medoff (1989), Schmidt and Zimmermann (1991). Descriptive statistics on all control variables are provided in Table 2. *DEMOG* denotes the demographic control variables for marital status, children, and geographic region.[20] The second set of control variables ($WORK$) refers to workplace-related characteristics such as firm size, firm ownership, and tenure.

We also control for time-changing observable industry characteristics (IND) by including the size of the industry (measured in terms of output Y) and equipment and plant capital intensity ($Cap_{Equ;Plant}/Y$). To capture industry-level technological change, we include research and development intensity ($R\&D/Y_{jt}$) as an input-based industry-level technology measure. However, the three panel dimensions also allow us to include a full set of industry-specific time trends that capture industry-level technological change over and above common macroeconomic trends accounted for by μ_t. We employ these trends as an alternative to industry-level research and development intensity in a robustness check.

To control for as much unobserved heterogeneity as possible, we make use of the three dimensions, i, j, and t, in our panel data and decompose the error term into industry fixed effects τ_j, time fixed effects μ_t, individual fixed effects ι_i, and a remaining error term ϵ_{ijkt}.[21,22]

[18]Our empirical model builds on Geishecker and Görg (2008) but goes further by incorporating heterogeneous tasks into the model.

[19]The specification allows for within-individual variation in the task measure $TASK_k$ — as described in Eq. (1) — if individuals change the occupation.

[20]We do not control for age as age together with individual fixed effects and time dummies would result in perfect collinearity.

[21]Industry fixed effects are not perfectly collinear with individual fixed effects since individuals can change industry. For these cases, industry fixed effects control for level differences in our time-changing industry variables such as output or offshoring.

[22]Since we combine micro-level and aggregate data we calculate cluster-robust standard errors applying the sandwich formula proposed in White (1980) and Arellano (1987).

Table 2. Descriptive statistics.

	Notes	Low- and high-skilled		Low-skilled		High-skilled	
		Mean	SD	Mean	SD	Mean	SD
WAGE	0/1	17.30	8.06	15.20	5.25	21.99	10.79
D: Married	0/1	0.76	0.43	0.74	0.44	0.79	0.41
D: Has children	0/1	0.57	0.50	0.56	0.50	0.59	0.49
D: Firm size <20	0/1	0.01	0.11	0.01	0.10	0.01	0.12
D: Firm size 20–199	0/1	0.09	0.29	0.10	0.30	0.08	0.26
D: Firm size 200–1999	0/1	0.27	0.45	0.29	0.45	0.24	0.43
D: Public firm	0/1	0.01	0.09	0.01	0.10	0.00	0.07
D: Firm owner not reported	0/1	0.01	0.10	0.01	0.10	0.01	0.10
Tenure	in years	12.00	9.29	12.56	9.39	10.77	8.94
Work experience full-time	in years	18.41	10.34	19.19	10.61	16.65	9.48
Work experience part-time	in years	0.23	1.11	0.18	0.99	0.34	1.35
D: Recent unemployment	0/1	0.02	0.13	0.02	0.14	0.01	0.11
D: High-skilled	0/1	0.31	0.46				
Production value Y	in billion euros	98.88	55.09	95.52	53.89	106.39	56.97
Cap_{Equ}/Y	in percent	54.84	15.28	55.53	15.42	53.29	14.86
Cap_{Plant}/Y	in percent	30.99	12.62	32.01	13.05	28.70	11.30
$R\&D/Y$	in percent	2.32	2.46	2.10	2.36	2.81	2.61
OS	in percent	6.53	5.11	6.29	5.16	7.09	4.94
Observations		13,695		9458		4237	

We control for the nature of job tasks of individuals by including our constructed interactivity and non-routine indices, respectively. By splitting the sample between low- and high-skilled workers we allow for heterogeneous task effects across skill groups. To capture the potentially heterogeneous wage pressure from offshoring across skill groups and tasks, we interact offshoring with the typical task content of workers' occupations ($OS \times TASK$) and estimate the model for the split samples of low- and high-skilled workers respectively.

Accordingly, the marginal effect of offshoring for the different groups of low- and high-skilled workers can be denoted as

$$\left(\frac{\partial \ln WAGE_{ijkt}}{\partial OS_{jt}}\right) = \lambda + \nu \times TASK_k. \tag{4}$$

Hence, we allow for heterogeneous effects of offshoring within skill groups depending on the corresponding non-routine or interactivity index. This captures the idea that actual measured offshoring may be expected to have stronger effects on workers carrying out tasks that are more easily offshorable, even within a given skill group. By splitting the sample between high- and low-skilled workers, we also make sure that any task-related heterogeneity in the offshoring effect is not already accounted for by education-related heterogeneity, which was the focus of previous empirical work (e.g., Geishecker and Görg, 2008; Liu and Trefler, 2008; Hummels *et al.*, 2011).

One particular concern with our empirical analysis is that offshoring may be endogenous to wages.[23] This would be the case if, for example, offshoring took place in high-wage industries in order to exploit the potential for cost savings abroad. As argued in e.g., Ebenstein *et al.* (forthcoming) and Geishecker and Görg (2008), simultaneity of industry-level offshoring and individual wages may be less of a problem as it seems less likely that industry aggregates are determined by individual labor market outcomes. However, depending on the within-industry correlation of wages, simultaneity may still persist.

Another source of endogeneity is an exogenous shock that affects both wages and offshoring simultaneously.[24] In order to deal with such unobservable shocks, we control for observed and unobserved industry-specific effects using time-varying observable characteristics (industry size,

[23]Another possible concern about endogeneity is the potential endogeneity of individuals' tasks (as stressed by Autor and Handel, forthcoming) since workers may readily switch between different sets of tasks depending on associated wages. However, in contrast to Autor and Handel (forthcoming), we do not look at within-occupation task variations. In our approach, every task intensity is linked precisely to one occupation. Arguably, we thereby miss a potentially important source of within-occupation wage differentials. However, individuals rarely change occupation and when they do they are more likely to choose occupations with a similar task content (see Gathmann and Schönberg, 2010) in order to minimize task-specific human capital losses. In our sample, only 470 year to year occupation changes (of 13,695 observations) take place between 1991 and 2006. We therefore consider simultaneity between wages and tasks to be of lesser concern when looking at task-specific offshoring effects. The importance of unobserved characteristics for determining initial occupational choices is taken into account in our model through the inclusion of individual fixed effects.

[24]For example, think of final product demand shocks that affect industries and that thus translate into differential skill demands and revenues. If offshoring involves fixed costs, then higher revenues may translate into more offshoring and a simultaneous skill and task demand shift.

capital intensity, research and development intensity), industry fixed effects, and in some specifications industry-specific time effects. Our identifying assumption is then that the unobservable shock would be correlated with these variables.[25] Still, this might not be enough to rule out all endogeneity concerns.

We therefore explicitly test the hypothesis that offshoring is exogenous to wages in our setting. In order to do so, we implement an instrumental variables estimation. In the first-stage estimation we regress the offshoring measure as dependent variable on individual and industry characteristics included in the empirical model, as well as a number of excluded instruments that determine offshoring but not individual-level wages in Germany. In the choice of instruments, we follow recent work by Hummels *et al.* (2011) and use industry-specific measures of trade costs and world export supply.[26]

Hence, these variables capture shocks to transport costs and worldwide export supply, which are important determinants of offshoring but which, arguably, are exogenous to German workers. Hence, while both types of variables should be strongly correlated with offshoring activity, they are not correlated directly with the residual in the wage regression. In other words, they are likely to be relevant as well as valid instruments.

Table 3 shows the first stage regression results for the excluded instruments and reports test results of instrument strength and orthogonality.[27] The regression is run for the full sample and separately for the subsamples

[25]One potential problem that remains (not only in our paper but in all of the literature) is that the exogenous shock may be specific to certain products within particular industries, i.e., there may be within-industry heterogeneity in the shock. We cannot address this issue with either our covariates or an instrumental variables approach, which are both based on industry-specific variables. This potential shortcoming should be kept in mind in the interpretation of results.

[26]Ad valorem and unit transport costs are obtained from the OECD Maritime Transport Costs data base (OECD, 2011) at the two-digit level of the Harmonized System (HS2) and refer to container shipments. We subsequently map transport costs to two-digit industries using Eurostat's concordance table and calculate the weighted two-digit industry averages with 1991 HS2 import values as weights. Clearly, maritime transport costs cannot capture costs of other transport modes such as air traffic. Nevertheless, their explanatory power for offshoring appears to be high. World export supply is calculated on the basis of data from UN Comtrade and then mapped to two digit industries utilizing concordances between five-digit SITC and two-digit industry codes (ISIC, rev.3).

[27]We only report coefficients of excluded instruments in order to save space. Full first stage estimation results are relegated to a separate Appendix to this paper, which is available from the authors upon request.

Table 3. Within-industry analysis: Exogeneity tests.

	Low- and high-skilled workers	
"First-stage" coefficients of excl. instruments		
ln(World Export Supply)	2.046	(0.485)***
Advalorem trade costs — export to USA	−44.936	(4.926)***
F-test	$F = 67.630$	$p = 0.000$***
Hansen J-statistic, overidentifying restrictions	$\chi^2 = 0.028$	$p = 0.868$
Durbin-Wu-Hausman, H_0: Exogeneity	$\chi^2 = 0.756$	$p = 0.385$
	Low-skilled workers	
"First-stage" coefficients of excl. instruments		
ln(World Export Supply)	2.224	(0.524)***
Advalorem trade costs — export to USA	−45.578	(5.813)***
Advalorem trade costs — export to Japan	6.835	(1.757)***
F-test	$F = 57.350$	$p = 0.000$***
Hansen J-statistic, overidentifying restrictions	$\chi^2 = 1.685$	$p = 0.431$
Durbin-Wu-Hausman, H_0: Exogeneity	$\chi^2 = 4.099$	$p = 0.043$**
	High-skilled workers	
"First-stage" coefficients of excl. instruments		
ln(World Export Supply)	2.737	(1.032)***
Unit trade costs — export JPN	−0.645	(0.127)***
F-test	$F = 13.610$	$p = 0.000$***
Hansen J-statistic, overidentifying restrictions	$\chi^2 = 0.447$	$p = 0.504$
Durbin-Wu-Hausman, H_0: Exogeneity	$\chi^2 = 0.126$	$p = 0.723$

Note: Standard errors in parentheses. **, ***significant at 5%, 1% error probability.

of low- and high-skilled workers. Given that we have individual-level data, a sample split between low- and high-skilled workers implies that the resulting industry structure differs between the subsamples. Accordingly, in the low(high)-skill sample offshoring activities of low(high)-skill intensive industries are over-represented, making necessary different sets of excluded instruments. Starting from the full set of available instruments (ad valorem and unit trade costs for exports and imports to/from USA, China, and Japan, as well as world export supply), we subsequently simplify the "first stage" model in order to maximize overall predictive power of excluded instruments while maintaining orthogonality.

Irrespective of whether we pool over all observations or split the sample between low- and high-skilled workers, F-statistics for the joint significance of the excluded instruments are always above 10, hence, problems of weak instruments are unlikely to be present (see Staiger and Stock, 1997). Instrument relevance is further indicated by the individual significance of the coefficients. This indicates that our instruments are important determinants of offshoring activity. The estimated coefficients also have the expected signs: world export supply is positively correlated with offshoring, while trade costs are generally negatively related. There is one exception, though, which is the cost of exports to Japan as a determinant of offshoring in the low-skill sample. In this particular instance, this may indicate that transport costs are in turn themselves determined by the level of offshoring, with high levels of offshoring to Japan or other countries in East Asia raising transport costs to East Asia.[28]

Based on these instruments, we can test the hypothesis of exogeneity of our offshoring measures in the second-stage regression. Note from the Durbin-Wu-Hausman test that for the pooled sample we are unable to reject the H_0 of exogeneity within reasonable confidence bounds. The same holds true for the sample of high-skilled workers. This implies that in these cases the OLS estimation is more efficient and, hence, preferable to the IV estimation. However, for the subsample of low-skilled workers we have to reject exogeneity of offshoring. In other words, while our empirical approach appears powerful enough to control for potential unobserved industry-specific shocks and while individual within-industry wage variation appears to be large enough to counter potential simultaneity in the sample of high-skilled workers (in which high-skill-intensive industries are over-represented), this is not the case for the sample of low-skilled workers. Hence, in what follows we therefore always split the sample between low- and high-skilled workers and use different estimation techniques for the two samples.

5. Within-industry offshoring: Estimation results

We now turn to the results of estimating various specifications of Eq. (3) for different task definitions. The main estimation results are presented in Table 4 for the interactivity and non-routine task index following the methodology proposed by Becker *et al.* (2013).

All specifications are estimated conditional on a large set of controls for observed individual heterogeneity as well as individual fixed effects

[28]The fact that offshoring and trade costs are jointly determined does not invalidate their use as instruments for our purposes. What is important in our context is that the instruments are exogenous to individual-level wages, conditional on other covariates in the model.

and industry, region, and time fixed effects.[29] The results presented in Column (a) refer to a baseline specification for low-skilled workers where potential endogeneity is ignored. In order to deal with potential endogeneity, we implement two approaches. Firstly, the specification in Column (b) includes industry-specific time dummies in order to capture time-varying unobserved shocks that may be correlated with offshoring. This specification is more robust to omitted variable bias as one potential source of endogeneity. Clearly, by including interacted industry-time dummies, all industry-level variables, including offshoring, are rendered collinear. However, one can still identify the parameter of the offshoring-task interaction, ν, in Eq. (3) as this only requires within industry-year variation of the task content. Comparing estimates of ν between Columns (a) and (b) of Table 4 shows that both estimates are very similar. Accordingly, for the identification of the task-specific offshoring effect, unobserved industry-specific shocks do not seem to play an important role. Rather, we suspect simultaneity of low-skilled workers' wages and offshoring to be of relevance.

We therefore further address the endogenity concern in a second approach by instrumenting for offshoring and the associated task-related interaction term. Our choice of excluded instruments is similar to the one employed for the exogeneity tests reported in Table 3. However, to instrument the task-related interaction term, we interact world export supply and one trade cost measure with the respective task index under consideration. As indicated by the Angrist-Pischke F-tests reported in Column (c-iv) of Table 4, our set of excluded instruments has sufficient predictive power in the two "first stages" and the test of the associated overidentifying restrictions does not indicate any violation of the orthogonality assumption.[30]

Both, the simple model specification that ignores endogeneity reported in Column (a) and the instrumental variables specification reported in Column (c-iv) of Table 4 show a similar pattern for the wage effect of offshoring. However, the overall negative wage effect is much more pronounced in the instrumental variables model. In both model specifications, low-skilled workers experience a wage reduction due to offshoring

[29]Coefficients on individual-level covariates take on the expected sign and are of the expected magnitude. To save space, coefficients are not reported but are relegated to a separate Appendix to this paper.

[30]Angrist and Pischke (2009) show how one can obtain modified first stage F-tests as the conventional ones are no longer appropriate if there are multiple endogenous variables.

Table 4. Within-industry analysis: Becker *et al.* (2013) classification.

	Interactive tasks				Non-routine tasks			
	Low-skilled			High-skilled	Low-skilled			High-skilled
	(a)	(b)	(c-IV)	(d)	(a)	(b)	(c-IV)	(d)
TASK	−0.0901		−0.0114	−0.0806	−0.0424		−0.1454	−0.1639
	[0.140]		[0.165]	[0.094]	[0.108]		[0.131]	[0.150]
Production value Y	−0.0002		−0.0012*	0.0012**	−0.0002		−0.0011*	0.0012**
	[0.000]		[0.001]	[0.001]	[0.000]		[0.001]	[0.001]
Cap_{Equ}/Y	0.0017		−0.0026	0.0049*	0.0018		−0.0025	0.0048*
	[0.002]		[0.003]	[0.002]	[0.002]		[0.002]	[0.002]
Cap_{Plant}/Y	−0.0045		−0.0018	−0.0066	−0.0048		−0.0015	−0.0065
	[0.004]		[0.003]	[0.005]	[0.004]		[0.003]	[0.005]
$R\&D/Y$	0.0096		−0.0043	0.0034	0.0095		−0.0028	0.0043
	[0.006]		[0.009]	[0.006]	[0.006]		[0.009]	[0.006]
OS	−0.0112*		−0.0369**	0.002	−0.0093**		−0.0456**	−0.0056
	[0.006]		[0.017]	[0.008]	[0.004]		[0.019]	[0.005]
$OS \times TASK$	0.0216*	0.0230***	0.0046	−0.0005	0.0123	0.0156**	0.0278	0.0102
	[0.011]	[0.009]	[0.020]	[0.018]	[0.008]	[0.008]	[0.018]	[0.007]
Observations	9,458	9,458	9,458	4,237	9,458	9,458	9,458	4,237
R^2	0.77	0.78	0.73	0.84	0.77	0.78	0.73	0.84
Industry-time effects	No	Yes	No	No	No	Yes	No	No
Angrist-Pischke F-test			$F = 31.83$,				$F = 22.49$,	
			$F = 64.09$				$F = 47.22$	
Hansen test of overidentifying restrictions			$\chi^2 = 3.352$				$\chi^2 = 3.677$	
			$p = 0.340$				$p = 0.299$	
Durbin-Wu-Hausman test of exogeneity			$\chi^2 = 5.401$				$\chi^2 = 4.695$	
			$p = 0.067$				$p = 0.096$	
Excluded instruments in column (c-IV):	Adv. Trade Costs: Export USA, JPN Adv. Trade Costs: Export *JPN* × *TASK* ln(World Export Supply), ln(World Export Supply) × *TASK*				Adv. Trade Costs: Export USA, CHN Adv. Trade Costs: Export CHN × *TASK* ln(World Export Supply), ln(World Export Supply) × *TASK*			

Note: Standard errors in parentheses. *, **, ***significant at 10%, 5%, 1% error probability. Regressions contain a full set of individual-level control variables as described in Table 2. All models with full sets of individual, time, industry, and region fixed effects.

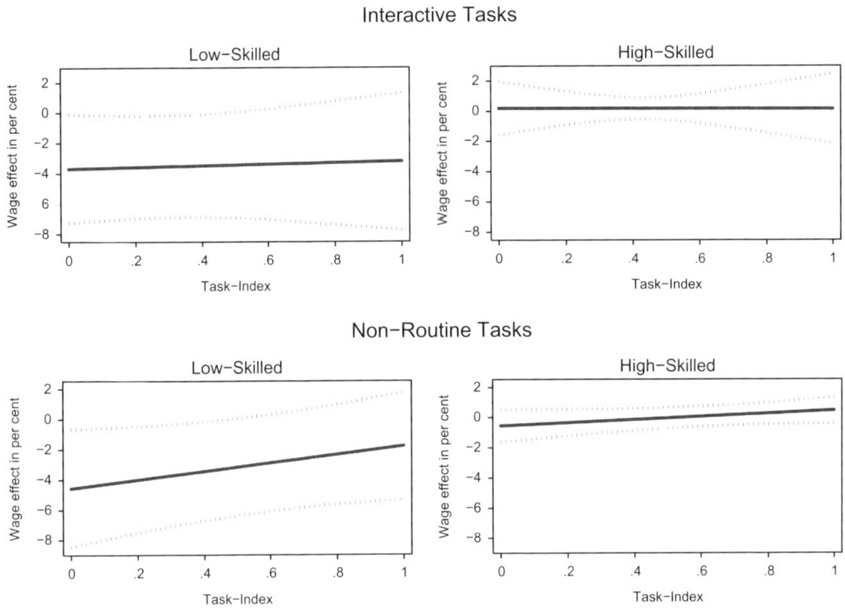

Fig. 4. Marginal effect of industry-specific offshoring with confidence band: Becker *et al.* (2013) classification.

which, however, becomes less severe the more interactive or non-routine occupational tasks become.

However, precision of the instrumental variable estimator is fairly low as not only offshoring but also the task-related interaction term has to be instrumented, resulting in rather large confidence bands around the marginal effect of offshoring as indicated in Fig. 4. Despite these complications, we find some support for our argument that tasks, in addition to skills, matter for the wage effect of offshoring. Thus, our results suggest that among the low-skilled, occupations with a high degree of interactive or non-routine tasks are somewhat shielded from the immediate negative wage impact of industry-level offshoring.

For high-skilled workers, however, as indicated in Column (d) of Table 4, we find no statistically significant wage effect of offshoring irrespective of the occupational task content of workers. Thus, although we observe high-skilled workers in occupations with low interactivity and low non-routine content, we cannot identify any immediate wage impact of industry-level offshoring.

6. Cross-industry results

We now turn to our second identification strategy. This is based on the idea that industry-specific offshoring measures may be a poor predictor of individual wages if individuals can potentially move between industries. Instead, we now look at cross-industry wage effects of offshoring. As discussed in Section 1, when allowing for worker mobility across industries, individual i's wages are not only determined by offshoring activity in the industry j in which i is employed, but also by offshoring activities in other industries $l \in J$, insofar as these activities affect the overall demand for labor that individual i faces.[31]

One way of approximating these wage effects of offshoring is to use weighted cross-industry measures of offshoring. In order to implement this, we build on Ebenstein *et al.* (forthcoming) and construct cross-industry offshoring by re-weighting industry-level offshoring measures (cf. Eq. (2)) with respect to industry employment within a given occupation L_{kj} as a share in total employment within the respective occupation L_k in 1991

$$OS_{kt} = \sum_{j=1}^{J} \frac{L_{kj}}{L_k} OS_{jt} \tag{5}$$

Thus, we allow for cross-industry effects of offshoring by making the identifying assumption that workers are reluctant or unable to change occupation k but readily switch between industries j. Accordingly, we re-estimate Eq. (3) substituting OS_{kt} for OS_{jt}.

$$\begin{aligned} \ln WAGE_{ikt} &= \alpha + \beta DEMOG_{it} + \gamma WORK_{it} \\ &\quad + \lambda OS_{kt} + \nu OS_{kt} \times TASK_k \\ &\quad + \theta OCC_{kt} + \rho R\&D/Y_{kt} + \tau_k + \mu_t + \iota_i + \epsilon_{ikt} \end{aligned} \tag{6}$$

where $WAGE_{ikt}$ denotes individual i's hourly wage in occupation k at time t.[32]

We now control for occupation-specific observable characteristics by including occupation-specific output and capital (OCC_{kt}) as well as R&D intensity that are constructed applying the same methodology as in Eq. (5). Occupation-specific unobservable characteristics are captured by a full set

[31] What is important is that no actual movement of workers is required to generate these cross-industry effects; the potential for movement suffices.

[32] We now have 61 clusters (occupations) instead of 21 (industries) in the previous analysis.

of occupation dummies τ_k. Since each occupation corresponds to exactly one time-constant task intensity $TASK_k$ in our data, we have perfect collinearity between the two variable sets. Accordingly, our occupation dummies also capture the respective main effect of interactivity and non-routine content. The main difference with respect to the estimation strategy used in Section 4 is that offshoring from several industries is now aggregated according to occupations' representation in the respective industries to capture cross-industry spillovers. Importantly, the weighted cross-industry offshoring measure still does not incorporate any (non-available) information on concrete task- or skill-specific offshoring costs or levels. Accordingly, similar to Section 4, we essentially rely on aggregated industry-level data to assess whether differential wage effects across different degrees of interactivity of non-routine content follow a pattern consistent with the offshorability of activities as postulated in, e.g., Blinder and Krueger (forthcoming). Again, we need to establish first whether occupational-level offshoring can indeed be considered exogenous to individual wages. Recalling the previous industry-level analysis, we established that endogeneity of offshoring seems to be mainly the result of simultaneity between offshoring and wages rather than that of industry-specific omitted variables. In the present cross-industry analysis we therefore expect less of an endogeneity problem as occupational-level offshoring is constructed as a weighted average of industry-level offshoring intensities, thereby introducing an extra layer between individual-level wages and aggregate offshoring figures. Or put differently, even if certain industries may raise their offshoring activities in response to contemporaneous individual wage increases, as long as there is sufficient variation in wage trends across industries, overall occupational-level offshoring will only respond by a fraction corresponding to the respective industries' occupational employment share.

To test for the exogeneity of offshoring, we again utilize measures of industry-level world export supply and industry-level trade costs and transform them into occupational-level variables applying the same weighting scheme as used in Eq. (5). Table 5 reports on the choice of excluded instruments and their relevance and validity. For the pooled sample as well as for the low-skilled and high-skilled samples our excluded instruments have high predictive power both individually and jointly, and coefficients have the expected sign, indicating that offshoring increases as world export supply increases and decreases as trade costs rise. Furthermore, our test of overidentifying restrictions does not indicate any violation of the orthogonality assumptions. Accordingly, our excluded instruments are

Table 5. Cross-industry analysis: Exogeneity tests.

	Low- and high-skilled workers pooled	
"First-stage" coefficients of excl. instruments		
ln(World Export Supply)	2.9575	(0.3953)***
Advalorem trade costs — export to USA	−35.1334	(5.5191)***
F-test	$F = 57.47$	$p = 0.000$***
Hansen J-Statistic, overidentifying restrictions	$\chi^2 = 1.721$	$p = 0.190$
Durbin-Wu-Hausman, H_0: Exogeneity	$\chi^2 = 0.803$	$p = 0.370$
	Low-skilled workers	
"First-Stage" coefficients of excl. instruments		
ln(World Export Supply)	3.459	(0.478)***
Advalorem Trade Costs — Export to USA	−38.268	(5.668)***
Advalorem Trade Costs — Export to China	−2.209	(0.651)***
F-test	$F = 45.43$	$p = 0.000$***
Hansen test of overidentifying restrictions	$\chi^2 = 2.711$	$p = 0.258$
Durbin-Wu-Hausman, H_0: Exogeneity	$\chi^2 = 0.524$	$p = 0.469$
	High-skilled workers	
"First-Stage" coefficients of excl. instruments		
Unit Trade Costs — Import USA	−0.634	(0.132)***
Unit Trade Costs — Import JPN	−1.052	(0.414)**
F-test	$F = 13.93$	$p = 0.000$***
Hansen test of overidentifying restrictions	$\chi^2 = 0.771$	$p = 0.380$
Durbin-Wu-Hausman, H_0: Exogeneity	$\chi^2 = 0.118$	$p = 0.731$

Note: Standard errors in parentheses. **, *** significant at 5%, 1% error probability.

relevant and valid. On this basis we perform a Durbin-Wu-Hausman test of the exogeneity of offshoring and cannot reject exogeneity in any of our three samples. For their superior efficiency, we therefore prefer standard fixed effects estimations over instrumental variable techniques.

Table 6 reports the parameter estimates applying the task classification scheme of Becker *et al.* (2013). Again, all estimates are conditional on a large set of individual-level control variables (see Table 2), individual fixed effects, as well as time, region, and occupation fixed effects.[33] We find a pronounced negative wage effect of cross-industry offshoring that is inversely related to the interactivity and non-routine content of workers'

[33]Coefficients on individual-level covariates take on the expected sign and are of the expected magnitude. To save space, coefficients are not reported but are included in a separate Appendix to this paper.

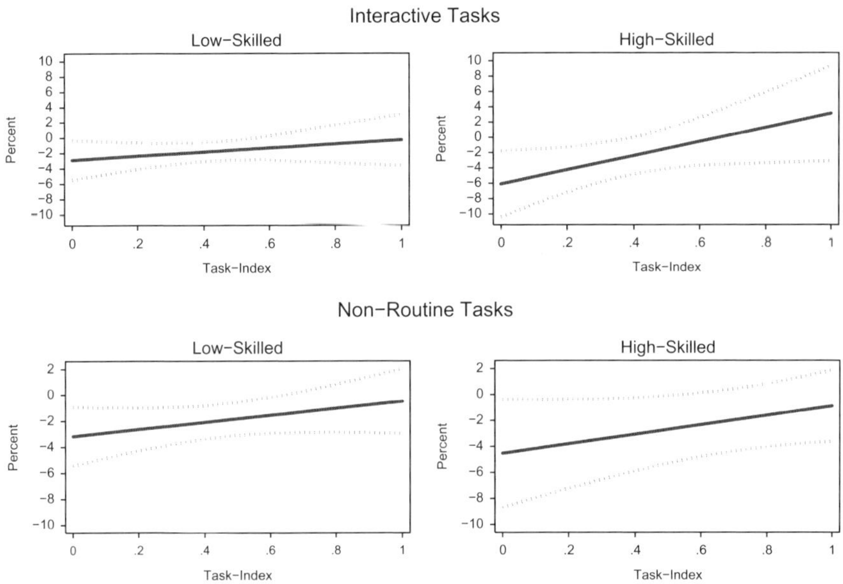

Fig. 5. Marginal effect of occupation-specific offshoring with confidence band: Becker *et al.* (2013) classification.

occupations. We provide a graphical representation of the marginal wage effect of cross-industry offshoring in Fig. 5. What becomes clear is that among low-skilled workers, occupations with low interactivity and low non-routine content experience significant wage cuts while occupations in the higher regions of interactivity and non-routine content are shielded from negative wage effects. Furthermore, after allowing for cross-industry effects of offshoring, we now also find statistically significant wage effects for high-skilled workers that are of similar magnitude and follow a similar pattern as those for low-skilled workers.

To sum up, we find evidence that offshoring mainly lowers wages for workers in occupations that are less interactive and have lower non-routine content. Moreover, this pattern is present for low-skilled and high-skilled workers alike. Our results suggest that indeed, irrespective of the education, a high degree of occupational interactivity or non-routine content shields workers from negative wage effects.

How large are these negative wage effects and how discrepant are they between the different occupational tasks? From the regression Table 6 this is difficult to infer. Instead we engage in a thought experiment and ask by how much hourly wages would have decreased had offshoring remained

Table 6. Cross-industry analysis: Becker *et al.* (2013) classification.

	Interactive tasks		Non-routine tasks	
	Low-skilled (a)	High-skilled (b)	Low-skilled (c)	High-skilled (d)
Production value Y	0.0004	−0.0018	0.0006	−0.0013
	[0.001]	[0.004]	[0.001]	[0.004]
Cap_{Equ}/Y	0.002	0.0053	0.0031	0.0037
	[0.004]	[0.009]	[0.003]	[0.008]
Cap_{Plant}/Y	−0.0036	−0.0209	−0.0034	−0.0162
	[0.004]	[0.017]	[0.004]	[0.017]
$R\&D/Y$	−0.0098	0.0439***	−0.0062	0.0460***
	[0.018]	[0.016]	[0.018]	[0.016]
OS	−0.0279***	−0.0531***	−0.0380***	−0.0471**
	[0.010]	[0.020]	[0.010]	[0.020]
$OS \times TASK$	0.0358	0.0805**	0.0494**	0.0407*
	[0.022]	[0.040]	[0.019]	[0.022]
Observations	9,458	4,237	9,458	4,237
R^2	0.77	0.84	0.77	0.84
Joint significance	$F = 7.34$	$F = 3.72$	$F = 9.11$	$F = 2.86$
$OS, OS \times TASK$	$p = 0.002$	$p = 0.032$	$p = 0.000$	$p = 0.067$

Note: Standard errors in parentheses. *, **, ***significant at 10%, 5%, 1% error probability. Regressions contain a full set of individual-level control variables as described in Table 2. All models contain a full set of individual, time, occupation, and region fixed effects.

constant at its 1991 value.[34] We do this separately for low- and high-skilled workers, and further distinguish between the types of tasks within skill groups by looking at the 10th, 50th, and 90th percentiles of the respective interactivity and non-routine content of occupational tasks. Table 7 presents the outcome of this exercise.

We find low-skilled workers in the bottom decile of interactivity to experience average cumulated wage cuts of 9% which is equivalent to a 1.3 Euro reduction in hourly gross earnings as compared to average wages in 1991. In comparison, low-skilled workers at the median experience wage cuts of 6% while low-skilled workers at the top decile of interactivity only experience wage cuts of less than 3.5%. Similarly, low-skilled workers in the bottom decile of non-routine content experience wage cuts due to offshoring of about 10% while low-skilled workers in the top decile have no significant wage losses. High-skilled workers generally have no statistically significant

[34]Note that to do so we assume that changes in offshoring intensity are essentially marginal.

Table 7. Cross-industry analysis: Economic significance calculations.

	Low-skilled			High-skilled		
Average hourly wage in 1991	15.00			21.00		
Interactive tasks						
	Percent		Euro	Percent		Euro
10th percentile	−8.52	(2.55)***	−1.28	−12.60	(4.91)**	−2.65
50th percentile	−5.79	(1.53)***	−0.87	−5.94	(4.43)	−1.25
90th percentile	−3.42	(1.80)**	−0.51	−3.01	(4.95)	−0.63
Joint significance	$F = 7.34$			$F = 3.72$		
OS, $OS \times TASK$	$p = 0.002$			$p = 0.032$		
Non-routine tasks						
	Percent		Euro	Percent		Euro
10th percentile	−10.87	(2.64)***	−1.63	−12.10	(5.22)**	−2.54
50th percentile	−7.32	(1.77)***	−1.10	−5.90	(4.20)	−1.24
90th percentile	−0.05	(2.74)	−0.01	−2.90	(4.58)	−0.61
Joint significance	$F = 9.11$			$F = 2.86$		
OS, $OS \times TASK$	$p = 0.000$			$p = 0.067$		
Model without task interaction						
	Percent		Euro	Percent		Euro
	−5.31	(1.57)***	−0.80	−6.80	(4.53)	−1.43

Note: Standard errors in parentheses. **, ***significant at 5%, 1% error probability.

wage losses due to offshoring, unless, they work in occupations belonging to the bottom decile of interactivity or non-routine content. For these high-skill occupations with very low interactivity and non-routine content we find wage losses from offshoring of around 12%.

To further corroborate the importance of the task dimension for the wage impact of offshoring, we run our model without the interaction of task and offshoring. Leaving this interaction term out and calculating the economic significance of offshoring allows us to assess the relevance of the interactions. As the table shows, we find a statistically significant negative effect of 5.3% for low skilled workers, and no impact for high skilled workers. By construction, these effects are uniform across tasks. Comparing this to our previous estimates shows that including the task interactions does indeed add important information to our analysis.

In sum, offshoring matters economically and can significantly reduce workers' wages. The effect, however, is heterogenous within skill groups and crucially depends on the interactivity and non-routine content of occupational tasks.

7. Robustness analysis

This section presents a number of robustness tests for the main cross-industry specification. For all of our tests we do not present the regression table here to save space. Instead, we proceed immediately to the calculation of economic significance, replicating Table 7 based on the new estimates.

In a first test, we expand Eq. (6) and apply an alternative set of technology controls. More specifically, we include occupation-specific time trends in addition to all time-varying industry variables (reweighted to the level of the occupation) included in the model. In a further test we exclude all individuals who have changed occupation during the sample period in order to focus on pure within-occupation changes. The calculated wage effects presented in Table 8 are similar for those two specifications compared to the ones presented in Table 7.

We also re-consider our offshoring measure. This is calculated based on offshoring activity within the industry in which an individual works. The idea behind this is, as pointed out above, that such a measure is likely to be most closely related to the actual concept of offshore outsourcing, i.e., that the production was carried out in the home country first and then switches to a location abroad. In comparison, imported intermediates from other industries may simply correspond to a switch from domestic to foreign suppliers. Still, we now also consider effects of imported intermediates from other industries by recalculating our offshoring measure using now the difference between imports from the own industry and imports of intermediates from other industries as an additional control variable.[35] In addition, we add controls for overall import penetration and export intensity. All of these measures are again reweighted to the level of the occupation. The results from this exercise are reported in Table 8. We can see that the economic significance of our preferred offshoring measure is hardly affected.[36]

A further set of robustness checks focuses on our task measure. Our analysis thus far uses task indices as outlined in Section 3 based on the

[35]This corresponds to the difference offshoring measure used by Feenstra and Hanson (1996).

[36]Note that all additional globalization indicators including the difference between broadly and narrowly defined offshoring are rendered statistically insignificant for the sample of low- and high-skilled workers alike.

Table 8. Alternative specifications: Economic significance calculations.

	Low-skilled			High-skilled		
	Percent		Euro	Percent		Euro
Occupation-specific time trends						
Interactive tasks						
10th percentile	−8.72	(3.39)**	−1.31	−14.03	(5.05)***	−2.95
50th percentile	−5.96	(1.98)***	−0.89	−6.11	(4.52)	−1.28
90th percentile	−3.56	(2.30)	−0.53	−2.62	(5.27)	−0.55
Joint significance	$F = 4.60$			$F = 4.11$		
OS, $OS \times TASK$	$p = 0.014$			$p = 0.023$		
Non-routine tasks						
10th percentile	−9.03	(3.11)***	−1.36	−9.72	(6.07)	−2.04
50th percentile	−6.75	(2.05)***	−1.01	−6.65	(4.14)	−1.40
90th percentile	−2.06	(3.37)	−0.31	−5.16	(4.52)	−1.08
Joint significance	$F = 5.42$			$F = 1.49$		
OS, $OS \times TASK$	$p = 0.007$			$p = 0.235$		
Reduced sample without occupation switchers						
Interactive tasks						
10th percentile	−9.44	(3.64)***	−1.42	−14.43	(5.13)***	−3.03
50th percentile	−7.44	(2.42)***	−1.12	−6.82	(4.71)	−1.43
90th percentile	−5.70	(2.51)**	−0.85	−3.46	(5.43)	−0.73
Joint significance	$F = 4.74$			$F = 4.24$		
OS, $OS \times TASK$	$p = 0.013$			$p = 0.020$		
Non-routine tasks						
10th percentile	−10.05	(3.17)***	−1.51	−12.01	(5.44)**	−2.52
50th percentile	−8.13	(2.46)***	−1.22	−6.49	(4.50)	−1.36
90th percentile	−4.19	(3.29)	−0.63	−3.81	(5.00)	−0.80
Joint significance	$F = 5.56$			$F = 2.49$		
OS, $OS \times TASK$	$p = 0.006$			$p = 0.094$		
Additional globalization controls						
Interactive tasks						
10th percentile	−7.62	(2.42)***	−1.14	−13.85	(4.57)***	−2.91
50th percentile	−4.84	(1.65)***	−0.73	−6.61	(4.09)	−1.39
90th percentile	−2.42	(1.98)	−0.36	−3.42	(4.73)	−0.72
Joint significance	$F = 5.29$			$F = 4.82$		
OS, $OS \times TASK$	$p = 0.008$			$p = 0.013$		
Non-routine tasks						
10th percentile	−9.96	(2.68)***	−1.49	−11.88	(4.79)***	−2.49
50th percentile	−6.12	(1.86)***	−0.92	−6.28	(3.88)	−1.32
90th percentile	1.75	(2.68)	0.26	−3.57	(4.64)	−0.75
Joint significance	$F = 6.93$			$F = 3.08$		
OS, $OS \times TASK$	$p = 0.002$			$p = 0.055$		

Note: Standard errors in parentheses. *, **, *** significant at 10%, 5%, 1% error probability.

classification strategy used by Becker *et al.* (2013). We now investigate how sensitive our results are to the definition of these task measures. Descriptive statistics for the alternative definitions of tasks are provided in Table 1.

A first test uses an alternative task classification, where we classify tasks into interactive/non-interactive and routine/non-routine, respectively, based on a list of 13 job descriptions that is available in our data set. This is the same set of questions that was first used by Spitz-Oener (2006). The questions are given in Table A2 in Appendix A. We then calculate a task index as described in Eq. (1) based on this classification. Based on this alternative task measure, we re-estimate Eq. (6). Results are presented in the top panel of Table 9. A look at the economic significance shows that the magnitude and pattern of the calculated wage effects is similar to our original results.

In a further robustness check we propose another alternative task index. Our definition of the task index in Eq. (1) implies, as in Spitz-Oener (2006) and Becker *et al.* (2013), that interactivity and non-routine content increase in the number of interactive or non-routine occupational tools or tasks. However, as the total number of tools or tasks, interactive/non-routine or not, varies across occupations, the proposed classification scheme could be distorted. Consider truck drivers as an illustrating example. Trucks are classified as tools that correspond to a task requiring geographic proximity (i.e., an interactive task). However, based on the task index used thus far, truck driving occupations might not be classified as very interactive as truck drivers may use few other tools than a truck.

As an alternative, we therefore use the task classification of Becker *et al.* (2013) but normalize by the total number of tasks used in the occupation (instead of the maximum number of interactive/non-routine tasks in any occupation). Thus, we construct modified indexes of interactivity and non-routine content based on the share of interactive (non routine) tasks in total occupational tasks

$$TASK_{zk}^{modified} = \text{Average}\left(\frac{\text{Number of } z - \text{tasks}}{\text{Number of total tasks}}\right) \text{of occ. } k, \qquad (7)$$

where k denotes the occupation and $z \in \{\text{non} - \text{routine, interactive}\}$ the task category.

The bottom panel of Table 9 reports the predicted wage changes due to offshoring according to specifications relying on these alternative task

Table 9. Alternative task indices: Economic significance calculations.

	Low-skilled			High-skilled		
	Percent		Euro	Percent		Euro
Task classification based on Spitz-Oener (2006)						
Interactive tasks						
	Percent		Euro	Percent		Euro
10th percentile	−8.60	(1.78)***	−1.29	−11.74	(5.35)**	−2.46
50th percentile	−7.11	(1.34)***	−1.07	−3.33	(4.37)	−0.70
90th percentile	−0.65	(2.68)	−0.10	2.43	(5.62)	0.51
Joint significance	$F = 14.11$			$F = 2.85$		
OS, $OS \times TASK$	$p = 0.000$			$p = 0.068$		
Non-routine tasks						
	Percent		Euro	Percent		Euro
10th percentile	−9.44	(2.01)***	−1.42	−11.47	(5.60)**	−2.41
50th percentile	−6.74	(1.32)***	−1.01	−3.32	(4.22)	−0.70
90th percentile	−0.85	(2.45)	−0.13	0.39	(4.92)	0.08
Joint significance	$F = 13.30$			$F = 2.33$		
OS, $OS \times TASK$	$p = 0.000$			$p = 0.108$		
Modified task classification, Eq. (7)						
Interactive tasks						
10th percentile	−5.20	(2.14)**	−0.78	−8.71	(4.71)*	−1.83
50th percentile	−5.35	(1.49)***	−0.80	−5.55	(4.72)	−1.17
90th percentile	−5.45	(2.14)***	−0.82	−1.39	(5.42)	−0.29
Joint significance	$F = 6.58$			$F = 3.39$		
OS, $OS \times TASK$	$p = 0.003$			$p = 0.042$		
Non-routine tasks						
10th percentile	−10.17	(2.47)***	−1.53	−13.96	(5.24)**	−2.93
50th percentile	−7.67	(1.72)***	−1.15	−2.80	(4.50)	−0.59
90th percentile	0.48	(3.04)	0.07	−1.17	(4.70)	−0.25
Joint significance	$F = 9.92$			$F = 4.55$		
OS, $OS \times TASK$	$p = 0.000$			$p = 0.016$		

Note: Standard errors in parentheses. *, **, *** significant at 10%, 5%, 1% error probability.

indices. We first focus on the interactivity index. While results are broadly in line with our previous findings for high-skilled workers, the negative wage effect for low-skilled workers is now essentially uniform across different degrees of interactivity.

This suggests that the initial task intensity measures based on the absolute number of tasks do capture some within skill-group heterogeneity for low-skilled workers that the measures using the alternative normalization do not. In fact, the correlation coefficient between the alternative interactivity index and the one obtained following Becker *et al.* (2013) is only 0.563 for low skilled workers.[37]

What our results suggest is that the total number of interactive tasks matters rather than their share in the total number of tasks, casting some doubt on whether the within-skill heterogeneity of offshoring effects can indeed be attributed to different degrees of interactivity. What seems to be important and what is at least implicitly captured in the initial interactivity index is the complexity of occupations as approximated by the total number of (interactive) tasks (cf. Antonczyk *et al.*, 2009).

In contrast, the choice of index does hardly matter for the results relying on the intensity of non-routine tasks (see the top panel of Table 9). This can be explained by the fact that the correlation between the alternative task index and the one calculated according to Eq. (1) based on Becker *et al.* (2013) is very large (correlation coefficient equals 0.90 for the low-skilled and 0.93 for the high-skilled). Thus, occupations will be classified very similarly according to their non-routine content irrespective of the classification scheme. Put differently, in occupations that use many non-routine tasks, that is in occupations that can, arguably, be described as rather complex, these non-routine tasks also account for a large share in the total number of tasks. Accordingly, we find the effects of offshoring to be very similar between the different classification methods for non-routine content.

Summarizing, we find the complexity of occupations as captured by the number of interactive or non-routine occupational tasks to play a mitigating role for the wage effect of offshoring. While the complexity of occupations is indistinguishable from the non-routine content (both are strongly correlated), our robustness analysis casts some doubt on the importance of pure interactivity of occupations for mitigating the wage effects of offshoring.

8. Conclusion

The paper analyzes the effects of offshoring on individual-level wages, taking into account the ease with which individuals' tasks can be offshored. Our

[37]For high-skilled workers for whom we find a wage effect that is smaller but at least weakly statistically significant when using the alternative interactivity index, the correlation coefficient between the two interactivity measures is 0.656 and thus significantly higher.

analysis relates to contributions such as Blinder (2006), Leamer and Storper (2001), Levy and Murnane (2004), and Blinder and Krueger (forthcoming), who postulate that there is only a loose relationship between the suitability of a task for offshoring and the associated skill level. Instead, these authors stress that the degree of offshorability depends on the relative importance of routine versus non-routine tasks or on the extent to which personal interaction is needed on the job.

For the empirical analysis we combine individual-level data and industry-specific offshoring measures and classify occupations according to their degree of interactivity and non-routine content. In line with earlier research, we find the within-industry impact of offshoring on individual wages to be rather modest or non-existent. However, we find substantial negative cross-industry wage effects of offshoring for low- and high-skilled workers. Furthermore, the magnitude of these effects strongly depends on the type of tasks workers perform. For instance, for low-skilled workers carrying out tasks with the lowest degree of non-routine content (which, arguably, are also the tasks that can most easily be offshored), increased offshoring between 1991 and 2006 accounts for a cumulative average yearly wage reduction of around 2400 euros (assuming 1500 annual work hours). For low-skilled workers with the highest degree of non-routine content, offshoring can merely explain an (insignificant) yearly wage reduction of about 15 euros.

Thus, in line with the arguments put forward in the literature, a higher degree of interactivity and, in particular, non- routine content can indeed shield workers against the negative wage impact of offshoring. Furthermore, this effect is present even after conditioning on workers' education.

Acknowledgments

The authors are grateful to two anonymous referees, the associate editor, and seminar participants in Aarhus, Copenhagen, Frankfurt, Kiel, Paris, Trondheim, and Essen for helpful comments on earlier drafts. Donnachad Krüger and Wadim Djatschenko provided excellent research assistance. Daniel Baumgarten thanks the Leibniz Association for financial support. Holger Görg gratefully acknowledges financial support through the European Commission as part of the 7th Framework Programme, Grant Agreement no. 244 552 (SERVICEGAP).

Appendix A. Task classification

See Tables A1 and A2.

Table A1. Classification of tasks following Becker *et al.* (2013).

	Non-routine tasks	Interactive tasks
Tools or devices		
Simple tools		
Precision-mechanical, special tools	x	
Power tools		
Other devices		
Soldering, welding devices		
Stove, oven, furnace		
Microwave oven		
Machinery or plants		
Hand-controlled machinery		
Automatic machinery		
Computer-controlled machinery		
Process plants		
Automatic filling plants		
Production plants		
Plants for power generation		
Automatic warehouse systems		
Other machinery, plants		
Instruments and diagnostic devices		
Simple measuring instruments		
Electronic measuring instruments		
Computer-controlled diagnosis		
Other measuring instruments, diagnosis		
Computers		
Personal or office computers		
Connection to internal network		
Internet, e-mail		
Portable computers (laptops)		
Scanner, plotter		
CNC machinery		
Other computers, EDP devices		
Office and communication equipment		
Simple writing material		
Typewriter		
Desktop calculator, pocket calculator		
Fixed telephone	x	
Telephone with ISDN connection	x	
Answering machine	x	
Mobile telephone, walkie-talkie, pager	x	
Fax device, telecopier		

(*Continued*)

Table A1. (*Continued*)

	Non-routine tasks	Interactive tasks
Speech dictation device, microphone		x
Overhead projector, beamer, TV	x	x
Camera, video camera	x	x
Means of transport		x
Bicycle, motorcycle		
Automobile, taxi		x
Bus		x
Truck, conventional truck		x
Trucks for hazardous good, special vehicles		x
Railway		x
Ship		x
Aeroplane		x
Simple means of transport		x
Tractor, agricultural machine		
Excavating, road-building machine		x
Lifting-aids on vehicles		x
Forklift, lifting truck		
Lifting platform, goods lift		
Excavator		
Crane in workshops		
Erection crane		
Crane vehicle		
Handling system		
Other vehicles, lifting means		
Other tools and aids		
Therapeutic aids	x	x
Musical instruments	x	x
Weapons	x	x
Surveillance camera, radar device		
Fire extinguisher	x	x
Cash register		x
Scanner cash register, bar-code reader		x
Other devices, implements		
Software use by workers with computers		
Word processing program		
Spreadsheet program		
Graphics program	x	
Database program		
Special, scientific program	x	
Use of other software		
Computer handling by workers with computers		
Program development, systems analysis	x	
Device, plant, system support	x	
User support, training	x	x

(*Continued*)

Table A1. (*Continued*)

	Non-routine tasks	Interactive tasks
Computer use by any worker		
Professional use: personal computer	x	
Machinery handling by workers with machinery		
Operation of program-controlled machinery		
Installation of program-controlled machinery	x	
Programming of program-controlled machinery	x	
Monitoring of program-controlled machinery	x	
Maintenance, repairs	x	x

Source: Becker *et al.* (2013). Items refer to the list of tools in the German Qualification and Career Survey 1998/99. The authors' strict classification is used.

Table A2. Classification of tasks based on Spitz-Oener (2006).

	Non-routine tasks	Interactive tasks
Training and teaching others	x	x
Consulting, informing others	x	x
Measuring, testing, quality controlling		
Surveillance, operating machinery, plants, or processes		
Repairing, renovating	x	
Purchasing, procuring, selling	x	x
Organizing, planning	x	x
Advertising, public relations, marketing, promoting business	x	x
Information acquisition and analysis, investigations	x	
Conducting negotiations	x	x
Development, research	x	
Manufacture or production of merchandize		
Providing for, waiting on, caring for people	x	x

Note: Items refer to the list of job descriptions in the German Qualification and Career Survey 1998/99. Whereas Spitz-Oener (2006) follows Autor *et al.* (2003) and creates five task categories, we aggregate them to measures of non-routineness and interactivity in order to ensure comparability with the Becker *et al.* (2013) mapping.

Appendix B. Supplementary data

Supplementary material associated with this article can be found in the online version at http://dx.doi.org.10.1016/j. euroecorev.2013.03.007.

References

Angrist, J., Pischke, J.-S., 2009. *Mostly Harmless Econometrics.* Princeton University Press, Princeton.

Antonczyk, D., Fitzenberger, B., Leuschner, U., 2009. Can a task-based approach explain the recent changes in the German wage structure? *Journal of Economics and Statistics*, 229 (2–3), 214–238.

Arellano, M., 1987. Computing robust standard errors for within-group estimators. *Oxford Bulletin of Economics and Statistics*, 49, 431–434.

Autor, D.H., Handel, M.J. Putting tasks to the test: Human capital, job tasks and wages. *Journal of Labor Economics*, forthcoming.

Autor, D.H., Levy, F., Murnane, R.J., 2003. The skill content of recent technological change: An empirical exploration. *The Quarterly Journal of Economics*, 118(4), 1279–1333.

Baumgarten, D., 2009. International outsourcing, the nature of tasks, and occupational stability: Empirical evidence for Germany. *Ruhr Economic Papers*, 108.

Beaudry, P., Green, D.A., 2003. Wages and employment in the United States and Germany: what explains the differences?. *American Economic Review*, 93(3), 573–602.

Becker, S.O., Ekholm, K., Muendler, M.-A., 2013. Offshoring and the onshore composition of tasks and skills. *Journal of International Economics*, 90(1), 91–106.

Biscourp, P., Kramarz, F., 2007. Employment, skill structure and international trade: firm-level evidence for France. *Journal of International Economics* 72(1), 22–51.

Blinder, A.S., 2006. Offshoring: the next industrial revolution?. *Foreign Affairs*, 85(2), 113–128.

Blinder, A.S., Krueger, A.B. Alternative measures of offshorability: A survey approach. *Journal of Labor Economics*, forthcoming.

Brown, C., Medoff, J., 1989. The employer size-wage effect. *Journal of Political Economy*, 97(5), 1027–1059.

Crinò, R., 2010. Service offshoring and white-collar employment. *Review of Economic Studies*, 77(2), 595–632.

DiNardo, J.E., Pischke, J.-S., 1997. The returns to computer use revisited: have pencils changed the wage structure too?. *The Quarterly Journal of Economics*, 112(1), 291–303.

Ebenstein, A., Harrison, A.E., McMillan, M.S., Phillips, S. Estimating the impact of trade and offshoring on American workers using the Current Population Surveys. *Review of Economics and Statistics*, forthcoming.

Feenstra, R.C., Hanson, G.H., 1996. Globalization, outsourcing, and wage inequality. *American Economic Review*, 86(2), 240–245.

Feenstra, R.C., Hanson, G.H., 1999. The impact of outsourcing and high-technology capital on wages: Estimates for the United States 1979–1990. *Quarterly Journal of Economics*, 114(3), 907–940.

Feenstra, R.C., Hanson, G.H., 2001. Global production sharing and rising inequality: A survey of trade and wages. Working Paper 8372, NBER.

Frick, J.R., Grabka, M.M., 2003. Imputation of item-non-response on income questions in the SOEP 1984 to 2002. Research Notes 29, DIW.

Gathmann, C., Schönberg, U., 2010. How general is human capital? A task-based approach. *Journal of Labor Economics*, 28(1), 1–50.

Geishecker, I., Görg, H., 2008. Winners and losers: a micro-level analysis of international outsourcing and wages. *Canadian Journal of Economics*, 41(1), 243–270.

Grabka, M.M., 2012. Codebook for the PEQUIV file 1984-2011 CNEF variables with extended income information for the SOEP. Data Documentation 65, DIW Berlin.

Grossman, G.M., Rossi-Hansberg, E., 2008. Trading tasks: a simple theory of offshoring. *American Economic Review*, 98(5), 1978–1997.

Haisken-DeNew, J.P., Hahn, M., 2006. Panelwhiz: a flexible modularized stata interface for accessing large scale panel data sets. Mimeo (⟨http://www.panelwhiz.eu⟩).

Head, K., Ries, J., 2002. Offshore production and skill upgrading by Japanese manufacturing firms. *Journal of International Economics*, 58(1), 81–105.

Hummels, D., Jorgensen, R., Munch, J.R., Xiang, C., 2011. The wage effects of offshoring: evidence from Danish matched worker-firm data. Working Paper 17496, NBER.

Jensen, J., Kletzer, L., 2010. Measuring tradable services and the task content of offshorable services jobs. In: Abraham, K.G., Spletzer, J.R., Harper, M. (Eds.), *Labor in the New Economy*, University of Chicago Press, Chicago, pp. 309–335.

Kohler, W., Wrona, J., 2010. Offshoring tasks, yet creating jobs? Working Paper 3019, CESifo.

Leamer, E., Storper, M., 2001. The economic geography of the internet age. *Journal of International Business Studies*, 32(4), 641–665.

Levy, F., Murnane, R., 2004. *The New Division of Labor*. Princeton University Press, Princeton.

Liu, R., Trefler, D., 2008. Much ado about nothing: American jobs and the rise of service outsourcing to China and India. Working Paper 14061, NBER.

Mincer, J., 1974. *Schooling, Experience and Earnings*. National Bureau of Economic Research, New York.

OECD, 1999. Classifying Educational Programmes: Manual for ISCED-97 Implementation in OECD Countries. OECD, Paris.

OECD, 2011. Clarifying trade costs in maritime transport. Working Party of the Trade Committee TAD/TC/WP(2008)10/FINAL.

Prasad, E.S., 2004. The unbearable stability of the German wage structure: evidence and interpretation. *IMF Staff Papers*, 51(2), 354–386.

Schmidt, C.M., Zimmermann, K.F., 1991. Work characteristics, firm size and wages. *Review of Economics and Statistics* 73(4), 705–710.

Spitz-Oener, A., 2006. Technical change, job tasks and rising educational demands: Looking outside the wage structure. *Journal of Labor Economics*, 24(2), 235–270.

Staiger, D., Stock, J., 1997. Instrumental variables regression with weak instruments. *Econometrica* 65(3), 557–586.

Statistisches Bundesamt, 1992. Klassifizierung der Berufe — Systematisches und alphabetisches Verzeichnis der Berufsbenennungen. Metzler-Poeschel, Stuttgart.

Statistisches Bundesamt, 2009. Volkswirtschaftliche Gesamtrechnung — Input-Output-Rechnung 2006. Fachserie 18, Reihe 2, Statistisches Bundesamt.

Wagner, G.G., Frick, J.R., Schupp, J., 2007. The German socio-economic panel study (SOEP) — scope, evolution and enhancements. *Schmollers Jahrbuch* 127(1), 139–169.

White, H., 1980. A heteroskedasticity consistent covariance matrix estimator and a direct test for heteroskedasticity. *Econometrica*, 48(4), 817–838.